THE GLOBAL THEME PARK INDUSTRY

Front cover images suplied by S. Anton Clavé. a) Animal Kingdom, b) Futuroscope, c) SeaWorld Orlando, d) Coney Island

THE GLOBAL THEME PARK INDUSTRY

Salvador Anton Clavé

www.cabi.org

CABI is a trading name of CAB International

CABI Head Office
Nosworthy Way
Wallingford
Oxfordshire OX10 8DE
UK

Tel: +44 (0)1491 832111
Fax: +44 (0)1491 833508
E-mail: cabi@cabi.org
Website: www.cabi.org

CABI North American Office
875 Massachusetts Avenue
7th Floor
Cambridge, MA 02139
USA

Tel: +1 617 395 4056
Fax: +1 617 354 6875
E-mail: cabi-nao@cabi.org

A catalogue record for this book is available from the British Library, London, UK.

A catalogue record for this book is available from the Library of Congress,
Washington, DC.

ISBN-13: 978 1 84593208 4

Translated by Andrew Clarke
Typeset by AMA DataSet Ltd, Preston, UK
Printed and bound in the UK by Biddles, Kings Lynn.

Contents

Acknowledgements   xi

Introduction   xiii

I. The Development of Theme Parks   1

1. The Social Origins of the Theme Park Concept   3
1.1. The Heritage of the European Garden Design   5
1.2. Lessons from the Universal Expositions   8
1.3. Amusement Parks' Entertainment Background   12
1.4. The Language of the Cinema   16
Case 1. The New World in Singapore, an Early 20th-century
         Amusement Park in Asia   18

2. Development and Categorization   21
2.1. The Invention of Theme Parks   22
2.2. The Nature of Theme Parks   27
      2.2.1. Definition and types   28
      2.2.2. The concept and the utilities of the themes   32
2.3. The Social Bases of Success   37
2.4. Synergies with the Media Entertainment Industry   41
Case 2. Efteling, the Best Childhood Memories for Everyone   43
Case 3. Huis ten Bosch, a Replica of the Dutch World in Japan   44
Case 4. Cedar Point, the Roller Coaster Capital of the World   45

3. Globalization of the Theme Park Industry   48
3.1. Location Tendencies of Theme Parks in the World   49
3.2. The Diversification of the Industry in the USA   56

3.3.   The Transformation of the Amusement Park
       Model in Europe   64
3.4.   The Growth of the Markets in Asia/the Pacific   72
3.5.   The Proliferation of Initiatives in the Rest of
       the World   85
Case 5.   The Recent Growth of the Theme Park Industry
          in Brazil   90

4.   **A Profile of Major Theme Park Operators**   **93**
     4.1.   The Role of the Large Operators in the USA   **94**
            4.1.1.   Disney's integral strategy   **98**
            4.1.2.   Six Flag's orientation to regional markets   **106**
            4.1.3.   The positioning of Universal as an operator of
                     destination parks   **112**
            4.1.4.   The consolidation of Cedar Fair as an operator
                     of regional parks   **121**
            4.1.5.   Anheuser Busch's corporate strategy   **124**
     4.2.   The Emergence of Regional Operators in the
            Rest of the World   **128**
            4.2.1.   The development of transnational groups
                     in Europe   **129**
                     (A) The Tussauds Group   **130**
                     (B) Merlin Entertainment   **131**
                     (C) Grévin et Cie   **133**
                     (D) Parques Reunidos   **136**
            4.2.2.   The diversity of operators in Asia/the Pacific   **137**
                     (A) Oriental Land   **138**
                     (B) Samsung Everland   **139**
                     (C) China Travel International Investment   **142**
                     (D) Village Roadshow Ltd   **145**
                     (E) Sanrio Company Ltd   **146**
            4.2.3.   The uniqueness of the CIE in Latin America   **147**
     Case 6.   The Family-run Europa Park   **149**
     Case 7.   A Chocolate-related Entertainment Destination in
               Hershey, Pennsylvania   **151**
     Case 8.   Suncity, Entertainment and Property Development in
               Malaysia   **153**

II.   **Theme Parks in the Entertainment Society**   **155**

5.   **Theme Parks and the Commercialization of Leisure**   **157**
     5.1.   Commercial Access to Entertainment   **160**
            5.1.1.   Consumption as a distinguishing factor of
                     contemporary leisure   **161**
            5.1.2.   The multiplication of themed leisure
                     environments   **166**
     5.2.   The McDonaldization Paradox   **170**

5.3. Disneyization as a Model 177
5.3.1. The components of Disneyization 180
5.3.2. Interpretations from postmodernity 183
Case 9. The Ecohistorical Parks of Grupo Xcaret 187
Case 10. The Globalization of Leisure and the
Sesame Street Characters 189

6. The Urbanism of Theme Parks and Spatial Innovation 191
6.1. The Urban Singularity of Parks 192
6.1.1. The spatialization of the imagination 193
6.1.2. Technology at the service of creation 195
6.2. The Corporative Urbanism of Leisure Complexes 198
6.3. Parks as a Referent for Planning 201
6.4. The Scope of Spatial Innovation 209
6.4.1. The privatization of development and the
challenge of the public use of space 210
6.4.2. The invention of the landscape and the
challenge of the identity of the territory 215
Case 11. The Creation of a Leisure Destination in Dubai 221

7. The Impact of Theme Parks 224
7.1. Parks in Regional and Urban Planning 225
7.2. The Effects on the Local and Regional Economy 233
7.2.1. The economic impact of theme parks 235
7.2.2. Parks and regional development 238
(A) Busch Gardens Europe
(Virginia, USA) 240
(B) Futuroscope (France, Europe) 243
7.2.3. Parks and tourist development 246
7.3. The Environmental Impact of Theme Parks 250
7.4. The Social and Cultural Effects of Parks on
Local Communities 257
7.4.1. Theme parks and social cohesion 258
7.4.2. The effects of parks on local culture 261
Case 12. Environmental Protection Measures in the
Redevelopment of Ocean Park 264
Case 13. The Grand Parc du Puy du Fou and the
Valorization of the Local Heritage 268
Case 14. The Enhancement of the Urban Landscape at
International Drive, Orlando 270

8. The Development of Theme Park Destinations 272
8.1. Theme Parks and Economic Development in Orlando 273
8.1.1. The role of Walt Disney World as a catalyst 275
8.1.2. Orlando besides the parks 283
8.2. Disneyland Paris and the Planning of Marne-la-Vallée 285

8.2.1. The creation of Disneyland Paris in
          Marne-la-Vallée   **291**
8.2.2. The role of Disney in Val d'Europe   **293**
8.2.3. The economic impact of Disneyland Paris   **297**
8.3. The Emerging Entertainment Economy of the
      Greater Pearl River Delta   **299**
8.3.1. Hong Kong's tourism and leisure project   **303**
8.3.2. Park development in the Shenzhen Special
          Economic Zone   **306**
8.3.3. The role of Macau in the tourism system of
          the Pearl Delta   **309**
Case 15. The Transformation of PortAventura into a
          Tourist Destination   **310**

III. **Fundamentals of Theme Park Development
       and Management**   **315**

9. **Factors Influencing the Development Process**   **317**
9.1. The Nature of a Theme Park as a Recreational Product   **318**
9.2. The Locational Factors in Theme Park Development   **321**
9.2.1. The size of the market   **322**
9.2.2. The characteristics of the place   **329**
9.2.3. The support of the public sector   **334**
9.3. The Business Environment as a Factor of Success   **337**
Case 16. Effects on Attendance of the Addition of a
          New Gate in a Multipark Destination   **341**

10. **Basic Principles of Theme Park Planning**   **343**
10.1. Project Development   **344**
10.1.1. The design of the master plan   **345**
10.1.2. The management of the development process   **348**
10.2. Project Viability   **351**
10.2.1. The planning of services and operations   **352**
10.2.2. The forecasting of operating measures   **355**
Case 17. Access for the Disabled at Disneyland Paris   **363**

11. **The Architectonic Design of a Theme Park**   **365**
11.1. The Form   **366**
11.2. Size and Capacity   **369**
11.3. Flows and Transport Systems   **370**
11.4. Components   **374**
11.4.1. The attractions and the shows   **375**
11.4.2. The services (food and beverages and shops)   **381**
Case 18. A Flow Management Model to Optimize
          Retail Profits at Universal Studios Hollywood   **383**

12. Management Strategies   385
   12.1. Operations Management   389
      12.1.1. The logistics of operations   391
          (A) Production   391
          (B) Procurement and distribution   392
          (C) Maintenance   393
          (D) Safety   395
      12.1.2. The documentation of processes   396
      12.1.3. Quality assurance   398
   12.2. Human Resources Management   400
      12.2.1. The hiring process   403
      12.2.2. Employee loyalty strategies   407
   12.3. Marketing Strategies   409
      12.3.1. Marketing plans   411
          (A) Product   412
          (B) Price   414
          (C) Promotion   415
          (D) Place   417
      12.3.2. The role of new techonologies   417
   12.4. Operators' Corporate Social Responsibility   419
   Case 19. The Safety of the Attractions at Six Flags Parks   424
   Case 20. The International Association of
           Amusement Parks and Attractions   426

Bibliography   429

Index   448

About the Author

Salvador Anton Clavé (PhD) is Senior Lecturer in Tourism Geography at the University Rovira i Virgili in Catalonia, Spain. His research interests have focused on leisure and tourism planning and development. He has authored and co-authored a number of books and many academic papers in this field. Currently, he is a director of the Tourism and Leisure University School and of the Science Park of Tourism and Leisure at the University Rovira i Virgili.

Acknowledgements

Writing this book would not have been possible without the collaboration and support of a great many people and organizations. First of all I would like to thank those anonymous referees of programmes for research at the Direcció General de Recerca de la Generalitat de Catalunya – Department of Research of the Autonomous Government of Catalonia – who have on three occasions awarded me with funds to carry out research periods in the USA in order to study the dynamics, evolution and impacts of theme parks. Without grants 1998BEAI400248, 1999BEAI00193 and 2001BEAI400048 from the Generalitat de Catalunya and my warm welcome by Briavel Holcomb at the Bloustein School of Planning and Public Policy at Rutgers, the State University of New Jersey in New Brunswick and, on several occasions, by Donald E. Hawkins and Kristin Lamoreaux at the International Institute of Tourism Studies at the George Washington University in Washington, DC, the research leading up to the writing of this book would never have materialized. I also wish to thank Nacima Baron-Yelles for providing me with perfect working facilities at the Institut Francilien d'Ingénierie des Services at the Université de Marne-la-Vallée, in France.

Some of the numerous people with whom I have come into contact when writing this book have played a determining role. Here I would specifically mention Michael D. Beyard, who, from his office in Georgetown provided me with access to some of the main corporations that operate theme parks in the USA and throughout the world. Similarly, without the collaboration of Frank P. Stanek, from Los Angeles, and of Richard M. Jackson, in Orlando, my ability to comprehend the phenomena associated with the development of theme parks would have been greatly limited. I also convey my thanks to the International Association of Amusement Parks and Attractions seated in Alexandria for having put all of their available resources at their documentation centre at my disposal. A great many others – management staff from parks, local and regional government professionals, and researchers – have received me at some time or another while devoting my time to the writing of this book. I thank all of you for responding to my needs for information, comment or guidance.

Thanks also to my colleagues of the Research Group into Territorial Analysis and Tourism Studies at the Department of Geography at the Rovira i Virgili University in Tarragona. I would like to make a special mention of Josep Oliveras – from whom I have received continuous support during the elaboration of this work – and of Jordi Blay – who has provided me with everything during fieldwork stays. I would also like to thank Xavier Culebras for preparing the figures I have incorporated into the text. Neither can I overlook the innumerable comments that have been made to me over the years I have devoted to the study of theme parks by the pupils and colleagues of the different universities at which I have had the chance to present the results of my research and from the professionals of the sector who have given me the possibility to debate my breakthroughs and appraisals concerning the social reality of theme parks with them. In this sense, I want to thank specifically the staff and management of PortAventura – particularly Lluis Rullan and Mercedes de Pablo – for their support and interest.

Although the structure and contents differ, this book has its precedent in a previous work I have written, which was published in Spanish by Ariel publishers of Barcelona, entitled *Parques temáticos. Más allá del ocio (Theme Parks. Beyond Leisure)* in 2005. I thank them for allowing me to use the previously published work as a basis for the drafting of this new book. Thanks also to Greg Richards and Julie Wilson because, aware of my work on theme parks, it was they who encouraged me to prepare this new work in the English language. Finally, I would like to thank most especially Andrew Clarke for his painstaking labour in preparing the translation of the new original manuscript into English. Logically, the final work has greatly benefited from the suggestions made by the reviewers. A task such as this requires time and dedication. This is why, in finishing, I would like to thank my friends, my family and, in particular, my wife María Angel, for their enthusiastic support and encouragement throughout the time I spent preparing the original.

Vila-seca, June 2006

Introduction

This book sets out to achieve three basic aims. In the first place it deals with defining and explaining the development and characteristics of the theme park industry on a global level and, from this point of view, offers the elements necessary for the understanding of their nature and functioning as spaces for entertainment with specific meanings. It is, above all, an explanatory book, containing real data as to the characteristics, the growth and the effects of the theme park phenomenon. Thus, it is a book whose primary aim is to try to understand why, as Tuan (1998) stated, theme parks are seen by their visitors as places through which to temporarily 'escape' from the conditions and worries of their everyday lives. In the second place, this book takes an analytical approach to the role played by theme parks in the social construction of space. Hence, on the basis of the analysis of its territorial effects, it deals with cultural trends, the dynamics of social change and local and regional development. It also presents the interests put into play by the agents participating in the development process of parks, the competitive instinct of the corporations that promote them and the strategic use they make of their resources and possibilities. Therefore, the book presents a debate as to the role of parks in the commodification of leisure and the social scope of their models of the creation of experiences. Finally, the third aim of this book is to look at the main conceptual, strategic and operative aspects which must be known about for the development and management of a theme park. An explanation is given as to the specificities that need to be taken into account during the planning stage, the conditioning factors that may affect their development, the characteristics and components of their layout as well as the main key aspects that contribute to the successful management and operation of a theme park.

This is a book which aims to arouse reflection and debate. Bearing their complexity and diversity in mind, it tackles the reality of theme parks. Its contents are set out along three principal axes: on the one hand, the theoretical reflection inherent in the academic work; secondly, the analysis of the reality on the basis of specific case studies; and finally, operative information, that is to say, the explanatory and informative elements, data, maps, tables and graphs that allow one to comprehend the reality of the activity rather than a mere interpretation thereof. This has in fact been a challenge, given the common practice in the study of theme parks of writing and interpreting while presenting hardly any data – very little empirical substance, that is to say.

Before moving on, I cannot fail to mention right from the outset that it has not been an easy task to deal with such matters taking theme parks as the 'object' of study. There are three reasons why this has been so. The first is that this book refers to a reality which – normally – in a great many parts of the world many people usually assimilate only in terms of 'I like it' or 'I don't like it'. Needless to say, in this sense, many people have their opinion of parks in their capacity as users – based, in addition, on something as difficult to argue with as their 'emotions' or their 'perception' – and that the interpretations made in this book may clash head-on with their most immediate intuition. Secondly, difficulties increase when, undervaluing their real territorial, economic, social and personal effects, it may be stated that a certain intellectual aversion exists to the scientific treatment of a subject, that of theme parks, and of consumerist leisure in general, which many academics tend to consider as either 'superficial' or 'little engaged'. Finally, a third difficulty is due to the fact that, in the same way as there are pro-park approaches, anti-park approaches also exist. To this end, we cannot forget that the academic contributions themselves to the analysis of theme parks made by French social theory and North American cultural studies have normally been highly critical of theme parks as artefacts of mass consumption, especially critical of Disney. However, the question that must be asked, as Marcus (1997) maintains, is whether the critical discourse that underlies the arguments put forward in academic books and journals (even in some semiological works with so much predication that they are cited in this book, such as Eco and Baudrillard) really goes beyond what an everyday conversation may provide.

Why Write a Book on Theme Parks?

Theme parks are liked by many people and this in itself is reason enough to try to understand why and to learn from them and interpret their effects. Their success defies the social scientists to assume a positive attitude and accept their existence, leaving aside merely ideological standpoints. Conversely, one must ask oneself what it is that leads our society to seek elements of escapism by means of parks and why they have become prominent elements of what Lefebvre denominates 'the second circuit of capital', that is to say, investment in real estate, urban development and the shaping of new social and economic elites (Gottdiener *et al.*, 1999). Similarly, one must also ask oneself why parks have managed to be, in fact, more meddlesome and subtle in their capacity for ideological penetration than any Marx or Mao could ever have conceived (Barber, 1996, 129). Understanding this requires serious study.

Posing a scientific discourse about theme parks therefore means trying to understand their meaning and function in the society of today and of the future. From this perspective, this book is an attempt at participating in the incipient tendency which Holt and Schor (2000, x) detect among academics of being increasingly attentive to the questions concerning the nature of society and consumption and of transferring such content to the channels pertaining to academic debate.

I agree with Lynch when he states that the field of the study of leisure and its practice cannot allow itself to bury its head in the sand and shun the kingdom of global, commercial and consumer leisure. To do so would, according to his standpoint, avoid most of what a huge number of people do in and for their leisure. There exists the need to be committed to the commercial and consumerism, to study them, understand them, influence and legislate them, and to make the most of the advantages they may offer (Lynch, 2001, 201). On the other hand, it cannot be forgotten that, in the same way as for Venturi *et al.* (1972), understanding the content of Pop messages in the Strip of Las Vegas and their means of projection 'does not mean that one need agree with, approve of, or reproduce that content', understanding the keys to a park's functioning, which are creations that appeal intelligently to our deepest emotions through elementary proposals, does not mean that their analysis should be the equivalent of predicating the universal exemplariness of the model of the creation of leisure experiences they pose.

The basic point which arises from this work is that theme parks cannot be only considered as mere spaces for entertainment and recreation or mere tourist attractions. Regardless of the size and scope of theme parks, they represent and give shape and sense to the societies in which they exist. By selectively interpreting the reality, transferring emotions and feelings from the personal to the commercial sphere and generating specific spaces of control and transgression, parks, in their capacity as organizations visited by millions of people each year, say a lot about us, about our cultural needs and imperatives, about our collective resignations and, of course, about our ideals and our frustrations. Now, as Barber (1996, 129) suggests, it should not be forgotten that theme parks as a metaphor are seated on theme parks as a material and spatial reality. It is in this sense, therefore, that studying the role of parks in the social construction of space acquires relevance. As Minca (1996, 2) says, space 'is acquiring unprecedented importance' in the evolution of social thought. This is so because it is the environment in which social groups – with their conflicts, tensions and dominations – materialize their preferences.

What is Known about Theme Parks?

Davis (1997) notes a variety of emphases, some contradictory, in the academic analysis of theme parks as of the mid-1970s in the USA. Initially, academic studies – largely focusing on Disney – were critical of theme parks as a characteristic result of North American economic policy. Intensely influenced by the popular radicalism of the end of the 1960s, Schiller (1973) was probably the first analyst to criticize the supposed stance of innocence and neutrality of Disney entertainment products. However, this approach is abandoned and, as of the 1980s forks into two currents. On the one hand, the social historians begin to tackle theme parks from the angle of the analysis of changes in consumer tendencies during society's leisure time and they take an interest, from this standpoint, in the history of theme parks (Adams, 1991). On the other hand, the interpretation of theme parks as narrative and textual scenarios becomes generalized. In this way, anthropologists and semiologists treat theme parks as supposedly paradigmatic spaces of the postmodern era (Eco, 1989).

The acceleration of consumption and its pre-eminence as an economic motor as of the 1980s, together with the manifestation of the crudest aspects of the structural crisis facing North American cities, arouses architects, urban planners, geographers and sociologists to take an interest – now as of the 1990s – in theme parks from the perspective of the relationships between social life and the production of space. From this point of view, theme parks are more than just leisure spaces. They become the physical expression of society's desires as to its preferences for the city and offer alternatives to the conventional processes of urban construction, which is moving towards the corporate privatization of spaces and, in short, the redefinition of social space. However, this approach has led to diametrically opposed results. Thus, whereas Rebori (1995a, 5–6) maintains that the study of Disney presents numerous ideas and examples of applications in the fields of planning, design, development and flow management, authors like Sorkin (1992a) use this same basis to criticize, by means of a journey through the principal scenarios of contemporary urban geography in North America (the 'analogical' cities of Atlanta, Calgary and Montreal, the West Edmonton Mall commercial area, the *exopolis* of Los Angeles or the utopia of Disneyland), the loss of public space or, at least, the confusion between the public and the private (Donaire, 1999).

In fact, one should not overlook the fact that the most relevant part of the bibliography existing to date on theme parks has mainly concentrated on Disney. This is logical when considering that authors with such prestige as Baudrillard (1998, 55) are capable of stating that 'if we believe that the whole of the Western world is hypostatized in America, the whole of America in California, and California in MGM and Disneyland, then this is the microcosm of the West'. In any case, Disney's dominance of the theme park industry brings about additional difficulties in the study of theme parks. As a symbol corporation of the process of the 'Americanization of the world', instigator of the expansion of consumer society and initiation rite of totalitarian capitalism (Ariès, 2002, 8–9), Disney has generated a multitude of critical interpretations (among the most significant those of Klugman, Kuenz, Waldrep and Willis in 1995 under the collective name of The Project on Disney, 1995), which have led to an impairment of the ability to interpret the theme park phenomenon beyond Disney. Thus, to cite one of the most recent in fierce argument against Disney's presence in France, Ariès (2002, 24) justifies such pre-eminence when he said that 'it has turned along with McDonald's, IBM, Microsoft and Monsanto into one of the most important symbols of the capitalist globalization taking place'.

Now, in the same way as Disney parks have been characterized as 'stupid' and 'plastic' and, in the beginning, Disneyland was dubbed a 'national monument to vulgarity' opposed to any manifestation of art and architecture, other professionals have validated its achievements to the extent that they give lessons to both planners and to architects who have crossed the frontiers of parks and have been useful in the design of public spaces (Rebori, 1995b). Without a doubt, the success of parks as regards visitor numbers, their corporate achievements in such diverse fields as the media, technological innovation, creativity of entertainment or the setting of urban standards and, of course, their particular narrative constructions and visions of society in themes such as gender, ethnicity and (local and global) history have made the Disney corporate conglomerate the favourite target of academics interested in the issue of theme parks. However, without denying Disney's role, neither can it be overlooked that the analysis of theme parks only on the basis of the Disney experience gives rise to considerable bias.

In short, therefore, the question of theme parks is approached taking into consideration the fact that, as Donaire (1999) maintains, these kinds of hyperreal spaces are 'the quintessence of post-industrial society and its tensions'. From this standpoint, Rebori (1995a), for example, upholds the view that theme parks are a feast for interdisciplinary studies. As for Davis (1997, 3), she bases her magnificent study on SeaWorld in San Diego from the perspective that parks can be considered emblematic of urban spatial problems. Likewise, in an article on the opposition to certain Disney projects in the USA, Warren (1996, 546) argues that theme parks are 'in fact a richly diverse landscape full of cultural contradiction not accounted for in theories of postmodern cities'. Parks, therefore, are seen to be significant from the point of view of the analysis of the relationship between society and space (Tuan and Hoelscher, 1997).

In any case, the growing literature on mass consumption and the development of recreational and tourist activities globally is giving rise to increased interest in the study of the social and urban implications of theme parks. So, for example, in Europe and from the angle of geography, Cazes (1988) even defined his study as the development of a new field of research. Nevertheless, it is also true that, besides a few excellent monographs on specific parks such as the one by Davis (1997) on SeaWorld or detailed analytical work on Disney's effect on the urban development of Orlando (Foglesong, 1999) among others, there is still a long way to go as regards the knowledge of theme parks as spaces of mass consumption. Issues such as their characteristics as a business, their effects on the strategies of the creation of corporate spaces for public use, the transformation of the local heritage and of the places themselves into standardized recreational products or the effect of their development on regional economies remain to be dealt with in depth.

How Was This Book Written?

Emulating landscapist Anne Whiston Spirn (1998, 4) I can say that the parks themselves and their immediate surroundings are the primary data for the drafting of this book. Photographs, sketches and field books containing notes written about sights, sounds, smells and thoughts are the first material source of the content of this work. Thus, still with the aim of offering a global overview of the reality of theme parks as places for entertainment with a great capacity to catalyse economic and territorial processes in their immediate surroundings, what is true is that the considerations I make are based on fieldwork periods in the USA, fundamentally in California, Florida and Virginia, and in Europe, in France, Germany and Spain. The effect caused on the territory by PortAventura, which was inaugurated in 1995, precisely the same year in which I finished my doctoral thesis on the tourist urbanization of the Costa Daurada (Gold Coast of Spain) (Anton Clavé, 1997), is without a doubt, in this context of references, what initially got me interested in the subject.

Therefore, the deliberations regarding theme parks that contribute to this book are as much based on the use of classic research techniques such as theoretical reflection and the analysis of indicators as that of personal document research concerning the principal places to which reference is made. As always, when the areas of theory and fieldwork are brought together and reality adopted as a laboratory, the number of questions is multiplied. In consequence, as is to be expected, it has proved more complicated to write this book than I could have imagined at first. Lanquar (1991, 4) neatly sums up some of the difficulties that derive from the very 'object' of writing. On the one hand, there is the peculiarity of scientific, technical and even commercial literature on this matter (with a great deal of knowledge amassed with the years of experience being kept as the property of the operating companies themselves and of design and planning consultants and therefore outside the circuit of dissemination of knowledge and know-how). On the other hand, there is the futility of much of the promotional and journalistic material, which, due to the rapid changes that affect the sector, is rendered quickly obsolete. Finally, as Spirn (1998) also maintains, given that the in-depth interpretation of a landscape requires local knowledge, there is the difficulty involved in the appreciation of complex and distant territorial realities.

On the other hand, despite inevitably having the Anglo-Saxon, and especially North American, reality as points of reference, it cannot be overlooked that this book on parks is written from a perspective of a peripheral academic tradition – in this case European geography. To this end it cannot be forgotten that studying theme parks from Europe means performing – as Keil (1994) shrewdly notes with regard to the differences that exist between the two urban realities – much reflection since the European and American social models, though similar, are not exactly the same. It may be timely to quote Baudrillard (1998, 123) at his most exquisite when he states that:

> [Europeans,] fanatics of aesthetics and meaning, of culture, of flavour and seduction, we who see only what is profoundly moral as beautiful and for whom only the heroic distinction of nature and culture is exciting, we who are unfailingly attached to the wonders of critical sense and transcendence, [find North America] a mental shock and a unique release to discover the fascination of nonsense and of this vertiginous disconnection.

It is as a result of these considerations that this book was construed with a unique structure. It consists of three parts. The first tackles the development process of theme parks. It reviews their background, it describes the process of their emergence in the USA as well as their organization as a leisure product, it analyses their international expansion from the 1950s to the present and it introduces the main operators. The second part deals with the role of parks in the social development of space and their importance from the viewpoint of the analysis of social reality. Thus, some of the main debates are concentrated on transversally covering the concern held by authorities, international organizations, economic agents and citizens' groups. Issues are scrutinized such as the nature of parks' productive systems in the context of post-Fordism and postmodernism, parks' effects on thought, contemporary urban practice and their impact on local and regional and tourist development and the role enjoyed by some park complexes in the creation of specific tourist destinations. The book is rounded off with a third part devoted to the question of the fundamentals of planning and management that are to be borne in mind for the development and establishment of a park. Furthermore, the book contains a bibliography and includes several brief analytical cases whose purpose is to illustrate, through the provision of solutions, how some specific theme parks have gone about achieving their own strategic and operative challenges.

Who Is This Book Written For?

To debate as to the role and social function of theme parks may help to facilitate the understanding of social and urban processes that are characteristic of both North America and Europe, Asia and, more incipiently, Latin America, such as the boom of shopping malls, the reconversion of heritage as leisure spaces, the gentrification of urban centres, the theming of consumption, the fragmentation of travel supply or the creation of gated communities – architectural spaces, all of them – which emulate the principles of design and operation of theme parks (Ritzer, 1999, 115).

On the other hand, it may also facilitate the proper interpretation of the future role of such spaces in a context in which, according to Holt and Schor (2000, vii–x), there are three factors that disquiet the current emergence of the consumer society. The first and most obvious is social inequality on any scale. Second is the growing transformation into a commodity of an increasingly large part of life and social relations, even of those aspects which until recently had been kept outside the market, precisely such as entertainment. In this sense, Ariès is quite to the point when he says that we are heading towards the 'commodification of the lived experience: the sale of affection, sensations and feelings' (Ariès, 2002, 218). Finally, the third is the rapid globalization of the world economy.

It should not be forgotten that criticism of today's entertainment society even involves actions of protest that find mechanisms of expression in popular anti-consumerism manifestos in the style of Naomi Klein's (1999) *No Logo* and which suggest the need to seek means to minimize inequality, escape from commodification and radically transform the meaning of globalization. Hence the need to render the knowledge of the patterns and mechanisms of consumption in a 'research schedule' and, especially, in this schedule to consider the demands, options and behaviour of developed society with regard to leisure. The problem according to Veal (1998, 260) lies in how to carry out more than purely descriptive investigation and develop a satisfactory theory that is linked to broader theoretical ideas. In any case, applicable to the subject of theme parks is Britton's (1991, 452) appraisal of the geographical study of tourism when he states that 'it requires a more rigorous core of theory in order to conceptualise fully its role in capitalist accumulation, its economic dynamics, and its role in creating the materiality and social meaning of places'. Only in this way is it possible to integrate his study into the front line of debate of the social disciplines.

Be that as it may, I believe, therefore, that it may be stated that through this book it is possible openly to comprehend the reach of the theme park phenomenon. I am of the understanding that through its study it is possible to learn about the pleasures and needs of today's society in developed countries and about leisure corporations' strategies as they strive to consolidate commercial access to emotions and feelings. 'Parkophilic' readers may discover, in short, that theme parks are, in addition to being a unique place for entertainment, a source of meaning and a suitable framework for the study of culture, space and technology. Opponents to parks in their capacity as privileged spaces of the reproduction of the capitalist system and paradigmatic examples of the renewed capitalist society, in which, as Debord (1967) announced, the spectacle is the great instrument of domination, may find this book helps their effort to understand the workings, dynamics and structures of the culture of global corporations and, therefore, a way to discover new useful tools to fight against them. All in all, paraphrasing Venturi *et al.* (1972), it should be acknowledged that, as humans, we can learn 'from Rome and Las Vegas and from looking around us wherever we happen to be'. When all is said and done, defenders and detractors compete in the market of ideas, attitudes and behaviours, and one as much as the other usually has valuable statements to make.

Lastly, I cannot help thinking that there is a wealth of information, knowledge and creativity that remains to be developed on the basis of the study of theme parks; important questions and approaches that have only been dealt with in brief. Therefore, new lines of research and study may open up both from within and from outside parks. At the end of the day, perhaps the most interesting thing about parks is that they convey to us the cultural, social and economic context of their development. In fact, this time paraphrasing Rifkin (2000, 298), while the wealthier are concerned with entertainment and creativity, millions of people live in poverty. My only hope is that the book will provide something different for those who are more knowledgeable of the subject and the odd novelty too – at least from an intellectual point of view – for those for whom the social and territorial implications of theme parks are quite unknown. Likewise, if the book inspires others to join in and contribute to the study of this kind of leisure space, I shall consider the time I have dedicated to this pursuit well spent. For all of the above it is my desire, just as for García Canclini (1995, 53), that this book should be read as if it were the start of a conversation between urban planners, geographers, anthropologists, psychologists, sociologists, economists and the citizens themselves, precisely as to 'what it means to be citizens and consumers'.

I The Development of Theme Parks

I fear that the productions of democratic poets may often be surcharged with immense and incoherent imagery, with exaggerated descriptions and strange creations; and that the fantastic beings of their brain may sometimes make us regret the world of reality.

(Alexis de Tocqueville, 1835)

The concept of theme park cannot be detached, nowadays, from the idea materialized by Walt Disney when on 17 July 1955 Disneyland opened its doors in California. In fact, as Lanquar holds (1991, 11), with Disney came the birth of 'supermarkets of leisure, places for the production and consumption of free time, a flat-rate price, integrating technology and modern management and the arts and spectacles'. In any case, there is a whole world of theme parks beyond Disney. Because of that, this first part of the book analyses the dimensions and processes that have shaped the present system of theme parks throughout the world. Chapter 1 deals with the historical, cultural and social foundations on which today's reality of theme parks is built since the pre-modern fairs. Chapter 2 characterizes the emergence of theme parks as specific leisure spaces and their fundamental features are set out. Chapter 3 tackles the question of the progressive worldwide expansion of the phenomenon since the 1950s to the present, especially regarding the intensification of their growth dynamics in Europe and in Asia as of the end of the 1980s and the early 1990s, just when in the USA the development of the industry saturated the market. Finally, Chapter 4 explains the role played in this process of internationalization and generalization on a global scale by the main operators, the large corporations – led by Disney – and other, smaller-sized operators. Both the one and the other are shaping the industry in the USA as well as in Europe and in Asia/the Pacific.

1 The Social Origins of the Theme Park Concept

The great European garden is an idealized world separated from both nature and the city . . . Human beings have always been tempted to envisage a world better than the one they know. The literature on Eden, paradise, or utopia is vast . . . After all, Heaven itself had its gate, guarded by Saint Peter, and only a small proportion of souls could enter.

(Yi-Fu Tuan and Steven D. Hoelscher, 1997)

Beyond their present role as pure manifestations of commercial leisure and despite the consideration by some in intellectual discourses – with no empirical foundation, however – that they are 'second class leisure facilities' due to their mass, artificial and consumerist nature (Lynch, 2001), theme parks are a cultural creation. The starting date of the theme park industry is usually put at 1955, the year in which Disneyland opened in Anaheim, California. This consideration, generally accepted in spite of being arbitrary (for example, Efteling, the Dutch theme park based on popular children's tales, opened its doors in 1952), is based on the fact that Disney was configured from the beginning as a recreational model and was enthusiastically emulated, imitated and envied by a great number of agents and corporations. Theme parks are necessarily associated, therefore, on the basis of the above, with the entertainment and leisure of the masses, consumption and, as of the 1970s, the stimulation of the tourist activity. However, notwithstanding their date of foundation, as regards being a cultural manifestation, theme parks have explicit precedents in another type of phenomena of popular culture. In fact, their origins can be traced back to European fairs of medieval origin. Along the way, theme parks have incorporated conceptual and operational breakthroughs that have been successively innovated in other kinds of leisure facilities and activities.

As can be seen in Table 1.1, for Botterill (1997, 146) theme parks as areas for recreation correspond to the very characteristics of contemporary society, which he denominates late-modern, in the same way as fairs and amusement parks were the recreational responses to the leisure needs and the relations of dominant power in pre-modern and modern societies. Thus, according to Botterill,

> across time and space, people have created a place within which they gathered in large numbers to participate in ritual, entertainment, amusements and spectacles, while consuming and exchanging foods, goods, and services. The theme park is the contemporary manifestation of fairs, carnivals, and amusement parks – a class of cultural phenomena which I will refer to as the amusementscape.
>
> (Botterill 1997, 1)

Table 1.1.   Social evolution of the amusement-scape (from Botterill, 1997).

	Pre-modern	Modern	Late-modern
Social characteristics			
Dominant place	Rural	Town	City
Production base	Agrarian	Industrial	Service/symbolic
Orchestration	Church/monarchy	Company/state	Corporation/media
State formation	Colonial	Nation	Transnational
Bridging voice	Tradition/church	Reformer/sponsor	Advertiser
Relations	Communal	Impersonal	Corporation with face
Identity	Birth/craft	Production	Consumption/pleasure
Market	Local	National	Global
Communication	Oral	Mass-mediated	Promotional culture
Group	Family/guild	Class	Fragment/other
Self	Animistic	Individual	Cultural subject
Power	Force	Alienation	Hegemony
Characteristics of the recreational scenario			
Form	Fair	Amusement park	Theme park
Primary case	Saint Bartholomew's Fair, London	Coney Island, New York	Walt Disney World Resort, Florida
Place	Street	Seaside	Suburb
Boundary	Open	Semi-open	Enclosed
Time	Religious calendar	Seasonal	Year-round
Motivation	Religious festival/ exchange of goods	Profit/civilizing/ amusement	Dividends/jobs/pleasure
Purpose	Expression	Education/culture	Entertainment
Audience	Pilgrim/peasant	Working class	Middle class
Orchestration	Community	Monopoly	Oligopoly
Transport	Foot/horses	Trolleybus	Car/plane
Mode	Allegory	Fact	Hyperreality/simulacra
Product	Made by	Made for	Consumer/promotion
Mocks	Church/monarchy	Genteel culture	Everyday/technology
Animal symbol	Pig	Elephant	Mouse
Chronology	1500–1850	1850–1960	As of 1960

The amusement parks that have sprung up both in Europe and the USA as of the 19th century reconstruct the fragments of the old fairs' 'manufacturing', by means of their rides, places for the entertainment of the masses of workers. In parallel, the coming of universal expositions showed how it was possible to create simulated geographies as stages for mechanical rides that were more in keeping with amusement parks. Finally, the appearance of the cinema and the mass media offer new perspectives of entertainment, new languages of communication and new ways (scenic and dramatic) of grasping reality.

Parks contain formulas for the creation of stages and landscapes that evoke the tradition concerning gardening and the domestication of nature, which is so characteristic of Western culture. Not in vain, as Capel claims (2000, 66), 'a garden is a refined construction . . . an image of paradise on earth [which] is progressively made accessible to aristocratic and bourgeois groups and then to the population in general'. In short, parks feed from the formally urban concept of universal expositions, from the ability to satisfy humans' leisure needs through 'manufactured' systems fitting of amusement parks, from fragmented language, scenes, characteristic of cinematography and of the effect of representing the world that has inherited the most classic garden tradition. Furthermore, theme parks are not just a complicated system of escape from the daily routine but are also places with a didactic vocation and signification. This is why they incorporate modern buildings, sanitized surroundings, advanced technology and purpose-planned and built areas – like gardens since the classic epoch – to create spectacle, pleasure and coercion (Sorkin, 1992b, 208).

In any case, Sudjic's (1992) statement could be applied to theme parks, when he referred to universal expositions saying that parks would be to the town 'the same as fast food outlets to a restaurant': an instant of massive doses of popular culture, congestion and spectacle that leaves the client hungry for more; a superficial mixture of the mundane and the fantastic allowing one to lose sight of the banality of the modern town; a place to sit down and drink, attend shows and shop, be entertained and work, see and be seen; in short, a microcosm in expansion.

1.1. The Heritage of the European Garden Design

Ouset (1986a, 67) states that 'most contemporary works devoted to the history of parks and gardens do not really evoke the conditions of the appearance of recreation parks'. In this respect, Samuelson and Yegoiants (2001) in their book on American amusement parks are explicit when stating that 'the roots of the modern inception of the American amusement park began in sixteenth century Europe' when, in French public gardens, sports activities started to be pursued and, progressively, places for refreshment and entertainment were incorporated and later when, with the industrial revolution at the end of the 18th century in Great Britain, the gardens of inns and hostels appeared and were developed in the form of complex landscapes where theatre plays were held, concerts, fireworks and, later, illuminations and balloon rides.

Mitrasinovic (1996, 3) shares this view, due to not only a genealogical criterion as in the case of the aforementioned authors but also a conceptual one. For him, a park, like a garden, is a complex symbolic space from a social and cultural point of view. There, the treatment of the landscape serves to construct, in an idealized way, an unreal space. In this sense, says Mitrasinovic, in the same way as the structures of Versailles or Chantilly 'reflect Descartes's Meditations, Pascal's Pensées, the power of Louis XIV', contemporary theme parks are like 'mirrors of infinity' showing images of collectivity that allows the reconstruction/reassumption of each one's place in the universe. Of the same opinion are the contributions by Young and Riley made at a Colloquium on the History of the Architecture of the Landscape of Dumbarton Oaks (Young and Riley, 2002), in which they review, among other things, the background to and variations of today's theme parks compared with the gardens of the 18th century.

Robillard (cited by Lusignan, 1993) is likewise explicit when stating that amusement parks, though they owe many of their characteristics to fairs, have their roots in the characteristic 18th-century English pleasure gardens. 'Amusement parks', says Robillard:

> owe to 'pleasure gardens', their concerts, balls, picnics, the spirit of baroque festivity transported from the great European courts to a public park offering a unified atmosphere with their dreamy montage, their engine rooms, their fabulous gardens, their theatrical spirit, their masquerades, their illuminations, their fireworks and a decorative style often inherited from the rococo.

Mangels (1952) is of the same understanding in his classic history of the outdoor entertainment industry when, in the middle of the 20th century, he states:

> the modern American amusement park is of comparatively recent development, but for more than three hundred years elaborate outdoor amusement centres have existed in several European countries. Known usually as 'pleasure gardens' they were remarkably similar to those of today in their general layout and variety of entertainment.

In their beginnings, the concept of a 'park' was applied to spaces that the European kings and aristocracy recreated and redesigned for the enjoyment of their leisure time. Lanquar (1991, 9) cites, along these lines, the Tuileries or Versailles in Paris. Lusignan (1993) goes even further back in time and cites the park of Hesdin in the 14th century in the domains of the Duke of Bourgogne in France, a place where wild animals roamed free but also an area in which a variety of attractions were located, ranging from a maze to a supposed predecessor of today's chamber of horrors. In the 18th century, these royal gardens and parks were opened up to the public. One of the categories of park that take part in this process is the aforementioned 'pleasure gardens'. These are places for leisure and attractions that sprung up in most European towns as of the 18th century and during the 19th century where – paying for them – one could enjoy a series of attractions that were a direct derivation of those that were common in the royal gardens.

The first European 'pleasure gardens' located in the outskirts of towns date from the 17th century. The most characteristic are Vauxhall Gardens (initially called New Spring Garden when created in 1661, and renamed Vauxhall Gardens in 1728, with an entry fee from 1730 and until 1859, the year in which it closed with a firework display) and Ranelagh Gardens (1690) in London. A century later, Ruggieri (1776) and Tivoli (1795) gardens were designed, later moved to Copenhagen (1843), and the Prater in Vienna (1766). Some of them are still kept today as gardens, while the Prater, as we shall see later on, has become one of the most characteristic amusement parks in Europe and Denmark's Tivoli has been turned into a theme park. These parks symbolize the democratization of the aristocracy's ludic pursuits. It was in 1793 that the first public zoo opened in France, on the lands of the old Jardin du Roi in Paris (Coltier, 1985). Around them the spirit of courtesan parties was adapted to the growing European bourgeoisie's need for leisure.

Concerning this, Capel (2000, 71) affirms that the very theatrical and scenographic nature of the courtesan and aristocratic garden of the 18th century gives rise to an intimate relationship between space and festivity:

> On the one hand, the theatre as a garden, that is to say, theatrical action performed in a garden . . . On the other hand, the garden as a theatre in which the action of the privileged owners and visitors is carried out.

Moreover, from the ludic point of view and according to Botterill (1997), during the 19th century, gardens, a legacy of aristocratic and bourgeois constructions and a manifestation of domesticated nature, were considered as being curative, educative, a source of artistic inspiration and a manifestation of the power of humanity over nature.

Linked to colonial and industrial lifestyles, these parks continuously observed the world and transplanted within their domains the flora and the fauna of the most varied regions of Europe and, in particular, from the Orient. They simulated the landscapes from other regions in one specific place. At the same time they evolved in the direction of zoological gardens, centres open to the public that performed the functions of the display, acclimatization and study of wild animals. This discourse, in fact, is well dissected by Davis in her study on the SeaWorld parks, which not only implicitly link their design to the concept of a park but also have, as a theme, nature itself, in this case, marine life. 'Seaworld's spectacular nature' says Davis, 'is a medium that connects customers to nature and, in the ordered theme park world, to each other and to themselves. In this way, it both continues and revises the quasi religious nineteenth-century tradition of nature as a self-discovery and gives domination of nature a gentle, civilized face' (Davis, 1997, 35).

Even so, it cannot be forgotten that, with industrialization, the creation of parks and gardens became a reaction to urbanization. Nature, whether in its pure state or domesticated, becomes an urban phenomenon and society tries to get closer to it either by preserving it, incorporating it into the cities or through its recreational use. Linked to the ideals of Romanticism, nature is observed as something curative and educative, 'God's visible smile on mankind', in the words of William Cullen Bryant (cited by Nye, 1981, 63). Outside towns and cities, Yellowstone (1872) symbolizes the bid to preserve natural areas and open them up for public enjoyment. At the same time, in the towns themselves the opening up of empty areas for the enjoyment of the emerging middle classes was under way:

> In 1812 Philadelphia landscaped five acres of the east bank of the Schuykill River. In this same century, Central Park was designed by F.L. Olmsted and Calbert Vaux in 1858 to furnish New Yorkers with a 'harmonizing influence' and 'to cultivate among the community loftier and more refined desires'.
>   (Nye, 1981, 63–64)

This, however, is another tradition. Finally, authors like Samuelson and Yegoiants (2001) also affirm that the roots of North American amusement parks are in the characteristic 'picnic groves' of Atlantic coast holiday 'resorts'.

For Burns (1988), 'picnic groves' are the American equivalent of the European 'pleasure gardens'. Based on the American tradition of landscapes, 'picnic groves' changed as of the early 19th century from recreational meeting places to veritable beach resorts. In 1859, 12,000 people met at the Martha's Vineyard Camp Meeting one Sunday in August. Current resorts like Newport on Rhode Island, Long Branch in New Jersey or Saratoga Springs in New York were developed as the train made them more accessible in the 1830s. They were places that were initially reserved for the elite and little by little became frequented by the masses. On their premises, adult-oriented entertainment took place, animals were exhibited and games for children were promoted. Rather than a classic reference of amusement parks, Coney Island itself was, in the 1850–1860 period, a bathing resort with areas that more closely resembled European 'pleasure gardens' than the later amusement parks.

1.2. Lessons from the Universal Expositions

According to Canogar (1992, 19) 'carnival, fairs and markets fused in the 19th century arriving at the new formula of industrial exhibitions. Such precedents served as conceptual models that were to enjoy an undeniable major role in the later development of universal expositions'. Universal expositions appeared, from the mid-19th century, as areas for the representation of modernity and progress (see in Table 1.2, for the purposes of illustration, the official name of the expositions prior to the Second World War). Unlike conventional fairs, whose main function was to exchange goods,

Table 1.2. Universal expositions prior to the Second World War (from Canogar, 1992).

Year	Venue	Name	Dimensions (ha)	Visitors (millions)
1851	London	Great Exhibition of the Works of Industry of All Nations	10.4	6
1855	Paris	Exposition Universelle des Produits de l'Industrie	13.6	5.1
1862	London	International Exhibition of 1862	10	6.2
1867	Paris	Exposition Universelle	50	11
1873	Vienna	Weltausstellung Wien	250	7.2
1876	Philadelphia	Centennial Exposition	175	10.1
1878	Paris	Exposition Universelle	70	16
1879	Sydney	International Exhibition Sydney	6	1.1
1880	Melbourne	International Exhibition	19.2	1.3
1888	Barcelona	Exposición Universal de Barcelona	N/A	N/A
1889	Paris	Exposition Universelle	90	32.2
1893	Chicago	World's Columbian Exposition	278	27.3
1900	Paris	Exposition Universelle	69.2	6.1
1904	St. Louis	Louisiana Purchase Exposition	508	19.6
1906	Milan	Esposizione Internazionale	100	5.5
1910	Brussels	Exposition Universelle et Internationale	88	13
1911	Turin	Esposizione Internazionale d'Industria e de Laboro	98.8	4
1913	Ghent	Exposition Universelle et Industrielle	123.6	11
1915	San Francisco	Panama–Pacific Exposition	254	18
1929	Barcelona	Exposición Internacional de Barcelona	120	n/a
1933	Chicago	A Century of Progress – International Exhibition	169.6	48.7
1935	Brussels	Exposition Universelle et Internationale de Bruxelles	125	20
1937	Paris	Exposition Internationale des Arts et Techniques dans la Vie Moderne	100	34
1939	New York	New York's World Fair	486.4	44.9

universal expositions were aimed at encouraging consumption, ideological persuasion based on the idea of progress and the dissemination of technological breakthroughs.

According to Adams (1991, 21), the 1893 universal exposition of Chicago is fundamental in understanding the step from amusement to theme parks. In fact, according to Zukin (1995, 56), together with the one held in 1939 in Flushing Meadows, the Chicago exposition shaped Walt Disney's idea of creating 'a place for people to find happiness and knowledge'.

Chicago's was a magnificent event (covering 278 ha, it occupied three times as much space as its predecessor, Paris in 1889) which projected – *avant la lettre* – the future development of illusory areas as theme parks. The extraordinary landscape of a macro-city – White City – was created with over 400 buildings, which, made of perishable materials, for the first time ephemerally represented a function instead of just housing it (in the fifth month of the exposition and before its closure, the buildings started to crumble). Canogar (1992) says that:

> the uniformity of the neo-classic style bestowed an image of authority and order to the architectural group which dramatically contrasted with the chaos of the city of Chicago. More importance had been given to the superficial effect of the buildings than to the exhibitional content of the different galleries.

On the other hand, at the universal exposition of Chicago, hygiene and sanitary systems were established – for the first time at an event of such characteristics – and, as in today's parks – with the dual function of transport and a ride – internal transport systems were developed within the exposition itself. These include mechanical walkways that moved at a constant speed allowing the masses to move in disciplined fashion, for example, and the public access by tram to the exposition. In fact, the exposition was a laboratory for experimentation with new forms of transport. Finally, Chicago's was, according to Botterill (1997), the first universal exposition that implemented a large-scale international advertising campaign. In conceptual terms, the universal exposition of Chicago did not represent an escape from the city but, fundamentally, like theme parks of today, an idealization and amplification of it. The themes behind the exposition were enlightenment, national pride and progress. The exposition was pure movement and mechanical technology. The urban aspect of the exposition was ideal for the creation of a meeting place that was conducive to art, inspiration, education, social participation, trade and good living.

According to Nye (1981, 65), the basis of the success of the universal exposition of Chicago was the Midway Plaisance, a kilometre-and-a-half-long walk full of shops, shows and games run by private enterprises, which can be considered the seed of the availability of these elements at today's parks (Nye, 1981, 64–65). The Midway Plaisance, with representations of a street in Cairo, a Persian palace, a Turkish village, a Japanese bazaar, Kilauea volcano, a Viennese café or, among other things, a scale model of the Eiffel Tower, was a concession to popular taste in contrast to the grandiosity and refinement of White City (Adams, 1991, 68). Canogar (1992) says, referring to this, that 'the proletariat of Chicago, intimidated by the grand ideological messages of the rest of the exposition, felt far more relaxed in the Midway Plaisance'. In fact, its takings were the principal cause of the positive economic result of the Chicago exposition.

The Midway Plaisance housed, furthermore, the Ferris wheel, the exposition's fundamental icon: a wheel that reached the height of 18 floors with a structure weighing 1080 t, on which during the exposition 1,453,611 people rode in exchange for 50 cents for a 20-min thrill. It was the first great machine exclusively for ludic and commercial purposes. It was the first recreational icon that fully captured the imagination of North Americans. The Midway Plaisance offered, therefore, a new set of sensations for the emerging middle-class North Americans who had witnessed, through fantasy, the illusory possibility of discovering the whole world. For the first time, as Zukin (1995) points out, the architecture and representations reduced the realizations of the universal culture to a few tourist signs. Its success made it, furthermore, a fundamental model for future leisure precincts. At each successive universal exposition, the spectacles were more mechanized. Canogar (1992) says that 'the mechanical attractions were favoured by the proletariat classes, the social group with greatest contact with machines in factories'.

The success of the universal exposition of Chicago proved the existence in the USA already since the end of the 19th century of millions of people willing to pay to be entertained and, if necessary, even travel. Railway and tram companies, breweries, local entrepreneurs and a wide variety of corporations entered, as of the early years of the 20th century, what one observer of the time denominated fairground/amusement park hysteria.

As for the universal exposition of New York of 1939, it used the future as its main thread. The organizers decided to create a futuristic landscape. The creation of atmosphere and space is this exposition's great contribution to today's concept of a theme park. As Canogar (1992, 73) says, 'the exposition was conceived as a total experiment where the tiniest detail would contribute to creating the fantasy of the future'. To achieve this, it was most important for the buildings 'to look' modern rather than being really novel. What was most relevant was the general orientation rather than the architectonic details. The buildings were aerodynamic, sculptural, capable of captivating at a mere glimpse. Canogar (1992, 74) states that, in fact, the exposition was 'a Las Vegas at an embryonic stage . . . A place where the pavilions did not exist so much to shelter as to communicate . . . A new architecture of mass communication was being formalised within the precinct of the New York exposition.'

A white sphere, Perisphere, together with a 183-m-high needle-shaped tower, Trylon, anticipated the future which the exposition evoked. The sphere symbolized the values of democracy, capitalism and international trade. Inside it there was a complex diorama called 'Democracy', which transported the spectator to a day in a city in the year 2039. But the most frequented spectacle was Futurama, a gigantic mobile diorama that transported the 27,000 daily visitors through a futuristic landscape of 1960 along a 480-m-long circuit in 15 min. It was the origin of the packetization of visitors on 'dark rides' that later evolved in theme parks. The interesting thing is, apart from the operational aspects, that 'Democracy' was inspired, from the urban point of view, by Ebenezer Howard's garden city models, whereas Futurama drew its inspiration from the utopian models of Le Corbusier, both of whom were designers possessing absolute faith in the virtues of technology. In addition, both aimed to contribute a global vision (the city controlled through design and the architect's eye) that would put an end to the confusion that was so common in urban life – something which, in their very design, is very much taken into account by theme parks today as regards ordered, controlled areas that are set apart from the chaos of the environment. It is not surprising, in any case, that the two architects have been considered fundamental from the point of view of totalitarian architectural projects or by corporations like General Motors, also interested in efficiently mobilizing large numbers of people.

Finally, the universal exposition of New York signals a last milestone from the perspective of theme parks. For the first time, the organizers had the explicit aim of facilitating the implantation of a market of a mass consumption so as to boost the city's industrial production, which had been paralysed since the stock exchange crash of 1929. It was this, the exposition, which, ideologically, catapulted domestic electrical artefacts as elements of daily welfare. The figure of spectator, characteristic of previous expositions, became synonymous with that of consumer. As of this moment, says Canogar (1992, 83), 'the new consumer no longer invested his money in a useful instrument, rather in the image of a social position, prestige, or lifestyle that that object granted'. Later, consumer culture reached the theme parks, not just from the point of view of the park as a place to consume but as a place of representation. Thus, just to cite one example, producers of everyday consumer items like Carnation bought the rights to sell, promote and market at Disney in exchange for helping to run one or another ride (Davis, 1997, 22).

1.3. Amusement Parks' Entertainment Background

Botterill (1997) distinguishes two moments in the step from pre-modern fairs as recreational scenarios to amusement parks. Until the second half of the 17th century, fairs were, fundamentally, like carnivals, moments linked to the religious calendar at which the celebration brought together nobles and craftsmen, clergy and farmers. As of this moment, the progressive formation of bourgeois groups and the incorporation of knowledge into the values that were prized by such social groups transformed the sense and contents of fairs. The dominant social groups built new forms of political organization such as the nation-state, they based their enrichment on a renewed use of private property as an instrument for the generation of profit and gradually created, thanks, among other things, to progressive technological advances and the demographic explosion, markets that allowed them to mass-produce. These social groups, in their search for elements of distinction and for the identification of their capacity for success, in the end eliminated the fair as a classic recreational area and produced new specific environments to satisfy their need for leisure. New areas appeared, such as gardens and spas in the sea (in this case for curative purposes); the theatre was banished from the streets to new, distinguished buildings and street entertainment ensured its survival in the form of travelling circuses. Moreover, at the end of the 18th century and the beginning of the 19th, the social organization of work facilitated the appearance of entrepreneurs of entertainment who 'produce for the people' what was previously self-generated. In this way, the public uses and habits associated with entertainment were, in fact, privatized.

In short, at the end of the 19th century the entertainment area ceased to be known as a fair (a concept linked to notions like market and feast) and took on the name of park (a concept linked to notions like public area and recreation). As Botterill (1997) mentions, the step from fair to park reveals the depth of change. The 20th century was, in fact, the period of conceptual and material creation of areas for public recreation. Juxtaposing the word 'park' and the concept of entertainment, pioneer entrepreneurs in the business of amusement parks take advantage of (and prevaricate over), at the end of the 19th century, the movement that associated the idea of a park and that of public space. Furthermore, they located their product in the orbit of the new instruments (of planning) that allowed people to 'escape' from the tribulations of everyday life. Once again in the words of Botterill (1997, 78), it does not cease to be 'ironic that at a period in history when the amusementscape would be completely enclosed, privatized, and commodified, it should come to be known as a "park" (or public space)'.

Fairs are, without a doubt, the spatial and recreational formulas that preceded amusement parks. In the step from fairs to amusement parks, what is also observed is the evolution from the scenarios of entertainment 'produced by' communities to the scenarios of entertainment 'produced for' individuals (these latter attain their greatest size with theme parks). Fairs were in the 18th century, and are today, an area concentrating traders, non-permanent food, drinks and amusement establishments. The entertainment was obtained through spectacles showing strange animals and humans, wild animals, minstrels and magicians, automats, acrobats, singers, musicians and dancers and theatre plays. They were, unlike amusement parks that 'manufactured' the sensations as in the 19th century, areas of shared experiences. Without a doubt, the availability of electricity, mechanical breakthroughs, changes in the distribution of personal and family time associated with work and free time and the development first of the railway and later motor transport favoured the creation of amusement parks as specific areas for recreation.

An additional aspect is that amusement parks rapidly turn into places for the masses. With them is born the philosophy of volume or, technically speaking, the search for economies of scale that allowed the adjustment of operational costs to the spending power of the working class. Indirectly, the need to generate a product for the masses caused the consequent generalization of the demand for them. At the beginning of the 20th century, the progressively higher income, transformation undergone by the working classes of the larger towns and cities from manufacturing industries to the services, reduced working hours counterbalanced by more free time, improvement in urban public transport systems, electricity and the appearance of new mass communications systems such as the radio did the rest (Adams, 1991). Thus became constituted, as Nye (1981, 65) points out, parks that were never a place for rest, but rather places for one to participate, with noise, jostle, light, colour and activity, intensified places where you could identify 'the full sense of humanity'.

In the USA, amusement parks reached their greatest splendour during the first decade of the 20th century, with Coney Island (promoted from the start, among others, by George Tilyou, failed buyer of the Ferris wheel exhibited at the universal exposition of Chicago of 1893) as one of its most complete, most studied and best-known manifestations. In reality, there were four parks that enjoyed different degrees of success and mixed trajectories (Sea Lion Park, 1895; Steeplechase Park, 1897; Luna Land, 1902; Dreamland, 1911) in an area that, in fact, was initially a collection of rides that ended up being separated into different parks. The Coney Island parks were located in the most promising metropolis in the world at the time when they were developed, and placed beside the sea and so touched by the mystique of the sea's curative properties. Coney Island is, according to Canogar (1992, 66), 'a technological paradise constructed for the amusement and escapism of the city of New York's immigrants at the beginning of the 20th century'.

From the moon to the depths of the sea, Coney Island turns the world into something beyond the day-to-day, a spectacle lived through simulated landscapes and shows. Dioramas and images catch your eye while the mechanical rides cause new bodily sensations (Weedon and Ward, 1981). The oriental architecture, the indiscriminate use of electric light and the pre-eminence of mechanical equipment imitated the Midway Plaisance (Canogar, 1992). Technology usually used in the workplace becomes technology for leisure and changes habits and behaviour. Technology, illusion and psychology come together to create a cultural product that bases its ability to attract on its alternative character to everyday life and its irreverence towards established culture. Botterill (1997, 93) is radical when he states that, in short, 'Coney structured leisure practices acceptable to the new middle class, and provided exotic substitutes for foreign travel for the working class'.

Ouset (1986b) identifies American amusement parks with his use of the expression Luna-Park, which, though specific to the Coney Island park, would end up becoming a generic term as of the 1920s to define mechanical amusement parks. Among the rides of these parks, the big wheel could not be left out (a tradition started at the universal exposition of Chicago), or imaginary, scenic train rides (the first of which took place at the universal exposition of Buffalo in 1901, a trip to the moon), or exotic cities (for example the Venetian canals of Sea Lion Park in Coney Island), extraordinary shows such as the fire at Dreamland Park (also on Coney Island) or roller coasters. The precedent of this type of ride is also European. It was the adaptation of slippery ice surfaces, which had existed since the 17th century in Russia and which became popular throughout Europe as of the 19th century.

In any case, the evolution of amusement parks cannot be separated, in the initial stages, from the emergence of the railway network. In some cases, the tram companies themselves acted as agents in the development of parks at one of the terminals that they managed. They are the so-called 'trolley-parks' (Burns, 1988), which allowed companies, first in New England but later more generalized, to keep passenger numbers up during the weekends. The instrumental nature, keeping train line revenues up, meant that, when it was possible to gain revenue with other lines, the railway companies quickly forgot about the parks, selling them, at best, to circus companies or as places for travelling fairs. This time, for this type of park, marked the beginning of a process of degradation, quickly leading to their loss of popularity and to closure.

In Europe, the first and main manifestation of the American tradition of amusement was Blackpool Pleasure Beach, founded in 1896 by G.W. Bean after a period spent residing in the USA, where he observed the growth of the phenomenon. In addition to Blackpool, characteristic of this tradition of places for entertainment are the piers located at coastal spa resorts. Now, there is a tendency to also consider the existence of a characteristic European tradition that derives from the pleasure gardens and, more concretely, from the use in such gardens of multiple mechanical vehicles of entertainment. Ouset (1986b) argues, to this effect, that a clear difference exists between European amusement parks, direct descendants of the gardens of the 18th and 19th centuries, and the American parks, veritable artificial areas, both due to the importance given to the mechanical rides and to resorting to fiction or theming. To give a specific example, Bakken park, which still exists near Copenhagen as a theme park, opened in 1583 as a garden for public use. The characteristic example of this European tradition is the Prater of Vienna, with rides like wooden Ferris wheels and one of the first roller coasters set in extraordinarily pleasant surroundings.

The Prater of Vienna is a good illustration of the European tradition of amusement parks (O'Brien, 1981). Sited on the outskirts of the old town, it was originally a private hunting ground for the imperial household on the banks of the Danube, half an hour from the palace, which, in 1766, Joseph II opened to the public in the form of a park for the Viennese. The area was gardened and concessions were immediately given to set up drinks and food stalls as well as rides, entertainment and shows featuring exotic animals. In one section it later housed the universal exposition of 1873. The sector given over to entertainment in the Prater is, since its beginnings to the present, the 'Wurstelprater'. Destroyed during the Second World War and rebuilt in the same style, the rides and services of the Prater, located on public land, are, unlike what happens at North American amusement parks, operated under licence by numerous agents. Deeply rooted in Viennese popular culture, the Prater is also a reference point for the city, with rides that have become family traditions, such as the miniature tramway inaugurated in 1928. To visit the park, still today, means being able to do a multitude of activities, from the rides to sports activities, eating or dancing. Unlike other metropolitan places of entertainment, like the aforementioned Coney Island in the case of New York, the Viennese 'have maintained a balance between the enjoyment of nature and the pleasures of an amusement area' (O'Brien, 1981, 82).

Between 1930 and 1950, the popularity of amusement parks began to slump, first in the USA and later in Europe. The 1929 crisis and the Second World War were key in this process of decline, especially in the USA. According to Rebori (1995a, 2), at this time, most parks fell victim to a gradual loss of affluence. In addition to the changes in people's lifestyle and parks' loss of ability to create distinction, the poor maintenance and management, together with a growing bad reputation as being dirty, unsafe places, led to the loss of their role in the imagination of the popular culture of the working classes. Even so, today over 600 amusement parks subsist in the USA alone, and their ability to attract lives on (O'Brien, 1994).

1.4. The Language of the Cinema

As Lanquar reports (1991), after opening Universal Studios in Hollywood in 1915, for 25 cents Carl Laemmle promoted a visit to the film studios between scenes, even selling picnics in the precincts. The appearance of the spoken cinema and the consequent need for silence on the sets interrupted this initiative, which only picked up again as of 1963, with coach visits beneath the studios. Such visits became, in 1964, the basis for Universal Studios' theme park in Los Angeles and, beyond the bounds of the park, the embryo of one of the biggest corporation of parks in the world as regards the number of visitors. Now, this is the anecdotal aspect of the relationship between parks and the cinema. In fact, it is not just that precedents of parks can be found in the visits to film studios themselves but it is the language of the cinema that is incorporated into the system of presenting the reality of parks: hence, today, one of the reasons for their success.

The strategy of unifying themes which is so particular to parks is nothing more than the result of transferring the concept of the stage and its ability to produce thrills to the building of a place for public use. Furthermore, as Nye (1981, 67) states, parks' theatrical elements, inspired by the cinematographic concept of the stage, have been powerfully amplified by the tendency towards 'happenings' or animations undertaken by appropriately disguised park employees. The new dimension of theme parks is,

therefore, the juxtaposition of the concept of attraction and that of communication by means of the image (the set) and animation (thematic performance). Universal Studios, even before Disney, had already understood
this when they considered that cinema production itself, with its sets,
techniques and studios, could be the object of a visit and of entertainment
(even of a cultural and pedagogical nature, elements that are being increasingly recovered by theme parks, unlike amusement parks). On the other
hand, it cannot be forgotten that Walt Disney was a man of the film industry (Bryman, 1995), specialized, moreover, in the art of animation. Rebori
(1995b, 2) states, to this effect, that, already with his first park, Disney 'capitalized on America's fascination with film and television, by incorporating
them into the marketing and design of his parks'. Visitors to theme parks
can be considered, therefore, as the audience of an experience which, like
cinematography, takes place via scenes and sets in the framework of fantasy
surroundings of a multidimensional nature. As in the parks, the cinema
reshapes reality in the form of a spectacle.

This is so much so that, according to Botterill (1997), Disney's main
contribution to the leisure industry through parks was the means of transforming the cinema into a fair format: 'through circulating stories first
through cinema and television then onto the park, Disney revitalized the
fair for modern audiences. This process also increased the circulation of
symbolic commodities, and created synergy between media forms.' Without Disney's professional involvement in the cinema and, in particular, as
an illustrator of comics, things would have turned out quite differently.
The initial designers of the park in Anaheim were, in fact, animators, who
created, as in the cinema, a series of scenes along which people had to
move in a system of well-controlled flow. This was so much so, for example, that the average visitor spent at Disney, even in its early stages, one
hour per themed area, the same average length of time as an episode of a
television series. The parks' relationship with the cinema necessarily
implied the total theming of the milieu, not just the rides. Indirectly, on the
other hand, it stimulated consumption since it disguised the commercial
nature of the products and characters, which were naturally integrated
into the environment (Smoodin, 1994).

It cannot be forgotten, on the other hand, that the domination of the
audio-visual media in developed Western societies determines people's
perception of what is 'ordinary' and what is 'extraordinary'. This is what
happens in a cultural context that may be referred to, as in Urry (1990,
101–102), as the 'three-minute' culture. That is to say, the media have
'educated' people to constantly change the forms and places of leisure
and pleasure. Consequently, the consumption of leisure time is becoming
increasingly less a time for the strengthening and upkeep of the collective
memory (leisure 'produced by', in fair style), finally becoming a time for
the acquisition of immediate pleasure (leisure 'produced for', in park style).
Theme parks are established as extraordinary places that are perfectly
adapted to these new cultural habits produced by the media. Sorkin (1992b,
208) says to this effect that 'Television and Disneyland operate similarly,

by means of extraction, reduction and recombination to create an entirely new, antigeographical space.' The result is a highly regulated, completely synthetic vision that provides a simplified, sanitized experience.

On the other hand, it is not just that the language of the cinema conceptually conditions the design of theme parks, but it is the cinema itself that changes, from its beginnings, into a fundamental component of recreational areas. The universal exposition of Paris in 1900 widely spread the possibilities of the cinema. Over 5000 people attended the projections of the Lumière brothers every day. At the Universal Exposition of Paris, 50 years before Walt Disney's Circorama, Raoul Grimoin-Sanson had already come up with a circular building whose inside circumference was to house an endless screen, the Cineorama, where, for the four projections for which it worked, it showed panoramic images simulating being in a balloon over Paris, Nice, Biarritz, Tunis, Southampton and Barcelona. The cinema is, in fact, as parks will be, an instrument for entertainment and – why not? – knowledge. Venturi *et al.* (1972) cite, along the lines of this argument, a comment to Morris Lapidus in *Progressive Architecture* of September 1970 which certainly explains the advantage acquired by parks by associating their contents with the idea of knowledge that is implemented in the cinema as entertainment. Lapidus says:

> People are looking for Illusions; they don't want the world's realities.
> And, I asked, where do I find the world of Illusion? Where are their tastes formulated? Do they go to museums? Do they travel in Europe? Only one place – the movies. They go to the movies. The hell with everything else.

In any case, as will be seen, today the relationship between the industry of the parks and the cinema is also due to the fact that many of the major corporations that operate theme parks come from or are closely linked to the film industry and the mass media. In short, as Ren (1998) maintains, theme parks are, like advertising, characteristic products of consumer culture based on making profits from the production of meanings. The only difference between theme parks and the rest of the classic products of this economy of signs is their location in concrete places. Thus, it may be considered that theme parks are, therefore, a product based on signs and space.

Case 1. The New World in Singapore, an Early 20th-century Amusement Park in Asia

The amusement park industry in colonial Singapore arose from the opportunities offered by a burgeoning urban population. As a major Asian port of the British Empire, between the 1920s and 1930s Singapore was increasingly exposed to a wide variety of commodified spectacles, such as world fairs and trade exhibitions, which are closely associated with the development of amusement parks. The New World amusement park, opened in 1923, introduced the modern consumption and the popular entertainment culture that had emerged in Europe and in the USA around the turn of the century to colonial Singapore during the interwar period. As a precedent, there is only in Singapore the Happy Valley Park, which was founded in 1921 and ceased to operate after fewer than 10 years in business. Another internal influence for the New World amusement park was the Malaya Borneo Exhibition of 1922. In terms of external influences there were Shanghai's Great World and New World, established in 1912 and 1917, respectively, as multi-storeyed entertainment palaces that provided every day a variety of Chinese entertainment at the lowest possible price, with the largest variety of shows.

As Wong and Tan (2004) point out, the New World was first conceived and founded by two Chinese brothers, Ong Boon Tat and Ong Peng Hock, as part of a land speculation exercise. In 1938, when the park was already well established and the configuration and programmes and structures were in place, they entered a joint venture with the Shaw Brothers, moguls of Asia's film industry. The success of urban amusement parks in Shanghai was the reason why the Shaw Brothers decided to join the venture with the Ongs. In 1958, the Ongs completely relinquished their ownership to the Shaw Organization. In fact, at that time the Shaw Brothers owned and operated other amusement parks and entertainment facilities in Malaya's major cities. Today, the New World amusement park is a vacant site awaiting redevelopment.

The creation, development and evolution of the New World amusement park reveals the uniqueness and modernity of Singapore during the interwar period. It received an influence both from the Shanghai eclosion of entertainment venues and from the popular consumer culture in the West. The park was situated on the outskirts of Jalan Besar, a zone away from the developmental pressures of the central area. The development of the park was planned initially by the Ong brothers as part of one of the earliest attempts to drain comprehensively a large tract of a swamp area, in a context in which Singapore was receiving an increasing number of migrants and the middle- to upper-income households fled to suburbs in all directions around the city. The park was conceived as a value-adding leisure attraction as well as an attempt by the Ongs to diversify their assets by venturing into a nascent leisure and entertainment industry. The municipal council view the plan as an opportunity with little outlay by the colonial government to transform an otherwise flood-prone area into prime land for development.

At the beginning, the business format of the park was modelled on fairs and exhibitions, with staged shows and performances as the major attractions drawing in the masses. Tropical weather made under-the-sky night-out activities pleasant and, in fact, it maintained an open fairground-type configuration throughout its existence. In 1932, New World was rebuilt and expanded into a full-scale urban amusement park with new structures and buildings, which added complexity to the layout of the park as well as to its entertainment programmes. From then, the entertainment blueprint was firmly established, with the creation of an idealistic setting for a wider spectrum of class enclaves within one precinct. As Wong and Tan (2004) state, New World:

> offered variety and choice and non-stop offerings that could not be found in traditional cultural and entertainment venues. It was a crucible of new cultural forms, as old contents transformed to meet changing popular taste, and new ones were introduced to suit the diverse crowds.

Activities were commercially driven and audience-oriented. Thus, some were hybridized while others were emulated and transformed. Mass entertainment revealed the need to be aware of all identities as consumers were drawn from within the multiracial migrant society of colonial Singapore. New World was, in this sense, a modern cosmopolitan and non-segregated urban space in a colonial society. At the park, 'the vulgar coexisted with the refined, the low with the high, the ethnic with the contemporary' (Wong and Tan, 2004).

The history of the New World amusement park offers a new route for understanding the evolution of the modern leisure industry around the world in a colonial context. The park gives the opportunity to see the current development of entertainment facilities in Asia in the frame of a long-term process that interrelates urban planning and design, class niches, mass audience, cultural entertainment, popular practices and modernity.

2 Development and Categorization

[T]ourists had hitherto flocked to 'original' sites because they simply had no choice in the matter.

(Julian Barnes, 1998)

Davis (1997) is of the opinion that, due to its structure, its components and its conception, a theme park, despite being linked to the different traditions referred to in the previous chapter, differs significantly from its predecessors, in particular, from amusement parks. Similarly to Botterill (1997), he argues that a theme park is a cultural product of entertainment that corresponds to the needs of late-modern capitalist society and only makes sense in this context. Sorkin (1992b) is also explicit along these lines when he states that Disney evolves the ancestral concept of a fair to the limit. For him, a theme park changes the original idea of a 'celebration of production' characteristic of medieval fairs and festive encounters into a process of 'production of celebration' – of spectacle – peculiar to contemporary capitalist society. This fundamental condition symbolizes the basic difference that may be established between theme parks and conventional amusement parks (Weinstein, 1992). As Ritzer (1999) would say, a theme park is, in fact, one of the cathedrals of consumption characteristic of contemporary society. Even so, authors like Nye (1981) consider that theme parks satisfy the same utilities as their amusement park predecessors: play, escape, liberation, fantasy, emotion and a family day out.

A theme park can be characterized as a symbolic microcosm with a distinctive identity that proposes a complete emotional experience, a place of entertainment which has been provided with its own homogeneous semiotics (Mitrasinovic, 1996), which is intensely commercial and closely linked to the production of media images. Moreover, unlike other entertainment installations, a theme park regards and conveys its inauthenticity as normality. As Donaire (1999) says, a theme park is, literally, a utopia for consumption. It is not only, therefore, a place produced 'for' leisure, like the traditional amusement parks, but a place of fiction that bases its existence on the materialization of a fantastic narration through shapes, volumes and performances. It considers itself an 'alternative world', which is organized like a sequence of scenes in a film. It represents, therefore, a harmonious spectacle that can be seen, heard and lived in a different way from how life is lived conventionally.

SeaWorld is, for example, a park based on shows with and of animals. The progress of the killer whale Shamu is the object of adoration, the dolphins add amusement, Clyde and Sea is a show with sea lions while the waterski show is a sports show in purest North American style. It is all very epic, very diaphanous, very clear, very luminous. To this must be added the display halls of the different marine species, some of them in very clear aquarium format like the ones of the sharks, while others are interactive as in Key West, others are assertive, like the one that alerts us to the risk of extinction of manatees, and there are even others in the form of rides like Wild Arctic. Appropriately themed conventional rides have been added, like that of Atlantida – in Orlando – or a roller coaster, which, despite subtracting placidity from the park, situates it in a more multidimensional concept of entertainment. Here, as in other parks, visitors regard themselves as fictional co-stars (Zukin, 1995).

Besides the concept, from an operational and design point of view, according to Botterill (1997), what singularizes a theme park is its 'emphasis on control, the narration and its strategic integration in a matrix with other communication media and recreational and travel pastimes'. Lusignan (1993) reproduces a definition of Six Flags from the concept of a theme park, according to which it is a place 'in which the purpose of each detail, of both the concept and operation, is to contribute to the creation of an atmosphere of amusement and dreams'. It is also a place that has been fully designed and highly coordinated to incite consumption through the illusion of an emotion. So, whether it be 'SeaWorld, Disneyland, or Six Flags Over Texas, the theme park carefully controls the sale of goods (food and souvenirs) and experiences (architecture, rides, and performances) "themed" to the corporate owners' proprietary images' (Davis, 1997). This has clearly been, according to the same author, 'Disney's major contribution to the industry and perhaps to American culture'.

This chapter establishes, in the first part, the context and the conditions of the appearance of theme parks in the mid-20th century. In the second part, there is an explanation as to the nature of theme parks from the point of view of their fundamental singularity, the theme concept. Finally, some of the parameters of parks' recent evolution are stressed as regards their recreational format for consumption.

2.1. The Invention of Theme Parks

The North American socio-economic context from the end of the Second World War until the oil crisis of the 1970s, the period denominated by

Harvey (1990) as Fordist–Keynesian, can be characterized as a stage of the 'democratization' of access to consumption and of the dominance of the myth of the nuclear family. The urban context also takes on its own dimensions. European models of zonification disappear and the 'street culture' gives way to 'suburban culture'. Thus, urban and metropolitan centres join in chaos and degradation while a phase of suburban housing explosion is begun, led by the generation of the 'baby boom' seeking a new town environment for their families to grow up in. The city becomes diffuse and, just as in the interwar period the 'square' as a commercial space replaces department stores and towns' and cities' high streets, in the mid-1960s the suburban 'malls' become the dominant spaces for consumption.

In addition to unprecedented increased productivity, the growing mobility that dominates all aspects of modernity is key in the transformation process of post-war North American society. With universal access to the car, in the surroundings of towns motorways become areas concentrating consumption and entertainment and camping becomes a new form of recreation. In this process, access to new, varied modes of consumption becomes an indicator of status. Furthermore, leisure as a space of personal time freed from work starts to compete with the 'pleasure' generated by commercially 'produced' recreational activities to fill this leisure time. In this context, the appearance of the television as a generalized consumer object revolutionizes the cinema and entertainment industry. In fact, this new phase of transformation of North American society has been characterized as the arrival of a new stage in the idea of North American popular culture. It is in fact at the beginning of this period that Disneyland is built, on the outskirts of Los Angeles, in an easily accessible place from the freeway exit road but far enough away to retain its character of being an 'alternative world' (Findlay, 1992).

It is common knowledge that, with Disneyland, the concept of theme park materializes as it is known today. However, it cannot be forgotten that authors like Samuelson and Yegoiants (2001) are precise when stating that, 'contrary to popular belief, Walt Disney did not invent the theme park'. More concretely, according to these authors, what he created was not technically a theme park in the strict definition of the term (that is to say, with a single structuring theme) but a new genre of park that separately presents specific themed areas. For them, theme parks in the sense of parks based on just one theme existed long before Disneyland. Thus, rather than Disney, other parks ought to be considered when speaking of the first thematic facilities. Certainly the first of them in the USA must have been Knott's Berry Farm, currently operated by Cedar Fair, which was born as a sales point for forest fruit and between 1920 and the early 1950s was gradually converted by Walter Knott into a theme park. Likewise, the different parks devoted to Santa Claus should be borne in mind (Holiday Land, Santa Claus Land, Santa's Village, Santaland USA and Santa's Workshop) and those devoted to children's tales (Storybook Lands, Wisconsin Dells and Idlewild Park) which flourished in the USA between the 1940s and the 1950s.

This is an interesting appreciation that leads us to consider two key aspects in the discussion as to the origins of theme parks: first, the concept of theme as a basis of the idea of a theme park; and secondly, the idea that a theme park is a new genre of park in that its structure, organization and operational system differ from those of their forerunners. In fact, when Disneyland is spoken about as being the 'first' theme park, this is especially because, despite the fact that prior to its existence there may have been other parks with a structuring theme, it materializes for the first time and synthesizes the characteristics pertaining to the new type of parks which have ended up being called theme parks – more due to the incorporation of themes than to the existence of a single structuring theme. To this end, according to Botterill (1997), Disneyland would be a theme park because, in it, its designer, Walt Disney, and his team transform their talent and experience as comic illustrators to build 'credible illusions', emotive characters and emotionally pure drawings in landscapes for entertainment.

Unlike fairs and amusement parks, and parallel with gardens or even universal expositions, theme parks are, therefore, entertainment landscapes created by architects and planners with a concrete narrative intention. They are thus a cultural creation, in which the landscape and the relationship between spaces are fundamental and the requirements for transport, movement and mobility are studied to perfection. Also they are fortresses separated by trees and structures from the surrounding area. The purpose is to remove from the interior landscape of the park any reference to outside. This is so much so that, when in 1963 Sheraton requested from the town council of Anaheim permission to build a 22-storey building, Disney appealed on the grounds that such a building might lead to the possibility that visitors to the park would not manage to forget the outside world (Bryman, 1995). Finally, a 16-storey hotel was built and the municipality forbade tall buildings in the vicinity of Disneyland.

Also, unlike their predecessors, later theme parks are organized to make profits not just through consumption in the park and the rendering of services such as catering for weddings, parties and conventions but also thanks to brand consumption, which their visitors do inside and outside the parks. Parks are places for profit for the corporations – generally linked to media groups – who own them. In this sense, in their book on the history of North American amusement parks, Samuelson and Yegoiants (2001) speak of amusement parks surviving today as places where visitors can leap – to be entertained – into the past of more than 50, 60 or 70 years instead of falling victim to the continuous bombardment of images featuring theme parks' own television and cinema personalities.

As has been indicated, the bases of the currently acknowledged concept of theme park were set out by Disney in Anaheim. However, the first demonstration of Disney's interest in the creation of a park was simultaneous to the building of its new studios in Burbank, California, in 1939 (see Weinstein, 1992). The idea at the time was to create a small play area for children, little bigger than 3 ha in surface area, beside the film studios where photographs could be taken with their favourite cartoon characters.

In 1952, the idea of disposing of a small play area next to the studios had led to a proposal to develop a park valued at 1.5 million dollars in an area of almost 65 ha of orange trees in Anaheim, half of which it was to occupy initially. The elements which inspired and catalysed the change were, according to Samuelson and Yegoiants (2001), Disney's visit to the Chicago Railroad Fair of 1948–1949 and his stopover at Henry Ford's Greenfield Village in Dearborn, Michigan, a park given over to showing the achievements of the great inventors. Furthermore, the move from Burbank to Anaheim responded to Burbank's local administration's refusal to allow its development.

Disney's first idea for his park was based on simply building a pleasant place to present his characters, improving the standards of cleanliness and control of traditional amusement parks. In this respect, Walt Disney's aversion to Coney Island is well known. His parents would go there during the 1920s and Disney regarded it as physically and symbolically disagreeable (Weinstein, 1992). When setting up his own park, he eliminated all 'sideshows', games of chance and animals from his concept and placed more emphasis on the aspects of theming and landscape design. He also got rid of beer and hot dog stands, he improved salubrity and introduced subtle ways of controlling agglomerations of visitors. There can be no doubt that the opening of Disneyland on 17 July 1955 was to have a definitive effect on the park concept.

However, at that time, the idea seemed not to enthuse anyone whatsoever. Both the Californian financial world and his own executives were fervently opposed to the project. Moreover, without his brother Roy's support, Walt Disney had to found WED Inc. to plan, design and administer the park. In order to finance it, Disney resorted, in addition to his own funds and the concession of the building of some amusements to other corporations, to the signing of a contract with the American Broadcasting Company (ABC) – the only television network that accepted his idea and the smallest-scale network at the time. This circumstance was to be particularly relevant in the future. As a consequence of its initial link with the television market – which was also in its beginnings at the time – from the start Disneyland received much coverage in the media until it even became the operations centre of Walt Disney for television. Indeed, according to Adams (1991), Disney went as far as moulding the design of the park to its media potential. This is so much so that, in fact, the park was conceived as a mirror of the fragmented structure of the television, with half-hour- and hour-long spectacles that transport their spectators to illusory worlds in different times and places. Furthermore, this initial alliance between park and television meant it was possible to witness television and the media's ability to create synergies in order to attract visitors to the park.

This is how Disneyland was shaped as a model for successive theme parks as regards the structuring of space. It was fashioned as a place cut off from the real world with different themed sectors. The themes were based on folklore, tales, the history of America, children's literature and carnival.

The arrangement of the themes in space guaranteed fantasy. Moreover as indicated, the proposal for the use and running of the park was linked to the segmented nature of television entertainment – which was born in the same era. So, in the case of Disneyland, the visitor enters a kind of 'distribution point', which is at the end of Main Street and decides, in front of Sleeping Beauty's castle and as if using a kind of remote control, whether to visit Adventureland, Frontierland, Fantasyland or Tomorrowland. As of this point, the visit takes place through a succession of scenes and images. The changes in time and space that are rendered possible on the television screen and are a common element of cinema products take place materially in theme parks by just moving from one themed area to the next (Adams, 1991). This is, basically, the most profound change established between the conventional amusement park and a theme park.

Following the initial success of Disneyland, Six Flags Over Texas, located between Dallas and Forth Worth, a good, well-financed project whose technical design was done by Randall Duell and Associates, was the second successful theme park to open, in 1961. With intense rides as the main attraction, the park was a success both as regards the number of visitors and financially right from year one. The six flags which its name alludes to represented the six themed areas it contained, Spain, France, Mexico, the Confederation, the USA and the Republic of Texas, that is to say, the six political powers and forms of state that had dominated Texas since the arrival of the Europeans in America. This park was followed by its namesake, Six Flags Over Georgia in 1967. Well situated on the communications axes and with easy access by car from the main towns, putting emphasis on exciting rides, cleanliness, thorough maintenance and good theming and with novel characteristics such as the 'pay-one-price' access ticket, professional shows and relaxing picnic areas, the Six Flags parks broadened and improved upon the original concept of Disney. In fact, it was the success of Six Flags that formed the foundations for the expansion of the business of theme parks in the USA as of the 1970s. If Disney invented the concept, the Six Flags parks of the first era put their finger on the formula.

However, expansion and generalization were not immediate. First of all, the owners of amusement parks questioned the suitability of the Disney design. Without popular rides and with a large amount of space that was not generating direct income, they were of the opinion that the model would be certain to fail. On the other hand, as Adams (1991) reports, between 1955 and 1967, the date of the opening of Six Flags Over Georgia, there were other initiatives that resulted in failure. This is the case of Denver Magic Mountain, which was to open in 1958 but was never built due to problems of financing; Pleasure Island near Boston, which had to be rescaled as a small, conventional amusement park; Pacific Ocean Park in Santa Monica, with high operative costs which brought it into bankruptcy; and, perhaps the most famous flop, Freedomland, a park built in the heart of the Bronx in New York, designed by an ex-Disneyland director, inaugurated in 1960 and closed down in 1964. In any case, what the first steps of the new business of theme parks demonstrated was that the size of the investment required to develop them was only possible if their developers were large corporations. Traditional family operators of amusement parks remained outside the sector.

Finally, it cannot be forgotten that Disneyland's opening day was a disaster: an excess of visitors, who were not handled properly; several of the park's initial 11 rides did not work properly; the staff, who had not yet been trained, were not sufficiently attentive towards the public; and unfavourable weather conditions, in particular, the heat that melted the asphalt, did the rest. In fact, the press qualified it a fiasco (Adams, 1991). Now, Disney learnt from this first day's failure and adjusted the park to a model that has proved to be a success. In fact, the new genre of parks created by Disney is not that of the year of inauguration but the one which, having been touched up, was in full functioning and performance in the mid-1960s. Thus, during the decade after its inauguration, Disneyland adjusted basic elements such as access control. It also introduced a pay-one-price admission system to the park (a system thought up by Six Flags and which is today widespread in the sector) instead of the system of price-per-ride with which the park had been inaugurated, it began to conceive 'pre-entertainment' areas as queue management systems, it promoted the 'desire' for souvenirs among its visitors, it emphasized security and safety. It progressively increased the number of rides. It institutionalized, in short, the idea of interminable improvement and novelty that characterizes consumer culture. Also, from the beginning it was interested in finding out its visitors' opinions and was able to construct a halfway house between people's desires and its idea of business. For example, in the opinion of Botterill (1997), it realized the public's desire for mechanical rides but maintained its vision of contextualizing them by means of a theme. This is the case of Space Mountain, Bobsled or Splash Mountain. In short, the medium-term success of Disneyland in Anaheim stimulated a complete new cycle of the growth of theme parks and its essential idea was replicated and, in some aspects, improved upon, initially in the USA and later abroad.

2.2. The Nature of Theme Parks

Leaving aside other conceptual and operational questions, the most immediately perceptible difference between an amusement park and a theme park lies in the fact that, whereas amusement parks present numerous attractions in a relatively small area, each of which has a specific price, theme parks present a small number of attractions in a large-scale, landscaped environment – which does not generate revenue directly – at a generally unique price (Zukin, 1995). But, in contrast, this environment is meticulously designed to handle visitors so that they are entertained and, especially, so that they spend money in an orderly, safe, relaxed atmosphere (Nye, 1981). This is the case, for example, of Universal Studios' park in Orlando, Islands of

Adventure. It is an intense, dense, compressed park like a page in a colour comic. It seems that it is dominated by a kind of *horror vacui*, a fear of empty space, and hence the texture, colour, intensity and power of designed space, beyond the rides and shows. Below we define the concept of the theme park and then discuss the role of theming as a distinguishing basis of this type of recreational facility.

2.2.1. Definition and types

According to Tourism Research and Marketing (TRM, 1995), historically, making a precise definition of the concept of theme park has been avoided due to the existence of multiple similar formats that hinder such a task. Moreover, the definitions that have been made have generally been seen to be incomplete or inaccurate. They often do not allow the specific differentiation of theme parks from other types of recreational park. Thus, for example, Coltier (1985, 24) defines a theme park as 'a closed universe whose purpose is to succeed in the encounter between the dreamy atmosphere it creates and the visitor's desire for *dépaysement*'. The means to achieve it is the theme (Wong and Cheung, 1999). This is why some authors choose to define parks on the basis of a series of characteristics (see, regarding this, the attempts at characterization by Chassé, 1993a; Milman, 1993; Sánchez, 1998; Jones *et al.*, 1998). In general terms, no characteristic taken individually suffices to differentiate a theme park from other attractions but all of them are necessary. To this end, below we present a characterization that allows one to positively identify theme parks as ludic places consecrated to distraction, evasion, imagination, knowledge and play on the basis of a series of criteria and differentiating them from other parks and recreational areas. Theme parks are recreational areas, therefore, where the following characteristics can be observed:

1. They have a thematic identity that determines recreational alternatives.
2. They contain one or more themed areas.
3. They are organized as closed spaces or with controlled access.
4. They have a great capacity to attract families.
5. They contain enough rides, shows and systems of movement to create a visit that lasts on average some 5 to 7 h.
6. They present atmospheric forms of entertainment (musicians, characters or actors who perform in the street 'free of charge').
7. They have an important commercial vocation (fundamentally food and beverages and shops).
8. They have high levels of investment per unit of ride or show capacity.
9. They have high-quality products, service, maintenance and standards of cleanliness.
10. They manage their productive and consumer processes centrally.
11. They incorporate technology as much in the production processes as in those of consumption.

12. Generally, though exceptions do exist, they have a single ('pay-one-price') admission system.

On the basis of these general characteristics, several types of theme parks can be distinguished (Table 2.1). There are two basic criteria to establish the typology of parks: (i) the size, which can be evaluated by the number of visitors, the surface area that they occupy, the number of employees they have or the necessary investment for their development (all of which are closely related variables); and (ii) the dominant markets according to their origin. Because of their operational and design implications, the use of these two criteria is one of the most common ways to categorize parks, especially because of the fact that they distinguish between urban, regional and destination parks. These criteria are less clearly related when dealing with niche parks. However, this typological categorization may be purely illustrative since, depending on other variables, significant variations may occur in each of the types of park. There are, in fact, other categorizations that can be made. They deal with the seasonal nature of parks, the type of dominant rides, contents, the ownership of the park and their turnover (for further information, see Lanquar, 1991; Braun, 1993; Anton Clavé, 2001).

Destination parks are those that have been specifically designed to attract a large number of visitors coming from places located at middle and long distance and who spend a night at the said destination with the main aim of visiting the park (often for more than one day). Generally this type of park includes accommodation and other attractions in the product mix so as to encourage staying overnight. Most Disney parks, together with some of Universal's, can be considered destination parks. They are parks that are usually very sensitive to economic, social and political variations that affect the consumers' susceptibility to travel. The larger ones usually require investments of over €1000 million and generate over 5 million visits a year. They are intensely themed parks, with different areas in which the main attractions and brand images are located.

Table 2.1. Types of theme parks (from author's own research).

Type	Investment (million €)	Visitors (million)	Attractions	Demand
Destination	Over 250	From 3.5	Over 55	Tourist demand can reach over 50%
Regional	Between 100 and 250	From 1.5 to 3.5	35–50	Tourist demand up to 25%
Urban	Between 80 and 100	Between 0.75 and 1.5	25–35	95% from the immediate urban areas
Niche	Between 10 and 80	Up to 0.75	Variable	Variable

Regional parks have been designed to attract a significant number of visitors during a few hours per day. Most visitors to this type of park come from areas located some 100–200 km away. Among them we should also consider some parks located in tourist destinations such as PortAventura, which, though not places of destination, become parks that are visited by a significant percentage of tourists due to their location in a tourist region and their tourist appeal. The principal operator of this type of park is, without a doubt, Six Flags. Other parks such as those of SeaWorld in the USA, Europa Park in Europe or Ocean Park in Hong Kong belong to this category. They are characterized by the strength of their rides and shows, although their theming is not as intense as in the previous type mentioned. In some cases, such as Six Flags or SeaWorld, theming evokes the operator's corporate concept.

Thirdly, there are parks of a local scope, parks visited almost exclusively by residents of the immediate urban area. Six Flags is also the dominant operator of this kind of park. They are highly ride-oriented and their theming is more limited. They are closer, therefore, to conventional amusement parks. Isla Mágica in Europe, Elitch Gardens in the USA and Enchanted Kingdom in the Philippines are good illustrations of this sort of park.

The creation of destination parks and the increase in the demand for regional parks by means of the flows of tourists are only possible through the intense development of a wide variety of rides with the aim of increasing the length of stay at the park. For this, night-time entertainments are especially needed (ranging from firework displays to *son et lumière* shows) and special events and the location of new recreational facilities in their surroundings. Peripheral developments may include hotels, commercial areas, water parks and other theme and/or recreational parks and their integration within larger-scale mixed projects (including cinemas, simulators, family entertainment centres (FECs), restaurants and residences). This is also, in fact, a fundamental difference between theme parks and their amusement park predecessors. Basically, what parks try to develop today is a complete holiday experience. To do so, they develop accommodation systems and areas for night-time entertainment. The hotels, moreover, lead to an increase in the per capita revenue for the park, since visitors usually go there on more than one day. In addition, this type of park can be integrated within rehabilitation projects for urban, peri-urban or run-down areas. This is the case, for example, of the Osaka seafront (Universal Studios Japan).

The main reasons that justify the dynamic of the integration of parks in environments of leisure and consumption are, in short, of an operative and financial nature, namely:

• Ensuring a good length of stay (7 h for several days).
• Creating overnight stays through the diversification of the market.
• Developing comparative advantages by broadening the market.
• Inducing return visits.

- Generating revenue by taking advantage of the demand for the principal attraction.
- Increasing the value of the land.

In an inverse sense, but along the same lines of creating destinations, covered parks are arising in commercial areas, among which we can cite the best known, which are those in West Edmonton Mall in Canada, Lotte World in Seoul and Mall of America in Minneapolis. In addition, it may be said that, in suburban environments throughout the world, amusement parks are designed as integral parts of commercial complexes (Madrid Xanadú, for example).

Finally, there exists one last specific type of park which is harder to classify given the variability of their demand, depending on characteristics such as the urban or rural location of the park and its argumental content. We refer to niche parks, small-sized recreational areas given over to a specific theme receiving 0.75 to 1 million visitors at most, with a limited number of attractions (normally 20 at most) and costing some €10 million. In urban environments, they normally become urban entertainment centres. In the event that they are located in rural areas with a certain ability to attract, they may attain significant numbers of tourists. Some such parks are, in the USA, Holyland Experience, which was inaugurated in February 2001 in Orlando, recreating the life of Jesus Christ and the Holy Land (Sargent, 2001) or the Bonfante Gardens in California, whose aim is to educate visitors as to horticulture and the role played by trees in everyday life. Sesame Place, in the north of Philadelphia, oriented at boys and girls of between 2 and 13 years of age, which reproduces the famous Sesame Street characters, can also be categorized as a niche park. Again notable, along such lines, are the multitude of parks which, as we shall see, are being developed in Europe on this same level and to the same scale.

On the basis of this characterization, a theme park can be considered a system of representation of changeable scale whose purpose is entertainment and consumerism. For Ren (1998), a theme park is, more specifically, the landscape resulting from a cultural representation: a place where knowledge and technology are applied to the creation of a new form of organization of production based on signs and space. Based on this, parks are planned in order to materialize a commercial atmosphere in which the basic management principle is that of getting visitors to move, have a good time and spend. To do so, according to Adams (1991) parks like Disney embrace 'control, exclusivity, minute planning, and fastidious sanitation to actualize a segregated promised land of perfection where technology solves all of civilization's problems and at the same time engineers entertainment extravaganzas'. More generally, parks offer a model of the creation of a system of social order – clean, safe and regulated – in an overcrowded space. In such a landscape, the social relations of production are rendered structurally invisible whereas the presence of the processes aimed at consumption are magnified. Thus, the very organization of the park segregates maintenance and supply work, which are kept hidden so as not to distract the visitors from their participation in a ludic and pleasurable act. In addition, reinforcing the perception of the park as a place for entertainment, the process of production is disconnected from the process of consumption. In this context, the theme park as a means of institutionalizing the conversion of symbolic capital into productive capital is done via an appropriate structuring of the narrative it offers, that is to say, the theme.

2.2.2. The concept and the utilities of the themes

The fundamental issue which gives a park its character is its physical and symbolic structuring around a theme (Samuelson and Yegoiants, 2001). The aim of theming is to facilitate the organization of a complex, recreational proposal around a single conceptual resolution. The theme must refer to a story, an argument, which the visitor will assimilate during his visit in a progressive process of identification. The physical, landscape and aesthetic characteristics of the surroundings provide the forms. For this, park designers use a wide variety of artefacts, ingredients, styles, architecture and exhibitions. Theming means, therefore, providing a product with content and establishing the symbolic need to consume it. A theme is, from this point of view, the seminal basis of the forms and contents of a park and the most relevant part of the visitor's experience. Chazaud (1998) has determined the following characteristics concerning what constitutes good theming:

1. The theme must be sufficiently rich to allow a *mise-en-scène*. The semantic field of the theme must be well defined.
2. The theme, which must be adaptable to a visit, an animation or an entertainment, has to be declinable and able to be broken down into sub-elements. It must be able to facilitate an approach by scenic and dramatic stages.
3. The theme must provide identity, a suitable image for the chosen place and positive differentiation from other parks.
4. The theme must give cohesion to the whole and to the marketing strategy, positioning, media presence, space organization and animation.

The realization of a park's themed contents can be done in three different ways (Wong and Cheung, 1999):

*   Through a single theme throughout every aspect of the park, as in the case of Warner Bros.
*   Through easily identifiable sub-themes in different areas or nodes of the park, as is the case of Disneyland with Frontierland, Adventureland, Fantasyland, Discoveryland and Main Street USA.
*   Through transitional themes, that is to say, themes that are created on the occasion of special events which are only running during concrete periods of time, as is the case of Halloween in many parks worldwide.

In any case, the theme must fulfil the aim of offering conceptual identity and formal coherence to the product. Hence, taking it yet further, the theme can be spoken of from three perspectives: as an argument, as an organizational foundation and as a marketing strategy. This is why it must be said right from the start that the production of a themed environment is very costly and requires the centralized control of a great many factors.

1. The theme as an argument. A theme is an argument that gives content and structure and provides all the elements of a recreational product or facility with discourse and form. In a park, each thematic node and each attraction is created not just in respect of a desirable objective image but in respect of an account, a specific narration which runs transversally throughout the whole project and substantivates all of its components. Theming implies, therefore, establishing the bases of functioning in the time and space of the universe that is created or recreated. As Swartzman (1995) states, theming is to do with the use of the story, spectacle and technology in the creation of an atmosphere of entertainment that fosters a fantasy, location or idea. This is why theming implies creating special atmospheres and causing specific emotional responses from the consumers. Despite seeming paradoxical, what is expected of theming is that it should be 'authentic' in its strategy to respond to the imaginary expected by the visitor. For this, according to Mongon (2001a,b), it is necessary not to intellectualize the argumental discourse but to have a special devotion to detail and apply it universally in the area that is the object of action. Therefore, it follows that what is fundamental in a theming process is, in addition to the choice of theme, its effective physical materialization (Brill, 1993). The seminal argument is expressed through the forms and volumes.

2. The theme as an organizational foundation. In order to achieve its narrative and symbolic objective, the development of a theme park involves systematizing the organization of the production and consumption processes in such a way that its recreational suggestion appears to the consumer's senses as a complete, closed, self-sufficient universe. The narration proposed by each park requires flows in specific sequences. Hence all parks control the movement and behaviour of their visitors. Following the rules of the park, maximum enjoyment is ensured for the maximum number of people. The music and the images incite in the visitors their own particular feelings and emotions. The rides and attractions regulate the rhythm of affluence of the people in the areas of movement. The standardization of productive processes generates standards in the visitors' responses which are only perceived when somebody transgresses them. Botterill (1997) is explicit when he states that through the use of technology, in Disneyland, the cultural experience is served in a routine, efficient, rationalized and perfectly timed way. Thus, the running of a theme park translates, operatively, into precise procedures which, according to Ritzer (1996):

- Maximize the efficiency of processes – both productive and consumer.
- Allow offering an easily quantifiable and valuable experience in economic terms and from the consumer's point of view.

- Facilitate the precise compliance of the expectations the users place in the product supplied.
- Allow the control of the elements that come into play in the production process, in the product and in the act of consuming the elaborated product.

In fact, there are two main effects of theming as an organizational foundation: the packetization of the experience and the guarantee of productive efficiency. Packetizing means, according to Ren (1998), eliminating the imprints of the social relations of production that make the running of the park possible, standardizing the appearance of all objects and keeping the purity of the products that are made available to the consumers. Thus, for example, a park's services area is never on view to the visitor or the workers' physical appearance simulates, by means of their uniforms, order, safety and security, friendship and cleanliness as well as distinguishing one from another in accordance with their roles and characteristics. Guaranteeing efficient production means properly managing the control of mass affluence and productivity. From the point of view of the park, the ultimate purpose of its narrative discourse is to naturalize the act of consuming, that is to say, the appropriation of the contents and suggestions of the park. The opening times, the attractions and the shows are constituted as an orderly system of flow management which turns visitors into consumers via the use and symbolic acquisition of ingredients of free access (having paid the entrance fee, of course), but also through the incorporation into this process of use and acquisition of new objects and goods (food and commercial items), for which payment is required. The more successful the transformation process, the greater the park's revenue and productivity. The proper planning of the configuring elements of the park implies, therefore, ensuring the production of consumers.

3. The theme as a marketing strategy. Finally, the theme provides the park with its singularity and, therefore, conditions, in the framework of some specific thresholds for each case, their ability to attract (Mongon, 2001b). According to the function of the singularity, exceptionality or symbolism of each theme, the possibility of getting access to one or another market varies. It should not be forgotten that one same content can be themed in different ways in accordance with the interest in seducing one or another visitor. As Chaspoul (2001) points out, theming can be done in kitsch register, like some casinos of Las Vegas, or on the basis of a cultural register, as in the case of certain parks with historical or patrimonial arguments (from Puy du Fou in France to Malay Village in Singapore). In any case, the benefits of theming are, in this context, as follows (Wong and Cheung, 1999):

- The creation of an initial perception of quality.
- The increase of the rates of frequentation.
- The generation of greater added value.
- The coordination of merchandizing products and the increase in spending on shopping by the visitors.

- The achievement of a competitive edge thanks to the differentiation and greater recognition of the park.

Therefore, theming is not an exercise of mere fantasy and/or decoration, though doubtless the colours, the music and the decorative details reinforce the thematic treatment of the imagined reality in parks. Thus, for example, SeaWorld stands out not just due to its scientific–environmental content and its concern for nature, but also, and especially, thanks to the freshness of its atmosphere, the pastel colours, the marine scenes and the succession of shows with marine species. Theming is, in fact, a process of the physical and social construction of a type of reality which, being imaginary, magnifies the characteristics of contemporary society: a creative exercise which mixes imagination, technical capabilities, artistic concepts and the visitors themselves through a dynamic in which the aesthetic variables are fundamental.

In its details, theming involves 'attempting to construct the reality of goods or places on the basis of nostalgia and amnesia, or partial memory and partial forgetting' (Archer, 1997), all of this with a deep epic or dramatic sense. This is the case, for example, of Universal Islands of Adventure. It is an intense, diaphanous park with clearly differentiated themed areas in which the best things are the density, compression, colour and forms. The shows and especially the shops and food and beverage points are numerous. They almost go unseen, such is the theming, but are omnipresent. In addition, it is a park that makes no effort to disguise its inauthenticity since, in fact, it themes fantasy, adult and children's comics, legend, the cinema and cartoons. Though it does make spectacular use of technology in the case of the Spiderman ride, others such as 'Poseidon's Fury' make direct use of storytelling (verbal narration) as a form of expression.

Recurring themes in existing parks are, in fact, comics (Asterix Park), the future and science (Epcot), history (Isla Mágica), children's tales (Efteling), the world of toys (Legoland), travel (PortAventura), nature (SeaWorld), the cinema (Warner Bros), local mythological culture (Dragon World in Singapore) or music (Six Flags New Orleans). Table 2.2 contains the attributes of the different groups of themes that theme parks have developed to date, according to Wong and Cheung (1999).

Table 2.3 specifies the themes that it is understood will dominate in the future development of theme parks in the USA according to the operators themselves. In any case, it highlights the range of possibilities, from local identity to pure entertainment. In fact, some parks built as symbols of local culture and their content are directly linked to the identity of where they are located. This is the case of the South-east Asian living museums such as Taman Mini in Indonesia or China Folk Culture Villages in Shenzhen (Hitchcock *et al.*, 1997). In another sense, Disney's most recent park in the USA has also included many special local flavours from the California heritage. It has, for instance, a thematic area, Paradise Pier, which evokes the traditional 'boardwalks parks'. Amusement parks

Table 2.2. Attributes of different groups of themes (from Wong and Cheung, 1999).

Type	Attributes
Adventure	Excitement and action
	Frightening
	Mysterious
	Thrill rides
Futurism	Advances in society and technology
	Discovery
	Exploration of science and technology
	Laser
	Robot
	Scientific
	Science fiction
International	Flavours of the world
	International village
	Miniature replicas
	Scenic spots
	World expositions
Nature	Animals
	Floral displays
	Horticultural gardens
	Landscaping
	Marine life
	Natural wonders
	Ocean
	Wildlife
Fantasy	Animation
	Cartoon characters
	Childhood enchantment
	Children's play park
	Fairy tale
	Magic
	Make-believe
	Myths and legends
History and culture	Aboriginal
	Authentic
	Cultural heritage
	Ethnic appeals
	Gold rush
	Historical ambience
Movie	American Wild West show
	Comedy
	Motion picture
	Show business
	Stunt show

Table 2.3. Themes that will appear in the future development of theme parks in the USA according to park operators (from Milman, 2001).

Contents	Degree of accord (on a scale of 1 to 5)
Interactive adventure	4.18
Fantasy and mystery	3.82
Movies and TV shows	3.69
Science fiction/futuristic	3.60
Space	3.45
Nature/ecology	3.44
Educational	3.32
Seasonal themes	3.20
Sports	3.11
Storybook themes	3.06
Food	3.06
Science	3.00
Cultural and demographic diversity	2.92
History	2.73
Transportation	2.68
Ethnic themes	2.67

have become, in this case, the motif of the theming of one specific theme park. For this purpose, it has white roller coasters, which, though looking old and made of wood, are in fact made of steel. So, commemoratively, the park evokes Playland Park of San Francisco, Looff Pier, Lick Pier and others of Santa Monica, the Pike in Long Beach and other parks in California, in addition to Coney Island.

The choice of a theme for a park is of vital importance. To the extent that it is evocative, it will attract visits. In fact, McClung (1991) has shown that the theme is one of the basic factors of choice by tourists when visiting a park. In addition, there is an important correlation between themes and specific segments of demand. Hence the themes are normally transversally popular and hence the success that media and branded products have as bases for theme parks. Conversely, and for certain parks in highly localized cultural contexts, this is also the basis for the success of certain aspects of traditional popular culture. In other words, for a theme to be successful, it must be installed in the collective memory of the population to be attracted.

2.3. The Social Bases of Success

High per capita income, the re-emergence of leisure time and the arrival of paid holidays gave amusement parks new energy and, especially, new orientations in the 1950s. Thus, places for entertainment recovered their previous popularity of the beginning of the 20th century. In any case, the concept changed. So theme parks took over from amusement parks as icons of the latest thing in recreational spaces as of the 1950s. Theme parks became popular because they are clean, orderly and safe and they are family-oriented and develop in accordance with the tendencies of contemporary society and culture. Such are the foundations of their success. Moreover, '(f)ilm, television, and the automobile, which previously had done much to take patrons away from the amusement park, now began to bring them back to the theme park'. (Rebori, 1995a, 2).

Thus, using the possibilities of the concept of the Hollywood set, borrowing motifs from fairs, carnivals, children's literature and history, reconstructing in miniature everyday landscapes of popular culture and the unconscious, the simple idea of entertainment through the ingenuity of the rides has become, with theme parks, something very different from what their predecessors had developed. As Sorkin (1992b, 226–227) maintains, the result has been a montage, a factory of aggregated visual images where their logical structure is of no importance. Zins (1993) proposes four reasons of opportunity that explain the consolidation and especially the growth of the diversification of the development of theme parks. They are:

- Curiosity and the population's growing interest in the most diverse themes.
- The prioritization of leisure and education in the population's system of values and their increasingly high level of instruction.
- The technological possibilities for the presentation of the themes.
- The increase in short trips of an 'enriching' nature.

He also stresses four factors that may constitute, in the medium term, a threat to this process of the development of the activity. Specifically, they are the following (Zins, 1993):

- The competition between thematic products (from parks to museums, theatres and so on, places of interest, etc.).
- The competition between leisure and educational alternatives linked to new technology and communications media (for example, virtual tourism via television or the Internet).
- The search for authentic experiences among certain segments of the demand.
- The rapid obsolescence and the short life cycle of thematic equipment.

In fact, as parks have become generalized, they are also ceasing to be exceptional places for families to visit. Hence parks tend to put forward strategies that avoid this perception. They attempt to be conspicuous. In order to achieve this, the larger parks resort to developing brand concepts and media images. This is obviously the case of Disney or Universal. Also Six Flags in the USA benefits from the use of brand concepts, although they belong to another corporation, Warner Brothers in fact, a subsidiary of AOL Time Warner. In general terms, as of the 1980s, parks turned into nuclei of vast recreational complexes. Operators began to develop complete urban entertainment districts. To this end, parks have been enthusiastically supported by local, regional and state authorities. In this way, a process of corporate development has been consolidated, which, on occasion, has cloned the same elements in differentiated cultural surroundings and contexts. Finally, as of the early 1990s, there has also been a tendency towards the creation of niche parks, normally small in scale though conceptually very well defined, offering distinction and therefore having more than enough ability to attract even from outside their sphere of influence. In all cases, the challenge is to suitably orient the contents that ensure parks' ability to attract. Specifically, HTR (1999) lists, for Europe, the following five key contents: roller coasters, water, educational content, nature and virtual animation.

Milman (2001) proposes several key factors that are going to influence the immediate development of North American theme parks according to the opinions of their operators in the USA. As can be seen in Table 2.4, what stands out is the sensitivity of this type of facility to the factors that affect the market, especially consumers' preferences and the dynamics of the general economy. In this respect, it cannot be ignored that theme parks are products which are especially consumer-oriented. Hence the quality of service, represented in the table by means of the employee factor, and demographic dynamics, which condition the adaptation of the entertainment 'mix' supplied by each park to certain concrete segments of

Table 2.4. Factors that would have an impact on the future of theme parks in the USA according to park operators (from Milman, 2001).

Factor	Perceived importance (on a scale of 1 to 5)
Customers	4.34
Economic forces	4.13
Employees	3.88
Demographic forces	3.79
Competitors	3.73
Entertainment alternatives	3.62
Technological forces	3.57
Local communities	3.36
Sociocultural forces	3.27
Political/legal forces	3.05
Suppliers	2.72
Special interest groups	2.67
Trade associations	2.66

demand, are also of great relevance, ahead, even, of competitors' strategy, leisure alternatives (which, though important, are less so) or even technological dynamics.

In greater detail, Wootton and Stevens (1994) cite ten key social tendencies which, according to the International Association of Amusement Parks and Attractions, have more or less relevant implications for the development of the activity. They are:

- Cocooning: today's technology offers a great possibility of consuming domestic entertainment services (fundamentally television, video and electronic games). This tendency forces approaching the challenge to get people out of the house.
- Fantasy adventure: people tend to take limited risks by consuming safe experiences. They want to flee from the daily routine but be safe in the knowledge that their 'escapade' will be exciting and interesting.
- Small indulgences: people want to find economical means of satisfying their desires.
- Ergonomics: the desire to be acknowledged individually involves an increase in the demand for services and products designed to satisfy personal motivation.
- Vigilante consumer: this trend reflects consumers' distrust towards large companies and the government. In addition to the demand for quality, people do not want to be taken in by advertising and demand responsibility in business.
- Staying alive: people are health-conscious. They eat, drink and live differently in order to ensure greater longevity.
- Ninety-nine lives: we seek services that expand in time thanks to the flexibility that they offer when being able to do different things.
- Cashing out: a growing number of people question the values that lead them to excessive work. There is a return to a simpler life and an idealization of non-urban culture.
- Down-ageing: older people tend to want to ensure the youth of their body and mind.
- SOS (save our society): there is growing concern for ethical, educational and environmental values, in addition to the quality of life.

In this context of change, Formica and Olsen (1998) maintain that the business of theme parks is today subject to two basic challenges: demography and technology. With regard to demography, they consider that parks cannot limit themselves to specific age and interest groups but must consider broadening their scope of attraction to all potential segments. Regarding technology, parks are in the dilemma, expressed by Robinett (1998), of directing the development of entertainment in such a way that the application of technological utilities (in the style of virtual reality, electronic interaction, three-dimensional (3D) or surround sound) does not lead to a progressive anaesthesia of people's senses, especially those of young people, in respect of other, less sophisticated, more expensive possibilities of entertainment. Other conditioning factors of parks are the new emphasis on disposing of educational experiences during the holidays and the limitations of the international capital (highly significant if it is borne in mind that operators need large investments not just to become consolidated but also to survive). So they claim that, in the present context, parks cannot survive just from the entry tickets and traditional revenue generated through food, beverages and commerce, but they must be conceived as veritable multi-purpose entertainment centres, including special restaurants, theatres, sports facilities, stages for concerts and sets where they can produce cinema films. In addition, they can even be considered as places that can accommodate other activities than just entertainment. This concept would be close to the idea of Futurascope or – an even clearer example – Jewelry City, a South African park where, in addition to entertainment, they have developed a research and development (R & D) centre for the jewellery industry.

2.4. Synergies with the Media Entertainment Industry

The main operators of North American parks are linked to media conglomerates. Wolf (1999) uses the word 'synergy' to define the strategy of the corporations that have been devoted to entertainment as of the 1990s. According to him:

> Companies were no longer interested in merely being the biggest studio or the most successful TV network. They have to be more. Theme parks, cable networks, radio, consumer products, books, and music, all became prospects for their potential empires. Medialand was gripped by merger mania. If you weren't everywhere . . . you were nowhere.

Lanquar (1991) explains the question of the presence of the film industry in the business of theme parks on the basis of three principles. For him, the large film companies are obliged to diversify their business and use equipment and studios to 'get better known by the public and, on the other hand, add supplementary income to their turnover', especially taking into account the very dynamics of the industry, in which, in the 1980s, a time of important expansion of the theme park industry and of the restructuring of the supply, on average, only 40% of the income from a film was coming from being shown at cinema studios. With the cinema, television became a means of vital importance from the operators' point of view.

The relationship between theme parks and the entertainment industry is, on the other hand, a fundamental element when understanding the strategy of the main operators of being present in places other than the USA. There is a dual aim: to find new business opportunities in the parks sector (D'Hauteserre, 1997) and, above all, to boost their image as producers of universally disseminated entertainment services and products (Duncan, 1998). It cannot be ignored that, for these companies, parks provide the context for the recreation and dissemination of the products stemming from films (Davis, 1997). Reproducing their own production and consumption landscapes, parks generate, in the end, specific icons and symbols, which they universalize through the operating companies. In Davis's opinion, the cultural capital that theme parks spatialize is, in any case, infinitely more expandable than other investment modes. Now, the cases of the two major park operators, Disney, paradigmatic, and Universal, in Disney's wake, have specific characteristics that set them apart.

The linking of the parks to a few media conglomerates results, therefore, in a dynamic of 'branding', from the English 'brand on', an expression which designated the tool used by cowboys to mark their livestock with a red hot iron. Just as for the livestock, in which the iron identifies each head of cattle, 'branding' aims to psychologically link the experience of each person with the product consumed (Ariès, 2002, 164). As Zukin (1995) states, for the case of Disney, the parks are not just the most important tourist destinations of the end of the 20th century and do not merely represent a topical image of America but, especially, they symbolize a way of life. The logic behind 'branding' lies in two principles. First, it allows one to differentiate between functionally equivalent products through the symbolic content associated with them. Secondly, thanks to flexible production systems, it facilitates customization (and therefore increases the consumer's ability to choose) despite still being mass products (Holt and Schor, 2000, xx–xxi).

'Every kid wants to hold a piece of the cartoon world between his or her fingers – that's why licensing of television and movie characters for toys, cereals and lunchboxes has spawned a $16.1 billion annual industry.' This is what Naomi Klein (1999) says when explaining the business of the enterprises devoted to family entertainment, but also, their need to:

> extend their television and movie fantasies into real-world experiential
> extravaganzas . . . Back in the 1930s, Walt Disney, the grandfather of modern
> synergy, understood the desire to crawl inside the screen when he
> fantasized about building a self-enclosed Disney city and remarked that
> every Mickey Mouse product or toy doubled as an advertisement for his
> cartoons.
>
> (Klein, 1999, 145)

Parks respond, therefore, from the point of view of the operators who have interests in the entertainment industry, to the need to 'create a destination', a place to be visited where entertainment is mixed up with consumption and the contents are with the media. Parks, especially those of Disney and Universal, obey, when it comes down to the essentials, the dissemination of a far more important purpose than the creation of an entertainment area – the physical materialization of a brand experience. Again, in the words of Klein (1999, 190), 'never mind Disney World; Disney has launched the *Disney Magic* cruise ship and among its destinations is Disney's privately owned island in the Bahamas, Castaway Cay'. In short, these corporations, especially Disney, are creating branded products for all ages in life and in any format, from maternity to adult life, from dolls to interactive areas given over to sport, from spectacles to book collections (Ariès, 2002, 168–175).

Case 2. Efteling, the Best Childhood Memories for Everyone

Efteling opened in 1952. The park then consisted of a Fairy Tale Forest. It comprised some 65 ha of nature, including water gardens, a playground, tennis courts and football pitches and portrayed ten fairy tales: Sleeping Beauty's Castle, Snow White and the Seven Dwarfs, the Frog Prince, the Magic Clock, the Chinese Nightingale, the Talking Parrot, Longneck, the Gnome Houses, Mistress Holle's Well and Little Message. It was based on an idea proposed by the mayor of the Dutch town of Loon op Zand. He wished to build a playground around the sports field that had been set up in the early 1930s by two Catholic priests. There were 222,941 visitors in the first year and an entrance ticket was €0.36. (See the history of the park at http://www.efteling.nl.)

Over the years, new characters, attractions, rides and shows have joined the Fairy Tale Forest, including the first roller coaster in 1981. Moreover, in 1992 the Efteling Hotel opened – followed by the Efteling Dreamland Hotel – and 1995 was the year of the official opening of the Efteling Golf Park's 18-hole course and distinctive clubhouse. In 2004 the Efteling Museum was opened and the new Efteling Internet site was launched. Nevertheless, what Efteling offers are the best memories of childhood. According to Van Assendelft de Coningh (1994) 'there are very few Dutch people who do not get a warm feeling inside when they hear the word "Efteling"'. More than four out of five people over the age of 10 have been at least once and the average number of visits is four. Dutch visitors make up more than 75% of the total. Everyone in the Netherlands has pictures, images and songs from Efteling, which are stashed away in the deepest recesses of their minds. Efteling changes but childhood memories anchored in traditional European fairy tales remain the character of Efteling. In 2000, the year's theme, 'Efteling brings back your happiest moments', underlined the importance that Efteling attaches to the way in which visitors experience the park. Moreover, for instance, in 2005, when the 200th anniversary of Hans Christian Andersen's birth was celebrated throughout the world, Efteling paid special attention to him. In the Efteling Museum there was an exhibition on the Andersen fairy tales that Efteling has reproduced, and the Efteling Hotel opened a suite dedicated to the famous Danish fairy tale writer.

Efteling has become a part of the Netherlands' cultural heritage. Nevertheless, it has adapted its strategies to the common theme park management procedures in order to stay well positioned in the European market. In 1999, the park was divided into four themed realms, the Fairy Realm, the Travel Realm, the Adventure Realm and the Alternative Realm, to adapt it to coherent themes and more practical operation practices. The same year was the first time that Efteling opened to the public for 21 days in the winter. In 2000 Efteling opened the Pardoes Promenade and Efteling Village Green. The following winter, Efteling followed the success of the first occasion. New in 2001 was the spectacular 'Efteling on ice' show, which is performed three to four times a day throughout the season. In 2002, Efteling celebrated the fact that it had been in existence – as an amusement park initially and as a theme park since the 1980s – for 50 years. The two biggest anniversary novelties were the PandaVision attraction, which has been brought about in collaboration with the WorldWide Fund for Nature, and the Efteling Theatre, where the Wonderful Efteling Show was staged with world-famous magician Hans Klok. Other special anniversary activities were a jubilee exhibition, a documentary and the book *Efteling, Chronicle of a Fairy Tale*, which tells the 50-year history of the park. Optimal managing and decision making has transformed a sports playground designed back in the 1930s into one of the best theme parks in the world, all without losing its character as a producer of childhood memories.

Case 3. Huis ten Bosch, a Replica of the Dutch World in Japan

The Huis ten Bosch website (www.huistenbosch.co.jap) explains that during the summer of 1979 Yoshikuni Kamichika, the founder of Huis ten Bosch, went on his first trip to Europe. The natural splendour of the Mediterranean Sea reminded him of Omura Bay. Kamichika pondered upon the possibilities of turning the latter area into a unique place. At that point he thought of the small island of Dejima, an artificial island in the harbour of Nagasaki, from which only the Dutch were allowed to conduct trade during Japan's period of national isolation (1600–1868). He conceived the idea of building a 'modern Dejima'. Kamichika visited the Netherlands and learned about the Dutch tradition of reclaiming land from the sea. The fact that the land development was carried out in harmony with the environment, using natural rocks instead of concrete, impressed him. It was then that Kamichika decided to build a town – designed for everyday living – in Japan that combined Dutch city planning with Japanese technology.

   A first step towards the realization of this project was the construction of a small 10-ha town called Nagasaki Holland Village in 1983, with an initial attendance of around 2 million. It is now the site of rides and amusement for children, some 40 min by boat from the port of Huis ten Bosch. In October 1988, the construction of Huis ten Bosch started. A network of over 6 km of canals was created, replicas of famous Dutch buildings were built and over 400,000 trees and 300,000 flowers were planted. Huis ten Bosch (named after Queen Beatrix of the Netherlands' official residence) has become a place where nature and classic Dutch architecture are in harmony. In order to capture the charm and beauty of a 17th-century Dutch town, numerous historical landmarks were duplicated and in 1992 Huis ten Bosch opened its gates. The total costs of the project were $2.5 billion. Bricks were imported from the Netherlands to build and pave the place. It incorporates facilities where Dutch students of Japanese from the University of Leiden spend their year abroad, three enormous hotels and a residential section that offers holiday homes in 17th-, 18th- and 19th-century Holland. There are future plans to open a university, for South-east Asian students predominantly.

Nevertheless, as Hendry (2000b) points out, although apparently a theme park, Huis ten Bosch is described by publicity leaflets and is in fact one of the world's largest resort cities. It is a planned development area of 152 ha of land that contrasts largely with the lack of planning in the city of Kyoto. It is owned by the Nagasaki Holland Village Company and was raised in its first stage with the help of nearly a hundred corporate stakeholders, including many banks and local transport companies, such as Kogyo Bank and Nagasaki Motor Bus (Jones, 1994). Plans included building a city that could serve as a model for Asian urban planners. The chief idea of the company was, in short, to build a future world and the park is a way to make it possible. In this context, a key feature of Huis ten Bosch is its environmental policy and especially its treatment of waste water in three stages at its own water processing plant. The recycled water is used for watering plants within Huis ten Bosch and is also used for cooling systems and sanitary installations. Only clean, natural gas is used in heating and air-conditioning systems. Excess energy is recycled as much as possible. This has boosted the thermal efficiency of Huis ten Bosch to 70%. So Huis ten Bosch offers some interesting paradoxes. At first sight, Huis ten Bosch appears to be a 17th-century Dutch town. Below ground, however, a high-tech tunnel system, over 3.2 km in length, contains networks for communication, energy and water supply. Also at first sight, Huis ten Bosch appears to be a theme park. Nevertheless it is also a planned urban development.

Huis ten Bosch corporation also has two other facilities: a wildlife resort, Nagasaki Bio Park – where visitors interact with animals from all over the world – and an 18-hole golf course designed by Jack Nicklaus that offers amazing views of Huis ten Bosch and Omura and Sasebo Bays below. The course's country club is a replica of a Dutch castle which is located in the small town of Middelburg in the Netherlands.

Case 4. Cedar Point, the Roller Coaster Capital of the World

Samuelson and Yegoiants (2001) consider Cedar Point the most successful traditional park to have survived the 20th century in North America. From a resort that was declining by 1950, it has become a destination park. Its history incorporates all the evolutionary stages of the amusement park industry in the USA, from its beginnings as a resort, the expansion of rides and attractions during the 1920s, deterioration between the Depression years and the immediate post-war period, the decline of big city parks in the 1950s, the advent of the new theme park concept due to Disney's development and the ownership of many parks by a few corporations – among which is Cedar Fair Ltd, the world's second biggest operator of regional parks.

Cedar Point is the second-oldest amusement park in North America. Its history began in 1870 as an amusement resort when Louis Zistel, a German cabinetmaker from Sandusky, opened a small beer garden, dance floor, bathhouse and children's playground on the Cedar peninsula on Lake Erie. Zistel's company closed that same summer even though during the 1880s many people visited it each day to go sailing, bathing, fishing or picnicking. Two Sandusky businessmen realized the commercial potential of Cedar Point and in 1887 the Cedar Point Pleasure Resort Company was formed, and the development of the place as a major resort started. By 1890 Cedar Point was known as the Coney Island of the Midwest and the first of the multitude of roller coasters that the park hosts arrived in 1892. Up to his death in 1931 and under the direction of George A. Boeckling, a businessman from Indiana who acquired the resort in 1897, Cedar Point was transformed successfully into a major Midwest recreation area. After his visit to the Saint Louis World Fair in 1904, the landscape of Cedar Point changed dramatically and the resort entered a golden age. The year 1906 saw the opening of the 600-room Breakers Hotel and it was defined as an amusement area, known as Amusement Circle. Newer attractions were continuously added and faster rides were incorporated. By the 1920s, Cedar Point was a well-established resort, with people arriving at the park from across the Midwest by train (with a ferry connection from Sandusky) and by steamboats from places such as Detroit, Toledo or Cleveland (about 60 miles away).

After the hard times of the Great Depression and the Second World War – the only bright spot was that the huge Coliseum built in 1907 at Cedar Point hosted some of the greatest names of big-band sound and entertainment during the 1940s – the Cedar Point resort was in a deplorable condition, physically deteriorated and on the verge of bankruptcy. Despite the improvements that were made and, especially, the refurbishment of the Amusement Circle, in the mid-1950s a group of investors headed by George Roose became interested in the Cedar Point property and in 1956 they announced plans to raze the park and put up housing using the waterline residential areas of Fort Lauderdale as the model for the new development. Public opposition was strong and the Governor of Ohio announced that if necessary the state would acquire the property and operate it as a state park rather than lose it to residential development. In 1957 Roose announced new plans to redevelop Cedar Point as one of the Midwest's finest amusement parks, the 'Disneyland of the Midwest' (Samuelson and Yegoiants, 2001). Capital improvements were made, including a new marina. The new owners saw to it that a causeway connecting the park to Sandusky was completed. With Emile Legros and having the positive Disneyland model of amusement culture in mind, George Roose was responsible for Cedar Point's turnaround (Hildebrandt, 1981). Modernization began and, as the rebuilding took place, attendance and profits increased. Roose and Legros borrowed freely from Disney both ideas and management but they did not try to duplicate the extensive theming, choosing instead to concentrate on rides. So, rapidly, during the 1960s Cedar Point started to become a coaster mecca or the roller coaster capital of the world. Many major coasters, the quintessential rides, have been put in place there up until today (Francis and Francis, 2004).

It is without any doubt that one of the bases for the success of Cedar Point is its roller coaster orientation, in fact the purest symbol of the amusement park industry, according to Hildebrandt (1981). It began early and was accelerated from the 1960s. The first roller coaster at Cedar Point was the sensational Switchback Railway. It was opened in 1892. In 1902 a 46-foot-high coaster, Racer, made its debut. In those times, roller coaster technology was rapidly changing and in 1908 the Dip the Dips Scenic Railway was added. Four years later saw the start of the quicker Leap the Dips and a few years later the new Leap Frog Scenic Railway replaced the Dip the Dips. In 1929 Racer was replaced by the Cyclone roller coaster, described as one of the finest ever constructed in the Midwest. The first large new wooden coaster set in the park after its refurbishment in the late 1950s was Blue Streak in 1964. Since then, the new greatest coasters have been Cedar Creek Mini Ride in 1969, Corkscrew in 1976, the massive Gemini racing coaster in 1978, Junior Gemini in 1979, Disaster Transport in 1985, Iron Dragon in 1987 and Magnum XL-200 in 1989. A major wooden track coaster was launched in 1991 named Mean Streak. Then came Raptor (1994) and Mantis (1996) and the ultimate Millennium Force (2000), a hyper-coaster 310 feet tall that travels at 93 miles per hour. Currently, among many other carousels, spinning rides, calm rides, children's rides and water rides, the park boasts 16 roller coasters, including three of the top ten steel roller coasters in the world.

As Hildebrandt (1981) points out:

> Cedar Point succeeded in its rebirth because the times were right; because it was located on land which could be further redeveloped; because its management was quickly to capitalize on the new amusement park philosophy developed by Walt Disney; because it continued to stress the kind of ride-oriented participation experience people liked; because it managed itself exceedingly well.

In consequence, Cedar Point has become one of the top amusement/theme parks in America – drawing over 3 million guests during its approximately 130-day operating season. It is an updated amusement park with a modern theme park philosophy and operation tools. Moreover, founded as a resort, it is already a contemporary resort offering numerous hotel facilities, including the historic Breakers Hotel and Breakers Express with over 800 guest rooms, two other hotels including the Radisson and the Sandcastles Suites Hotel, a recreational-vehicle (RV) campsite, a water park, a marina, a beach, children's areas, a mini-golf course and a go-kart racetrack (see http://www.cedarpoint.com).

3 Globalization of the Theme Park Industry

In the late nineties, the pitch is less Marlboro Man, more Ricky Martin: a
bilingual mix of North and South, some Latin, some R&B, all couched
in global party lyrics. This ethnic-food-court approach creates a One World
placelessness, a global mall in which corporations are able to sell a single
product in numerous countries without triggering the old cries of
'Coca-Colonization'.

(Naomi Klein, 1999)

In recent decades, the theme park industry has undergone marked expansion worldwide. During the 1980s, the development of theme parks
became internationalized. If until then theme parks merely represented a
highly capitalized response to the entertainment needs of the generation
of the 'baby boom' in the USA and Canada, as of this moment they turned
into a business which, in order to continue to grow, resorted, in addition
to diversification towards other areas of entertainment, to internationalization. However, internationalizing the business of theme parks requires,
among other things, disposing of urban societies with large-sized urban
agglomerations and high income levels. In the mid-1980s, certain areas in
Asia and Western Europe met these conditions. It was the Disney Corporation that initiated the process of the creation of new international markets with the opening of its first Tokyo park in 1983 and the Paris one in
1992. As Dicken (1992, 143) points out, through this strategy Disney seeks,
fundamentally, economies of scale and coordination (cited by D'Hauteserre,
1997, 19). Nevertheless, what happened in Asia and in Europe is not the
same. There is no need to say that meanwhile, in the rest of the world, the
development of theme parks is taking place at a very slow pace in very
specific locations.

Table 3.1 synthesizes some of the main ideas that will be dealt with in
this chapter. In this third millennium, different processes of evolution are

Table 3.1. Dynamics of theme park development by world region (from author's own research).

	USA–Canada	Europe	Asia/the Pacific	Rest of the world
1950	Start			
1960	Development	Start		
1970	Expansion	Development	Start	
1980	Maturity	Expansion	Development	Start
1990	Concentration	Adaptation	Expansion	Development
2000	Diversification	Repositioning	Selective growth	Expansion

being experienced, each with its own rhythm of development. It may be observed that, in the USA and in Canada, the maturity of the market has brought about the concentration of a great many of the parks in the hands of just a few operators and the rise of diversification and international expansion strategies among the main corporations. In Europe, where a state of market maturity has not yet been attained, there currently exists a dynamic of adjustment and repositioning of the system of theme parks which is linked to its population singularity (distribution of the system of settlements), social singularity (patterns of consumption) and economic singularity (differences in the distribution of income). In Asia/the Pacific, however, an intense expansion process is being produced in which only certain areas and certain park formats are participating. In the rest of the world, the development process is not yet significant and, though expanding, its scale will be minimal during the next decade. Even so, tendencies hint at significant growth in countries like China, India, Mexico and Brazil and the most dynamic in the Indochina peninsula (Thailand, Singapore and Malaysia especially) and Indonesia.

3.1. Location Tendencies of Theme Parks in the World

Table 3.2 summarizes the principal magnitudes concerning the recent evolution of the theme park industry in the world according to data from Economics Research Associates (ERA). The ERA definition of a theme park for this purpose is a gated attraction that contains rides and/or shows in a themed environment, offers a pay-one-price ticket for its guests and attracts at least 500,000 annual visits. It is estimated that in 2005 there were 362 theme parks in the world. They are mainly located in Asia (35%) and the USA and Canada (31%). In all, they generate 606 million visits. While Asia/the Pacific has undergone significant growth in the last 5 years, increasing from 119 to 127 parks and from 188 million visits to 233, the situation in the USA and Canada has remained more stable. In visitor numbers, the world's number one region is Asia/the Pacific,

Table 3.2. Principal magnitudes on theme parks, 2000–2005 (based on Camp and Aaen, 2000, and ERA, 2003).

	Number of parks			Number of visits (millions)			Revenue (billion $)		
	2000	2005[a]	% 2005	2000	2005[a]	% 2005	2000	2005[a]	% 2005
USA–Canada	112	113	31.2	226	229	37.8	6.762	7.133	47.2
Europe	83	92	25.4	101	113	18.6	2.208	2.486	16.4
Asia/the Pacific	119	127	35.1	188	233	38.4	4.416	5.024	33.2
Rest of the world	28	30	8.3	30	31	5.1	0.414	0.475	3.1
Total	342	362		545	606		13.800	15.118	

a. Estimated figures.

obtaining numbers in 2005 even above those of the USA and Canada. Of the $15.2 thousand million invoiced by the industry according to ERA, nearly half (47%) was generated in the USA and Canada despite possessing only a third of parks. Greater per capita consumption inside parks by visitors in the USA and Canada explains the difference that can be observed between the three indicators. In 1990, according to the same source, the number of parks worldwide was 230, the total number of visits was 309 million and revenue was 7.9 thousand million dollars.

Table 3.3 allows us to go into greater depth as regards the different behaviour concerning visits and revenue in the different regions of the world. Braun's (1993) appreciation is valid, according to which relative per capita indicators are significantly higher in the USA and Canada than in the rest of the world. Thus, the number of visits to American parks is double the rate for the rest of the world, being 50% above the number of visits received by European parks and 10% above that of the parks in Asia/the Pacific. Therefore, with regard to the number of visitors, a certain convergence between the results of the USA and Canada and those of the Asia/Pacific region may be observed. Revenue per park is also substantially higher in the USA and Canada than in the other regions. Some of these results are due to the different behaviour of the consumer visitor to theme parks in the USA from that in the other regions. So, whereas in North American parks per-visitor expenditure is on average above $31, in European and Asiatic parks, the figure is between $21 and $22. In parks located in the rest of the world, per visit expenditure, at $15.3, is below half of what is made at North American parks. Quite different management systems, which obey different expectations by consumers, also explain the relative differences between each of the indicators. For example, Universal Studios Japan (Osaka), with a daily capacity for 58,000 and, therefore, twice that of PortAventura (Salou), disposed, at the time of its inauguration in 2001, of a restaurant seating capacity of just

Table 3.3. Principal indicators concerning theme parks, 2005[a] (from author's own research based on ERA, 2003).

	Visits/park (millions)	World = 100	Revenue/ park ($1000)	World = 100	Revenue/ visit ($)	World = 100
USA–Canada	2.03	121.6	63,124	151.1	31.15	124.8
Europe	1.23	73.6	27,022	64.7	22.00	88.2
Asia/the Pacific	1.83	109.6	39,559	94.7	21.56	86.4
Rest of the world	1.03	64.8	15,833	37.9	15.32	61.4
World	1.67		41,762		24.95	

a. Estimated figures.

6000, only 1000 more than that available at the Mediterranean park. Conversely, these restaurant facilities were permanently open and at the disposal of the public from 10 in the morning until 10 at night. Such differences have to do, therefore, with the singularities that are particular to the specific consumer culture of the Japanese and the Europeans.

Asia/the Pacific is the region with the highest forecast growth for the forthcoming years. The opening of Disney and Universal in this market as well as the profound transformation of the economy and of consumer patterns in China would back such predicted evolution. Evolution in Europe will be marked by the prospects of new developments in Russia and in Central European countries, which, to date, despite their population critical mass and due to the very nature of their potential markets, do not have theme parks. A second influence on such evolution will be the generalization of the phenomenon through small and medium-sized parks, especially in countries like France and Austria. In this sense, it cannot be forgotten that in 2002, for example, more roller coasters were built in Europe (22 in 16 parks) than at any other time in history (Benz, 2002). Latin America is not involved in the expansion process whereas the USA and Canada are at a stage of stability, which is linked, as will be seen later, with the state of market saturation, as well as other circumstantial factors.

Even so, as can be seen in Table 3.4, the USA and Canada was the second region in the world in terms of market growth during 1993–2005 if considering visits to the top ten theme parks each year. Only the Asian region is ahead. However, any consideration concerning the evolution of demand must be made with great caution given the theme park sector's sensitivity to happenings that may upset consumers' normal assurance, as, in fact, was patently demonstrated for the case of North America by the events of 11 September 2001. This was corroborated by the change to visitor numbers between 2000 and 2001, which fell, in the USA and Canada, considering that only the ten biggest parks appearing in

Table 3.4. Evolution of the number of visitors to the top ten theme parks of each region and of the 50 main parks in the world, 1993–2005 (in millions of visitors) (based on *Amusement Business* data).

	USA–Canada	% Change	Europe	% Change	Asia/the Pacific	% Change	Latin America	% Change	World[a]	% Change
1993	69,550		36,817		53,218		15,000		213,511	
1994	67,300	3.2	35,050	−4.8	62,292	17.0	15,400	2.7	222,057	4.0
1995	76,400	13.5	38,218	9.0	55,144	−11.5	13,950	−9.4	224,931	1.3
1996	80,973	6.0	40,100	4.9	58,103	5.4	13,700	−1.8	233,145	3.6
1997	84,611	4.5	42,350	5.6	59,656	2.7	14,807	8.1	242,868	4.2
1998	82,191	−2.9	39,766	−6.1	54,895	−8.0	16,720	12.9	233,395	−3.9
1999	81,650	−0.7	42,220	6.2	58,300	6.2	15,521	−7.2	240,217	2.9
2000	86,600	6.1	42,600	0.9	58,315	0.0	15,165	−2.3	245,118	2.0
2001	79,923	−7.7	42,973	0.9	65,146	11.7	15,214	0.3	250,515	2.2
2002	78,216	−2.1	41,330	−3.8	69,132	6.1	15,785	3.7	250,951	0.2
2003	77,571	−0.8	40,135	−2.9	68,120	−1.5	15,393	−2.5	247,062	−1.5
2004	83,240	7.3	41,240	2.8	68,850	1.1	15,360	−0.2	252,400	2.2
2005	85,527	2.7	42,150	2.2	65,030	−8.5	11,959	−22.1	253,081	2.2

a. Figures corresponding to visitors to the world's 50 principal parks.

the table are considered, by 7.7%. The effect was so great that it was not until 2005 that there was any clear recovery in the direction of the figures for 2000. Similarly, severe acute respiratory syndrome (SARS) in 2003 and, especially, the natural disasters that hit the region in addition to the recessive nature of the Japanese economy led to a significant decrease in 2005 in comparison with 2004 in Asia/the Pacific. Leaving aside Europe's greater stability, Table 3.4 highlights, in any case, the small scale of the Latin American market, which is also subject to intense interannual fluctuations, with visitor numbers far below the norm in 2005, especially in the Brazilian parks, which has had an effect on the continent's parks as a whole.

Table 3.5 allows us to observe the regional distribution of theme parks of the world with over 3 million visits in 2005, according to *Amusement Business*. The source includes some parks such as Blackpool Pleasure Beach, in England (6 million visits), and Adventure Dome in Las Vegas (4.5 million visits), in the USA, which are, without doubt, unusual in comparison with the rest. In any case, the data provided show, in the first place, that just 17 parks receive over 5 million visits and only 18 parks are visited by between 3 and 5 million people in the whole world.

It would therefore be relevant to point out that the very large, large and medium-sized parks are, in this order, the exception to the world park landscape. Only the USA and Asia/the Pacific are capable, today, of having a minimal number of this kind of facility. On the other hand, as can be seen in Table 3.6, of the 17 parks with over 5 million visits, nine are operated by Disney (the four with over 12 million visits each year and four of the five parks with between 8 and 12 million visits), in addition to Disney California Adventure with 5.83 million visits in 2005, and three parks by Universal Studios (between 5.7 and 8 million visits). This statement allows the hypothesis to be made that, in fact, the world distribution of the very large and large facilities is basically the result of these large corporations' competitive strategies in today's scenario of market globalization. This affirmation can be complemented by the fact that, leaving aside the Hong Kong park, only one Disney park is visited by fewer than

Table 3.5. Regional distribution of theme parks with over 3 million visits, 2005 (from author's own research based on *Amusement Business*).

Visitors	USA–Canada	Europe	Asia/the Pacific	Rest of the world[a]	Total	%
Over 12 million	2	–	2	–	4	11.4
From 8 to 12 million	3	1	1	–	5	14.3
From 5 to 8 million	4	1	3	–	8	22.9
From 3 to 5 million	10	6	2	–	18	51.4
Total	19	8	8	–	35	100.0
%	54.3	22.8	22.8	–	100.0	

a. Latin America.

Table 3.6. Main world theme parks with visitor numbers, 2005 (in million visits) (based on *Amusement Business* and IAAPA data).

Order	Park	Country	Visits 2005	Year of opening
1	Magic Kingdom at Walt Disney World, Lake Buena Vista, Florida	USA	16.160	1971
2	Disneyland, Anaheim, California	USA	14.550	1955
3	Tokyo Disneyland	Japan	13.000	1983
4	Tokyo Disney Sea	Japan	12.000	2002
5	Disneyland Paris, Marne-La-Vallée	France	10.200	1992
6	Epcot at Walt Disney World, Lake Buena Vista, Florida	USA	9.917	1982
7	Disney-MGM Studios at Walt Disney World, Lake Buena Vista, Florida	USA	8.670	1989
8	Disney Animal Kingdom at Walt Disney World, Lake Buena Vista, Florida	USA	8.210	1998
9	Universal Studios Japan	Japan	8.000	2001
10	Everland, Kyunggi-Do	South Korea	7.500	1976
11	Lotte World, Seoul	South Korea	6.200	1985
12	Universal Studios at Universal Orlando	USA	6.130	1989
13	Blackpool (England) Pleasure Beach	England	6.000	[1896]
14	Disney's California Adventure	USA	5.830	2001
15	Islands of Adventure at Universal Orlando	USA	5.760	1999
16	SeaWorld Florida, Orlando	USA	5.600	1973
17	Yokohama Hakkejima Sea Paradise	Japan	5.300	N/A
18	Universal Studios, Hollywood, Universal City, California	USA	4.700	1964
19	Adventuredome at Circus Circus, Las Vegas	USA	4.500	1985
20	Busch Gardens, Tampa Bay, Florida	USA	4.300	1959
21	SeaWorld California, San Diego	USA	4.100	1964
22	Tivoli Gardens, Copenhagen	Denmark	4.100	1843
23	Ocean Park	Hong Kong	4.030	1977
24	Europa-Park, Rust	Germany	3.950	1975
25	Nagashima Spa Land, Kuwana	Japan	3.800	1964
26	Paramount's Canada Wonderland Maple, Ontario	Canada	3.660	1975
27	Knott's Berry Farm, Buena Park, California	USA	3.470	1920
28	PortAventura, Vila-seca/Salou	Spain	3.350	1995
29	Paramount's Kings Island, Kings Island, Ohio	USA	3.330	1972
30	Efteling, Kaatsheuvel	Netherlands	3.300	1952
31	Liseberg, Göteborg	Sweden	3.150	1923
32	Morey's Piers, Wildwood, New Jersey	USA	3.130	1969

Continued

Table 3.6. *Continued.*

33	Cedar Point, Sandusky, Ohio	USA	3.110	1870
34	Gardaland, Castelnuovo del Garda	Italy	3.100	1975
35	Santa Cruz Beach Boardwalk, California	USA	3.000	1907
36	Six Flags Great Adventure, Jackson, New Jersey	USA	2.968	1972
37	Six Flags Great America, Gurnee, Illinois	USA	2.852	1976
38	Six Flags Magic Mountain, Valencia, California	USA	2.835	1971
39	Hersheypark, Hershey, Pennsylvania	USA	2.700	1907
40	Busch Gardens Europe, Williamsburg, Virginia	USA	2.600	1975
41	Suzuka Circuit, Suzuka, Japan	Japan	2.600	1962
42	Bakken, Klampenborg	Denmark	2.600	1583
43	Happy Valley, Shenzhen	China	2.600	1997
44	Alton Towers, Staffordshire	England	2.400	1924
45	Window of the World, Shenzhen	China	2.390	1995
46	Dollywood, Pingeon Forge, Tennessee	USA	2.360	1976
47	Six Flags over Texas, Arlington, Texas	USA	2.310	1971
48	Six Flags México, Mexico	Mexico	2.279	1982
49	Camp Snoopy at Mall of America, Bloomington, Minnesota	USA	2.200	1992
50	Paramount's Carowinds, Charlotte, North Carolina	USA	2.130	1973

☐ Parks in the USA–Canada
☐ Parks in Europe
☐ Parks in Asia/the Pacific
☐ Parks in the rest of the world

5 million, the Walt Disney Studios Park in Paris. Finally, only six of the 17 parks receiving over 5 million visits are not operated by these two companies. In addition to the aforementioned park in Blackpool are three parks in Asia, Everland and Lotte World in South Korea (with over 6 million visitors each in 2005) and Yokohama Hakkeijima Sea Paradise in Japan (5.3 million visitors in 2005), and SeaWorld in Orlando (5.6 million visits in 2005).

The two series of maps in Figs 3.1 and 3.2 allow us to see the evolutionary parameters of the world distribution of facilities with over 3 million visits. Figure 3.1 clearly shows the decided incorporation of Europe and Asia/the Pacific into the world market of large theme parks between 1988 and 1992, as well as a slight substitution and consolidation process of parks with an increase in frequentation in the USA, fundamentally on the east coast and around the large industrial metropolises. Figure 3.2 illustrates, in the first place, the consolidation in 1998 of the European (Western) and

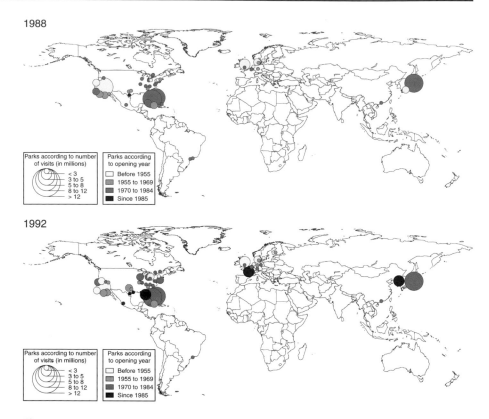

Fig. 3.1. Evolution of world location of the main theme parks, 1988–1992 (from author's own research based on *Amusement Business* and IAAPA data).

Asiatic (Japan/Korea fundamentally) markets and, already in 2005, the rescaling of the capacity to attract of different parks that cease to show such marked disequilibria as those observed in the previous map, in addition to the absolute consolidation, as will be seen later, of four large foci of theme parks in the world, California, Florida, Western Europe and Japan/Korea.

3.2. The Diversification of the Industry in the USA

As can be seen in Table 3.7, today the USA and Canada have nine theme parks receiving over 5 million visits per year. All nine are located in Orlando and Los Angeles, and make up the main theme park tourist destinations in the world. Six of them are operated by Disney, two by Universal Studios and the remaining one is a SeaWorld park, operated by Busch Gardens. On the other hand, in the main they are recent parks within the context of the activity's short history. Thus, five of them were started up after 1985 and, in fact, only one pre-dates the 1970s. It is Disneyland

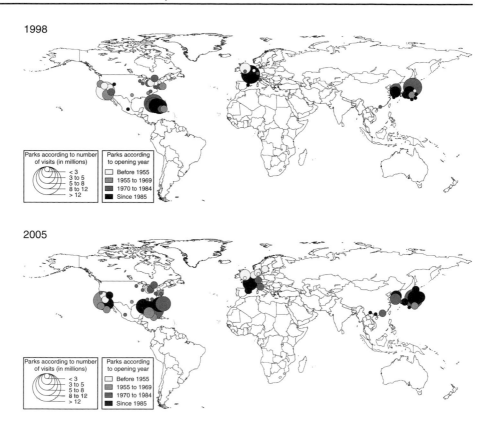

Fig. 3.2. Evolution of world location of the main theme parks, 1998–2005 (from author's own research based on *Amusement Business* and IAAPA data).

(14.5 million visits in 2005) in Anaheim, which, as is well known, was inaugurated in 1955. Among the most recently founded parks, two Disney and one Universal Studios park date from post-1998. All of these parks together generate 80.8 million visits – that means a third of all visits to the 50 main theme parks in the world. This figure gives one an idea of the scale of the business in the USA, of the role of the main corporations, especially Disney's, and of the importance of the activity in Orlando.

The ten medium-sized parks that appear in Table 3.7, with between 3 and 5 million visits per year, combine the characteristics of regional parks with a certain tourist capacity to attract. These parks are operated by some of the major North American leisure corporations, barring three cases, Morey's Piers in New Jersey (3.1 million visits in 2005), Santa Cruz Beach Boardwalk in California (3 million visits in 2005) and Adventuredome (4.5 million visits in 2005), the indoor park incorporated into the Circus Circus hotel in Las Vegas. Within this segment, most parks belong to Anheuser Busch and Cedar Fair/Paramount Parks, each with two facilities. Also appearing is the Universal Studios park in Los Angeles, which, depending on the circumstances, may also be cited for some years in the

Table 3.7. Theme parks in the USA–Canada according to visitor numbers, 1992 and 2005 (in million visits) (based on *Amusement Business* and IAAPA data).

Order	Park	Visits 1992	Visits 2005	Year of opening
1	Magic Kingdom at Walt Disney World, Lake Buena Vista, Florida	12.1[a]	16.2	1971
2	Disneyland, Anaheim, California	11.6	14.5	1955
3	Epcot at Walt Disney World, Lake Buena Vista, Florida	10.6[a]	9.9	1982
4	Disney–MGM Studios at Walt Disney World, Lake Buena Vista, Florida	7.6[a]	8.7	1989
5	Disney Animal Kingdom at Walt Disney World, Lake Buena Vista, Florida	–	8.2	1998
6	Universal Studios at Universal Orlando	6.7	6.1	1989
7	Islands of Adventure at Universal Orlando	–	5.8	1999
8	Disney's California Adventure, Anaheim, California	–	5.8	2001
9	SeaWorld Florida, Orlando	4.1	5.6	1973
10	Universal Studios, Hollywood, Universal City, California	4.8	4.7	1964
11	Adventuredome at Circus Circus, Las Vegas	N/A	4.5	1985
12	Busch Gardens, Tampa Bay, Florida	3.0	4.3	1959
13	SeaWorld California, San Diego	4.0	4.1	1964
14	Paramount Canada's Wonderland, Maple, Ontario	2.3	3.7	1975
15	Knott's Berry Farm, Buena Park, California	3.9	3.5	1920
16	Paramount's Kings Island, Kings Island, Ohio	3.3	3.3	1972
17	Morey's Piers, Wildwood, New Jersey	1.4[d]	3.1	1969
18	Cedar Point, Sandusky, Ohio	3.1	3.1	1870
19	Santa Cruz Beach Boardwalk, California	3.0	3.0	1907
20	Six Flags Great Adventure, Jackson, New Jersey	3.1	2.9	1972
21	Six Flags Great America, Gurnee, Illinois	3.1	2.8	1976
22	Six Flags Magic Mountain, Valencia, California	3.2	2.8	1971
23	Hersheypark, Hershey, Pennsylvania	1.7	2.7	1907
24	Busch Gardens Europe, Williamsburg, Virginia	2.1	2.6	1975
25	Dollywood, Pigeon Forge, Tennessee	1.8	2.4	1976
26	Six Flags over Texas, Arlington, Texas	3.0	2.3	1961
27	Paramount's Kings Dominion, Doswell, Virginia	2.2	2.2	1974
28	Knott's Camp Snoopy, Bloomington, Minnesota	2.5[c]	2.2	1992
29	Paramount's Carowinds, Charlotte, North Carolina	1.3	2.1	1973
30	SeaWorld Texas, San Antonio	1.5	2.1	1986
31	Paramount's Great America, Santa Clara, California	2.3	2.1	1976
32	Six Flags over Georgia, Atlanta	2.6	2.1	1967
33	Silver Dollar City, Branson, Missouri	1.8	1.9	1960
34	Casino Pier, Seaside Heights, New Jersey	1.5[d]	1.7	1938

Continued

Table 3.7. *Continued.*

35	Six Flags New England, Agawam, Massachusetts	1.0[c]	1.7	1940
36	Six Flags Marine World, Vallejo, California	1.9	1.5	1964
37	Dorney Park, Allentown, Pennsylvania	1.2[c]	1.5	1884
38	Wild Adventures, Valdosta, Georgia	–	1.5	1996
39	Six Flags Fiesta Texas, San Antonio	2.0	1.5	1992
40	Legoland California, Carlsbad	–	1.4	1999
41	Cypress Gardens, Winter Haven, Florida	0.8[b]	1.4	1936
42	Six Flags St. Louis, Eureka, Missouri	1.8	1.4	1971
43	Six Flags Astroworld, Houston, Texas	2.0	1.3	1968
44	Knoebels Amusement Resort, Elysburg, Pennsylvania	1.0	1.3	1926
45	Six Flags Darien Lake, Darien Center, New York	1.0	1.3	1968
46	La Ronde, Montreal, Quebec	1.2	1.2	1967
47	Kennywood, West Mifflin, Pennsylvania	1.2	1.2	1898
48	Six Flags America, Largo, Maryland	N/A	1.2	1981
49	Six Flags Elitch Gardens, Denver, Colorado	0.8[c]	1.2	1890
50	Lagoon, Farmington, Utah	1.0	1.1	1886

a. Author's estimation.
b. Data for 1991.
c. Data for 1993.
d. Data for 1994.

bracket of parks receiving over 5 million visits. In general terms, they are parks that were developed during the initial onslaught of the activity in the USA in the 1950s and 1960s. So only three of them were inaugurated later than 1970. They are located both in the country's major metropolitan areas, as well as in states such as California and Florida, and are associated, therefore, with significant tourist activity.

Below the 3 million visits mark, there are 31 parks with over 1 million visits per year and, despite not appearing in Table 3.7, over 50 parks with visitor figures greater than 500,000. The parks of between 1 and 3 million visits are basically regional and urban parks located in the surroundings of larger metropolitan agglomerations. Of these, 14 are operated by Six Flags, the segment's dominant operator. Also significant is Cedar Fair/Paramount Parks' and Anheuser Busch's prescence. Nine of the parks in this segment are independent and one has been developed by the European group Lego, currently belonging to the Merlin Entertainment Group. The parks receiving between 2 and 3 million visits, those developed during the 1970s and the early 1980s, correspond to the second stage in the growth of the activity in the USA, stimulated by the success of corporations such as Disney. They are parks, on the other hand, that were developed, in a significant number of cases, by corporations which, as we shall see in the next chapter, abandoned the sector during the second half of the 1980s. Conversely, the parks with 1 to 2 million visits are dominated by those developed prior to the 1970s and, in particular, the theme parks, which, like Dorney Park (1.4 million visits in 2005) or Elitch Gardens (1.2 million visits in 2005), are the inheritors of old amusement parks or recreational resorts initially developed before 1955 and, in some relevant cases, even as early as the 19th century. In this case, both parks associated with the metropolitan dynamics of the country's major cities and parks linked to classic tourist and holiday development processes in the USA are identified.

As a result of the theme park implantation process in the last 50 years, in the USA today, most metropolitan areas that are, due to population numbers, capable of sustaining a theme park have one (Robinett, 1992). In these areas the market is ensured, the parks are located in spaces where the price of the land at the time of implantation is economic and the system of motorways guarantees accessibility. Fitting into this category are metropolises such as Atlanta, Buffalo, Chicago, Cleveland/Columbus, Dallas, Denver, Houston, Los Angeles, Louisville, San Antonio, San Francisco, St. Louis, Sacramento and Washington, DC, and fundamentally urban states such as New Jersey, New York and Ohio. They are home to parks receiving between 1 and 4 million visits a year made by the citizens that, in general terms (80%), reside within 2 h of the park. To illustrate this, it may be said that it has been estimated that, today, over 80% of Americans live in the proximity of a park operated by Six Flags (the second biggest operator of parks worldwide according to visitor numbers).

An important part of existing principal American regional parks was developed between the implantation of Disneyland in Anaheim, California, in 1955, and the end of the 1970s. Characteristic examples of such park facilities are Silver Dollar City in Branson, Missouri, founded in 1961 (which recreates the lifestyle, culture and history of the Ozark region in 1890 and received 1.9 million visits in 2005), or Six Flags Great America in Gurnee, Illinois, founded in 1976 (which commemorates the bicentenary of the foundation of the USA and had 2.8 million visitors in 2005). It was also between the 1950s and the 1970s that some old amusement parks dating from the end of the 19th century or the early 20th were redesigned to adapt to American society's renewed leisure habits after the Second World War. This is the case, for example, of Hersheypark, founded in Hershey, Pennsylvania, in 1907 (2.7 million visits in 2005), which today has several themed areas, or Santa Cruz Beach Boardwalk, founded in California in 1907 (3 million visits in 2005), which was an old beach amusement park, which today not only houses themed areas like Neptune's Kingdom but, keeping on a wooden roller coaster from the year 1924, has been catalogued as being historical patrimony by the state of California.

Disney's establishment of its first park in Florida in 1971, Magic Kingdom (16.2 million visits in 2005), marks a point of inflection in the evolution of the theme park industry in the USA, conditions future trends concerning the location of such facilities and introduces the concept of destination park. The continuous growth of Disney facilities in Florida made this corporation absolute leader and dominant company in the sector during the 1980s, transforming, as it set out to do, the content of a visit to a theme park into a holiday experience. In fact, the development of new parks as of the 1980s tended to concentrate in Florida – which became the characteristic destination of this kind of tourism in the USA – and ceased to be dominated by parks of a regional nature. This situation of Disney's absolute primacy remained until Universal Studios' implantation in Florida in 1989 with the inauguration in Orlando of a replica of its Californian park, Universal Studios Florida (6.1 million visitors in 2005). Thus, despite the differences in size between the two companies, rivalry between Disney and Universal in Orlando allows us to speak of the end of the Disney monopoly of the 1980s and the start of an oligopoly, in which leadership is shared by the two companies as of the 1990s (Braun and Soskin, 1999). As regards the growth of medium- and small-sized parks, it has progressively slowed down since the 1980s. This must be interpreted in the context of a certain maturity within the theme and amusement park industry in the USA.

Figure 3.3 helps to illustrate the major trends of park location in the USA from the 1980s to the present. In concrete terms, three main axes of change can be observed: first, the consolidation of Florida, but also California, as regions for the location of large destination parks and, in consequence, of smaller-sized parks, which, without destination parks, would probably find it difficult to subsist; secondly, the existence of adjustment processes in the surroundings of large metropolitan agglomerations in the northern half of the east coast and the Great Lakes area; and, thirdly, the existence of circumstantial changes in the rest that can be explained in accordance with local dynamics beyond the scope of the general parameters concerning the location of this kind of facility. Each of these tendencies is explained in greater detail below.

In addition to the large facilities developed in Florida, a trend is observed as of the 1980s in the USA to locate new parks in the south. This is the case, for example, among the main cases, of the two parks that were inaugurated in San Antonio, Texas, in 1986 (SeaWorld Texas) and in 1992 (Six Flags Fiesta Texas), totalling some 2 million visits per year. They are parks of reduced size. The opening of Disney California Adventure in Anaheim (5.8 million visits in 2005) has changed the tendency to concentrate the large parks in Florida, whereas, in the rest of the USA, the situation is characterized by the presence of small and medium-sized parks.

The progressive saturation of the market has led, in the USA and Canada, to the search for new business opportunities. Thus, for example, in addition to diversifying the recreational contents around their parks through developing hotels, the creation of veritable ludic and tourist complexes in the style of Universal City Walk and Disney Village and complementing their offer with brands in Hard Rock Cafe or Rainforest Cafe style, the major corporations have begun to develop urban entertainment centres in the most important metropolitan agglomerations. So,

Fig. 3.3. Evolution of the location of the main US theme parks, 1986–2005 (from author's own research based on *Amusement Business* and IAAPA data).

almost at the same time as Disney opened its first Disney Club in Thousand Oaks, California, in February 1997, in March the first Gameworks was inaugurated in Seattle as a result of an agreement between Universal, Sega and Dreamworks. Later, in 1998, the first DisneyQuest was inaugurated in Downtown Disney, a Disney style themed interactive family entertainment centre with much emphasis on the use of high technology. According to Jones *et al.* (1998) it could be held, therefore, that the situation of the theme park industry in the USA may be defined by the following four key words:

- Maturity: the rise in the number of visitors to the top ten parks in the USA and Canada was 24% between 1992 and 2005. Even so, significant fluctuations occurred between 2000 (86.6 million visits to the top ten parks) and 2005 (85.5 million), having witnessed a drop to 77.5 million in 2003. Over half of the growth enjoyed by the great parks (8.6 million visits) is as a result of the integration of new parks into the system and not of the increase in per capita frequentation levels to parks. In 2005, global frequentation to all theme parks surpassed the 330 million visits mark. This figure leads one to understand that almost 100 million visits take place at the country's innumerable parks receiving less than 500,000 visitors. Large park corporations like Six Flags are in the process of redefining their portfolios of facilities (in 2004 they sold the Six Flags Worlds of Adventure park in Ohio to Cedar Fair and, in 2005, they initiated the closure and sale of Six Flags Astroworld in Houston). Likewise, CBS sold the Paramount parks division to Cedar Fair in 2006, while Universal, as in fact Six Flags too, has withdrawn from the investments it began in Europe in the 1990s.

- Consolidation: the growth experienced by the sector, frequentation and business figures are stable. Global revenue and per visit income between 2000 and 2005 have grown by 5.5%, while per park income has increased by 4.5%. Frequency figures remain stable, on average slightly over 2 million visits per park among those receiving over 500,000 annual visits. Such dynamics have been accompanied by a rise in sales in the parks as well as increased entrance fees (greater than the rate of inflation). The main inter-annual variations are due to the results of the larger-sized parks, whose frequentation figures are easily affected, be it due to negative occurrences such as terrorist attacks or natural disasters or, conversely, by events that have a distinct driving nature such as, in 2005, the celebration of the 50th anniversary of the creation of Disney. Nevertheless, it is observed that frequentation to regional parks below the 3 million visits mark stabilized between 1992 and 2005. Indeed, two parks have continued to receive the same number of visits, 12 have seen a drop in numbers and 13 have enjoyed a rise. Circumstantial, operative or management issues, in each case unique, would help to explain these dynamics.

- Diversification: the sector is diversifying, with new products designed for specific niches in the market that materialize in the form of small-scale parks such as Discovery Cove (operated by Anheuser Busch in Orlando), with nearly 275,000 visitors a year. In parallel, the large parks have become veritable leisure complexes, with medium- and long-duration integrated entertainment possibilities and holiday opportunities. Just as Lanquar (1991, 34) foresaw at the start of the 1990s, today the future of parks in North America is protean. There are a multitude of possible formulas based on a few basic ingredients, which are entertainment, sports, leisure, technology and culture. Consequently, it may be predicted that, in the future, different evolutions will differentiate regional and urban parks from destination parks. Moreover, various new opportunities will arise for small-sized parks and markets.

- Tourist destination: a large number of the main theme parks to be developed during the last decade have been destination parks. In these cases, the orientation of their location in the southern states has been of importance. In addition to Florida, south California and, more recently, Texas, are the states where destination parks are being located. In this way, the development of theme parks in North America has ceased to be an activity aimed at selling a 7-h experience and has turned a visit to a theme park into a holiday experience. Indirectly, a consequence of this evolution has been the greater susceptibility of the markets to sensitive issues such as the feeling of safety, security and risk and the increase in the price of crude oil.

3.3. The Transformation of the Amusement Park Model in Europe

Despite not reaching the characteristic scale of the American market (with per capita visit numbers at 0.8 in the USA and an average maximum of 0.3 in Europe, with marked contrasts between the European countries), the European theme park market may be considered, at least in the West European sector, as being consolidated. Unlike the USA and barring the case of Disneyland Paris, in Europe medium- and small-sized parks dominate. As can be seen in Table 3.8, currently the European theme park industry has two parks with over 5 million annual visits, Disneyland Paris (10.2 million in 2005) and Blackpool Pleasure Beach (6 million visits in 2005), and six parks with over 3 million visits: Tivoli Gardens, Europa Park, PortAventura, Efteling, Liseberg and Gardaland. These figures illustrate the global dimension of the European market. It is essential to acknowledge, along these lines, that the characteristics, magnitude and location of the potential demand in Europe condition the possibilities of the development of the sector (Camp, 1997). This is an especially critical factor with regard to operations that aspire to welcome more than 3 million visits a year. This was, for example, how those in charge at Tussauds, one of the principal European leisure attraction operator groups, saw things when they stated that Disney solved the problem of the limited dimension of the market areas in Europe by choosing Paris as the site to establish, as it has some 300 million potential visitors less than 3 h away (Hill, 1999). This is also why the European park structure, especially in the more mature regions of the centre and the north of

Table 3.8. Recent evolution of visitor numbers to the top ten European theme parks, 1995–2005 (in millions of visits) (based on *Amusement Business* data).

Order	Park	1995	1996	1997	1998	1999	2000	2001	2002	2003	2004	2005
1	Disneyland Paris, Marne-La-Vallée	10.7	11.7	12.6	12.5	12.5	12.0	12.2	10.3	10.2	10.2	10.2
2	Blackpool (England) Pleasure Beach	7.2	7.5	7.8	6.6	6.9	6.8	6.5	6.4	6.2	6.2	6.0
3	Tivoli Gardens, Copenhagen	2.4	3.1	3.2	2.8	3.1	3.9	3.9	3.8	3.3	4.2	4.1
4	Europa-Park, Rust	2.5	2.5	2.7	2.7	3.0	3.0	3.1	3.3	3.3	3.3	3.9
5	PortAventura, Vila-seca/Salou	2.7	3.0[a]	3.0	2.7	3.0	3.1	3.3	3.3[a]	3.1	3.1	3.3
6	Efteling, Kaatsheuvel	2.7	3.0	3.0	2.7	3.0	2.9	3.1	3.0	3.2	3.2	3.3
7	Liseberg, Göteborg	2.2	2.4	2.5	2.5	2.6	3.0	3.1	3.1	2.8	3.0	3.1
8	Gardaland, Castelnuovo Del Garda	2.5	2.4	2.7	2.7	2.8	2.9	2.9	2.9	3.0	3.1	3.1
9	Bakken, Copenhagen	2.4	2.1	2.1[a]	2.0[a]	2.3[a]	2.5	2.5	2.8	2.7	2.5	2.6
10	Alton Towers, North Staffordshire	2.7	2.7	2.7	2.5	2.8	2.4	2.3	2.5	2.5	2.4	2.4

a. Estimated.

Europe, is characterized by the establishment of numerous small recreational facilities.

The above shows, therefore, a dynamic of smaller dimensions than in the rest of the world, though with relatively more positive growth rates of revenue indicators. Thus, the number of parks in Europe grew between 1990 and 2005 from 62 to 92, the number of visits from 61 to 113 million and revenue from $1104 to 2486 million. Comparatively, the number of parks in Europe has increased by 48.4% as against 57.4% worldwide, and the number of visits has grown by 85.2% as against 96.1% globally. Conversely, revenue has gone up during this period by 125.2%, substantially higher than the 74.7% for the whole world. European parks receive, on average, fewer visits per park than the world average (1.23 compared with 1.67) and, though per visit income is lower ($22 per visit in Europe as against $24.95 worldwide), it rose by 22.2% between 1990 and 2005 whereas the global average has slightly decreased, by −2.4%. Finally, precisely due to the lower number of visits in Europe, per park income, which is at $27.02 million on average for Europe in 2005, grew between 1990 and 2005 by 51.7% in comparison with 11% growth globally.

According to Robinett and Braun (1990), the explanation as to the difference in results between Europe and the rest of the world, the USA in particular, is a result of the 15–20 years' difference between the two areas in the activity taking off. However, there are other, more relevant reasons, such as the lower levels of investment and expenditure on marketing by European parks compared with the American ones, the different European holiday model, the role of the big travel operators in the creation of preferences among the demand and, especially, the European amusement park tradition, which would explain in greater detail Europe's singularity in the theme park market on a world scale. Valls and Mitjans (2001) noted that, while in the USA society is quick to take up the consumption of leisure products and services, in Europe, the appearance of tour operators that ensure, as an exceptional element of free time, the journey and stay at economical prices from central and northern Europe to the Mediterranean leads to a slower incorporation by European society of the consumption of leisure services such as theme parks.

As can be seen in Table 3.9, prior to the opening of Disney in Europe in 1992 and the progressive appearance of new recreational facilities during the 1990s, there was an important concentration of medium- and small-sized amusement parks in the continent's more densely populated area: France, Germany, the Benelux countries, the countries of the north and the Baltic and Great Britain. The existence of these parks is perfectly appreciable from Fig. 3.4, in which it can be seen that the oldest parks are located along the North Sea–Baltic Sea axis, whereas those immediately prior to Disney are found on the so-called 'European banana' (the most populated area of Western Europe between the Liguria and the London area). Besides its predecessors of the 19th century and the early 20th (Tivoli Gardens, working in Copenhagen from 1843, or Alton Towers, opened in

Table 3.9. Opening dates of a selection of European theme parks (from own research).

Park	Location	Country	Year of opening
Bakken	Copenhagen	Denmark	1583
Tivoli Gardens	Copenhagen	Denmark	1843
Grona Lunds	Stockholm	Sweden	1883
Blackpool Pleasure Beach	Blackpool	UK	1896
Pleasureland	Southport	UK	1912
Liseberg	Göteborg	Sweden	1923
Alton Towers	North Staffordshire	UK	1924
Efteling	Kaatsheuvel	Netherlands	1952
Madurodam	The Hague	Netherlands	1952
Bobbenjannland	Lichaart	Belgium	1961
Duinrell	Wassenaar	Netherlands	1965
Phantasialand	Brühl	Germany	1967
Legoland	Billund	Denmark	1968
Holiday Park	Hassloch	Germany	1971
Alton Towers	Alton	UK	1974
Europa Park	Rust	Germany	1975
Gardaland	Castelnuovo Del Garda	Italy	1975
Six Flags Belgium	Wavre	Belgium	1975
Hansa Park	Slerksdorf	Germany	1977
Heide Park	Soltau	Germany	1978
Thorpe Park	Chertsey	UK	1979
Futuroscope	Poitiers	France	1986
Chessington World of Adventures	Chessington	UK	1987
Frontierland	Morecambe	UK	1987
Parc Astérix	Plailly	France	1989
Walibi Schtroumpf	Moselle	France	1989
Mirabilandia	Ravenna	Italy	1992
Disneyland Paris	Marne-la-Vallée	France	1992
PortAventura	Vila-seca/Salou	Spain	1995
Warner Bros Movie World	Bottrop	Germany	1996
Legoland Windsor	Windsor	UK	1996
Isla Mágica	Seville	Spain	1997
Terra Mítica	Benidorm	Spain	2001
Warner Bros Movie World	Madrid	Spain	2002
Legoland Deutschland	Gunzburg	Germany	2002
Walt Disney Studios Park	Marne-la-Vallée	France	2002

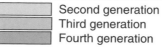

Predecessors   Second generation
First generation   Third generation
   Fourth generation

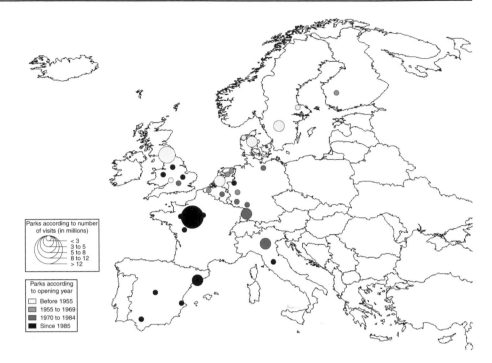

Fig. 3.4. Location of the main theme parks in Europe, 2005 (from author's own research based on *Amusement Business* and IAAPA data).

Great Britain in 1924), the first generation of today's theme parks in Europe was developed during the 1950s and 1960s. In their early days, they were landscaped amusement parks operated by family businesses with hardly any rides or services and, in any case, with a limited ability to capture demand. Examples of this type of park are Efteling (later renewed), which began operating in the Netherlands in 1952, or Phantasialand, which opened in Germany in 1967.

A second generation of parks played an important role in the expansion of this phenomenon in the 1970s. During this period, development continued to take place, but in Central and Northern Europe. Medium-sized parks appeared, basically operated by families. This is the case of German parks like Heide Park, in Soltau, which was started up in 1978 by Jurgen Tiemann, or Europa Park, opening in 1975, property of the Mack family (Lanquar, 1991). The latter got under way after the inheritor of the seventh generation of this lineage of manufacturers of machinery and games decided to transform a test area bought at the end of the 1960s in the surroundings of a castle to build an amusement park. In any case, they are strictly regional parks, that is to say, according to HTR (1999), with mixed demand, with over 50% of regional origin and less than 15% tourist demand.

In this context, the announcement in the mid-1980s of the future opening of a Disney park in Europe caused, as has already been indicated, renewed development of the activity in the last 15 years and a series of strategic decisions by investors and operators. Overcoming the economic crises of the 1970s and a notable increase in leisure time and family income accompanied this new boom in parks. Much of the development took place in France, with the creation of Mirapolis, Zigofolis, Futuroscope, Parc Astérix and Big Bang Schtroumpf (currently named Walygator Park) during the second half of the 1980s. Regarding this, Brown and Church (1987) speak of the 1980s as a period of expansion for the development of theme parks in Europe, both as a result of the creation of new parks and due to the multiplication of investments in existing parks. Moreover, the second half of the 1980s saw the replacement of Germany by France as the main theme park development area. It was the third generation of theme parks in Europe.

In this regard, Jones *et al.* (1998) consider that the announcement and the later opening of Disneyland Paris had a significant impact on at least six key points in the European system of parks:

- The expansion of the theme park business throughout Europe and the materialization of the multipark destination concept.
- The education of the market as regards the product's characteristics, the quality of the experience and the payment of a single entrance fee for a day of quality entertainment.
- The establishment of a market price of reference for the theme park market.
- The creation of a market through creative marketing plans and illustrating to competitors the use of effective marketing techniques.
- The improvement of management expertise in the European theme park business via the training of park management, which, in the future, may enhance the performance of the European parks business as a whole.
- The need for adequate positioning in the market concerning Disney strategy.

Thus, Disneyland Paris saw the inauguration of the fourth generation of parks in Europe. They are facilities developed by transnational companies, which introduced new operation methods, concepts and quality standards. Furthermore, as a result of this new generation of parks, those already in existence embarked on intensive reinvestment campaigns with the aim of developing new attractions and services that would generate revenue and repositioned themselves on the market. Efteling in the Netherlands was especially aggressive in this sense (see Van Assendelft de Coningh, 1994). Alton Towers in the UK, Europa Park in Germany, Parc Astérix in France and Gardaland in Italy followed in the wake. Fundamentally, it is a question of increasing the capacity of attractions and shows and broadening food and beverage services and commercial activity. Also, these parks decided, in order to increase the market, to develop holiday and/or recreational spaces nearby and include the parks within further-reaching tourist, hotel and commercial projects. The first stage of development really took off in the 1990s, with the development of hotels in Disneyland (seven hotels), Efteling, Europa Park (hotel and guest house), Liseberg Viking Hotel, Legoland, Alton Towers and Parc Astérix. A second wave of development since 2003 has brought more accommodation to Phantasialand (hotel and guest house), PortAventura (three hotels), the Liseberg Hotel Kärralunf, Disneyland Resort Paris (four partner hotels), Europa Park's Tipi Village, the Alton Towers Splash Landing Hotel, Blackpool Pleasure Beach's Big Blue, Colosseo Hotel at Europa Park and Eftelings's Dreamland Hotel (PricewaterhouseCoopers, 2004).

Repositioning, renovation, reinvestment and remarketing are a few key words that describe the present situation (see also Jones *et al.*, 1998). Parks like Alton Towers in England (2.4 million visits in 2005), Efteling in the Netherlands (3.1 million visits in 2005) and Gardaland in Italy (3.1 million visits in 2005) have changed in ways such as increasing the capacity of the attractions and shows or improving the provision of services to visitors like restaurants and shops. Thus, compared with previous leisure experience, which was commercially lacking and quasi-public (characterized by low admission fees), today parks are characterized by the facilities' greater orientation to the market, price increases and the redefinition of the demand. In fact, as of the last development stage, in Europe one may speak of a clear diversification process by the industry, whose main trait, in the words of Koranteng (2002), is the advent of a hiatus in the development of traditional theme parks in Europe based on roller coasters of immense proportions, in comparison with current expectations that highlight the goodness of investing in quiet, educational parks, providing entertainment, fundamentally urban, medium-sized, covered and conceptually linked to museums. This can be seen through the following:

1. The multiplication of the supply of unique products and the territorial generalization of small and medium-sized parks. Many proposals for the development of theme parks that exist today in Europe are on a small scale (between 250 and 750 thousand visits per year). A good example of this is the Ravensburger Spielelandpark, near Ravensburg in Germany. It covers 23 ha and has a capacity to attract nearly 300,000 visitors a year, primarily oriented at 2- to 12-year-old children. The park, with a high technological component, is configured as an interactive play space, with puzzles, films and attractions located in a highly pleasurable landscaped setting.
2. The multiplication of improvement processes, expansion programmes and investments along the lines of: (i) creating veritable recreational complexes like that of PortAventura in Spain, which, in addition to other recreational facilities, has started up three hotels since 2002; (ii) developing new business opportunities, like opening at Christmas, for example, as parks like Tivoli Gardens have done since the year 2000 or Liseberg, in Göteborg; (iii) incorporating thrilling attractions in

conventional parks (for example, the first 'flying' roller coaster, inaugurated in Alton Towers in 2002); and (iv) designing new attractions with a high technological component (for example, in Thorpe Park, the Pirates 4 D experience, inaugurated in 1999).

3. The growing valuation of local identity as an argument for the development of parks. A considerable number of themed projects today in Europe are clearly oriented at creating themed spaces based on heritage. Such operations can become emblematic in terms of symbology, image and cultural consumption where they are located. The Grand Parc du Puy du Fou is without doubt the characteristic point of reference for this trend. In this context, entertainment, in European parks, has increasingly more elements of informal education and instruction.

4. The diversification of the concept and of the formats. In addition to conventional parks, in Europe new products are being developed. As a paradigmatic example of this, see Autostadt, the car city that Volkswagen inaugurated in June 2000 in Wolfsburg, integrating, in a corporate visitor centre, the latest technological breakthroughs with museum-like presentations aiming to generate physical, emotional and intellectual sensations among its visitors (Gilling, 2001). This initiative joins Opel Live and is followed by Delivery and Event promoted by BMW. On the other hand, other projects currently being developed are based on educational concepts that can be easily covered by the media such as life or health (Bostnavaron, 1999).

5. The introduction of themes and formats based on the countryside and the environment (Hachache, 1999). In this sense, the bid by the Labyrinthus parks in France is clear. Also significant is Le Parc du Vegetal project located in Anjou, opened in 2005. It is a reconversion of an old golf course into a park, combining education and entertainment for a family public. At an estimated cost of €70 million, the project is the result of an agreement between the Département de Maine et Loire and a private initiative. It hinges around the area's agricultural image. It clearly evokes the California Bonfante Gardens in the USA. Annual demand is estimated at 0.5 million visitors during the initial phase, reaching the 1 million mark after 7 years.

6. The incorporation of Central European areas in the theme park market. Despite having still low levels of income, the area is attractive to operators due to the unregulated labour market, its tradition as regards entertainment, the demand for facilities with North American traits and the availability of economical land.

In any case, it cannot be forgotten that European demand for parks is growing and that the potential for growth through new parks or by improving existing parks' capacity to attract is still important (see McEniff, 1993; Jenner and Smith, 1996). In this regard, there is one point of interest that may be pointed out concerning the future dynamics of theme parks in Europe, which is the support given by the European public sector to such facilities. In this sense, it is paradigmatic that one of the

French successes with medium-sized theme parks is an initiative which was originally promoted 100% by a public administration with the aim of providing a medium-term response to a region's stagnant economy. This was Futuroscope. Similarly, the aforementioned Vulcania project in the Auvergne is also an initiative of the Regional Council (Conseil Régional d'Auvergne, 1999) or, in Spain, the recent development of Warner Bros Movie World in Madrid took place with the support of a company whose capital was provided by the Autonomous Community of Madrid, Arpegio. On another scale (not dealing in this case with a theme park), Dinópolis, in Teruel, has also arisen as a result of a regional public initiative to boost the economy of a deprived area.

In rounding off, according to Camp (1997) and HTR (1999), some weaknesses may be identified in the present structure of the theme park sector in Europe. They are as follows: errors in the consistency of the themes, unplanned growth, Europe's lack of know-how, a scarcity of expert corporations, the absence of specialized operators, low investment levels, high degrees of competition, the dependency of local markets, modest per capita expenditure, overlapping spheres of influence, labour costs and legislation that hinder the adaptation of human resources to peaks and troughs in demand, limited available land, restrictive territorial planning regulations, investors' lack of confidence and the prudent stance of the financial markets.

3.4. The Growth of the Markets in Asia/the Pacific

Since the beginning of the 1990s, Asia/the Pacific has become the theme park sector's main market of the future (Robertson, 1993). This is both due to the spending power and patterns of consumption in countries with a notable implantation of such facilities like Japan or South Korea and due to the possibilities of expanding into other markets like China and a series of countries in southern Asia, from India to the Indochina peninsula passing through Indonesia. This is so much so that, in 2005, Asia/the Pacific as a whole had over 125 facilities receiving more than 500,000 visitors a year. This figure is even higher than for the USA. It represents, between 2000 and 2005, a world quota of 35% of parks of this nature. During this period, visitor figures to parks in the region increased from 188 million to 233 million, and world market share increased from 34.5% to 38.4% in 2005. This has meant an increase in visitors per park, set at 1.83 million people in 2005, slightly above the world average, as well as a slight increase in per park revenue, which stood at $39.56 million in 2005, some five per cent below the world average.

However, in spite of the increased number of parks, and especially visits, the Asian market is becoming characterized by a fall over the last decade in per visitor income. Thus, between 2000 and 2005, per visitor income for theme parks in Asia/the Pacific fell from $23.49 to $21.56, some 13.5% below the world average. In fact, this trend had already been observed during the previous decade and persisted during the first 5 years of the new millennium. So, whereas in 1990 per visitor income at an Asian park stood at $30 (compared with the $23.3 average income globally), in 2000, per capita income had dropped to $23.49 (compared with the $25.3 world average) (Camp and Aaen, 2000). Economic reasons, the saturation of the principal markets and the opening of new markets with populations with still average income would explain this particular process. However, according to Jones *et al.* (1998), factors such as the growing level of expenditure on entertainment among the region's social groups enjoying higher incomes, the different countries' policies of economic support and the development of a multitude of joint public/private incentives should allow one to continue to have confidence in this market.

As can be seen in Table 3.10, with almost 45 million visitors to just the top five parks (Disneyland Tokyo, Disney Sea Tokyo and Universal Studios Japan in Japan and Everland and Lotte World in South Korea), Japan and South Korea are, as has been mentioned previously, the main theme park market in Asia/the Pacific. Among the remaining five, which represent 18.3 million visitors, are three Japanese parks (Yokohama Hakkejima Sea Paradise, Nagashima Spa Land and Suzuka Circuit) and two in China (Ocean Park and Happy Valley), one of which is in Hong Kong. The two parks in China represent just 6.6 million visits, slightly over 10% of the total number of visitors to the top ten parks. However, this result is significant of the emergence of China in the field of theme parks, especially, as we shall see later on, in the Pearl River Delta region. However, Japan's role is preponderant. Of the 65 million visits occurring in the region's top ten parks, 44.7, that is to say, 69%, are to Japanese parks. It is clear that first Disney's and then Universal Studios' penetration into this market, with 33 million visits in 2005, accounted for 51% of attendance at Japan's top-ranking parks. Figure 3.5 illustrates the location of the main parks in Asia/the Pacific.

The huge growth in the number of theme parks in the region today is being fomented by growing consumer purchasing power in many parts of South-east Asia. According to Hannigan (1998), the economic situation of Asia/the Pacific may be characterized as follows: an expanding economy, increased free time and a growing middle class. To this end, it has been estimated that, in 2010, the middle class in South-east Asia will reach the figure of 800 million. In cities like Bangkok, this will account for 20% of families. Thus, as a result of the growth of the issuing market of the region's main countries, most Asian communities and places are actively seeking to increase their share in the tourism industry (Kotler *et al.*, 2002). As Teo and Yeoh (2001) state, in fact, 'with money in their pockets and time to spare, many Asians are looking for amusement within Asia'. Moreover, within the current international trend towards shorter but more frequent vacations, many places within 2 hours' travel of major metropolitan areas have found new opportunities. Nevertheless, critical public infrastructure

Table 3.10. The recent evolution of attendance at the top ten theme parks in Asia/the Pacific, 1995–2005 (in million visits) (based on *Amusement Business* data).

	Park	1995	1996	1997	1998	1999	2000	2001	2002	2003	2004	2005
1	Tokyo Disneyland, Japan	15.5	17.0	17.3	16.7	17.4	16.5	17.7	13.0	13.2	13.2	13.0
2	Tokyo DisneySea, Japan	–	–	–	–	–	–	4.0	12.0	12.2	12.2	12.0
3	Universal Studios Japan	–	–	–	–	–	–	9.0	8.0	8.8	9.9	8.0
4	Everland, Seoul-Do, Korea	7.3	8.0	9.1	7.3	8.6	9.1	9.0	9.3	8.8	7.5	7.5
5	Lotte World, Seoul, Korea	5.0	5.2	6.3	5.8	6.1	7.2	7.4	9.1	8.5	8.0	6.2
6	Yokohama Hakkejima Sea Paradise, Japan	6.0	6.9	6.6	5.7	5.7	5.3	5.1	5.1	5.3	5.1	5.3
7	Ocean Park, Hong Kong	3.3	3.8	3.7	2.9	3.3	3.2	3.0	3.4	3	3.8	4.0
8	Nagashima Spa Land, Kuwana, Japan	3.6	3.5	3.5	3.2	n/a	4.5	3.9	2.5	n/a	3.8	3.8
9	Suzuka Circuit, Japan	n/a	3.5	2.6	3.2	3.2	3.0	2.9	2.7	2.7	2.6	2.6
10	Happy Valley, Shenzhen, China	–	–	–	n/a	n/a	n/a	n/a	n/a	n/a	n/a	2.6

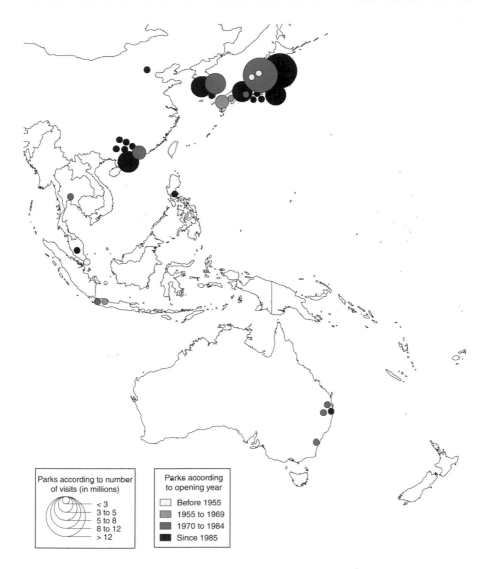

Fig. 3.5. Location of a selection of the main theme parks in Asia/the Pacific, 2002 (based on *Amusement Business* and IAAPA data).

is not yet in place in many parts of the main and most populated countries such as China and India.

Such a situation is leading to intense growth in the entertainment industry throughout the region, which is based on the importation of Western formats and concepts, theme parks among them. In fact, their links with other kinds of facility associated with consumer leisure, and in particular shopping malls, has been key in the eclosion of the development of theme parks as of the 1980s. As the number of malls grew and competition got fiercer, it was no longer enough to have restaurants, fast-food outlets, bars and cafes. Later, musical fountains, cinemas, ice rinks and even zoos were added. Then, to please the children, came amusement parks. Thus, the mall had transcended shopping; it had become a theme park. Consequently, several Asian cities are becoming 'tourism hubs', Bangkok, Singapore and Kuala Lumpur among them, and theme parks are central in their strategy.

Currently, the development of theme parks is being shaped by a mixture of global and local influences. In fact, consultants have to take into account the specificities that are characteristic of Asiatic consumers (Kazdoy, 2005). It cannot be forgotten, as Hannigan (1998) remarks, for example, that in different places in Asia 'location is governed by the practice of feng shui, a combination of architecture, metaphysics, science and parapsychology which aims to harmonize the placement of humanly constructed structures in nature'. So, with the exception of Disney and Universal, few of the themed developments are directly developed or franchized by the biggest international players. Indeed, most of them are being capitalized by corporate conglomerates and local or regional millionaires independently or in collaboration with state bodies. In many cases, government participation and involvement in creating conducive conditions for investments and providing incentives are the main factors that attract private entrepreneurs to invest in the leisure and entertainment industry. Hence, developments are usually carried out on the basis of the know-how of North American companies like Duell Corporation, Landmark, International Theme Park Services or Forrec. There also exist ventures such as Intra-Asia Development, a US-based company which developed and operates a park in the city of Weifang, in Shandong Province, the Weifang Fuhua Park.

Asia/the Pacific is, therefore, a clear example of how globalization allows a mixture of strategies, capital and know-how of multiple origins (including the emerging countries in the Pacific themselves). This is illustrated, to cite one example, by Discovery World, a theme park costing over $170 million, which the Taiwan Yue-mei International Development Corp. and Korea's Samsung Corp. have developed in Taichung, on the west coast of Taiwan. The planning and development of the park were in the hands of Forrec, a company in Toronto, which in turn coordinated a specialized team in which the companies Architectura from Vancouver, BRC Imagination Arts in Burbank, California, and LHA Architects, a firm of architectural consultants in Los Angeles (O'Brien, 1999; Emmons, 2002b), participated. According to Hannigan (1998), the growth of the leisure entertainment industry in the Pacific region has also been propelled by the proclivity of the nations of the region to invest in neighbouring economies.

The development process has also produced a mixture between global and local culture. In fact, as Teo and Yeoh (2001) maintain, 'local money has implications for the creation of identity in the parks'. According to them, three types of local agent exist who participate in such a dynamic:

governments, local communities and private companies. Sarawak Cultural Village is an example of state initiative. It is a living museum of the seven major ethnic groups dwelling in Sarawak. In Singapore, Malay Village has become a focal point of celebration for the whole nation as Malays celebrate the breaking of the fasting month at the Village. Likewise, the Chinese Garden, again in Singapore, is the venue for the Autumn Festival. It forms an integral part of the park's desire to be as much a part of the local as of the tourist landscape. Private companies, however, try to generate profits by applying some of the Disney traits to their theme park business. This is the case of Mines Resort City – which includes the Mines Wonderland theme park – in Kuala Lumpur. It is a park developed by Tan Sri Lee Kim Yew, which, like Disney, sells a lifestyle rather than a product. In general terms, eight models of theme parks can be established for Asia/the Pacific. Two of them, the 'local model' and 'the buffet model' have been previously defined by Hannigan (1998). It is noteworthy that a great many of them base their theme on culture, in its various modalities:

1. The 'Aboriginal model'. This is the exception rather than the rule. This is the case of the Tjapukai Cultural theme park in Cairns, Queensland, which is partially owned by the local Aboriginal community and attempts to provide an 'authentic' introduction to the life, culture and language of the Tjapukai tribe.

2. The 'local model', within which the theme park is developed around local culture. In Asia public investors such as the state have preferred to valorize traditional elements of local culture in cultural theme parks. Shaw and Williams (2004) indicate that, in these cases, 'at its most extreme, local tradition, lifestyles and culture may be compressed into the themed space and presented in an easily recognized way for visitors'. In fact, many parks tend to 'accentuate themes peculiar to their culture and location as a way to differentiate themselves from competitors' (Chang *et al.*, 1996). There are two other purposes: first, turning parks into tourist attractions to capture the tourist dollar and, secondly, to cater to the sense of identity of the multifarious ethnic groups in the region. This is the case of Splendid China and China Folk Culture Villages, which hold miniaturized national landmarks and authentic replicas of typical dwellings and cultural displays of 21 minority groups (Oakes, 1998).

3. The 'natural model'. Asia likes theme parks that offer reproductions of the natural world. This may be partly because of the potential disappearance of the real things, such as primary rainforests or many species of wildlife, from tigers to bears. So, in consequence, there is the creation of artificial indoor jungles in Malaysia or safari parks in Shenzhen or Singapore. This is the case of the AgroTourism Resort in Penang, Malaysia, a themed destination that juxtaposes a water park and a nature and wildlife reserve.

4. The 'buffet model', within which the visitor is given a mixture of attractions covering both global and traditional culture, as, for example,

Kyongju World Tradition Folk Village in South Korea. Here, visitors are able to choose from various world cultural zones such as the South Pacific, Europe or America as well as visiting an educational and recreational centre themed around Korean history (Hannigan, 1998).

5.   The 'wonderful world model'. Typical of one of the most important Japanese traditions of theme parks and currently being developed in China, it is a kind of park that focuses its interest on the representation of foreign countries and cultures. In fact, for the case of Japan, Hendry (2000a) distinguishes two kinds of *tema paku* or theme park: the *gaikoku mura* or foreign villages and the *yuenchi*, corresponding to the English meaning of the expression 'theme parks'. So, in Japan there are parks like Canadian World, Glüks Königreich (a German village), Marine Park Nixe (a Danish village), Tazawako Swiss Village, Roshia Mura (a Russian village), Parque España or Huis ten Bosch One (a Dutch village), as well as Nijinosato (which has British, Canadian and Japanese sections) or the Maruyama Shakespeare Park, among others. In addition to lacking rides, what these parks have in common is 'an extraordinary degree of attention to detail and authenticity, most including museums and displays about the people and cultures represented and several offering food, drink and goods imported directly and advertised as unavailable elsewhere in Japan'. Most of them capitalize on the Japanese fascination with the West (Raz, 1999). In other parts of the region, an interesting project is the Asia–Pacific Family Centre, which is planned for a northern suburb of Beijing.

6.   The 'global model'. This is the extension of the American theme park model as represented by the Disney Corporation in Japan and Hong Kong and as it has been adapted by many other parks around the area. Sceptics argue that the local markets are not big enough to sustain really huge American-style parks. However, several smaller experiences do exist. Thus, for example, Australia Dreamworld was developed by a local entre-preneur, John Longhurst, who hoped it would become Australia's answer to Disneyland. Without belonging to the large North American park corporations, this is also the case of Malaysia's main theme park, Sunway Lagoon, located in Bandar Sunway resort, near Kuala Lumpur. As Teo and Yeoh (2001) point out, in Sunway Lagoon, 'divided into a waterpark and a dry park, simulacra and fantasy characteristic of Disney are liberally used'. Even so, in this case, the local culture becomes evident in the park to the extent that 'fully-clothed Muslims frolic in the water of the Surfwave Pool'. One could also include within this typology those parks which, like some of the ones in Chinese cities such as Shenzhen, Shang-hai and Guangzhou more recently developed by North American consul-tants, incorporate a diversity of cultural referents, such as medieval knights and Wild West gunslingers.

7.   The 'high-tech model'. Includes parks based on the display of tech-nology such as Space World or Suzuka Circuit in Japan. Operated by Nippon Steel, Space World was developed in a former steel mill. It was opened in 1990. Among other attractions, it boasts a space shuttle, a

museum of space science and several futuristic rides. In addition, a Space Camp is operated under licence from the US Space Foundation, offering 2- and 4-day programmes for youngsters. Like Space World, Suzuka Circuit – a motor sports resort established in 1961 – which includes a theme park, a Grand Prix circuit and a resort, also provides educational programmes.

8. The 'simulacra model', characteristic of parks like Kurashiki Tivoli Park, which reproduces the reality of other already existing theme parks, like, in this case, the Danish park Tivoli.

Table 3.11 lists the opening dates of a selection of the region's most significant theme parks today. It is representative of the different traditions and of the different degrees of evolution of the industry in each country, with a long-standing tradition in countries like Japan, which, on the other hand, connects with other cultural manifestations like gardens, amusement parks and universal expositions, and a still very recent historical journey in an emerging country like China, passing through the emulation of North American cultural patterns as in the case of Australia. So, for example, in Indonesia, the theme park craze may have started in 1971 when Tien, the late wife of President Suharto, had the idea of Taman Mini Indonesia Indah – a reproduction, in miniature, of the thousands of islands that make up the sprawling archipelago of Indonesia. In any case, different countries' traditions vary in accordance with a series of cultural, social and economic factors that affect their development process. Also, as the operators themselves acknowledge, it is a region that currently has specific regional markets in each country.

In Japan, the main concentrations of parks are in the Kanto region, on the outskirts of Tokyo and near Osaka and Kobe (Jones, 1994). They are the two biggest urban areas in Japan. In the south of the island of Kyushu attractions are also being developed. According to Jones (1994) the first Japanese theme park was opened in 1965, the Meiji Museum Village. This is a heritage centre which consists of a reconstruction of a Meiji village and features the culture, lifestyle and architecture of the period. There were, previously, several amusement parks and gardens that were used as leisure places in a traditional way. The second major park development was built in 1975 and, in 1983, three theme parks opened, Tokyo Disneyland among them. Since then the latter has been Japan's most popular theme park and has generated a multitude of new initiatives. Since the end of the 1980s, the main Japanese industrial and service corporations have shown an interest in the theme park industry and there has been a virtual explosion of leisure-oriented theme parks throughout Japan. Many of them often have promotion and direct financial backing from the local authorities in whose areas they are located. Joint projects shared between several companies have been common in order to develop small and medium-sized parks. However, problems concerning their design, operation and funding and their poor results have triggered caution in certain Japanese enterprises.

Table 3.11. Opening year of a selection of Asia/Pacific theme parks (from author's own research).

Park	Location	Country	Year of opening
Toshimaen Amusement Park	Tokyo	Japan	1925
Haw Par Villa	Singapore	Singapore	1937
Yomiuri Land	Tokyo	Japan	1949
Suzuka Circuit	Suzuka	Japan	1962
Nagashima Spa Land	Kuwana	Japan	1964
Meiji Museum Village	Inuyama	Japan	1965
Jaya Ancol Dreamland	Jakarta	Indonesia	1967
Seaworld	Gold Coast	Australia	1971
Ocean Park	Hong Kong	China	1971
Expoland	Osaka	Japan	1971
Taman Mini Indonesia	Jakarta	Indonesia	1971
Toei Uzumasa Film Village	Kyoto	Japan	1975
Everland	Kyonggi-do	South Korea	1976
Siam Park	Bangkok	Thailand	1979
Dreamworld	Gold Coast	Australia	1981
Little World	Inuyama	Japan	1983
Nagasaki Holland Village	Nishisonogi	Japan	1983
Tokyo Disneyland	Tokyo	Japan	1983
Australia's Wonderland	Sydney	Australia	1984
Lotte World	Seoul	South Korea	1985
Huis ten Bosch	Sasebo	Japan	1985
Beijing Amusement Park	Beijing	China	1986
Seoul Land	Seoul	South Korea	1986
Splendid China	Shenzhen	China	1989
Sanrio Puroland	Tama	Japan	1990
Space World	Kyushu	Japan	1990
Warner Bros Movie World	Gold Coast	Australia	1991
Sanrio Harmonyland	Kyushu	Japan	1991
China Folk Cultures	Shenzhen	China	1991
Enchanted Kingdom	Manila	Philippines	1992
Window of the World	Shenzhen	China	1995

Continued

Table 3.11. *Continued.*

Happy Valley	Shenzhen	China	1997
Future World	Shenzhen	China	1999
Universal Studios Japan	Osaka	Japan	2001
Tokyo Disney Sea	Tokyo	Japan	2002
Hong Kong Disneyland	Hong Kong	China	2005

A good indicator of the magnitude of this phenomenon in Japan is the fact that the most visited theme park in the world is Disneyland Tokyo. The opening of Tokyo DisneySea, which received 4.7 million visitors in its first year, has strengthened the role of the Disney Company in the region. The start-up of Universal Japan in Osaka equally confirmed just how attractive the Asian market is for international park operators. As for South Korea, it houses two of the most visited parks in Asia, one of them, Lotte World, the biggest covered theme park in the world. These parks may be compared to Tokyo Disneyland or Ocean Park in Hong Kong, though, since they are located on the outskirts of the city of Seoul, they are not usually frequented on an international level. Steady internal demand ensures their commercial success.

According to Ren (1998), the 1990s experienced veritable theme park development 'fever' in China. According to the data he possesses, during the first half of the decade, over 300 parks were constructed. A report printed in *The Economist* in November 1999 indicated that in China, during the second half of the 1990s, over 2000 recreational attractions were built, ranging from children's to theme parks. Emmons (2002a) reports that in China there were approximately 400 parks at the start of the new millennium at an average cost of $12 million. Furthermore, an interesting fact is that, following common practice in the countries of South-east Asia, in China, malls are increasingly incorporating elements that are typical of theme parks, from covered roller coasters to artificial ski slopes. Korean and Taiwanese companies in addition to Chinese and North American ones are participating in the construction and development of a multitude of attractions. Most are built and operated by means of a one-sided agreement between the Communist Party of China and foreign capital, principally coming from Hong Kong, Taiwan and the USA.

The main development areas are the Pearl River Delta (Guangzhou, Zuhai and Shenzhen) and the outskirts of Hong Kong (where in 2005 Disney's Chinese park was started up), Shanghai (where Disney is studying to set up a new park) and Beijing (see Ap, 2003). There are also a variety of initiatives in continental China. Thus, significant projects have already been developed in Beijing (World Park and Chinese Ethnic Culture Park), Chengdu (World Landscape Park and Wonderland of the

Southwest) and Kumming (Yunnan Nationalities Villages), all of a marked cultural nature (whether dealing with Chinese ethnic minorities or world heritage). Beijing Amusement Park has been running since 1987. It was the result of a Sino-Japanese joint venture. They are parks receiving between 0.5 and 1.5 million visits a year. For all of the above, according to some analysts, this country is turning into 'the market of theme parks of the new millennium' (Zoltak, 1998). Despite the slowness of the development of the projects and the lack of certain support infrastructures hindering their materialization and commercial success, the size of the potential Chinese market (a sixth of the world population, low indices of ageing, motivation, a 5-day working week since 1994 and a growing per capita income – crucial for the take-off of the entertainment business and of tourism) gives rise to many, varied expectations among companies, not just in the most dynamic coastal areas but throughout the country. The main problems of Chinese parks are their limited recreational value, given their passive nature and scarce theming (most only manage to get average stays of between 2 and 4 h), in addition to under-maintenance, access difficulties for visitors, little reinvestment, unsafe/insecure conditions and low quality. On the other hand, the arrival of Disney in Hong Kong prompts visitors to expect higher standards of service and an excellent quality facility.

In any case, from the point of view of yield on investment, per capita income at existing parks in China is currently at a third of what is usual at parks in North America. Per capita expenditure stands at between $3.5 and 12.3. Admissions are the main generator of revenue, representing between 80 and 90% thereof. Investment per park is estimated at being far lower than in Japan and the USA, however, standing at between $12 and 74 million. For all of the above reasons, for the moment development is not leading to the emergence of China's own entertainment industry (Yoshii, 2002). Thus, at the 'China Theme Park Forum on Development' (Emmons, 2002a), it was made clear that the park market in China is characterized by:

- The misconception by investors that merely constructing them will guarantee a successful transaction.
- The common practice of copying theme parks that have enjoyed success.
- Excess supply.
- The scarce consideration of the capacity of innovations to provide the parks with distinction and uniqueness.
- The limited understanding of customers' expectations.
- Low value for money, which restricts return visits – most parks only receive the one visit.

In the countries of the Indochina peninsula, the development of theme parks has arisen out of the incorporation of recreational elements

and attractions into malls in large cities in the 1980s with the aim of setting them apart and lengthening consumers' stays there. The attractions have overtaken trade, and a kind of theme park, which is usually
incorporated in other recreational and commercial facilities, has become
generalized. So, for example, in Bangkok, ingenious ways are needed to
persuade shoppers to stay put once they have arrived. At the Seacon
Square Mall, which opened in 1994, the fourth-floor amusement park
has a roller coaster, a Ferris wheel, a monorail and a Land of Water, with
rides on boats. Leoland Central City, also in Bangkok, opened in 1995
with seven types of swimming pool and a '7 Traveltron' simulator theatre,
which jerks and wobbles to make the onlooker feel part of the attraction.
This is also the case of the Philippines, where S.M. Prime, a shopping-
mall developer, is using a theme park to attract shoppers to what it
says will be the world's largest mall, which it is building on reclaimed
land in Manila Bay. In fact, these initiatives form part of city marketing
strategies of places like Jakarta, Manila, Bangkok, Singapore or Kuala
Lumpur, among others, whose strategic targets include becoming gate-
ways for the entry of tourists to the region. This is why they offer a great
many incentives to larger theme park operators and recreational developers and why these operators continuously probe these markets (Yoshii,
2002).

According to analysts, the phenomenon is reaching its greatest
expression in the capital of Malaysia, where one of the many grandiose
schemes for the city involves privatizing a stretch of Kuala Lumpur's
Klang River. With the construction of Linear City, a ten-storey tube-like
structure will snake on stilts above the river for a mile and a quarter
(2 km). In addition to the predictable shopping malls, this enormous tube
will contain 108 restaurants; a jazz club; an aviary; and a collection of
hotels (linked by cable car), apartments and offices. Its theme parks will
include NatureWorld, a reconstructed rainforest stalked by robotic rubber
dinosaurs; SportsWorld, which will offer rock-climbing, scuba-diving and
ice-skating and CyberWorld, where monsters and villains can be hunted
with laser guns.

Though there is a sufficiently sizeable middle class among its 800 mil-
lion-plus-strong population, the development of the theme park industry
in India is lower than in the rest of the countries of the area. Amusement
facilities and particularly theme/amusement parks are nevertheless growing in India, which has more than 200 family entertainment centres and
more than 50 local and regional amusement parks. However, consultants
like Spiegel, president of Theme Park International Services, have stated
that India is probably 10 to 12 years from being able to support a theme
park of the size of Disneyland (Powers, 2006). The challenges faced are
the improvement of infrastructure, the protection of trademark and copyright interests, more favourable government regulations, great mass transportation systems and adequate waste removal systems, among other
things. Nevertheless, in 2006 Turner Broadcasting System, a Time Warner
company popularly know for its animated Channel, Cartoon Network,

announced plans to launch two innovative, world-class, Western-standards theme parks in India based on Indian kids' channels Cartoon Networks and Pogo. The objective is not only to entertain but also to help build the media brand faster in India. They estimate that, in this country, the leisure industry, including family entertainment centres, malls, multiplexes, water parks and amusement/theme parks, has a market of around 30 million people. Both parks – Cartoon Network Townsville and Planet Pogo – will be built in Delhi. There, the per capita income is twice the national average. As in many other parts of Asia/the Pacific, this development combines local and global interests. The developing team comprises Canada-based Forrec for architecture, Management Consultants from California as operational consultants, Hong Kong-based MVA Hong Kong Ltd as traffic consultants, TÜV (Technischer Überwachungsverein) from Germany to measure and monitor quality and Scotland-based EuroPools for water management.

According to Hannigan (1998), the evolution of the theme park industry in Australia can be traced back to the early part of the 20th century with the Luna Park in Sydney and in Melbourne. However, the first real theme park, Dreamworld, developed by local businessman John Longhurst to the south of Brisbane on the Gold Coast, was inaugurated in 1981. Australia's Wonderland opened in Sydney's western suburbs in 1987. It was developed by Taft Broadcasting, an Ohio television and media company, which, in the 1970s, came into the park business in order to dispose of a vehicle through which to show the cartoon characters whose licence it held. In 1982, Taft had built, prior to its Australian park, Canada's Wonderland on the outskirts of Toronto. Both parks were sold during the second half of the 1990s to Asian companies, Dreamworld to the Singapore shipping magnate Kua Phek Long and Wonderland to the owner of Malaysia's Sunway City park. The development of parks in Australia has concentrated on the east coast, where most of the population is concentrated as well as the prime tourist destinations. In the area of the Brisbane Gold Coast corridor, at the end of the 1980s, Warner and Village Roadshow undertook the development of the Warner Village Theme Parks, comprising SeaWorld, Movie World and Wet 'n Wild Water Park. In parallel, old amusement parks such as Luna Park in Sydney reopened in 2003. However, given its scarce demographic volume and the recent failure of the Fox Studios' park, which opened in 1999 and closed in 2001, investors tend to inject cash into other types of recreational and consumer facilities instead of theme parks. This is the case of Tropical Fruit World, Currumbin Sanctuary and Cable Sports World.

In conclusion, some critical points may be made concerning the current structure of the theme park sector in Asia/the Pacific. First, it should be pointed out that the opening of Disney in Hong Kong need not necessarily affect its competitors negatively: rather, the opposite. It may well stimulate, as it did in Japan, the development of new initiatives and the enhancement of existing ones. In any case, one must be aware, in the first place, for the case of Asia, of the regional character of the predominant markets. So there is a particular need, for the parks in Asia/the Pacific as a whole, to take Teo and Yeoh's (2001) recommendations for the parks of Singapore in the sense that part of their future success will lie 'in knowing the markets and in being quick to respond to taste changes'. Secondly, from such an angle innovation is key in maintaining continuous demand in the short term. Thirdly, Asian parks must be able to extend the length of visitors' tourist stays. To this end, a process of the incorporation of theme parks in more complex leisure operations that include other recreational attractions and activities as well as accommodation is observed, as has happened in the USA and in Europe. This is the case of the aforementioned Sunway Lagoon. Without a doubt, the development of the theme park industry is still growing. Initiatives are many and they clearly include operations that integrate everything from theme parks to malls through hotel resorts, as is the case of redeveloped Sentosa Island in Singapore. Differences between countries and the uses by the population of this kind of facility are, on the other hand, notable: hence the operators' interest, at this time of growth, in having greater knowledge of the market to allow consolidation, cooperation and innovation in the industry. Nevertheless, the reality is that knowledge as to the state of the theme park industry in the different parts of the region is still greatly unbalanced and limited.

3.5. The Proliferation of Initiatives in the Rest of the World

The main hot spot of growth in the theme park industry in the rest of the world is Latin America. There are indications of expansion such as the arrival of Six Flags in Mexico in 1999, the positive evolution of the Corporación Interamericana de Entretenimiento and the initiatives pursued in Brazil with the support of the administration. However, the differences between countries and their political, economic and social instability hinder the homogeneous development of regional parks and, barring Mexico, the start-up of parks with fundamentally tourist purposes. On the other hand, globally speaking, in Latin America there is a prevalence of traditional amusement parks. An important percentage is accounted for by family businesses, whose concept is in line with the atmosphere of a fair or carnival.

As can be seen in Table 3.12, in 2005 the Latin American park to receive the highest visitor numbers was Six Flags Mexico, with 2.2 million visits. Six Flags' arrival in Mexico took place in 1999 with the purchase of the Reino Aventura park, founded in 1982 and located in the federal capital. The management of Six Flags has provided the park with the corporate style of the North American company and has served to introduce to Mexico the common standards of North American theme parks. For consultants such as Economics Research Associates (ERA), such a presence forces the other park operators in Latin America to

Table 3.12. Attendance in the principal ten theme parks in Latin America, 2005 (in million visits) (from *Amusement Business*).

Order	Park	Country	Visits 2005
1	Six Flags Mexico, México DF	Mexico	2.279
2	Playcenter, São Paulo	Brazil	1.650
3	La Feria de Chapultapec, Mexico DF	Mexico	1.533
4	El Salitre Mágico, Bogotá	Colombia	1.485
5	Hopi Hari, São Paulo	Brazil	1.305
6	Plaza de Sésamo, Monterrey	Mexico	0.960
7	Selva Mágica, Guadalajara	Mexico	0.862
8	La Ciudad de los Niños, Mexico DF	Mexico	0.810
9	Parque da Monica, São Paulo	Brazil	0.575
10	Valle Fantástico, Puebla	Mexico	0.500

incorporate international quality standards (O'Brien, 2001b). La Feria de Chatapultapec, also in Mexico City, was the second park in Mexico in 2005 for visitor numbers. Since 2001, it has been completely controlled by the Corporación Interamericana de Entretenimiento (CIE), owner of a further ten facilities in Mexico and Latin America and, therefore, the sector's Latin American leader. CIE also owns the main Mexican theme park outside the federal capital, Selva Mágica, in Guadalajara. The success enjoyed by the Salitre Mágico park in Bogotá, opened in 2000 and also the property of the Mexican group, is also noteworthy. As can be observed in Fig. 3.6, parks also exist in Mexico at tourist destinations like Acapulco and Cancun. It is interesting to point out, in this latter case, the existence of thematic ecological and water parks belonging to the Xcaret Group – Xcaret, Xel Ha, Garrafón – with over 750,000 visits a year.

As can be seen in Table 3.13, among the top six most visited parks in Latin America in recent years are two in São Paulo, Playcenter – Brazil's most traditional theme park, founded in 1973, 10 miles from the city centre – and Hopi Hari. As of the end of the 1980s, Brazil has experienced a growing appearance of themed facilities, among them, the Parque da Monica, an indoor theme park located in a shopping mall – also in the São Paulo metropolitan area. Now, as in the case of Mexico, frequentation of parks in Brazil remains moderate and there are great inter-annual instability and relatively low growth rates. In the rest of Latin America, the small regional parks set around big cities like Buenos Aires and Bogotá dominate.

Outside Latin America, there are different realities and diverse initiatives in all four corners of the world. Regarding Africa, park consultants and promoters (O'Brien, 2001a) maintain that, barring a few existing developments like Dadda in the old part of Tunis or the children's

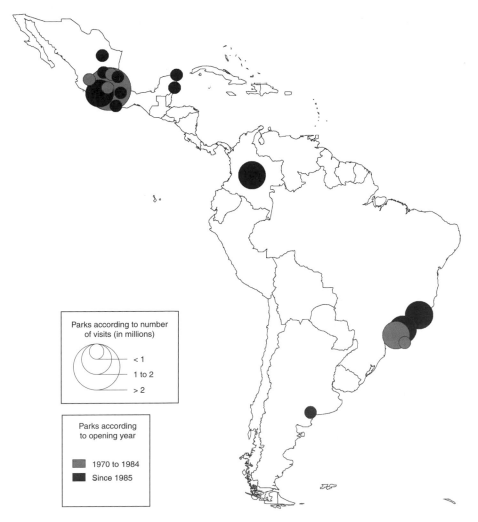

Fig. 3.6. Location of the main theme parks in Latin America, 2005 (from author's own research based on *Amusement Business* and IAAPA data).

amusement parks that exist in Islamic cities and resorts in North Africa, the development of such initiatives is necessarily linked to the creation of tourist destinations in the countries of the Mediterranean coast to cover European family-type demand. Issues such as the region's political instability, the state of the economy and the unlikelihood of the local population visiting this type of recreational attraction condition all kinds of development. Thus, Forrec designed a small park for the Tunisian tourist corporation, Polina Holdings, of half a hectare in size on the outskirts of Tunis, Carthago Adventureland, linked to an integral tourism and recreation project with the idea of attracting some 600,000 visitors a year. As for South Africa, there are some consolidated parks such as Gold Reef City

Table 3.13. Recent evolution of attendance at the most visited theme parks in Latin America, 1995–2005 (in million visits) (based on *Amusement Business* data).

Park	1995	1996	1997	1998	1999	2000	2001	2002	2003	2004	2005
Six Flags Mexico, Mexico DF[a]	3.4	2.9	3	2.7	2.7	2.1	2.6	2.5	2.5	2.1	2.3
Playcenter, São Paulo	2.3	2.1	2	2.1	1.8	1.5	1.8	1.8	1.6	1.7	1.6
La Feria de Chapultapec, Mexico DF	1.4	2.0	1.7	2.1	2.3	2.8	2.7	2.9	2.8	2.7	1.5
El Salitre Mágico, Bogotá	–	–	–	–	–	1.6	1.6	1.5	1.5	1.6	1.5
Hopi Hari, São Paulo	–	–	–	–	–	1.9	2.0	2.2	2.0	2.1	1.3
Selva Mágica, Guadalajara	1.3	1.6	1.6	1.8	1.8	1.8	1.8	1.9	1.9	1.9	0.9

a. Until 2000, Reino Aventura.

and the Lost City in the Suncity recreational complex in Johannesburg and Ratanga Junction in Capetown, as well as recent initiatives like Africa The Park, a project developed by ITEC Entertainment Corporation in Johannesburg with a forecast frequentation of over 2.5 million a year. The park aims to entertain the family public and is founded on the precise presentation of African cultures (Nevin, 2005). In general terms, as Swarbrooke (2002) suggests, the reasons that explain the scarce presence of such facilities in Africa are:

- A lack of recognition of the potential role of inbound cultural tourism.
- Relatively low levels of economic development and unequal distribution of wealth, which often limit the potential domestic market for attractions.
- Inadequate infrastructure to support the development of attractions.
- Political and/or economic instability, which discourages the substantial investment required for the development of attractions.
- An emphasis in tourism policy and tourism marketing on 'traditional' natural attractions such as beaches and wildlife.

In the Near East and the Arabian Peninsula, Dubai is playing a major role in a large-scale touristic dynamization process also involving the consequent planning of parks like Dubailand. Other emirates and countries in the region such as Qatar, Bahrain, Abu Dhabi and Oman, to mention a few, are beginning to emulate the dynamic of Dubai and it is plausible to imagine a process of the growth of theme parks associated with the creation of tourist, recreational and commercial infrastructures. Other reasons would explain the incipient development of theme parks – to date – in Saudi Arabia, where over the last 5 years several parks oriented towards the region's dominant social classes have been planned and, in some cases, started up. Thus, JPI Design, an entertainment architecture studio from Ontario, was chosen in 2001 by Mersal Entertainment to draw up the bases of Adventure World, a theme park based on the most popular tales from around the world among Arabs and covering 14 ha in Mersal Village, a tourist destination located on the outskirts of Jeddah on the Red Sea coast. There already existed a themed attraction in Jeddah, Jungle Land, which is to be incorporated into the new park as one of its 12 thematic areas. In parallel, CT Hsu International, an Orlando-based company of architects, has designed another 15 ha park, Al Shallal Festival, again in the surroundings of Jeddah, for Fakieh Poultry Farms, one of the biggest fast food corporations in Saudi Arabia. Also, the Saudi chain of hotels, Alhokair & Sons Group, opened a theme park in 2001 near Riyadh airport aimed at the regional market, families from the Persian Gulf and resident expatriates in the area known as Alhokairland. The park includes five themed areas corresponding to as many world regions, in addition to a further three themed sections: Malland, given over to trade and food and drink, Abcarino, an educational area for children, and a convention centre.

Case 5. The Recent Growth of the Theme Park Industry in Brazil

Precursors of the theme park industry in Brazil date back to the beginning of the 20th century with the development of the Parque Fluminense in Rio de Janeiro. Inaugurated in 1899 and having a roller coaster as its main attraction, in 1900 it incorporated different components imported from the Paris international exposition of the same year. However, in spite of the existence of initiatives such as the amusement park installed at the 1922 Universal Exposition – with a great variety of attractions, including cinemas, theatres, roller coasters and dance halls – or the development of a leisure area at the Parque do Ibirapuera during the 1950s on the occasion of the festivities to commemorate the fourth centenary of the city of São Paulo, Brazil's first amusement park did not start functioning until the beginning of the 1970s (Salomao, 2000). Playcenter was located in the São Paulo area and its main attraction was a roller coaster. Currently, following renovation works done in 2002, it has over 30 attractions and covers a surface area of 11 ha.

In any case, the development of the industry did not take place until the beginning of the 1980s. In fact, for many years the Brazilian military governments considered the amusement industry a superfluous sector of the economy and the importation of such kinds of products was prohibited. Thus, it was not until the Collor government at the beginning of the 1990s that the veto was suspended. In 1989, ADIBRA, the Brazilian Association for the Amusement Industry, was founded, whose aim is to boost the growth of the industry. The expansion of the industry in the 1990s was contributed to, in addition to the lifting of the veto on importation, by the commitment made by the sectorial Chamber of Tourism of the Ministry of Trade and Industry with the aim of professionalizing the sector and obtaining fiscal incentives, the reduction in the tax on industrialized products promoted by the first government of Cardoso already in the early 1990s, the new national policy to stimulate tourism, economic stability, the opening of lines of finance by the National Bank of Economic and Social Development and, especially, changes to tax laws (Paes de Barros, 1996). As a result of this new context of development, during the 1990s, an expansion process got under way, a consequence of which was the implantation of the theme parks that appear in Table 3.14. A progressive growth process can be observed, with facilities of a small and medium size often linked to the existence of malls. In fact, due to several financial problems, Terra Encantada, which, at the time of its planning was presented as the largest theme park development in the whole of Latin America, became, after just a short while, a commercial leisure centre with cinemas, bars and shops. Also, it ceded part of its surface area to Estácio de Sá University.

Parallel to the development of theme parks, the leisure industry has also developed in other related fields. Thus, in 1985, the first Brazilian water park was inaugurated in Ceará, The Beach Park – currently one of the biggest tourist complexes in the north-east of the country – and, in

Table 3.14. Principal theme parks implanted in Brazil as of the 1990s (based on de Araújo Rodrigues, 2004).

Park	Location	Opening year	Year of closure	Average visitors (million)	Observations
Beto Carrero	Penha (Santa Catarina)	1991		0.6	US$190 million initial investment for an area of 61 ha divided into seven themed areas. Promoted by private investor Joao Batista Sergio Murad.
Parque da Monica	São Paulo	1993		0.6	Located in the Eldorado Shopping Center on a 1 ha surface area. Aimed at the under-12s. Promoted by Mauricio de Souza Produçoes.
Parque do Gugu	São Paulo	1997	2002	–	Located in the Shopping Center Market on an area of 1.2 ha. In 2003, it was replaced by the new Mundo da Xuxa Park.
Terra Encantada	Rio de Janeiro	1998	2001	–	US$240 million initial investment whose purpose was to build the biggest theme park in Latin America. In 2001, it was turned into a commercial leisure centre.
Magic Park	Aparecida do Norte (SP)	1998		0.2	US$80 million initial investment for an area of 10 ha divided into nine themed areas. Promoted by Park Inn and Previ.
Parque da Monica	Rio de Janeiro	1999		0.4	Located in the Cité América Shopping Mall. Following the same model as the Parque da Monica in São Paulo.
Hopi Hari	Vinhedo (São Paulo)	1999		1.8	US$160 million initial investment for a surface area of 76 ha divided into five themed areas. Investors were the Grupo Playcenter, operator of Brazil's first attractions park and five pension funds.
Mundo da Xuxa	São Paulo	2003		N/A	Promoted by the popular TV presenter Xuxa and targeting the under-10s. It is located on the site that was abandoned by the Parque do Gugu in the Shopping Center Market in São Paulo.

1991, the first indoor water park was inaugurated in São Paulo, The Waves, though it closed after 4 years. On the other hand, in 1998, the North American franchise Wet 'n Wild set up in São Paulo, followed a year later with the inauguration of a new park in Rio de Janeiro. The country's main water park – Hot Park – is located at the classic thermal spa of Caldas Novas, in the state of Goiás (see Lopes, 2002).

4 A Profile of Major Theme Park Operators

> The whole world is made to pass through the filter of the culture industry.
> (Theodor W. Adorno and Max Horkheimer, 1944)

The destination of 69.7% of the 232.4 million visits made during 2005 to theme parks with a frequentation of over 2.5 million was a park operated by one of the large North American entertainment corporations. In greater detail, 41.6% of the visits made to the biggest parks in the world were to parks belonging to the Walt Disney Company. In fact, 24 of the 42 parks that received more than 2.5 million visits during 2005 are run by Disney (nine parks), Universal Studios (four parks), Anheuser Busch (four parks), Six Flags (three parks), Cedar Fair (two parks) and Paramount Parks (two parks). Moreover, in May 2006, Paramount Parks became the property of Cedar Fair. On the other hand, among the other most frequented parks in the world, there are eight in Europe (29.55 million visits), seven in Asia (32.03 million visits) and only three in North America (8.83 million visits). These parks are run under different formulas, whether through independent companies, regional corporations devoted to entertainment or multi-sectorial groups with interests in the business of leisure.

In any case, the diversity of operators that participate in the business of theme parks and the existence of two kinds of dynamics are significant. The first, of a global nature, is led by a few operators, in particular Disney and, to a lesser extent, Universal, whose main players are the majority of the most visited parks in the world. Both companies are the only two corporations with clear transnational positioning with a presence in the Asian markets and, in the case of Disney, Europe. In fact, competition between Disney and Universal on a global scale became, according to Rubin (1997), a spectacular process in the thematic entertainment industry during the 1990s. Despite that, the situation of one and the other is unequal, as can be seen in Table 4.1. The second dynamic is of a regional nature and presents

Table 4.1. Transnational positioning of Disney and Universal, 2005 (based on *Amusement Business*).

	Disney		Universal	
	Parks	Visits (million)	Parks	Visits (million)
USA	6	63.3	3	16.5
Asia/the Pacific[a]	2	25.0	1	8.0
Europe	2	14.2	–	–
Openings 1998–2005[a]	4	28.2	2	14.1

a. Does not include Hong Kong Disneyland.

differences in each part of the world. Thus, in the USA, the integration of parks into just a handful of companies is keeping the existence of independent parks to a minimum and the consolidation of alliances with media conglomerates has turned the parks into instruments for marketing corporate brands (Stevens, 2003). In Europe, the first corporations are emerging, which, being well consolidated in some European countries, are proposing transnational strategies in the regional and local theme park sector while keeping important, independent, regional parks of reference. They are, on the other hand, corporations that do not exclusively operate theme parks but incorporate another type of visitor attractions among their facilities. In parallel, in Asia/the Pacific, the processes of transnationalization are still in their early days, except in the cases of the development of large parks by the big North American companies, whereas, in Latin America, there is only one large corporation operating parks, which is linked, as in the case of North American operators, with the media and entertainment industry. Besides, in Europe, Asia/the Pacific and Latin America there is a dominance of independently run parks.

4.1. The Role of the Large Operators in the USA

Control of the business of theme parks in the USA is currently in the hands of a few large corporations, namely the Walt Disney Company, Six Flags, Universal Studios, Anheuser Busch and Cedar Fair. In 2006 Cedar Fair bought the Paramount Parks division from CBS Corp. These companies absorb a large percentage of visitors and revenue and set the trend with regards to the technology to implement, the rides to develop (high-definition films, simulators or virtual reality) and the new entertainment alternatives to be designed, in and outside theme parks. As Davis (1997, 22) points out, only a few small local parks, in some cases survivors of old pre-Second World War amusement parks, remain in the business.

This dynamic is the result of a process of concentration helped by the market, which is becoming generalized in the USA in the different areas of family entertainment. The same thing happens, for example, in the business of family entertainment parks with Palace Entertainment. Established in 1998 after the initial acquisition of four independently owned family entertainment companies, it has become the largest family amusement and water park operator in the USA, with 38 facilities that include such features as go-kart racing, video game arcades, laser tag and bumper boats. It receives over 12 million visitors annually and is ranked among the top ten amusement and theme park chains by *Amusement Business* since 2003. Palace Entertainment owns Boomers, Castle Park, Silver Springs, Malibu Grand Prix, Mountasia and Speedzone family entertainment parks in California, Texas, Florida, Georgia and New York. The firm has been on a buying spree as of late and has rebranded all of its acquired facilities and probably will be in the next level of theme parks in a few years. In fact, as Stevens (2003) remarks, 'the key to future attraction development will be in creating and controlling intellectual properties and brands. Companies develop unique experiences incorporating themed retail and entertainment with powerful brands that cannot be duplicated.' Also, according to Stevens (2003), 'this is the emergence of what has become known as "corporate lands"'.

As can be seen in Table 4.2, the number of visitors to the attractions of the main North American theme park operators grew nearly 55% between 1994 and 2005. Between these dates, the number of visits increased from 137.7 million to 211.2 million. At the same time, it can be observed in Table 4.3 that the number of facilities operated by all corporations (including, in addition to theme parks, amusement parks, water parks and animal parks, for example) has grown from 36 to 75, i.e. 108%. Three questions of interest can be highlighted with regard to growth during this last period:

1. The growth in the number of facilities has taken place via the acquisition of parks (the case of Six Flags or Cedar Fair). Only a part of the growth has been as a result of the construction of newly built parks (principally Disney and Universal), whether in the USA or in other parts of the world. Paramount Parks – owned by Cedar Fair since 2006 – and Anheuser Busch remain stable for this period.
2. The growth in the number of visits and facilities has taken place through dynamics of diversification, which includes the development and operation, together with actual theme parks, of water parks, parks with animals and other attractions integrated within the recreational areas that the corporations have developed in the surroundings of theme parks (it is significant that, of the 32 Six Flags facilities, only 21 are actual theme parks).
3. An inflection occurs in the growth trend as of 2002. In fact, that year signals the maximum number of visitors and number of facilities in the group of principal North American corporations, with 226.9 million visits and 83 parks. The decline can be explained by two points, a slight stagnation in internal demand and the general dynamics of disinvestment in Europe

Table 4.2. Evolution of the number of visitors to the main North American theme park operators, 1994–2005 (in millions of visits)[a] (based on *Amusement Business* data).

Operator	1994	1995	1996	1997	1998	1999	2000	2001	2002	2003	2004	2005
1 Walt Disney Attractions	65.2	75.6	81.0	86.0	87.0	89.2	89.3	94.7	96.5	96.7	101.0	106.0
2 Six Flags Inc.	21.8	24.3	25.9	25.6	38.1	47.5	48.8	51.2	50.5	48.2	33.2	35.1
3 Universal Studios[b]	12.3	12.7	13.8	14.3	18.5	20.9	23.8	31.2	31.1	31.0	29.2	26.0
4 Anheuser Busch Theme Parks	19.9	19.8	20.0	20.7	20.4	19.5	20.2	20.7	20.1	20.0	20.1	21.2
5 Cedar Fair Ltd	5.9	7.1	6.9	13.4	13.7	13.5	14.0	14.3	14.9	14.6	14.6	14.8
6 Paramount Parks[c]	12.6	13.3	13.4	12.8	12.9	12.3	12.0	12.2	13.8	13.6	13.1	13.4
Total	137.7	152.8	161	172.8	190.6	202.9	208.1	224.3	226.9	224.1	211.2	216.5

a. Includes all facilities operated by each corporation, whether theme parks, amusement parks, water parks, animal parks or other attractions.
b. Previously Music Corporation of America (MCA).
c. Owned by Cedar Fair since 2006.

Table 4.3. Evolution of the number of facilities of the main North American theme park operators, 1994–2005[a] (based on *Amusement Business* data).

	Operator	1994	1995	1996	1997	1998	1999	2000	2001	2002	2003	2004	2005
1	Walt Disney Attractions	7	8	8	8	9	9	9	11	12	12	12	13
2	Six Flags Inc.	9	11	12	12	31	35	36	38	40	40	32	31
3	Universal Studios[b]	2	2	2	2	5	5	5	6	7	7	5	5
4	Anheuser Busch Theme Parks	10	9	9	9	9	9	10	10	9	9	9	9
5	Cedar Fair Ltd	3	5	5	7	8	8	10	12	9	12	12	13
6	Paramount Parks[c]	5	6	6	6	6	5	5	5	6	6	5	5
	Total	36	41	42	44	68	71	75	82	83	86	75	76

a. Includes all facilities operated by each corporation, whether theme parks, amusement parks, water parks, animal parks or other attractions.

b. Previously MCA Corp.

c. Owned by Cedar Fair since 2006.

by Universal, Six Flags and Paramount. At the beginning of the new millennium came an end to the state of euphoria running through some corporate headquarters with the idea that, given an apparent slowing down of the US market, especially for large-scale theme park development, there was an opportunity to develop the potential in the European markets, as occurred in the early 1990s.

As a result of this process, in Table 4.4 it can be observed that, despite the increase in the number of visitors, between 1994 and 2005 there was a significant decrease in the number of visitors per recreational facility. This is especially clear with the companies that have experienced the greatest expansion or that have incorporated the greatest number of other attractions, such as water parks. Thus, Disney went from receiving 9.3 million visits per park in 1994 to 8.1 million in 2005, Six Flags from 2.4 million to 1.1 million and Cedar Fair from 2.0 million to 1.1 million. After withdrawing from Europe, Universal managed to obtain a frequentation per park close to the 6.2 million of 1994. However, there have been ups and downs – from 7.2 million in 1997 to 4.2 million in 1999. Evidently, questions of circumstance influence the final figures. Nevertheless, also well known are the so-called 'cannibalization' processes of demand which have taken place with the opening of a new park adjacent to a pre-existing one.

The dynamic of loss of visitors per park is especially significant in the case of Six Flags and Cedar Fair. Here, it can be explained by the constant incorporation of a great many small-sized parks into the chain and, most relevantly, by the time – from 2 to 3 years – that is required for the process of redesigning the parks that join the chain. In fact, there is evidence that the effects of such incorporation on the overall number of visitors are not immediate, though, the results are positive in the medium term. Finally, the figures for Busch and Paramount have remained far more stable. The reason is the conservatism of these corporations, which is translated into the non-increment in the number of facilities and the concentration of their businesses on a type of establishment whose characteristics, scale and processes they are highly familiar with. The results of visitors per attraction also offer a clear differentiation between corporations managing large parks or parks located in multipark destinations and corporations specializing in regional and local parks. Disney and Universal, with per-park visitors at 8.1 and 5.4 million, are among the first.

4.1.1. Disney's integral strategy

According to D'Hautaserre (1997), due to the intangible assets it develops, its ability to create new, imaginative media consumption products and its sophisticated imagineering skills, Disney has become the park operator par excellence. Due to its vast resources, its financial capacity, its ability to recruit the top professionals and its commitment to high levels of quality and customer service, it has become, furthermore, a reference for the

Table 4.4. Visits per attraction among the main North American park operators 1994–2005 (in millions of visits)[a] (based on *Amusement Business* data).

	Operator	1994	1995	1996	1997	1998	1999	2000	2001	2002	2003	2004	2005
1	Walt Disney Attractions	9.3	9.5	10.1	10.8	9.7	9.9	9.9	8.6	8.0	8.1	8.4	8.1
2	Six Flags Inc.	2.4	2.2	2.2	2.1	1.2	1.4	1.4	1.3	1.3	1.2	1.0	1.1
3	Universal Studios[b]	6.2	6.4	6.9	7.2	3.7	4.2	4.8	5.2	4.4	4.4	5.9	5.2
4	Anheuser Busch Theme Parks	2.0	2.2	2.2	2.3	2.3	2.2	2.0	2.1	2.2	2.2	2.2	2.4
5	Cedar Fair Ltd	2.0	1.4	1.4	1.9	1.7	1.7	1.4	1.2	1.7	1.2	1.2	1.1
6	Paramount Parks[c]	2.5	2.2	2.2	2.1	2.2	2.5	2.4	2.4	2.3	2.3	2.6	2.7
	Total	3.8	3.7	3.8	3.9	2.8	2.9	2.8	2.7	2.7	2.6	2.8	2.8

a. Includes all facilities operated by each corporation, whether theme parks, amusement parks, water parks, animal parks or other attractions.

b. Previously MCA Corp.

c. Owned by Cedar Fair since 2006.

rest of the industry. With the development of Walt Disney World in Orlando during the 1980s, Disney materializes, in addition, the multipark resort destination concept. The parks and resorts division is one of the Walt Disney Company's four main divisions, together with the following other business segments: studio entertainment, consumer products and media networks. In all of these cases, the aim of the company is to produce entertainment experiences based on quality creative content and exceptional storytelling.

Since it was founded in 1923 as Disney Brothers Studios (in 1929 it changed its name to Walt Disney Productions), the Walt Disney Company has been one of the main entertainment companies in the world. Walt Disney, comic illustrator and founder of the company together with his brother Roy, directed the first Mickey Mouse animation in 1928. In 1937 Disney studios produced the first full-length cartoon, *Snow White and the Seven Dwarfs*. Disneyland opened in Anaheim in 1955, a year after the debut on ABC of the weekly series by the same name. Until 1960, Walt Disney Productions owned just 34.5% of the park. In 1966, Walt Disney died, 5 years prior to the opening of Walt Disney World in Florida and the death of his brother Roy. In 1971, with the opening of Magic Kingdom in Orlando, the company's true growth process began in the business of theme parks. Magic Kingdom was, in fact, qualitatively different from the theme parks that had existed until then. The fundamental difference lay in the fact that it had been designed right from the start as a destination park, to which visitors could plan a complete holiday instead of a day trip (Kurtti, 1996). Its location on the outskirts of Orlando is explained because the city had all of the conditions Disney was looking for in order to locate its second park in the USA: that is to say, an emerging metropolitan area in the early 1970s (fed by the development of high technology and aerospace industries, related to the also recent installation in Florida of the Kennedy Space Center), its location at the intersection of several freeways (greatly used by tourist flows by road towards holiday destinations on the Florida coast), the availability of large areas of land at a reasonable price so as to allow the company to prevent the chaotic growth that had come about around Disneyland in California, the support of the administration and a pleasant climate.

Following Roy Disney's death, Roy E., his son, became the company's major shareholder. In 1980, Walt's son-in-law, Ron Miller, became president. With the arrival of Michael Eisner (who came from Paramount) as chief executive officer (CEO) and Frank Wells (who came from Warner Bros and who died in 1994), as president, the Disney Corporation began, as of the mid-1980s, a stage of innovation and prosperity after a period of something of a crisis during the first half of the decade (see Grover, 1997). During the 1980s, Disney opened the 'Experimental Prototype Community of Tomorrow' (Epcot) parks (1982), Tokyo Disneyland (1984) and Disney–Metro-Goldwyn-Mayer (MGM) Studios (1989), launched the Disney Channel (1983) and Touchstone Pictures produced its first film (1984). In 1986, the corporation changed its name to the Walt Disney Company and in 1987 opened its first shop in Glendale, California. In the 1990s it opened

Disneyland Paris (initially Euro Disney, in 1992), bought Miramax (1993) and purchased Capital Cities/ABC (today ABC Inc.) (1996) and the Internet service company Starwaver (1998). That same year saw the start-up of Animal Kingdom in Orlando. In 1999, together with Infoseek, it launched Go.com (currently Walt Disney Internet Group). In 2000, Bob Iger became the new president of the company. In 2001, Disney expanded its first theme park in Anaheim in the shape of Downtown Disney and Disney's California Adventure. The company also formed a joint venture with Wenner Media and took a 50% stake in the entertainment magazine *US Weekly*. It later bought Fox Family Channel, which it renamed ABC Family. In 2002, it opened Walt Disney Studios in Paris and Tokyo DisneySea. In 2003 Disney exited from the sports world by selling the Anaheim Angels and in 2005 it sold the Mighty Ducks of Anaheim, a hockey team. On the other hand, in 2005 it got Hong Kong Disneyland under way. Nevertheless, amid all this, the company has endured financial turmoil for several years across nearly all of its industries. So, following a spell with results that were deemed below par by a large number of its shareholders, a public confrontation with Roy Disney, the founder's nephew, and the announcement of a takeover by the media giant Comcast, a cable company, which never materialized, Eisner – who had enjoyed huge success in the 1980s and early 1990s – was not re-elected as chairman and was replaced by George J. Mitchell. Robert A. Iger was elected president. In January 2007 John E Pepper Jr. was elected chairman.

The company's strategy concerning parks is characterized by three principles: increased frequentation, increased length of stay by visitors to parks and increased visitor expenditure. To achieve this, in addition to increasing the existing parks' capacity to attract and creating new operative systems such as 'fastpasses' to avoid queue-associated problems and improve customer satisfaction, since the 1980s Disney has embarked upon an intensive process of the expansion–concentration of its parks in the USA in Florida and California and the opening of parks (with the participation of other companies) outside the USA in urban regions that can allow the harnessing of multimillion visitor numbers annually (above 10 million visits). Leaving aside one of Disney's early operations in Japan in the shape of Dreamland Park, which opened in Nara in 1960 (Nye, 1981, 74, n. 14), a process of internationalization took place, materializing in 1983 with a park in Tokyo in which the Walt Disney Company has a management contract and only takes part in the rights generated through sales. The second park outside the USA was located in Paris in 1992. Here they also have a minor share (39%). Such set-ups recur with second parks both in Japan, DisneySea (2001), the property, like the first, of Oriental Land Co., and in Paris, Walt Disney Studios (2002), with the same make-up of shareholders, as well as in Hong Kong. This latter park allows Disney its first significant penetration into the world's most populated country.

Table 4.5 summarizes Disney's resources in the Parks and Resorts division. It includes the two water parks the company has at Walt Disney World Orlando, Blizzard Beach and Typhoon Lagoon. In addition to

Table 4.5. Parks and resort properties owned by the Walt Disney Company, 2005 (from company reports).

	Ownership (%)	Parks/ships/other	Hotel rooms	Workforce
Walt Disney World (Florida)	100	Magic Kingdom Epcot Center MGM Studios Animal Kingdom Blizzard Beach Typhoon Lagoon	24,000	54,000
Disneyland (California)	100	Disneyland California Adventure	2,224	18,700
Disneyland Paris	41	Disneyland Paris Walt Disney Studios	5,760	12,000
Tokyo Disneyland	Licence only	Tokyo Disneyland DisneySea Tokyo	1,006	20,700
Hong Kong Disneyland	43	Disneyland	1,000	N/A
Disney Cruise Lines	100	2 ships	5,200	3,000
Disney Vacation Clubs	100	7 resorts	1,568	1,300
ESPN Zone	100	8 restaurants	–	2,400
Total			40,758	112,100[a]

a. Excludes 1300 imagineers and workforce in Hong Kong Disneyland.

theme parks, the Parks and Resorts division also includes the world-class Disney Cruise Line, seven Disney Vacation Clubs, ESPN Zone dining locations and Walt Disney Imagineering, which is responsible for the design and creation of all Disney attractions, resorts and real-estate developments.

Table 4.6 shows the evolution of visits to Disney theme parks worldwide. As can be seen, the US parks and resorts have suffered in the past few years, largely because of a weak tourism market brought on by the 11 September 2001 terrorist attacks on the USA. Just when the Florida parks started to bounce back, a string of hurricanes that plagued Walt Disney World in Florida during the summer and early autumn of 2004 caused both attendance and revenue to fall short of expectations.

It is significant, in any case, that despite the company's internationalization process in 2004 it is estimated that 49% of the Parks and Resorts division's income comes from Disney World in Orlando and 24% from the resorts and hotels in the USA, also mainly located in Orlando. To date, Disneyland in California represents 14% of the business of the division, whereas 10% derives from other holiday and leisure activities, among which are the Disney Cruise Lines. In spite of the high frequentation achieved, for the Walt Disney Company the European and Asian parks only represent 3% of its total revenue. In Tokyo, moreover, the Disney Corporation has no shares in the parks. In Paris and in Hong Kong it does hold some shares in the parks. In greater detail, Table 4.7 shows Disney's participation

Table 4.6. Evolution of visits to Disney theme parks 1994–2005 (in millions of visits) (based on *Amusement Business* data).

Park	1994	1995	1996	1997	1998	1999	2000	2001	2002	2003	2004	2005
Magic Kingdom at WDW	11.2	12.9	13.8	17	15.6	15.2	15.4	14.8	14	14	15.2	16.2
Disneyland Anaheim	10.3	14.1	15	14.3	13.7	13.5	13.9	12.4	12.7	12.7	13.4	14.5
Tokyo Disneyland	16	15.5	17.0	17.3	16.7	17.4	16.5	17.7	13.0	13.1	13.2	13.0
Tokyo DisneySea	–	–	–	–	–	–	–	4.0	12.0	12.2	12.2	12.0
Disneyland Paris	8.8	10.7	11.7	12.6	12.5	12.5	12.0	12.2	10.3	10.2	10.2	10.2
Epcot at WDW	9.7	10.7	11.2	11.8	10.6	10.1	10.6	9.0	8.3	8.6	9.4	9.9
Disney–MGM at WDW	8	9.5	9.9	10.5	9.5	8.7	8.9	8.4	8.0	7.9	8.3	8.7
Disney Animal Kingdom at WDW	–	–	–	–	6	8.6	8.3	8	7.3	7.3	7.8	8.2
Disney's California Adventure	–	–	–	–	–	–	–	5	4.7	5.3	5.6	5.8
Walt Disney Studios Park	–	–	–	–	–	–	–	–	2.8	2.2	2.2	2.2
Hong Kong Disneyland	–	–	–	–	–	–	–	–	–	–	–	2.2 [a]

Parks in the USA–Canada
Parks in Europe
Parks in Asia/the Pacific

a. Opened in September 2005.
WDW, Walt Disney World.

Table 4.7.   Participation by the Walt Disney Company in European and Asian theme parks (from company reports).

	Investment (million $)	Shares (%)	Rights over entrance fees (%)	Participation (%)	Rights to F&B, M (%)	Special Events Rights (%)	Others (%)
Tokyo Disneyland	0	0	10	4	5	5	4
Disney Sea Tokyo	20	0	10	4	5	5	4
Disneyland Paris	581	41	5	5	2.5	N/A	1
Walt Disney Studios Paris	91	41	5	5	2.5	N/A	1
Hong Kong Disneyland	315	43	10	10	5	5	2.5

and rights in the parks outside the USA. Whatever the case, the Disney process occurs in all areas of the company and has the specific support of Walt Disney International, the centre of Disney's business development and growth around the world. They are responsible for providing administrative support and coordination for Disney's 45 global offices, promoting coordination and encouraging synergies between individual businesses and expanding the business, especially in the key growth markets identified by the company (China, India and Russia). For instance, Walt Disney International supported the launch of Hong Kong Disneyland.

These results illustrate, therefore, at least three points that are relevant from Disney's point of view: on the one hand, the role played by revenue that is not directly linked to the parks (be it hotels or other holiday products) but is associated with the image of entertainment that is characteristic of the parks and the Disney factory's other products; secondly, the importance of conceiving their parks as multi-purpose areas capable of generating a high volume of revenue which is not as a result of either entrance tickets or their visitors' direct consumption; and, finally, the relevance of the parks not just as generators of income but, on an international level, as exporters, by means of a brand, of a style of life and consumption. In this regard, Disney's corporate capacity to create a lifestyle outside the USA became clearly manifest when, to announce Disney's settlement in Hong Kong, a reporter with the *Evening Standard* wrote that 'Hong Kong buys into Disney's magic world' (Colquhoun, 1999).

Continuing with this idea, it cannot be forgotten that, parallel to the business of theme parks, Disney owns television channels and cable communications media, film studios and consumer products such as sports teams, publications and shops. Some of Disney's well-known brands in these fields are ABC TV, ABC Radio Network, ABC Family, ESPN (80%),

Toon Disney, Disney Channel, Soap Net, A&E Television (37.5%), LifeTime (50%), Walt Disney Pictures, Touchstone Pictures, Miramax, Dimension, Buena Vista Home Entertainment, Buena Vista Music Group, Theatrical Productions, Hollywood Pictures, Disney Cruise Line, Disney Vacation Club, Hyperion and the Disney Stores. In fact, it is present in all key business areas in the entertainment sector: television and cable media conglomerates, film production, parks and resorts and other holiday products, as well as consumer products. With regard to this, see Table 4.8. It is significant to note that, in 2005, the Parks and Resorts division represented, according to available data, approximately 28% of the company's total revenue and 23% of the operating income.

In fact, Disney's maximum aim is to create the concept of an integral product for all facets of its potential consumers' lives. The clearest manifestation of this was represented by the development of Celebration (Rymer, 1996), a newly constructed city built for 20,000 people on the outskirts of Orlando, founded in 1994. Although it was sold to Lexin Capital in 2004, Celebration was the materialization of the aesthetic and ethical idea of a city according to Disney ideology, a peaceful, pleasurable place, bicycles without padlocks, music in the streets and Neighborough Electric Vehicles to get around internally, a city which:

> is not an organic creation, built painstakingly over many years by a combination of trial and error, the wrangling of competing interests, and human beings coming together in shared civil engagement. Rather it is a predesigned construction from beginning to end, a carefully planned commercial venture, part living space, part theatre, for those who are willing to pay an admission fee.
>
> (Rifkin, 2000, 117)

It should be mentioned in closing that, after a certain stabilization at the beginning of the decade of 2000, the Walt Disney Company recovered its growth rate between 2003 and 2004. Thus, as can be seen in Table 4.9, the Media Networks and Studio Entertainment divisions had improved their revenue and operating income results by 2003. As for the Parks and Resorts division, it exceeded its record revenues of 2001 in 2004. Even so, operating income is still significantly below that obtained in 2000.

Table 4.8. Financial results of the Walt Disney Company by business segments, 2005 (in million $) (data from the company).

	Revenue	%	Operating Income	%
Media Networks	13,207	41.3	3,209	62.5
Parks and Resorts	9,023	28.2	1,178	22.9
Studio Entertainment	7,587	23.8	207	4.0
Consumer Products	2,127	6.7	543	10.6
Total	31,944	100	5,127	100

Table 4.9. Evolution of the main financial indicators of the Walt Disney Company, 2000–2004 (in million $) (from the Walt Disney Company 2004 Annual Report).

	2000	2001	2002	2003	2004
Revenue	25,325	25,172	25,329	27,061	30,752
Media Networks	9,836	9,569	9,733	10,941	11,778
Parks and Resorts	6,809	7,004	6,465	6,412	7,750
Studio Entertainment	5,918	6,009	6,691	7,364	8,713
Consumer Products	2,762	2,590	2,440	2,344	2,511
Segment operating income	4,112	4,005	2,822	3,174	4,488
Media Networks	1,985	1,758	986	1,213	2,169
Parks and Resorts	1,615	1,586	1,169	957	1,123
Studio Entertainment	126	260	273	620	662
Consumer Products	386	401	394	384	534

Growth is also the dominant issue in the Consumer Products division, which has surpassed its maximum operating income though it is below the best year in the 2000–2005 period as regards revenue. Specifically referring to the Parks and Resorts segment, it should be highlighted that Disney parks have a clear tourist destination component, which, though a reinforcement at times of economic plenty, is also a threat under less favourable economic circumstances. Thus, for example, given that approximately 50% of visitors to Disney in Orlando and 25% of the visitors to Anaheim travel by air, it is hardly surprising that the attacks of 11 September 2001 caused a 20–25% drop in the number of visitors to Walt Disney World and a 5–10% decrease at Disneyland. This had a notable effect on the company's annual results, more so when bearing in mind that, in the business of theme parks, any downward variation implies a large fall in commercial margins during the harder times. Also, the saturation of the North American market itself and the instability of the other markets make it very risky to undertake investments. In the more general field of entertainment, the progressive consolidation of large media groups in the USA like AOL Time Warner, Viacom or News Corp/Fox, among others, and, in addition to NBC Universal, has conditioned the company's business opportunities in a global context of recession like that of the early years of the new millennium.

4.1.2. Six Flags' orientation to regional markets

The background of Six Flags Inc. lies in an independent chain of regional parks, which, following Disney's example, first developed in 1961 with what today is Six Flags over Texas. Its founder, Angus Wynne, was a businessman dealing in oil and local real estate. The name evokes the flags of the six countries that had had rights to the historical territory of Texas prior to its joining the USA in 1842. Wynne was the first operator to introduce the concept of theming to parks that were fundamentally oriented towards the regional and metropolitan market, until that time mainly amusement parks. It was its acquisition by Bally and its later shaping as a corporation exclusively devoted to the business of theme parks which provided it with its potential in the sector of regional parks in the USA as of the mid-1980s.

In 1982, the Bally Manufacturing Corporation bought the Six Flags Inc. parks. Bally was an entertainment company with interests in the business of the casinos of Atlantic City, Las Vegas and Reno, the design, manufacture and sale of equipment, gaming machines and video games, as well as in the fitness sector. It also bought Great Adventure in Jackson, New Jersey, a park built in 1974 which was, until then, the biggest park not to have been developed by Disney in the USA (in fact it was a park divided into two sectors, a safari and the thematic area). In 1984, it acquired the Great America Park from the Marriot Corporation, in Gurnee, Illinois. With seven parks (Great Adventure, Six Flags Magic Mountain, Six Flags Texas, Six Flags Mid-America, Six Flags Great America, Six Flags Georgia and Astroworld), in the mid-1980s, Bally was, barring Disney, the giant of the theme parks sector in the USA. However, in 1987, it sold all of its properties to the Wesray Corporation. According to Adams (1991), the reason for the sale was that the theme parks business, not being dominant in the global interests of the company, demanded excess resources in capital investments, operations and management. The seasonal nature of the business in the USA, as well as the fluctuations due to such things as the weather or economic circumstances, created burdens which the company was not willing to bear. As a result, Six Flags consolidated, in the shape of Wesray, as a corporation solely given over to the ownership and management of theme parks.

In 1991, Six Flags was acquired by Warner Brothers Entertainment (today part of AOL Time Warner), which, in this way, consolidated its presence in the business of theme parks in the USA. Since the mid-1970s, Warner had already had specific relations with Six Flags with regard to promotion and marketing. In 1995, Time Warner sold its 51% share of the stocks to Boston Ventures, a financial company, which was owner of the Six Flags parks for 3 years until they were bought by Premier Parks.

Premier Parks, initially TierCo, was a company devoted entirely to real estate and got into the business of theme parks in 1983 with the purchase of 50% of Frontier City in Oklahoma City, a small park that had been inaugurated in 1958. In 1989, Kierkan Burke, then company chairman, was appointed CEO and, as of that moment, the then TierCo diversified its portfolio in the direction of the entertainment industry. After buying the remaining 50% of Frontier City in 1990 and the incorporation of a water park, also in Oklahoma, and another small theme park in Maryland, in 1994, the company adopted the name of Premier Parks. In 1995, it acquired Funtime Parks Inc., with which it incorporated another three parks into its portfolio in the USA (Geuga Lake in Cleveland, Wyandot Lake in

Columbus and Darien Lake in Buffalo). Between 1996 and 1997, it completed its expansion in the USA with the purchase of Elitch Gardens in Denver, Waterworld USA in Sacramento and Concord, Great Escape and Splashwater Kingdom in Albany, Riverside in Springfield and Kentucky Kingdom in Louisville. It also negotiated a management contract with Marine World in Vallejo, with an option to buy. The purchase of the Six Flags parks in 1998 turned Premier Parks into the main operator of regional parks and transformed a company which in 1990 had just one theme park into one of the main reference points in the industry. With this acquisition process, Premier not only bought 12 Six Flags facilities but, above all, a brand. In fact, in the year 2000, Premier Parks decided to keep the Six Flags brand as a reference to the company. Today, the company uses the Six Flags brand at 24 of its attractions. It must be taken into account that, having been present in the entertainment market since the 1960s, in the USA Six Flags as a brand has a high degree of recognition. In the 16–24-year age range, this recognition is comparable to that enjoyed by such brands as Disney, Nike or McDonald's.

Six Flags' strategy at the end of the 1990s and the beginning of the new millennium was to continue with the diversification of opportunities and the expansion of markets and presence both in the USA and outside, always in the regional parks segment (Gilling, 1998). The main actions of this strategy of expansion were the purchase of classic parks with results below what was expected of them and their improvement and adaptation. In 1999, it acquired Reino Aventura in Mexico and between 2000 and 2002 Wild Waves and Enchanted Village, SeaWorld Ohio, White Water in Atlanta and SplashTown Waterpark, and Jazzland in New Orleans in the USA and La Ronde in Montreal in Canada. The acquisition of Reino Aventura could be understood, furthermore, as Six Flags' springboard into the Latin American market.

Table 4.10 shows the financial results of the improvements carried out on a selection of parks in which Six Flags/Premier Parks acted between 1992 and 1998. A higher number of visits, a longer length of stay at the park, greater revenue and higher profit margins are the results of the process. The global result was a 70.2% increase in the number of visitors (from 5.318 million to 9.053 million), a 90.7% rise in income (from $137 million to $261 million) and in earnings before interest, taxes, depreciation and amortization (EBITDA) of 355.7% (from $23 to $104 million). In greater detail, the corporate administration of the company understands that, as a long-term effect on the improvement process, there must be an increase in per capita spending of $5 to $6 per person (from $2 to $3 as a result of the increase in the price of the entrance ticket, $2 coming from increased sales encouraged by the incorporation of comic characters into the parks and from $1 to $2 for the increase of food and beverage sales). In any case, the company is capable of promoting the internal growth of each park through improved management, that is to say, the increase in the number of visitors, the increase in per capita income and strict control over expenditure. For this, Six Flags invests each year in new attractions,

Table 4.10. Results of improvement and reinvestment in a selection of Six Flags theme parks (from Crédit Lyonnais Securities (USA) Inc. Report EQ027-02).

	Year of purchase	EBITDA in the year of purchase (million $)	Margin (%)	EBITDA 2000 (million $)	Margin (%)
Six Flags America	1992	0.1	1.0	10.1	27.7
Six Flags Darien Lake	1995	4.6	24.9	16.6	38.2
Six Flags Elitch Gardens	1996	Negative	–	13.6	36.9
Six Flags New England	1996	1.5	7.9	33.7	48.6
Six Flags St. Louis	1998	10.4	19.5	20.5	39.9

it broadens the marketing and sponsorship programmes, increases the number of presold tickets (groups, season tickets, etc.), uses pricing strategies to maximize income through tickets according to the degree of use of the park, adds and improves restaurants and shops, and holds special events.

Between 1998 and 2004, Premier Parks/Six Flags was also intensely active in Europe, specifically with the purchase of six parks that the European group Walibi had in France, Belgium and the Netherlands: Walibi Rhone Alpes, Walibi Schtroumpf and Walibi Aquitaine in France, Walibi Wabre and Bellewoerde in Belgium and Walibi Flevo in the Netherlands. Walibi had been created in 1975 for the development of Walibi Wavre in Brussels by Eddie Meeus. When it was bought by Premier Parks, Wailibi was the most important leisure group in Europe, with over 18 million visits in 1994 (TRM, 1995). In 1998, Premier Parks also bought Warner Bros' parks division in Europe, including ownership of the German park and the building and management contract and the licence to the new park at that time being built in Madrid. The Warner Park in Australia remained outside the purchase. The acquisition also included an agreement as to the long-term rights of use (until 2023) of the Looney Tunes, Hanna-Barbera, Cartoon Network and DC Comics' characters for Europe and Latin America, including Yogi Bear, Scooby-Doo and the Flintstones. In this way, Premier consolidated a situation whose precedent was the fact that, until the merger with Premier Parks, Six Flags had been operating, as has already been said, since the 1970s with a licence to use Warner Bros characters in the USA and Canada. It must be pointed out, however, that the agreement for the USA and Canada (until 2053) specifically excludes the Las Vegas metropolitan area.

In 2004, Palamon Capital Partners acquired Six Flags' European division for 200 million dollars, excluding the group's participation in Warner Bros Movie World Madrid. In this way Six Flags Holland, Six Flags Belgium, Bellewaerde Park, Walibi Lorraine, Walibi Rhône Alpes, Walibi Aquitaine and Warner Bros Movie World in Germany have come to make up European group Star Parks. With these transactions, Six Flags has minimized its presence in the European markets, which at the beginning of the 21st century represented some 20% of its total revenue.

In fact, between 2003 and 2005, the company started a strategy of selling its facilities, contrasting with its characteristic dynamic of purchasing during the 1990s. Thus, in addition to the sale of the European parks, in order to focus on proven markets, in 2004 it sold Six Flags Worlds of Adventure to Cedar Fair for $145 million. This is a significant case since, in 2001, Six Flags bought the adjacent theme park SeaWorld Ohio, with the aim of merging them, and invested $40 million, whose principal effect was a 42% increase in the number of visits. However, despite the increase of 2001, the figures for 2002 were only slightly over the 2 million visits mark. Also, in 2005 the company announced the closure and sale of Astroworld in Houston. Declining attendance, the expiration of a parking-lot contract and rising real-estate values in the area explain the decision. It does not signal a move towards selling other parks to real estate. In fact, there are currently no plans to sell Six Flags SplashTown, which also operates in Houston. The company expected as well that the closure of Astroworld would drive incremental visitors to other Six Flags parks in Texas.

In summary, Six Flags' portfolio of parks in 2005 is as seen in Table 4.11. Despite Six Flags New Orleans sitting under 12 feet of water during the flooding of the city in September 2005 in the wake of Hurricane Katrina, the company has plans to rebuild the park. In addition to the parks and in spite of this not constituting its main business strategy, they own a campsite with 700 spaces, and 440 recreational vehicles available for daily and weekly rental and a 163-room hotel at Six Flags Darien Lake. Table 4.12 outlines the make-up of Six Flags' parks with over a million visits between 1997 and 2005. Moreover, 2006 saw the opening of the Six Flags Great Escape Lodge and Indoor Waterpark, which is located across from the Great Escape and Splashwater Kingdom. In addition to a 200-suite hotel, the facility features a 38,000 square foot indoor water park. The facility is owned by a joint venture in which Six Flags hold a 41% interest. Six Flags Theme Parks Inc. owns directly and indirectly all parks excluding Six Flags over Texas and Six Flags over Georgia, which are owned by Six Flags Inc.

The Six Flags parks present the usual mechanical rides of most amusement parks in a themed context. They operate in the main only during a period of the year which, in general terms, spans from Memorial Day until Labour Day (weather conditions and influences of the school calendar explain each specific case). Over 85% of frequentation and sales take place during the second and third quarters of the year. Most North Americans reside within 200 km of a Six Flags park and the company is present in 34 of the 50 principal metropolitan areas of the USA. Six Flags, like the North American theme parks industry in general, has wrestled with the constraints of a difficult economic environment and, in 2003 and 2004, unusually poor weather affecting multiple major markets for extensive portions of their operating seasons. In 2005, as can be seen in Table 4.13, there was a recovery in attendance. Consequently, in 2005

Table 4.11. Main characteristics of the Six Flags properties in 2005 (from company reports).

	Location	Type	Primary market (million people)	Secondary market (million people)	Site (acres)
Six Flags Magic Mountain	Los Angeles	Theme park	10.6	17.7	262
Six Flags Hurricane Harbor	Los Angeles	Water park	10.6	17.6	
Six Flags Marine World	San Francisco	Theme park	5.7	10.7	135
Six Flags Waterworld	Concord	Water park	7.6	11.3	21
Six Flags Waterworld	Sacramento	Water park	3.2	10.9	14
Six Flags Elitch Gardens	Denver	T&W park	2.9	3.9	67
Six Flags over Georgia	Atlanta	Theme park	4.8	7.8	290
Six Flags White Water	Atlanta	Water park	4.8	7.8	69
Six Flags Great America	Chicago	T&W park	8.8	13.5	324
Six Flags Kentucky Kingdom	Louisville	T&W park	1.5	4.8	59
Six Flags New Orleans	New Orleans	Theme park	1.6	3.1	140
Six Flags America	Baltimore	T&W park	7.4	12.4	523
Six Flags New England	Springfield	T&W park	3.2	15.8	263
Six Flags St. Louis	St. Louis	T&W park	2.7	3.9	503
Six Flags Great Adventure	Jackson	Theme park	14.3	28.1	2279
Six Flags Hurricane Harbor	Jackson	Water park	14.3	28.1	
Six Flags Wild Safari	Jackson	Animal park	14.3	28.1	
Six Flags Darien Lake[a]	Buffalo	T&W park	2.1	3.1	978
The Great Escape Splashwater Kingdom[b]	Lake George	T&W park	1.1	3.2	351
Wyandot Lake	Columbus	Water park	2.2	6.8	18
Frontier City	Oklahoma City	Theme park	1.3	2.6	113
White Water Bay	Oklahoma City	Water park	1.3	2.6	21

Continued

Table 4.11. *Continued.*

	Location	Type	Primary market (million people)	Secondary market (million people)	Site (acres)
Six Flags over Texas	Arlington	Theme park	5.7	6.8	187
Six Flags Hurricane Harbor	Arlington	Water park	5.7	6.8	47
Six Flags Fiesta Texas	San Antonio	T&W park	2.0	3.6	216
Six Flags Splashtown	Houston	Water park	5.1	6.3	60
Wild Waves and Enchanted Village	Seattle	Water park	3.5	4.6	66
La Ronde	Montreal	Theme park	4.3	5.8	146
Six Flags Mexico	Mexico City	Theme park	N/A	30	107

a. Includes the Six Flags Darien Lake Hotel and Camping Resort.
b. Includes the Six Flags Great Escape Lodge and Indoor water park.
Primary market: permanent resident population in millions within 50 miles.
Secondary market: permanent resident population in millions within 100 miles.
T&W park: theme park with free water park.

revenue rose 9.1% above 2004 and the total adjusted EBITDA was
$307.2 million.

The fragmentation of theme parks' potential markets makes an operator like Six Flags especially competitive, with purchasing power, economies of scale regarding management matters, a very light corporate
administration both at the level of parks and for the company as a whole,
possibilities of agreements with other large corporations concerning
sponsorship, the ability to offer top-level work posts for managers, possibilities of optimizing the use of its attractions at different parks rota-
tionally, access to capital markets and clear referents to transitional
popular culture like the Warner Bros characters and other comic figures.
The finalization of the diversification and expansion policy started in the
1990s and concentration on a selection of markets also materialized in the
company's plans to create multipark destinations combining theme parks
and another type of attraction as well as developing new, unique attractions in already existing parks.

4.1.3. The positioning of Universal as an operator of destination parks

Universal Studios has become consolidated in the last decade as Disney's
prime competitor in the field of theme parks and multipark destinations. Its first venture into the business dates from the 1960s, when, like

Table 4.12. Recent evolution of visits to Six Flags theme parks with over a million visitors 1997–2005 (in million visits) (based on *Amusement Business* data).

Park	1997	1998	1999	2000	2001	2002	2003	2004	2005
Six Flags Great Adventure, Jackson, New Jersey	3.700	3.420	3.800	3.500	3.560	3.250	3.150	2.800	2.968
Six Flags Great America, Chicago, Illinois	3.100	2.905	3.100	2.875	2.900	2.700	2.575	2.300	2.852
Six Flags Magic Mountain, Valencia, California	3.400	3.070	3.200	3.300	3.200	3.100	3.050	2.700	2.835
Six Flags over Texas, Arlington	3.100	2.819	2.750	2.775	3.000	2.675	2.600	2.200	2.310
Six Flags Mexico, México DF, Mexico	–	–	2.300	2.750	2.670	2.525	2.450	2.150	2.279
Six Flags over Georgia, Atlanta	2.800	2.321	2.550	2.400	2.400	2.250	2.100	1.950	2.050
Six Flags New England, Springfield, Massachusetts[a]	1.270	1.590	1.600	2.000	1.950	1.875	1.750	1.500	1.695
Six Flags Marine World, San Francisco, California[a]	1.100	1.831	2.100	2.100	3.120	1.900	1.725	1.450	1.537
Six Flags Fiesta Texas, San Antonio	1.800	1.490	2.451	2.200	2.075	1.875	1.700	1.400	1.442

Continued

Table 4.12. *Continued.*

Park	1997	1998	1999	2000	2001	2002	2003	2004	2005
Six Flags St Louis, Missouri	1.800	1.556	2.059	1.900	1.860	1.750	1.675	1.350	1.377
Six Flags Astroworld, Houston, Texas[b]	2.100	1.900	1.900	1.825	1.775	1.800	1.700	1.400	1.330
Six Flags Darien Lake, Buffalo, New York[a]	1.400	1.520	1.704	1.625	1.640	1.525	1.460	1.250	1.275
La Ronde, Montreal, Quebec	–	–	–	–	1.200	1.350	1.250	1.200	1.254
Six Flags Elitch Gardens, Denver, Colorado[a]	1.500	1.500	1.600	1.525	1.500	1.500	1.350	1.050	1.155
Six Flags America, Baltimore, Maryland[a]	0.985	1.170	1.700	1.600	1.620	1.550	1.425	1.150	1.180

a. Parks belonging to Premier parks in 1997.
b. Closed permanently since October 2005.

☐ Parks in USA–Canada
▨ Parks in the rest of the world

Table 4.13. Evolution of selected Six Flags financial data, 2001–2005 (in million $) (from company reports).

	2001	2002	2003	2004	2005
Revenue	1028.5	1012.8	1007.3	998.6	1089.7
Admissions	569.7	556.9	548.6	534.1	587.9
Merchandise and other	458.8	455.9	458.7	464.5	501.7
Operating costs and expenses	829.1	787.5	818.3	845.8	906.3

MCA Inc., it created the Universal Studios Tour of Universal Studios Hollywood, a 2-h visit to the company's film studios (Kaak, 1992). Today, in addition to Universal Studios Hollywood, Universal owns two theme parks in Orlando, Universal Studios Florida and Islands of Adventure and holds 24% of Universal Studios Japan. Between 1998 and 2004, at a time of intense competition with Disney globally, it was a shareholder of Universal Mediterranea in Spain (including the theme park, Universal PortAventura, the Costa Caribe water park and the PortAventura and El Paso hotels), where it still, under licence, holds on to the brand and the merchandizing. It is also proprietor of the Universal Experience in Beijing, the Universal City Walk in Hollywood (extended in 2000), Orlando and Osaka, the Wet 'n Wild water park in Orlando and 50% of Universal Orlando, Universal's resort, where the Portofino Bay Hotel, the Hard Rock Hotel and the Royal Pacific Resort are located. Also, at the Universal City Plaza in Hollywood, in addition to its head office, it is the owner of two hotels, the Sheraton–Universal Hotel, ceded under licence to Sheraton, and the Hilton Hotel. See, in Table 4.14, the evolution of frequentation to each park.

Universal's film studios were created in 1912 when Carl Laemmle, a German immigrant, who had got into the film business when exhibiting in Chicago in 1906 and as a distributor and producer in New York in 1909, changed the name of Nestor Studios, which he had acquired in Hollywood in 1911, to incorporate the name 'Universal'. The doors of Universal City opened in 1915 as a place that was completely devoted to film production. Having created, among other films, some of the mythical horror movies of the 1930s (*Dracula*, *The Mummy* and *Frankenstein*), Laemmle retired in 1936, selling the studios to the Standard Capital Company. In 1946, Universal merged with International Pictures and in 1952 the company was bought by Decca Records. The purchase of Decca by MCA Inc., a process which began in 1958 and was finalized in 1962, gave way to a period of unprecedented growth and diversification for Universal and also signalled the start of its venture into the business of theme parks.

MCA (Music Corporation of America) was created in Chicago in 1924 by Jules C. Stein and William Goodheart with the aim of representing music groups. At the end of the 1930s, the company represented almost two-thirds of all groups in the USA. In 1936, Stein contracted 22-year-old Lew Wasserman, who, 10 years later at the age of 33, became company

Table 4.14. Evolution of the number of visitors to Universal theme parks 1994–2005 (in millions of visits) (based on *Amusement Business* data).

Park	1994	1995	1996	1997	1998	1999	2000	2001	2002	2003	2004	2005
Universal Studios Japan	–	–	–	–	–	–	–	9.0	8.0	8.8	9.9	8.0
Universal Studios Orlando	7.7	8	8.4	8.9	8.9	8.1	8.1	7.3	6.8	6.8	6.7	6.1
Islands of Adventure	–	–	–	–	–	3.4	6	5.5	6	6.1	6.3	5.8
Universal Studios Hollywood	4.6	4.7	5.4	5.4	5.1	5.1	5.2	4.7	5.2	4.6	5	4.7

☐ Parks in the USA–Canada
☐ Parks in Asia/the Pacific

president, now based in California since 1937 and having consolidated interests in the business of representing film artists. It was Wasserman who decided in 1949 to start producing television programmes. He started production in 1952, including an agreement with Alfred Hitchcock, turning Wasserman into the company's major shareholder. In 1954, for the first time in the history of MCA, revenue through television (almost $9 million) exceeded the revenue generated through commission for representing artists. At the end of the 1950s, MCA had become a consolidated television production company. In 1958, long-term strategic investment was undertaken with the purchase of the studios of Universal Pictures for some $11 million. In the process, it absorbed Decca Records Inc. (owner of 90% of Universal Pictures). However, in 1962, the US Department of Justice forced MCA to decide whether it wished to continue as a representative of artists or as a television production company. The company decided to concentrate on producing films under the name of Universal Pictures and to diversify its revenue in fields that were not linked to entertainment. To do so, it bought Columbia Savings and Loan in Denver, Colorado, and the Spencer Gifts network of retail shops in 1968. In 1964, continuing Laemmle's pioneering initiative, the company once again allowed visitors to the filming of its movies, creating the embryo of Universal's first theme park, the Universal Studios Tour.

Until the 1970s, MCA's revenue basically depended on television programmes. It was not until the production of films like *Jaws* or *Airport* that its television successes started to have their counterpart on the cinema screen. Thus, in the mid-1970s, for the first time in the company's history, the revenue generated by the cinema outstripped that of television. At the same time, at the beginning of the 1970s, Universal Studios Hollywood had already become one of the biggest tourist attractions in the USA. In addition to the use of the sets as theme park attractions, it had incorporated an office complex, a hotel, restaurants, an amphitheatre and, of course, the scenes where many of MCA's productions were filmed. Also, in 1973 MCA bought Yosemite Park and Curry Company and won the exclusive concession of the Yosemite National Park operation rights. In addition, the company bought the publishing companies G.P. Putnam's Sons and Grosset & Dunlap, as well as ABC Records and Jove Publications. At the beginning of the 1980s, MCA principally produced cinema films, television series, LPs and books, as well as having an interest in retail distribution in other sectors. In 1981, it bought some 170 ha in Orlando, where, at the end of the decade, it opened its second theme park, initiating direct competition with Disney in Orlando itself. In 1986, it bought 50% of the Cineplex Odeon Corporation, a company devoted to showing films. In 1987, it bought a New York television network and in 1988 a substantial part of Motown Records.

In 1991, the Japanese electronics company Matsushita bought MCA for $6.1 thousand million. Four years later, Seagram, the Canadian company, world leader in the alcoholic beverages sector, paid the Japanese $5.7 thousand million for MCA and, in 1996, changed the name MCA for that of Universal Studios (in this way reclaiming its tradition as one of the oldest film producers), in addition to selling the Putnam Berkeley publishing house. In 1998, Universal acquired 45% of USA Networks and merged its Cineplex Odeon studios with the Sony Studios, giving rise to Loews Cineplex Entertainment. Furthermore, Seagram bought Polygram and, combining its potential with Universal's music divisions, created the Universal Music Group, consolidating the company in a leading position in the business. In December 2000, Vivendi Universal was created with the fusion of Seagram, Canal + and Vivendi. That same month, the new company sold Seagram's wine and alcoholic beverages business unit.

Vivendi was a French company, created by imperial decree in 1853 as Compagnie Générale des Eaux, devoted to providing urban public services. Between 1980 and 1998, it internationalized and diversified its interests towards sectors such as waste, energy, transport, construction, telecommunications, multimedia-format educational publications, television, the Internet and the property business. It was known as plain Vivendi only after 1998. With the acquisition of Seagram for $34 million, Vivendi was also positioned in the field of entertainment. Vivendi wanted to articulate a strategy of the creation of synergies in three areas: the integration of contents, diagonal marketing and the optimization of distribution networks. Its aim was to strike up synergies between distribution channels (the Internet, pay-per-view television and telephony) and the contents (video games, the cinema, music, education and literature) in such a way that all of the entertainment-oriented business lines achieved greater value. In this way, it wanted to define and expand the Universal brand as a leader in film production and the production and distribution of television programmes and to become a world reference for issues concerning theme parks and resorts.

As Vivendi Universal, the company continued its process of growth with the purchase in 2001 of mp3.com, the first Internet music supplier, and American publisher Houghton Mifflin and, in 2002, it purchased USA Networks Inc.'s cinema and television assets. Also in 2002, Vivendi Universal restructured its business units, establishing a new company denominated Vivendi Universal Entertainment (VUE) integrating Universal Pictures Group, the division devoted to the production and distribution of cinema films, Universal Television Group, which operated four cable television channels in the USA and had interests in several international television channels, and Universal Parks and Resorts. In fact, VUE fundamentally integrated the company's North American interests in the field of the cinema, television and theme parks. VUE left out other subsidiaries of Vivendi Universal in the area of entertainment, the media and telecommunications such as Vivendi Universal Games (99%), Canal + (100%), Universal Music Group (92%), Cegetel Group (70%) and Maroc Telecom (35%), with which VUE had a clear capacity to create synergies. In 2002, Universal Parks and Resorts' contribution to VUE's turnover amounted to 14% or €871 million, of which the parks accounted for between 45 and 50%. In addition to the parks, hotels and city walks, in 2002 Universal Parks and Resorts also included the chain of shops and online services of Spencer Gifts (700 shops in the USA, Canada and the UK), which was sold in 2003.

Midway through 2002, Vivendi Universal's top executive, Jean Marie Messier, lost the confidence of the shareholders after confirming a result of a €13,597 million loss the previous year. Vivendi Universal's results and financial crisis and its slump on the stock exchange led to the sale in October 2003 of Vivendi Universal Entertainment to the National Broadcasting Corporation (NBC) television group, sister company of the General Electric conglomerate of companies. With this sale, as expressed by the editorial in *Le Monde* on 4 September 2003, Vivendi Universal beat a retreat, 'offering General Electric the possibility of constituting, with its sister company NBC, the world communications giant it dreamt of becoming'. Since October 2003, 80% of Vivendi Universal Entertainment has belonged to NBC. The remaining 20% is the property of Vivendi Universal. NBC is in turn the property of General Electric, the North American industrial complex created in 1892 as a result of the merger of Thomson–Houston and Edison General Electric.

General Electric is a corporation with interests in sectors as diverse as aeronautics, the distribution of electricity, financial services, nuclear reactors, domestic appliances, health equipment, plastics, insurance, machinery, communication or media materials, among others. In 1919, General Electric and Westinghouse created the Radio Corporation of America (hereafter RCA). In 1926 RCA created NBC in order to produce quality radio programmes. Antitrust legislation caused General Electric to sell its part of RCA in 1930. In 1939, NBC started its first regular television service and in 1941 it was awarded its Federal Communications Commission commercial television licence. The same year, the nucleus of the future American

Broadcasting Company (ABC) was created based on one of the two radio companies that were the property of NBC. In 1986, General Electric again incorporated RCA (with NBC), buying it for $6.4 thousand million, though it sold the radio division the following year. Today, NBC is the principal mainstream television channel in the USA. It operates on 29 stations and has over 220 affiliates. It has interests in cable television channels, including among others MSNBC (with Microsoft) and economics news channels such as CNBC (with Dow Jones), and participates in other television channels (A&E, Paxson Communications, ShopNBC, Bravo and the History Channel among others). Moreover, it owns Telemundo, the second Hispanic television channel, with some 25 stations, in the USA. With sales for 2002 of $7149 million, NBC represented approximately 5% of General Electric's total sales (valued at $130,685 million in 2002).

The sale of part of Vivendi Universal Entertainment to NBC gave rise to the creation of NBC Universal, one of the biggest media groups in the world, valued at $43,000 million. As Mulard (2003) states, with the NBC operation, it acquires the means to rival the large global communications corporations. NBC was, in effect, says Mulard, 'the last of the four big American channels that was not in alliance with a film production company whereas Universal was one of the odd ones (along with Sony) that was not associated with a mainstream channel'. It cannot be forgotten that Twentieth Century Fox has Fox Channel and cable television, that Warner studios, who have a cable network with HBO and CNN among others, created WB and that the channel ABC is the property of Disney and CBS of Paramount-Viacom. In short, with its alliance with VUE, NBC is gaining, as regards strategy and results, on its main competitors: Viacom, AOL Time Warner, Fox and Disney. NBC Universal generated total sales in 2004 of $12,886 million, or 8.6% of General Electric's total revenue. This figure is close to the income forecast by the company when acquiring Universal, which was set at some $13,000 million, with earnings before interest, taxes, depreciation and amortization (EBITDA) close to $3000 million and an operating margin of 20%. In fact, the profit generated by NBC Universal in 2004 was $2558 million, 12% of the total for General Electric. Furthermore, it cannot be forgotten that potential synergies had been identified deriving from the operation valued at between $400 and 500 million, considering both savings in costs and the growth of income.

As would be logical, parks are seen, in the context of the operation between General Electric and Vivendi Universal, as privileged spaces where multiple synergies on a promotional level can materialize. Concretely, the new NBC Universal considers parks as places to hold events of the NBC chain, television programmes and promotions of the different chains of the new company. In fact, this has been the strategic value of Universal's theme parks, whichever business corporation to which they may have pertained and regardless of their own profitability as businesses. In short, parks have been a privileged means to increase the value of the Universal brand. This is why their part in the business of the group so notably increased during the 1990s, making use of their own capital but also, especially, via collaboration with other companies. For example, of the $2.1 thousand million involved in developing Universal Studios Escape in Orlando, the company only used $500 million of its own capital and got the remainder through joint ventures (it acted similarly in Osaka). Also, Universal receives significant revenue from management contracts and the royalties it receives from the parks of which it is not the owner (for example, the case of PortAventura in Spain). More concretely, the mechanisms of growth activated for Universal's parks division during the last decade have been:

- In the first place, in the USA, the constitution of a pole of entertainment in Orlando, a joint venture together with Blackstone Financial Group. In the area of its first park, Universal carried out the construction of a second park, Islands of Adventure (the design of which was assisted by Steven Spielberg), which opened its doors in 1999, integrating them into a single recreational destination, today's Universal Orlando. The project has implied the opening of a replica of California's Universal City Walk and the development of three hotel complexes in collaboration with the Rank Group and Loews Hotels.
- In the 1990s, Universal started its Asia/Pacific expansion. Thus, in 1994, as MCA Development, it developed Porto Europa, a theme park located in Wakayama, Japan, which recreates Europe. However, the fundamental milestone in its expansion is the opening in 2002 of Universal Studios Japan in Osaka, with 35 million inhabitants living less than 150 km from the park. This is a joint venture with the Rank Group, the city of Osaka and local businesspeople and is the centrepiece of the remodelling of the Osaka waterfront.
- Complementarily, the company has renovated Universal Studios Hollywood, which is at the same time a theme park and a cinema studio, with new attractions and theming such as the Nickelodeon Blast Zone or a monumental recreation of Egyptian ruins. Also, in 2002, architect Jon Jerde, the creator of City Walk in 1993, doubled the surface area of his creation.

It cannot be forgotten, on the other hand, that in 1998 Universal became the first American corporation in the leisure sector to be present in Beijing, with the start-up of Universal Studios Experience Beijing as the centrepiece of a large regional commercial complex, the Henderson Center, developed by Henderson Land Development Co. Ltd, a Hong Kong company (O'Brien, 1998). In Europe, however, Universal has not kept hold of the 37% stake in PortAventura it held between 1998 and 2004, selling its share to La Caixa, a Catalan savings bank and partner in the park, for $30 million. Universal began to transform the park into a destination, Universal Mediterranea, with the opening in 2002 of two hotels and a water park, in addition to the only Universal Studios shop in Europe. Nevertheless, after NBC's entry into the group, Universal Studios abandoned its position as shareholder in Europe, even though PortAventura has kept the licence to Universal characters.

4.1.4. The consolidation of Cedar Fair as an operator of regional parks

Davis (1997, 23–24) maintains that the evolution of the business in the USA has shown that only organizations with a large financial capacity can sustain industry growth processes, especially as regards large parks, due to their high financial costs and, once they are functioning, the operating costs. This reality has led to a scenario dominated by just a few corporations, which were shaped in the 1980s. It was during this decade that Disney became consolidated as the only corporation capable of maintaining a significant growth rate and new investments, whereas Universal was starting its activity in Orlando and, on the other hand, other traditionally important groups disappeared. This is the case of Taft Broadcasting, the Marriott Corporation, the Bally Manufacturing Corporation and Harcourt Brace Jovanovich (HBJ). In this context, with Anheuser Busch Paramount became one of the principal beneficiaries of the changes in ownership that came about. In 2006, Cedar Fair made an important move in this process of concentration with the acquisition of Paramount Parks, the parks division belonging to CBS Corp. With this, Cedar Fair, which has developed its portfolio of parks basically through purchases made as of the 1990s, has become the third biggest park operator in the USA – and consequently in the world – with visitor numbers (28.2 million in 2005) only behind those of Disney and Six Flags. With this purchase, Cedar Fair has also become the second operator of North American regional parks. Table 4.15 shows the recent evolution of the results in visitor numbers of Cedar Fair parks (including those of Paramount) between 1997 and 2005. They are very stable regional parks.

As Lyon (1987) reports, Cedar Fair Ltd was created in 1983 when Cedar Point Inc. was acquired by an investment group comprising the Munger family, S. Pearson Inc. and Lazard Frères & Co. The company's base theme park is Cedar Point, on Lake Erie, Ohio, founded as a theme park in 1965, although it has a background as not just a traditional amusement park (with three roller coasters already in 1920) but even, as far back as 1870, as a coastal resort to which attractions were added as of 1897 when it was bought by an entrepreneur from Indiana, G.A. Boeckling (see a description of the park's origins in Hildebrandt, 1981). Hence, often the park is evoked as a magnificent example of the successful conversion of a classic amusement park into a theme park. Keeping its historical tradition as a point of concentration of roller coasters, today it is the park with the greatest density in the world of such rides.

Until 1992, the company did not undertake the expansion process that came about with the purchase of Dorney Park, California, a park that was initially developed as a resort in 1884. In fact, until then, Cedar Point could be considered an independent park enjoying very good results. It later acquired Worlds of Fun in 1995 and Knott's Berry Farm in 1997 (located in the surroundings of Disneyland and Universal Studios in California, it is the only one that stays open year-round and, like Cedar Point, has a hotel). Knott's Berry Farm is one of the USA historical parks, which dates from

Table 4.15. Recent evolution of visits to Cedar Fair theme parks 1997–2005 (in millions of visits) (based on *Amusement Business* data).

Park	1997	1998	1999	2000	2001	2002	2003	2004	2005
Paramount's Canada Wonderland[a]	2.860	3.025	2.975	2.975	2.975	2.826	2.628	3.420	3.660
Knott's Berry Farm	3.650	3.400	3.600	3.456	3.589	3.624	3.479	3.510	3.600
Paramount's Kings Island[a]	3.300	3.400	3.325	3.200	3.350	3.182	3.278	3.510	3.330
Cedar Point	3.200	3.400	3.300	3.432	3.100	3.250	3.300	3.170	3.110
Paramount's Kings Dominion[a]	2.270	2.325	2.210	2.150	2.250	2.092	2.100	2.180	2.220
Paramount's Carowinds[a]	1.850	1.875	1.900	1.900	1.850	1.850	1.770	2.010	2.130
Paramount's Great America[a]	2.250	2.050	1.875	1.800	1.750	1.820	1.911	1.930	2.070
Dorney Park	1.300	1.300	1.400	1.260	1.510	1.600	1.400	1.430	1.500
Geuga Lake[b]	1.300	1.300	1.200	1.700	2.750	2.150	1.500	0.680	0.700
Valleyfair	1.200	1.200	1.000	1.050	1.100	1.050	1.100	1.040	0.990
Worlds of Fun	1.100	1.200	1.000	1.000	0.900	0.940	0.880	0.890	0.800
Michigan's Adventure	–	–	–	–	0.430	0.420	0.480	0.470	0.550

a. Owned by Cedar Fair since 2006.
b. Operated by Six Flags until its purchase by Cedar Fair in 2004.

1920 and was operated from 1940 by the Knott family until it was bought by Cedar. Its history, as Adams (1991) indicates, started with a property growing woodland fruit, to which, during the era of the Great Depression, a restaurant service was added, which served special fried chicken which was later to become famous. As of 1940, new land was added to the plantation, which filled up with attractions until it had become a true park of attractions.

Moreover, Cedar Point owns Valleyfair and in 2001 it completed the purchase of Michigan's Adventure, a small, family-oriented park attracting some 400,000 people per year. The company's newest park before the purchase of Paramount Parks is Geuga Lake, acquired in 2004. Nevertheless, it is a park with an attendance that remains far below the company's original goal of 1.5 million. In 2006 Cedar Fair purchased one of the best-known theme park groups in the USA, Paramount Parks, which had been put up for sale by its owner company, CBS. Cedar Fair's acquisition implies the generation of significant synergies as regards costs and capital, a reduction of the company's risk by diversifying its presence in North American markets and the creation of new growth opportunities (including the development of new attractions as well as other components on the land bought, which had not to date been developed by Paramount, a total of 939 acres). Also, with this purchase, Cedar Fair acquired the rights to use the Nickelodeon brand. Table 4.16 includes the main financial indicators of Cedar Fair and Paramount Parks in 2005.

The origin of Paramount Parks goes back to the purchase by Paramount Parks of the King's Entertainment Company (KECO) during the second half of the 1980s. In turn, KECO goes back to the parks created and operated, as of the 1970s, by Taft Broadcasting. Kings Island, which opened in 1973 in the north of Cincinnati, was Taft Broadcasting's first park. Taft Broadcasting was a television and media firm that also owned another classic amusement park in the area, Coney Island. Its interest in the park business lay in disposing of a vehicle to show off the Hanna-Barbera cartoon characters like Yogi Bear or the Flintstones. This park was followed in 1975 by another, newly created park, Kings Dominion, on the outskirts of Richmond, and the purchase of a small park in North Carolina, Carowinds. Both transactions took place with the participation of the Kroger Company, which withdrew from the parks business in 1981. That same year, at a cost of CA$122 million, Taft Broadcasting built Canada Wonderlands in the surroundings of Toronto. In 1982, theme parks generated 36% of Taft's income and 28% of its profit. In 1987, it also built a Wonderland park in Australia. KECO, created as an independent company following the division of Taft's attractions, took charge of and managed all of the parks of Taft Broadcasting between 1984 and 1986 (Lyon, 1987). Taft finally sold the parks division because, in spite of the increased invoicing since the early 1980s, operating costs (maintenance and high-level management) and financial costs (principally reinvestments) were, in fact, depleting the company's profits, which went from 22.4% in 1982 to 17.4% in 1984 (Adams, 1991). Following a series of changes of ownership, KECO was acquired by Paramount Parks. Meanwhile, KECO had won a contract to manage the Great America Park in Santa Clara (sold by Marriot to the city of Santa Clara). The acquisition of this set of parks was useful for Paramount, then dependent on Viacom, to situate itself in

Table 4.16. Comparison between the results of Cedar Fair and Paramount Parks in 2005 (from company reports).

	Cedar Fair	Paramount Parks
Attendance (millions)	12.738	12.397
In-park revenue per capita ($)	37.68	34.23
Revenue (million $)	568.7	423.1
EBITDA (million $)	194.4	110.4
% margin	34.1	26.1
Capital expenditure 2002–2005 average (in million $)	61.7	44.1
% of revenue	10.8	10.4

the market of theme parks, rubbing shoulders with the other big film and television producers and entertainment products.

In 2000, Viacom acquired CBS Corporation for $23 billion. Viacom became one of the world's largest media companies, with pre-eminent positions in broadcast and cable television, production and distribution of television programming, radio and outdoor advertising, film production and distribution and publishing. However, despite being the sixth biggest chain of parks in the USA, with over 13 million visits in 2004, the parks division's sales were at just $413 million in 2004, with EBITDA of $108 million. In 2005 Viacom agreed to split its assets into two publicly traded companies. Paramount Parks was included in the resulting CBS Corporation in a specific Parks and Publishing division, which, in 2005, it is estimated would generate 5% of the company's EBITDA. At the end of 2005, CBS revealed plans to sell its Paramount theme park division in late 2006. The assets of Paramount Parks bought by Cedar Fair for $1.24 billion in cash are the five theme parks of the company in the USA and Canada, including Paramount Canada's Wonderland, Paramount's Carowinds, Paramount's Great America, Paramount's Kings Dominion and Paramount's Kings Island. Table 4.17 summarizes the main characteristics of the current company's theme parks.

Furthermore, Cedar Fair is proprietor of water parks in San Diego and Palm Springs, in addition to those located at Cedar Point, Knott's Berry Farm and Worlds of Fun. Two of them are operated as Knott's Soak City (in Cedar Point and Palm Springs). Cedar Fair also owns and operates the Castaway Bay Indoor Waterpark Resort in Sandusky, Ohio. Finally, Cedar Fair owns restaurants, marinas and hotels. Cedar Point includes a separately gated water park, four hotels with about 1400 rooms, the Cedar Point Marina, the Castaway Bay Marina and Camper Village, which includes lake-front cottages, cabins and RV sites and Knott's Berry Farm, which opens year-round and includes a seasonal water park as well as a Radisson hotel with 320 hotel rooms. Also, the transaction that led to the ownership of Geuga Lake includes the Woodlands Hotel and Silverhorn Camping Resort. Finally, when Cedar Fair acquired Knott's Berry Farm in 1997, the park came with rights to a children's playground themed around Charlie Brown and Snoopy characters. Since that time, Camp Snoopy has been replicated at Cedar Point, Worlds of Fun and Michigan's Adventure. Cedar Fair also manages Camp Snoopy at the Bloomington Minnesota's Mall of America, an indoor amusement park, until 2017. The rights to Snoopy were acquired simultaneously with the acquisition of Knott's Berry Farm.

4.1.5. Anheuser Busch's corporate strategy

Anheuser Busch controls over 45% of the US beer market and is one of the biggest enterprises in this sector in the world. For the company, the parks have a tangential interest (they help to promote a family image of the Budweiser brand of beer). Anheuser Busch started its activity in the

Table 4.17. Main characteristics of the Cedar Fair theme parks in 2006 (from company reports).

	Location	Foundation	Acquisition	Site (acres)	Rooms
Cedar Point	Sandusky, Ohio	1870	1870	365	1540
Valleyfair	Shakopee, Minnesota	1976	1978	160	–
Dorney Park and Wildwater Kingdom	Allentown, Pennsylvania	1884	1992	200	–
Worlds of Fun and Oceans of Fun	Kansas City, Missouri	1973	1995	350	–
Knott's Berry Farm	Buena Park, California	1920	1997	160	320
Geuga Lake and Wildwater Kingdom	Cleveland, Ohio	1888	2004	670	100
Michigan's Adventure	Muskegon, Michigan	1988	2001	235	–
Kings Island	Cincinnati, Ohio	1972	2006	453	–
Canada's Wonderland	Toronto, Ontario	1981	2006	295	–
Kings Dominion	Richmond, Virginia	1975	2006	264	–
Carowinds	Charlotte, North Carolina	1973	2006	246	–
Great America	Santa Clara, California	1976	2006	180	–

entertainment business with the creation of sophisticated guided itineraries in the botanical gardens beside the Pasadena brewery in 1903. In 1904, moreover, it sponsored an attraction based on the countryside of the Tyrolese Alps for the Saint Louis Universal Exposition. Later, at the Tampa facilities, the company developed a garden which was included in a tour around the brewery facilities together with a beer-tasting session. During the 1970s the Tampa amusement park expanded with a zoological garden. In 1959, the company had already created the subsidiary Busch Entertainment and in 1966 it opened another park in Los Angeles, which did not make a profit.

As a brewery, Anheuser Busch was founded in 1852 in Saint Louis and its top brand, Budweiser, was created in 1876. With brands like Budweiser, Bud Light, Busch, Michelob, Red Wolf Lager, ZiegenBock Amber and O'Doul's, among others, it has agreements with companies in Europe, Asia and Latin America and products on sale in over 80 countries. The company's international expansion intensified during the 1980s and 1990s, just when it also showed its initial interest in developing its first theme park outside the USA, namely, today's PortAventura in Spain. Actually, Budweiser was introduced into Japan and England in 1984 and, in order to increase its international presence, acquired shares in breweries in Mexico, China, Brazil and Argentina between 1993 and 1996 and in Chile at the beginning of 2001. Furthermore, the company has other subsidiaries devoted to a wide variety of businesses, such as international investment, aluminium recycling, grain processing, communications and marketing, property development, road and rail transport and containers, which are principally linked to global business needs and the different product development cycles of the company concerning beer.

Anheuser Busch's first successfully completed initiative in the parks business was with the conversion of Tampa Busch Gardens at the beginning of the 1970s into a park devoted to Africa. Its configuration as an operator of parks came about via the *ex novo* construction of its first park, currently Busch Gardens Europe, near Williamsburg, Virginia, in 1974. The addition of new attractions in one or another park led to increased visitor numbers. Both parks, with their own particular atmospheres and scenes continue to have the power to attract all segments of the public, especially the adult and senior citizen public. The original portfolio of parks was rounded off in the 1970s with the acquisition of Sesame Place, a children's theme park in Langhorne, Pennsylvania.

In 1989, Anheuser Busch bought the four parks of SeaWorld, Cypress Gardens and Boardwalk and Baseball (closed in 1990) from HBJ. In 1977, HBJ, whose interests lay in the sector of publications, had bought the three parks that SeaWorld Inc. had in San Diego, Orlando and Cleveland, to which it added a fourth in San Antonio. SeaWorld had begun its activities in 1964. They were entertainment parks based on shows related to marine animals and educational presentations. In 1985, it also bought Cypress Gardens in Florida, a botanical park dating from the 1930s, which also included shows with animals. Finally, in 1987, it opened a park devoted to sport, Boardwalk and Baseball, again in Florida. In 1989, its owners ranked it in second place after Disney. Nevertheless, in the same year, they put them up for sale. The official version, according to Adams (1991), said that the reason was the need to reduce the debt that the company had incurred with the option to purchase that its principal business received in 1987 from British press baron Robert Maxwell. The fact is that its properties formed the basis, as we shall see, of a second division of parks in the heart of the Busch Entertainment Corporation, created in 1979, helping to form, by means of this sale, the current scenario of park corporations in the USA. Table 4.18 shows the results in visitor numbers for Anheuser Busch's parks portfolio. The important role played by the three SeaWorld parks stands out, receiving 11.8 million visitors in 2005.

In 1989, Anheuser Busch pulled out of the commitment it acquired after having won the Government of Catalonia's tender for the construction of a Recreational and Tourist Centre in Vila-seca/Salou, Spain, which was to include a theme park (what was to become PortAventura). With time, of

Table 4.18. Recent evolution of visits to Anheuser Busch, 1997–2005 (in millions of visits) (based on *Amusement Business* data).

Park	1997	1998	1999	2000	2001	2002	2003	2004	2005
SeaWorld Florida	4.900	4.900	4.700	5.200	5.100	5.000	5.200	5.600	5.600
Busch Gardens Tampa Bay	4.200	4.200	3.900	5.000	4.600	4.500	4.300	4.100	4.300
SeaWorld California	3.990	3.700	3.600	3.600	4.100	4.000	4.000	4.000	4.100
Busch Gardens, Europe	2.500	2.400	2.300	2.300	2.700	2.600	2.500	2.400	2.600
SeaWorld Texas	1.740	1.700	1.700	1.700	1.800	1.600	1.700	1.800	2.100
Sesame Place	0.850	0.900	0.800	0.800	0.830	0.800	0.780	0.800[a]	0.800[a]
Discovery Cove	–	–	0.180	0.270	0.271	0.276	0.270[a]	0.270[a]

a. Estimated.

the parks purchased from HBJ, Anheuser Busch has only kept the SeaWorlds. They are highly suitable parks for the Busch strategy to continue to attract an adult public, thanks to water shows and botanical gardens. As of the first moment, they took hold as a separate division in the heart of Anheuser Busch. In 1999, it started up a niche theme park, Discovery Cove, in Orlando, with a capacity for just 1000 visitors a day. It is, in fact, a second park for SeaWorld in Orlando. SeaWorld in Ohio, which had an average of 1.7 million visits at the end of the 1990s, was sold to Six Flags in 2002. In addition to theme parks, the company owns two water parks, Adventure Island in Florida and Water Country USA in Virginia. In addition to the parks, through its subsidiary, Busch Properties Inc., Anheuser Busch owns the Kingsmill Resort and Spa in Williamsburg which offers world-class recreational amenities and accommodation close to Busch Gardens and Water Country USA. Other visitor attractions owned by Anheuser Busch are the five existing Budweiser Brewery Tours, the Anheuser Busch Center and the St. Louis Grant farm. As can be observed in Table 4.19, although the corporation's income was diversified, the company's seven theme parks and two water parks are a minor fraction of Anheuser Busch's business portfolio. In 2004, it contributed $173 million in operating profit to the parent company.

To this end, theme parks may be understood, from the point of view of Anheuser Busch, as places for children and young people to socialize with the world of beer and as showcases of the company's beer brands to adult guests. In addition, the parks are useful for the company to display its commitment to the environment and the well-being of the citizens (Benz, 2002). The company's commitment to conservation was formalized in 2003 with the creation of the SeaWorld and Busch Gardens Conservation Fund, a non-profit foundation that supports wildlife and habitat conservation,

Table 4.19. Gross sales by Anheuser Busch by business segments 2002–2004 (million $) (from company reports).

	2002	%	2003	%	2004	%
Domestic Beer	12,562.9	77.1	12,997.5	76.9	13,371.6	75.4
International Beer	713.6	4.4	797.0	4.7	1,015.1	5.7
Packaging	2,072.0	12.7	2,093.6	12.4	2,276.8	12.8
Entertainment	858.6	5.3	923.9	5.5	989.3	5.6
Other	92.8	0.6	74.4	0.4	75.4	0.4
Total	16,299.9	100	16,886.4	100	17,728.2	100

education, research and animal rescue worldwide. In 2004, the fund gave more than 50 grants, totalling $500,000. Two parks opened environmentally themed gift shops in 2005. Sales will directly benefit the Conservation Fund.

4.2. The Emergence of Regional Operators in the Rest of the World

Whereas in the USA and Canada five companies operate the majority of the main 50 parks, most theme parks in the rest of the world are independent. Even so, since the 1990s, symptoms have been observed that allow one to speak of the appearance of groups and corporations which, on a regional level, integrate theme parks and recreational attractions within one firm and, occasionally, one brand. The process, though incipient, has begun to have its consequences in Europe, where four corporations with transnational interests exist and include over 80 attractions, 18 of which are medium- and small-sized parks – parks, in any case, with visitor numbers in general below the 2 million visitors per year mark. That means that the large-sized parks continue to be operated, in the majority, independently. Similarly, the emergence of parks in China has not led to the appearance of large operating groups, and neither did this occur in its time in Japan, Korea and, in general, in South-east Asia, with a longer trajectory in the industry and some large parks. In this region, generally speaking, parks are exploited independently by family businesses and corporations, which, in a large percentage of cases, have, however, interests in other industrial fields. In fact, barring the presence of the large North American operators Disney and Universal in Japan and China, the role of corporate groups is quite minor. The same situation exists in Latin America, where just one large corporate park operator can be identified. It is the Mexican company Corporación Interamericana de Entretenimiento SA, which has interests, in the style of the North American corporations, not just in exploiting the parks but, in general, in the Spanish-speaking media, artistic and television industry.

4.2.1. The development of transnational groups in Europe

The European theme park industry has traditionally been characterized by a high degree of fragmentation (Brown and Church, 1987). It is estimated that nearly 85% of European parks are independent. Nevertheless, a generalized tendency exists towards the consolidation of corporate groups and towards the integration of parks into tourist and leisure conglomerates. In greater detail, of the ten major theme and attraction parks in Europe in 2005, only Disneyland Paris (10.2 million visitors in 2005) and Alton Towers (2.4 million visitors in 2005) belong to any of the main theme park and leisure corporations on a worldwide level. Besides Disney's presence in Europe, with 13.8 million visitors in 2005, Tussauds (which operates Alton Towers) is, in fact, the main European park operator chain. The remaining ten biggest parks in Europe belong to entrepreneurial groups with a variety of characteristics, ranging from family businesses, such as the Mack family in the case of Europa Park (3.95 million visitors in 2005) in Germany, to financial entities such as the Catalan savings bank La Caixa, such as PortAventura (3.35 million visitors in 2005) in Spain. It should be pointed out that the company that operates the park in Blackpool (6 million visitors in 2005) in Great Britain, Blackpool Pleasure Beach, also exploits a second amusement park in Southport, Pleasureland. Moreover, Merlin Entertainment, which since 2005 has become one of the top worldwide theme and leisure parks groups, acquired in 2006 the Italian Gardaland (3.1 million visitors in 2005).

Even so, during the 1990s and the beginning of the first decade of the new millennium, multiple changes in ownership took place in existing parks, which has led to the present make-up of the European park groups today. Table 4.20 shows, along these lines, the main operating corporations of theme and leisure parks in Europe including, among other indicators, their country of origin, the number of attractions they run (including theme parks as well as other types of facility such as water parks, museums and aquariums) and the total number of visitors thereto. They are the Tussauds Group, Merlin Entertainment/Legoland Parks, Grévin et Cie and Parques Reunidos. The Disney Company is a shareholder in Euro Disney SCA, owner of Disneyland Paris and Walt Disney Studios, again in Paris, whose main results are presented in Chapter 8. Unlike what happens in the USA, noteworthy for the case of Europe is the diverse nature of leisure facilities run by the different groups. Complementarily, it should be noted that important corporations exist devoted to exploiting other types of facility that do not include proper theme parks. Such is the case of Aspro Ocio. It is a group of companies founded in 1991 which reports to the Luxembourg-based investment group Leisure Resources International Ltd, which exploits water parks with participative attractions, wildlife parks (with shows featuring dolphins, sea lions, parrots and birds of prey), botanical and ornithological parks and state-of-the-art aquariums in Spain (12 parks), France (eight), Switzerland (one), Portugal (one), Great Britain (two), Martinique (one) and Belgium (one). Finally, worthy of mention is the presence of transnational

Table 4.20. Theme/leisure park corporations in Europe, 2005 (from author's own research).

	Main owner	Country of origin	Attractions in other countries	Attractions	Visitors (million)
The Tussauds Group	Dubai International Capital (Emirates)	Great Britain	Germany, Netherlands, USA, Hong Kong	11	13.8
Merlin Entertainment[a]	Blackstone Group (USA)	Great Britain	USA, Germany, Finland, France, Spain, Netherlands, Ireland, Belgium, Denmark	33	12.2
Grévin et Cie	Compagnie des Alpes (France)	France	Netherlands, Germany, Switzerland, Great Britain, Belgium	20	9.7
Parques Reunidos[b]	Advent International (USA)	Spain	Belgium	16	7.5

a. In 2006, Merlin Entertainment acquired Italy's top theme park, Gardaland, including the 247 room Gardaland Resort Hotel. Merlin Entertainment also added three new Sea Life Centres to its portfolio and a water park in Milan.
b. In 2006, Parques Reunidos started an international expansion with the acquisition of several facilities in Europe and Latin America. In 2007, Advent International sold Parques Reunidos to the British company Candover.

investment and venture capital companies among the owners of the main operator groups of European theme and leisure parks.

(A) The Tussauds Group

Tussauds is one of the main operators of recreational attractions in the world. Its name is usually associated with the world-famous wax museums of the same name. It dates back to 1802, when Madame Tussaud brought her waxwork collection to London. However, its business as an operator of recreational attractions is broader. Altogether, the group attracts some 14 million visitors to its different facilities each year. In addition to four theme parks and to the Splash Landings hotel, Europe's first indoor water park hotel, the group owns a third of the London Eye (the most popular fare-paying attraction in the UK), and one of London's Madame Tussaud's urban leisure facilities (2 million visitors per year), the Madame Tussaud's in Amsterdam, New York, Las Vegas and Hong Kong and Warwick Castle. Today, the Tussauds Group belongs to Dubai International Capital, which purchased the group from Charterhouse Capital Partners in 2005 for $1.5 thousand million. This acquisition has taken place at a time when Dubailand is being built in the United Arab Emirates, a leisure project valued at $5 thousand million, which will be developed in phases between 2007 and 2018 and, in addition to theme parks, foresees the construction of a Formula One Grand Prix racing track. On the other hand, it could be added that Dubai International Capital also has interests in Jumeirah International, which has an international portfolio of unique, luxury hotels, including the Carlton Tower London and Burj Al Arab.

Tussauds embarked on the management of theme parks when the group was bought in 1978 by S. Pearson and Son, then the owner of Chessington Zoo. After making an investment of £18 million, the Zoo was reopened in 1987 as a theme park under the name of Chessington World of Adventures. Three years later, in 1990, for £60 million Tussauds bought Alton Towers, the leading theme park in Great Britain. In 1995, at the time of the opening of PortAventura in Spain, Tussauds was the main shareholder, with 40% of the total, which was sold in 1998, Tussauds ceasing to participate in the operation of the park. This transaction coincided in time with the purchase of the group, as part of Pearson, by Charterhouse Development Capital. That same year, the group bought Thorpe Park and in 2001 again undertook new international expansion with the acquisition of Heide Park in Germany. Altogether, the group generates an annual turnover of approximately £200 million, with EBITDA that can be put at £70.6 million for 2004.

(B) Merlin Entertainment/Legoland Parks

In 2005, the US private-equity firm Blackstone Group bought, through its affiliate company Blackstone Capital Partners IV, the leisure parks operated by Merlin Entertainment ($182.3 million) from Hermes Private Equity and the four Legoland Parks theme parks and the 176-room hotel in Denmark held by Danish toymaker Lego ($459.2 million). Purchases turned the group into the second largest leisure and theme park company in Europe for visitor numbers, with a combined attendance in 2005 of over 12 million and the ninth largest entertainment operator in the world. With the acquisition of the Italian theme park Gardaland and the opening of new Sea Life Centres, and the water park in Milan, in 2006 Merlin Entertainment became the first visitor attraction operator in Europe.

Blackstone is one of the US private-equity firms that see Europe's fragmented leisure parks sector as ripe for consolidation and growth. As can be seen in Table 4.21, both groups' results were, when acquired by Blackstone, satisfactory. It was founded in 1985 and has raised a total of approximately $34 billion for alternative asset investing since its formation. Other investments by Blackstone in the leisure sector have included Universal Studios in Orlando and Six Flags. In addition to private-equity investing, the

Table 4.21. Merlin Entertainment performance measures, 2004 (from company reports).

	Visitors (millions)	Turnover (million)	EBITDA (million)
Merlin Entertainment	6.3	£44.9	£14.5
Legoland parks	5.6	172.2 euros	36.3 euros

business core of the group concentrates on private real-estate investing, corporate debt investing, marketable alternative asset management, corporate advising and restructuring and reorganization advising. During the last decade, the group has met with success in several European ventures in many sectors, especially in the UK and Germany.

In 2006 Merlin operated 37 attractions under the Sea Life, Dungeon, Legoland, Gardaland and Earth Explorer brands, including three marine sanctuaries (Table 4.22). It also operated 2 resort hotels, Legoland Billund and Gardaland Resort Hotel. Based in Poole, Dorset, it is the first visitor attraction operator in Germany and the second in the UK. It also holds the world's biggest aquarium brand, Sea Life. It was formed in 1998 when venture capitalist company APAX and J.P. Morgan Partners acquired the attractions division of Vardon. It was sold in 2004 to Hermes Private Equity. Its success is based on the strategy that it is customer-led and locally focused. It has strong ecological roots and is involved in high-profile research/conservation projects. In fact, Merlin was the first major commercial partner for Greenpeace. The company employs around 1000 staff during the peak season. It is averaging EBITDA to sales of around 30%.

The Legoland theme parks, currently one of the company brands, have their own particular history. They were created by the Lego Group, a company founded in 1932 by the Kirk Christiansen family in Billund, Denmark. This is well known as one of the top toy-producing firms in the world and among the five most consolidated brands in Europe (nearly 300 million people have at some time played with lego blocks). The Legoland parks represented the company's strategy to show consumers of Lego products the values it wishes to convey through its products. Today, there are Legoland parks in Billund (Denmark), Windsor (Great Britain), Carlsbad (USA) and Gunzburg (Germany), with joint visitor numbers totalling 5.6 million (Table 4.23). Legoland Billund was the first Lego

Table 4.22. Merlin Entertainment brands, 2006 (from company reports).

	Number	Locations
Sea Life Centres	22	Blackpool, Brighton, Scarborough, Weymouth, Birmingham, Great Yarmouth, Loch Lomond (UK), Timmendorfer Strand, Berlin, Oberhausen, Dresden, Nuremberg, Speyer, Konstanz, Königswinter, Munich (Germany), Helsinki (Finland), Disneyland Paris (France), Benalmádena (Spain), Scheveningen (Netherlands), Bray (Ireland), Blankenberge (Belgium)
Marine Sanctuaries	3	Gweek, Oban, Hunstanton (UK)
Dungeon attractions	5	London, York, Edinburgh (UK), Hamburg (Germany), Amsterdam (Netherlands)
Earth Explorer	1	Ostend (Belgium)
Legoland	4	Denmark, UK, USA and Germany
Gardaland	1	Italy
Water park	1	Milan (Italy)

Table 4.23. Characteristics of Legoland Parks, 2004 (from company reports).

	Country	Date of opening	Opening days per year	Visitor numbers (in millions)
Legoland Billund	Denmark	1968	215	1.53
Legoland Windsor	Great Britain	1996	215	1.37
Legoland Carlsbad	USA	1999	300	1.42
Legoland Deutschland	Germany	2002	215	1.45

park, for which 42 million blocks were used in its construction. It is situated 3 h from Copenhagen and just an hour and a half from Germany. In addition to toys, the company produces television programmes, educational material, books, video games and computer game software. In 1992 the company inaugurated its first shop, the Lego Imagination Center, in Minneapolis, and this was followed by a second in 1997 at Walt Disney World in Orlando.

(C) Grévin et Cie

Grévin et Cie operates several attractions in France, the Netherlands, Germany, Switzerland, Belgium and Great Britain. The corporation's best-known theme park is Parc Astérix, created in 1984. In fact, Parc Astérix was the name of the company until 2001, when, having started the process of growth and the incorporation of new facilities, it was renamed Grévin et Cie. As can be seen in Table 4.24, Grévin et Cie has based its growth on the low-cost acquisition of several family recreational facilities, first in France and, as of 2001, in Europe, which have often continued to be operated by the same agents. This is the case, for example, of Bagatelle, a regional theme park located near Lille and started up in 1956. Since 2002, Grévin et Cie has belonged to the French group La Compagnie des Alpes. La Compagnie des Alpes was created in 1989 by the French public company Caisse des Dépôts et Consignations Développement, with the aim of acquiring and managing ski slopes. In 2002 it went into the leisure parks business through Grévin et Cie. Considering both divisions, today La Compagnie des Alpes is the number one operator of leisure facilities in Europe. In addition to the attractions that appear in Table 4.24, the group, which was privatized in 2004, operates 14 ski destinations in France, Italy and Switzerland. The two activities are, on the other hand, complementary in time, since the peak period spans from December to April for the ski resorts and from April to October in the case of the leisure parks.

In 2006, La Compagnie des Alpes signed a protocol with Palamon Capital Partners for the acquisition of five of the seven parks belonging to Star Parks (Walibi Lorraine in Metz, France, and Warner Bros Movie World in Bottrop, Germany, were not included in the agreement). Star Parks was constituted in 2004 following the acquisition by Palamon

Table 4.24. Acquisitions by Grévin et Cie (number of visitors in millions) (from company reports)[a].

	Country	Date of acquisition	Visitors 2004	Type of attraction
Parc Astérix	France	–	1.8	Theme park
Le Grand Aquarium de Saint Malo	France	1998	0.4	Wildlife park
Musée Grévin	France	1999	0.7	Ludic attraction
France Miniature	France	1999	0.2	Ludic attraction
Bagatelle	France	2000	0.3	Amusement park
Dolfinarium Harderwijk	Netherlands	2001	0.7	Wildlife park
Avonturenpark Hellendoorn	Netherlands	2002	0.3	Amusement park
Fort Fun	Germany	2002	0.5	Amusement park
Mini Châteaux	France	2002	0.2	Ludic attraction
Aquarium du Val-de-Loire	France	2002		Wildlife park
Parc aquatique du Bouveret	Switzerland	2003	0.3	Water park
Panorama Park	Germany	2003	0.1	Amusement park
Pleasurewood Hills	UK	2004	0.2	Amusement park
Planète Sauvage	France	2005	–	Wildlife park
Wailibi Belgium and Aqualibi	Belgium	2006	1.3[b]	Theme park + water park
Bellewaerde Park	Belgium	2006	0.8[b]	Amusement park
Walibi World	Netherlands	2006	0.9[b]	Amusement park
Walibi Rhone Alpes	Netherlands	2006	0.4[b]	Amusement park
Walibi Aquitaine	Netherlands	2006	0.3[b]	Amusement park
Bioscope[c]	France	2006	–	Theme park

a. In 2006, Grévin et Cie also acquired the theme park La Mer du Sable in France.
b. 2005
c. In the case of Bioscope, 2006 refers to the opening date of the park.

Capital Partners, a British investment group, of the European division of Six Flags (except Warner Bros Movie World Madrid). Founded in 1999, Palamon Capital Partners is a partnership investing in middle-market European businesses in engineering, financial services, communications, software services, business services and consumer-related sectors. The origin of Star Parks' parks goes back, principally, to the creation of the Walibi group, of Belgian origin, between the 1970s and the 1990s. Walibi Wavre in Belgium opened its doors in 1975. In 1982 it incorporated Walibi Rhône Alpes, in 1990 the group bought the Bellewaerde Park, also in Belgium, and in 1991 it completed its portfolio of parks with today's Walibi World in Amsterdam and the Walibi Lorraine and Aquitaine parks in France. In 1998, the group was acquired by Premier Parks, which was also bought that same year by the North American group Six Flags. Thus, the Walibi parks came to belong to the largest group of regional leisure parks in the world. Complementarily, in 1999 Warner Bros Movie World opened its doors in Bottrop, Germany, under Six Flags' management. The same year, the parks of the Walibi group were renamed the Six Flags European Division. When in 2004 the private-equity firm Palamon Capital Partners took over the seven parks of the Six Flags European Division, the group was renamed under the brand Star Parks. With this transaction, moreover, La Compagnie des Alpes became proprietor of the Walibi brand, which is well known and appreciated by Europeans. Of today's visitors to the group's parks, 95% reside less than 2 h away. This operation also means that the French company is tending to balance out its main lines of business, the management of ski resorts and leisure parks. Moreover, also in 2006, Grévin et Cie acquired the theme park La Mer de Sable in France.

The aim of La Compagnie des Alpes has been to take advantage of its management experience through the operation of attractions that are giving below-par results. Hence its strategy regarding acquisitions is steered mainly at regional parks and attractions which have been on the market for 10 years or more, which are well established in the market and are primarily family-oriented, not just towards adolescents. In fact, to date, the French company has given priority to the purchase of already existing facilities in densely populated and/or tourist areas. However, currently it is also committed to the development of Bioscope, a ludic and pedagogical theme park focusing on humanity and the environment, in Alsace, at a cost of €60 million, which enjoys the collaboration of the region's public institutions.

Prior to the acquisition of the five Star Parks parks, amusement parks generated 22% of the leisure division's total revenue, whereas the wildlife and water parks accounted for 16%. Attractions brought in 10%, while Parc Astérix represented 52%. Due to the dynamics of the integration of new facilities, Grévin et Cie's management strategy has shifted, in order to obtain such results, towards the cultural integration of the parks into the region where they are located, the integration of new attractions but preserving the identity of each place, the reduction of seasonality when possible (for example, in the case of the aquariums) and the diversification of risk via geographical diversification. In 2005, the Grévin et Cie's turnover was €137 million. Altogether, the 15 parks and 14 ski resorts belonging to La Compagnie des Alpes generated sales of €375 million with a net profit of €27 million.

(D) Parques Reunidos

Parques Reunidos operates water parks, animal parks such as dolphinariums and wildlife parks of a themed nature, amusement parks like the one in Madrid (which it themed) and other unusual attractions (see Table 4.25). It grew mainly during the 1990s, based on the materialization of well-defined

Table 4.25. Evolution of frequentation at Parques Reunidos attractions 1998–2005 (in millions of visitors) (from company reports).

	Park	1998	1999	2000	2001	2002	2003	2004	2005
1	Parque de Atracciones de Madrid	1.780	1.610	1.410	1.300	1.380	2.160	1.710	1.690
2	Madrid Zoo	0.825	0.861	0.798	0.794	1.040	1.140	0.964	0.977
3	Aquopolis de Madrid	0.218	0.214	0.232	0.221	0.298	0.323	0.235	0.257
4	Aquopolis de Torrevieja	0.139	0.141	0.142	0.152	0.172	0.193	0.161	0.157
5	Aquopolis de Sevilla	0.202	0.192	0.211	0.185	0.186	0.225	0.217	0.196
6	Aquopolis de Vila-seca	0.323	0.341	0.366	0.346	0.316	0.340	0.302	0.298
7	Aquopolis de Cullera	–	0.093	0.086	0.092	0.094	0.122	0.108	0.101
8	Aquopolis San Fernando	–	–	–	0.057	0.182	0.256	0.160	0.141
9	Aquopolis Huelva	–	–	–	0.051	0.066	0.080	0.065	0.054
10	Madrid Cable Car	0.189	0.184	0.198	0.181	0.252	0.300	0.231	0.220
11	Selwo	–	0.022	0.316	0.301	0.288	0.206	0.198	0.183
12	Selwo Marina	–	–	–	–	0.119	0.276	0.258	0.242
13	Valwo	–	0.084	0.090	0.085	0.094	0.970	0.066	0.063
14	Benalmádena Cable Car	–	–	–	0.067	0.202	0.200	0.205	0.195
15	Oceanogràfic	–	–	–	–	–	1.530	1.530	1.210
16	Bobbejaanland	–	–	–	–	–	–	0.781	0.662
	Total	3.68	3.75	3.85	3.84	3.97	7.45	7.19	6.64

strategies of acquiring already existing parks. Its origins date back to 1967 with the constitution of the company Parque de Atracciones Casa de Campo de Madrid SA. The sole shareholder of Parques Reunidos, since 2004, is venture capital firm Advent International. Founded in 1984, Advent International, located in Boston, finances companies in a variety of industries around the world. In the case of Parques Reunidos, Advent International has much potential as a consolidator in a highly fragmented European market, with the objective of transitioning the business into a diversified pan-European leisure operation. In fact, Advent International's strategy since joining Parques Reunidos has been to optimize operating efficiencies while leveraging the company's leading position in Spain as a platform from which to grow through acquisitions across other leisure markets in Europe and more recently also in Latin America.

A fundamental milestone in its configuration as one of the main Spanish operating groups of leisure parks in Europe was the acquisition of the Madrid Zoo in 1997 and the two wildlife park projects, which were unfinished at the time of the purchase, Selwo and Valwo in 1999. Through these parks, Parques Reunidos introduced the recreational concept of wild-life parks in Spain. In addition to the Parque de Atracciones de Madrid, the company operates seven water parks in Spain, both in metropolitan areas and in tourist destinations (Vila-seca, San Fernando de Henares, Sevilla, Torrevieja, Cartaya, Villanueva de la Cañada and Cullera). The water parks generate a very high margin for the company, over 40% of the EBITDA. Parks such as the one on Catalonia's Costa Daurada – Gold Coast – obtained a per visitor income of €15.64 in 2002. This is only lower, within the group, than the income received by the Parque de Atracciones de Madrid (16.81) or Selwo (19.63). Furthermore, the company operates two cable cars (Madrid and Benalmádena), the Selwo Marina in Benalmádena and the Oceanogràfic in Valencia in the City of the Arts and Sciences complex. The latter is one of the group's star attractions, an underwater city covering 110,000 m² containing 42 million litres of salt water. The group's total turnover for 2004 was €84.6 million and the growth of the EBITDA reached 35% in 2004. Complementarily, the group exploits a leisure Internet portal, several gastronomic complexes and a wide range of à la carte animation services. Likewise, since 2004 it has incorporated a park outside Spain, Bobbejaanland, in Belgium, and in 2006 it became the majority shareholder of Bo Sommerland water park in Norway. Moreover, also during 2006, Parques Reunidos acquired Mirabilandian in Italy, the Aquarium of Mar del Plata in Argentina, Marineland in France and the operation of Warner Bros in Madrid. Unlike other companies, Parques Reunidos operates most of its attractions under administrative concessions by local authorities.

4.2.2. The diversity of operators in Asia/the Pacific

The presence of the large North American theme park operator corporations is limited in Asia/the Pacific. The many existing initiatives that make the region the area of the world with the greatest growth in the market of theme parks are developed, in general terms, at a local and/or regional level and often with the collaboration of the public institutions on different territorial scales (from the municipal to the state), be it as investors or as agents collaborating in other private initiatives. Teo and Yeoh (2001) point out, moreover, that the 'theme park owners in South-east Asia are clearly cognisant of their dependence on regional markets, namely Singapore, Indonesia, Malaysia, India, Taiwan, Japan, Korea, China and Hong Kong'. To this end, one cannot speak of large Asian corporations operating theme parks, but rather of numerous private initiatives that not only set themselves apart from the North American case but are even some way away, as regards integration, from the situation observed in Europe.

Table 4.26 shows the characteristics of some theme and leisure park operators in Asia/the Pacific. They are Oriental Land, the owner of the two Disney parks in Japan, Everland, belonging to the Korean group

Table 4.26. Theme/leisure park corporations in Asia/the Pacific, 2005 (from author's own research).

	Parent companies	Country of origin	Parks	Visitors (million)
Oriental Land	Keisei Electric Railway Co. Ltd Mitsui Fudosan Co. Ltd	Japan	Tokyo Disneyland, Tokyo Disney Sea	25.0
Samsung Everland	Samsung Corporation	South Korea	Everland, Caribbean Bay, Animal Wonder World	8.9
China Travel International Investment	China Travel Service Holdings HK Ltd	China	Splendid China, Chinese Folk Culture Villages, Window of the World	3.7
Village Roadshow Ltd	Village Roadshow Corporation Pty Ltd	Australia	SeaWorld, Movie World, Wet 'n Wild, Aussie Farm Tour	2.6
Sanrio Company Ltd	–	Japan	Sanrio Puroland, Sanrio Harmonyland	1.2

Samsung and owner of the most visited theme park in Asia after those of Disney and Universal, China Travel International Investment Hong Kong Limited, one of Asia's biggest tourist services companies including tour operation, hotels, theme parks, passenger and freight transportation, golf clubs and infrastructure investment, Village Roadshow, the main Australian entertainment group and theme park owner and operator, and Sanrio Company Ltd, the leading Japanese maker of character toys such as Hello Kitty. They are five operating companies with very different characteristics setting them apart. In fact, they illustrate a reality, that of Asia/the Pacific, with scarcely any transnationalized corporations, which may be defined due to the presence of initiatives of very different scale and characteristics.

In this sense, many other examples may be cited: (i) recreational developments based on cultural assets that are promoted by government bodies, such as Sarawak Cultural Village in Indonesia; (ii) parks belonging to individual entrepreneurs, such as the Mines Resort City in Kuala Lumpur, developed by Tan Sri Lee Kim Yew; (iii) large corporations from outside the entertainment industry like Kumagai Cumi Co. in Japan, a civil engineering company, which participates in the development of Beijing Amusement Park; (iv) real-estate companies such as Shunde Jiaxin Realty Development Co., which has created a theme park featuring Snoopy in Guangdong; (v) tourism companies that go into the theme park business, like the Shanghai-based company China Pan Tourism Industry Development Co.; or, even, (vi) North American corporations that participate in the process of the growth of the Asian market through specific initiatives such as the Intra-Asia Entertainment Corporation, whose headquarters are in California, owner of the Weifang Fuhua Amusement Park in the Chinese province of Shandong.

(A) Oriental Land

The Japanese company Oriental Land Co. was established in 1960 with the aim of reclaiming land off the coast of Urayasu, developing commercial and residential land and constructing a major leisure facility to contribute to the nation's culture and welfare. Reclamation work was completed in 1975. In 1979, Oriental Land and Walt Disney Productions concluded an agreement concerning the licensing, design, construction and operation of Tokyo Disneyland Park. It accomplished the original mission of the company. Since then, Oriental Land has become the partner of Disney in Japan. Under licence, Oriental Land owns and operates the Disneyland facilities in Japan in Uraysu-shi, Chiba, approximately 10 km from the centre of Tokyo. Oriental Land also has interests in the retail business and since 2002 has operated the Disney stores across Japan. E Production was also established for the management of entertainers and in 2003 the company established OLC/Rights Entertainment for the management of copyrights. Keisei Electric Railway Co. Ltd is the major stakeholder of Oriental Land Co. Ltd, controlling 20.43% of voting rights. Mitsui Fudosan Co. Ltd controls 15.96%.

The success of Tokyo Disneyland, which opened in 1983, prompted the desire to develop new assets. So, in 1996, Oriental Land and Disney concluded a new agreement concerning the licensing, design, construction and operation of the new Disney theme park, Tokyo DisneySea, which opened in 2000, and the current Tokyo DisneySea Hotel MiraCosta, also operational in 2001. Tokyo Disneyland and Tokyo DisneySea make up the Tokyo Disney Resort, a totally integrated entertainment destination that expands the concept of a theme park to a theme resort. It is located on some 200 ha of land and encompasses a number of distinct facilities. In addition to its theme parks, the resort features nine themed zones of shopping, dining and entertainment facilities, including about 130 shops and restaurants, at Ikspiari. The resort also offers two Disney hotels and five official hotels. The Disney Resort Line monorail system, operational since 2001, connects the various resort facilities.

The company generates revenue through its four business divisions: theme parks, retail business, entertainment and commercial facilities and other business. Table 4.27 includes the main operations of each business segment, the main affiliates and other companies conducting each business during 2005 and the revenue obtained during the fiscal year.

(B) Samsung Everland

Samsung Everland is an independent subsidiary company of Samsung, one of Korea's most enduring and respected corporations, having supported development since its foundation in 1938 (see the report 'Consolidated Financial Statements for the Interim Period Ended September 30, 2004' in www.olc.co.jp). Today, Samsung is engaged in several major business areas: electronics, machinery-related industries, chemistry, financial services and other industries, including hotels and resorts, communications,

Table 4.27. Outline of Oriental Land group, 2005 (from company reports).

Activity	Companies	Revenue (million yen)	Operating income (million yen)
Theme parks	• Management and operation of theme parks		
	Oriental Land Co. Ltd		
	• Management and operation of Tokyo DisneySea Hotel MiraCosta		
	Maihama Resort Hotels Co. Ltd	129,237	9,739
Commercial facilities	• Management and operation of Ikspiari		
	Ikspiari Co. Ltd		
	• Management and operation of Disney Ambassador Hotel		
	Maihama Resort Hotels Co. Ltd	10,711	925
	• Management of Camp Nepos		
	Oriental Land Co. Ltd		
Retail business	• Management and Operation of Disney Stores Japan		
	Retail Networks Co. Ltd	10,467	511
Other	• Management of Palm and Fountain Terrace Hotel		
	Maihama Resort Hotels Co. Ltd		
	• Management and operation of monorail		
	Maihama Resort Line Co. Ltd	5,874	145
	• Operation of employee cafeterias		
	Bay Food Services Co. Ltd		
	• Management and operation of themed restaurants and others		
	RC Japan Co. Ltd and 13 other companies		

medical services, academic foundations and educational organizations among others. Samsung Everland, founded in 1963, is Korea's leading company in the leisure and resort business. It covers a broad range of businesses, including catering and food services, building assets, energy, golf course operation and management, environmental development and landscape architecture management. It has 1570 employees and generated US$1136.9 million in sales during the 2004 fiscal year.

Samsung Everland was established in 1963 as Dongwha Real Estate. In 1967 it changed the company name to JoongAng Development Co. The Everland theme park opened with the name Yong In Farmland in 1976. In 2006 Everland made a leap forward as a world-class resort. It has raised the level of theme parks in Korea one step higher through a number of quality certifications and awards. In 1996 Caribbean Bay, an indoor and outdoor water park, opened – the first of its kind in the world. Caribbean Bay is not only Korea's first water park, but also the world's biggest water park, with linked indoor and outdoor areas. Since 2005, it has also operated the thematic zoo Animal Wonderworld. Moreover, Everland is full of festivals throughout the year, and manages golf courses. Starting with the Anyang Benest Golf Club in 1968, Samsung Everland has launched five golf clubs and guided Korea's golf culture, offering outstanding golf clubs and services. Anyang Benest Golf Club is known to lead the pack in Korea, Gapyeong Benest Golf Club, which opened in September 2004 was modelled on Anyang Benest, and Dongrae Benest Golf Club constitutes the 'Benest' brand. Along with these three golf clubs, two others, namely Seven Hills Golf Club and Glenross Golf Club, symbolize the best-quality golf courses offering sophisticated services, which appeal to many golfers in Korea. In 2005, the company laid a firm foundation for making four golf clubs globally competitive by holding one of the major golf tours in Korea, KPGA Korean Tour 'Samsung Benest Open Golf Tour' in Gayeong Benest Golf Club.

To develop entertainment and recreational activities, currently Samsung Everland has a number of operating divisions (see http://www.everland.com):

1. The Food Service and Distribution division, which strives to nurture an advanced food and beverage culture suited to the ever-changing food consumption styles of the public, is committed to creating a new food and beverage culture with globally competitive services.

2. The Service Academy is a service education/consulting institute designed to provide a creative service culture based on the company's spirit of service, which always puts customers first. Since its opening in 1994, the Service Academy has educated 430,000 people from about 800 institutions and is now emerging as a pre-eminent HRD (human resource development) centre in Asia in both quality and quantity.

3. The Everland Culinary Academy, which opened in June 1997, has pursued improvement in food and beverage quality and productivity, while assuming the role of inheriting the tradition of Korean food and making it globally competitive.

4. The Turf and Environment Research Institute, which cherishes the environment and pursues 'green living' and 'green leisure'.
5. The Food Research Institute is a comprehensive food and beverage institute which develops high-quality food materials of private brands and conducts total quality guarantee and safety analysis activities.

Moreover, Samsung Everland builds green living spaces and restores damaged ecosystems through environment-friendly development projects in landscape architecture and environment restoration. Achievements in the landscape business include the Incheon International Airport in Yeongjongdo, the World Cup Main Stadium, the Shilla Hotel in Jeju Island, Noble County and other representative buildings in Korea.

(C) China Travel International Investment

China Travel International Investment (CTII) is a company specialized in the investment and management of tourism and related business. It is a consumer services company in the fragmented Chinese travel industry. Its parent is state-owned China Travel Services Holdings, which owns 58.95% of the total shares. CTII is a leader in travel agency and related services in China. It has over 70 years' experience in operation and management in Hong Kong. Nowadays it owns a comprehensive network of travel, transport, leisure, entertainment and hospitality resources in Hong Kong, Macau and the Pearl River Delta Region. It has developed the following businesses (Table 4.28): the processing of travel permits for residents in Hong Kong and Taiwan visiting China, hotel management in Hong Kong with a total of 1350 rooms and an average occupancy rate of 90.5% (since 1992 CTII has bought four hotels, built the Metropark Hotel and sold its Hotel Grandeur Macau), investment in three theme park operations in Shenzhen, golf course management, tour operation in Hong Kong, China and overseas, coach operation in Hong Kong and Guangdong, a 29% stake in a Hong Kong–Macau ferry service, investment in a power plant, and a freight forwarding business in Shanghai and Hong Kong. In 2005 CTII opened the Zuhai Ocean Hot Spring Resort. It was purchased in 2002 and rebuilt with the development of a 950-room resort hotel, a golf course, water sports and hot spring clinic facilities. The resort is virtually competition-free in the Pearl River Delta. It is located between the two special administrative regions of Macau and Hong Kong and the area is a popular destination for the Chinese and visitors to the region. Excluding its loss-making golf course, the largest profit contributor at 38% in 2004 was the Shanxi Weihe power plant, followed by the travel business at 29%, transportation at 19% and hotels at 14%.

CTII owns 51% of three theme parks in Shenzhen. Overseas Chinese Town company (OCT), a sister company controlled by the CTII's ultimate parent, owns the remaining 49%. OCT also owns 100% of another completed theme park in the vicinity, Happy Valley. The four parks combined drew more than 5 million visitors. Table 4.29 shows the combined results of the three CTII theme parks in Shenzhen. Annual visitors in recent years

Table 4.28. Business segments of CTII (from company reports Ju and Li, 2005).

	Turnover 2004 HK$ (in millions)	Operating profit 2004 (in millions)	Profit contribution 2004	Assets
Travel, leisure and entertainment			29%	
Theme parks	380	136		Splendid China (51%) China Folk Culture Village (51%) Window of the World (51%)
Tour operation	1935	232		China Travel Service Ltd China Travel International Ltd China Travel Net HK Ltd
Golf club	43	−12		Shenzhen Tycoon Golf Club
Leisure resort	−	−		CTHK (Zuhai) Ocean Spring Co.
Hospitality			14%	
Hotels	373	111		Hotel Concourse Hotel New Harbour The Metropole Hotel Metropark Hotel
Investment holdings			38%	
Infrastructure	−	311.2		Shanxi Weihe Power (51%)
Transportation			19%	
Freight	1857	55		CTS (Cargo) HK Ltd SCT (Cargo) HK Ltd CTS International Trans Co. Ltd (76%)
Passenger transportation	213	98.1[a]		CT Tours Transportation SHK Ltd Shun Tak-CTXI Ltd (29%) China Travel Express Ltd (70%)

a. Including associated operating profit from ferry services.

are only about half of those at the beginning of the 1990s, when tickets were selling at about a third of today's price. A major asset in the area that also affected the results of the CTII parks was the opening of the new Hong Kong Disneyland in September 2005. Nevertheless, while Hong Kong Disneyland may draw some visitors from CTII theme parks, the overall effect should be positive for the company because it will help the company's passenger, tour and hotel businesses. In any case, CTII parks target a different segment of visitors from Hong Kong Disneyland.

Table 4.29. Main performance indicators of CTII theme parks in Shenzhen (from Kwong, 2005 data).

	1990	1991	1992	1993	1994	1995	1996	1997	1998	1999	2000	2001	2002	2003	2004
Annual visitors (million)	3.30	4.01	7.36	7.21	6.13	5.82	4.99	4.53	3.71	4.01	4.57	4.48	4.12	2.78	3.73
Operating profit (HK$ million)	79	78	120	109	58	83	107	61	82	72	159	158	126	66	136
Ticket per visitor (HK$)	40	36	26	33	28	35	92	96	98	92	95	95	97	196	102
Profit margin (%)	59	54	63	46	34	41	23	14	23	20	37	37	31	22	36

(D) Village Roadshow Ltd

Village Roadshow is the main Australian-based entertainment group. It was founded by Roc Kirby in 1954 as one of the first drive-in cinemas. It entered film distribution in the 1960s and film production in the 1970s. In the 1980s, Village Roadshow was a pioneer in the development of state-of-the-art multiplex cinema complexes. In the 1990s, Village Roadshow sought to further strengthen its position by diversifying into complementary media and entertainment businesses. This included the purchase and development of theme parks and the purchase and integration of the Triple M and Today radio networks to create Austereo Group Limited. Today, Village Roadshow operates core businesses in cinema, movie production, film distribution, radio and theme parks. While creating strong and diverse earnings streams, these businesses are also complementary, targeting a similar customer demography and providing significant cross-promotional opportunities. The main shareholder of the company is Village Roadshow Corporation. The Kirby family and Graham Burke control their stake through their 100% ownership of it. The company has also had a historically strong relationship with Warner Brothers. So, for instance, in 2005 Warner owned 50% of the Village Roadshow theme parks and granted Village Roadshow exclusive theatrical film distribution rights in Australia, Greece and New Zealand and they were partners owning 25% of the Australian Pay TV Movie Network, among other things.

In 2006 Village Roadshow acquired all of Warner Bros' interests in their jointly owned Australian theme park venture for US$ 194 million. The transaction involved Village Roadshow acquiring the companies which hold the interest of Warner and Warner's share of associated bank debt. In any case, it will continue to partner Warner Bros in theme parks in Australia via a long-term licensing agreement. The transaction also provides for Village Roadshow to explore theme park opportunities in Asia with Warner Bros. As a result, currently with three theme parks on Australia's Gold Coast, Paradise Country–Aussie Farm Tour experience and the exciting evening dinner show, Australian Outback Spectacular, Village Roadshow is the country's largest theme park operator. More than 2.5 million people per annum visit the three parks, Warner Bros Movie World, SeaWorld and Wet 'n Wild Water World. It is also 50% owner of SeaWorld Nara Resort, a 405-room hotel adjacent to SeaWorld. With direct monorail access to SeaWorld, this secluded and luxurious resort enjoys the reputation of being Australia's number one theme park holiday destination, only minutes from Marina Mirage, a centre for world-class shopping and dining, and Surfers Paradise. Village Roadshow also owns the Warner Roadshow Studios. They are located next to the Warner Bros' Movie World theme park. Over the last 16 years the studios have been home to countless feature films, telemovies, TV series and mini-series. All facilities are located within 20 km of each other on Australia's Gold Coast. As reported in Table 4.30, it can be estimated that parks generated about AUS$160 million in revenue in the fiscal year ended 30 June 2005 and AUS$45 million of earnings before interest and taxes (EBIT), representing an overall margin of 28%.

Table 4.30. Main results of Village Roadshow theme parks, 2004/05 (from Farrell and Watson, 2005).

Theme park	Year opened	Attendance (millions)	Adult ticket price (AUS$)	Average spend per ticket (AUS$)	Revenue (million AUS$)	EBIT (million AUS$)
SeaWorld	1971	1.2	56	50	60	20
Movie World	1982	1.2	56	54	63	14
Wet 'n Wild	1984	0.8	36	20	15	6
Paradise Country	2005	0.1[a]	–	–	–	–
Other						
Nara Resort					20	4
Movie Studio					2	1

a. Expected.

Originally opened in 1971, SeaWorld was associated with Village Roadshow in 1992. It is the company's largest and oldest park and has become Australia's prime marine park. SeaWorld Research and Rescue Foundation is an independent, non-profit-making organization supported by SeaWorld. With Movie World Park, which consists of a number of movie-themed attractions on a surface area of 100 ha, both parks are most lucrative. In both cases, since 1997 international attendance levels have declined because of the Asian crisis. Adjacent to Movie World is a small film and TV studio, which includes sound stages, water tanks and editing suites and which makes up an integral part of the theming. Wet 'n Wild is a themed water park ideally suited to the tropical climate of the Gold Coast. Attendance levels have shown continuous improvements over the last decade because of the domestic market. Paradise County is the newest and smallest park. It has no rides and caters primarily for the pre-booked international market that seeks an Australian country and farm experience. It is located next to Movie World. Adjacent to SeaWorld, the Nara Resort was opened in 1988 and enjoys occupancy in most years of around 75–80%. During 2005, Village Roadshow developed Australian Outback Spectacular, a unique and fun-filled evening dinner show representing the grandeur of the Australian outback, located between Movie World and Wet 'n Wild (see http://www.village.com.au). In addition to the above, Village Roadshow is conducting a feasibility study on a new theme park on Singapore Sentosa Island that would require an initial investment of AUS$20–40 million.

(E) Sanrio Company Ltd

Established in 1960, the principal businesses of the Japanese Sanrio Company are the manufacture and sale of social communication gifts (91.5% of company sales in 2005), the manufacture and sale of greeting cards, the operation of family-oriented restaurants, the publication of books and magazines, the production, promotion and distribution of movies and the planning and operation of theme parks (around 0.5% of company sales). Sanrio is a leading maker of character toys. The most popular among them is Hello Kitty, which celebrated its 30th anniversary on 1 November 2004 and was the child ambassador of UNICEF in Japan in 1994. The company obtained a consolidated income of $995 million in the tax year ending in May 2005, of which $68.6 million were generated by the two theme parks it operates in Japan (Sanrio Puroland, an indoor theme park running since 1990 in Tama City, Tokyo and Harmonyland, which opened in Oita in 1991).

The operation of the theme parks is done through two subsidiary companies, Sanrio Puroland Co. Ltd and Harmonyland Co., 100% and 95% property of Sanrio Company Ltd, respectively (see http://www.sanrio.com). Both theme parks are viewed strategically by the company in the medium-term business plan, together with a greater presence of its products worldwide, licensing and increased sales. In order to improve the results of the parks – whose operating costs exceeded income in 2004 and 2005 – Sanrio foresees, in the short term, increasing the number of visits (standing at 892,000 in Sanrio Puroland and 340,000 in Harmonyland in 2005) and raising per-consumer expenditure (5179 yen in Sanrio Puroland compared with 4559 yen in Harmonyland in 2005), as well as diversifying revenue sources such as content revenue and advertising functions (the outside revenue obtained by the two parks together in 2005 stood at 1070 million yen). In addition, a reduction in general services costs is contemplated and a decrease in depreciation expenses to allow an improvement in the economic and financial situation. To achieve this, Sanrio Puroland is counting on the opening of 'Kitty's House' and the introduction of new shows featuring such popular characters as Usahana, which should bring about the harnessing of international visitors. As for Harmonyland, it has the possibility of expanding its sphere of influence to South Korea, as well as other improvements affecting operational aspects and contents. In any case, it is worth highlighting the character of the two parks, which feed from the popularity of Hello Kitty and the other characters created by Sanrio. In the case of Harmonyland, which is out of doors, in addition to the attractions and events, the park teaches visitors about Oita's natural environment and cultural heritage.

4.2.3. The uniqueness of the CIE in Latin America

The Corporación Interamericana de Entretenimiento (CIE) is the leading out-of-home entertainment company in Latin American, Spanish and US Hispanic markets. It is the largest live event producer in the Hispanic world, manages several venues, including Mexico City's racetrack of the Americas, and owns and operates several theme and amusement parks in Latin America. CIE also owns and operates seven radio stations in Argentina and has film production and distribution interests. CIE has a vertically integrated business model producing contents (events, games, horse racing), managing venues (stadiums, arenas, trade and exhibition centres, theme parks, zoos, race tracks, amphitheatres, theatres and auditoriums) and developing services, such as sponsorship, ticket sales, food and beverage operation and souvenirs and merchandising sales. The company has three operating divisions: entertainment, commercial and services (Table 4.31). It has subsidiaries in Mexico, Argentina, Brazil, Chile, Panama, Colombia, the USA, Spain and the Netherlands.

CIE is Latin America's leading operator and developer of theme parks, with more than 10 million visitors yearly. It operates 11 amusement parks in five cities: Mexico City, Guadalajara and Acapulco in Mexico, Bogotá in Colombia and Fort Lauderdale in the USA. It also has projects in Chicago (USA), Puebla and Guadalajara (Mexico). CIE focuses on serving the low/medium-income social groups. They are parks that are open for 365 days a year. Visitors' average stay at the parks is 4 h. The parks are visited four times per year as a rule. CIE came into the theme park business in 1997 with the purchase of 50% of the capital pertaining to Grupo Mágico, Mexico's main theme park developer in the 1990s, with five units in

Table 4.31. Operating divisions at CIE (from company reports).

	Activity	Revenue contribution (%)	Revenue (million $) 2003	Operating income (million $) 2003
Entertainment	• Live entertainment (Mexico, Argentina, Brazil, Chile, Spain, USA) • Venue operation • Gaming • Amusement parks (Mexico, Colombia, USA)	77	5124.5	812.4
Commercial	• Sponsorship and advertising (music, amusement parks, movie theatres, naming rights, overpasses, airports, skywalks, venues, ticketing, corporate events, radio, rotational advertising) • Food, beverage and merchandising	13	875.9	112.4
Services	• Ticketing (Mexico, Argentina, Chile) • Teleservices	10	686.3	137.6

Mexico City and Guadalajara, and it progressively expanded its operations in other Mexican cities, such as Acapulco. In 2001, CIE also acquired the rights to operate La Feria de Chapultepec (1.53 million visitors in 2005), Mexico City's most popular leisure park. In 2003, CIE took up the operation of México Mágico, a theme and educational park located next to Planeta Azul in Mexico City displaying architectural models concerning the history of Mexico. In 2004, the company's two parks in Bogotá were reinaugurated. By means of this expansion process, the Corporación Interamericana de Entretenimiento has become not just an operator of reference in Latin America but also one of the leading groups worldwide as regards visitor numbers (Table 4.32).

In 2002, CIE formed a partnership, through Grupo Mágico, its theme park subsidiary, with ZN Mexico II, a private capital fund, and the Mills Corporation, one of the USA's most important promoters of shopping malls, for the funding of the Wannado City project in the Sawgrass Mills shopping mall, with over 30 million visitors a year, in Fort Lauderdale. Wannado City is a new recreational concept designed by CIE, whose aim is to build other such facilities in other American metropolitan agglomerations. It is a covered theme park valued at $45 million, targeting 4- to 11-year-olds, where they will be able to pursue educational and entertainment activities in tune with the slogan 'At Wannado City, kids can do what they Wannado!' This is the first incursion into the North American market by a Latin American theme park company. A second project to be developed exists in Gurnee Mills, also operated by the Mills Corporation, in Chicago.

Case 6. The Family-run Europa Park

Europa Park opened its doors in 1975 in Rust, a German town located next to the French-Alsatian and Swiss borders. Since then, the park has

Table 4.32. CIE parks (from company reports).

Park	Country
La Feria de Chapultepec, Mexico DF	Mexico
Selva Mágica, Guadalajara	Mexico
El Salitre Mágico, Bogotá	Colombia
Divertido, Mexico DF	Mexico
Cici de Acapulco	Mexico
Planeta Azul, Mexico DF	Mexico
Perimágico, Mexico DF	Mexico
Cici Bogotá, Bogotá	Colombia
Naucali Mágico, Mexico DF	Mexico
Divertido, Guadalajara	Mexico
Wannado City, Fort Lauderdale	USA

become an international leisure destination. The combination of accurately shaped themed areas, exciting rides, dazzling shows, modern leisure technology, fascinating architecture and generous flowered gardens in a unique place with a 550-year-old castle transforms the visit into a relaxing, entertaining and enriching experience (see http://www.europapark.de). The park, one of the top five in Europe in visitor numbers, with a mean approaching 4 million per year, is also ranked amongst the most beautiful in the world. It is the second attraction in Germany after Cologne cathedral. Today the park features 12 areas themed after various countries across Europe. Its 170 acres offer more than 100 attractions, including Europe's tallest roller coaster and three hotels with more than 4128 beds. Since its beginnings, the park has invested €420 million without receiving aid from the public sector (Mack, 2005), and it employs 2800 people and generates some 8000 indirect jobs in the Freiburg region. The park is owned and managed by the Mack family.

As Schoolfield (2005) reports, the Mack family history in the amusement business dates back to the 18th century when in 1780 Paul Mack established the family's first official construction facilities for carriages and stagecoaches in Waldkirch, Germany. In the late 19th century, the Mack family started to build its first amusement products, such as organ wagons and saloon caravans for travelling showmen and circuses. By the first decades of the 20th century, they started to produce carousels for carnivals and wooden roller coasters. As of the 1950s, Franz Mack started to expand the family business in the USA, visiting amusement and theme parks, doing research, meeting clients and extending his company's reach. During these years he developed the idea to build a park in Europe. Nevertheless, it was in 1970, when he took a 2-week tour in the USA with his son Roland Mack visiting parks and taking field notes, that the Macks conceived the park. The park would provide guests with a one-stop shop of all that Europe has to offer. The opportunity was in Rust, located close to the Mack factory in Waldkirch, and the project could serve a dual objective: to create an entertainment destination and to showcase the Mack amusement product line (featuring the company's first permanent attractions).

Roland Mack and his younger brother Jurgen Mack own and manage the park. For them, being a family-owned business is one of the park's major strengths. Because of this, Roland has been preparing the rise of his sons, Michael and Thomas Mack, to Europa Park management. They started in the business as cabin boys and cabin characters in the park or at other amusement and theme parks worldwide, from Warner Bros in Australia to Busch Gardens in Virginia. Recently they have finally joined the management staff of the park to deal with challenges such as the operation of the park and its hotel management and expansion. As a family business, Europa Park is more organic than the traditional corporate structure. At Europa Park the goal is continuity and the maintenance of a quality identity. Without a doubt, the advantage of the family organization lies in the speed of taking and implementing decisions. Continuous training, a good work atmosphere and motivation are fundamental in this context. Also without a doubt, the close relationship of the park's ownership with the Mack Rides attraction producers in Waldkirch, one of the leading manufacturers of attractions worldwide, which has produced more than 90% of the park's attractions, is a key element for the success of the company.

Until now, the Mack family has developed not just an entertainment product that is broadly known in Europe and throughout the world, but moreover and especially an image of a brand associated with quality, emotion and innovation. Though almost imperceptible, the process has been continued along its 30 years of experience. Innovation has been fundamental in this process. In addition, it has led to the diversification of the business, not just in sectors such as the hotel and catering, which is managed by the family itself, but also television production, consultancy and commercial activity. Currently 16% of clients spend over 1 day at the park. This means that, in 2004, the park's hotels had close to 320,000 overnight stays. At the same time, the park organizes almost 1000 events a year, for which ten conference halls are available with a capacity of nearly 2300 people simultaneously. However, families – who represent 90% of visits – are the park's main centre of interest: hence the commitment, too, to innovation in attraction-related matters. Proof of the success of this philosophy is the huge response by the demand for the 4D cinema screen inaugurated in 2003 – which projects a fantastic film about nature (produced in collaboration with the WorldWide Fund for Nature in Germany). In any case, continuous innovation is the essence of the Mack family's project (Mack, 2005).

Case 7. A Chocolate-related Entertainment Destination in Hershey, Pennsylvania

In 1883, Milton Hershey established the Lancaster Caramel Company, which quickly became an outstanding success. Fascinated with German chocolate-making machinery exhibited at the 1893 World's Columbian Exposition, in 1894 Hershey decided to produce sweet chocolate as a coating for his caramels. He bought the equipment for his Lancaster plant in Pennsylvania and started to produce a variety of chocolate creations. Excited by the potential of milk chocolate, which at that time was a Swiss luxury product, Hershey developed a formula to produce and sell it to the American public. In 1903 he began the construction of the Hershey Chocolate Company, which was to become the world's largest chocolate manufacturing plant. It was completed in Lancaster, Pennsylvania, in 1905. With mass production, Hershey was able to transform the once luxury item for the wealthy into a product affordable to all. Today, the Hershey Company is the leading North American manufacturer of chocolate and non-chocolate confectionery and grocery products. Hershey's products are exported to over 90 countries and net sales are around $4 billion.

From the moment he developed his factory, Milton Hershey envisioned a complete, new community around it (Jaques, 1997). He planned a model town for his employees, which had to include comfortable homes, an inexpensive public transportation system, a quality public school system and extensive recreational and cultural opportunities. So he built a park to create a more pleasant environment for workers and residents and, in 1907, Hersheypark was opened as an ideal spot for picnicking, boating and canoeing. The park provided a shady retreat for thousands of people without being crowded. The original main buildings, a rustic bandstand and pavilion, served as a stage for vaudeville and theatre productions. Immediately, new attractions and rides were added. The first was a merry-go-round. Then, each season, new attractions were added to Hersheypark and by 1945 there were more than two dozen 'amusements and fun devices', and the original carousel was replaced by the one that is still in use today. The year 1971 saw the beginning of the conversion of the amusement park into one of America's most popular theme parks. The pay-as-you-ride policy was replaced with a one-price admission plan. As a result, currently Hersheypark encompasses a 110 acre clean and green theme park with more than 60 rides and attractions – including ten roller coasters, eight water rides and more than 24 kiddie rides. Moreover, the park includes in the one-price admission entrance to Zooamerica North American Wildlife Park, an 11-acre walk through zoo with more than 200 animals and plants native to North America. Currently, Hersheypark employs more than 250 full-time and 3000 seasonal employees. In 2005 it received 2.7 million visitors.

At present, the Hershey Entertainment Group owns and operates not only Hersheypark and Zooamerica North American Wildlife Park but several sports facilities, such as the Giant Center, a new arena that opened in 2002, the Hersheypark arena, opened in 1936, and the Hersheypark stadium and the Star Pavilion at Hersheypark stadium, opened in 1996. It also operates as a franchise the Hershey Bears, an AHL (American Hockey League) affiliate of the NHL (National Hockey League) Washington Capitals. In 2001 the firm expanded with the purchase of the Dutch Wonderland theme park in nearby Lancaster, Pennsylvania. This is a family entertainment complex opened in 1963 that now features 25 rides on 48 acres, plus attractions like Discover Lancaster County History Museum and the Old Mill Stream Campground. The Group also owns and operates several resort facilities, including the Hotel Hershey, built in 1933 by Milton Hershey, the Spa at the Hotel Hershey, opened in 2001, the Hershey Lodge, offering 665 rooms including 28 suites and more than 100,000 square feet of meeting, banquet and exhibition space – recognized as Pennsylvania's largest convention resort – opened in 1967, the Hershey Country Club with two private courses built in 1930 and 1970, plus the Spring Creek Golf Course (designed specifically for junior players), and the Hershey Highmeadow Campground, established in 1963. Finally, the Group owns the Hershey Nursery, founded in 1905, which offers landscape design and maintenance for both commercial and residential properties, and Hershey Cleaners, founded in 1908, which offers a wide variety of services and amenities, including private and commercial laundering and dry cleaning, sale of uniforms and linen, embroidering and tailoring, and the preservation of special garments. The legacy of Milton Hershey is also alive at Hershey Gardens, a botanical treasure opened as a 3.5 acre rose garden in 1937 and expanded to its current 23 acres by 1942. Also in Hershey there are other attractions, such as Hershey's Chocolate World, the Hershey Museum and the Hershey Trolley Works.

As is explained at the Hersheypark website (www.hersheypa.com), to manage all its entertainment holdings, in 1927 Milton S. Hershey separated his chocolate manufacturing operations from his other businesses and founded Hershey Estates, now known as Hershey Entertainment and Resorts Company. Its mission was to become one of the world's premier entertainment and hospitality companies by creating experiences. Prior to this, in 1909, he created a deed of trust establishing the Hershey Industrial School for orphaned boys, later renamed the Milton Hershey School. The Hershey Trust, as trustee for the Milton Hershey School, owns Hershey Entertainment and Resorts Company. In addition, the Hershey Trust owns the majority of the voting stock of the Hershey Company, a publicly held company. Today, the profits generated by these entities perpetuate the Hershey Trust, which in turn funds the Milton Hershey School. Currently, Hershey Entertainment and Resorts employs about 1400 full-time employees and 4500 seasonal and part-time employees.

Case 8. Suncity, Entertainment and Property Development in Malaysia

The Suncity Group of Companies began its operations in 1986. It is a part of Sunway City Berhad, which was incorporated as a private limited company under the Malaysia Companies Act in 1965. It was converted into a public limited company in 1995 and assumed its present name in 1996. The company was officially listed on the Main Board of the Kuala Lumpur Stock Exchange the same year. The principal activities of Sunway City Berhad are property development and investment holding (see http://www. sunway.com.my/suncity). The principal activities of the subsidiary and associated companies are:

- Property development and investment.
- Operation of hotels, theme parks and related activities.
- Provision of recreational club facilities.
- Operation of travel, tour business and related activities.
- Operation of a medical centre.

Sunway City is well known for its highly successful Bandar Sunway township (Klang Valley) in Petaying Java. Key investment properties include the Sunway Pyramid shopping mall, Sunway Lagoon Theme Park and Sunway Lagoon Resort Hotel, a family recreation club in the heart of Bandar Sunway. Bandar Sunway was developed on the concept of a 'resort living within the city'. Sunway Lagoon is the key tourist icon of Bandar Sunway. It has international-standard rides and attractions and annual visitor numbers reaching 1 million. Rides are regularly upgraded and new entertainment facilities introduced to constantly provide visitors with an enriching leisure experience. Suncity Group has also brought the same fun-filled experience to Ipoh at the Lost World of Tambun. Sunway Travel, a tour and travel operator, is the other leisure and entertainment activities company operated by Suncity Group. Complementing Sunway Travel's business is Sunway International Vacation Club's membership scheme, which offers flexible holiday accommodation packages tailored to its members' dream holiday.

II Theme Parks in the Entertainment Society

We are gravely suspicious of any tendency to expend less than the
maximum effort, for this had long been a prime economic virtue.

(John Kenneth Galbraith, 1958)

Theme parks are cultural creations that offer an opportunity to reflect on
the ways in which leisure and entertainment are becoming a fundamental
factor of economic, social and territorial development in contemporary
societies. Their influence on the processes of the social construction of
space is growing as they integrate commercial areas, hotels and entertainment areas into their corporate complexes as a strategy to increase their
business opportunities. Hence, though some authors have defined them
in terms of 'ageography' (Sorkin, 1992a), a multitude of analysts, planners
and property developers have held, conversely, that theme parks can be
considered places of innovation concerning planning matters regarding
the use of land, the management of energy flow, transport and communications, design and construction, the management of water and waste or
even the conservation of an area (Rebori, 1995b).

Theme parks are, in fact, one of the clearest spatial manifestations of
contemporary corporate capitalism (Atkins *et al.*, 1998). In addition, they
symbolize the role of the leisure and entertainment industry as potential
catalysts of development in the world economies in the near future
(Molitor, 1999). This part of the book attempts to explain why. In order to
do so, we perform an analysis reflecting on the key factors governing the
success of theme parks as places of entertainment (Chapter 5), which is
followed by an analysis of urbanism and the spatial implantation of parks
(Chapter 6) and a reflection on their spatial impacts (Chapter 7) and con-
cludes with an analysis of the development process of three of the world's
principal theme park destinations (Chapter 8). It cannot be forgotten, in
short, that, beyond people's ideological preferences, parks are increasingly

emulated in the processes of city building or the organization of activities in the territory. In fact, words like 'Disneyization', 'Disneyfication' or 'Disneylandization' are, as Mitrasinovic (1996) observes, common expressions to describe the expansion and application of the conceptual and constructive principles of parks outside their limits, to express the emblematic use of architectural styles out of context and to signify the *ex novo* generation of specific spatial and visual systems, often nearing hyperreality. Further, theme parks also symbolize the primacy of consumption as a formula for organizing social relationships (Rifkin, 2000).

This part of the book, on the other hand, tackles some of the concerns of postmodern European schools of thought and of some of the specialists on Anglo-Saxon cultural studies. However, there is a need to indicate that the analysis carried out allows the establishment of a certain distance with respect to the well-known discourses on the culture of the masses by French post-structuralist and post-Marxist thinkers, such as Baudrillard and Lyotard, and, especially, their epigones in the English language. The former and the latter often interpret the generalization of theme parks in the setting of a universal crisis of paradigms and convictions. Contrarily, below, it is fundamentally a question of understanding how reality is construed socially and, especially, how it materializes in urban forms that have territorial, economic, environmental and social repercussions that are evident in the contexts in which they occur. To approach in this way the question of the role of theme parks in today's entertainment society doubtless allows the introduction of 'heterodox' questions as well as the accentuation of the contradictions that exist between discourse and reality.

5 Theme Parks and the Commercialization of Leisure

Sightseeing is a substitute for religious ritual. The sightseeing tour as secular pilgrimage. Accumulation of grace by visiting the shrines of high culture. Souvenirs as relics. Guidebooks as devotional aids.

(David Lodge, 1991)

The changes in productive processes that took place during the last decades of the 20th century have led to significant changes in the ethics of the population of developed countries in such a way that it has ceased to focus on the world of work and its attention has shifted to play, leisure and culture (Rifkin, 2000). Along with this change, free time has come to be as fundamental as thinkers such as Dumazedier (1962) had foreseen. The result of this process is the consolidation of a new social and cultural order, which Debord (1967) qualified in terms of the society of the spectacle, one of whose main traits is the commercialization of leisure time and the production of specific places for its consumption (Miller *et al.*, 1999). One of the clearest exponents of this new order is the development of theme parks. However, theme parks are but one of the concrete manifestations of this phenomenon.

The transformation of the productive processes is impregnating how leisure is experienced, leisure which has not just increased in quantity, diversity and in ease of access, but is being taken in new directions, recovering classic meanings. It may be necessary to recall, to this end, that the Greeks used the word *scholé* to refer to free time, this word also meaning learning. As Csikszentmihalyi (2001, 19) recognizes, 'it was considered natural to use free time for the development of the mind and to gain greater knowledge of the world'. In fact, the new culture of free time, whose foundations lie in a society based on knowledge, productive innovation and a renewed learning capacity, boosts the development of new dimensions in the field of leisure, from things ludic and festive to the creative, even going as far as educational, voluntary and charitable and environmental. In the words of Cuenca (2001), it may be held, therefore, that, with the new millennium, 'new conception of things, new uses and new ways of being in the world lead to what could generically and globally be called a new citizenship'.

The renewed primacy of leisure has led to the disappearance of the limits between high culture and mass culture, has taken culture to the kingdom of leisure and, once there, has undifferentiated culture and tourism, art, education, the media, architecture, shopping and sport. In the same way as Valls (1999) states, 'what surrounds leisure takes on enormous proportions, lights up and tints all that is not leisure. If labour, the productive factor, has been the factor to have founded contemporary society, now its backbone is leisure.'

This new conception of leisure (which attempts have often been made to understand – as will be discussed in this chapter – from paradigms such as post-Fordism or postmodernism) involves the consumption of products that generate experiences and emotions. Leisure has become a consumer product and, therefore, an object of production and commercialization, which is fully integrated in the most conventional systems of the functioning of capitalism. Corporations devoted to entertainment, tourism and culture are making an effort to create recreational products and amenities. Two apparently contradictory alternatives give form to these needs. The first is the bid to create products based on the specificity of places and their authenticity. The second is the one that tends towards artificiality and imitation as a final referent for all recreational experience. Richards (2001) observes tendencies in both senses in the emergence of cultural industries based on experience. This means an evolution with regard to the common practices of communication characteristic of the conventional procedures of the presentation of culture, in which creativity plays a most important role. In addition, they fully incorporate culture and entertainment into the circuit of consumption. In short, it allows the generation of leisure products and recreational attractions that meet the following conditions: first, to generate value; secondly, to generate a competitive edge in the places where they are established; thirdly, to create processes; and, finally, to detach the processes of development from the existence of resources.

The process of developing theme parks occurs, therefore, in a scenario of the transformation of the role of leisure in society, which may, in summary, be characterized by:

1. A new value of free time as a central component of contemporary developed society.
2. The dominance of consumption as a fundamental element of leisure in developed societies.
3. The leadership of a few, large leisure enterprises on a worldwide scale with enormous financial capacity and technological and telematic possibilities.

4. The diversification of recreational content.

5. The incorporation of issues related to leisure into all facets of life.

6. Consumers' acceptance of high components of theatrical authenticity in the consumption of recreational products.

7. The demand for high levels of comfort, safety and security and environmental aesthetics in leisure products and facilities.

Based on these parameters, the development of theme parks has become a global phenomenon. Parks are being built in all corners of the planet. Tokyo Disneyland introduced the world of Disney to Asia, and Disneyland Paris brought about the thematic conversion of European amusement parks. Mexico and Brazil are notable for their incipient emergence of parks, and Magic Parc, Chak Wak and Carthageland indicate their expansion in North Africa. This is why the reflections made by park consultants regarding the potential future growth of the industry globally are more than optimistic. For example, Jones *et al.* (1998), of Economics Research Associates, consider that, though in 2010 82% of the world's population will be living in developing countries, the figure that should be considered in order to evaluate the future potential of the activity is that 20% of that population will have sufficient income to be able to consume the theme park product. That will mean close to a thousand million people and would explain, in their opinion, the important current expansion of theme parks in Asia.

The reason for this expansion process is dual. First, according to D'Hauteserre (1997), is the stabilization of the North American demand for parks as of the 1980s. Facing this situation, theme park operators, since they cannot separate their production means – the parks themselves – from their potential consumers, have had to set up in new markets as this is their only means of achieving growth. Secondly, besides the strategies of the big corporations, parks have demonstrated that cultural capital (that is, the capital that is invested in the production of cultural forms) has become a resource for accumulation and that their capacity to penetrate the market can in fact be infinitely more expandable than other kinds of investment. That would explain the multiplication of initiatives and their attachment to the media entertainment industry. Park operators create their own landscapes of production and consumption and generate specific icons and symbols that they popularize via the mass media they control. In short, theme parks spatialize the forms and contents of the mass media culture. MacDonald and Alsford (1995) summarize, in this sense, the reasons for the continued success of theme parks (see Shaw and Williams, 2004):

1. High-quality visitor services which satisfy the needs of the contemporary superficial tourists who consume signs and places.

2. Multisensory experiences, including simulated environments, interpretations and performances, state-of-the-art films, themed exhibits and eating places.

3. A highly structured experience.

4. The constant reinvention and upgrading of experiences with the latest technologies.

To this end, it should be considered that, for their purposes, theme parks use both their own references, which Ortiz (1994) denominates 'international-popular culture', that is to say, 'transnational symbols of a multilocalized imaginary that television and advertising bring together' and elements belonging to the cultural circuit, defined by García Canclini (1995) as 'historical-territorial', that is to say, all knowledge, habits and experiences organized over several eras in ethnic, regional and national territories that are especially manifest in historical heritage and traditional popular culture. The former are linked to the creation of myths and images through the cinema, the media and brands and are dominated by large commercial corporations. The latter refer to the symbolic cultural production of a territory that becomes integrated in the markets and communications procedures that are typical of a globalized economy. In this sense, it is significant that in recent years some of the main new clients of commercial events such as the annual Exhibition of the International Association of Amusement Parks and Attractions are museums that want to break out from the traditional mode.

In addition to being mechanisms for the accumulation of capital, theme parks allow one to see that globalization goes beyond economics and is fundamentally based on things cultural (Norcliffe, 2001, 23). As Nogué and Vicente (2001, 15) point out, globalization:

> inevitably embraces a whole range of aspects of the reality surrounding us and our every day life, directly or indirectly, which are affected by it: geopolitics, the universalisation of some languages, culture in its broadest sense (aesthetic trends, artistic movements, clothing and wardrobes, consumer habits) and even the homogenisation of some landscapes (especially western ones).

Castells (1998) considers that globalization and the technological revolution have been able to transform the three basic pillars on which society is based: the means of producing, the way of life and the shapes that governments adopt. Following his reasoning, it could be said, for the case of theme parks, that, through entertainment, globalization has homogenized consumer systems and preferences.

5.1. Commercial Access to Entertainment

Based on the Frankfurt School, MacCanell (1976) and Jameson (1984), Harvey (1990) links leisure with consumption. To do so, he develops the concept of 'symbolic' or 'cultural' capital, originally introduced by Bourdieu (2000), as a factor that can explain the emergence of leisure as an activity of reference in contemporary society. In accordance with this perspective, leisure and, especially, consuming leisure products emphasize individual differentiation and create distinction. Thus, consumption can be understood, as Baudrillard (2000) mentioned at the end of the 1960s, as a logic of meanings, a structure of exchange and differentiation and a system of productive forces. Harvey therefore updates one of the most consistent theories concerning the relationship between social class and leisure, at the end of the 19th century formulated by Veblen (1953). According to Veblen, motivation to consume leisure products is not subsistence but rather the generation of distinction between people (Ritzer, 2001).

To the extent that the consumption of leisure products and facilities has become democratized, symbolic differences have been established that express distinction (see Tomlinson, 1990). Wherever you travel, whatever you consume, the facilities you frequent indicate things – meanings – about the users and consumers. Taste, however, like society, evolves. Moreover, it is not universal and unique for all cultures. Corporations like Nike, Wal-Mart, Microsoft and McDonald's have turned into 'the planet's best and biggest popular education tools, providing some much-needed clarity inside the global market's maze of acronyms and centralized, secretive dealings' (Klein, 1999, 441). In a world which is today, in the words of Barber (1996, 136), in fact a market where everything is for sale and there are no common goods or public interests and where everyone is equal as long as they can afford the price of admission to what they wish to consume, leisure products are elements that feed from and feed back into the dynamic of consumption.

In this context, entertainment is not just a field of activity but a necessary ingredient to understand the running of the economy and society in the present phase of capitalism. This is so much so that the civilization of leisure praised by Dumazedier (1962) translates, according to Wolf (1999), into the introduction of the values of leisure in the conventional production and consumption processes. Thus, for example, the concept of 'experience' is today required by all productive sectors. Through the creation of brands that suggest lifestyles, the big corporations incorporate into their products not just human and technological capital but also, and especially, symbolic capital. It is simply that entertainment explains that a market relationship is not just limited to the sale of goods and services but can lead to experiences. The production of leisure products and facilities (including tourism, culture, games and the media) catalyses this dynamic and becomes fully integrated, in consequence, in the business of the experience economy.

5.1.1. Consumption as a distinguishing factor of contemporary leisure

Modern use of free time through concrete leisure practices began during the Industrial Revolution. As Britton (1991, 452) stated, neo-Marxist interpretations concerning leisure outline a genealogy of free time as a consequence of the productive organization of the capitalist system. Leisure would be, from this point of view, a necessary component of the system because, in the words of Lefebvre (1976), it allows the workforce to recover but also because 'a leisure industry exists, large-scale commercialization of specialised spaces' which in turn, generates a new social division of work and provides new landscapes. According to Rojeck (1985), there are four characteristics that define the organization of leisure in modern capitalism: privatization, individuation, commercialization and pacification.

Cuenca (2001, 63) refers to Corbin (1993) in order to explain the existence of the three cultural traditions that make up leisure time as it is produced today. The first is the English, which develops parallel to the generalization of therapeutic baths, thermal and spa resorts and the discovery of beaches. The second is the French, which, as a consequence of the image projected by Paris after the first universal expositions, incorporates happiness, pleasure and spectacle into the idea of leisure and imposes holidays as a necessary, personal break in everyday life. The third is the North American, which conceives leisure as a time of individual happiness earned at work thanks to democracy, which is quickly perceived as consumption time.

The transformation of the perception of leisure time and of the use made of it as a consequence of the social organization of work after the Industrial Revolution is, therefore, a key explanatory factor – in the archaeology of knowledge – of the emergence of leisure facilities, among which are theme parks (Anton Clavé, 1998). A fundamental question is that, unlike the Mediterranean festive model, characterized by 'a deep rooting in the society in which it takes place, as it is a profound, processual experience' (Cuenca, 2001, 93), English, French and North American traditions of leisure, which became gradually dominant and confluent as of the Second World War, incorporate the commodification of the use of leisure time into their proposed uses of free time. The practices that have evolved have turned leisure (including cultural consumption, tourism and entertainment) gradually into a product of consumption (Roberts, 1999).

In the words of Csikszentmihalyi (2001, 23), developed contemporary societies have learned to 'subcontract' leisure out to professionals as a mechanism to avoid drudgery, forgetting that much of what is accessible to us by buying it not so long ago was free of charge. This is a generalized dynamic in other areas of activity in the current phase of capitalism. Rifkin (2000, 7) is radical when he states that it is possible to identify:

> a long-term shift from industrial production to cultural production . . .
> Global travel and tourism, themed cities and parks, destination entertainment centres, wellness, fashion and cuisine, professional sports and games, gambling, music, film, television, the virtual worlds of cyberspace, and electronically mediated entertainment of every kind are fast becoming the centre of a new hypercapitalism that trades in access to cultural experiences.

As a consequence, Rifkin (2000, 8) continues:

> cultural rituals, community events, social gatherings, the arts, sports and games, social movements, and civil engagements all are being encroached

upon by the commercial sphere. The great issue at hand in the coming years is whether civilization can survive with a greatly reduced government and cultural sphere and where only the commercial sphere is left as the primary mediator of human life.

Along these same lines, for authors such as Willis (1993), entertainment is the commercialized alternative to fun.

The arrival of leisure on the market responds, furthermore, to the fact that, as Wolf (1999) says, 'The [economic] value of each leisure moment is increasing.' Leisure products and commercial facilities respond to the need for each leisure moment to be high-quality, to offer guarantees and to respond to its potential consumers' expectations. In a context of complex use of available time (which in tourism is translated, for example, into increased short journeys to nearby destinations), a multiplication of recreational supply, potential consumers' increased expectations and increasingly high income per family unit, the existence of commercial leisure products and facilities allows one to get access, by consuming, to a multitude of varied experiences which would otherwise be impossible, since, in themselves, they would require, outside the market, special preparation conditions (for example, a visit to a natural area) or highly specific vocational aptitudes (for example, knowing the characteristics of a certain species of animal). Commercial products and facilities mediatize access and satisfactorily simplify the fulfilment of individuals' desires to be, do and know.

Along these same lines, though more critically, Ariès (2002, 215) holds that the emergence of 'industrial' leisure is based on the exploitation of the current crisis of individual and collective identities brought about by capitalism. This crisis translates into the gradual subjection of all spheres of human life to the domain of things commercial: in short, to the commodification of the experience of life, which is on the way to being acquirable just like any other good or service. Though argued in the form of a novel, authors like Houellebecq (2002) present interpretations of this kind concerning the present and future of the commercialization of human relations in developed contemporary societies. According to Rifkin (2000), the consolidation of the industry of experiences is the last evolutionary stage of capitalism. The process began, according to his interpretation, with the commodification of the land, was followed by the commercialization of craft production and has continued with the arrival on the market of the more conventional family and community functions.

Nowadays, the goods that are produced, the services that are exchanged and the cultural experience shared by people, in which framework one may find the content of the recreational activities they carry out, are in the process of commodification. The existence of large corporations exclusively devoted to culture and entertainment is not alien to this. Transnational media companies:

> are using the new digital revolution in communications to connect the
> world and in the process are pulling the cultural sphere inexorably into the

> commercial sphere, where it is being commodified in the form of
> customized cultural experiences, mass commercial spectacles, and
> personal entertainment.
>
> (Rifkin, 2000, 8)

Some authors have defined this dynamic as 'post-Fordist consumption' due to its relationship with current processes of capitalist production that allow the customization of production according to the consumer's tastes, yet maintaining highly automated processes.

Today's domination of industry in cultural production, the generalization of entertainment as a specific form of the consumptive use of leisure time by large contingents of people and the symbolic content associated with the process of consumption have led, as a consequence, to the appearance of new criteria on taste and style and new sensitivities. As Sontag (1961, 304) mentions, 'the beauty of a machine or of the solution to a mathematical problem, of a painting by Jasper Johns, of a film by Jean-Luc Godard, and of the personalities and music of the Beatles is equally accessible'. In all cases there is, anyway, a constant need to get greater, new, different or better pleasure. What is significant about the process is that the differentiation between individuals and social groups is rather given by the symbolic and immaterial contents of the products they consume than by the goods and services actually consumed: in short, by the 'experience' they can add, via consumption, to their everyday lives.

To this end, Ogilvey (1990) warns that consumers today do not ask themselves as often 'What do I want to *have* that I don't have already?'; they are asking instead 'What do I want to *experience* that I have not experienced yet?' Individuals buy, therefore, through leisure, a lifestyle, a statement of taste or the manifestation of possessing a certain cultural and symbolic capital (Britton, 1991, 454). Technological capacity has allowed the production for the masses of apparently customized consumer products, which also incorporate continuous improvements and innovations: hence individuals' need to desire more and more the latest goods and gain access to experiences in order to maintain – through consumption – a lifestyle which is, paradoxically, guaranteed by commercial and entertainment corporations. Such corporations design structures, like theme parks among many others, which – like a mirage – attend perfectly to the symbolic needs of their users but which have, in short, an absolute commercial vocation. Associated with this process, the corporations themselves transform their shops and establishments into branded environments with specific contents. An advertisement at the exit of the Zion National Park in Utah sums up the feeling of consumption as a means for the 'subcontracting' of leisure to professional corporations and, by means of this, to obtain status. It says, 'You've seen the park. Now experience it.' It invites you to go to an Imax cinema where you can get the feeling of having 'lived' an adventure in the park.

Though this contrasts with the real importance of the generalized use of commercial leisure facilities among the populations of developed countries, Roberts (1999) observes that academic literature on leisure is plagued with criticisms of the consumption culture which – as has been explained so far – dominates it: hence also, with certainty, the generalized criticisms by numerous academics of its most characteristic amenities, theme parks. Roberts comments, along these lines, that 'commercialism has been accused of filling people's free time with mere amusements and diversions . . . creating endless insatiable desires that leave people unfulfilled and restless . . . and turning people into passive receptacles of entertainment to which no critical response is possible' (Roberts, 1999, 178). It is undeniable that that has happened. However, it is also undeniable that mere criticism has served little to advance both academically and collectively.

Conversely, it may be useful to observe the dominance of consumption as a distinguishing feature of contemporary leisure in the way that García Canclini (1995) proposes of 'reconceptualizing consumption, not as a simple scenario of pointless spending and irrational impulses but as a place which provokes thought, where much of economic, socio-political and psychological rationality in societies is organized'. As Rifkin (2000, 265) points out, 'themed cities, common-interest developments, entertainment destination centres, shopping malls, global tourism, fashion, cuisine, professional sports and games, film, television, virtual worlds, and simulated experiences of every kind represent the new stage of capitalist development'. What it leads one to think, in any case, is that paying for it, commercial entertainment, that is, shifts leisure from the cultural sphere to the market and, in doing so, radically transforms the key concepts of how Western civilization is run.

It should be admitted straight away that consumption is an activity with a low moral and intellectual qualification. The word 'consumption' is often associated, according to García Canclini (1995), with futile expenditure and irrational compulsion. Therefore, in order to understand the role and rationality of consumption, it may be necessary to start from an intellectually more elaborate definition such as that proposed by García Canclini himself: 'consumption is the set of sociocultural processes in which the appropriation and use of products is carried out'. This characterization may help us to see that, when consuming, people choose goods and appropriate them in a process which, implicitly, defines what is considered valuable, which integrates individuals into society and the way that things pragmatic are combined with things for enjoyment.

From a more closely reasoned point of view than that of ideological criticism, Castells (1998) maintains that consumption 'is a place where class conflicts, brought about by the unequal participation in the productive structure, continue apropos of the distribution and appropriation of goods'. Based on this, and linking these considerations to the condition of consumption as a social practice associated with the creation of lifestyles, it can be understood that 'the logic that governs the appropriation of goods in the form of objects of distinction is not that of the fulfilment of needs, rather the scarcity of such goods and the impossibility for others to have them'. Therefore, through consumption 'part of the integrative and communicative rationality of a society is constructed' (García Canclini, 1995, 61). What can happen, as Klein (1999, 130) says, is that, 'dazzled by the array of consumer choices, we may at first fail to notice the tremendous consolidation taking place in the boardrooms of the entertainment, media and retail industries'.

In short, it is the political condition of consumption as a space of conflict which gives relevance – both from a social and from an academic perspective – to the consumptive dimension of contemporary leisure time and, especially, the proliferation of recreational products and facilities that are only accessible via the market, theme parks among them. Through them, individuals do not just consume but acquire life experiences, 'bits of identity' in the words of Ariès (2002). Klein (1999) refers to Susan Sontag to admit that we are living in the era of shopping and that, therefore, 'any movement that is primarily rooted in making people feel guilty about going to the mall is a backlash waiting to happen'. Furthermore, as Klein herself admits, whereas some Westerners 'sweat over what kind of shoes and shirts are most ethical to buy, the people sweating in the factories line their dorm rooms with McDonald's advertisements, paint "NBA Homeboy" murals on their doors and love anything with "Meeckey"'. This paradox is nothing other than the result of the persuasive and competitive strategies of the big companies that offer consumer products during leisure time: companies which, as we have seen in previous sections, strengthen their impacts by combining different cultural and entertainment services such as film studios, television networks, shops, parks and mass consumption products, among others. Analysis of the patterns of consumption during leisure time should explicitly examine, on the one hand, the connection between cultural production and the production of space. On the other hand, it also ought to allow an exploration of the relationship between the structures of production and social domination.

5.1.2. The multiplication of themed leisure environments

Individuals and groups build their identities through the signs and values that can be attributed to their choices of consumption. Changes in the social organization of free time, the emergence of the 'new' economy of services, information and experience, the changes in the collective appreciation of time, and technical innovations applied to leisure mean that individuals can satisfy their expectations both through mass consumption and through individualized consumption (Urry, 1990). As Lynch (2001) comments, it is often considered that what is available as pre-packaged passive, non-productive, market-provided leisure is a type of expression of 'second-class' leisure, in which the consumer would be an element that does not actively come into the production of his own experience. However, to date there is no empirical research to allow making such an assumption. On the contrary, what there is, is a progressive process of the generalization of the different types of spaces which, in one way or another, package and commercialize leisure. In fact, as Ritzer (1999) states, in commercial leisure there is nothing new which – at least in previous formats – has not existed since the middle of the 20th century. What is really new is the generalization of the use of what he calls 'means of consumption' or, put another way, spaces for recreational consumption.

Valls and Mitjans (2001) propose the hypothesis that the organization of leisure industries in a certain place is a consequence of the structure of its inhabitants' leisure types and that, as a result, it is from this perspective that the successful development of theme parks in the USA since the 1950s should be contemplated. Thus, authors such as Díaz (2000) maintain that the initial success enjoyed by theme parks in the USA would be assured by questions such as the fact that the cities are not very structured, the distances separating them are large, few places exist to interact, life focuses on convenience and is governed by regulations and brands are important. Contrarily, in Europe, the cities are more structured, the distances between them are short or medium, there are many opportunities to interact, life focuses on needs and decision making and personal relations are more important than brands. In Asia, despite the notable differences and geographical, economic and political contrasts, theme parks emerge from the shaping of consumer societies on a regional level. For the case of Japan, Raz (1999) uses as a basis the fact that 'consumption plays an important role in Japanese life, shaping tastes, desires, lifestyles, and ultimately identities', to the extent that popular culture, consumption and leisure are confused in Japan as much as or more than in the USA – and, to a lesser extent, in Europe.

Tyrell and Mai (2001) affirm, complementarily, that consumers in developed societies currently carry out more leisure activities than some years ago, although, inevitably, such activities have a shorter duration. The time available for each of them is limited but the spending power available for them is high. Urry (2002) refers to the concept of 'three minute culture'. Smith (2006) associates such patterns of consumption with practices that are characteristic of a new kind of tourist that he calls 'new leisure tourists'. They are escapist, need constant stimulation, fun and entertainment and may prefer representations to reality. They want to get emotions from sanitized, comfortable and glamorized experiences. Due to this, commercial leisure facilities have mushroomed at the disposal of the consumers, and frequentation to commercial leisure facilities has become generalized in the last 20 years in the USA, Europe and Asia.

Smith (2006) states that 'contrary to predictions that leisure time would increasingly take place within the home, it seems that new leisure consumers are more interested in going out than staying in'. In fact, since the 1980s, the recreational attraction industry has been one of the most dynamic in the context of tourist development, to the extent that their development has become generalized worldwide. These facilities have been considered by authors such as Ritzer (1996) as some of the new 'cathedrals of consumption', at which 'consumer religion' is practised. It is a 'religion' with a complex liturgy that incorporates play, health, fun, leisure, travel, learning, information or the strengthening of middle-class values (Barber, 1996, 128). They are hybrid enclaves of leisure and consumption – which some authors consider non-spatial and ahistorical – which, according to postmodern thinking, possess components of 'hyperreality', defined by Eco (1989) as extra-authenticity (Boniface and Fowler, 1993) or fake authenticity (AlSayyad, 2001). They are theme parks, media landscapes, heritage sites, centres for scientific divulgation, zoological gardens, corporate visitor centres, aquariums and also commercial centres, water parks, cruises, casinos and even club and sports organizations' stadiums with a media presence, which also become 'cathedrals of consumption' (see Ritzer, 1999; Stevens, 2000).

In this respect, it is significant that, in France, several types of recreational leisure facilities have grouped together in one association (see Bennet and Huberson, 2005): the Syndicat National des Espaces de Loisirs, d'Attractions et Culturels (SNELAC). It includes actual theme parks (Disneyland Paris, Parc Astérix, Futuroscope), aquariums (from Océanopolis to the Aquarium de La Rochelle), as well as water parks (Aqualand, Marineland, Océanile), zoos (from la Cité des Insectes to Donjon des Aigles and le Jardin des Découvertes) as well as other cultural spaces such as museums (such as the Ecomusée d'Alsace), science parks (like La Cité de l'Espace), leisure sports parks (like Transmontagne) and gardens (like La Bambouseraie in Languedoc-Roussillon): a broad variety of scales, contents and formats, which, despite generating clearly different facilities (see Puydebat, 1998), respond to society's commercial need for leisure (Parent, 1998), even reaching the commercialization of nature in order to predispose it for tourist and recreational consumption. This is the case, for example, of the Eden Project in Cornwall, proposed by architect Nicholas Grimshaw, who, using geodesic domes, has designed the biggest covered botanical gardens in the world. Needless to say, the orientation to the market of natural values is nothing but a logical step in the progressive integration of natural resources and culture into the world of commerce (Davis, 1997, 237). In fact, a number of heritage sites offer a version of history which focuses on entertainment rather than education. So, in consequence, museums are becoming more and more like theme parks as they are offering to consumers a more entertaining experience than a genuine cultural interaction or authenticity.

Extending Gottdiener's (1997) ideas, Shaw and Williams (2004) recognize a typology of themed spaces that range from the original theme park through to the theming of different tourism landscapes. All of them clearly illustrate the success of invented spaces centred on signs that locate tourist places (Boorstin, 1964). They recognize three main subsets of themed spaces: theme parks (and related attractions), themed environments and themed landscapes:

1.   Theme parks. The increasing experimentation with the original theme park concept has produced a variety of offshoots. So the theme park concept may include, according to Shaw and Williams, different types of invented

and commodified spaces such as 'cultural theme parks' like those developed in many parts of South-east Asia, such as Singapore's Haw Par Villa; 'specialized theme parks', which aim to be representative of any cultural, social or media singularity, like the proposed Dracula Park in Romania; 'heritage parks' that use theme park technology, styles of presentation and virtual reality, like the Ironbridge Museum at Telford; nature theme parks that sell unique experiences based on the concept of biodiversity and a sustainable world, like Xcaret in Mexico; and, of course, 'attractions theme parks', or, as the authors define them, Disney-type theme parks, based on attractions, performances and characters as a way to develop a unique and complete personal experience.

2. Themed environments. These are spaces of everyday life that use theming concepts and technologies and become themselves visitor attractions appealing to the consumer experience. There is, first, the worldwide emergence of global branded restaurants and cafeteria chains like Starbucks and, especially, themed shopping malls or, indeed, mega-malls with themed attractions inside, like the well-known West Edmonton Mall in Canada. Other themed environments may include museums and art galleries, festival market places like the Quincy Market in Boston and, although the authors do not refer to it, this category may include some of the other cathedrals of consumption analysed by Ritzer (1999), such as casinos or cruise ships. All of them are spaces of illusion with speciality shopping, restaurants and entertainment where private space is carefully constructed, themed and regulated.

3. Themed landscapes. Theming technologies may give uniqueness to everyday life landscapes using components of the popular culture, especially television programmes, films or also, to some extent, literature. Some fictional events and images generate character for places that private and public stakeholders may use to develop the whole space as a visitor attraction, constructing the tourist gaze upon the place and creating a new or unique destination through place marketing. Places and spaces acquire meanings from these imagined worlds (Herbert, 2001). Shaw and Williams (2004) recognize, in this sense, that the most recent example of the creation of theme landscapes from literary fiction has been from the making of J.R.R. Tolkien's *Lord of the Rings* on location in New Zealand.

In short, applying Urry's (1990, 104) dichotomous classification concerning the nature of tourist spaces, it may be stated that they are, in all cases, spaces that are subject to the collective tourist gaze (as opposed to the romantic), modern in their design and conception (as opposed to the historical nature of other attractions) and inauthentic. They are spaces, on the other hand, in which spectacle takes priority. They may also be precursors of the type of spaces that may be established in the future. As Wolf (1999) states, 'maybe the next step in this evolution is to put housing next to the stores and megaplexes and call it a small town. People living, working, shopping, and consuming entertainment in one place.' In fact, today, some such spaces have already conquered emblematic parts of cities for commercial leisure. This is the case of Inner Harbor in Baltimore, a well-known, classic example of the recreational and commercial tertiarization of a seafront. It has, moreover, several implications from the point of view of the substitution of urban fabrics. Thus, in this case, the areas adjacent to Inner Harbor are being reconverted into a large recreational marina; the historical districts such as Fells Point have changed scenically to welcome tourist activities, creating a clear differentiation between the streets to be used for recreational purposes and the rest; and, finally, there is a clear intention to spatially segregate the commercial leisure space from the rest of the city centre.

According to Britton (1991), here we should consider the thesis by Zukin (1991) according to which the creation of commercial leisure spaces and, among them, themed spaces is not just reshaping corporations' productive investment and citizens' consumption practices but is, fundamentally, creating a new form of capital, cultural capital, which, as it requires a fixed, precise location for its development, has the capacity to create new urban, regional and international poles of growth. The result of the process of commercializing leisure time is, therefore, the creation of spaces of consumerism that hinge on commercial entertainment facilities, which may range from commercial centres to theme parks through urban centres reoriented towards recreational consumption, like the aforementioned Inner Harbor in Baltimore. These places cause new developments in the service activities and sustain new urban growth: that is to say, they create spatial complexes that structure new territorial production (human and material) and consumption relations.

5.2. The McDonaldization Paradox

With capitalism maturing, between the end of the 19th century and the end of the 20th century, there was an improvement in strategies of standardization, efficiency, rationalization and routinization in the productive processes of goods and services. These, now commonly called Fordist strategies, aimed to ensure the uninterrupted flow of production and consumption. As Ritzer (1996) describes it, Fordism presents precise characteristics. First, it means the mass production of homogeneous articles. Secondly, it implies stiff production mechanisms such as, in the case of industry, the assembly line. Thirdly, it requires the adoption of routine labour procedures. Fourthly, increased productivity derives from large-scale production and intensive, routine working days. Lastly, given that standard goods and services are produced, it leads to the homogenization of consumer habits.

Since the 1980s, however, it has been usual to refer to the crisis of the Fordist production system. The term post-Fordism, which we use to describe the new situation, alludes to the crisis of line production, standardization and homogenization, which were replaced by criteria of singularity and specificity. Like Fordism, post-Fordism had a series of peculiar characteristics.

Ritzer (1996) also sums them up as follows. First, there is a decline in interest for series production products and greater preference for more specialized articles, especially high-quality, prestigious ones. Secondly, the more specialized products require shorter production lines, giving rise to smaller, less productive systems. Thirdly, thanks to the introduction of new technology, it has been possible to incorporate more flexible, more cost-effective production systems. Fourthly, it is said that post-Fordist production systems demand much more of the workers in terms of creativity, commitment and dedication than their predecessors. Finally, the greater specialization in the workplace is reflected in the more specific demands made by society.

The transfer of this process to leisure, tourism and cultural production results in the crisis of *massification*, market segmentation and the transformation of the productive, organizational and spatial processes. Companies incorporate new production technology and new information management systems, like global decision systems or computerized booking systems. New technology is shaped as an essential part in the process of replacing tourist packages – created under assembly-line criteria – with new modular products that are sensitive to the specific needs of the different segments of demand. As for the people, they compress and customize their moments of fun, free time and culture into increasingly more concentrated doses. Given that they dispose of income, they require of companies the satisfaction of increasingly more concrete expectations that represent a break away from the daily routine. In their role as consumers, they wish to experience novelty and familiarity, excitement and reassurance at the same time. Cuvelier (2000) states, for example, that during the 1990s, we witnessed the advent of self-organized tourism, which, essentially, means the end of the Fordist model.

Now, despite the changes that have affected the systems of rendering leisure services, what is true is that theme parks are a perfect illustration, in today's scenario of the commercialization of free time to which we referred in the previous section, of the functioning of a highly rationalized management system aimed at large contingents of visitors. It cannot be forgotten that theme parks are usually conceived integrally on the basis of a single design and a global conception, which ensures both the quality of the experience they aim to supply and the ability to control all of the elements that come into play in the process of the production and consumption of that experience.

Thus, theme parks, as well as other mass commercial leisure spaces, ensure the feeling of singularity in their visitors' recreational experiences through the organization of a system which, though allowing choice, is organized like an assembly line. Grady Larkins, set designer at Big Bang Schtroumpf, declared in this respect that:

> a theme park is at the same time a place for distraction, a place of culture, a place of advanced technology, an immense supermarket, all in an ever ludic atmosphere. In the same way it is a city whose organization (transports, roadways, services . . .) are controlled by computer, like a ballet, a

timepiece . . . Nothing is left to chance when satisfying [the visitors']
desires at the right moment.

(Cited in Eyssartel and Rochette, 1992)

So, for example, the control of the image that the park conveys ensures
that the users' perception with regard to the symbolic values of the product
is unanimous and exact. Therefore, the entertainment areas or thematic
nodes will have to be identified by a characteristic scenery, characters
and products on sale and cannot be subjected to variations derived from
cultural influences. In the same way, at certain attractions, it may be prohibited to take photos. Whoever does so runs the risk of having their roll
of film confiscated. This is the case, for example, of the 'behind the scenes
tour' at Magic Kingdom. Divulging the contents of the operative part of
the park would imply violating the enchantment as well as revealing the
business's operative elements to the competition.

Ritzer (1996) has proposed an interpretation of the underlying paradox between a productive context which has come to be qualified as
post-Fordist and recreational spaces that are highly routinized, by means
of the concept of McDonaldism or McDonaldization. Thus, on the basis of
the example of tourist packages, Ritzer and Liska (1997) maintain that,
although Urry's (1990) thesis of transition from Fordism to post-Fordism
in tourism is right (in the sense that highly standardized trips are on the
decline), it is also true that tourist packages continue to be one of the
choices of preference of the demand and continue to be closed products.
In fact, organized trips in groups are designed to offer predictability and
efficacy: that is to say, something that does not bring up any surprises
even if it means minimal contact with the people, culture and customs of
the countries visited. Along these same lines, tourists feel reassured when
they know the daily schedule before the day begins and perhaps even
before the trip itself is under way. Concretely, therefore, Ritzer and Liska
(1997) state that, though it may be more flexible than its predecessors
described by Urry (1990), any organized trip is still highly routinized.

Taking the original work by Ritzer (1996), there are three factors that
explain the McDonaldization of the productive processes associated with
the creation of leisure time: first, large corporations' material interests,
especially in striving towards targets and economic ambitions (higher
profit and lower costs); secondly, it is the child of our sociocultural
environment and has been born due to the fact that the phenomenon
has been considered a valuable means to an end in itself; and, finally,
McDonaldization is advancing in leaps and bounds because it has synto-
nized with several changes that have taken place in our society, in particular, the generalization and multiplication of possibilities of leisure and
the need to satisfy large contingents of people.

McDonaldism shares a number of characteristics with Fordism, in
particular the dominance of homogeneous products, strict techniques
and technology, standardized working routines, the lack of qualification,
the homogenization of work (and of the customer), series labour and the

homogenization of consumption. There are references, therefore, to the concept of the scientific organization of work as conceived by Taylor at the beginning of the 20th century; to the Ford assembly line; to the construction of series housing; to the large commercial centres; and, obviously to the first McDonald's founded by the McDonald brothers. The most important and interesting argument by Ritzer is, in any case, that the flexibilization of the productive processes is a consequence, at least in part, of its own scientific organization.

The bases of the success of McDonaldism are fourfold. Ritzer's words can be used, when applied to a McDonald's establishment, in order to explain them:

> First, McDonald's offers *efficiency* . . . it offers the best available means of getting us from a state of being hungry to a state of being full . . . Second, McDonald's offers us food and service that can be easily *quantified* and *calculated* . . . Third, McDonald's offers us *predictability* . . . Fourth and finally, *control*, especially through the substitution of nonhuman for human technology . . . The humans who work in fast-food restaurants are trained to do a very limited number of things in precisely the way they are told to do them.

In short, efficiency, quantification, predictability and control are the four ingredients of Ritzer's (1996) thesis. They are, also, four of the basic ingredients of some of the theme parks' own operation processes.

In fact, it can be stated that the McDonaldization thesis is useful to explain the basis of the operative system of parks (see a detailed analysis of this in Bryman, 1999a). In parks, there are strict systems of control over visitors (directing flows, surveillance of behaviour via closed-circuit television (CCTV), creative queue management, etc.), their workers (strict codes of appearance, the obligation to 'appear to be' happy, the strict differentiation and stratification of the work posts, etc.) and the physical space (purposely recreated in accordance with the park's thematic purpose, sanitized, ordered according to a design proposal, etc.) (Fjellman 1992; Archer, 1997). Control is necessary from the point of view of the company's success. In a park, everything is programmed. One could even speak, in fact, of parks as panoptic systems in Bentham (1979) style.

For Ritzer and Liska (1997), if McDonald's is the paradigmatic example of the rationalization of society as a whole, theme parks are a model for the tourism and leisure industry. In order to explain this they take the example of Walt Disney World. The park must receive, feed, move and entertain – all of this in irreproachable conditions of security, safety and cleanliness – large contingents of people. To achieve this, the park must be efficient in many ways but, especially in the handling of large flows of visitors each day on a relatively small, well-taken-advantage-of surface area. To do so, parks are continually making adjustments, having been started up, modifying circulation, densifying and de-densifying areas, recalibrating rides and food and beverage areas, planning new areas, etc. The range of prices – from the day ticket to season tickets – and the abundant signage concerning waiting times illustrate the quantification factor. What happens in the park must also be highly predictable. Visitors must not be unpleasantly surprised if they take the wrong decision as to where to go or what to do. Finally, technology dominates human decisions: not so much or just because of the presence of numerous mechanical and electronic attractions but also because of the strict technological control of the processes and routines to be performed both by the workers and by the visitors in order to ensure the park's satisfactory running. In short, the aim is to control the client. To do so, parks are based, in their conception, on a mechanical perception of personal motivations (Ariès, 2002, 112). For this it is also necessary to study in detail and set up models of use of the parks like those developed by Kemperman (2000a).

For the purposes of illustration, the process may be described as Ritzer (1996, 51) explains for the case of Disney:

> At Disney World and Epcot Center in Florida, for example, a vast highway and road system funnels many thousands of cars each day into the appropriate parking lots. Once the driver has been led to a parking spot (often with the help of information broadcast over the car radio), jitneys are waiting, or soon will arrive, to whisk family members to the gates of the park. Once in the park, visitors find themselves on what is, in effect, a vast (albeit not self-propelled) conveyor belt which leads them from one ride or attraction to another. One may get off the larger 'conveyor system' to enter one of the local systems that move people to a particular attraction . . . The speed with which one moves through each attraction enhances the experience and reduces the likelihood that one will question the 'reality' of what one sees. In fact, one is often not quite sure what one has witnessed, although it 'seems' exciting.

The whole system has been created to handle large contingents of people as efficiently as possible.

In order to do so, theme parks centralize the production processes through technologically smart systems and have permanent information on each business unit. It is important to stress, in this regard, the importance of the availability of information and quantitative and qualitative statistics as to visitor numbers and sales for decision taking in the short, medium and long term (Lanquar, 1991, 105). They usually have central control systems that are used as operations centres for everything to do with lighting, sound, security, surveillance, the management of the buildings and emergency systems as well as for logistics-related matters such as stocks, invoicing and the staff's concrete needs. Thus, for example, theme parks incorporate real-time control systems (RTCS) to assign their human resources to the needs of the facility (Thompson, 1999).

The system receives information in real time concerning visitor numbers according to the tickets registered. Based on this, taking other data into account such as the weather conditions, the kind of day (depending on the season, if it is a working day or a weekend) and predictions as to the numbers of groups that will be visiting, among other things, the system continuously updates a precise forecast of the volume of business that will be done during the day. Complementarily, based on the information available, again in real time, on the number of visitors at each sales point and each ride, the system provides the taking of decisions concerning matters such as flow and queue management. Furthermore, using the predictions that the system performs for the development of business during the day, the RTCS allows the optimization of the use of human resources adjusting them to the needs at any given time during the day. In fact, the system recommends when extra operators are needed, when operators should change position in order to maximize the profits for the organization or when it is possible for them to take a break.

On the other hand, the construction of a comprehensive themed environment, a package of routines and a set of possible choices mean that visitors' needs are predefined and potentially sorted out prior to entering the park. They know in advance what they will find. At the extreme, there is no need to worry even about oneself in a park, or the children, or anything. Everything is done by the park operator through control protocols and the application of previously defined solutions to problem scenarios. The greater the level of conformity to visitors' expectations of the park's programme, the more the value of the park increases as a system and as a business: hence the park's need to guarantee the fulfilment of expectations. This is why even the photographic souvenir system is rationalized, whether by facilitating the purchase of photographs at the park's rides or via the classic 'picture spot' signposts. As a consequence, all family albums contain the same photos but with different subjects in them. And the visitor, prior to going to the park, knows what to expect from it and which are the symbolic elements of reference that 'mustn't be missed'. The park's programme increases its efficiency and, above all, the feeling of value the visitor acquires, who has the impression of being in the right place. Conversely, any feeling of incertitude and, especially, insecurity decreases the park's ability to attract and has direct effects on visitor numbers (Lanquar, 1991, 110–112).

Finally, theme parks' human resources managers have clear indications as to the qualities and characteristics the employees must possess. Normally, they must be clean, pleasant, relaxed and smiley and must treat each visitor as if they were their own personal guest. They have a basic mission from the point of view of the park as a product since the *mise-en-scène* of the park requires commitment by its hundreds or thousands of workers. The park's capacity to 'enchant the world' lies with them. Hence the importance of corporate training at each park so that the workers can identify with its values and discipline. Control over the employees is, therefore, most intense (see, concerning this, The Project on Disney report (1995) entitled *Inside the Mouse. Work and Play at Disney World*). In all, certainly, it is the only way to ensure discipline, especially considering their profile and demographic characteristics. This characterization contrasts with the ideal type of work that is typical of service activities, according to post-Fordist approaches: little to do with flexible, initiative-based and intellectually versatile labour dynamics. Normally flexibility is limited to the rota systems, conviction is reduced to standardization and versatility depends on park management needs.

An example of this is Busch Gardens in Tampa. In the park there are 3500 people working. Of those, about 190 hold a management position, 850 work full-time throughout the week and the rest are seasonal. It is difficult to cover all positions. There is much competition since not too much training is required prior to joining, and everything, from fast-food chains to hospitals, competes for the same segment of workers. What they seek are normally students who live in the nearby area (60% of workers in the park live less than 5 miles away) and who are responsible and politically correct (at the entrance to the personnel selection area a sign warns, for example, as to the incompatibility of getting a job in the park and drug taking, as well as advising that, prior to taking up the position, a test is done which can detect drug consumption up to 90 days earlier). As Zukin (1995) maintains, the model gives rise to internal stratification and disparities.

Lastly, it cannot be forgotten, as Weber's theory of rationalization indicates, that the process of McDonaldization often leads, with the routinization of the productive processes, to irrationality (Ritzer, 1996). Thus, the expenditure of families in the park, generally uncalculated, turns what *a priori* should have been an economical visit into a highly costly one. In some cases, what was foreseen as being a time of freedom has turned into a moment of pure commercial leisure. The irrationality towards which McDonaldized activities lead was dealt with in an article in *The Washington Post* entitled 'How I Spent (and Spent and Spent) my Disney Vacation'. Its author, Bob Garfield, took his family, consisting of four members, to Walt Disney World or, as he called it, Expense World. As Ritzer (1996, 125–126) reports, the 5 days of holiday for the four cost $1700, $551 and 30 cents of which corresponded to entrance tickets. Conversely, Garfield calculated that over the 5 days they had less than 7 h of pure amusement. The rest of the time was spent going around by bus, 'queuing up and schlepping from place to place'. The 17 rides they went on amused them for a total of 44 min.

It is significant, on the other hand, that the Disney company has invented negative choices of consumption for those who wish to express their disagreement. Each area of Disney has its Disney Villains Shop with products for 'naughty boys and girls'. Visitors with anti-Disney sentiments can express them by consuming a negative Disney line of products. With this, what is achieved is in fact that every visitor to Disney is a consumer. Therefore, the first guarantee parks offer is that of satisfying expectations. In the end, controlling the client means just that: 'being able to hold and direct his or her attention and manage the minuscule details of each person's life experiences' (Rifkin, 2000, 103).

Neither can it be forgotten that, towards their visitors, parks are also a new modality of a space of control (Warren, 1994, 560). In fact, like other leisure facilities, such as commercial centres, casinos and cruises, they have many characteristics which Goffman (1970) denominates 'total institution'. One could even speak about them from the analytical perspective of what Foucault (1979) considers a 'closed space'. They are moralizing environments

whose structure is one of segregation and of control. The main difference
with regard to Goffman's institutions is that, in parks, control is exercised
subtly and tenuously. Visitors do not perceive and are unaware that they
are being controlled. Nevertheless, their control is necessary for the good
running of the facility. In fact, parks aim to generate their own specific
urbanity. As Zukin (1995) says, still without repressive police systems,
parks have created a culture of civility and security and safety which is
characterized by the fact that inside them arms, the homeless, illegal beverages and drugs are forbidden. Even so, as in other moralizing total institutions and in spite of the efforts made by those running them, such
alternative practices are on the increase. And it is not just a question of
breaking the parks' internal regulations such as taking your lunch in
with you despite being forbidden, but of making parks concrete scenarios
for normally forbidden social conduct. Though this is a topic that has
not been studied in much depth, Ariès (2002, 152–162) is explicit when
indicating episodes of intolerance and violence, while Warren (1994,
555–559) describes situations ranging from the consumption of alcohol
and drugs to increase the stimulant effects of certain rides to moments of
sexual violence and abuse.

In short, the McDonaldization thesis has become an interpretative
alternative to those analytical schools derived from the theories of regulation that try to explain the recent changes in the productive processes
only as part of the transition from Fordism to post-Fordism. Ritzer (1996)
has presented McDonaldization as an essential process in the modern
world. Ritzer's thesis is that McDonaldization and its 'modern' characteristics will not just be maintained in the future but will extend its influence at an accelerated pace throughout society. Two elements give rise to
the need to maintain McDonaldism as a dominant organizational system
of the production of commercial leisure time for large contingents of people: the need to control the internal processes and the need to give visitors
guarantees. Indirectly, McDonaldization constitutes, therefore, a criticism
of post-Fordism. In addition, bearing in mind that, from a social and cultural point of view, post-Fordism as a productive state of late capitalism
would correspond to postmodernity, McDonaldism is also, in fact, a criticism of postmodernism as a metanarrative to understand society. All of
this, of course, may be controversial, as can be demonstrated, for example,
by the critical readings of Ritzer's approaches as presented by Alfino *et al.*
(1998). Nevertheless, even in these cases recognition is given that theses
on McDonaldization are valuable in order to comprehend the processes
that effectively articulate the production and the consumption of leisure
services (Kellner, 1999).

5.3. Disneyization as a Model

Theme parks exemplify the success of consumer culture. Technology applied
to their design, operation and management is becoming generalized in other

leisure and tourist products and facilities. This is why, despite the existence of genetic and cultural factors that condition their development in different parts of the world, a process of the internationalization of their implantation and of the incorporation of their most characteristic practices has arisen in other leisure products and facilities. Therefore, some general tendencies can be established which transversally dominate the leisure time of the societies of developed countries. These tendencies are, fundamentally, the following four:

1. The creation of private commercial leisure spaces with cultural contents. Parks are cultural creations equivalent to a painting, a photograph or a film. They are codified places of performance which have been created to be 'passed through'. Along the way, they allow one to 'observe' an imaginary content with its own meaning, which transmits precise values and attempts to be complete, to propose a coherent world adjusted to the time during which it is visited. Their existence is based on a single significant attribute of the people, that is, their capacity to consume and manifest, by consuming, their social status. This consumption is done, on the other hand, in spaces that can be qualified as corporate. This is so much so that Sorkin (1992b) speaks of parks as the first 'copyrighted urban environments'. In fact, parks have their own rules, vocabulary and even, in some cases, currency. In them, all is protected by copyright legislation.

2. The manufacture of simulations that dilute the distinction between what is real and what is imaginary, what is real and what is false. This responds to the need of part of contemporary society to seek pure simulacra whose attraction lies precisely in recognizing their existence as just that, a simulacrum. In parks, the natural world perishes before the primacy of the artificial. Willis (1993) cites the case of a mother at the Disney Resort Hotel who comments without turning a hair – with a small snake before her with which her children were playing – 'Don't worry, it's rubber.' Her opinion is directly related to the perception that, in short, a real snake would not make sense in a Disney park. Outside parks, reality itself is manipulated in an effort to construct the recreational or tourist space that the visitors expect to find (Dietvorst, 1998, 15). Thus, for example, the aesthetics of the town of Santa Fe were invented for reality to represent what was dictated by the imagination as to what ought to be seen in Arizona. The paradoxical reaches such an extreme that when we travel to a place which maintains its absolute vernacular integrity, where people also buy things, we remember Disneyland (Scully, 1996).

3. The strict separation between production and consumption in material and, especially, symbolic terms. Rybczynski (2001) describes Downtown Disney, in the new resort of Anaheim, California, as an eclectic blend of architectural styles:

> Arts and Crafts next to – and under – the hotel; slightly farther away, art deco. Many buildings are distinctly 'scenographic'. The balconied Jazz Kitchen looks like something from New Orleans, a flamboyant Cuban nightclub is a Miami transplant, and the Rainforest Café resembles a Mayan temple.

On the other hand, ESPN Zone, the multiplex and a monorail station are abstract modern designs, more in the 'architecture' category.

The overscaling, the warping, the decoration serve to generate universes that are directly and solely identified as consumer spaces. Despite the fact that people work in theme parks, the work appears to be hidden by the ludic dimension of the architecture and the symbolic narration it presents. It is the oversignification of the function through the construction (Venturi *et al.*, 1972). Complementarily, we should not forget, in this context, the appearance of corporate visitor centres of the widest variety of goods (from Kellogg's or Hershey in the USA to Volkswagen or Heineken in Europe).
4.   The concealment of the fact that leisure has turned into consumption time through the creation of fantasies. The architecture in theme parks serves to tell stories. As Dunlop (1996) affirms, parks' architecture serves to hide and stimulate what visitors do when they go to a park: consume. In this context, we should not lose sight of the fact that the large commercial centres themselves tend to incorporate entertainment, creativity, instruction, events and technology. They are spaces that attempt to create affective relationships with the consumers, to make demand loyal, to set themselves apart from e-commerce, to promote convenience and fellowship, to favour the pleasure of shopping and to promote the image and values of brands through theming, the development of services with added value, pedagogy, welfare, event planning, the development of ludic spaces and the personalized relationship. A good example is the firm Décathlon's park on the outskirts of Lille or its North American equivalent and predecessor Recreational Equipment Inc. in Seattle: a space for initiation into sports which is in turn a test lab at the international head office of the sports clothing and accessories firm. These spaces incorporate the Anglo-Saxon concept of 'fun shopping' or window-shopping and have in the urban entertainment centres their clearest manifestation (see Beyard *et al.*, 1998).

Bryman (1999b) has tried to interpret these tendencies through the definition of the concept of Disneyization. He proposes it as a complementary thesis to that on McDonaldization put forward by Ritzer (1996). He admits, however, that he does not under any circumstances wish to suggest that Disney parks may have brought about the practices he identifies as characteristic of Disneyization but, simply, that the success of Disney parks has facilitated, within the framework of favourable social and cultural conditions, their generalization and assimilation. In fact, theme parks have a special relationship with the sensitivity of the mass commercial culture of the era. As Eyssartel and Rochette (1992) point out:

> as a 'metabolic' cultural medium, the theme park is related with television, which also juxtaposes sequences of images without the zeal to know whether such syntax organizes its intelligibility. Like the theme park, television, despite consisting of a series of sequences, may only be fully perceived as a continuous flow. In each case this is due to the effect of a strange catalysis between the compacting and fractioning born of the universes of completely new feelings.

This is the context of the success of the parks and the field of dissemination of their cultural practices.

It must not be ignored, in this regard, that in Asia, while the big transnational corporations, especially Disney, propose and develop amusement parks of a global nature:

> public investors such as the state have preferred to valorise traditional elements of local culture in cultural theme parks for two purposes: on the one hand, tourist gazing of the parks allows the nation to benefit from the tourist dollar; on the other, such parks pander to the sense of identity of the multifarious ethnic groups in the region.
>
> (Teo and Yeoh, 2001, 145)

This is the case of Splendid China in Shenzhen, of Sarawak Cultural Village, the living museum of the seven ethnic groups dwelling in Sarawak, and of Dragon World in Singapore. By doing so, the state invents a landscape of nostalgia on which to build a sense of national identity, while international tourism is introduced to native culture in a context of commercialism and commodification. This is Hendry's (2000b) assumption when he claims that, in Asia, theme parks are a source of self-identity and compares some Japanese theme parks to Western historical parks or heritage centres. Furthermore, he maintains that there are important areas of overlap between education and entertainment and, indeed, between museums and theme parks, at least for the Japanese case.

5.3.1. The components of Disneyization

The principles applied by Disney in particular, and by the theme park industry in general, have become generalized to such an extent that they are progressively dominating broader aspects of individuals' practices of consumption in developed societies. In fact, it has been commonplace to speak – with heavily loaded negative ideological connotations – of ideas such as the 'Disneyfication' of society (see Warren, 1994, for example). Ritzer and Liska (1997) have put forward the term McDisneyization to express the fusion of principles of the organization of work that are typical of McDonaldism with the principles of organization of the consumption of leisure typical of Disney. The main components of the concept of Disneyization suggested by Bryman (1999b) are theming, the dedifferentiation of consumption, the merchandising (which means the promotion of goods in the form of or bearing copyright images and logos, including such products made under licence) and the emotional labour. It derives from an intellectual tradition that is highly contrasted with that of Ritzer. So, while the concept of McDonaldization has something to do with the theory of rationalization, that of Disneyization has to do with the social theories of consumption. Moreover, if the former is rooted in the nucleus of contents of 'modern' society, the latter has come to be general associated with the theses that attempt to explain the 'postmodern' character of consumer society. Even so, the continuities between both concepts are many. Bryman (2003) himself has explained that McDonald's restaurants fit the notion of Disneyization well.

Dunlop (1996) makes it clear that thematic architecture has always existed. The temples were built as places where divinity lived, cathedrals as the cities of heaven, town and city halls as spaces of reference for the community, palaces and gardens procuring a cosmic order, cities seeking a certain symbolic sense (Scully, 1996). Even the suburbs have sought references in literature, in culture or in art by means of the names of their streets. What theme parks do, therefore, is revive architecture as a narration that aims to create a complete world, a special place, a new land in an architectural and urbanistic model. In short, building in a theme park is always subordinate to a script. Everything starts with a story. The script is the creative technique that serves to coordinate the work of the designers and technicians to ensure that everyone is committed to the same project. It is not necessary for visitors to follow the plot. The story ensures that all visitors will recognize at least some of the sensations and experiences offered to them. At Disney's California Adventure, for example, some will recognize the smell of the wines of Robert Mondavi, whereas others will identify the reddish asphalt of the roads that go to High Sierras (Rybczynsky, 2001). Theming, therefore, serves to give coherence to the variety of attractions and atmospheres of a park and to put the accent on the created universe rather than on each of the emotions.

On the basis of this, Mitrasinovic (1996) holds that theme parks are hybrids that cross the strict limits of what is cultural, social, economic, philosophical, political and scientific. Baudrillard (1983) also proposes that, in parks, there is no clear limit between reality and its representation. Now, when Bryman (1999b) speaks of the dedifferentiation of consumption, he refers to the difficulty of distinguishing between consumer activities that are characteristic of different spheres: cultural, commercial, tourist or leisure. Parks have but one purpose: communication, circulation and consumption. That is what they were designed for. That is why they are full of shops and food and beverage points – which, of course, represent significant parts of their revenue – and which, more recently, in the wake of Walt Disney World in Orlando, have incorporated other facilities for the commercial consumption of leisure, such as hotels and other accommodation, sports facilities and even real commercial areas such as Universal's City Walks.

Besides the parks themselves as objects of consumption, the commercialization of goods bearing the image or the corporate logos of the operators are characteristic. This is a field in which Disney – given the popular media scope of its image and cartoon characters – is dominant, not just through its parks but through its shops, and into which other operators such as Universal Studios and Six Flags try to enter by means of specific licences that link them to other media characters of transnational popular culture. Klein (1999) points out that the commercialization of merchandising objects has become generalized, even to other corporations, whether service or industrial. Disney, according to Bryman (1999b), has stood out because of knowing by intuition the huge possibilities of doing business through it. Such is its importance that designers decide upon the creation of new products to put on sale in accordance with their capacity to maximize the consumer's propensity to buy them.

Finally, Bryman (1999b) agrees with Ritzer (1996) when considering that McDonaldized work tends to be dehumanizing and alienating. However, that would lead one to consider that work in theme parks, in their capacity as McDonaldized spaces, presents the same characteristics. It is true that there is very strict control but it is also true that workers are expected to have a certain emotional capacity and commitment. Empirical evidence, such as that gathered by Lewis and Clacher (2001, 174) concerning the management of problems and customer complaints at three English theme parks, indicates that the commitment to the quality of the service and the increase in satisfaction can only be achieved through strict compliance with the established procedures and also through the assignation of greater employee initiative and communication between all those involved in a given problem. The management of human resources at parks goes, therefore, beyond characteristic Fordist control and has connections with the instrumentation of processes of adhesion and commitment to and recognition of the company and the visitors (Raz, 1997). It should not be overlooked, in any case, that employment in parks ranges from reception and animation to food and beverage and recreation, passing through mechanics, electronics, gardening and security. Therefore, the chances of pursuing a professional career if there is a bond between company and employee are many. The most favourable analyses of Disney maintain, for example, that, thanks to this, the company inspires commitment and motivation from its employees and this means that the rate of turnover of employees is significantly lower than in the rest of the industry (Rebori, 1993).

On the other hand, themed experiences are increasingly dominating people's everyday lives. This is the process which Bryman (1999b) identifies with the concept of Disneyization. However, it can be observed not just in that parks are or are not Disney parks but through the generalization, on a global scale, of other themed recreational facilities. This includes: restaurant chains and hotels that are themed (see, for example, the Olive Garden Italian food restaurants or the Luxor Hotel in Las Vegas); the large shopping malls that contain themed areas of rationalized consumption (as happens at West Edmonton Mall in Canada, the best known, internationally disseminated case); airports that try to adopt themed contents (like the proposal of a theme park at London's Gatwick airport); or historical places and living history museums that develop attractions and shows with a clear themed tone. Gottdiener (1997) has studied this in some depth. Now, what must be highlighted is that the important thing is not the fact in itself but the magnitude and the degree to which the process has become generalized.

It must be noted, however, that theme park operators are increasingly taking into account the specificity of things local as a key element for their competitiveness. The recent history of the development of theme parks demonstrates that cultural and linguistic differences that exist between places cannot be overlooked (with regard to this see the Disney experience in France by Grover, 1997). This is how, for example, the directors of Universal Studios have appreciated it when stating that the main challenge of Universal Studios Experience Beijing is, precisely, the adaptation of the product to the cultural sensitivities of the Chinese (O'Brien, 1998). The bond with things local is, on the other hand, one of the main trends observed in the development of parks in the short and medium term (Jones *et al.*, 1998). Along these lines, one could highlight a range of initiatives, from European ones like La Cité de la Bière in Armentières to the numerous parks in South-east Asia (small in scale and highly diversified in their contents), focused on historical and cultural themes of their location (Robertson, 1993). With regard to this, Teo and Yeoh (2001) report the case of Bandar Sunway (Sunway City) in Petaling Jaya, near Kuala Lumpur, the capital of Malaysia, the first international-standard theme park in the country, attracting 35,000 visitors a day. Although there is theming, merchandising and a Disney culture of excellence, local culture makes its presence felt in the park and among visitors. Therefore, there is a need to bear in mind the dialectics that are generated by globalization from two angles:

- The exportation of the cultural contents that are characteristic of the mass communication circuit.
- The reification and commercialization of the cultural contents that are characteristic of the historical–territorial circuit.

5.3.2. Interpretations from postmodernity

Considering the importance of the components that are typical of Disneyization as described by Bryman (1999a), as well as the inclusion of the concept in the framework of theories on consumerism, theme parks have often been presented as emblems of postmodernism (Fjellman, 1992). Inspired, along with many others, by the work of Derrida (1972), Jameson (1984), Lyotard (1984) and Foucault (1988), postmodernism 'implies resistance to rigid, categorical formulations, the search for new ways to interpret the empirical world and the rejection of ideological mystification' (Nogué and Vicente, 2001, 24). For Rojek (1993), there are four points that characterize postmodern leisure: first, that it is fundamentally equivalent to a consumer activity, in which issues proper to modernity, such as authenticity and autorealization, are irrelevant; secondly, that it is based on the generalized process of the dedifferentiation of society; thirdly, it establishes its own working rules beyond state regulations or socially accepted morals; and finally, that postmodern leisure exalts fictitious, dramaturgical values, that is to say, that the show and spectacle dominate. However, as Warren (1994) maintains, much postmodern literature has shied away from detailed ethnographic investigation and has preferred to 'take a broader sweep' so that it may be stated, for example, that in very few cases do postmodern interpretations on theme parks 'include empirical observations concerning the behaviour of the customers in a park'.

From this perspective, there are indeed elements that allow the association of theme parks with a postmodern characterization of society (see Bryman, 1995). The main reasons for this are, among others, that:

1.   Parks symbolize the confusion between images and forms and compress, in the way mosaics do, time and space (Rojek, 1993). Donaire (1999) holds that, rather than a utopia, parks are also 'uchronias' in which the universe is located at the intersection of the presents, the pasts and the futures they represent. With no hierarchies, with no boundaries and with no priorities, they juxtapose what is real and imaginary, the past and the future, science and history, legends and tales. It is a stationary journey (on the scale of real journeys) but is accelerated to the scale of the park, where the attractions 'attract' like magnets and bring about anxiety when not visited with celerity. Time, in a park, becomes space. Seven centuries of the history of Paris at the Parc Astérix, the journey from the islands of Polynesia to Imperial China at PortAventura, the conquest of the infinite at Futuroscope are examples of such compression. Distances disappear in exchange for immersion into the scene. As in a video-clip, to go around a theme park is to blend different music and tales. Everything is dense and fragmentary. As in videos, a space has been created by plundering images from everywhere and arranging them in a defined scripted order for them to be well read by the consumers, who feel they are the stars of their own script.

2.   As has been mentioned, parks express the concept of dedifferentiation clearly and in a multitude of ways. There is no differentiation between consumption and entertainment and there are no limits defined between units and modalities of consumption. Disney Animal Kingdom is a good example of this. It is, as stated in the headline of an article in the *San José Mercury News*, a facility that seeks to provide 'Ecotourism manufactured for mass affluence'. The terms of the paradox are of such magnitude that there is no need to render them, but merely to contemplate them. This is possible, in fact, only, in a context of consumers' dedifferentiation and acceptance of theatrical authenticity as a system of life and play. In Europe, for example, the Ruhr region has redirected its industrial crisis by transforming its factories into places for culture and entertainment, with presentations of light and colour at the Thyssen steelworks, music festivals at a former electrical power plant or an artificial ski slope opposite a coking plant and billowing smokestacks.

3.   As simulacra, parks blur the limits of reality and build hyperrealities. This is the case with Disney's California Adventure. As described by Rybczynski (2001):

It is about California, of course, but past and present bear upon each other in complicated ways . . . It is both about California and in California, it refers to the past yet is about today, it contains a portion of real vineyard and a real bakery next to a fake oceanfront and a simulated – but geologically accurate – mountain.

According to Eyssartel and Rochette (1992), parks' uniqueness is juxtaposing disparate worlds beyond any diachronous continuity and synchronic contiguity. In this sense, they are emblematic of an era of the dissolution of forms, in which art is mixed with play (Eco, 1986). This is also the case in the Phoenix Seagaia complex in Miyazaki, Japan, where up to 10,000 people every day can enjoy an artificial beach with smooth waves for the family to bathe in and crests of up to 3 m for surfers.

4. Finally, theme parks are paradigmatic places of the emerging post-tourist interested in activity, play, consumption, recognition and even knowledge itself. The more affluent, better-educated, more travelled and more experienced consumers as well as the older ones are becoming constrained by complicated lifestyles and are seeking leisure offers that are in touch with their needs. Stevens (2003) maintains concerning this that there are four emerging tendencies in the development of visitor attractions to be borne in mind:

- The development of destination attractions that offer a comprehensive range of services and facilities for entertainment, shopping, eating and all other aspects of leisure.
- The creation of new destination attractions with year-round operation that appeal to different markets at the same time and are used by policymakers as a 'kick-start' tool to develop new tourism economies everywhere.
- The progressively full integration between shopping and entertainment in a context of polarization of retailing activity within the entertainment and enjoyment aspects of leisure.
- The emergence of a number of specialist destination management companies operating on a worldwide basis, leading to the further globalization of the industry, as well as the homogenization of consumer choices.

Now, according to Bryman (1995), if dealing with the fundamental concepts of the theory on consumerism, it must be admitted that the tone of theme parks is clearly not postmodern concerning:

1. The acceptance of the idea of technological progress, which underlies its most conventional materializations (despite often distorting history to give continuity to certain events). Francaviglia (1999) explains, with regard to this, that the themed area of Frontierland, in Disneyland, perpetuates the expansionist conception that has been prevalent in North American ideology since the end of the 19th century and its relationship with the idea of progress, illustrated via the railway, steamboats and the mine train. Paradoxically, while the integration of the West of the USA was a

large-scale planned military, economic and infrastructure-related operation, it is presented as the result of the innovator, pioneer spirit of its individual players.

2.   The acceptance of metanarratives concerning the goodness of capitalism, of enterprise, of the traditional nuclear family and of participation in
technological progress. Much has been written on the ideology of Disney
parks. As Ariès (2002, 22–23) says, each detail is conceived to contain a
message. Each themed area in Disney conveys one of the great North
American myths. This is so much so that visitors can quickly recognize
their contents because they have patterns of interpretation. Magic Kingdom constructs a mythical structure, with themes that penetrate the
American conscience. Another case, SeaWorld, is also significant. Davis
(1997) holds that it is an announcement of the benefits that a multinational
corporation can offer society as a whole. In fact, parks are instruments for
the conveyance of the message of North American world dominance
(Schaffer, 1996).

3.   The Fordist nature of the system of organization of production and, in
particular, the non-existence of elements of informality, belief in the
workforce's decision-making capacity and structural flexibility characteristic of post-Fordism in the organization of work. On the other hand, as
has been seen, this is highly routinized, structured and presents high
doses of predictability.

4.   Parks' doubtful linkage to the domain of hyperreality. Going to an
extreme, parks are nothing more than the spatial materialization of individuals' most diverse fantasies. The power of consumer culture and great
technological capacity characteristic of today's society do the rest. This
can be clearly illustrated on the basis of a questionnaire carried out by the
journal *Amusement Business* at the end of 1999 on a series of creative
designers from different parks, in which they were asked about their ideal
theme park. Dale Mason, attraction development director at Universal
Creative, replied saying that it would be an underwater leisure complex
in the Great Barrier Reef in Australia. Bob Rogers, founder of BRC Imagination Arts, said Hogwarts School from the Harry Potter books, while,
among many others, Dennis Speigel, president of International Theme Park
Services, Inc., spoke of a park that is totally directed at the Far West experience. Doubtless, should they materialize, one could speak of hyperreality, but in their creators' minds parks are only fantasies, which, thanks
to some corporations' financial capacity and society's being in tune with
such fantasies, may become, given the right conditions, simply realities
(Valenti, 1997). This leads us, in any case, to another debate which has
been dealt with in depth from the angle of culture and philosophy, that of
authenticity (see Urry, 1990). As Münch (1999, 136) says, it is possible to
ask oneself, even, whether the triumph of the entertainment culture represented by parks means the end of 'authentic' culture.

Therefore, it may be concluded that, given their characteristics, theme
parks are fully integrated in a society – today's – which is relatively different

from its modern predecessor in the use of leisure time and its high tendency towards conspicuous consumption. Parks symbolize, therefore, the state of social, economic and cultural transition in which advanced capitalism is found. The new consumer opportunities, the incorporation of technology into production and the globalization of media entertainment are casting doubt as to what is effectively happening to the ways people relate. Changes are fast and global. Now, it is also true that continuity exists between the means of production and consumption established in the modernity of classic Fordist production systems and current times. Thus, beyond the coherence of the interpretative framework which postmodernism provides with regard to certain characteristic aspects of theme parks and the emergence of a consumer culture which has overpowered leisure time, it may be maintained that theme parks are a phenomenon rooted in modernity and that attend to mass consumption, which involves rigid structures and puts the accent on rationalization. From this perspective, therefore, the hypothesis may be considered and assessed that Disneyization, like McDonaldization, is a modern phenomenon that continues to be of importance in a world which has, in some interpretations, been considered postmodern (see Ritzer and Lika, 1997). Both concepts can be useful to understand theme parks from the concrete angles of production and consumption. In fact, Harvey (1990) already considered that postmodernism is not a discontinuity in respect of modernism: rather, it deals with different manifestations of the same underlying dynamic. Therefore, the apparent paradox may be considered as having a 'modern' system of production which is projected in some forms of consumption, which, from some perspectives, belong to and can be interpreted from postmodernity (regarding this, see Storey, 1998).

Case 9. The Ecohistorical Parks of Grupo Xcaret

The Mexican Group Xcaret is made up of the Xcaret, Xel-Há and Garrafón ecohistorical theme parks, all located in the Mexican Caribbean. It develops research programmes through Vía Delphi, the company that administers its dolphinariums and is in charge of the operation of the Parque Ecoturístico Cañón del Sumidero in Chiapas. Each year, its different facilities receive over 2 million visitors and it has a staff of some 2600 employees. Based in the Mexican state of Quintana Roo, it sets its sights on the tourist recreation market through the development and management of unique, sustainable, natural theme parks. Complementarily, it aims to play a relevant role in the world as a consultant in the design, development, commercialization and operation of natural theme parks and to become an exemplary enterprise as regards sustainable development. The values that the Grupo upholds are authenticity, solidarity, loyalty and productivity. The Group is studying projects in Mahahual, Quintana Roo, Cabo San Lucas, Baja California Sur, and Miami, Florida.

Xcaret, the Group's first park, was inaugurated in 1990 (see www. xcaret.com.mx). In 1984 architect Miguel Quintana Pali bought from a group of Mexican business people 5 ha of land in the surroundings of a small cove of the Mexican Caribbean – which is the meaning of the Mayan word Xcaret – with the idea of building a private residence. Upon preparing the land and witnessing the beauty of the spot, he changed his mind and started to conceive the project for the development of a nature theme park open to the public. To do so, he partnered with brothers Oscar, Marcos and Carlos Constandse. At the same time, he got into contact with the National Institute of Anthropology and History (Instituto Nacional de Antropología e Historia), so as to reconstruct all of the vestiges of the Mayan pyramids and buildings found in the area. For over ten centuries, the place had been a Mayan port and ceremonial centre. Today, the park – commercially known as a sacred paradise for nature – covers 80 ha, 75 km to the south of Cancún and offers a multitude of recreational possibilities, like swimming, snorkelling in the underground river, lagoon or at the beach, visiting the butterfly house, the aviary, the botanical gardens or the reef aquarium, seeing endangered mammals like jaguars and manatees or being a spectator of a host of Mexican-themed night-time shows. The park includes five restaurants offering local and regional specialities and a hotel operated by Occidental Hoteles. At present, it is the number one destination for visitors to Cancún, Playa del Carmen and la Riviera Maya.

After Xcaret, the same group developed Xel-Há, a thematic water park with a natural aquarium, and which, like Xcaret, allows one to enjoy natural attractions, ecological attractions and water activities in rivers, lagoons, natural pools and ancient caves bathed by the underground rivers that flow into the Caribbean Sea. In 1998, Grupo Xcaret took charge of Parque Garrafón, on Isla Mujeres, which at the time had a greatly deteriorated natural environment. That year, renovation work started on the park and to protect the reef. In conjunction with the Instituto Nacional de Antropología e Historia, Punta Sur was revamped in order to offer a unique panoramic visit and access to the archaeological vestiges of a Mayan temple. During the widening of the track leading to Punta Sur, a new area of coral was discovered. This area, which is protected, is today an ideal place to discover and observe animals in the wild and has countless sea urchins, tropical fish and different species of coral and rays. Finally, Parque Ecoturístico Cañón del Sumidero, in Chiapas, also managed by Grupo Xcaret, allows one to explore the region's natural surroundings – one of the most important natural and cultural monuments in Mexico – by carrying out open-air activities in an atmosphere of respect and promotion of environmental culture. Prior to opening, the Fondo Chiapas and Grupo Xcaret negotiated federal resources to the tune of over 120 million pesos for a waste-water treatment plant. Today, the Group also contributes to the permanent cleaning of the navigable section of Cañón del Sumidero.

According to Córdova Lira (2005), the parks of Grupo Xcaret are administered within the framework of a system whose main characteristics are the capacity to generate utilities and its own technical knowledge, participation in the solution of social problems in the local, regional and national spheres and the duty to preserve the ecological bases through the protection methods and the rendering of services. Consequently, all of the Quintana Roo parks have been accredited as 'socially responsible companies'. In addition, they have been classified among 'the best companies to work for' in Mexico, and Xel Há notably appears among the top 20 to work for in Latin America, according to the Great Place to Work Institute. Also, the Instituto Nacional de las Mujeres de México highlighted Xcaret, Xel Há, Garrafón, Via Delphi and the Grupo Xcaret companies with the award of the title 'Gender Equality Model'. Also, from the point of view of the environment, the Group will implement in its parks continuous diagnostics and environmental monitoring strategies, biological pest control, the sustainable use of water and the integral handling of solid waste, among other things.

Despite the existence of critics who insist that, though the Group's discourse is committed, its practice is barely sustainable (for further information, see Adelson, 2001), other aspects that illustrate Grupo Xcaret's management style are: the development of its own scientific research and conservation programmes, environmental education and scientific dissemination, alliances with different university bodies, with the UNAM (Institute of Limnology and Geophysics Institute) and with the University of the Caribbean (funding of the sustainable tourism and telematic engineering degrees), responsible management of mass tourism, community development, including actions that range from free visits by over 8000 students a year to the city of Chemuyil's urban planning, where a large number of Xel-Há employees live. More particularly, with regard to research, the Group is in the process of joining the National Register of Scientific and Technological Companies (Registro Nacional de Empresas Científicas y Tecnológicas) and has obtained research funds from the Naval Research Office (Oficina de Investigación Naval), which reports to the US Navy. Via Delphi has one of the most important research programmes in Latin America as far as dolphins and other sea mammals are concerned. In any case, on 2 October 2004, Grupo Xcaret signed their adherence and commitment to the articles of the Charter of the Earth. This turned it into the first business group in Mexico to have taken this initiative.

Case 10. The Globalization of Leisure and the Sesame Street Characters

Sesame Place is a theme park located in Langhorne, Pennsylvania. It is operated by Busch Entertainment Corporation, the entertainment division of Anheuser Busch. Sesame Place first opened in 1980 near the Oxford Valley Mall and initiated the expansion of the commercial complex in the vicinity. The original park was 3 acres in size and featured play areas and large computer labs where kids could colour in their favourite Sesame Street characters. Since then the park has expanded to 16 acres. Currently, Sesame Place includes a variety of rides, shows and water attractions, specially suited to very young children. Two of the more popular attractions at the park include Sky Splash and Vapor Trail. Sky Splash is a large raft water slide. Vapor Trail is a roller coaster catering to the tastes of young thrill seekers, even as young as 3 years of age. The entire Sesame Place crew struts down Sesame Street twice a day in the 'Rock around the Block' parade, which features all of the Sesame Place characters, large floats, dancers and lots of music. Families can even have breakfast with the Sesame Street characters an hour before the rest of the park opens. This is not, however, included in regular admission. Elmo's World is the newest attraction in the park. It features dry rides for young children.

Sesame Place derives its theme from the Sesame Street television programme and characters like Big Bird, Elmo, Ernie and Bert. Sesame Street is an educational American children's television series designed for preschoolers, combining education and entertainment shows. More than 4000 episodes of the show have been produced in 36 seasons, which distinguishes it as one of the longest-running shows in television history. The original series has been televised in 120 countries, and more than 25 international versions have been produced. Moreover, because of its positive influence, Sesame Street has earned the distinction of being the foremost and most highly regarded educator of young people in the world. Because of its international appeal, there are also several international Sesame Street themed locations around the world, including Tokyo Sesame Place in Japan, Parque Plaza Sésamo in Monterrey, Mexico, and inside the Hopi Hari theme park in São Paulo, Brazil. A Sesame Place park also existed in Irving, Texas, from 1982 to 1984, closing its doors due to poor attendance and a large number of water parks competing for its business (for more information see www.sesameplace.com and also Sesame Place and Sesame Street in http://en.wikipedia.org).

6 The Urbanism of Theme Parks and Spatial Innovation

> We can enjoy and even admire the well made wax fruit and silk flowers, but the pleasure that they generate lies in the recognition of their artistic prowess, not on being taken in by them. In our day-to-day life we all prefer real fruit and flowers.
>
> (César Pelli, 1999)

According to Warren (1994), when Disney opened its first park in 1955, not only did it give rise to a new form of entertainment but also it sowed the seed of a new vision of the city. Because of their capacity for innovation and their meticulous planning, Disney parks have been the subject of debate and application among planners and urban designers (see Rebori, 1995b). There have been several reasons for this. First, the ways of organizing the space of theme parks have had an influence on the design of areas – tourist and holiday resorts (Rebori, 1995c) – and have encouraged the creation of a new architecture of entertainment (Huxtable, 1997). As Minca (1996, 152) states, the success of this architecture is based on a 'philosophy of reconstruction and recreation'. Secondly, beyond classic tourist facilities, parks have also set standards for the leisure industry as a whole – including museums and theatres and the like – and have been useful for the design of other facilities that are halfway between consumption and entertainment as commercial areas (Crawford, 1992). Finally, parks have surpassed the limits of entertainment and recreation and even urban planning has incorporated some of their solutions. Going to an extreme, whole towns, like Seaside in Florida, have been designed in Disney style (Zukin, 1995). Thus, in addition to offering an alternative to traditional amusement parks, parks have presented the bases of an urban proposal that can be characterized, according to their followers, by their good aesthetics, by their running in line with what is expected and by the feeling of comfort that their users perceive. It is a proposal that also banishes crime, drugs, corruption, poverty, racial conflict and, in short, all of the problems that are characteristic of urban life, from crossing their frontiers.

This chapter is given over to the debate as to the influence of theme parks in the conception, design and development of urban areas. This is an influence that has proved to be more than notable in the case of North America but has also become generalized thanks to a process of 'hegemonic' implantation, in the Gramscian sense of the word, in the rest of the world. As we shall see, however, the model of parks does have its limitations. The reactions of the citizens of each place to the presence of solutions fit for theme parks to solve their cities' problems has forced planners to adapt to local social and cultural conditions and, sometimes, even to give up their projects. The chapter starts with a section that aims to characterize the urban dimension of theme parks. This is followed by a look at the translation of their design principles to their corporative leisure environment, increasingly more common among medium- and large-sized theme parks. The third section aims to look into the extent to which the experience of theme parks has been used in urban, dynamic processes of territorial development of a general nature. This is a section which, necessarily, must refer to the urban dynamics occurring in the last 50 years in developed countries, especially, but not only in the USA, and especially as to the fashionable debate over a compact or a diffuse city. Finally, the last section attempts to denote the limits of the proposals for spatial innovation that theme parks carry out.

6.1. The Urban Singularity of Parks

Eyssartel and Rochette (1992, 38) propose a definition of theme parks that is useful for the purposes of this chapter. They say of them that they are 'urban spaces with a commercial vocation', where the resources of architecture, art and technology (especially communications technology) are at the service of a coherent 'cultural creation' (in its broad sense). This is why, as Rybczynski (2001) admits, they so impress. Unlike conventional towns and cities, parks aim to recreate 'atmospheres', including sounds and smells. This is also why it is normally difficult to explain a park's ambience in words. In short, a theme park 'is a space which has not been made in order to be described but rather to be experienced and lived *in situ*', a place in which architectural shapes have an evocative and invocative power (Eyssartel and Rochette, 1992). However, no matter how fantastic, it would be naive to think that the 'creation' of a theme park can be done without taking into account, among other things, the safety requirements that are implicit for mass frequentation or the need for an object to remain in good condition after being put to the test by thousands of visitors touching it to see if it is real. Parks are, in fact, the result of precise formulas of planning and design of space whose aim is to propose a certain way of consuming leisure time. They are, in short, one of the possible categories of leisure places to which Lefebvre (1976) referred: places for consumption in its pure state, which require, in order to fulfil their purpose, highly standardized production mechanisms and a multitude of stimuli aimed at the visitor–consumer.

There are two paradoxes that traverse the urban condition of parks: first, that, despite being productive places, they tend to mask the production processes so as not to condition the consumptive use their visitors make of them; and, secondly, that, due to the necessary existence of commercial establishments and premises inside them, they seem to have the attributes of a public place. The imaginary character of parks is their main means of hiding the productive nature and private ownership of the space. Their theme is the fundamental factor that sets them apart from other urban areas.

It cannot be forgotten, finally, that, as in the case of modern gardens, parks have a closed format and a clear desire for internal order that has nothing to do with the order/mayhem outside. The 'vocation' of parks is to be worlds apart. Their marketing would support this idea. You enter the park and you 'live' differently once you are there. Parks are based on this inside–outside dichotomy and their planning would support this. This is, on the other hand, an essential idea in order to comprehend the capacity of parks to act as laboratories for urban design and experimentation and, therefore, as reference points for planning models. This is for two reasons: first, because design and experimentation are done with no constraints of any kind; and, secondly, because the inability, when it exists, to adapt parks' urban solutions to real towns and cities is a direct consequence, precisely, of their state of being an imaginary world.

6.1.1. The spatialization of the imagination

As is noted by Minca (1996), the Michelin Guidebook on Disneyland Paris describes the park as if it were describing a city. Nevertheless, despite its urban structure and the suitability of the description given by the Guidebook, a park, including Disneyland Paris, is a reality that has been programmed by its creators and which, therefore, only tangentially incorporates active social and historical remains, which are characteristic, on the other hand, of cities. One initial question to be considered is, therefore, that a theme park is a place to which the comments of Venturi *et al.* (1972, 149) can be applied when they state that 'total design is the opposite of the incremental city that grows through the decisions of many'. Total design fundamentally implies conceiving 'a messianic role for the architect as corrector of the mess of urban sprawl; it promotes a city dominated by pure architecture and maintained through "design review"'. Thus Ariès (2002, 69) can argue, for example, that Disneyland Paris rests on the ignorance of geography. Disneyland Paris, he says, reinvents nature in accordance with its needs and its social ghosts. For him, for example, Disneyland Paris does not adapt to a territory; rather, it transfigures or disfigures it. Little do the over 100,000 trees planted in Disneyland Paris matter to him since they simply act to decorate. They respond to the needs of the total design.

Total design allows the creation of tourist and recreational urban realities which, unlike traditional tourist areas, which are the result of the slow adaptation of the original spatial forms to the new functions carried out by tourism and leisure activities, are little prone to pre-existing spatial organization, and theirs has a spatial logic which is hardly linked to outside what takes place within the corporative space. From such a perspective, theme parks would be, as regards materializations of total design and in accordance with Shields's (1991) terminology, a type of place on the margin. In them, what matters is the discourse that is conveyed through the design elements that shape the recreated landscape – the fronts of Victorian houses, Sleeping Beauty's castle, the rounded shapes of Toontown or the masculinity of Frontierland, in the case of Disney parks. Conversely, in incremental cities, the elements are juxtaposed and amalgamate and become meaningful in accordance with a hierarchy that is acquired on the basis of the social relationships that dominate urban life. It is evident, therefore, that the Main Street in Disneyland Paris does not possess the attributes of the place it simulates being (Donaire, 1999).

Thus, parks represent a specific type of urbanism of illusion and of emotion that lies at the crossroads of the tourist industries, culture industries and country planning (Eyssartel and Rochette, 1992). They are at the same time constructed places and cultural creations. As regards the latter, they express themselves, precisely, through architectural, landscape and scenic design. The linking of images, constant play with steps, the miniaturization of decorative elements, the realism of the elements, the special effects, the use of water and the manipulation of the experiences one will encounter along the way are ways to create emotions via architecture and urbanism. It cannot be ignored, therefore, that, basically, they pick up on an idea that was neatly solved by the painters and engineer architects of the 17th and 18th centuries: an idea which, in the words of Eyssartel and Rochette (1992), consists of:

> enclosing a meaningful universe in an ordered space . . . establishing the rules of composition in accordance with those that govern the visual arts of an era and of a culture . . . mobilizing all of the techniques used to create wonderful festive effects . . . stimulating intellect at the same time as emotion is globally worked on through spectacles that simultaneously appeal to one's sense of sight, hearing and sometimes smell . . . articulating the *mise-en-scène* of places of live spectacles.

The difference from gardens lies in the fact that parks commercialize this idea, offering it to broad sections of the population so that they can experience it during their free time.

As in Las Vegas, in parks, urbanism is rather a matter of communication than of architecture. Therefore, the key elements of parks are the visual motifs they incorporate. The function of the aesthetic design of parks is twofold: to modulate the rhythm of the visitor's 'journey' through the park via the aesthetics of the points of view and, secondly, to explain their narrative plot. Once again, both functions were already characteristic of the gardens of the 17th century. The only difference is that, if in those days the decoration of the gardens made reference to the theatre, today, the make-up of parks does so to the cinema. The very use of gardens as theatres in those days and that of theme parks as sets for the making of films today reflects these relationships of equivalence. What is important is that they should create a landscape of fantasy, seeking 'effects'. This is why Sorkin (1992b) was bold enough to say that Disneyland is 'the place where the ephemeral reality of the cinema is concretized into the stuff of the city'.

Given that it is a 'cultural creation', the imaginary landscape of each park is specifically oriented at certain social groups that may be stimulated by it. This is why parks profusely use the most generic references of the collective memory and, especially, of the media. So, in general, parks express, mediatize and symbolize cultural referents related to science, exploration, sport, nature, the imagination, the cinema. For example, a show at Epcot strengthens the feeling of patriotism through an account of the history of the USA, with a highly contrasted teleological meaning based on the idea of personal and collective progress. The account starts with the arrival of the pilgrims in the Mayflower and ends with a chant to America as a model of freedom. Hence, as Zukin (1991) points out, it should be no surprise that most visitors to Disney are white, middle- to upper-class, with clear ideas about their historical and social referents and who trust in social progress. The architecture of Epcot, the reconstructions of the past and the inventions of the future in just one precinct do the rest. In other words, the constructed space capitalizes on the narrative symbolism of the place and instrumentalizes it to generate, through itself, business opportunities.

Due to all of these considerations, parks do not fit in with the historically learned conventional concepts of urban form and function. But that is because they respond to a type of spatial order in which narration takes precedence over function. Continuing with the same example, it is not that Epcot, like the rest of parks, does not have any urban value, but, rather, that it is different and, above all, it is especially or mainly for certain social groups, such as those cited above, who recognize and accept its symbolism, despite the fact that intellectuals, academics and architects generally reject it.

6.1.2. Technology at the service of creation

In spite of creating imaginary worlds, the designers of theme parks use, very precisely and in controlled fashion, concepts and relations learned in the functioning of conventional urban reality. Also, as in the case of gardens, the design of the routes to be followed by the systems of movement, of the visuals and of the uses define the imaginary. Put another way, the design of the imaginary world of parks lies in the well-thought-out organization of space. Moreover, it is efficient in respect of the emotion it should arouse in its visitors and also of its operational needs. Often, in this latter sense, there is talk of the passages and tunnels that criss-cross beneath Disneyland (Sorkin, 1992b). In fact, they are a metaphor of the design needs of a park and the discipline demanded in their gestational period.

From the point of view of their relationship with the visitors, as Rebori (1993) mentions for the case of Disney, there are three design elements that ensure that the aim of arousing emotion be fulfilled: order, enclosure and context. These three fundamentally technical elements are essential in order to make the imaginary world of parks an intelligible, comfortable and satisfactory place for their users–visitors.

1. Order is the deliberate grouping of uses, elements and references. This can be figurative or symbolic in parks. The organizational axes, the flux of directional movement, the limits constructed and the landmarks allow the different elements of the park to connect and relate. The relationships that are struck up between them are the basis of the order perceived by the users–consumers and, in turn, facilitate and direct movement. To provide an example, the entrance corridors to the parks and their landmarks of reference (the train station and the castle at either end of Main Street at Disney parks) serve this purpose: that of generating order and directing movement.
2. The enclosure of parks allows users–visitors to conceive, understand, relate to and experience the place. Parks are conceived as a texture of interrelated solid and empty spaces. The main referents of solids are the buildings and the network of streets and squares are those of the empty spaces. Based on this, different interrelated factors contribute to the establishment of the closure systems according to climate, the available space, the market segments or the culture of the place. Ratios of size, form, height, architectural characteristics and the sense of continuity define each space in accordance with the aim of the park, the needs of the users–visitors and the conditions of the place. A further two elements help understand and set limits to the space when the precedents are insufficient: the consistency of the ground and the landmarks. The scale, the handling of the subspaces and the changes of level give rise to additional effects.

Thus, for example, parks usually accept, with regard to size, that the maximum area for a reasonable, all-embracing public urban space should be no greater than 60–150 m or that the optimal visual effects are created when the height of a building does not exceed the immediate width of the street by a factor of 3:1 or 4:1 at most. Likewise, perception is optimal if, being virtually homogeneous, structures do not vary by more than 25%. The most satisfactory forms are simple ones. Architectural subdivisions and details facilitate the perception of space in manageable sectors and allow the identification of elements that grab the interest of the different users–visitors. The space of the parks must also offer a clear sensation of continuity, though not of monotony. The alternation of lines in the shaping of the ground creates disjunctive structures and specific elements of the landscape. The landmarks have effects equivalent to unification and central focalization. Dealing with scale, which is determined by the previous factors, is basic when generating aesthetic pleasure. Thus, for example, in order to achieve this, the façades in Disney parks' Main Street are on a scale of 5/8 compared with their real size. It is an effect that gives rise to intimacy. Furthermore, scale decreases with height. It is 90% at street level but 60% on the third floor. The creation of subspaces through landscaping, seating, the changes in ground level and the constructions help the psychological need to set limits to space. They generate more private spatial structures without generating the perception of solitude. In a similar way, changes in level create aesthetic and psychological well-being.

3. Context is the grouping of elements in space, which contributes as much to its unique shape as to providing the place with some meaning. Put another way, context is formed by the human and social characteristics that give it meaning. This is what leads to two places never being equal. This is the most difficult characteristic to achieve through the total design of parks: hence the attention to detail and the hyperabundance of elements to ensure that the thematic aspects can be assimilated. However, it cannot be forgotten that normally the details refer to utopian or familiar versions in respect of the place to which they refer. In incremental urbanism, on the other hand, context arises from social and cultural heritage. Therefore, the context can only be created figuratively, combining the ideals of the intellectual contents with the cultural and social desires and expectations of the visiting users. That is why, in parks, activity, diversity and vitality are magnified as instruments to improve the 'visitor's experience'.

Therefore, the design of an imaginary world goes beyond just the theme; it is a technical procedure whose aim is to:

1. Establish or maintain a well-structured atmosphere.
2. Establish a meaning for the place.
3. Minimize conflict and maximize urban order.

Basically, then, the aesthetics of parks rely on technical design. They are places that aim to welcome, distract, instruct and establish a social relationship with their visitors. Zukin (1995) sums this up well when he states, concerning Walt Disney World, that the park:

> exemplifies visual strategies of *coherence*, partly based on uniform and behavioural norms of conformity, and partly based on the production of set *tableaux*, in which everything is clearly a sign of what it represents in a shared narrative, fictive or real . . . Disney World also uses a visual strategy that makes unpleasant things – like garbage removal . . . invisible.

Thus, despite the fact that parks belong to the world of production, their design, both as regards the thematic and the technical aspect, infers that this is not so.

6.2. The Corporative Urbanism of Leisure Complexes

As of the creation of Walt Disney World in Orlando at the beginning of the 1970s, the companies operating theme parks have developed veritable leisure complexes in their immediate surroundings, places concentrating recreational, commercial, tourist and, in some cases, residential activities. Such developments were proposed by Disney in Orlando, not just to increase the firm's profit and to control the shape and rhythm of growth around the park (after verifying what had occurred in the surroundings of Disneyland in California, where a multitude of low-quality establishments had sprung up), but also, as Walt Disney said himself, to explore the transfer of the solutions provided in his park to matters such as mobility and the general planning of urban development (cited in Rebori, 1993). Leisure complexes are, therefore, the first area outside the parks themselves where their principles of composure and order are applied. The implications that this has had for the entertainment industry in general and for the creation of a specific architecture of leisure establishments have been fundamental. This is so much so that the planning of corporate space surrounding the parks through tourism and commercial and entertainment functions must be considered among park operators' contributions to town planning, spatial innovation and territorial planning.

The aim of corporate leisure complex designers is that of creating, in a more open environment than that of the parks, multifunctional spaces which, like the parks, differ from other existing alternatives not just in their structure but also in their narrative content. Everyone is impressed by the thematic spaces, perfectly organized atmospheres and coherence between the forms and functions that are typical of these complexes. The criteria respond in so far as possible to the aim of providing segments of specific demand with singular experiences. For this, in the same way as the parks, these places incorporate the concept of a theme as a design basis. However, there has been a certain evolution in their use. While themes were initially used to recreate exotic atmospheres, today they are used to create atmospheres that make sense in themselves or because of the fantastic stories they represent (concerning this, see Branch, 1990a, b). This is how, for example, in the case of Disney, the different architects who have worked for the company and have buildings and facilities in the resort have interpreted it (among them Michael Graves, Robert Venturi, Helmut Jahn, Robert A.M. Stern, Arata Isozaki, Charles Gwathmey, Robert Siegel and Bernardo Fort-Brescia). Moreover, this is how they have converted the Disney property in Orlando into a kind of open-air museum of architecture. These architects, who have worked freely and with an agreed financial arrangement with the company to create buildings, have normally made use of architectural forms from the past and they have applied fantasy to them with no other reference to either time or space. In short, the referent that delimits Disney property and indicates its territorial reach is the use of a theme.

Given the success of its pioneering initiative in Orlando, the creation of corporate leisure areas has been reproduced by Disney both in Japan and in

Paris and has recently been used as a reference point for the reformulation of Disneyland in Anaheim and/or the planning of their park in Hong Kong. In the same way as in Orlando, one fundamental factor in the success of the development of this type of urbanistic process around the park has been the support of the public sector. However, the dynamics of creating corporate spaces is not restricted to Disney. Take Universal Studios' Universal City Walk in Los Angeles, which has without a doubt been as significant a contribution as that of the concept of a resort by Walt Disney World. Inaugurated in 1994, it was conceived, in its initial stages, as a 450-m-long commercial street connecting the film studios, the park, the Cineplex Odeon cinema complex and the Universal Amphitheater, a place for open-air concerts. Today, many of the visitors to the park use it as an area of transition between the car park and the park. The residents of Los Angeles use it as an urban entertainment centre, especially between 5 and 11 in the evening and the younger population until 2 in the morning. The concept has been reproduced in Florida at Universal Orlando. For Jon Jerde, its main designer, the important thing about the City Walk is its uneven, chaotic interior area – along the lines of Los Angeles, the city it simulates – which induces experiences in people. To do so, despite being a purely commercial area, its creators have used fundamentally urbanistic techniques and concepts. Later, Disney formally reinvented the idea in Downtown Disney. Likewise, the above-mentioned reconversion of Disneyland in Anaheim into a resort has once again taken up the aim of converting Downtown Disney into the urban entertainment centre of Anaheim.

The concepts of a resort and of an urban entertainment centre are, in fact, two of the main contributions of theme parks to the creation of an architecture and urbanism of entertainment. The possibilities of the application of one and the other are conditioned, fundamentally, by questions of size. So the concept of a resort is more broadly possible in Disney, thanks to the territorial dimensions of its property. In a far smaller urban space, Universal has developed the concept of an urban entertainment centre. Development on Disney property is extensive and the different elements it incorporates are carefully located. Universal in Orlando is far denser. The availability of space for Disney (the more than 11,000 ha that Walt Disney secretly bought in the 1960s) and the characteristics of this area (available water, level topography, the absence of property development) help this. Visually, there is a predominance of open spaces and a clear linearity between the recreational equipment. The treatment of the landscape and gardening is generalized. Universal is far less natural. Its landscape is more urban, metallic in the material used and angular in its forms. At Universal, there are car parks that are made of concrete, which do not exist at Disney. The space restrictions, both in surface area and in the urban nature of the environment (Universal is in the city of Orlando, whereas Disney is located in the adjacent counties of Orange and Osceola), make this necessary, in addition to a different thematic concept and orientation. Making a metonym, Disney recreates a natural landscape while Universal recreates an urban landscape.

Though these are perhaps the most notable and best-known experiences, the development of corporate leisure areas in the surroundings of the parks has become generalized. An unpublished report by the International Association of Amusement Parks and Attractions (IAAPA) in 1992 already mentions that one of the main trends and development strategies in the sector is the incorporation of parks into large-scale leisure complexes. Likewise, Jones *et al.* (1998) consider as one of the main medium-term trends in the development of parks their integration into mixed projects of larger dimensions. In fact, the development of these corporate areas is taking place in such a generalized manner, especially at medium-sized and large parks both in the USA and in Europe (where existing parks are reconverting into leisure complexes, while newly created parks already include them in their plans) and Asia. In fact, it could be said that, today, many of the medium-sized and large theme parks are already designed with the aim of promoting recreational and entertainment complexes that will turn into magnets of development (see Anton Clavé, 1996).

Taking their generalization into account, authors such as Scheer (2000) have even been bold enough to model from a time perspective the relationships that are established between the elements of what he calls a 'leisure and business complex', that is to say, the park and its corporate leisure surroundings. Scheer (2000) establishes four baseline hypotheses, which, summarized, are as follows:

- Hypothesis I. The theme park is the dominant attraction and normally the first to be built. Its ability to attract decreases since this is transferred to the other elements that emerge in the complex as it develops.
- Hypothesis II. The internal spatial organization of the complex is polynuclear; it contains a great variety of differentiated elements. Each element is normally characterized by having a monofunctional structure and representing a specific supply. The essential elements of the complex are: one or more theme parks or similar, hotels and conference centres, a variety of sports facilities, recreational and leisure facilities, shopping centres, areas of housing and reservation areas like car parks, camps and protected areas.
- Hypothesis III. The project takes place in different characteristic stages. After the theme park, the major investment, the other attractions successively integrate into the project. During the process, a chronological order to finish the complex is observed.
- Hypothesis IV. The projects are integrated into specific plans concerning the use of an area with the aim of generating growing profits for the surrounding region and greater regional distinction. Prior to starting the project, the surrounding region does not usually dispose of a diversified tourist and service structure. The facilities take on growing importance due to their spin-off effects.

In terms of the evolution of the complex, according to Scheer (2000) two evolutionary principles can be distinguished: first, the theme park's relative loss of ability to attract in the framework of the leisure and business complex; and, secondly, the falling growth rates of the complex as a whole during its development. The evolutionary model may be organized in four stages. There are two premises that explain this: their progressive integration into the host region and the growing interconnection between each one of the elements of the complex. These assumptions are summarized in Fig. 6.1:

- Stage I: Formation of the focal point.
- Stage II: Internal connection.
- Stage III: External connection and internal differentiation.
- Stage IV: Construction of the complex and regional integration.

According to Scheer (2000), the lesson to be learned from corporate leisure areas is their creators and planners' capacity to transfer the design concepts applied inside the parks to open, multifunctional, productive areas. Moreover, through corporate leisure complexes, and on the basis of the experience inside theme parks, this way of going about things has been transferred to other types of places. Progressive incorporation has taken place in specific facilities, such as shops, restaurants, cinemas, malls, family leisure centres, hotels, golf courses and a whole range of recreational facilities. The results, however, can be quite varied in formal, aesthetic and structural terms. The differences between Disney and Universal in Orlando are a good illustration of this.

Without the integration of parks inside recreational leisure centres and the ability to use this means to experiment with solutions to urban problems, the role of the theme park in the reflection on the social construction of the area would be equivalent to what can be done with regard to their immediate predecessors, gardens or universal fairs. It is the creation of corporate leisure areas and the use that is later made of their advances that make it possible to debate the role of parks in urban planning in general. It cannot be forgotten, however, that in spite of their appearance as public places, leisure complexes around parks are corporate places: that is to say, places where the being inside–being outside dichotomy also works symbolically and operatively – spaces, on the other hand, that have the same conditions of the absence of a relationship with the characteristic pre-existing territorial structure of parks and which, necessarily, require the building of a 'cultural' sense of place.

6.3. Parks as a Referent for Planning

In an intense, critical article on the influence of Disney on contemporary urbanism, Warren (1994) acknowledges the company's relevance concerning this matter when beginning with the following statement:

> Consider a list of the most formidable design influences on the North American city: Ebenezer Howard, Daniel Burnham, Frederik Law Olmstead, Le Corbusier, Robert Moses, Jane Jacobs, Mickey Mouse. Mickey Mouse? Strange though it may seem, this Walt Disney Company spokesrodent has

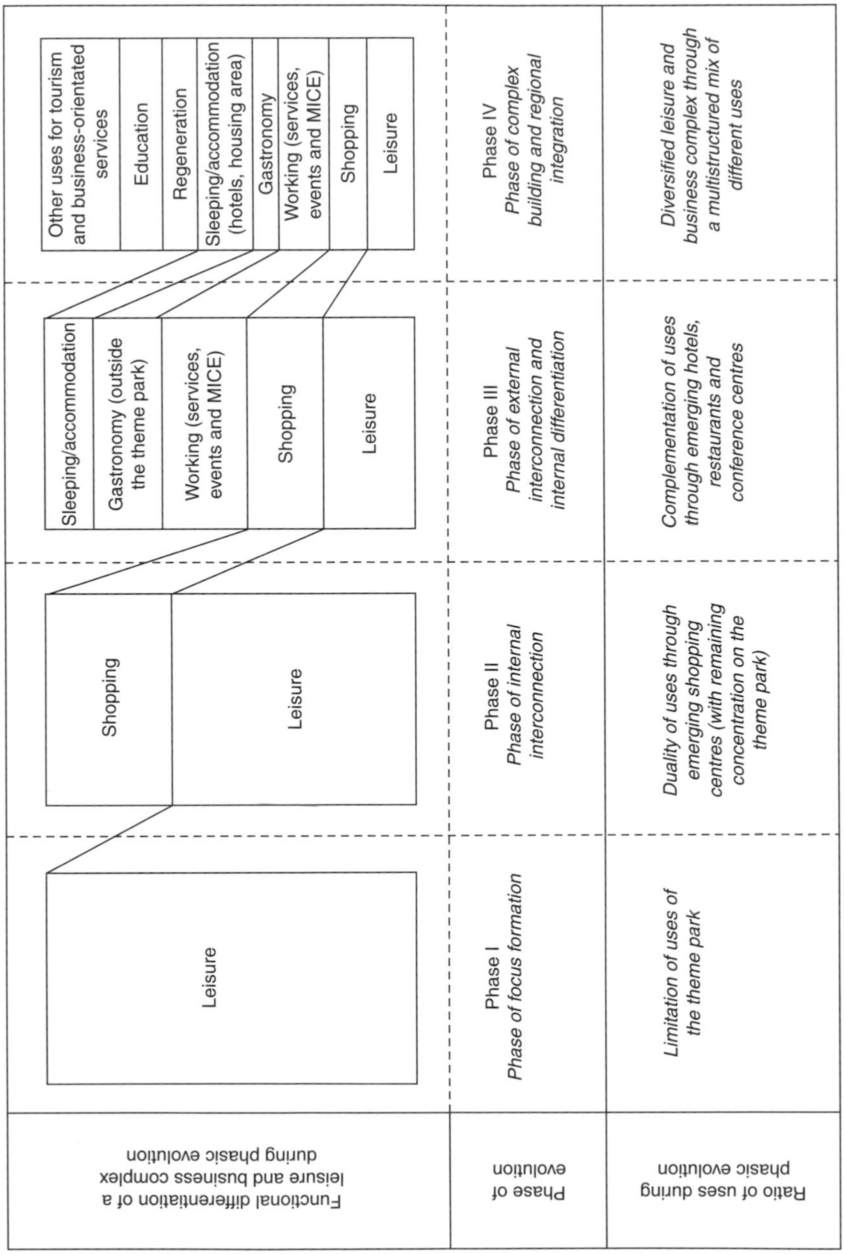

Functional differentiation of a leisure and business complex during phasic evolution	Phase of evolution	Ratio of uses during phasic evolution
Leisure	Phase I *Phase of focus formation*	*Limitation of uses of the theme park*
Shopping / Leisure	Phase II *Phase of internal interconnection*	*Duality of uses through emerging shopping centres (with remaining concentration on the theme park)*
Sleeping/accommodation, Gastronomy (outside the theme park), Working (services, events and MICE), Shopping, Leisure	Phase III *Phase of external interconnection and internal differentiation*	*Complementation of uses through emerging hotels, restaurants and conference centres*
Other uses for tourism and business-orientated services, Education, Regeneration, Sleeping/accommodation (hotels, housing area), Gastronomy, Working (services, events and MICE), Shopping, Leisure	Phase IV *Phase of complex building and regional integration*	*Diversified leisure and business complex through a multistructured mix of different uses*

Fig. 6.1. The diversification of uses in corporate leisure and business complexes (from Scheer, 2000).

become the somewhat frivolous symbol of an entirely serious new urban style: the city built in the Disney image. Millions of dollars have been spent by planners, architects, and others who consciously look toward Disney as an expert on the creation of liveable public space. Suburban shopping malls, inner city festival markets, small town main streets, residential neighbour-hoods and, in a few cases, whole cities have been shaped according to the lessons of Disney theme parks.

Theme parks and, in particular those of Disney, have gained recognition by numerous professionals as creative experiments of interest for urban planning, territorial organization and the management of the masses. Already in 1963, James Rouse, promoter of well-known – and debated – operations of a certain style of urban renovation in the USA, such as the city of Columbia in Maryland and the renovation of the port of Baltimore and Quincy Market in Boston, said, at a class at the Harvard Graduate School of Design:

> I hold a view that may be shocking to an audience so sophisticated as this, and that is, that the greatest piece of design in the USA today is Disney-land . . . I find more to learn in the standards that have been achieved in the development of Disneyland than in any other single
> piece of development in the country.
>
> (Cited by Spirn, 1998, 238)

Other professionals and analysts have coincided in their opinions (see Rebori, 1995b). Thus in 1979, urbanist David Brinkel declared that Walt Disney World was the most imaginative and successful project of urbanism as regards planning issues in the USA. Evidently, he was not just speaking of the amusement park but the whole of the Disney property:

> Roads are built, means of transport, lakes, golf courses, campsites, horseriding centres, businesses and hotels. And all of this constitutes the best managed urban place in the USA, everything is more in harmony there than in any other American urban setting.
>
> (Cited by Eyssartel and Rochette, 1992)

Even critical authors like Zukin (1995) admit that observing Disney property in Orlando allows one to learn about a range of fields: theme parks, urban planning, service activities and symbolic economy.

It cannot be forgotten, in order to understand the reason for these considerations, that, as was indicated at the beginning of this chapter, what Disney was aiming for when developing his property in Orlando was to offer urbanistic solutions and not just the creation of a leisure area. More concretely, when commencing the operation at the beginning of the 1960s, Disney did not just have the idea of developing in Orlando an imaginary world of entertainment-oriented parks and recreational facilities but his aim was basically to create comfortable places for everyday life. Epcot was to be Disney's urban experiment. More than Magic Kingdom, it is the initial ideal that Walt Disney had of Epcot that sets the difference between developing spatial innovation via the parks and proposing urban solutions beyond them. However, Epcot was not developed as Disney had foreseen, as an 'Experimental Prototype Community of Tomorrow', that is, as an urban utopia where he could put his ideal of a town into practice. This ideal was to combine the incorporation of the most important technological advances concerning urban matters with a profound humanistic reflection on the dimensions and functions of the town in order to make it habitable and comfortable. The company's evolution redirected what Epcot was to be, which was finally inaugurated at the start of the 1980s as Disney's second theme park in Orlando (Zukin, 1995). In any case, it is the reflection that surrounds Epcot and the way the company's later development has taken place which turned Disney – and by extension the other operators of theme parks – into an element for debate on planning issues.

Paradoxically, or perhaps precisely because of this, theme parks appeared in the USA at a time when the crisis in its urban model hit rock bottom. Cities like Los Angeles and Miami are two examples of the (sub)urban reality of extensive motorways and peri-urbanization into which the birth and initial development of theme parks in the USA as of the 1950s are contextualized. With no traditional centre, these cities can only be apprehended as fragments. They are unstructured cities in which there is no coincidence between built form and identity (Zukin, 1991). They are the result of a reality that can be explained by several factors: the emergence of individual motorization as of the end of the Second World War, the zonification and programming undertaken in the 1950s and 1960s, the crisis of urban centres, the abandonment and relocation of industrial areas and the popularization of certain urban and architectural ideals and trends, among which was that of housing property in the form of a characteristic typology of house and garden. Consequently, there is a domination of landscapes lacking characteristic collective and institutional urban elements that contribute, generally, to causing pleasurable experiences among people. As Sorkin (1992a, xii) says, this type of city 'eradicates genuine particularity in favour of a continuous urban field, a conceptual grid of boundless reach'. In the 1950s and 1960s, the protagonist was the 'urban sprawl'. Currently, it is the appearance of suburban cities on the outskirts of existing metropolises. They are the 'edge cities', as defined by Garreau (1991). Ibelings (1998, 88) describes the result as a heteropolis, 'a city without form or plan, without structure or centre, where even the architecture seems to be characterized mainly by an absence of distinguishing marks, by neutrality'.

The existing urban fabrics of today in the USA are nothing but series of adjacent structures that form a kind of continuous urban area, with no interrelation, either formal or functional. The North American suburb is an area, moreover, that is not prepared for the pedestrian urban experience. Space is and must be seen quickly from the car: hence the signposting competing to indicate the different structures in the arteries where they are concentrated. As a consequence, the experience of public space is very limited. Architect Jon Jerde, creator of the Universal City Walk of Los Angeles, clearly expressed this at a conference at the National

Building Museum of Washington in 2001. The use – and the very existence – of common space is the principal deficit of the North American city. Thus the principal challenge facing architects in the USA is to design experiences for places that do not dispose of them. These experiences are designed on the basis of the acceptance of the suitability of the traditional European urban model: compact, cultural and multifunctional. The definitive solution would be to go back and put all of these functions together as they once were and not segregate spaces according to activities.

Nevertheless, facing the past, present and future dominance of suburban non-differentiation, the alternative that has been activated has not had the result of a renewed boost to the development of European-style cities but has been directed at creating pieces of total design halfway between what is architectural and what is urbanistic. Theme parks would be one such space. Malls, resorts, designer housing estates and industrial estates would be along the same lines. There are two questions of an ideological nature that justify their existence, as regards islands of urban design, as a response to the crisis of the traditional city in the USA: first, the acceptance that consumption is, in the USA, as well as an addiction, a system of cultural interaction; and, secondly, the persuasion that the human experience is an event that can also be designed or, through an example, the assumption that the sense of place of the Plaza di Spagna in Rome may be created through an architectural project and a narrative content, the theme.

Therefore, the contribution made by theme parks to the necessary reflection as to the urban reality concerns five aspects. The first, aesthetic, refers to the visual order of things. The second, structural, concerns the dimensions of the urban elements and the possibility of being able to navigate them without the need for a motorized form of transport. The third, functional, refers to the use made of the buildings and the urban fabric. The fourth, social, affects the need to create safe places. Finally, content poses the question of the identity of the place. Probably the Main Street of Disney parks synthesizes these five contributions. Indeed, in a traditional American city, Main Street was a place with an aesthetic value, of intuitively conceivable dimensions, with a mixture of functions and with a sense of place, the authentic soul of the city. In greater detail, the following considerations can be taken into account:

1. In many cities, good visual order has been replaced by visual chaos, created by commercial signage and the infrastructure. The result is the loss of identity and image. Conversely, through visual order, individuals gain information as to the places and references that allow them to satisfy their needs. In addition, it generates a sensation of pleasure and rhythm. The importance of visual order and the role that parks have played in the establishment of their value is observed, for example, in International Drive in Orlando. Whereas in the area of the city it is characterized by congestion and chaos, in the area of Orange County this same way is free of advertisements and infrastructure. The reason is the adhesion, in this sector, to the standards aspired to by Disney in the planning of the

public thoroughfare. Universal Studios, however, due to its expansion from its present emplacement towards the International Drive area, is managing urban aesthetics improvement programmes with the International Drive Chamber of Commerce.

2.   Faced with the generalization of the automobile, shopping malls and the horrors of urban redevelopment and improvement programmes during the 1950s and 1960s, theme parks highlight the fact that the size of human settlements is fundamental from an urbanistic point of view. From the present perspective, Disneyland was a notorious gamble in that it proposed the pedestrian use of space at a time when the automobile was king in the USA. According to Dunlop (1996), today it represents the potential for change that the Americans would like and has served as a source of inspiration both for the renewal of the urban centres of small localities, such as dozens of shopping malls throughout the USA. In any case, the domination of the automobile has led to the loss of significance for public places such as streets and squares to the extent that they have lost their ability to become places for relating to one another.

3.   The organization of space in Main Street contrasts with the idea that the zonification that is common in the urbanistic practices at the time of the suburban expansion has given rise to the generation of places lacking identity and the capacity for relations. Contrarily, readopting the European style of urban centre – which is still maintained today in spite of inevitable peri-urban expansion – suggests the mixture of uses in just one space and, even, in one single building as a solution to relational problems.

4.   Theme parks can be characterized as areas of control: not only of the processes that guide the patterns for the entertainment of their visitors–users but also of the social dynamics in which they develop. The visitors constitute part of the product that they themselves consume and, therefore, their characteristics and behaviour matter to the park operators. The idea that the urban spaces must be safe has had a multitude of derivations in the dynamics of the urban development of developed and, even, less developed countries. The most radical has been the creation of exclusive communities segregated by security systems from their neighbouring areas. Softer strategies of control have been implemented by numerous improvement and redevelopment organizations of city centres, among others the Business Improvement District of Times Square in New York.

5.   Theme parks usually have architectural programmes in which the buildings and facilities are ordered in relation to one another with the idea of shaping a place as a whole. The aim of this is to create the very sense of the place, not just recreating a thematic script but attempting to create identification between the function carried out and its form and location in space. It is due to all of the above that parks' plans include criteria and proposals that tend to entertain the possibility that parks may work as public places: that is to say, places with which the users–visitors establish a relationship of empathy and of identification beyond the proposal emanating from the offices of the designers.

On the basis of the experience of the USA, parks can be characterized, therefore, as places that allow, though not classically, the collective interaction of their visitors–users – places, moreover, that, in the style suggested by Jerde, aim to have a sense of place. So, despite there not being a sense of collective memory among all visitors to the park at any given moment, there does exist among them the illusion of having the ability to get access to it. To do so, collective memory is replaced by corporate identification. Parks and their leisure surroundings appear, in this context, as illustrations of what could be a comfortable urban form and they symbolize the struggle against the tyranny of the private automobile and the sense of place. However, they introduce, as we shall see later on, a crucial confusion between place and market. In addition, despite the differences of context, such pretensions are exported by the parks in their dynamics of global expansion towards Europe, Asia and other parts of the world. The idea that, from the point of view of its structure, a park should be a dense, pedestrian area, apt for interaction and with a sense of place is reaffirmed when North American consultants, professionals and tourists apply the concept to describe the Rambla of Barcelona. A theme park is not, therefore, merely a question of thematic aspects but also of form and function. What is interesting to underline, therefore, is that, when generalizing territorially, parks do not just export a model of entertainment but also the model of a town: or, more appropriately worded, an alternative to the urban problem of the North American society.

Things being as they are, parks reach Europe and Asia with this twofold condition: not just as places of fantasy and entertainment but also as ordered spaces of dimensions that are acceptable to the human experience – places that are capable of providing an experience of quality public use and, as such, 'mock' towns that can manage to occasionally and momentarily substitute for the 'real' public experience (Darling, 1978). Now, it should not be forgotten that, despite appearing to be a public place, as Stern (1992) discussed, parks provide good spaces only for those who pay for them. Only in this case does a park satisfy a need unfulfilled in everyday life: a need that is decreasingly available in the places where we live, that of being safe and at ease, even among strangers in a public place, 'to have a sense of a town or a city, to have a choice and variety'. This is one of the keys of parks' success and, of course, one of their limitations – as we shall see in the next section. Their contributions to urban questions, both from the point of view of being a pure form of a city for consumption and from the point of view of their innovations concerning urban design, must be understood, therefore, from the perspective of the context in which they appear.

Beyond what their progressive implantation demonstrates, the success of their procedures can be observed to the extent that, both in the USA and in Europe and Asia, 'history that haunts our landscapes is being aestheticized, and at the same time desocialized and artificialized' (Augé, 1995). As Augé (1995) says, 'our towns have been turning into museums (restored, exposed and floodlit monuments, listed areas, pedestrian precincts), while at the same time bypasses, motorways, high-speed trains and one-way systems have made it unnecessary for us to linger in them'. In this way, just as analysts such as Eco and Baudrillard acknowledge, 'the fictitious becomes reality' and reality tends to imitate the imitation. This is what is happening with numerous historical centres in Europe, where the preservation of the constructed landscape dominates the use of the urban functions, or with the transformation into a museum of rural authenticity in many Asian parks such as the Korean Folk Village or Miniature Park, near Jakarta, or with the creation of entire cities that attempt to emulate the aesthetic criteria and urban *mise-en-scène* typical of parks such as Seaside in Florida. The idea of social harmony that presides over any of these activities becomes magnified by their own urban structure. Needless to say, on the other hand, theme parks are becoming points of reference for entire cities, the most extreme case being Las Vegas. Also, they are having a direct influence on the very transformation of contemporary post-industrial cities into complex places for leisure and recreation (Hannigan, 1998).

On the basis of these observations it may be held that theme parks play a role in the dynamics of social construction of urban space. Ariès (2002, 177) says, concerning this, that parks are the forerunners of the cities of the future, places where, moreover, tensions are visually articulated between what is public and private, what is global and what is local and the market and the place. However, an important aspect is that parks are the product of a corporation whose aim is to make people's lives as pleasurable as possible and this is why everything must be clean, efficient, attractive and friendly. Conversely, the city is the product of several agents, which, via their interactions, determine its form and function. Each agent is responsible for a part of the whole. What is fascinating is that parks idealize urban space and by doing so create a new ideal of public space. The question to ask oneself is if, with this, parks render irrelevant all that which lies outside them or, conversely, their realizations are just that, an ideal. In the end, as we shall see in the next section, what is important is not the lessons but the problems, the limitations and the shortcomings of the real world to achieve the same results. In short, as Sorkin (1992a) maintains, theme parks and, along with them, the corporate spaces that are developed around them invoke 'an urbanism without producing a city. Rather, it produces a kind of aura-stripped hypercity, a city with billions of citizens (all who would consume) but no residents.'

Finally, it must be said, paraphrasing the considerations expressed by Mullins (1991, 326) with regard to tourist towns, that the parks and the corporate spaces surrounding them are relevant from the point of view of the history of urbanism because they 'represent a new and extraordinary form of urbanization because they are cities built solely for consumption'. Thus, whereas the processes of mass urbanization that occurred during the last centuries took place in general in response to production and commercial needs, tourist areas, and among them parks, emerge as places strictly for consumption: in addition, consumption for relaxation, recreation and amusement. It is not the consumption associated with basic needs, such as housing, education or health. It cannot be forgotten, in short, that parks allow one to think of leisure and tourism as catalysts of urban processes to date unknown. The clearest urban expression of the mass consumption of leisure lies in the order and architecture of the theme parks.

6.4. The Scope of Spatial Innovation

The application of proposals made by theme parks on urbanism and spatial planning has a lot to do with individuals' social and political choices and the answers that corporate capitalism gives to collective needs. Beyond concepts and formal and design instruments, it cannot be forgotten that underlying such proposals are some fundamental questions regarding the way in which societies are organized in order to produce space. From this perspective, it is indispensable to approach two key subjects in respect of the implications of the generalization of the social production of space as with parks: in the first place, the social and collective sense of the processes of urban development and, secondly, the ability of the 'new' spaces (pertaining to total design, if they allow themselves to be so classified) to generate collective identity. There is no need to say that all of these questions, which set limits to the suitability of parks as development models, are also aspects which the creators and planners of parks themselves have considered.

A fundamental consideration when replying to these questions is that the urban nature of parks is fictitious. As fundamental as their condition of mock city is that, though maintaining a public usage and imitating the urban space in its forms, a theme park is a private conception and under private management. It is a space, in short, which, according to Augé (1995), cannot be defined by the identity or by the relationships struck up by its inhabitants but by the absence of memory and of society. Conceptually, parks refer to the idea of the privatization of development and to the identification of the citizen with the consumer. This is, in fact, a growing identification and a tendency that appears irreversible nowadays. This is so much so that, as García Canclini (1995, 29) states, in today's society:

> men and women perceive that many typical questions of citizens – where do I belong and what rights does this give me, how can I get informed, who represents my interests – are answered more through the private consumption of goods and of the mass media than through the abstract rules of democracy or collective participation in public spaces.

While the citizens languish, the territory fills with corporate places for consumerism, theme parks, holiday resorts, heritage centres or malls. But, to continue with a question inspired by García Canclini (1995): are these places not becoming significant places for the new generations that mark them, that utilize them and include them in their own history? This is certainly a difficult question to answer.

6.4.1. The privatization of development and the challenge of the public use of space

When, as in the case of Disney, the operators of theme parks undertake the development of residential areas, it is not just that the parks become referents for urban planning, but they themselves make tangible, material proposals for development. The most relevant case in this respect – which will be studied below as an illustration – is the building of the town of Celebration in Orlando by Disney in 1994. However, let it be said as of this moment that the phenomenon is not exclusive to the USA or to Disney. Many parks around the world have realizations or plans that include the idea of creating residential urban areas. Needless to say, in this sense, that Celebration was sold in 2004 by The Celebration Company, a subsidiary of the Walt Disney Company, to Lexin Capital, a New York investment firm that owns and operates residential and commercial developments in various USA markets, including Florida and Washington DC.

In the case of Orlando, a series of laws dating from 1967 made by the state of Florida allowed Disney to dispose of its own unit of government, the Reedy Creek Improvement District (RCID), from the start. The reason was Disney's interest in directly intervening in the creation of a town. It is to this intention of Walt Disney himself to which reference needs to be made in order to understand the development of Celebration. It has already been indicated that, when Walt Disney presented his project in Florida, not only did he intend to build a theme park and ensure the control and profits of neighbouring entrepreneurial activity but he also wanted to contribute solutions to the problems that pressed the urban society of North America. Epcot (Experimental Prototype Community of Tomorrow) was to be the materialization of this initiative: a community of some 20,000 people that was completely regulated, with infrastructures controlled by a central system and strict codes of conduct. In his last promotional film produced before his death, he described Epcot as 'a new model of a city', which could influence the shape of urban life in the future (cited in Rebori, 1993). Epcot was to be a town for 20,000 permanent residents, of radial design, whose downtown was made of glass buildings, residential areas, manufacturing areas and cultural districts connected by an ultra-modern transport system. It would show the latest technology of the home and city and would not give cause for marginality. Visitors would pay to see it (Fjellman, 1992, 155).

However, according to Zukin (1991), the company considered that the construction of a residential community meant too much responsibility. Moreover, part of the technology that Disney would have required to materialize its plan was not yet available at the end of the 1960s or it was too expensive even in the event that other industrial corporations were to sponsor Disney for the building and fitting of specific constructions. Finally, an early incursion by Disney into property at Lake Buenavista, which did not work well due to misunderstandings between the permanent and the holidaying residents, discouraged the project. Without a doubt, on the other hand, the death of Walt Disney meant that the plans for Epcot were totally reconsidered and that the project was carried out in the easiest way for the company, a theme park (in spite of having been, on the other hand, the main justification for the creation of the RCID). None the less, Walt Disney's basic ideas for Epcot were retained by Michael Eisner and considered when, in the 1980s, the company embarked on an important process of diversification and wished to take advantage of its experience in the design of spaces, the management of groups, transport and entertainment. It is in this context that the development projects for hotels, resorts, malls and office buildings on the property in Orlando multiplied, with the Disney Development Company being created specifically for this purpose.

On the other hand, and despite being less well known, it is interesting to note that, parallel to the development of their properties and leisure complexes and the commissioning of prestigious architects for their buildings, as of the 1980s the Disney company became committed to projects that were not directly linked to its existing parks and gained experience in the 'real' world. It developed consultancy projects like the Johnson Space Center in Houston and the Gene Autry Western Heritage Museum in Los Angeles (Warren, 1994) and advised cities such as Long Beach, Seattle and Anaheim. Disney offered knowledge and know-how on matters such as theming, merchandising, traffic and the management of the masses. Paradoxically, Disney offered solutions which the company had experienced inside its parks for problems that occurred outside, even when, outside its own parks like Disneyland in Anaheim, it had been unable to control these very problems. With these initiatives, Disney once again took up in the 1980s practices with regard to which it already had experience, although it had developed less intensely, due to its participation as a consultant for the Universal Exposition of New York in 1964 and the solution to Las Vegas's traffic problems with a monorail in 1960.

In this context, Michael Eisner took up Disney's idea of creating a community, though taking another look at its bases. Eisner's aim can be summed up as creating 'a community of the future with yesterday's values' (cited in Rebori, 1993). This was Celebration: a city for 20,000 residents designed in 1988 in accordance with the principles of traditional urbanism, which Disney had revived in its Main Streets, and inaugurated in 1996 (see a description of the project in Didier, 1999). A pedestrian town with a coherent structure of streets and squares that avoid 'sprawl', there are no fences. It is not a closed community like those that are distorting urban revitalization in the USA. There is no corporate police. There are, on the other hand, mixed uses of space and of buildings, for example apartments over the shops in Main Street.

Celebration was the materialization of the aesthetic and ethical idea of what a city should be like according to Disney ideology. It is an extraordinarily pleasant place, with a density and blend of functions at the points of greatest hierarchy and centrality. It seeks its 'false' identity in the reproduction of architectural styles for residents' buildings and in the prestigious architectural firms for the public buildings such as the post office and the cinema. It attempts to create an atmosphere of a better life than the one lived in conventional suburban developments, but also better than that of similar developments of closed communities that have proliferated. Calm streets lined with trees, free of advertising hoardings, bicycles without padlocks, vast areas of open spaces in the form of parks, communal buildings, squares and Neighborough Electric Vehicles (electric cars) to get around the neighbourhood are details which illustrate the result of Disney's proposal of total design for urban applications. The question to be asked, however, is whether Celebration is a model for urban renovation schools such as New Urbanism would have it, or whether it represents, precisely, the failure of real urban America. The appreciation by Ibelings (1998, 77) is droll in this regard, when he states that 'Celebration is a reanimation of the ideal American suburb in a form that never existed anywhere . . . but which strikes everybody as familiar.' It is the result, once again, of the application of the utilities of parks to the total design, in this case, of a town (Charmes, 2005).

In material terms, Celebration can be defined fundamentally as a pedestrian environment that aims to rediscover the civic life of 50 years ago. Thus, functional activities such as garages are located behind houses. The fronts are meeting places, for riding a bicycle or for walking. However, the most up-to-date information technology has been incorporated, computerized systems that make homes 'smart'. From a social point of view, the residents in Celebration acquire, in fact, not just a house but also a 'lifestyle package' when purchasing their home. They customize their choice with a greater or lesser presence of technology, the type of atmosphere they wish to experience (grid style, suburban, cul-de-sac or curving streets) or the format of the house. The project took into account the future development of common institutions of reference that would have to be developed based on community projects, willingness or the proprietors' commitment. In this sense, the project took into account the design of the means to avoid Disney's well-known inability to give individuals the capacity to take decisions: not just for the creation of a sense of place but also for the purposes of establishing a community. For this, the project understood that a town is not just its structure and design (which is what Disney highlights) but also the relationships that are established among its citizens and with its institutions (Rebori, 1993). From this perspective, Celebration attempted to get reasonably close to reality. To solve matters like the vote and issues concerning social participation, Disney even detached from its field of management the RCID, 5150 acres that were returned to the jurisdiction of Osceola County.

Celebration represented the culmination of Walt Disney's dream, a completely controlled, private urban community, conceived on the basis of values like the family and enterprise with an absence of problems of ethnic and class differences (Archer, 1997). Paradoxically, Celebration strived to be a model of authenticity consciously created by 'the founder company of illusion', a model of public space designed from the depths of capitalism, an attempt to solve urban life returning to the social bases of the concept of a community by means of the construction of a panoptic system, a proposal of a town that is based on the purchase by its residents of a branded lifestyle (see some of these criticisms in Klein, 1999, and Ariès, 2002). Nevertheless, despite the importance that Celebration had as a Disney idea and the role it played as a company property and real estate project, as of 2004, Celebration was not a Disney asset. On the other hand, in spite of any criticism, since all brands openly imitated Disney, their existence should not be disdained. In fact, despite her critical approach to what she calls 'branded cities', Naomi Klein (1999, 155) says that:

> though wired with every modern technology and convenience, Celebration is less futurism than homage, an idealized re-creation of the liveable America that existed before malls, big-box sprawls, freeways, amusement parks and mass commercialization. Oddly enough, Celebration is not even a sales vehicle for Mickey Mouse licensed products; it is, in contemporary terms, an almost Disney-free town – no doubt the only one left in America. In other words, when Disney finally reached its fully enclosed, synergized, self-sufficient space, it chose to create a pre-Disneyfied world – its calm, understated aesthetics and the antithesis of the cartoon world for sale down the freeway at Disney World.

Even so, although Celebration has helped popularity to be gained by the neo-traditional current of New Urbanism, which fights against suburban automobile-oriented developments and whose principles are being applied in the renovation of the urban fabric and buildings of American town and city centres, it is an urban artefact that pertains to the same category as City Walk. Though very different from the 'common interest urbanisations' expressly designed with walls, fences and entrance doors to restrict access, a fundamental ambiguity exists as regards its approach, which is fittingly reported by Scully (1996): 'if towns need the presence of indigent poor as well as of physically and mentally unfortunate citizens in order to sustain instincts of decent humanity in everyone else, how can such factors be designed in?' In short, Celebration looks like traditional towns in form and reminds its inhabitants as to the values of urbanity even if they have purchased not just a house but a whole lifestyle. However, the less fortunate members of society continue to live in half-destroyed towns and cities.

The sovereignty of things public disappears, then, around Celebration. Now, it cannot be forgotten that Celebration is no exception. What happened with this has become generalized since the 1980s in the USA and the 1990s in Europe and Asia. The processes of converting space into a good have multiplied, sometimes even with the drive of a public authority which is increasingly more directed at practices of public enterprise. Thus, society lives and relates in branded buildings and spaces. This is so much so that, in his analysis of New York and Tokyo, Cybriwsky (1999) establishes the following common trends regarding the design of public spaces and the changing behaviour as to how they are used. He takes as places for study Times Square, South Street Seaport and Battery Park City in New York and Yebisu Garden Place, Teleport-Daiba, Makuhari

New Town and Minato-Mirai 21 in Tokyo–Yokohama. His observations indicate:

1. The growing privatization of spaces which at the time were clearly in the public domain.
2. A growing watch over public spaces and controlled access in order to improve security.
3. The increasing use of designs that use simulations in theme park style and the rupture of connections with local history and geography.

What is happening? As Rifkin (2000, 207) indicates, the activities that used to take place in the public arena have shifted to private areas and have become a good for sale. Feasts, festivals, parades, ceremonies, sports and entertainment are better in private places than in that common cultural good, the public arena, an open space where people got together, communicated and were committed in cultural matters. 'In short, public space has changed from a meeting place, the heart of social life, into a highly regulated domain', where every individual demands safety and security (Ibelings, 1998, 66). If until then public spaces satisfied the social needs for relations of a private nature, today it is private areas that 'put on sale' the satisfaction of the private needs of leisure time. The places – squares and streets – have met a competitor, markets – malls, activity parks and, of course, theme parks. That is well generalized in the USA but not solely there. It is no coincidence, therefore, that in 1984 architect Charles Moore wrote an article in the Yale architecture journal *Perspecta* whose title said, 'You Have to Pay for the Public Life' (cited in Rebori 1993). This is what authors such as Mackenzie (1994) have denominated privatopia: a progressive process of social, economic and political dislocation provoked by the creation of spaces – territories – voluntarily cut off from their surroundings. 'Entire neighbourhoods, new cities in poor and rich countries respond to these characteristics, each with its own institutions, specific social control mechanisms, private law enforcement forces, a well delimited environment' (Nogué and Vicente, 2001, 138–139).

Further, following the evaluation made by Foglesong (n.d.) of Walt Disney World as a case of privatized urban development with over 20 years' existence, he comes to the following conclusions concerning the dynamics of privatization that are becoming generalized:

- It makes an efficacious urbanism policy possible.
- It facilitates political strategies of economic growth.
- It imposes development costs on the outside public.
- It reduces the capacity of the local public sector to plan growth.
- It causes contrary reactions when the problem of the management of growth becomes manifest.
- It gradually erodes power relations.

According to Sorkin (1992a), there are three characteristics that distinguish this new situation. The first is the disappearance of all stable relationships between things urban and the physical geography and local culture, the loss of specific links with the space. The second is the obsession with security and the proliferation of surveillance systems and segregation. The third is the domination of simulations of the past as a replacement for the present and as a way of giving urban value to the new. Such dynamics recur in a diversity of territorial and cultural contexts. This is shown, for example, by the planning – since the 1980s – of a number of projects for theme parks as a development strategy in Malaysia. Cartier (1998) examines, in this respect, the evolution of tourist activity in the city and the state of Melaka, from its origins in the attraction of the cultural landscapes associated with the port tradition of Malaca on the Malay peninsula until the development of new capital-intensive tourist activities, such as, in particular, golf resorts, theme parks and ecotourism parks. Such projects develop in parallel with the building and development of large transport infrastructures, once protection programmes and the turning of historic heritage sites into museums has been undertaken. That is due to the fact that, from the Malaysian state's point of view, 'the conservation status of historic landscapes limits their development potential and, in the era of megadevelopment projects, marginalises their significance in the state's tourism profile'. In fact, the development of theme park projects 'is also a strategy by which to engage in related property development schemes'. Thus, for example, the largest-scale project, Baba Nonya Heritage Village, 'blends the leisure theme directly into a residential development and so blurs the distinction between home and tourism, substituting authentic landscapes of Melaka town with themed copies'.

6.4.2. The invention of the landscape and the challenge of the identity of the territory

The processes of privatizing urban development are increasingly more manifest in all societies. In addition to segregation between groups and the loss of citizens' ability to intervene, privatization also involves the spatial fragmentation and the detachment of the urban pieces from the territory where they are implanted. In the case of parks, their simple spatial representation, viewing them through either aerial photographs or satellite images, already expresses their isolation and relative discontinuity with their surrounding areas as a distinguishing feature of territorial character. As Eyssartel and Rochette (1992) describe, what is around them is 'the often amorphous ordering of suburban confines, crossed by large communications axes. Some of them end up at the park as if this were their sole purpose. Inside, dense, complex order.'

This is why the analysis of the urbanism of parks leads one to ponder whether it may be considered that, with regard to invented landscapes, they generate new territorial identities. In fact, in spite of the lack of heritage, parks are concerned, as we have already seen, with proposing an identity – via their narrative – for the area they organize. On the other hand, parks' technical capacity to create 'spaces with contents' has been transferred to the rest of the area both in the creation of new places and as regards the valorization of pre-existing historical places (Montpetit, 1993). Now, real experience demonstrates that both the one and the other processes have their limits: the limits that have been imposed by citizens' intervention in the dynamics of development and the different consideration the concept of 'identity' has for one person and another. In simple terms, 'identity' equals the 'historical, social and environmental inertia' of the place in the case of the citizens who try to intervene in the development processes and, contrarily, equals 'structuring argumental content' in the case of the corporations that are trying to develop urban fabrics in their corporate spaces.

Augé (1995) considers theme parks as places to be classified as 'non-places'. According to his characterization, 'non-places' are places that that are built in relation to purposes such as transport, trade and leisure, which, unlike anthropological places, which create organic social relations, only generate solitary contractuality. They are places whose peculiarity is that they are defined partly by the words and texts they offer us:

> their 'instructions for use, which may be prescriptive ('take right-hand lane'), prohibitive ('no smoking') or informative ('you are now entering the Beaujolais region'). Sometimes these are couched in more or less explicit and codified ideograms (or road signs, maps and tourists guides), sometimes in ordinary language.
>
> (Augé, 1995, 96)

The differences between places and 'non-places' are, for Augé, fundamentally three. The 'non-places' cannot be considered as identifying, relational and historical places. That means that they are places for which people feel no vernacular attachment, that appeal directly to the conscience of each individual through the experiences they propose and which present themselves as a text that recalls the dominant collective imaginary.

The traditional landscape is the result of the cultural projection of a society in a certain space in all its material, spiritual, ideological and symbolic dimensions and incarnates the experience and aspirations of societies (Nogué, 2000). Conversely, parks' 'invented' landscape is, despite the differences that may be seen between some and others, an indication of universal equivalence in which each place becomes a destination and each destination can be in any place (Sorkin, 1992a). The function of one and the other is different. That of parks is a cosmology which, as all cosmologies, 'produces effects of recognition'. The visitor knows how to 'read' the landscape because it corresponds with an imaginary that is 'experienced' in accordance with the usual protocols of consumption. If in parks the landscape becomes a good, perhaps the reflection that should be made as to their identity is precisely on the basis of the question as to whether society can imaginatively reconquer consumption as a place of cognitive value, useful for thinking and acting significatively, refreshingly, in social life – as García Canclini (1995, 71) proposes.

What implications does this reconquest have in the context of the progressive invention of landscapes even outside the parks? In other words, how can the spatial innovations proposed and popularized by parks be socially interpreted when, on the one hand, corporate privatization of space even for public use is condemned and, on the other hand, there is reproach for new towns or residential, commercial or leisure areas that do not offer, because they have not designed it, the space for the concentration of cafes, hotels and businesses that are typical of traditional squares and urban centres. Moreover, how can the replica of the mock be conceptualized, of the 'supposedly' identity-less space, whether it is the reproduction Europa Park makes of Walt Disney World on the Alsatian border (with over 3 million visitors a year) or, in Los Angeles, the replica of Rodeo Drive just a few blocks from the 'supposedly' authentic street? In short, how can we conceptualize, from this analytical perspective, the controversy surrounding the urban renewal of Times Square in New York? (See Zukin, 1995, and Berman, 1997, for further information on this.)

In short, today's practices of urban development and the preservation of heritage are applying the creative practice of the parks to the logic of the creation of places, because it is not just a question of the peripheral creation of malls or of resorts: it is also a question of the commercial reconversion of the historical centres. Augé (1995) is explicit in this regard when he states, for the case of France, that:

> every settlement aspires to be the centre of a significant space and of at least one specific activity . . . Every town or village not of recent origin lays public claim to its history, displaying it to the passing motorist on a series of signboards which add up to a sort of 'business card'. Making the historical context explicit in this way, which in fact is quite a recent practice, coincides with a reorganization of space (the creation of bypasses and main motorway routes avoiding towns) that tends, inversely, to short-circuit the historical context by avoiding the monuments that embody it . . . The dated monument is cited as a proof of authenticity which ought in itself to arouse interest: a gap is opened up between the landscape's present and the past to which it alludes. The allusion to the past complicates the present.

On this basis, what there may be is the artificial recuperation of constructions and structures with no function. The result is the creation of environments which, in spite of being supposedly real and having their identity, are scenographically inauthentic, though economically viable.

This is the case, for example, of the Singapore River thematic zone, one of the 11 thematic zones identified by the Singapore Tourism Board that are the object of tourist promotion. Savage *et al.* (2004, 224) insist that concern exists that modernization and tourism may suppress:

> the River's place uniqueness as it changes into a waterfront not unlike those found in many Western cities. It is vital that specific policies are put in place to ensure that indigenous (or 'local') landscape elements of thematic areas like Singapore River do not give way to the modern (often equated with the 'global') if Singapore is to have a sustainable urban tourism programme.

There are concerns that were already noted by Chang (2000) in an article significantly entitled 'theming cities, taming places', which deals with the case of the historical district of Little India, also in Singapore. In this case, the tourist use and the theming of the space produced a decline in traditional Indian activities, displacement of the local communities and simplification of the image of their own identity. Nevertheless, on the other hand, it has generated, as a reaction, a new dynamics of the reassertion of the identity of the Indian community.

Basically what there may be is, as Ibelings (1998, 65) points out, a paradox. Large parts of the world today are easily conceivable and easily visited, at least for people of developed societies. However, this is only possible with a fleeting visit that does not muster up any bonds of affinity, like those that are produced when one 'is' from a place or 'has a relationship' with the people of that place. The answer is the preparation of the places to respond to the visitors' expectations. Parks have done so by inventing themselves as 'worlds apart'. When their techniques are transferred 'outside' their walls, what there is is the need to create identities that are adapted to the needs of visits: identities that could be denominated phenotypic (as opposed to genotypic). This context, furthermore, is supported by the fact that, even in the 'real' world, that is to say, outside the parks, the tourist accepts and celebrates inauthenticity. As Nogué (2000) indicates:

> the tourist is perfectly aware of the unreal component of the tourist experience . . . We shall have to seriously consider, in this new scenario, what kind of territorial identities we will be capable of creating and what landscapes-as-symbols will act as the drive belt between the past, the present and the future.

The limits are set by society and its stakeholders. As an example of this, below are two cases of landscape touristic and thematic reinvention which have been contested by the local populations. The first concerns the Disney company and refers to the ability of the citizens of Seattle to paralyse a proposal made by the corporation, which aimed, not just to reinvent the landscape of the town but also, by doing this, to change its identity. The second refers to the theming of patrimonial values as a strategy for the development of tourism in Singapore and is the crux of the debate on the growing 'commodification' of authenticity in Asia.

As Warren (1994) states, Disney arrived in Seattle in order to advise as to the reconversion of the Seattle Center. This ageing civic and entertainment area had been built on the occasion of the 1962 universal exposition. Since then, it had become a heterogeneous public place, with a science museum, opera, sports facilities, gardens, open-air concert areas and amusements. Disney had, at the end of the 1950s, already acted as consultant for the shaping of the place for the development of the exposition. In the 1980s, both the local authorities and the management of the Seattle Center considered that Disney could again help them to reformulate the area. For this, Disney designed a project which was to become its first and biggest incursion into town planning outside Disney property. In fact, Disney not only offered a proposal to redesign the landscape but also the development, financing and operations. Negotiations began in 1986. Three years later, and following a promising start, Disney abandoned the project. There were two fundamental reasons: (i) Disney's inability to create designs for the Seattle Center that came into line with the residents' wishes and needs; and (ii) Disney's apparent lack of willingness to remedy this situation by seeking the opinion, or taking it on board when offered, of local agents.

Discussions started in Seattle by its residents' organizations hinged around the adequacy of the Disney designs for the planning of their public spaces. Their dissatisfaction with Disney began even prior to knowing precisely what Disney was proposing for the Seattle Center. When Disney presented three alternatives, this just led to further arguments and they received criticism from all angles, especially for their dysfunctionality, lack of attractiveness and the inexpressiveness of Seattle's social and ethnic diversity and, therefore, of its character. In addition, the existing buildings in the 30 ha of the Center had to be, for all three alternatives, demolished. The disappointment with Disney's plans turned into rage. Disney again raised one of the plans but the population of Seattle, in spite of the commissioning costing the town half a million dollars, continued to be irrevocably disenchanted with the proposed 'design'. Furthermore, the development of the plan did not cost the $60 million that had initially been quoted and considered assumable but $335 million. This forced the town to charge an entrance fee to the precinct in order to finance its development.

The Seattle Center was finally renovated without Disney. Its current configuration, unlike what Disney had proposed, has incorporated the efforts of the numerous architects, planners, designers and other citizens that explicitly rejected the Disney project, considering it as being autocratic and forced from without. The principal cause for opposition was that the proposals did not manage to capture the local culture and suitably incorporate the ethnic diversity of the town's social groups. The end result has preserved the character of the centre, the one so loved by its inhabitants, sometimes chaotic and comprising groups ranging from the homeless to opera fans, without this reducing the possibilities of a middle class which is the norm. In the words of one homeless person who filled in a questionnaire during the planning process, it can be summed up in the following way: 'Thank you for having me and other individuals to be part of the [Seattle] Center' (cited in Warren, 1994).

Similarly, in Singapore, a compulsory reference in this debate is the transformation of the historical Haw Par Villa, a garden that was conceived in 1937 with the aim of presenting Singapore's cultural diversity, into a theme park in the 1990s after it was purchased by the government of Singapore in 1985. Today the park – named Dragon World – introduces itself as 'the only Chinese mythological theme park in the world'. Yeoh and Teo (1996) explain that this transformation is coherent with the emphasis on developing 'new and 'different' modes of commodified leisure pursuits for Singaporeans and tourists. The remaking of Haw Par Villa drew upon the old moral landscape of Chinese myths and legends, but embellished these with 'new cultural elements enhanced by the possibilities and plausibility of technological innovations'. The park packages and reinvents local tradition and discloses that 'culture, like any other commodity, can be transferred, transplanted, miniaturised and embellished to create landscapes of spectacle'. The transformation of the gardens into a theme park in fact symbolized the conversion of 'an eccentric folk icon into a standardised theme park that illustrated the "Asian way" with modern technology' (Oakes, 1998). This is so much so that the transformation of the park was considered an example of 'American cultural imperialism in Oriental disguise'. The process also meant the end of free access to the traditional gardens and the transformation of the original landscape.

Besides the fact that the park has not enjoyed the success expected of it, it is true that its development strengthens the discourse concerning modernization in Asia and, particularly, the need to preserve cultural identity in a context of globalization. Thus, after its Disneyization, huge financial losses were incurred and the company rethought its strategy. Finally, Dragon World 'reverted to the idiosyncratic landscape that the original owner had designed it to be and which Singaporeans had valued because of the moral lessons the park had offered to the local people' (Teo and Yeoh, 2001). In the same way, in Asia some parks become the vehicle for the celebration of local festivities. This is the case in the Malay Village and in the Chinese Garden in Singapore.

So Xie and Wall's (2003, 112) conclusion can be applied to what has happened in Singapore regarding the use of identifying elements for the development of tourist attractions. According to them, 'commodification of cultural expressions can be interpreted as a means of marking identity and a step in the finding of the true self through the appropriation of heritage'. It seems distinctive of these dynamics that modernization, 'rather than constituting a straight path ahead, instead assumes a more complex form in which the global is tailored to the local and vice versa'. In this way, 'rather than completely undermine and replace local cultures', identification is possible of a 'global trend towards "staged" and "reconstructed" authenticity, wherein traditional crafts, dances, foods etc, are artificially preserved and reconstructed'. Within the Asian area, it is an especially significant process in multi-ethnic states like Indonesia, Malaysia or Singapore (Sofield, 2001). At the heart of this dynamic lies a continuum of paradoxes that moves, as Swain (1989) has shown for the case of the folk villages of Hainan in China, though not solely, between the following opposite poles: spontaneity versus commercialism; economic development versus cultural preservation; cultural evolution versus conversion into a museum; ethnic autonomy versus state regulation; and mass tourism versus sustainable cultural development. More particularly, for the case of Asia, Teo and Yeoh (2001) hold, along these same lines that 'while Southeast Asian theme parks may appear to be commercially viable and internationally appealing, and akin to the universal Disney product, they also communicate and respond to the various impulses of what is often construed as "local"'.

Case 11. The Creation of a Leisure Destination in Dubai

Dubailand is an entertainment complex under development in Dubai located along the Emirates Road and the Dubai–Al Ain Road, which will provide easy access from Abu Dhabi, Al Ain, Dubai and Sharjah. It will be located 60 min from Abu Dhabi, 10 min from Dubai Airport and 20 min from Sharjah. Dubailand is the vision of Dubai's Sheikh Mohammed bin Rashid Al Maktoum. It is managed by the Dubai Development and Investment Authority (DDIA) to secure Dubai as the premier tourist destination for the Middle East. The goal of Dubailand is to attract 15 million tourists to Dubai by 2010, not only from surrounding countries but also from Europe and Asia. Dubai now receives close to 6 million tourists a year, although it is one of the growing destinations according to figures from the World Tourism Organization.

Dubailand is being created to appeal to the widest audience of tourists, covering all age groups, nationalities and activities. On a longer-term basis, Dubailand is seen as a way to phase out Dubai's dependence on oil revenues by establishing a sustainable economy through higher value-added services. The venture is expected to attract approximately 200,000 visitors daily and cost $20 billion. The project is the same size as the developed area of Singapore, and Dubai as a destination can be compared nowadays with Orlando or Las Vegas because of its fantastical and unique architecture. Currently, hotels – including the famous Burj Al Arab – are some of the most luxurious in the world. Moreover, sumptuous shopping malls are attracting tourist consumers, and world-class events like the Dubai Shopping Festival, first held in 1996, are supporting a large influx of people. In 1989 the Dubai Desert Classic, a PGA tour tournament, teed off and in 1996 the Dubai World Cup was inaugurated, the world's richest horse race. In 2001, adjacent to what is today the Dubailand site, construction of the Palms got under way, the world's largest man-made islands, comprising residences, entertainment venues and hotels visible from space. The development of a second artificial island complex called the World has also been started (see http://www.dubailand.ae).

The Dubailand project was officially announced in 2003. Dubailand includes 45 mega-projects and 200 sub-projects. On completion, Dubailand will be twice the size of Walt Disney World in Florida, making it the biggest theme/amusement park in the world. Dubailand is being built in four phases, each of which will take 5 years. The first of the four phases, comprising the development of Dubailand, will be completed in early 2008, since the developers decided to extend the park by 50%, consequently postponing its completion date. Completion of the final phase is targeted for some time between 2015 and 2018. Dubailand is seen by its designers as a city and therefore, like a city, they expect it to continue to grow and develop beyond the four-phase plan. As its chief executive Salem Bin Dasmal points out, 'Dubailand is a brand new city' (Robathan, 2005). Nowadays, Dubailand is the biggest entertainment, leisure, tourism and urban project in process in the entire world. The development is also stimulated by the growth of Emirates, the airways carrier, and the construction of new airport facilities.

Dubailand LLC – a subsidiary of parent company Dubai Holdings – is funding infrastructure such as the roads, parking facilities, water and electricity for Dubailand. The land itself is being prepared and serviced by the government. Private investors and developers fund the individual projects – some of which are based on concepts developed by Dubailand – according to basic financial and attendance projections. Every project has a contractual obligation to be developed with certain quality, health and safety and environmental standards and within a certain time frame. According to the owners, in 2005, around 80% of phase I was sold to investors, with 19 projects capitalized. This private reaction towards the project has been positive and Dubai has exceeded the $4.9 billion private investment figure it expected for the entire project by collecting approximately $6 billion from the private sector for the first phase alone. Through the project, Dubai is giving leisure opportunities to an *ex novo* destination that is building a type of 'man-made, designed authenticity'. The strategy is conceived from the top, addressed to high value-added segments in a new kind of 'mass luxury' expectations and promoted on a worldwide scale. It shakes off all pre and post prejudices and conceptions. Dubai is going to build the biggest, the largest, the tallest and the most expensive in the leisure and entertainment industry. It is a fashionable brand and little concern has been expressed regarding its environmental, social and economic sustainability (Knipe, 2005).

The various projects being built in Dubailand have been categorized into six themed zones (Table 6.1) or worlds which focus on a different aspect of the Dubailand experience. These six separate worlds have been conceived to facilitate and to help manage the development, but they will probably merge.

Table 6.1. Planned theme zones in Dubailand (from Robathan, 2005).

Zone 1. Attractions and Experience World (13.9 km^2**)**
  The Attractions and Experience World will feature a critical mass of themed, large-scale attractions, using the latest technology for thrills and safety. Its largest theme park will act as an anchor, attracting visitors and encouraging the growth of visits to other attractions. It will contain a total of 16 projects (Aqua Dubai, Astrolab Resort, Aviation World, Snowdome (Dubai Sunny Mountain Ski Dome), Dubai Wheel, Dubailand Theme Park, Falcon City of Wonders, Fantasia, Giants World, the Global Village, the Islamic Culture and Science World, Kids World, Legends-Dubailand, Planetarium, Space and Science World, Tourism Park), several of them still at the concept stage.

Zone 2. Themed Leisure and Vacation World (29.7 km^2**)**
  The Themed Leisure and Vacation World will consist of appealing retreats designed to respond to the growing international demand for quality vacation village residences, resort hotels and wellness retreats. It will include several

Continued

Table 6.1. *Continued.*

fitness and stress-management-focused facilities and will offer unique creative concepts, such as themed resorts, providing visitors a chance to experience faraway exotic locales without leaving Dubailand. It will contain a total of six projects (Andalusian Resort and Spa, the Indian Theme Resort, LEMNOS Women's World, the Nubian Village, the Silver Street Resort, Thai Express Resort).

Zone 3. Eco-Tourism World (130 km²)

The Eco-Tourism World will comprise a series of nature- and desert-based attractions integrated within their desert parkland surrounds. Its experiential and cultural activities will have broad appeal and its vast number of exquisite and unique offerings will no doubt encourage long stays and repeat visits. It will contain a total of seven projects (Al Barari, Dubai Heritage Village, Life World, Pet Land, Safari Park, Sand Dune Hotel, Tropical Village) in around a third of Dubailand on the outside of the development.

Zone 4. Sports and Outdoor World (32.9 km²)

The Sports and Outdoor World will include a mix of sporting venues that will incorporate a dynamic programme of international rugby, cricket and other sports tournaments as well as extreme sports activities. It will contain a total of five projects (Dubai Autodrome and Business Park, Dubai Sports City, Extreme Sports World, Golf World, the Plantation Equestrian and Polo Club), four of which have been capitalized. Dubai Sports City is the anchor project, which will encompass four major stadiums set to host international events. Dubai golf city is a themed community with five designer 18-hole golf courses.

Zones 5 and 6. Downtown (1.8 km²) and Retail and Entertainment World (4.0 km²)

The Downtown, and the Retail and Entertainment World will be the gateway to Dubailand – a mixed destination offering a variety of retail, dining and entertainment facilities. It will feature popular family entertainment components such as cinemas, bowling, street entertainment, computer-based games centres, themed restaurants and nightclubs. As shopping is one of the essential activities undertaken by tourists on vacation, this world will provide a critical mass of retail facilities providing a wide variety of global brands, but also unique boutiques and discount stores. It includes the Mall of Arabia, which will be the world's largest shopping mall, a City Walk and the Great Dubai Wheel – the world's largest observation wheel. It will contain City of Arabia, Dubai Bazaar, Dubai Outlet City, Restaurant Complex, Teen World, Virtual Games World, including high-rise hotels and a dinosaur-themed theme park called Restless Planet, which will incorporate more than 1000 animatronic dinosaurs, artificial volcanoes and themed rides.

7 The Impact of Theme Parks

They are temples to modernity, our secular churches in which the values of play, health, fun, travel, leisure, and the American way are sanctified in a painless liturgy that draws together entertainment, information, and an effortless hint of instruction.

(B.J. Barber, 1996)

Since its opening in 1964, SeaWorld has played a key role in turning San Diego, in the USA, into a tourist destination of the first degree and, in particular, in the reorganization of the city's urban structure. According to Davis (1997), though San Diego's economic growth had traditionally hinged around military expenditure, the location of federal institutes of research and science and the real estate activity, as of the end of the Second World War its development has included a new axis: tourism activity. In this context, SeaWorld has provided San Diego with an easily identifiable landmark. With a population approaching 2.5 million inhabitants, tourism is today one of the city's three main sources of revenue, together with the manufacturing industry and the armed forces.

San Diego's transformation into a tourist destination was, in the mid-20th century, a planned option. This option involved a major role for the SeaWorld park. Its location and development took place with the collaboration of both the city's public and private agents. Both considered SeaWorld as the ideal promoter of a unique image of the city, linking the beach, its main attraction, with a certain idea of commitment to the environment. Thus, thanks to SeaWorld (and to a lesser extent, more recently, to the Wild Animal Park), San Diego, which even then had enjoyed a certain tradition as being a holiday destination since the end of the 19th century, has positioned itself touristically not just as a sunny paradise of blue skies with the added value of its multiple colonial vestiges and its proximity to Mexico, but, fundamentally, as an environmentally friendly tourist destination.

SeaWorld is, in fact, Mission Bay's key attraction and hence San Diego's. Its location was planned at the beginning of the 1960s and its development enjoyed the benefits of an agreement between the park and the local administration as regards the concession of the land, the park's fiscal obligations towards the city and its possibilities of expansion. Though the initial agreement referred simply to the construction of a facility to display marine life and perform educational functions, the park was seen by the local administration right from the outset as being a productive activity with great potential to favour the development of a new concept of city. In fact, while SeaWorld was becoming established, in the mid-1960s, in the old marshes of Mission Bay, the hotels in the centre of San Diego and its commercial establishments, from department stores to small shops, began to flag. They could not face up to the new reality of Mission Bay promoted by the local administration and the relocation of commercial activities from the centre to Mission Valley. The then desired effects on the urban dynamics started to make themselves felt. In parallel, the traditional working-class residential neighbourhoods, the military bases and industrial activities remained spatially segregated from the tourist sectors.

In fact, SeaWorld in San Diego is probably one of the first theme parks – if not the first – in the world, since, during its development stage, it was seen not just as a recreational business – the fundamental nature of this type of park from its promoters' point of view – but also as an instrument of a city's urban policy. Moreover, its potential impact had the dual effects of generating not only a facility with the ability to boost local economic development but also, fundamentally, a mechanism for territorial reorganization and the creation of a new image of the city.

The ability of parks like SeaWorld in San Diego to generate external economies, to create an image and to catalyse the location of economic activities forces one to think of theme parks from the point of view of their effect on territorial and urban development. The large surface area they occupy and the infrastructural needs involved also make one contemplate their role in regional and urban planning. Bearing these statements in mind, below we shall first consider the role played by parks as elements for generating new areas of centrality. Then their economic effects on a local and a regional level are discussed, their use as tools for development is approached and their capacity to play a relevant role from the point of view of a place's dynamics of tourism is assessed. To do so, a few specific territorial realities are reviewed, principally dealing with medium-sized parks. The last section in this chapter is given over to discussing parks' environmental and social impacts.

7.1. Parks in Regional and Urban Planning

Today, theme parks, whatever their size, are viewed by public administrations, both in the USA and in Europe and Asia, as tools for executing strategies of economic growth, productive diversification, renewed spatial equilibrium and even the valorization of parts of the territory. Obviously, there do exist parks with negligible effects on the territory, especially if they are small in size, profoundly oriented towards urban and metropolitan markets and with scarcely any influence in terms of urban strategy. In these cases, the administrations deal with responding to the needs that the day-to-day running of the park generates in the city (for example, the management of conflictive traffic points) and the remaining private agents try to take advantage, with no collective strategy, of the externalities that arise because of the existence of the park.

This is the case, for example, despite being a medium-sized park operated by one of the sector's major corporations, of the Busch Gardens park in Tampa, Florida. It is a park covering 135 ha with an adjacent water park measuring a further 10 ha, which is visited by almost 4 million people a year. It generates some 3500 jobs in the high season, 200 of which are perennial. With regard to management, despite the fact that Busch Gardens has continuously acquired land around the park as a reserve for potential expansion or diversification processes over the next 10–20 years, in fact there is no concrete initiative or materialization that brings resort-type developments to mind. On the other hand, neither has the park generated special economic activity beyond the typical hotels, commercial establishments and fast-food outlets located at the main access points to any North American town with establishments of greater or lesser quality, depending on the importance of the avenues in the park's surroundings.

Busch Gardens' relative inability to dynamize the territory of Tampa is due, first and foremost, to the operating corporation's productive orientation, its main activity being brewing beer. It does not have such an intense vocation for the development of spaces for entertainment (with the exception of the Busch Gardens park in Virginia) as that of operators like Disney or Universal. Secondly, due to the characteristics of the municipality itself, which is not strategically motivated by tourist development and entertainment activities and which, in general terms, positively values the moderate nature of Busch Gardens' activity in the city in that it does not give rise to excessive traffic and noise problems. In fact, fundamentally, the park is viewed in Tampa as being a 'good neighbour', giving adolescents and young people their first employment, rather than a key element of urban strategy: in this respect, something similar to the consideration that other activities may have, such as a McDonald's, a large hospital or sports and educational facilities. Thirdly, the characteristics of the park, which is not, and does not aim to be, a destination park, as local demand accounts for a third of all visits and visitors from the metropolitan area (up to 2 h away) account for a fifth. Located just over 100 km from Orlando, its visitors from elsewhere are tourists who are either not in Tampa and come to the city to spend a day at the park or, if they are in town, have come for other reasons than the parks. Therefore, in the case of Tampa, Busch Gardens bases its entrepreneurial dynamics on its tradition as a park, on the know-how of the Busch corporation and on the locational rent, which means being a complement of Orlando and the nearby beaches of the Clearwater district. Tampa does not for the moment, however, intend to use the park to propose something new for the city.

It is becoming more and more common, nevertheless, especially when proposing a new development, for parks to integrate into a concrete territorial and productive strategy. In this sense, it is evident that theme park developments have served, in most cases, to catalyse broader urban and territorial operations. Certainly one of the clearest examples of this is Disneyland in Paris, which is developed in the framework of the project to create a specific sector of a new city to the east of Paris, Marne-la-Vallée. This operation includes commercial centres, a business park and housing in surroundings which 10 years previously consisted merely of wheat fields and now, with the construction of infrastructures and the activation of the real-estate market, forms part of the urban scenery of the periphery of Paris. Now, there are other cases on different levels and with different scales. It should be borne in mind, however, that the development of parks in these conditions depends to a great extent on the social context of reference in which the investment is being made, which is very different in the USA, Europe and Asia, and of the more or less dominant position held, respectively, by the company behind the project and the authorities involved in territorial strategy. The results may be quite different and examples exist for each of the possible cases. Thus, for example, negotiations with Disney for the development of the park in Paris were done directly by the French government and that meant that the project could avoid, in Marne-la-Vallée, dynamics of social exclusion in residential areas to be developed that have arisen in other places, such as Florida. This demonstrates, on the other hand, that 'capitalism is not a monolithic force that operates alone universally'; rather, it adapts to the designs of each part of the world in accordance with power relations and social dynamics (concerning this, see D'Hauteserre, 1997, 28–29).

The interesting thing about this is, as Lazzarotti (1995) points out, that the emergence of leisure facilities, theme parks included, has important spatial implications, both due to their induced effects and due to the fact that, as they are often located in peri-urban areas, they imply a new conception of the urban structure, which, furthermore, in the case of theme parks, is specifically and strategically thought out. It is not surprising that leisure facilities end up generating a very positive image of the space where they are situated in such a way that some peri-urban areas cease to be rather unstructured places from a territorial and social point of view, becoming positively acknowledged from without. Thus, as Barrado (1999) says:

> even when it is only on the basis of an axial structure directed by the major communications paths, the forms of spatial production involved in such facilities advance from the city, in a star shape, towards increasingly peripheral areas but whose distance is rarely measured in distance but in time.

Disneyland Paris is a magnificent example of the use of a recreational facility, in this case, an entertainments complex including the Disney parks, to generate urban attraction capacity and minimize the distance factor from the centre of the metropolis or, even, in this case, from neighbouring Dutch, Belgian, French, German and Swiss metropolises. The 'good' image Disney generates, the 'Disney effect', which Zukin (1995) mentioned for the case of Orlando, is crucial from the point of view of the location of new activities there, whose basic characteristic is its peri-urban nature. In this way, what was a place set aside from market tendencies becomes a production space. One should not lose sight, on the other hand, as Barrado (1999) notes, of the fact that, in the peri-urban setting, parks seek 'the unfinished state, still being modelled, with no identity or clear references for the inhabitants of the metropolis, still free of the weighty sociospatial inertia and controls of consolidated urban environments'.

Theme parks' strategic instrumentation as elements for territorial and urban planning, therefore, offers the possibility of creating new areas of centrality. Perhaps one of the clearest and most interesting examples regarding this is that which occurred with the development of the first real recognized theme park, Disneyland in California. The orange trees surrounding Disneyland at the end of the 1950s had, by the early 1990s, become areas for the location of suburban housing, commercial establishments and, above all, decidedly themed motels and restaurants. As Walsh (1992) reports, agricultural use, which in 1955 represented 72% of the over 348 ha of the sector of the city where Disneyland was located (see Fig. 7.1), was reduced to just 12% in 1990, the predominant use by this time being by hotels/motels, which represented 26% of the total (even more than the surface area occupied by the park, which was 16%, and by parking, 17%).

Anaheim is a city located 40 min from the centre of Los Angeles, with a population of over 300,000 inhabitants and three axes of growth: the tourism favoured by Disneyland and, as a complement, the Convention Centre; the dynamic urban expansion in the form of a diffuse city which is characteristic of the south of California; and the aerospace companies. Towards the 1990s, however, cities like San Francisco, San Diego and Las Vegas were starting to become important rivals, both in capturing leisure tourism flows and from the point of view of conventions. They were all cities that had enjoyed success in their own particular repositioning process. In parallel, California as a recreational destination as a whole was starting to lose ground to dynamic Florida, which the Disney company itself had helped create. An added problem for Anaheim was, on the other hand, that its structure is an urban one, typical of the diffuse suburban North American model, with very little ability to attract.

However, in the early 1990s, Disneyland, the first piece of the Disney empire as regards parks, had become a kind of nostalgic curiosity (Czarnecki, 2001). Moreover, it made no strategic sense, either for the Disney corporation, which saw how the park's possibilities had stagnated, especially compared with the results they were obtaining from the well-planned Disney facilities in Orlando, or for the city of Anaheim itself, which was losing strength as a characteristic south Californian tourist destination.

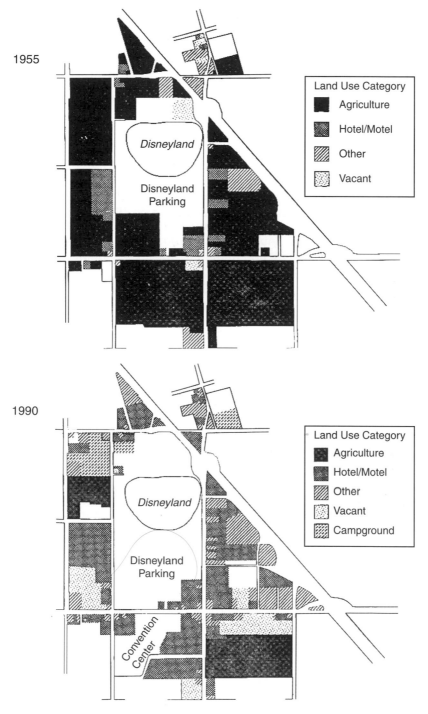

Fig. 7.1. Evolution of the uses of the land around Disneyland in Anaheim, 1955–1990 (from Walsh, 1992).

According to Sorkin (1992b), the frustration was twofold: first, because of the revenue that Disney ceased to receive to the benefit of the nearby establishments that accommodated its visitors (data by the same author indicate that in the first 10 years Disney took $273 million compared with the $555 million taken by the others); and, secondly, because, unlike what happens at other Disney properties, especially in Florida, the image of its immediate surroundings was one of complete chaos and scarce aesthetic value.

It was at the beginning of the 1990s that Disney's interests coincided with those of the city of Anaheim. The city had already developed some improvements by itself with an aim to increase convention and business-related tourism and attract private investors, but the initiative lacked ambition (a total of $55 million invested in 1994). Its bottom-line approach was to work to get visitors to choose Anaheim as their central holiday point in the south of California. Based on these needs and the acceptance of Disney's preponderant role in Anaheim, a public–private collaboration agreement between the two organizations was proposed. The aim for the city was to use the agreement with Disney to turn Anaheim into a high-quality urban destination via the aesthetic renovation of its urban environment and the use of landscaping techniques. Moreover, it was essential to manage to reorganize the traffic inside the city. This was a basic requirement to make it more attractive. The main problem was that, until then, the development processes of the 1970s and 1980s had not been properly handled, leading to aesthetically ugly, unpleasant urban landscapes. Obviously, the improved aesthetic quality of the Disney surroundings was also a basic target for the park itself. One of the main objectives of the agreement was simply or fundamentally to make the city and, in particular, the surroundings of Disney, that is to say, the Anaheim Resort District, aesthetically more pleasing: concretely, as the promotional literature for the city of Anaheim read, a destination for both residents and tourists, a meeting point for the whole world and an exuberant pedestrian gardened district. Landscaping, infrastructures and signage were the three key elements involved. Disney wanted, moreover, to expand its California park following its own Florida model.

Based on the framework agreement, two plans were developed in parallel that affected the Disneyland scene, including the park itself. Both plans turned the Anaheim Resort Project into the public–private project of greatest scope in the USA (see Fig. 7.2). The first, the Disneyland Resort-specific Plan, affected 196 ha and the second, the Anaheim Resort-specific Project, covered a further 220 ha. The project was none other than to facilitate the rebirth of Anaheim as a Californian tourist destination. In short, Disneyland and the city of Anaheim came to an agreement to collaborate in an ambitious plan which, according to its promoters, was to redefine the south California holiday experience. For this there was also intense participation by the community, with public talks, meetings and sessions with the planning teams, and also a creative, mixed funding system, allowing tackling the project's financial needs without

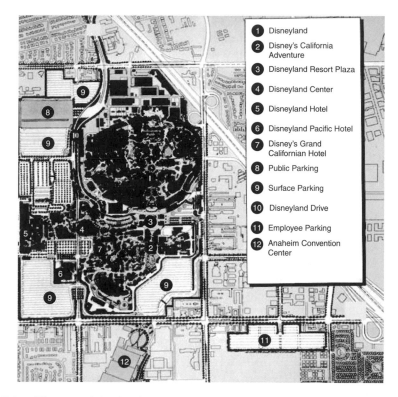

Fig. 7.2. Diagram of the Anaheim resort area (from City of Anaheim).

Table 7.1. Hotels in the Disneyland Resort in Anaheim (from company reports).

	Opening	Rooms
Disneyland Hotel	January 1998	990
Paradise Pier Hotel	December 1995	502
Grand Californian	March 2001	750
Total		2242

having to increase taxation on residents (Lockwood, 2000). The initiative also contemplated the scheduling of additional developments for the establishment of new hotel beds and of other businesses linked to receiving visitors. Over 2000 rooms are now operated by Disney itself (Table 7.1).

Cooperation (started in 1994 and valued at over $4.2 thousand million) between Disney and the city of Anaheim, in California, allowed the transformation of the surroundings of Disneyland into what has come to be called the Anaheim Resort District (Lockwood, 2000). This operation has involved the construction of a second theme park, Disney's California

Adventure, within the framework of the Disneyland Resort, the expansion of the Convention Centre, the embellishment (landscaping, signage, infrastructure, transport, etc.) of the park surroundings and the addition of new access points via the Interstate I-5 (by the California Transport department and with direct access to the new Disneyland Resort's 10,000-space parking facilities). Furthermore, according to the municipality of Anaheim, the project, which means the Disneyfication of this sector of the city, must involve an annual contribution to the municipal funds of $6 million and has taken place without increasing the taxes paid by the city's residents.

The main development axis of the Anaheim Resort has been the expansion of Disneyland and its conversion into the Disneyland Resort (Ault and Wiktor, 2001). The initiative was completed in 2001 with the opening of Disney's California Adventure, a park covering 22 ha located on what had been the Disneyland car park. Today's complex, with Disneyland, Disney's California Adventure, Downtown Disney, the Disneyland Hotel, the Disneyland Pacific Hotel and the new Grand Californian Hotel, has favoured a new situation of Disney dominance and leadership in Anaheim. The cost of the project, which recreates the main elements of Californian lifestyle, rose to $1.4 thousand million. Currently the entrances to the two parks are set one in front of the other in a pedestrian square, from which one can gain access to Downtown Disney in the style of Universal's City Walks or Disney Village in Paris.

An important aspect of the collaboration between Disney and Anaheim was the open conception of Downtown Disney. Downtown Disney aims to be, in fact, a 'real' urban experience that is both useful to visitors to the park and to residents and tourists. It also aims to be an urban space for the adjacent Anaheim Convention Center, which has also been renovated and enlarged. Although in fact the result is somewhat forced, bearing in mind Anaheim's diffuse suburban reality, Downtown Disney is, in effect, the closest thing to an urban centre the inhabitants of the area actually have. It is designed to be able to receive between 35 thousand and 70 thousand visitors a day. The space includes Disney-related establishments (ESPN Zone and World of Disney) but also others that are not (AMC Theaters and House of Blues).

In addition to things involving Disney, the project has involved the enlargement of the Anaheim Convention Center, which received a million visits in 1999. Completed in 2001, the enlargement has meant a 40% increase in capacity. With an auditorium seating 8000, the centre became the biggest on the west coast of the USA. The result is that in 1999 they already had reservations for the year 2018. A final section of the Anaheim project involves an investment of $100 million to renovate the old Anaheim Stadium in the Edison International Field baseball ground, where the Anaheim Angels play. The adjacent Stadium Promenade is where numerous new restaurants have set up. Finally, the Anaheim Resort-specific Project incorporated regulations governing the future as regards the size and layout of the buildings and guidelines for the redesign of roads and the landscaping of the streets. In fact, the boulevards that already existed around Disney were redesigned and landscaped with the idea of providing them with their own citizen-oriented identity and consistent character and making the identification of streets and their functionality an easier task.

For Anaheim, the project has meant the start of a new stage. The existing hotels have undergone considerable renovation, inside and out, and new hotels rooms have been built (including the 750 at the Grand Californian). The project created almost 30,000 jobs during its execution and a further 8000 permanent jobs in the city of Anaheim itself, once up and running. What is relevant in this case is that the theme park's expansion has favoured the configuration of an area of specific centrality in the suburban stagnation of the south of Los Angeles. Once again, the configuration of a precise idea for a project has been fundamental for the urban renovation undertaken under the protection of the development of a theme park.

The case of Disneyland in Anaheim illustrates the fact that, though not studied in such depth as residential peri-urbanization (or suburbanization in the case of North America) and as the creation of functionally central urban spaces in the surroundings of major cities (Garreau's edge cities, 1991), the peri-urbanization of leisure functions has been increasingly important over the last 50 years. Of course, there are precedents in the peri-urban location of gardens and amusement parks characteristic of European cities dating from the modern era. But what is really significant is that mass entertainment facilities, in the USA as of the 1950s, in Europe as of the 1970s and in Asia as of the 1980s, are located in peri-urban areas. Even the cinema, which had traditionally been a fundamentally urban leisure experience, 'associated with a night-time walk and evening leisure pursuit is now associated with the car, fast roads, large car parks and the malls' and therefore with peri-urbanization (Barrado, 1999).

7.2. The Effects on the Local and Regional Economy

Public authorities, from local to state government, tend to perceive theme parks as machinery for economic development. It is understood that they are conducive to new investments, create jobs and generate revenue in local and regional economies beyond what they turn over. Also, according to Lanquar (1991), parks affect consumption, the added value of nearby tourist services, capitalization and, on a national accounting level and in the event that parks are capable of attracting international tourism, the balance of payments. Moreover, on occasion, parks catalyse processes of economic development, especially if, when being conceived, it was decided to propose complementary activities – tourist, recreational or of another kind – with which the park might have synergies.

Their progressive use as an instrument for economic dyamization forces one to explicitly consider the question of their impact on the local and regional economies, or, in other words, the magnitude of the production

relationship established between parks and their immediate surroundings. This question, furthermore, is often behind the justifications made
by technicians, politicians and operators when considering the development of a theme park.

Despite the importance of this aspect, which is usually known on the
basis of indirect indicators, in scientific literature there are no precise
evaluations as to the magnitude, the scope and the scale of this impact.
There do exist, however, partial estimate approaches concerning future
impact, which the parks themselves or the administrations where they are
located usually commission at concrete moments during their development and, in general, with the aim of justifying their proposals regarding
employment and the generation of income. However, it is clear that the
impact is more than notable, especially depending on the characteristics
of the local and regional economies where the park is located. On some
occasions, such incidence has been witnessed negatively as a result of
dynamics leading to a park's closure. This is what happened in Nashville,
Tennessee, when Garland Entertainment decided to close Opryland (a
park receiving some 2 million visitors a year) in December 1997 and
tourist activity fell way below even the worst predictions.

On the other hand, the question that needs answering from the point
of view of the role of parks in local and regional economies is whether
their implantation can act as a basis for a global local and regional model
of economic development. Even in places like Orlando, in which a superficial reading may lead one to think that parks explain their whole economic dynamics, what happens is that, parallel to the symbolic economy
of parks, there is a very powerful material economy in certain industrial
and services sectors. To what extent theme parks have catalysed or conditioned this process in the case of Orlando is still today a subject for discussion (see Zukin, 1991, 1995). In any case, besides Disney and Orlando,
there exist significant experiences of multi-sectorial economic dynamics
created initially on the basis of services having a theme park as a significant element. Such dynamics tend to be complemented by important
urban expansion and by the attraction of certain basically clean industrial
activities and of advanced services beyond those necessary for the
entertainment business.

Despite the fact that theme parks' effects on local and regional economies are normally regarded positively, a great many critical opinions cannot be forgotten, however, which, notwithstanding what they represent as
regards the creation of jobs and income, insist on underlining the low
occupational quality and the seasonality of much of the work they generate
and, consequently, the low salaries associated therewith. Each country's
labour laws determine, in any case, the types and modalities of hiring and
condition the management of human resources in accordance with the
intensity with which workers' rights are protected. In general, in Europe,
labour legislation, which is more protectionist towards the worker, and
the presence of the unions in the process of collective negotiation prevent
the facilities that park operators enjoy in other contexts.

Other indicative figures of the characteristics of the jobs provided by theme parks are, according to an IAAPA survey, that 41.9% of park employees in the sample are 19 years of age or under, 61.3% were first-time employees and the turnover rate for seasonal work was 31.3%. At Disney, which according to authors like Rebori (1993) inspires commitment and motivation in its workers, in the mid-1990s, this figure was 24%.

What is true is that parks reinforce a model in which strong internal labour stratification arises, with normally temporary workers on low salaries performing maintenance, security and safety and customer service tasks and, on the other hand, highly qualified posts with good possibilities in the future, which may reach a ratio of 9:1. Thus, according to Lanquar (1991), in Europe parks create one permanent position for every 16 seasonal posts. In the USA, the ratio is 1 permanent position to every 8/12 seasonal ones. Both kinds of position work via differentiated circuits corresponding to Atkinson's (1984) concepts of a primary (permanent) and a secondary (temporary) labour market. This criticism, on the other hand, is not just applicable to parks but to the whole of the tourist, entertainment and commercial consumer services industry. The structural organization itself of work in such occupations contributes to strengthening or minimizing this situation in each place and for each specific activity (Fainstein and Gladstone, 1998, 33). Given that for their development parks often receive important incentives and aid from the authorities, from the point of view of public policies, another point that should be borne in mind has to do with the cost involved in each work post. In this sense, it is estimated that, in the case of Disneyland Paris the cost was some 200,000 francs per permanent position.

7.2.1. The economic impact of theme parks

The Association des Chambres Françaises de Commerce et Industrie report (ACFCI, 1993) considers three types of economic impact of parks on a local and regional level: impact generated during the construction phase, that generated during the operation phase and that generated in terms of image. The former are the effects of the action of constructing the park, limited in time, on the local and regional companies responsible for the different stages of the project and on local and regional administrations in the form of charges and taxes. The second set stems from the expenditure of their visitors both in and outside the park and from the running of the park. Finally, the latter, whose nature is qualitative and difficult to quantify, are those impacts deriving from the condition that the park may acquire as a catalyst, in the short and medium term, of new economic activity.

Economic theory distinguishes three groups of impact: direct, indirect and induced. The total impact is the sum of the three effects. The most commonly used technique to determine it is Leonfief's input–output model. It is a traditional procedure in disaggregate analysis by sectors of the effects of changes in final demand of certain goods and services (Fletcher, 1989). Its main advantage is the possibility of obtaining a differential multiplier for the different sectors that interrelate in a specific area. However, it does have some drawbacks when operatively considering its elaboration. The main one is the need to have detailed statistical information concerning the intersectorial relationships of the geographical area where the park is located. When analysing the impact of tourist facilities in their operation phase, the case may arise, moreover, in which total expenditure by visitors does not exactly match the quantification of the direct impact of the demand in the geographical area of reference (Stynes, 1997).

In spite of the generalized use of the input–output model in the study of regional economics and in the analysis of the impact of tourism and recreational activities on cities, regions and specific states, especially in the USA as of the 1980s (Sasaki *et al.*, 1997), its use in analysing the impact of theme parks, for both the construction and the operation phases, has, to date, been rare – this despite the high degree of interest the results might bear for the parks themselves and for local and regional administrations that back their development in order to justify their investment plans and political decisions regarding them. Nevertheless, there are parks like SeaWorld, in San Diego, that periodically draft internal reports concerning how the company is positive for the city, due, among other things, to the return they provide in taxation, non-profit-making activities, projects, clean-ups and educational activities.

Specific analyses exist which, using other methodologies, attempt to get close to the same kind of quantification of multipliers. For instance, a study by Grévin Development on the economic impact of Grévin parks in France shows that 1 euro of initial investment generates a total investment of 1.4 euros and that 65% of investment expenses ends up in the hands of local entrepreneurs. An internal report by Universal Studios (Blair and Rush, 1998) estimates that the contribution made by the complex to the economy of central Florida between 1988, when construction began, and 2001 was $51,370 million. This estimate includes the impact generated by the film and television production activities carried out by the company in Orlando, over two-thirds of all production being done in the centre of Florida with an annual expenditure by Universal Studios of over $120 million. Table 7.2 summarizes the estimated economic impact due to the presence of Universal Studios in Orlando. It highlights the magnitude of the effects generated by visitors to the park. The figure is highly sensitive to the evolution of the market. It is based on estimated per capita expenditure outside the parks of $267.

On this same theme, for the case of Spain, the ad hoc study carried out in order to quantify the impact of PortAventura in 1995 (COCIN, 1996) is well known. As can be seen in Table 7.3, it allowed estimates that total tourist expenditure in the five municipalities in its immediate surroundings (Salou, Vila-seca, Cambrils, Tarragona and Reus) was 20,755 million pesetas in 1995, representing 15% of total expenditure generated by

Table 7.2. Estimated economic impact of Universal Studios on the economy of central Florida, 1988–2001 (from Blair and Rush, 1998).

	Absolute value (million dollars)	%
Construction of Universal Studios Florida	3,970	7.7
Salaries, maintenance and infrastructures in Universal Studios Florida	5,870	11.4
Film production	2,980	5.8
Visitor expenditure	38,550	75.1
Total	51,370	100

Table 7.3. Economic impact of PortAventura on the local economy in its first year of functioning (1995) (from COCIN, 1996).

	Absolute value (million pesetas)	%
Agriculture and fishing	781.5	3.8
Industry and construction	4,328.5	20.9
Trade and repairs	1,580.6	7.6
Hotel and catering	6,584.3	31.7
Other services	7,480.4	36.0
Total	20,755.3	100

tourism in the area. Also, the study calculated that, although only 50% of the visitors to PortAventura that stayed overnight due to visiting the park did so in the immediate tourist area, during 1995 the park generated an additional 1.6 million plus in overnight stays – mainly at hotels – in this area.

Sasaki *et al.* (1997) performed a complete study of the economic impact of parks during their construction and operation phases using the input–output model for the case of Space World, the theme park developed by Shin-Nippon Steel in Kitakyushu, Japan, on a 33 ha plot of disused industrial land. The park, themed on the universe from the point of view of entertainment and education, is visited by 2 million people each year. Although the analysis was done in a highly specific social, political and economic context (with important regulatory measures concerning limits to imported foreign products) and takes 1990 as its year of reference, its conclusions provide some interesting evidence concerning the differentiation established, in terms of intersectorial relationships, between the construction phase and the operation phase of a theme park and regarding the role and the problems involved in economic development processes based on this type of entertainment facility. Table 7.4 shows, in absolute values, the total magnitude of impact during the construction phase and during the operation phase, without differentiating the part of the impact that remains in the regional economy from the rest.

Table 7.4. Economic impact of Space World in Japan (in thousands of pounds) (based on Sasaki *et al.*, 1997).

	Construction phase		Operation phase	
	Income	Jobs	Income	Jobs
Initial investment/direct impact	177,360	1,711	95,220	3,968
Indirect impact	76,689	573	35,928	1,318
Induced impact	69,156	462	47,796	1,921
Total	323,205	2,746	178,944	7,207

Greater importance can be seen in terms of income during the construction phase, though its effect on occupation is greater during the operation phase. On the other hand, it is seen that, while in the construction phase induced impact is less than direct impact, exactly the opposite occurs during the operation phase.

More in-depth analysis of the results of direct intersectorial impact brought about by the construction and development of a theme park indicates that the construction, real estate, energy, services and machinery groups of activity are more important during park construction, and services, commerce and transport are during operation. If indirect and induced impact is considered, it can be seen, however, that service activities are benefit most, even during the construction phase.

The results of the research clearly show, therefore, that, in order to gain the maximum advantage from the development processes of a theme park, not only must emphasis be placed on the 'tangible' sectors of activity (the construction sector) but it must also be placed on the 'intangible' sectors of activity, such as the management, organization and training of the workforce. In the case of Kitakyushu, such a statement translates into the implantation of a university in the area aimed at leisure activities, where enterprises and academics facilitate the production of a greater local effect of intersectorial relationships that are established based on the process of constructing and exploiting the park. It is clear that further studies of this nature for different social, economic and political realities, as well as for different-sized parks, would allow us to refine the scope of the observations made. In any case, using more qualitative systems, in the next section some results seen in respect of the impact of other medium-sized parks on the local and regional economy are considered, especially in terms of their contribution to the configuration of a new model of economic development.

7.2.2. Parks and regional development

Results available to date in the case of some medium- and small-sized and of most of the large parks, normally associated, in this case, with the development of multi-purpose recreational attractions, indicate that some parks may contribute notably to arousing the quantitative and qualitative development of the local and regional economy. This may be why, as Warren (1994) indicates, the choice of including the implantation of a theme park within a strategy of economic development driven by public administrations only arises when no alternative exists. It is important to point out, in any case, that the configuration of a development model on the basis of a theme park has, in the first place, as its main conditioning factor, the very success and continuity of the park as a recreational and entertainment business. This is why it is generally accompanied by complementary programmes and projects of an urbanistic, recreational, touristic or even industrial nature, which favour the creation of networks of businesses and interests based on the good image the establishment of a park usually causes for the place.

On the other hand, there is an ostensible difference between the parks that, either of their own accord or as the business strategy of their promoters – whether private, as in the case of Busch Gardens in James City Co., Virginia, or public, as in the case of Futuroscope in Poitiers, France – have been conceived as poles of activity (sometimes, as in the two cases presented below, even multi-sectorial, that is to say not strictly recreational or touristic) and those in which the parks are strictly kept as a recreational supply for the inhabitants of the regional or urban area of influence, as happens in Europe, for example with Europa Park or Phantasiland in Germany, or in the USA with most parks operated by Paramount, for example Kings Dominion, on the outskirts of Richmond. In these cases, also given that they do not lead to development projects of entertainment spaces in their immediate surroundings, the capacity of such parks to generate specific local development dynamics is greatly limited.

In short, it may be stated that parks may be considered instruments for regional development not just when they imply the net creation of activity (which they all do) but fundamentally when, as in the cases to be presented below, the capturing of production activities has been favoured – of service or industrial activities, research, commercialization or residential activities for the area where they are located. From this perspective, parks help to configure a new productive base or to reconfigure the existing one in the place and region where they are located. However, that would depend as much on the organization, funding and running of the facility as on the vitality of the economic fabric of the place where it is located. This is so much so that sometimes parks may cause effects on a rather more national or international than on a local or regional level. It is from this point of view, therefore, that there may be criticism that the choice of a theme park as a development instrument hinders the chances of other alternatives, which may be subjected to less competence in overall terms but which may be less risky in terms of the continuity of the business, less dependent on investor operations that can normally only be undertaken by large corporations that do not tend to have close links with the territory and which, in short, could generate better job opportunities in the area where they are set up (Fainstein and Gladstone, 1998).

It is noteworthy that there is a harnessing of new activities, and this is what sets parks apart as a basis for the configuration of a differentiated local and regional development model: not so much the production of 'tangibles' as the rendering of services based on an 'intangible' element, as is the claim made by the theme park. Accepting the consideration of a park as a cultural phenomenon, it may be stated, therefore, that, in these two cases, it must be understood that it is culture – or a certain form of culture, if you like – which acts as the motor of development in regions in which parks manifest themselves as being fundamental for new productive organization. It is clear, however, that such a consideration has its limitations. It is necessary to see how the territory proves capable of responding to the needs of services and goods that the park requires – that is to say, how it establishes synergies with it and to what extent it takes on the condition of dependence. These factors, in any case, will also depend on the specific conditions of each place and on the activity's general economic and locational trends at the time the park is implanted. In this regard, as Zukin (1991) states, it cannot be forgotten that Disneyland's success in California coincides with the expansion of the suburb as an urban form of everyday life characteristic of the North American society and with the mass shift of activity and population towards the south-west. Something similar will happen to the success of Walt Disney World in Florida, which, 15 years after its Californian predecessor, appeared at the time of greatest expansion of the leisure-oriented service economy. Neither can it be forgotten that parks increase and bring about the broadening of the recreational opportunities of the resident population.

Below we illustrate parks' capacity to generate an economic base for regional development through two examples of well-known medium-sized parks, both located in rural settings. The first, Busch Gardens in James City Co., in the USA, catalyses a development process on the basis of the business idea fostered by its promoters. In this case, the local public administration, practically non-existent at the time of its implantation, takes advantage of the synergies that the creation of the park represents and uses it for intense economic dynamization, not just of the city but, in collaboration with the neighbouring municipalities, especially Williamsburg, of the region. The second, Futuroscope, in France, is a magnificent example of public intervention aimed at creating a multifunctional attraction whose medium and social milestone of reference is a park but which, using it appropriately, proposes going beyond the simple creation of a strictly recreational facility.

(A) Busch Gardens Europe (Virginia, USA)

The dynamic generated by Anheuser Busch in James City Co., Virginia, as of the construction of the park, started in 1971, of Busch Gardens the Old

Country currently Busch Gardens Europe (with visitor numbers of between 2.5 and 3 million a year) is representative of the capacity parks have to generate development processes. This is an area with very small-scale local administrative jurisdictions in which, in three neighbouring administrations, James City Co. itself, Williamsburg and York County, a tourist destination known as Colonial Virginia's Historic Triangle has been shaped. Altogether there are some 125,000 inhabitants, a third of whom live in James City Co. This destination's main attractions, set in natural surroundings managed by the National Parks system, are Williamsburg itself, one of the best-preserved colonial towns in the USA, bringing 7 million people to it each year, a million of whom purchase an entrance ticket to experience its attractions, Jamestown, the first British settlement in the USA, and Yorktown, one of the battlefields of the American revolution. It is a place of transit on the way to the seasonal beach holiday destinations on the coast of Virginia, in particular Virginia Beach, over 100 km away, one of the state's main coastal locations, with over 400 thousand inhabitants. It is located 45 min from Richmond and 2.5 h from Washington, DC.

The distance in time of over 30 years since the establishment of the Busch Gardens park in James City Co. provides an interesting perspective in terms of valuing its effects in the medium term. It is important to stress right from the start that Anheuser Busch not only develops a park but promotes a corporate space that includes a holiday and sports area, the Kingsmill Resort in the neighbouring municipality of Williamsburg and an industrial area. On the other hand, it is the park that promotes the creation of the local administration of James City Co. This can be explained by the characteristics of the administrative organization on a local level in the USA. However, it is relevant from the point of view of seeing how at present, this local administration, despite having been created as a result of the park's establishment, is capable of efficiently managing the challenges that the park's existence has generated 30 years later.

Anheuser Busch's bid to locate its activities in James City Co. implied an important improvement to the provision of infrastructures, the settling of the resident population and, in general terms, the modernization of this until then profoundly rural area of Virginia. The theme park, the brewery (it must be remembered that Anheuser Busch is, first and foremost, a brewer) and the industrial park were from the outset and until the early 1980s the main driving force of economic development of James City Co. locals highlight, in this regard, Anheuser Busch's corporate culture as a key factor in the process. It would appear that it is not so much the location of the facility as the business strategy of creating a node of multi-sectorial activity which has facilitated the shaping of a solid productive base for development. This corporate commitment is the reason why there has been state and federal investment in the area's infrastructure. It is also due to Anheuser Busch's capacity as a corporation that the Kingsmill Resort is home to PGA golf tournaments. According to Horne (personal communication, 1998), who has firm views on the subject, success is not just because there is a park but because the corporation that operates the park has interests in the area and is deeply committed to it: encouraging productive initiatives but also making donations to schools or participating in local charity initiatives. All of the above offer security to corporations that relocate to this area since they can offer their employees guaranteed welfare and quality of life despite being in what was, until a few decades ago, a deeply rural area. The success of tourism in the area is indicative, in this case, of quality of life. Furthermore, the park and the dynamics generated by the Anheuser Busch corporation have favoured the generation of a certain pride in the place.

Regarding this, a parallel may be drawn, though on another scale and dimension, with the effect of Disney's corporate leadership in Florida. As in the case of Disney, in which one often speaks of a hypothetical 'Disney effect' which has stimulated companies to locate in Orlando, Horne indicates that the Busch Corporate Industrial Park offers status, services and protection to the over 170 industrial enterprises that are established there. It gives an image of quality and this is why the industrial enterprises, on the basis of the image the park generates, the recreational opportunities that its development has given rise to and the quality of the area as a space for residence, especially the Kingsmill Resort – also developed by Anheuser Busch – decide to move their regional corporate headquarters there. Other areas of industrial and commercial estates have been designed to house other initiatives that wish to relocate to the area, such as the James River Commerce Center and Stonehouse Commerce Park.

From the point of view of regional development, apart from being a lucrative business for the corporation operating it, the park has become the standard of the process rather than its fundamental axis. The political strategy of the local administration, which was highly dependent on Anheuser Busch's needs in its early stages but not at present, refers, in addition to tourism, to prioritizing the location of commercial and high-technology industrial and information activities. In fact, the local administration receives more through the taxes coming from the brewing activity and industrial activities than from the park. Another thing is real-estate development. From the production point of view, 30 years after its inauguration, the park, though still important for the area given the diverse economic activity present, no longer has the relevance of being a fundamental activity as in its beginnings and due to the effects of image. The park, in short, has put James City Co. and the Williamsburg area, in the words of Hershberger (personal communication 2000), 'on the map': hence its strategic importance from the point of view of a model for regional development.

On the other hand, from the tourism standpoint, the dynamic of James City Co. cannot be separated from the general context of Colonial Virginia's Historic Triangle. Today, the area as a whole has more than 10,000 hotel rooms and a growing timeshare sector. If up until the 1970s the only reference in this area was Williamsburg (restored by Rockefeller as of 1926 and running as a tourist attraction as of the 1930s), after the park was started up there was a progressive diversification and generalization of the historical theme. Given that the historical attractions of James City Co. do not have the power, distinction and tradition of Williamsburg Colonial, a veritable themed space with public streets and privately managed buildings for use as recreational attractions, the role and effect of the Busch Gardens park and the adjacent water park operated by the same corporation confer on it an important presence in the area. This is why all of the administrations of the Historic Triangle work together on promotional material. Added to these, as of the mid-1990s, are Virginia Beach (seeking to diversify its tourism model of sunshine and beach) and the town of Norfolk (an urban tourist destination).

The result is that there has been a progressive packaging of the offer in such a way that multidimensional proposals are made incorporating aspects of entertainment like the park, historical aspects, activities and relaxation. In this way, the park is shaped, therefore, as a key element in the catalysis and maintenance of tourist development, especially at a time when the area was witnessing how stays were getting shorter and shorter. Today, an especially good position is being consolidated concerning golf tourism. The reason, according to Hershberger (2000), in addition to the existence of 18 golf courses that put the area among the top 25 destinations in the USA, is the area's geographical location vis-à-vis the large metropolitan markets of the east coast and the holiday routes heading out towards Florida from the north. The new Conference Centre in Williamsburg, added to the three existing convention spaces in the area, as well as the 24 hotels targeting this market, aims to catalyse new dynamics and promote the arrival of new segments of demand.

(B) Futuroscope (France, Europe)

Robillard (1993) says, and the example of James City Co., founded on Anheuser Busch's corporate strategy, corroborates this, that 'it is clear that, in technopolises, play and work are not opposed values'. Furthermore, when locating, technology companies tend to look for places with leisure possibilities. This has been the driving principle of the political strategy that gave rise to Futuroscope in France. Despite responding to a diametrally opposite process to the one observed in Virginia, they have several points in common: the multifunctionality of the initiative, the clear option of tourist development and the creation of an image as a strategy in order to capture other companies, investments and infrastructures. As in the case of James City Co., the element to catalyse the process is a theme park but the will of its promoter, in this case the public administration, is also to promote a multifunctional development model. So, in the case of Futuroscope, initially the idea was to provide a showcase for technology for the inhabitants of the Département but, by 1985, the Vienne General Council accepted that 'the Futuroscope pavilion was integrated in a larger complex, comprising an entertainment area, an educational area and an activity area'. In this case, as in the previous one, it is observed that a theme park integrated into a development strategy can lead to the generation of a whole range of new forms of productive activities, including, of course, tourism. In fact, Futuroscope can be considered a significant experience of the creation of culture-based techno-polises in Europe.

Futuroscope, the European image park, is located near Poitiers (10 km). It is an excellent placement from the point of view of harnessing demand, being just 10 km from the exit from the A-10 motorway, which goes from Paris south, and connected by TGV (with its own station, which was inaugurated in 2000, putting it just 1 h 20 min from Paris and 2 h from Marne-la-Vallée). The project was fostered by the General Council of the Département of Vienne – the local public administration – which favoured new dynamics of development. In this way, it is an unusual park. It opened its doors in 1987 in the framework of a high-technology development project. Jacquin (1993) characterizes the magnitude of the park's economic impact on the local and regional area on the basis of four axes of reference:

1. It is a project aimed at saving the Département de la Vienne from its economic lethargy. The president of the departmental General Council, René Monory, its creator and promoter, considered Futuroscope fundamentally as being an instrument of economic promotion which would help to attract grey matter and state-of-the-art technology to a still basically rural area of late-1980s France. The aim was to sketch a way out from the Département's agrarian base founded on the creation of a technological attraction. Monory (1992) himself defines it as a concept of dynamic leisure for the regeneration of the local economy with an aim to 'transfer knowledge to the Département and create another new knowledge'.

2. A high-technology complex founded on the synergy of three activities: leisure, training, production. For the creation of the technological attraction and in order to create a specialization for the territory and set it apart from other areas of France, the Département encourages a line of specific activities dealing with a central theme: the processing of information. The uniqueness of the project consisted of dealing with this matter from the three directions of leisure, training and production. To do so, 1200 ha of land was set aside, 200 for the leisure park and the remainder for other activities.

The training area comprises:

- A pilot University Institute that is an innovator on subjects related to computing, communication and image.
- The National Distance Learning Centre.
- The International Prospective Institute.
- The Observatory of Social Change in Western Europe.
- A university focusing on communication and physics.
- The National School of Mechanics and Aerotechnics (in Poitiers since 1948).

The productive area comprises the following:

- The Congress Centre.
- The Area of Advanced Telecommunications.
- An office area, initially comprising 10,000 m^2 in the first year and a further 15,000 m^2 yearly. At the beginning of the year 2000, over 100 companies were located here, generating over 3500 jobs.
- An area of accommodation and catering services.

The park, though a space for leisure, was initially conceived as a space for the presentation of the different existing systems of projection (Kinemax, Omnimax, 3D, 360°, dynamic cinema, etc.), a historical explanation of communication and leisure (via specific attractions).

The aim was to create synergies: the congress centre benefits from the recognition of the park, the Advanced Telecommunications Area attracts colloquiums, which help to improve the levels of occupation of the hotel establishments, and the dynamics of the whole – of a marked technological nature – favours the training centres.

3. A progressive project which is the result of decentralized territorial cooperation. The idea of Futuroscope forms part of the Département de la Vienne's long-term strategic dynamics, which began in 1983 with the consensus of the politicians of the Département as regards concentrating budgetary effort on just one project and a specific – not peripheral – area of its territory. The region and the state only take part in the project in a supporting role once it starts to prove its reliability and feasibility.

4. The idea that the success of the park is a springboard for the development of the place as a whole. The park is a high-technology, unvulgarized product, which was highly differentiated from other existing amusement parks in France at the time of its opening. This has favoured a growing ability to attract among the French clientele both independent tourists and those who usually use the services of tour operators. The park's success has allowed the relaunching of the economic activity of the Département de la Vienne and has boosted the other associated activities through an important image and recognition effect. New companies have been created and, therefore, new jobs too. The success of the park is also thanks to a most accessible pricing policy, with regard to both access to the park and the prices of the hotels, run by themselves, which proves to be a big draw for school and other groups. The aim was to achieve the necessary critical dimension.

On the basis of these premises, Futuroscope, which was conceived right from the start as a pillar of regional economic dynamization and has been directly linked to public initiative, has favoured the location of computing, programming, informatics, telephony, cinematography, communication companies, etc. (Alcatel, France Telecom, Hewlett Packard, Imagine Production and Matra Communication among them) in its immediate surroundings. Given the characteristics of its foundation, both Futuroscope and the Département de la Vienne benefit from shared promotional strategies that lead to synergies between the two. Futuroscope's success, in terms of both business and development, has meant that numerous local administrations have tried to emulate it both in France and, in general, in Europe. Generally, however, they are more modest projects on the border between cultural, ludic and educational. Conversely, Futuroscope, even from the early 1990s has been turning into an 'incubator' project, evolving as much in the instructional as in the technological and ludic aspects. This is so much so that, because of its very configuration and immediate effects on the surrounding territory, it may be considered that around Futuroscope a ludic resort has arisen in that it offers complementary services to those of the visit to the park and that the number of visits is increasing progressively, and, whether or not these visitors go to the park on the second day or successive days, this brings about overnight stays in the immediate area.

7.2.3. Parks and tourist development

The ACFCI report (1993) on theme parks' economic impact showed, furthermore, that, in addition to the effects during the construction phase and during the operation phase, other, more qualitative types of impact could and should be considered related to their effect on the area's image and tourist development. When considering such impacts, it is commonplace to refer to what has occurred in Orlando, whose tourist system is based, precisely, on the development of theme parks, initially Disney and later SeaWorld, Universal Studios and others. What has happened both in America and in Europe proves, however, that a theme park does not necessarily imply the generation of an influx of tourism allowing the reconversion of a place's productive base, apart from the fact that, to some extent, parks generate influxes of visitors, depending on a variety of factors. In any case, the experience in Orlando, because of its magnitude and its results, is to date an exception in the world context.

The statement that theme parks have an effect on tourism is based on the fact that the decision taken by families to go to one is usually taken more in advance than the decision to go to other types of recreational facility like water parks. Nevertheless, as has been indicated on other occasions throughout this book, it is typical that, except at destination parks, it is the residents living within a maximum radius of 2 h who generate more than three-quarters of the visits to a theme park. Among them, of course, the tourists visiting the area may be included, many of whom, though tourists, go to the theme park as a complementary activity to their visit to the area and not as their main objective. In any case, it is clear that the parks may have helped to facilitate a tourist's visit to the area, but, as has been mentioned before, having a park does not automatically ensure an influx of tourists to the area where it is located. That will depend on several factors, which may act all together or separately. Clearly, if all concur, as occurs with destination parks, without a doubt the parks become poles of attraction and tourist dynamization for the area where they are established.

According to Jones *et al.* (1998), a theme park's capacity to attract and, therefore, to bring about a transformation of the economic base of the place where it is located basically depends on its magnitude, the quality of its recreational offer and its singularity. More concretely, for a park to have the capacity to attract tourism, it must fulfil a combination of the different requirements considered below:

• It must be unique, a place 'that has to be seen'. This means that the park operators have been capable of creating enough expectation for the potential demand to feel the 'need' to visit the park. This has been achieved by some parks on different scales. Without a doubt, the universal, vital media presence of Mickey Mouse in people's lives in their childhood means that a great many parents feel 'almost obliged' to take their children to a Disney park at least once in their lives. That would explain, leaving aside other aspects from those listed in this series of conditions, such as magnitude, quality or orientation towards the tourist market of the parks themselves, why, as can be seen in Table 7.5, frequentation by those not resident in the surroundings of Paris is greater than 50% at the French Disney park. However, on other scales, this is a task which can also be achieved if the park is linked to a certain 'unique' or 'singular' character in its immediate surroundings. So, although it does not generate international fluxes of tourists and the park is small or medium in size, the case may arise that it can generate significant flows of tourists if its content is sufficiently attractive in terms of events, integration into the natural environment or its actual architectural make-up. This is what happened, for example, until it was closed by its owners in 1997 in order to steer its activity back towards the mass commercial sector, to Opryland in Nashville, Tennesse.

Table 7.5. Demand for Disneyland Paris, 1993–2001 (from STI, 2002a).

Origin	1993	1995	1997	1999	2001
Total visits to the park	9,705,111	11,309,421	12,823,920	12,544,632	12,148,826
International demand	5,462,297	6,524,049	7,969,792	7,407,278	7,631,153
French demand from far away	1,884,025	2,416,166	2,709,790	2,708,590	2,452,919
French demand from nearby	2,358,789	2,369,206	2,144,338	2,428,769	2,064,754
Total visitors to the park	6,708,551	7,140,464	7,863,013	7,876,732	7,404,227
International demand	3,159,533	3,377,429	4,183,896	3,837,968	3,831,869
French demand from far away	1,248,014	1,548,527	1,693,619	1,747,477	1,610,373
French demand from nearby	1,301,004	2,214,211	1,985,498	2,291,287	1,961,985

- It must be of large dimensions and have a critical mass of attractions. It is well known that the dimensions of a park are not just conditioned by the size of the potential market around it but they condition, in fact, their capacity to attract. In short, potential visitors will travel from further afield to the extent that the recreational value offered by the park in terms of the number of attractions (including shows) is satisfactory enough to compensate for the distance friction effect they must overcome, as regards both travel time and cost. In order for a park to be able to attract significant numbers of international tourists, it is understood that the investment – as an expression of magnitude – must surpass $150 million.

- It must combine high technology and high levels of service and human quality. This was one of the elements that favoured the tourist success of Futuroscope at the beginning. A good choice of theme linked to technology, its uniqueness and significant quality of services and human aspects have brought about a notable tourist influx despite its being a medium-sized park. Daniéle Castan, Secretary General of Futuroscope in 1994, said as early as then in statements made to the *Gazzette Officielle du Tourisme*:

  The number of visitors has risen from 225,000 in 1987 to close to 2 million in 1993. And when 2 million people come to a Département, this does not happen without bringing about some changes in tourist development matters. La Vienne, therefore, has equipped itself: its diversity in hotel accommodation, catering, as well as the economic efforts made in the construction sector bear witness to this . . . The Département's landscape has been completely transformed over the last five years.

  In fact, as of the mid-1990s, over half of the visitors to Futuroscope stay overnight as tourists in the Département de la Vienne. The General Council of the Département de la Vienne itself took part in the construction of hotel establishments (up to 320 rooms between 1988 and 1992) with the purpose of facilitating the visit to the park and promoting visits to other attractions and places of interest in the region. After this initiative, it was private investors who took charge of the needs until in 1994 over half of the region's hotels were under 5 years old. In 1997, la Vienne, with 5500 rooms, had become the first Département in France for volume of growth of hotel supply.

- It must stimulate and facilitate overnight stays. For a park to have an effect on tourism, a critical variable is that the park itself should have its own or outsourced hotel rooms to offer its visitors when selling them the product. The concept of resort associated with the park inaugurated by Disney in Orlando aims to turn the park's recreational experience into a complete holiday experience. We have already seen the dimensions of Disney in Orlando as an operator of hotels. Also, one can refer to the incorporation of hotels in the holiday complex that is being built by PortAventura. This phenomenon, which has extended among most medium-sized European parks and is becoming generalized in the USA among the main park operators, can be explained by the profits that their visitors' overnight stays in their own facilities generate for them. According to Jones *et al.* (1998), a visitor that does not stay overnight generates just 20% of the income generated by one who does. For the purposes of illustration, it may be noted that, in 2001, clients of Disney hotels in Paris totalled 2,647,240, of whom 2,117,982 were non-French. This meant that hotel occupation at the hotels of Disneyland Paris for 2001 reached 85.5%, according to data supplied by the company. The impact of Disneyland Paris in its capacity as a park with the ability to attract tourists was not limited, however, to its own hotels. Thus, it is estimated that, in 2001, Disneyland Paris generated between 1.37 and 1.93 million overnight stays outside Disney hotels. Globally, Disney's net contribution to the hotel industry in Paris is consistent with the functioning of between 2600 and 4090 rooms with a mean annual occupation of 71.8% at the rate of two people per room at 80% of them and just one person at the remaining 20% (STI, 2002b).

- There must be complementary activities at the destination, whether it is understood that the destination is the holiday resort shaped around the park, which may offer a suitable combination of a variety of activities and facilities (hotels, meeting and congress facilities, commercial areas, restaurants, water parks, etc.) or if the destination is understood as the immediate surroundings where one may enjoy the beach (which is the concept of complementariety used by PortAventura) or the city (as in the case of Madrid for Warner or Paris for Disney). The figures shown in Table 7.6, in this last case, in fact demonstrate the importance played by the destination besides the park when stimulating overnight stays by tourists.

- It must be available for other purposes of media interest. This is a last condition that increases a park's capacity to attract tourists. The presence of the media is especially important not in terms of promotion but because of the consideration the park may be given as a space for the pursuit of other activities, ranging from television advertisements to widely disseminated social and sports events, like, for example in France or Spain, the biggest cycling competitions, whose start or finish usually takes place at a theme park.

Table 7.6. Disneyland Paris as a tourist destination, 2001 (from STI, 2002b).

Demand	Disneyland as sole destination (%)	Disneyland + Paris as destinations (%)	Disneyland + Paris + other destinations (%)
French from nearby	99	1	0
French from far away	83	14	3
International	64	26	10

According to the fulfilment of these conditions, the results may be more or less intense. The case of Walt Disney in Orlando is, due to its dimensions and tradition, the best known. However, small attractions can succeed: for example, the Polynesian Cultural Center in Hawaii, to mention quite a unique one, has also demonstrated an ability to attract among its nearly 1 million visitors a year a high percentage of tourists (Jones *et al.*, 1998). In any case, the impact of a park on tourism will generally depend, as has been seen previously, in addition to their proper operation in terms of marketing, on their singularity or singularization.

It is important to look at these conditions appropriately when considering any theme park development. This is especially relevant from the point of view of the support that can be given by the public administrations to such facilities. If what they pursue is the impact of the park on the tourist market, whether in terms of creation or restructuring, it will be necessary to integrate the park within a concrete tourist strategy, since a park by itself will be hard pushed to put such a programme into practice unless the park itself becomes – autarchically – a destination. A significant example of the consideration of a theme park as a central axis of a new tourist strategy is provided by the debated development of the new Disney park in Hong Kong.

7.3. The Environmental Impact of Theme Parks

The term environmental impact refers to the changes suffered by the environment when a project or activity is carried out. The change may be either a positive or a negative one. However, as Swarbrooke (2002) notes, in contrast to the case of their economic impact, the general view seems to be that theme parks have an overall negative impact on the environment.

Concern with the effects of the environmental impact brought about by development has grown as of the last quarter of the 20th century. During the 1980s a multitude of studies and reports, carried out to alert people to the planet's load capacity, put forward alternatives as regards the excessive consumption of resources and aimed at slowing down demographic growth. In 1987, the United Nations' World Commission on Environment and Development published the so-called Brundtland report, which demonstrated the will to draw up a strategy for sustainable development. As a result of this initiative, the United Nations Conference on Environment and Development, held in Rio de Janeiro in 1992, defined a series of global sustainability strategies. One of its conclusions was that development should be approached from a position of ethics in order to prevent certain communities or generations from benefiting more than others, since the earth's resources belong to humanity as a whole. This type of approach implies enormous difficulties for practical implementation and requires a change in the way the relationship between humanity and the planet is understood, the equitable redistribution of the costs and benefits of the use of resources and the preservation of the environment, as well as the eradication of one of the deepest-rooted principles of today's economic thinking: the belief that continuous growth is the only way forward.

Following Rio's influence, documents have appeared on an international level dealing with the need to boost the development of tourism and recreational activities in accordance with the principles of sustainability. Some of the most relevant documents drafted by international bodies like the United Nations, the World Tourism Organization, the European Union, the United Nations Educational, Scientific and Cultural Organization (UNESCO) and the World Travel Tourism Council are the following:

- The Charter for sustainable tourism, drafted at the World Conference on Sustainable Tourism in Lanzarote (1995).
- Agenda 21 for the travel and tourism industry (1996).
- The Berlin Declaration on biological diversity and sustainable tourism (1997).
- The Calvià Declaration on tourism and sustainable development in the Mediterranean (1997).
- The Rímini Charter drawn up at the International Conference on Sustainable Tourism (2001).

On the basis of documents such as these, fundamental criteria are established as to economic efficiency, understood as the maximization of social welfare and the minimization of the cost of the use of resources, such as:

- Treating the natural environment and the resources it possesses as natural capital.
- Acting in accordance with the principle of precaution.
- Using resources so that they do not transform environmental quality or do so within reasonable limits, measured by specific impact studies.
- Correcting the damage caused by development by means of development according to the 'polluter pays principle' (PPP).

Theme parks, like other tourist and recreational activities, involve the appropriation of space to the detriment of other activities or uses. To the extent that such appropriation implies urban development, the first and main impact they generate is as a result of the occupation of land. Lanquar (1991) proposes three criteria in order to evaluate the sense and magnitude of such an impact:

- The vulnerability of each space and, concretely, the possibility that their construction may involve the destruction of parts of the natural environment and, depending on size and nature, it may also be a source of pollution in terms of noise and air and water quality.
- The physical and ecological load capacity of the place where they are set up, particularly taking into account the intensity of the frequentation to the park at certain times of the year.

- The pressure induced by tourist activities and, in particular, by visitor flows generated by the park. The park may put a strain on local infrastructure. Moreover, theme parks' environmental impact must consider the inappropriate development outside them of buildings and structures and large, unsightly car parks.

In general terms, from this standpoint, it may be said that the impact caused by parks is therefore on a par with the impact brought about by other tourist activities. In fact, for example, given the size of parks and, therefore, the dimensions their effects may take on, in Europe, it is compulsory for any theme park development to undergo its corresponding Environmental Impact Assessment. An Environmental Impact Assessment constitutes a highly powerful tool as it forces the authorities to ascertain the consequences of the action of a project prior to taking the decision as to whether or not to see it through. Furthermore, its assessment must be made public, subjecting the said decision to public opinion. Its compulsory nature in the case of the European Union is a result of the conviction that the economic analysis of costs/profits falls short of the social suitability of a particular development. The precedent of the European Environmental Impact Assessment (EIA) is the National Environmental Policy Act (NEPA), which, at the end of the 1960s, constituted the formal birth of environmental law. Fifteen years after passing the NEPA in the USA, in Europe, European Directive 85/337/EEC was passed, introducing the technique of environmental evaluation in the area of the European Community. After the first years' experience of the application of the EIA, the European Union (EU) passed Directive 97/11/EC, modifying the previous one. These modifications concentrated on detailing in greater depth the contents of the evaluation and increasing the number of types of projects to be submitted to the EIA compulsorily, among which were, as has already been stated, theme parks.

The hypothesis could be put forward that the effects of environmental awareness concerning theme park development has passed through three stages. During the 1950s and 1960s, when environmental debate was truly incipient and prioritized a conception according to which the development of large-scale leisure facilities, especially in the USA, was seen as a factor of the democratization of society's recreational and consumer opportunities, no explicit criteria of analysis, management and prevention of environmental impact existed. In the 1970s and 1980s, as concern for the environment grew, it began to be appreciated how inadequate growth patterns – whether inside the park itself or in its immediate surroundings, as had happened in the area of Disneyland in Anaheim – can lead to the decadence of consolidated tourist destinations, and management practices started to be drawn up involving the exhaustive control of the use of resources in parks and around them. Also, some leisure facilities – especially those with contents and presenting attractions based on elements of flora and fauna – began to display their ideological – and commercial – commitment to the principles of sustainability in the use of resources on a global level (for further information, see the analysis of SeaWorld by Davis, 1997). As of the 1990s, together with the consolidation of green thinking among broad sectors of society and the appearance of alternative kinds of tourism reflecting the greater awareness and concern by tourists conscious of the problems of the environment, theme park operators not only incorporated environmental quality criteria into their facilities but parks were even developed that adapt the planet's environmental conditions into the theme – from Animal Kingdom in the USA to Sanrio Harmonyland in Japan and Xcaret in Mexico – explicitly expressing their commitment to sustainable development, even as a market positioning strategy, so as to prove their ability to satisfy new demand characteristics.

Taking this process of evolution into account, as well as the progressive establishment of efficient mechanisms of resource management (especially localized resources such as water) and of waste disposal – in accordance, that is, with the conditions of development of environmental technologies in the countries where they are located – the biggest causes for environmental concern and, as a consequence, the most generalized reasons for opposition by environment protection groups to the development of theme parks – when and if they bring them to the forefront of the debate – is the direct occupation of land for their development and the urban development processes that are usually carried out in their immediate surroundings. Another thing is the ecological footprint that may be brought about, from the point of view of the environment, by the consumption of energy. Illustrating this, to give just one example, are the allegations made by the environmental group Ecologistas en Acción in 1998 concerning the Environmental Impact Assessment report for the Warner Bros theme park project near Madrid. All of the allegations presented by the group involved the effects that the future occupation of the land due to the construction of the park would have. Thus, in general terms:

1. They warned as to the severe impact the park would have on its surroundings – due to its location and surface area – especially on the protected area of the Regional Park of the South-East and the Gózquez de Arriba nature reserve area. Concretely:

- Increased noise, atmospheric and light pollution.
- The disappearance of flora and fauna (nine autochthonous botanical species of the Iberian Peninsula exist in the area, living in the areas of gypsiferous scrub and grasses, and 11 threatened species on a national level, 43 considered of special interest in Spain and 11 catalogued as threatened in the Autonomous Community of Madrid).
- The visual impact on the landscape due to the building of constructions greater than 25 m in height.
- A permanent, severe impact on the palaeontological and archaeological heritage of the area.

2. They pointed out the inappropriateness of the proposed routes for the infrastructures to be built to provide access to the park by:

- Opposing the extension that crossed the protected area of the Regional Park of the South-east.
- Considering there was little to support the planning of an access road through an area of olive trees.
- Opposing the proposal to build an access road parallel to the Gózquez de Arriba nature reserve path. This would mean a strong, irreparable impact on the area as it would facilitate ease of mass access to a particularly fragile area.

3. They suggested that a protected area like the Regional Park of the South-east, put forward to become part of the European Union's Natura 2000 Network as a Site of Community Interest, ought to have a protection strip of at least 100 m around the whole perimeter, reaching 250 m in the areas of special value, as is the case of the Gózquez de Arriba Nature Reserve.

Things being as they were, the main reasons for conflict in this case were a result of the problems in assigning land use in an environment which, though metropolitan – south of the city of Madrid – has important natural value nearby (Barrado, 1999) and, especially, the coincidence of the northern boundary of the development with one side of the Regional Park of the South-East and the qualification of the whole area as an architectural zone declared a Site of Cultural Interest. In any case, it cannot be forgotten that, depending on the sensitivity of the park operators, they can find solutions to such problems. An added concern as regards parks' environmental impact was the effects their development might have in terms of the growth of built-up areas around them as a result of access infrastructures and property development and the rise in levels of frequentation to the area and thus greater pollution caused by transport systems. Concerning this, parks' environmental impact therefore depends on the suitability and adequacy of the process of urbanization. Less well known is the fact that urban pressure associated with low visitor figures can lead operators to even consider the closure of the theme park in favour of other activities (for the case of North America, see Burnside, 2005) and the revenue generated from the sale of the land. This is what happened, for example, to Six Flags Astroworld in Houston. Similarly, the closure in 1997 of Opryland USA in Nashville, which initially brought about a loss of over $50 million a year to the local economy, has led to the development of a 'high-end shoppertainment mall', Opry Mills, property of the Mills Corporation.

It is worth mentioning, however, that, paradoxically, parks appear to be models when it comes to landscaping inside their doors, but their teachings have hardly been applied by planners and promoters outside their doors. In this sense, there are some fundamental ambiguities. Indeed, whereas the pedestrian experience is fundamental within parks or leisure complexes, their surroundings are quickly destroyed by the intense use of the car, both by those who end up living there and by the millions of people that come to the park by car – precisely to walk through it. Moreover, needless to say, park workers usually reside at some distance from the park because, around them, the price of land (which has increased due to the influence of the park itself) makes it impossible for them to purchase or rent housing (due to the low salaries they usually earn). This leads to increased mobility and, moreover, and in a manner other than the environmental, generates added problems with the neighbouring local authorities, who have, among their biggest urban social concerns, the problem of providing accessible housing facilities for park workers.

As has been mentioned previously, another basic problem is the consumption of localized resources and, above all, the problem of the availability of water, especially in the case of parks located in dry climes. The figures concerning this are, on occasion, noteworthy. At Terra Mítica, for example, it was estimated that, though the demand for water made by the park was moderate – 4665 m^3/day of drinking water and 10,000 m^3/day of treated water – a spectacular increase to demand could be brought about precisely as a result of the urban growth induced by the establishment of the park (Martínez, 2001). This increase was cited at 85.8 hm^3/year in 2002 and 116 hm^3/year in 2012. These figures meant a real deficit in the supply of water in the area around the park of 45 hm^3 in 2002 and 75 hm^3 in 2012, which would have to be solved by bringing resources into the area from elsewhere. The park's ecological footprint as regards water, due to its effect on consumption by induced developments, ought to force the correct assessment of the environmental costs that a facility of this nature may cause if it is not suitably scaled in line with the physical capacity of the place where it is located.

In certain cases, the problem of water can find technical solutions, for instance through the implementation of saving strategies and the use of treated water. Regarding this, it is relevant to explain that, since 1978, Disney has experimented through the Water Hyacinth Project, with the use of flowers to eliminate water pollutants. The project was put to the USA Environmental Protection Agency and funded by among others, the National Aeronautics and Space Administration (NASA). In 1983, the Gas Research Institute joined the project, transforming vegetable waste into ethanol and other products. Likewise, other matters that give rise to an ecological footprint, such as the generation of waste, the emission of pollution into the atmosphere and the generation of noise, may have technical solutions. Normally they are problems of management that the parks often solve with existing environmental technology and by drafting specific protocols, such as treating and recycling water, replenishing aquifers, reducing the use of chemical fertilizers, thanks to the contribution made by the treated water, the establishment of intelligent, automatic irrigation systems to optimize the use of water, the separate gathering, collection and recycling of different sources of waste, using waste for the generation of energy and minimizing emissions through the burning of natural gas (cookers and heating) and oil derivates (transport) by means, in the latter case, of the adaptation of collective, non-pollutant internal and external transport systems (see, for example, Kurtti, 1996).

In this regard, it is known that Disney parks, and especially the one in Orlando, are sensitive to the natural environment. Thus, for example, in Orlando, the original plan includes a large conservation area, Reedy Creek Swamp. However, it cannot be forgotten that the existence of this area is of great strategic interest for the company since it works as a drainage surface for the area. However this may be, its conservation has allowed the regeneration of the habitat and wildlife of Florida's central wetlands and this has even gained acknowledgement by the Audubon Society. Furthermore, in 1993, Disney went still further with its commitment to the environment through an alliance with the Florida Department of Environmental Regulation and other agencies to set up the Disney Wilderness Preserve (3400 ha) to the south of its property. This process was encouraged by the existence of federal laws obliging the substitution of the wetlands where development was to be carried out. Even so, despite the Company's acknowledged environmental awareness, as the development of recreational and tourist facilities on Disney property accelerated as of the 1980s opinions have arisen questioning the suitability of the project to the area's load capacity, formulating criticisms concerning the impact generated (Murphy, 1997). The impact of the land occupation process is, from this standpoint, once again fundamental.

Anyway, the relations a park establishes with its surroundings as regards the environment may vary according to the place, the scale of the facility and the operating company. Though scarcely used, in order to provide a value, economic science has developed several instruments that allow the measurement in monetary units of the change brought about by an environmental impact: this is known as contingent valuation. In simple terms, the contingent valuation method consists of simulating a 'market of impacts', that is to say, by means of a questionnaire set for a representative sample of the population it aims to find out at what price the interviewee would be willing to accept the increase (or reduction) of an impact. For example, it would be possible to evaluate the social perception of the environmental impact of the development of a park in comparison with not building it. Applying the contingent valuation method, the differential effect of having the park or not would be described and the question would be asked as to whether the interviewee would be willing to pay a certain amount of money for the project. The result of the method is to obtain the 'value' of the impact according to the people.

From this standpoint, it cannot be overlooked that cases exist in which parks' capacity to transform the territory has been used, as a tool of territorial policy, to activate, especially but not solely in the case of Europe, environmental and landscape enhancement programmes. Thus, to quote a few examples, the development of PortAventura in Salou implied the closure of a solid domestic waste dump on top of which the park was built. As for Disneyland, its conversion into a resort was used to carry out important aesthetic enhancements and improvements to the system of environmental infrastructures in Anaheim. Then there is Universal's park in Osaka, which is part of a programme to reshape the city's port seafront area and to reintegrate the area into the pre-existing urban structure. Also, experience demonstrates that, contrary to what happened in Nashville, there are communities like Santa Clara, in California, which have opted to conserve a theme park precisely as a strategy of territorial management. Hence, Paramount's Great America, located on 100 acres of publicly owned land, represents one of the city's few chances of disposing of not only rides and attractions but also open space and landscaping.

From certain points of view, finally, one cannot fail to consider that the condition of a park as a place on the margin subject to integrated management offers the opportunity to consider theme parks, as Jones *et al.* (1998) do, as alternative solutions to the growing environmental pressure which will be brought about in the coming years by the flow of tourist trips to new destinations:

> A new role for theme parks is emerging. By their nature, they are designed to handle large numbers of people within a controlled space and with manageable impacts. In the future they will embody a greater educational function to introduce, interpret, and sensitize the overseas tourist to the environment and to the host community and its values. They can become a new gateway for host country tourism.

Rather than an attraction, parks could operate, therefore, as strategic visitor management tools. That implies, however, numerous changes, as much in the conception operators and consumers have of parks as in the environmental commitment of the authorities that promote and facilitate their development.

7.4. The Social and Cultural Effects of Parks on Local Communities

In addition to the appearance of documents internationally establishing the principles for the sustainable development of tourism and recreational activities, more recently declarations have begun to be made dealing with the need to approach the processes of touristic and recreational development in such a way as to minimize social and cultural impacts. This is the case of the Manila Declaration on the Social Impact of Tourism (1997) and the World Code of Ethics in tourism promoted by the World Tourism Organization (1999). This is because, for a development process to be sustainable, not only must it take place in harmony with the natural environment but it is also fundamental that it should arouse local participation in the economic processes it catalyses, in addition, of course, to generating economic benefits. This is a concern which, in fact, in general terms, was already included in North America's National Environmental Policy Act in the 1960s. Thus, in accordance with this regulation, environmental impact studies were already to consider not just the physical but also the human environment (people's welfare) and the relationship between the two. Also, preventing environmental impact should arouse people's welfare and wealth.

Depending on their characteristics, the nature of their operators and the place of implantation, theme parks can induce more or less severe impacts on social relations and the cultural identity of a local community. Below we deal specifically with two types of impact: those that involve parks' ability to generate new social dynamics and those that have repercussions on the cultural characteristics of places.

7.4.1. Theme parks and social cohesion

Generally speaking, the sustainable development of a theme park should provide different types of social benefits, (Swarbrooke, 2002) which aim to:

- Ensure a fair distribution of the costs and profits.
- Create jobs locally.
- Stimulate local enterprises, generate foreign currency within the country and inject capital and diversify in the local economy.
- Ensure that decision making is done after listening to all representatives of the local sectors.
- Instruct the local community as to the benefits of the resources they have and encourage them to preserve them.
- Contribute to the education and instruction of tourists and the personal enrichment of the local population.

One can in fact speak of the 4Es as a basic approach to solving satisfactorily the sustainable development of tourism and recreational activities in the social sphere (González Reverté and Anton Clavé, 2005):

1. Equality. Ensuring that all those participating in tourism have equal conditions and are treated fairly.
2. Equal opportunities, for both workers and tourists.
3. Ethics. The tourism industry must not deceive the tourists and must be honest when dealing with suppliers. As with governments, they must behave ethically towards residents and tourists.
4. Equality of treatment. It is essential for tourists to consider the people serving them as equals, with no feeling of superiority.

From the social point of view, therefore, implanting forms of sustainable development implies strengthening the local economy when facing macroeconomic upsets, minimizing the costs associated (especially those incurred by seasonality and the difference between workers' salaries in comparison with those of workers involved in other economic activities), attempting to spread the benefits generated by tourism among the local population and especially among the less favoured segments of the population, and protecting local companies against the competitive capacity of large international companies, who are only marginally committed to the destination. As Swarbrooke (2002) writes, the key point is often the extent to which the attractions reflect the needs and desires of the local people. Another issue is to observe how accessible they are to local people. Where attractions are seen to be out of keeping with the local area and locals are prevented from using them, as happens in several parts of the world, a sense of resentment towards the visitors is the most likely result. This is what happens with Xcaret, for instance, according to the Grupo Ecologista del Mayab (Mexico). With an entrance fee of 467 pesos per adult and 213 per child under 11, in an area where the minimum salary is just 37 pesos a day, the local population simply cannot easily enjoy the park.

Concerning the ability of theme parks to satisfy the expectations of the local population from a social angle, it is interesting to look at the case of the opposition by the local society of Virginia to the development of Disney America. Controversy broke out in Virginia in 1994 after Disney announced the project in 1993. Disney wanted to recreate the events of American history in a park covering 1200 ha, 6.4 km from the Manassas National Battlefield Park in Virginia, one of the main places given over to the remembrance of the Civil War, barely an hour from Washington, DC (see *NYT*, 1994): a place, on the other hand, with magnificent views and a pleasant natural setting, as General Lee declared in 1861. The plan met with opposition from both environmentalists and historians. As an element of discussion, the latter raised the question of the place's symbolic identity and the need not to trivialize it. Historians like David McCullough, among a great many other participants in the debate, declared that Disney's proposal was simply a sacrilege, that in a place to honour the past, as the company itself was announcing, what it would bring about was its ruin (cited in a special issue of the journal *Condé Nast Traveler* on the matter in September 1994).

Hawkins and Cunningham (1996) consider that this failure by Disney is a direct consequence of not drafting in the local citizens and influential figures in the process of the design of the park. Disney gained the support of local enterprise and authorities of Virginia, including a state incentive to the sum of $163.2 million in anticipation of the estimated effect that the project – valued at $625 million – would have had on the local economy. In addition to a park themed on the American cultural legacy, Disney proposed the development of 2500 residences, 1300 hotel rooms, recreational facilities and commercial areas. The park was to come into operation in 1998. However, it was the opinions as to environmental and social degradation and its consequent implications as to the identity of the place which the project would give rise to that ended up blocking the initiative. The main arguments against the project were an increase in traffic, the effects on the territory of the need for new infrastructures and the appearance of new, extensive residential developments around the park and, especially, in the area of the Manassas Battlefield, just 4 km from the proposed location for the park. An especially important factor of opposition was the perception by the inhabitants of Prince William County that, with this development, they would lose control of the future of the area. From the point of view of culture, in a few months over 20 groups opposed to the project were created, among which, with some 250,000 members, was the National Trust for Historic Preservation. In spite of the concessions that the Disney Company was willing to make (annual donations to historical preservation groups, contributing funds to improve the Manassas National Battlefield Park, donating a visitor centre to the area, committing itself to good environmental practices, conceding 36 ha of land for public facilities and limiting the number of vehicles going to Disney's America to 77,000 a day), opposition remained strong and, in September 1994, Eisner announced the withdrawal of the project.

This case, which was highly controversial in the USA, thus illustrates not just the need for theme park development to take into account the development expectations of the local population but also the importance of assessing its impact and that of its visitors on the local community culture. In this regard, all too often the real or perceived theme park impact is assessed only to the extent of whether jobs and visitor expenditure effects are enjoyed by the local people rather than outsiders. However, new attractions may introduce alien features and values that can be seen as a threat. In the aforementioned case of Disney, for example, the company was accused even in the USA of attempting to appropriate to itself corporately the culture of the place when it proposed developing near the Manassas Battlefield, the symbolic reference point of the American War of Secession, a park that set out to theme the history of the USA (*NYT*, 1994). The response by American historians and intellectuals to the project gave rise to a debate which was even dubbed 'the new civil war'. The conflict was based, in this case, on the opposition by activist groups on the grounds that staged authenticity replaced the genuine and, as a result, that, at its most extreme, places become 'wholly disattached from their social context, creating a sort of virtual reality' (Fainstein and Gladstone, 1998, 37).

From the standpoint of the local communities, there is an obvious risk: the fact that theming means inevitably packaging, interpreting, theatricalizing and simplifying – even obviating resources that are not directly involved in the main narrative object – in accordance with the precise expectation held by the customer. This is especially relevant in the case of theme parks with cultural content. It means, in such cases, according to neo-Marxist standpoints and the thought of the Frankfurt Critical School (Goytia, 2001), the creation of social mechanisms that cause the commodification of culture, its use for ideological purposes and its acceptance for consumption in capital accumulation cycles. Along these lines, for example, Amnesty International and other human rights groups charge that Splendid China, in Florida, which features more than 60 miniature versions of such famous Chinese landmarks as the Great Wall and the Forbidden City, portrays a false picture of social harmony and contentment among China's persecuted religious and ethnic minorities. So critics regard the park as a propaganda ploy, using make-believe and entertainment to polish China's image.

7.4.2. The effects of parks on local culture

Globalization – a process in which theme parks participate, notably through their use of brands and symbols of a transnational nature – goes far beyond things economic and rests, fundamentally, on things cultural (Norcliffe, 2001, 23). The construction of transnational symbols has created what Renato Ortiz denominates 'international popular culture'. Thus, popular culture consumers are able to interpret the quotations of a multi-locational imaginary brought together by television and advertising:

> the idols of Hollywood films and pop music, the logos of jeans and credit cards, the sports heroes of different countries and of one's own that play in another . . . Marilyn Monroe and the Jurassic animals, Che Guevara and the fall of the wall, the most widely drunk fizzy drink in the world and Tiny Toon may all be quoted or alluded to by any international advertising designer confident that his message will acquire meaning even for those who have never stepped foot out of their country.
>
> (García Canclini, 1995, 66–67)

In parallel, despite the globalization of information and convergence among countries concerning certain consumer habits, local and regional traditions and beliefs still persist. So, at the same time as the deterritorialization of processes, there are strong reterritorialization movements, represented, according to García Canclini (1995), by social movements that reinforce the local and also through media processes – regional radio and television stations, micromarkets, music and ethnic products – and the 'demassification' and 'ethnic mix' of consumption in order to engender local differences and the feeling of belonging to a place (García Canclini, 1995, 128). It is in this context, moreover, that, according to Klein (1999), the marketing of 'diversity' appears, presenting itself as the solution to all problems of world expansion. Instead of creating clear advertising campaigns for different markets, the campaigns sell diversity itself to all markets at the same time. This has two consequences:

1.   The redefinition of the sense of identity organized increasingly less through the sense of belonging to a place.
2.   The reinvention of 'autochthonous cultural assets' with the aim of turning them into commercializable, communicable goods.

According to Norcliffe (2001), Disney was a pioneer in this process in two main senses. First, he promoted the globalization of a sanitized and commodified popular culture, initially through animated films and, subsequently, through other entertainment media, marketed products and theme parks. Secondly, he helped to create a new discourse of globalization through a series of universally recognizable animated characters. 'This discourse has required deterritorialization, that is, the loss of normal links between a people and the territory they occupy.' In fact, he transmits ideological models that are representative of what could be called Western modernity: conceptions of democracy, liberty, welfare and human rights, which transcend the definitions of particular identities (García Canclini, 1995). Thus, in the same way as Disney bases its narrative on the legendary patrimony of Europe (from Snow White to Sleeping Beauty) but imported and re-exported to the whole world through its products, characters like Snoopy become a reference point of Universal Studios park in Japan, Warner Bros' characters colonize the recreational space of millions of people from Mexico to Australia. Consequently, at the end of the 20th century Hillary Clinton got the attention of the world by worrying that the export of American entertainment and consumer products was 'destroying indigenous cultures' (Holt and Schor, 2000, vii).

It must be noted, however, that, usually, transnational operators of theme parks are increasingly taking into account the specificity of the local as a key element for their competitiveness. However, whether attractions can actually pose a threat or whether the attractions themselves are modified by the indigenous culture is, as yet, a debate without conclusion. Thus, the recent history of theme park development clearly shows that the cultural and language differences that exist between places cannot be overlooked (for further information, see the cultural controversy generated by Disney in France in Grover, 1997). Bonding with the local is, in fact, one of the principal tendencies observed in the development of parks in the short and medium term (Jones *et al.*, 1998). So, in the case of theme parks, one may speak of a progressive interpenetration between the local and the global:

> Local reactions to global elements such as transnational corporations, the Olympic Games, foreign tourists, imported products and so on are necessarily conditioned by previous local experiences of such elements which collectively shape local impressions of what 'the global' represents. On the other hand the way a global agency behaves locally is also influenced by its previous experiences in that and other locales.
>
> (Norcliffe, 2001, 16)

More generally, the relationship between the global and the local leads to a process of the reification of local cultural forms and manifestations to adapt them to the demands of a market which is either global or is globally aware in so far as patterns of consumption are concerned. Thus, the operators know that they must offer a product in terms of a commodity to be consumed, discarded and replaced. Visitors purchase intangible qualities of restoration, status, lifestyle signifier, release from the constraints of everyday life or conveniently packaged novelty. As Britton (1991) states, it is interesting in these cases to use Jameson's notion of the 'warning effect': on the one hand, material and cultural objects, social activities and places are commodified and transformed into images of themselves for consumption; on the other hand, this transformation and consumption generate a 'flatness', where depth of appreciation, understanding and especially meaning are replaced with a 'new kind of superficiality in the most literal sense' (Jameson, 1984, 60). Illustrative of this is the controversy that arose from the proposal to develop the Dracula Park, in Romania (Jamal and Tanase, 2005).

Cultural impacts were a significant problem with the proposed park. Local civic action as well as domestic and international non-governmental organizations (NGOs) played key roles in opposing the proposed location adjacent to the medieval town and World Heritage Site of Sighisoara. Finally, the project was cancelled in 2006. Analysis reveals the complex interdependencies attributable to a diversity of stakeholders, issues ranging in scale and scope from the local to the global and the importance of enabling those who stand to be most impacted by the process – the local people with their local cultural background – to participate directly in the development decision making. Only in this way is it possible to follow the principles of the World Tourism Organization's Global Code of Ethics. Therefore, the reaction emphasizes the fact that cultural assets, activities and rituals are values in themselves, not objects we can reduce to a quantifiable standard and buy and sell in the market (Rifkin, 2000).

The development of theme parks – especially those with a cultural theme or which seek to take root in the identity of the place where they are located – translates, on the other hand, into the construction of ideological discourses in the heart of the local communities themselves. In this connection, some (small in size and highly diverse in content) parks in China may be highlighted which represent historical themes and ethnic diversity, such as the Chinese Ethnic Cultural Park in Beijing or Yunnan Nationalities Village in Kunming, among others. They are parks which, though aiming to demonstrate cultural diversity as a good, do not escape from controversy, precisely because of the stereotyped treatment of the identity aspects of the different ethnic groups (see Hitchcock *et al.*, 1997). Therefore, from a cultural point of view, conflict may prevail even in a case in which the development of the park is not led by large North American transnational corporations who introduce formulas of international popular media culture in different social contexts. The question that must be asked is, again, whether such initiatives respond to local expectations and needs.

One paradigmatic case in this respect is that of the Lost City, in South Africa. Promoted by South African entrepreneur Sol Kerzner on the Sun City site in 1992 as 'Africa's kingdom of pleasure, where fantasy becomes reality', it provides the visitor with a pre-packaged vision of exotic Africa that can be traced back to the colonial gaze and the imperialist project. The project invokes the genres of exploration, discovery and archaeology to validate colonial enterprise, uses techniques such as naming and mapping to appropriate space and renders the colonized land picturesque in accordance with Western aesthetic conventions. According to van Eeden (2004), all of these mechanisms 'reverberate in the cultural code of visitors to The Lost City precisely because of the mediatory role of popular culture such as films, which created the stereotypical visual lexicon by which Africa is recognized to this day'. The dilemma lies in the fact that, as van Eeden says, many tourists seem to prefer the clichéd statement and the romanticized image of other cultures. But the challenge for South Africans is to move beyond myth and stereotype and 'to engage with issues such as identity in a critical and sustained manner'.

Something different is the interest of the numerous parks in Asia – especially Japanese and, more recently, Chinese – in developing theme parks that represent foreign countries. It must be remembered that simulating a travel experience is also common in parks in North America and Europe (from Busch Gardens in Williamsburg to Europa Park in Rust, Germany). However, the Asians, unlike Westerners, are profoundly cultural and sometimes their parks do not even have any attractions. Cultural criticism (Mintz, 2004) has scorned Western parks' character of simulated travel and has tried to provide interpretations based on a supposed postmodern character of contemporary tourist and leisure practices. However, far more fruitfully, for the case of parks in Japan, Hendry (2000b) invites one to take a sceptical view of words like 'authenticity' and 'simulation' and demonstrates that they must be understood as constituting a more culturally anchored phenomenon:

> In Japan, as elsewhere, gardens are cultural interpretations of nature, and thus express a wealth of history and culture, in its sense of spiritual nourishment as much as anything else. In Japan the foreign culture theme parks have turned out to play a not dissimilar role.

Instead of essentializing these apparent efforts to essentialize culture, as a 'global' analysis might, Hendry proposes instead to examine them for the way in which they are wrapping 'culture' for local consumption.

Case 12. Environmental Protection Measures in the Redevelopment of Ocean Park

In 2005, the Ocean Park Corporation launched a project known as the 'Repositioning and Long Term Operation Plan of Ocean Park' (http://www.edp.gov.hk/eia/register/profile/latest/esb125.pdf). The project aims to redevelop the existing Ocean Park at Hong Kong, transforming it into a marine-based theme park, doubling the amount of attractions and establishing itself as a world-class and must-see destination. The project is largely located within the existing Ocean Park area at Aberdeen, and will extend to cover the existing bus terminus and part of the existing Hong Kong School of Motoring site, adjacent to the existing Ocean Park. Until 2005 Ocean Park was composed of three areas – the Lowland, the Headland and Tai Shue Wan. The main entrance of the Park is at the Lowland and there is another secondary entrance at Tai Shue Wan. A cable car system serves as the main mode of transport for visitors between the Lowland and the Headland.

Under the repositioning project, a new entry plaza with public transport interchange (PTI) and car parking facilities underneath will be constructed partly on the existing Hong Kong School of Motoring site. The new entry plaza will be provided with a direct pedestrian link to the proposed Ocean Park Station of MTRC South Island Line. Provision for a possible hotel development above the entry plaza will also be catered for.

The Lowland, which will be renamed the Waterfront, will be redeveloped, with the reconstruction and addition of new attractions and facilities, including a new aquarium, shark tanks, lagoons and new rides. The Headland, which will be renamed the Summit under the project, will be extended to cover part of the hill slope adjacent to Nam Long Shan. New attractions and facilities, such as the Ocean Dome Whale Stadium, a new Panda House, brand new theatres for shows, new rides and accommodation for new animals, will be incorporated. Some of the existing facilities, such as the Ocean Theatre and Pacific Pier, will be upgraded. Overall, the amount of attractions will be doubled under the project. The project will also include a new Summit Express (funicular train) in a tunnel to provide visitors with a weatherproof connection between the Waterfront and the Summit. Associated with the provision of new attractions, the facilities for the Park will also be upgraded. These facilities include administration offices, back-of-house facilities, service roads, utility services, life-support systems for animals, drainage, sewerage, waterworks, retail shops and restaurants. The existing cable car system will be retained as an alternative mode of transport between the Waterfront and the Summit for the visitors. The existing facilities at Tai Shue Wan will be cleared for other uses.

Upon completion of the project in 2010, it is envisaged that evening opening hours of the Park may be extended to 10 p.m., the number of attractions and rides will be doubled, some night shows are expected, though there will not be fireworks as one of the regular attractions, according to the preliminary design plan, and, apart from about 300 m at the Summit area, the funicular train will be operated within the funicular train tunnel. Works are due to start in 2006 and, before then, Environmental Impact Assessment (EIA) will have been undertaken, providing interactive environmental input for the design of the project. Environmental monitoring of the project will also be carried out during the implementation of the project.

Table 7.7 shows the potential environmental impacts associated with the construction and operation of the project. They have been identified in the preliminary EIA commissioned for the repositioning project. Mitigation measures to minimize potential environmental impacts are also indicated. In particular, according to the report, water quality impact from the modification of the existing boat jetty, spoil management and ecology are expected to be the key environmental issues during the construction phase. The key issues during operation would be noise impact, e.g. from fixed plants at the attractions, rides and funicular stations, and visual impact from the proposed above-ground structures. The EIA study indicates that the potential environmental impacts during the construction and operation of the project are not insurmountable. Moreover, the Ocean Park Corporation is committed to the full integration of environmental issues within the project design and construction, and to ensuring the adoption of the recommended protection measures for full compliance with environmental legislation and standards.

Table 7.7.   Possible impacts on the environment and protection measures to be incorporated in the project (from company reports).

Potential environmental impacts	Environmental protection measures

Construction phase

Air quality
- Dust from construction activities

Air quality
- Implement dust suppression measures set out in the Air Pollution Control (Construction Dust) Regulation

Noise
- Construction noise generated from construction activities

Noise
- Implementation of good site practices to limit noise emissions at source
- Use of quieter powered mechanical equipment
- Use of quieter alternative construction methods
- Use of noise barriers/enclosure

Water quality
- Construction runoff and drainage from land-based construction activities
- Sewage effluents from the construction workforce
- Modification of an existing boat jetty

Water quality
- Implement site practices as recommended in ProPECC PN1/94 Construction Site Drainage
- Install appropriate drainage facilities to control site runoff
- Provide adequate treatment facilities prior to discharge
- Provide proper toilet facilities

Waste management
- Construction and demolition materials
- Potential land contamination issues

Waste management
- Minimize waste generation and maximize waste recovery and recycling
- Sort and segregate waste for reuse and disposal
- Dispose waste to landfills only as a last resort

Ecology
- Direct impacts to undeveloped and semi-natural habitats including scrubland
- Indirect disturbance impacts to habitats and communities adjacent to works areas, including the Coastal Protection Area around the Headland
- Indirect impacts to aquatic communities resulting from sediment-rich site runoff and potential accidental spills of fuel/other chemicals

Ecology
- Avoid and minimize disturbance to any flora/fauna and habitats of conservation interest
- Mitigate unavoidable impacts
- Minimize indirect construction disturbance

Continued

Table 7.7. *Continued.*

Landscape and visual	Landscape and visual
• Impact on loss of scrubland in terms of landscape and visual value, eyesore of construction works, exposed slope surfaces and works areas	• Avoid and minimize disturbance to significant landscape resources such as Coastal Protection Area • Mitigate unavoidable landscape impacts through compensatory planting or transplantation • Use decorative screen hoarding and control night-time lighting
Cultural heritage	Cultural heritage
• Potential disturbance to historic buildings	• Avoid and minimize disturbance to historic buildings

Operation phase

Air quality	Air quality
• Impact from vehicle exhausts from nearby road networks, internal service roads and the proposed facilities	• Strategically design the entrances/exits and loading and unloading area to minimize queuing of vehicles. • Minimize idling emissions by providing instructions to drivers using PTI and loading and unloading bay to switch off the vehicle engines while waiting
Noise	Noise
• Operational noise from fixed plant, e.g. ventilation shafts, tunnel ventilation fans along the tunnel alignment for the funicular system and mechanical equipment at the cable car and funicular stations • Noise from Ocean Park operation including rides, shows, performances, cable car operations and traffic induced	• Use silencers, mufflers or acoustic shields for fixed plant • Use purpose-built noise barriers/enclosures • Use noise-tolerant buildings (e.g. office buildings) to act as noise screening structures • Orientate the performance stage to point away from the nearby noise sensitive receivers • Acoustic design of loudspeaker systems
Water quality	Water quality
• Storm-water runoff from hilly grassy land and concrete paved area, and waste-water discharges from the aquarium, tanks, pools, toilet facilities and restaurants to the public sewer	• Install appropriate treatment facilities

Continued

Table 7.7. *Continued.*

Ecology	Ecology
• Indirect disturbance impacts to habitats and communities adjacent to the Park, including Coastal Protection Area around the Headland	
Landscape and visual	Landscape and visual
• Style, layout, scale, material, colour and finishes of proposed facilities and structures, extent of planting areas	• Landscape planting for the project and reinstatement of planted areas
	• Aesthetic architectural form, colour and finishes of visible structures
Cultural heritage	Cultural heritage
• Indirect vibration impact on historic buildings	
• Potential visual impact on historic buildings	

Case 13. The Grand Parc du Puy du Fou and the Valorization of the Local Heritage

The culture and in particular the history linked to a place have been specifically adopted as a theme by certain parks. The development of culture-based theme parks is governed by the potential of the theme that sustains them, their size and especially their ability to attract in comparison with the available market areas in their immediate surroundings. Without doubt, the keys to the success of culture-based theme parks are respect for the specificity of the culture and the appropriate treatment of the basic theme:

1. Respect for the specificity of the culture. The challenge facing the recreational use of culture is to achieve a product development model that represents a compromise between the principles of proper conservation in terms of value, authenticity and identity and the interests of the tourist market. For this, carrying out interpretative plans on the basis of the resources–themes–markets paradigm once analysis has been performed as to the necessary agents–professions–funding for the development of the cultural facility of a recreational nature (Goodey, 1994) has proved to be of use. Procedures like this allow one to be transported from the façade to the atmosphere, from the monument to the landscape and from conservation to creative synthesis and make compliance possible, generally by means of the proper theming of the resource, with the communication demands required of the heritage in its capacity as a tourist product.

2. The appropriate treatment of the basic theme. The problem of theming often revolves around the issue of place identity. This, according

to Mongon (2001a), is a false debate since any intervention involves modification. Therefore, what is really necessary is to understand clearly the object and the objective of the process of theming. That implies, in the first place, a good choice of theme (since the option chosen simplifies the capacity to relate to other resources that also exist in the place) and is followed by applying the techniques available to make it easier for the public to enter the narrative discourse presented, that is to say, live experiences. Besides these requirements, theming implies taking care of the details and applying their foundations to any element of the whole, that is to say, universalizing the theme in the place in order to set it apart from any other. Hence the proper elaboration of a culture-based theming process, in addition to correct interpretation and communication of the resources, must involve regulations that help study and preserve it.

Such is the case of the Grand Parc du Puy du Fou in the French Vendée (de Villiers, 1997), with close to a million visitors a year. During the open season, its more than 35 ha is devoted, through street entertainment and shows, to remembering historical and legendary episodes and environmental characteristics of the Vendée, it has become a thematic cultural attraction of reference in Europe. It is managed by an association and has brought about the creation of 700 jobs. Furthermore, in the style of conventional theme parks, it has had notable direct and indirect effects on the local society, but it stands out due to having configured:

- A system of identifying the local population with the memory of the place by means of their (voluntary) participation in the show which deals with the park's *raison d'être*, the Cinéscenie.
- An educational centre for the region's inhabitants to pursue matters such as horse riding, falconry and cultural traditions that are dying out.
- A means to valorize the traditional industrial fabric of the region (95% of companies are art-and-craft-based).
- The demonstration that cultural products, when well designed and managed, are financially, territorially and socially profitable, even without economic aid from the public sector.
- The conversion of the surroundings of Puy du Fou into a centre for cultural innovation, a factory for the imagination on the basis of traditional culture.
- A system to integrate such a wide variety of aspects as recreational development, the conservation of heritage and international solidarity.

Cases like that of Puy du Fou allow one to illustrate that culture and, with it, heritage are not just an attraction but are an element of the collective memory of places and societies that can be preserved beyond their recreational use and become an engine for territorial development.

Case 14. The Enhancement of the Urban Landscape at International Drive, Orlando

From the standpoint of its territorial establishment the Universal park in Orlando offers a substantially different model from that of Disney. What is fundamental is that Universal Studios does not have the administrative sovereignty which Disney enjoys on its property. This is why, unlike Disney, Universal has been explicitly and intensely concerned with the problems of territorial and urban management in its immediate surroundings. Furthermore, the fact that the park is integrated into the city's urban fabric means that it must reach a consensus as regards its proposals with the needs and expectations of other urban agents, among whom are the resident population. This has led to numerous problems when proposing expansion. Thus, the step taken in the 1990s to cease to be just a theme park and to become a multi-purpose recreational complex gave rise to conflicts with neighbours' associations concerning three basic points: noise, the landscape and road access. It cannot be forgotten that between 14 and 16 thousand vehicles enter and leave Universal Boulevard every day. It was through close collaboration with the local administration and through zonification processes that these problems were solved.

The urban insertion of the park and its expansion zone make the issue of access points a key factor for the success of Universal. This is due to two reasons: first, due to its capacity; and secondly, because external access to parks often fails to have the aesthetic quality that would be desirable according to the company's standards. This is especially clear at International Drive, the main access artery to Universal Studios from the south, in the section of the road that corresponds to the city of Orlando. In order to overcome this situation, in the 1990s Universal Studios used the International Drive Chamber of Commerce as an instrument to put pressure on the administration and the owners of establishments and businesses located along this communications axis. Its ultimate aim is to achieve levels of aesthetic quality in keeping with those proposed by the park within. In other words, the intention is to reproduce pleasant surroundings outside the park: hence, for example, the interest of the Chamber of Commerce in enhancing all aspects that give rise to good visual conditions, like, among other things, appropriate signposting. The problem is that International Drive is 19 km long and a wide variety of private investments are being made in their thousands (today there are investors from a whole range of countries of origin, for instance from Japan, India and Brazil). On International Drive, there are over 25,000 hotel rooms and over 30,000 workers, most residing in Orlando. The area receives some 12 million tourists a year. It is, together with Lake Buenavista in the vicinity of Disney, the fastest-growing area with the greatest capacity to capture tourist investment.

Hence the Chamber works fundamentally with the city and county administration in order to favour a harmonious development of the area and for its sphere of influence to gain an attractive, positive image.

Its programmes at the end of the 1990s hinged around matters of security, the feeling of worth of employees, improved signage, embellishment, marketing and other issues related to the administration. It is interesting to note that the Chamber is funded by members' contributions and that, in order to carry out specific projects, it enjoys the position of an area of special taxation. So those operators that set up in the area within which the Chamber operates, once the projects have been completed, will have to pay for the aesthetic improvement work done. However, since these programmes are conducive to entrepreneurial success, investors are happy to pay up. Both the city of Orlando and Orange County are honorary members of the Chamber.

8 The Development of Theme Park Destinations

The world is changing very quickly. One point two billion people are
Chinese. Slow, gradual changes will not work. We need a revolutionary
transformation in all practices.

(John Lanchester, 2002)

Recreational attractions and among them, pre-eminently, theme parks are
often characterized as being key components in the system of tourism
(Benckendorff, 2006). The functions they undertake are basically to
arouse an interest in travelling to a specific destination and to provide
greater satisfaction of the visitor's expectations (Gunn, 1994). Hence, theme
parks and other recreational attractions are proliferating at tourist destinations. In a context of change in the motivations and behaviour of the
demand, of technological innovation within the reach of families, of the
increase of the middle classes in less developed countries and of consumers'
greater environmental awareness, their development allows tourist destinations to respond competitively to the new state of the tourist market.

Though often associated with metropolitan leisure dynamics, there
exist theme parks and large leisure complexes that bring together entertainment, accommodation, shopping and sports and/or cultural activities,
which have the ability to generate tourist flows. In certain cases, with the
creation of sufficient critical mass due to the concentration of attractions
and the actual size and scale of the recreational project, for some of their
visitors some theme parks can become tourist destinations in themselves.
The appearance of units of accommodation associated with parks in Europe
reaffirms this trend. However, only exceptionally do theme parks catalyse,
in their capacity as characteristic products, the creation of new tourist
destinations. For this to occur, there is usually a need, in addition to the
actual suitability of the parks with regard to their shows and attractions,
aggressive marketing strategies, often associated with corporate sponsors,

year-round operating systems, a highly diversified product make-up, as regards both contents and formats and target markets, for a clear territorial and brand identity and the creation of multi-purpose facilities. Thus, for example, the scale of the parks industry in Orlando, an exceptional example worldwide, has incited the development of one of the top local tourist destinations in the world as regards numbers of visitors.

This chapter precisely seeks to answer the question as to what are the development conditions of large theme park destinations with the capacity to generate expectations worldwide and/or of the large spheres of demand for theme parks of the world. It is clear that, as mentioned, the global reference point is Orlando. However, both in Europe and in Asia, there are, today, destinations with theme parks which, in the parks themselves, have a tool for the harnessing of tourist flows. Concretely, in addition to Orlando, we shall analyse the cases of Paris and the Greater Pearl River Delta. These are three thematic destinations led by large and medium-sized theme parks located in a context which, from the perspective of the touristic function of the place is multifunctional. In other words, they are destinations with diverse tourism opportunities and, in spite of the necessary isolated management of the parks, integrated. On the other hand, Orlando, Paris and the Greater Pearl River Delta are three places whose geographical scale of reference is not the local one. The parks shape regional spaces (central Florida, the Paris metropolis and the Hong Kong–Macau–Guangzhou conurbation) in which, furthermore, despite its importance, tourism is not the only activity of reference but, on the contrary, services and high-tech industry are dominant.

Though with notable cultural, political and institutional differences, the study of the world's large thematic destinations clearly shows, however, the strategic sense the development and establishment of theme parks has had for the different places and the different players – led by the private sector in some cases and with notable public participation in others. In addition to their suitable location in terms of market size, support from governments and administrations has been fundamental in all cases, however. Especially important has been the public commitment to the improvement and correct scaling of access points and communications axes. Needless to say, each of the destinations is at a different stage of development. The tendencies, expectations and opportunities of each are also different.

8.1. Theme Parks and Economic Development in Orlando

A mythical version exists of Disney's role in turning Orlando into one of the metropolitan areas in the USA with the greatest projection and capacity for growth (see Ward, 1997, for example). As Archer (1997) states, the idea that, prior to Walt Disney World, Orlando was a 'sleeping' city would suggest that it was merely 'awaiting' the arrival of Disney to act as an agent to modernize and grow. However, without minimizing the role effectively played by Disney in the city's development, it seems clear that growth in Orlando and consequently in central Florida was to be expected with or without Disney. In fact, studies carried out at the beginning of the 1960s by the Urban Land Institute clearly indicated that the I-4 Interstate Highway corridor between Daytona Beach and Tampa would become one of the six future megalopolises of the USA in 2000. Therefore, it seems that the decision taken by Walt Disney has had an influence – and has had far-reaching and irreversible consequences – but that it was a question of anticipation rather than stimulation.

Prior to Walt Disney's decision to develop its second theme park in Florida, Orlando was a city given over to agriculture, principally citrus fruits, an activity that was embarked upon around 1870 and was notably stimulated with the arrival of the South Florida Railroad in central Florida in 1880. The first radical change took place a few years before Disney took the decision to locate its second park in Florida. In 1956, the Glenn L. Martin Company of Baltimore, today Lockheed, bought some 17 km^2 in Orange County to build a missile manufacturing plant. This was the start of productive diversification in Orlando, in the shape of the high-technology military aerospace industry. The development of NASA's Kennedy Space Center near Cape Canaveral continued to boost this industry. Thus, although without a doubt the establishment and opening of Disney in 1971 turned tourism into the city's main activity, high technology continued to develop. Since the 1970s, the development of both sectors has shifted the farming of citrus fruits towards the south of the city. Agriculture has also played an important role in a significant process of industrialization. In this respect, it cannot be forgotten that already in 1942 two orange farming companies were the first to sell frozen concentrated orange juice. The following year they set up the well-known Minute Maid brand (Hood *et al.*, 1997).

So activities such as high technology, aeronautics, electronics and communications play a key role in the city's economic dynamics. This point is often overlooked when alluding to the competitive nature of the economic structure of Orlando. In fact, the parks have favoured numerous opportunities which are taken advantage of by companies and institutions to give a boost to other productive sectors with an even greater capacity than the tourism and entertainment activity itself to generate value. In fact, behind the highly visible entertainment industry and the worldwide well-known brand that also is Orlando, a $10 billion technology industry has grown up alongside the imagination, storytelling and customer service associated with the theme parks. So a number of strong, established industrial sectors are based in Orlando, such as advanced manufacturing, agritechnology, aviation and aerospace, customer support and administrative offices, digital media, energy and alternative fuels, film and television production, international business, life sciences and bio-technology, manufacturing, warehousing and distribution, modelling, simulation and training, photonics and software and hardware. In fact, Orlando is the headquarters (such as Darden Restaurants, Mitsubishi

Heavy Industries, AirTran Airways and Tupperware Brands Corporation) and site of customer service operations (such as Oracle, AIG, Hewitt and Associates, Siemens, Bank of New York, America Online, Walt Disney World Resort) of many major corporations. With more than 25 colleges and universities and more than 50 professional and technical schools, a skilled workforce and many educational and research facilities provide capacities and expertise to fulfil the needs of these corporations.

As a result, the city's growth process has been spectacular. With 337,516 inhabitants in 1960, the metropolitan area of Orlando (made up of Orange, Osceola, Seminole and Lake counties according to the 1990 census) doubled in size in 20 years, reaching 699,904. Fifteen years later it doubled again (1,410,877 inhabitants). Between 1995 and 2005, growth was at 34.7%, reaching 1.9 million inhabitants (of whom only just over 200 thousand are in the city itself). As is to be expected, such more-than-considerable growth over the last four decades has had its consequences, the main ones being the increased cost of land and cost of living (the cost of living composite index for Orlando in 2005 was 107.3 over 100 and the cost of housing 115.6 over 100), traffic jams and the overabundance of infrastructure. The most directly palpable benefits have been seen in the rise in occupation (with more than 1 million employees in 2005 and a rate of unemployment of 2.8% – below the average of 4.8% for the USA) and business activity (in 2005, 57,696 new companies set up in the Orlando metropolitan area). Finally, it cannot be forgotten that one of the main factors to have brought about such growth is the existence of a large amount of land available for urban development.

The result of this transformation process has, morphologically and functionally, created a fragmented city. Industry is located some 20–30 km around Orlando in an area set apart from the zone occupied by the tourist activity. The regulations governing the zoning of each county are most strict in this respect, as are environmental regulations. Companies' headquarters are in downtown Orlando. The south-west is urbanized for tourism purposes (the corridor between Disney and the city centre both along the I-4 and via International Drive). Now the touristic area is fragmented. Universal is 13 km from the city centre, while Lake Buenavista, the closest access to Disney property from the city, is 16 km from Universal. This landscape is completed with a series of satellite residential areas to the north and east, each with its own social and identity make-up.

8.1.1. The role of Walt Disney World as a catalyst

Table 8.1 reflects some of the highlights in the process of the establishment of the main theme parks in Orlando, including some of their predecessors. The city and surrounding metropolitan area today consists of over 80 attractions and more than 110,000 hotel rooms, 4500 restaurants, 80 golf courses and 250 local shopping malls and malls of regional scope. Also, the third biggest congress centre in the USA is located in Orlando.

Table 8.1. Chronology of the development of the main theme parks in Orlando (based on data from the Orlando/Orange County CUB).

1936	Opening of Cypress Gardens on the outskirts of Winter Haven, in the west of Orlando
1965	Following the purchase of almost 11,000 ha, Walt Disney reveals its intention to build a replica of Disneyland in central Florida
1967	The Kennedy Space Center Visitor Center in Cape Canaveral comes into service
1971	Magic Kingdom comes into service
1973	SeaWorld Florida comes into service
1975	Church Street Station comes into operation, an urban themed entertainment centre in the city of Orlando
1982	Epcot comes into service
1989	Disney MGM comes into service
1990	Universal Studios Florida comes into service
1997	Disney Village becomes Downtown Disney
1998	Disney's Animal Kingdom comes into service
1998	Universal Studios' City Walk comes into service
1999	Universal Islands of Adventure comes into service

Demand at the seven main parks in Orlando reached 60.4 million visits in 2005. That same year, visitor numbers to the Orlando metropolitan area were around 48 million. Over a third of all visitors to the city make a day visit. In 2005, tourism generated $28.2 billion in visitor spending, created 41% of the workforce of the counties of Orange, Osceola and Seminole (24% direct and 17% indirect and induced jobs) and an impact of $14.8 billion annual earned wages ($7.8 billion direct and $7.0 billion indirect and induced). Employment in leisure and hospitality in metropolitan Orlando was 191,100 in 2006, 19.9% of the total. The profits generated by tourism meant that resort tax collections in the counties of Orange, Osceola and Seminole reached over $154 million. Table 8.1 also highlights the role of the Walt Disney World Company as a catalyser of the process since the 1960s.

The process of the purchase by Disney of the land in Orlando dates back to the 1950s. For this, Disney used fictitious companies based in Florida, which bought the land without revealing its intentions (Kurtti, 1996). The average buying price was close to $81 per ha. With the acquisition of this land, Walt Disney pursued the control of developments in the periphery of the park so as to avoid the typical social and urban problems of North American cities and, at the same time, claim for itself any business opportunities that might arise around them. Initially, with the construction of Epcot, it also wanted to develop a model residential community, that is to say, create an urban model capable of proposing alternatives to the problems of the North American city. It was precisely this bid for urban innovation and experimentation that helped towards the government of the state of Florida getting involved in the creation of the Reedy Creek Improvement District (RCID) in the mid-1960s. This move included the state's concession to Disney of almost total sovereignty over the planning, management and development of its vast property (Sorkin, 1992b).

The original idea Walt Disney had for Epcot required urban planning legislature that was not necessarily in force in Orange and Osceola counties, where it had purchased its land. Consequently, a series of legislational regulations passed between 1965 and 1967 made it possible, right from the outset, for the Disney Company to be able to enjoy its own administrative body, the RCID, and thus most of the political powers that are normally vested in public authorities (Archer, 1997). This body deals with the regulation and the management of water, fire protection, the conservation of nature areas, the upkeep of roads and bridges, the zoning of land use and the administrative regulation of the area's urbanization. The RCID is, therefore, the planning and urban management authority on Disney property. Disney owns 98% of the land managed by the RCID and has 98% of the votes on the District's Board of Supervisors. Hence, it never opposes Disney projects. Its budget comes almost exclusively from the taxes Disney pays. In consequence, Orange and Osceola counties have no jurisdiction over Disney property.

Disney's administrative capacity through the RCID and its jurisdictional exceptionality are seen from a discriminatory standpoint by the communities and administrations of neighbouring counties. This is due to four main reasons: (i) unlike them, Disney has at its disposal mechanisms of territorial action like tax exemption and other systems that allow the funding of improvements to infrastructures and facilities; (ii) Disney banishes all residential and industrial uses and infrastructures that it does not wish to have on its property to its neighbouring counties. This has led, for example, to intense disputes between Orange County and the company. Thus in 1989 a court ruled that Disney should pay $14 million to improve the county's roads outside its property and for Orange County to accept the administrative powers of the RCID; (iii) Disney competes with neighbouring counties when locating its amenities (it cannot be forgotten that more than 20% of the total number of rooms in the metropolitan area of Orlando are located in Disney); and (iv) Disney has the advantage of being able to implement its strategies without any pressure from the residents, who have other interests. Indeed, it is the neighbouring counties that have to provide housing for Disney workers, most of whom are on low salaries.

Currently, the more than 11,000 ha that make up Disney property in central Florida are located in Orange and Osceola counties. In addition to four parks, the Disney property operates over 25,000 hotel rooms, two water parks, two campsites, over 80 swimming pools and recreational lakes, several golf courses and a variety of spaces for urban entertainment, such as Pleasure Island in Downtown Disney among others. Also, Disney property includes 3035 ha of land protected by the company for environmental conservation (Murphy, 1997). So Walt Disney World is, basically, a self-sufficient place on the outskirts of Orlando. Through the RCID, it oversees the whole area's planning and management process. The only thing that Walt Disney World does not have is its own airport. It could even be said that the development of Walt Disney World was privatized right from the start (Archer, 1996).

Initiated slowly, with just three fully planned resorts at the time of its opening (Fort Wilderness, Contemporary Resort and Polynesian Resort), the creation of a veritable holiday resort at Walt Disney World (WDW) became a priority for the company as of 1984. Between the inauguration of Magic Kingdom and the expansion of the complex, a second stage is etched which led to the inauguration of Epcot and of Disney Village in the early 1980s. In order to coordinate the resort creation projects, in 1985 the Disney Development Company was set up (a complete subsidiary of the Walt Disney Company), which took charge of the development of the projects beyond the park gates (see Marcy, 1994). Intending to capture all markets, Disney planned and developed accommodation opportunities (see Table 8.2) during the 1980s and 1990s, ranging from the luxury of the Grand Floridian Hotel to the lower-range complexes like the Caribbean Beach Resort, Port Orleans Resort and Dixie Landings Resort. Hence, Disney accommodation can be classified according to three categories: premium, moderate and economy. Also, in order to harness the conventions market, Disney promoted the WDW Dolphin Resort and the WDW Swan Resort. In the year 2005, DisneyWorld property hotels generated $1416 million. Their annual rate of occupation was 80.9% and the total revenue per occupied hotel room was $199.06. The revenue generated by hotels accounted for 34.6% of the total for the Walt Disney World complex.

In 1994 Disney created Celebration on an area covering over 1600 ha. In addition to the hotels and the residential town, one should add the three water parks (Blizzard Beach, River Country and Typhoon Lagoon), the 48 ha of Downtown Disney, a space for entertainment, commerce and food and beverage with three zones – Marketplace, Pleasure Island and West Side – and Disney's Wide World of Sports, a sports complex open since 1997, where teams from the top American leagues train.

Despite its self-sufficient nature, the development of Disney property has catalysed the growth of the surrounding area. Now, though good urban planning is characteristic of Disney property, the developments located around it have been far from harmonious as regards their aesthetics and far from efficient from a functional point of view. The Disney Company's political, administrative and financial autonomy within its property has allowed the creation of an out-of-the-conventional destination with very high standards of quality, but has shifted the urban problems it wished to solve to the outside. Thus, for example, in Kissimee and Lake Buenavista, areas adjacent to Disney property, hotel and business premises have developed in typical suburban American style. In fact, in the same way as it may be said that Disney has led the way in Orlando's

Table 8.2. Chronology of the creation of hotel rooms at Walt Disney World Resort, 1979–2004 (from Disney FactBook, 2004).

	Class	Opening	Rooms
Resorts operated by Disney			
Contemporary Resort	Premium	Oct. 1971	1,008
Polynesian Resort	Premium	Oct. 1971	847
Grand Floridian Resort and Spa	Premium	Jul. 1988	867
Caribbean Beach Resort	Moderate	Oct. 1988	2,112
Yacht Club Resort	Premium	Nov. 1990	621
Beach Club Resort	Premium	Nov. 1990	576
Port Orleans-French Quarter	Moderate	May. 1991	1,008
Port Orleans-River Side	Moderate	Feb. 1992	2,048
All-Star Sports Resort	Economy	May. 1994	1,920
Wilderness Lodge	Premium	May. 1994	727
All-Star Music Resort	Economy	Nov. 1994	1,920
Boardwalk Inn	Premium	July 1996	372
Coronado Springs	Moderate	Aug. 1997	1,921
All-Star Movies Resort	Economy	Jan. 1999	1,920
Animal Kingdom Lodge	Premium	Apr. 2001	1,923
Disney's Pop! Century	Economy	Dec. 2003	1,880
Campsites operated by Disney			
Fort Wilderness Campsites	–	Oct. 1971	784
Fort Wilderness Cabins	–	Oct. 1971	409
Subtotal operated by Disney			23,233
Resorts not operated by Disney[a]		–	6,278
Total at Walt Disney World Resort		–	29,811

a. Included are hotels operated by other companies near Disney Downtown Marketplace, plus Disney World Swan and Disney World Dolphin, which are also operated by other companies.

touristic transformation, it has also brought about the multiplication of initiatives that have not been solved following the control criteria that exist within Disney property. Also, Disney has generated specific needs in its surroundings as regards transport and housing infrastructures which have not been solved by the company. Hiaasen (1991), for example, has been highly critical of this reality.

The opening of Universal Studios in 1990 turned Orlando as a tourist destination into the scene of a battle of the giants between the two principal media and thematic entertainment corporations (Samuels, 1996, 7). In the wake of Disney, the construction of a complete holiday and recreational complex was also in Universal Studios' sights in the 1990s. Thus, in addition to inaugurating a new park adjacent to the one it had established in 1990 (see Corliss, 1999), in Florida it reproduced the City Walk idea which it had put to the test in its California park. With the City Walk, Universal Studios linked up the two parks, making an entertainment area with restaurants, retail establishments, nightlife facilities and 16 cinema studios seating 5000. Also, in the resort housing the two parks and the City Walk, Universal developed three hotel establishments: Portofino Bay Hotel (750 rooms), Hard Rock (650 rooms) and Royal Pacific (1000 rooms). Each one is 20% cheaper than the previous one. Universal's strategy during the 1990s was, therefore, 'to follow the formula' for success launched by Disney though 'changing the contents' and adapting to the specific conditioning factor of being 'a park in the city' and not having their own capacity to develop. Following Universal's arrival in Orlando, Disney reformulated its strategies, started to sell complete holidaying experiences using its hotels and incorporated new attractions, urged by the initiatives taken by Universal in its second park. Thus, though in a different style and in different conditions, while Universal reproduced Disney's keys to success, Disney began to take Universal's strategies into account (Rubin, 1997). In all, moreover, both operators were faced with the challenge to maintain a touristic dynamic which, while growing, has proved to be highly rewarding economically, and has been in a state of progressive maturity since the 1990s. In any case, rivalry between Disney and Universal during the 1990s meant that one could speak in Orlando of a situation of change from a Disney monopoly during the 1980s (Braun *et al.*, 1992) to an oligopoly with shared leadership by the two (Braun and Soskin, 1999).

Currently, including the SeaWorld park, in Orlando, seven large parks are up and running (four belonging to Disney, two to Universal and one to SeaWorld) and tens of other attractions. This has made Orlando the main competitor for Florida's classic holiday destinations – like the city of Miami itself – and one of the main tourist destinations in the world. Now, Orlando's consolidation as a theme park tourist destination, following two decades (the 1970s and 1980s) in which the only concern was to receive greater visitor numbers, forces one to question the capacity of the model. Today, what is important in Orlando, as in the parks themselves, is not just to attract greater demand, but, above all, to ensure return visits (Robinett, 1999). In the end, according to the city's Convention and Visitor Bureau, in Orlando it is being seen that an increase in supply cannot ensure an equivalent rhythm of increase in demand (Blank, 2000). What is more, numerous corporations such as Marriott or Disney and Universal are decidedly going into the timeshare property market. Concerning this, see the data in Table 8.3 on the evolution of lodging indicators in Orlando between 1979 and 2005 in terms of the growth in the supply of hotel rooms and variations in levels of occupation. There is little need to point out, on the other hand, the effects of the terrorist attack of 11 September 2001 with regard to visitor numbers or occupation and prices.

The question that has arisen is to what extent the growth in the affluence of visitors to the city and the parks can be maintained when, on average, the tourists only visit 1.4 parks per capita and, conversely, the length of their

Table 8.3. Evolution of tourist supply and demand in Orlando (from Orlando Convention and Visitor Bureau (CVB) Research Department).

Year	Number of hotel rooms	Rate of occupation (%)	Rooms occupied (in millions)[a]	Mean daily price ($)
1979	31,800	71.0	8.2	28.00
1980	32,200	70.0	8.3	34.00
1981	33,620	67.0	8.2	37.00
1982	33,763	69.0	8.5	40.00
1983	37,602	79.0	10.9	40.00
1984	44,530	68.0	11.1	52.00
1985	52,783	66.0	12.7	51.00
1986	57,696	70.0	14.7	52.00
1987	60,959	73.0	16.2	52.00
1988	61,558	76.0	17.1	53.00
1989	68,500	78.8	19.4	59.83
1990	76,260	75.3	20.0	66.20
1991	77,511	70.8	19.6	64.83
1992	78,929	74.1	21.5	63.82
1993	80,112	72.2	20.8	64.61
1994	82,287	71.3	21.1	65.62
1995	84,614	74.6	22.7	68.55
1996	85,994	80.1	24.8	73.04
1997	88,011	79.0	25.0	79.81
1998	92,014	74.6	24.4	82.12
1999	99,171	71.7	25.1	84.21
2000	102,838	72.6	26.7	89.83
2001	106,069	63.7	24.5	87.29
2002	109,784	62.6	24.9	88.02
2003	111,687	62.7	24.9	84.60
2004	112,981	70.9	29.1	86.80
2005	111,564	70.7	29.0	91.91

a. Indicates the total number of rooms occupied during the year.

holidays remains basically stable, if indeed it is not falling. In this respect, Braun and Milman (1994) showed that patterns of complementarity exist between parks and processes for substitution for one another are generalized. The maturity of Orlando's tourism model is equally observable when analysing the visitor numbers to the main parks as of the 1990s, as is reflected in Table 8.4. Without going into considerations in respect of the effects of the 11 September attacks on 2001 and 2002, it can be appreciated that, despite the increase in the number of large parks by two in 1997 and 2000, the maximum increment in demand achieved is a mere 9.4 million

Table 8.4. Visitors to parks of the main operators (in millions of visits)[a] (based on *Amusement Business* data).

	1997	1998	1999	2000	2001	2002	2003	2004	2005
Disney	39.3 (3)	41.7 (4)	42.6 (4)	43.2 (4)	40.2 (4)	37.6 (4)	37.8 (4)	40.6 (4)	42.9 (4)
Universal	8.9 (1)	8.9 (1)	11.5 (2)	14.1 (2)	12.8 (2)	12.8 (2)	12.9 (2)	13.0 (2)	11.9 (2)
Sea World	4.9 (1)	4.9 (1)	4.7 (1)	5.2 (1)	5.1 (1)	5.0 (1)	5.2 (1)	5.6 (1)	5.6 (1)
Total	53.1 (5)	55.5 (6)	58.8 (7)	62.5 (7)	58.1 (7)	55.4 (7)	55.9 (7)	59.2 (7)	60.4 (7)
Visits per park	10.6	9.3	8.4	8.9	8.3	7.9	7.9	8.4	8.6

a. The number of parks in parentheses.

between 1997 and the year 2000. Between these same two years, the number of visitors per park fell by 1.7 million. It is indicative, in this sense, that, whereas at the end of the 1980s authors like Braun and Milman (1990) refer to the effects of the economies of location to explain the expansion of the park business in Orlando, in the mid-1990s, authors such as Mason and Opperman (1996) were speaking of the competition between the parks of the same location in terms of the 'cannibalization' of the demand. This effect not only arises among the large parks but also concerns all of the other attractions.

The main motivations for visiting Orlando are leisure-related (76%). In 2004, the average stay of North American visitors spending a night in Orlando was 2.8 nights. Average expenditure was $1381 per party per trip. These visitors' average per family income was $70,649. Of these visitors, 58% visited the theme parks. International visitors (5.4% in 2004) spent 11.7 nights on average and spent a mean of $898 per person per trip in Orlando. Their reasons for coming were 82% leisure/recreation/holiday and the main activities they carried out were shopping (94%), dining (90%) and visiting amusement/theme parks (86%). Their mean income was $82,200 per family. The figures, however, also indicate that, in Orlando, tourist affluence does not just head for the theme parks. As can be seen in Table 8.5, almost 21% of domestic visitors to Orlando in 2004 came for business purposes. This figure is up almost 5% on that for 1993 and, in absolute numbers, there was double the number of visits to Orlando for this purpose in 2004. In 2004, professional visits brought about an economic impact of $3.1 billion (including the $315 million spent by exhibitors at the conventions centre). Their average spending was $722 per person per trip, their mean stay lasting 3.3 nights. Orlando's bid to increase this segment of visitors has been highly significant in recent years, with the execution of an improvement and expansion plan for the conventions centre linked to the expansion of Universal Studios in the city. This expansion is being funded by the Orlando Convention and Visitor Bureau (CVB) with the funds it obtains through the tourist tax paid by visitors. The Convention Center, located in the part of Orange County called International Drive, receives between 5 and 6 million delegates a year and generated some

Table 8.5. Travel to Orlando, 1993–2004 (based on data from the Orlando/Orange County CVB).

	1993		2004	
	Total	%	Total	%
Domestic	24,897,000	87.6	45,166,000	94.5
Leisure	20,053,000	70.5	35,162,000	73.9
Florida	12,183,000	42.8	17,672,000	37.0
Rest of the USA	7,869,000	27.7	17,491,000	36.6
Business	4,844,000	17.0	10,004,000	20.9
Florida	2,939,000	10.3	6,077,000	12.7
Rest of the USA	1,905,000	6.7	3,928,000	8.2
International	3,537,000	12.4	2,582,000	5.5
Total	28,434,000	–	47,748,000	–

$5 thousand million in the metropolitan area of Orlando between 1998 and 2003.

In Orlando, the public management of tourism is handled by the Convention and Visitor Bureau, a non-profit-making private organization with over 500 members, which has a contract with the administration basically to promote tourism and administer the conventions centre. To do so, it has available to it the funds collected from the resort tax (5% added to each tourist's spending when using any touristic service), from its members' contributions and from its own income through the rendering of services.

8.1.2. Orlando besides the parks

As has already been said, tourism in Orlando is the city's most dynamic activity. It produces the most jobs, generates more income in the form of taxes than the costs involved in its development and provides quality of life. Moreover, it acts on two intangibles: the development of committed labour ethics (young people come into the labour market through companies in which training is important) and the stimulus of residential mobility towards the city (especially among the younger population residing in other towns).The importance of tourism and, in particular, of theme parks has, on the other hand, boosted the growth of the cinema and television production industry. Thus, Orlando is the USA number three city for film production and Nickelodeon's headquarters. In parallel, as has already been mentioned, it has become one of the main destinations for congress and convention tourism, competing with classic US cities such as Chicago.

According to the Economic Development Commission of Mid-Florida, the development of tourism has a further two strategic implications for the city's economic dynamics and for those of the metropolitan area. In the first place, it sustains the airport and has led to the creation of new national and international lines and connections. This factor is of great importance from the point of view of attracting companies. Thus, today's Orlando International Airport, created in 1981 as a replacement for the Orlando Herndon Airport, has become the 14th biggest airport in the world, with 958 movements a day and nearly 32 million domestic passengers in 2005, in addition to which are 2.2 million international passengers. Secondly, congresses and conventions held and the arrival of executives in the city spending their holidays facilitates contacts between the organizations that promote the economy and companies that are potentially interested in setting up in Orlando. In this way, tourism is used in Orlando as a strategic instrument to communicate the opportunities the city has to offer to entrepreneurs and top managers. In this way, these economic promotion bodies aim to explain, without having to move from site, matters of interest to potential investors: matters such as the size of the market, access to suppliers, regulations governing trade, the nature of the job market, the demographic profile, labour, structural and development costs, the system of taxation, the price of the land or issues concerning logistics and the possibilities of funding, among many others. Also, by means of this strategy, investors can find out for themselves the role, singularities and characteristics of Orlando in comparison with rival, neighbouring cities such as Miami and Tampa, whose image as centres for the location of administrative and service or industrial activities is more consolidated than Orlando's, normally associated with greater or less exclusivity with the dynamics of the Disney theme parks, in particular.

In short, advantage is taken of the arrival of visitors in order to show that, as well as being a place with a pleasant image, Orlando is a good place to do business. In this way, an attempt is made to overcome the idea that a tourist destination cannot be a good place to carry out activities related to other sectors of activity. As Fjellman (1992) and Archer (1996) report, the result is that Orlando's image of being Disney headquarters and a holiday resort has proved useful for the location of international or regional headquarters of companies or for the attraction of an NBA franchize, which is important in symbolic terms and for the promotion of the city within the USA. As Zukin (1995) claims, companies are attracted to Orlando because Disney and the theme parks project a certain image of quality, cleanliness, absence of ethnic conflicts and well-being of the city, which means that potential investors or new residents will not have to worry about mundanities such as bad weather or safety and security. As a result, each week in Orlando, 103 successful new business establishments are set up and 314 new jobs are generated for the 1275 new adult residents coming to the city and its metropolitan area. As Zukin (1995) states, to a certain extent Orlando reiterates the mythology of Los Angeles: a young city, with employment both in industry and in the services and an image of leisure.

In any case, fundamental differences exist between industrial and touristic activities. The first is that, while the theme parks have generated

Table 8.6. Major industries in Metro Orlando, 2005 (from Metro Orlando Economic Development Commission).

	Establishments		Employees	
	No.	%	No.	%
Services	32,118	42.15	357,042	40.17
Retail trade	15,911	20.88	199,125	22.40
Finance, insurance and real estate	7,901	10.37	56,810	6.39
Construction	6,346	8.33	48,274	5.43
Wholesale trade	4,070	5.34	44,053	4.96
Transportation and communications	2,797	3.67	45,726	5.14
Manufacturing	2,341	3.07	51,938	5.84
Agriculture, forestry and fisheries	1,669	2.19	37,124	4.18
Public administration	1,518	1.99	40,746	4.58
Other	1,532	2.01	7,930	0.90

an image of the place, the defence, aerospace and high-technology industries have not. However, whereas industry has managed to attract the suppliers to the Orlando metropolitan area, helping to create a veritable industrial fabric associated with its development, the effects of the theme parks in the creation of a support industry has been more limited, barring their effects on the film and television industry. Thirdly, the average wage is somewhat lower in the leisure and hospitality industry ($5475 for the second quarter of 2005) than the mean for all industries ($8821). Indeed, industrial workers earned an average $11,244 in the same second quarter and workers in professional, scientific and technical services $13,327. Globally, the distribution of work and the economic activity of the main sectors are as reflected in Table 8.6. The city's main employers are Walt Disney World (57,000), Florida Hospital (14,667), Universal Orlando (13,000), Orlando Regional Healthcare (12,178), the University of Central Florida (8250), Central Florida Investments (7500), Darden Restaurants Inc. (7361) and Marriott International Inc. (6312). Other major manufacturers set up in the city are: Lockheed Martin Missiles, Siemens Westinghouse Power, Lockheed Martin Simulations Training and Support, Orlando Sentinel Communications, Oracle Corp and Northrop Grumman Electronic. In addition, Orlando has one of the most highly valued office real-estate markets in the USA.

8.2. Disneyland Paris and the Planning of Marne-la-Vallée

Euro Disney SCA owns and operates the Disneyland Paris theme park and resort. The park, opened in 1992, features 43 rides and attractions, restaurants, shops and live entertainment. It is Europe's top tourist attraction, drawing more than 10 million visitors a year. Ten years later, Euro Disney opened the gates of a second theme park, the Walt Disney Studios Park. It draws more than 2 million visitors per year. The company also runs seven hotels, two convention centres and the Disney Village entertainment complex, which links the parks with the on-site hotels. Euro Disney has also developed its own town, Val d'Europe, anchored by a shopping centre and a business park. Euro Disney pays royalty and management fees to the Walt Disney Company, which also owns 39.9% of the shares. Saudi Prince Al Waleed owns 10% and the rest of the shares are owned by several others. Due to its location, 32 km to the east of Paris, and its links via a great variety of transport systems, Disneyland Paris is situated in the centre of a potential market of 17 million people residing less than a 2-h drive or train journey away and over 320 million potential visitors less than a 2-h flight away.

In the early 1990s, according to its designers, Disneyland Paris had to be somewhat 'bigger and better than any Disneyland or Disney World'. It had to bear in mind, just as Grover (1997, 237) says, that the Europeans 'have grown up in the shadows of great monuments and cathedrals'. The project was lived with excitement in the company. It was the flagship of Disney in Europe. However, in the mid-1990s, Disneyland Paris had become, in the words, once more of Grover (1997, 235), its biggest headache since the 1980s. In this regard, Phillippe Bourguignon, CEO of Disneyland Paris in 1992/93, explains the bad results of the first years through the 14–12–9 equation. According to this, Disneyland Paris needed 14 million visitors per year, had a capacity for 12 million and got a demand of only 9 million (Bourguignon, 2005). Thus, due to the poor financial results obtained in the first 2 years, in March 1994 the possibility of closure was being considered. To solve this, a consortium of 60 banks announced an agreement to restructure the debt of a thousand million dollars owed by Euro Disney SCA – the company exploiting Disney's recreational complex in Paris – while Saudi Prince Al-Waleed Bin Talal Bin Abdulaziz Al Saud came in to buy nearly a quarter of the company shares for $247 million. During the 1990s, the idea of creating a new Orlando on the outskirts of Paris slowed down and the second park took longer to materialize than had been foreseen. However, at the beginning of the new millennium, Disneyland Paris had in fact become the main thematic tourist destination in Europe.

The company made several mistakes in its initial stages, which have been explained in depth (see Martí and Comas, 1994; Grover, 1997; Richards and Richards, 1998): among other questions, issues such as location, costs and construction schedule have been said not to have kept to what had been predicted; the limited provision of attractions (only 15 big attractions at the time of opening compared with the 45 in the California park); Europeans' tastes and preferences were not taken into due consideration with regard to food and beverages and consumption; the structure of admission prices to the park and hotels, which ended up being the highest in the world; and an erroneous concept of complementarity between the park and the city of Paris, a major urban tourism destination in Europe.

Analysts like Altman (1995) or Packman and Casmir (1999) insist, more-over, on the Disney Company's lack of sensitivity concerning European cultural specificities as a key factor which would explain Disney's waste of 'time, money and reputation' in the first stage of its European adventure. The recessive economic climate in the early 1990s in France did not help matters for the company. Since the mid-1990s, however, the situation has improved notably.

Thus, the principal positive aspects of Disneyland Paris with a view to the future are its leadership on a European level; the well-known Disney brand itself; the good operational results both from a commercial point of view and regarding costs control; and the potential for added value it is achieving and may obtain on the basis of the Val d'Europe development project. On the downside are the still greatly limited room for financial manoeuvre due to the amounts owed, the difficulty of maintaining results, increased financial burdens, the concentration of all operations in just one place, the royalties Euro Disney SCA must pay to the Walt Disney Company and the results themselves, which were below forecast for the first years of Walt Disney Studios' functioning.

As can be seen in Table 8.7, with some 12 million visitors, today's Disneyland Paris complex seems to have reached the threshold of maxi-mum frequentation. Though the opening of Walt Disney Studios was a strategy hatched in order to surpass this figure, the results obtained so far would indicate the contrary. A substitution effect has been brought about, which, on the other hand, has allowed an increase in repetition and, in another sense, a guarantee of high levels of occupation of the hotels year-round. In fact, the opening of the Walt Disney Studios has not trans-lated into an improvement in company results. In addition to the substitu-tion effect, the additional costs associated with its start-up and the low growth of the market during recent years have meant that Euro Disney SCA had to restructure its debt once again in 2005. Also, some marketing and sales strategies have had to be rethought and improvements to the hotels and attractions have had to be planned. Among them is the improvement of the experience offered by the two parks, the development of seasonal events, the improvement of the positioning of the hotels and the orientation of sales and marketing towards new visitors and new distribution channels.

In relative terms, 40% of visitors to the Disneyland Paris parks come from France, 19% from Great Britain, 16% from the Benelux countries, 8% from Spain, 6% from Germany, 3% from Italy and 3% from other countries. During the year, there is an average of 40,000 visitors a day to the park, of which 55% come to the resort by car, 15% by plane, 14% by train, 11% by coach and the remaining 5% by the railway system that serves the area around Paris, the RER. In 2004, theme parks represented 51% of the company's sales, whereas the hotels brought in 39%. In addi-tion to tourist activities, Euro Disney SCA obtains minimal income, which is set to grow in the coming years, from the development and management of the almost 2000 ha of land it has and, in the next few years, from the

Table 8.7. Euro Disney SCA operating results, 1992–2004 (based on company reports and *Amusement Business* and Bear Sterns data).

Park	1992	1993	1994	1995	1996	1997	1998	1999	2000	2001	2002	2003	2004
Visits to Park I[a]	7.0	9.8	8.8	10.7	11.7	12.6	12.5	12.5	12.0	12.2	10.3	10.2	10.2
Visits to Park II[a]	–	–	–	–	–	–	–	–	–	–	2.8	2.2	2.2
Total visits[a]	7.0	9.8	8.8	10.7	11.7	12.6	12.5	12.5	12.0	12.2	13.1	12.4	12.4
Per capita spending (euros)	56.6	40.4	39.7	35.2	37.8	38.3	39.3	40.7	42.2	43.1	42.7	40.7	40.1
Income[b]	396	395	349	376	409	452	464	460	459	476	526	508	531
Hotel occupation (%)	74	55	60	68.5	72.2	78	80.9	82.6	82.9	86	88	85	80
Hotel income[b]	190	262	234	270	295	330	365	352	370	387	412	417	405
Property income[b]	–	–	–	–	–	–	–	–	15	37	27	24	12
Other income[b]	–	85	49	51	50	53	69	108	115	105	106	99	100
Total income[b]	586	742	632	697	754	835	898	920	959	1005	1071	1047	1048
Operational costs[b]	370	516	430	418	432	480	501	503	531	549	609	639	664
Administration and general[b]	129	170	152	169	173	175	173	171	171	186	187	202	203
Depreciations and amortizations[b]	48	35	44	40	43	45	47	49	50	54	64	66	147
Royalties and management costs[b]	30	62	–	–	–	–	–	31	31	32	35	8	58
Total costs[b]	577	783	626	627	648	701	722	754	783	820	895	915	1072
Operating profit[b]	9	–41	6	70	106	134	176	166	176	185	176	132	–24

a. (million)
b. (million euros)

Val d'Europe residential property development, as well as the development of public, sports and business services. Also 9% of the company's income comes from the sale of other tourism and commercial services. To develop its activities, in 2004 Euro Disney SCA employed 12,162 people, leading to an expenditure of €336 million on salaries. Its own staff training system, in order to ensure quality, generated 54,535 days of instruction for the same period.

The development of Disneyland Paris was accompanied by strong progression in the hotel business during the 1990s. From 55% occupation in 1993, it has now risen, with variations, to over 80% in the new millennium. Conventions, company seminars and meetings have been especially important outside the high season and explain such results. Thus, some 1500 events are held each year at the two congress-oriented hotels (New York and Newport Bay Club), though there is demand for over 2000 annual events. Today, Euro Disney SCA has seven hotels (Disneyland, New Cork, Newport Bay Club, Sequoia Lodge, Cheyenne, Santa Fe and Davy Crockett Ranch), with 5800 rooms. Another 2033 rooms correspond to seven associated or recommended hotels with which the company has sales and marketing contracts (Elysés Val d'Europe, MyTravel Explorer, Kyriad, Résidence Pierre et Vacances, Holiday Inn, Marriot Vacation Club, Mövenpick Dream Castle). Table 8.8 shows the evolution of per-room and per visitor unitary income for the park between 2000 and 2004. With regard to per capita spending in the parks, it must be pointed out that mean spending in the new park in its first year of opening was €25 compared with the €45.3 of the first park.

As mentioned previously, in addition to being a recreational complex with two theme parks, hotels, the Disney Village and Golf Disneyland, Disneyland Paris is the key component of a territorial planning operation conceived by the French state as a means to re-equilibrate the east of Paris. Disneyland Paris is in fact a project born as a result of the establishment of the agreement signed on 24 March 1987 by the Walt Disney Company, on the one hand, and the French state, the Île-de-France

Table 8.8. Key indicators of income by activity (from company reports).

| | Theme parks | | Hotels | |
	Visitors (million)	Spending per visitor (€)	Rate of occupation (%)	Spending per room (€)
2000	12.0	38.1	82.9	165.4
2001	12.2	38.9	86.0	168.6
2002	13.1	40.1	88.2	175.1
2003	12.4	40.7	85.1	183.5
2004	12.4	42.7	80.5	186.6

region, the Seine et Marne Département, the Etablissement Public
d'Aménagement de Marne-la-Vallée and the Régie Autonome de Trans-
ports Parisiens, on the other. Disneyland Paris is, therefore, the principal
node of territorial polarity planned by the French administration, with a
leaning towards centrality on a regional, European and even transconti-
nental scale. Being connected by the TGV with the main European
metropolises and through the airport with the rest of the world strengthens this condition.

Thus, when Disney decided to undertake its European expansion process, it found that, thanks to this programme, in the area to the east of
Paris there is ample provision of land suitable for urbanizing, concrete
commitments to provide infrastructures by the state and appropriate legal
and administrative mechanisms to get a project under way with the drive,
commitment and support of the public sector (see a detailed explanation
of the support given by the administration in Lanquar, 1992, and Grover,
1997). In fact, Disney's location in Paris is justified, in the first place, by
the commitment made by the French public sector, which considers the
project as being of general interest, offers guarantees and simplifies the
negotiation process, with the appointment of an interministerial delegate
for the project. If you add to this the fame of the universal image of Paris,
the existence of an important communications network and the market area
obtained by a park located in Paris, any other proposed location would
have meant incurring opportunity costs (D'Hauteserre, 1997, 23).

Therefore, it may be stated that the success of and the prospects for
Disneyland Paris are not simply the result of the company's capacity and
its good choice of location in relation to the market, but they are directly
guaranteed by the development policies implemented by the French public administration. Without a doubt, these guarantees have also helped to
overcome the financial difficulties (Taylor and Stevens, 1995) the project
had in its early days and which were solved through financial restructuring in March 1994. Moreover, the commitment between the public sector
and the private sector has led, though with delays, to the creation of a
veritable recreational and commercial attraction, in which, as the news-
paper *Les Echos* headed a piece of news on 2 December 1998, the state
also makes its demands on the company to the extent of having 'per-
suaded' Disney 'to launch a second theme park'.

It cannot be forgotten, however, that, in spite of its results and strategic nature, the setting up of Disneyland Paris has been highly criticized,
especially at the beginning. Thus, Lipietz (1987), considered that it was
'a project of no public interest' regarding which neither the commitment
by nor the support of the French administration could be justified. Jacquin
(1993), moreover, characterized Disneyland Paris, in comparison with Futuroscope, as 'a prestigious operation of national importance with uncertain
and arguable economic results' and, along complementary lines, Alphandéry
(1993, 1996) qualified the project as unsustainable. Grover (1997) acknowledged, in another sense, that the French intellectuals spoke of the development of Disneyland in Paris as a kind of 'Cultural Chernobyl' (regarding

this, see Lanquar, 1992), while Ariès (2002) contemplates the park's installation process as the 'story of a nation's submission to Mickey'.

8.2.1. The creation of Disneyland Paris in Marne-la-Vallée

For the French state, Disneyland Paris is the spearhead of an operation of broader scope, as is the creation of Val d'Europe in sector IV of the 'new town' of Marne-la-Vallée (in the municipalities of Chessy, Coupvray, Bailly-Romainvilliers, Magny le Hongre and Serris). This operation also involves, in addition to the Disney complex, residential uses, a multifunctional international business park, an area of offices and a latest-generation regional mall. Until the establishment of the park, the process of urbanizing the 'new town' of Marne-la-Vallée to the east of Paris was only reaching sectors I and II. Disneyland Paris became a fundamental instrument for urbanization to get as far as sector IV.

The development of 'new towns' was planned in France during the second half of the 1960s. Five were foreseen in the Paris region (Evry, Cergy-Pontoise, Saint-Quentin-en-Yvelines, Melun-Senart and Marne-la-Vallée) and another four in the outskirts of Lille, Rouen, Lyon and Marseille. The Marne-la-Vallée 'new town' is the result of a planning process that began, in the Paris region, with the passing in 1960 of the Plan d'aménagement et d'organisation générale de la région parisienne and in 1965 of the Schéma Directeur d'Aménagement et d'Urbanisme de la région de Paris. In 1976, the Schéma Directeur d'Aménagement et d'Urbanisme de la région Île-de-France established the general development principles of the five Parisian 'new towns' and in 1994 the new Schéma Directeur de la région Île-de-France reconsidered some points of the urbanization process in order to save some spaces from being built upon.

The 'new town' of Marne-la-Vallée has been developed between 12 and 37 km to the east of Paris. It was constituted in 1972 in the space of 26 municipalities. It is 25 km long and between 5 and 10 km wide. It is an urban space that is still being consolidated, with a total surface area greater than that of the city of Paris itself (15,214 ha compared with the 10,500 ha of Paris). It is connected with the city via the A4 motorway (functioning since 1976), by line A of the RER (running since 1977) and by TGV (inaugurated in 1994). It is organized according to four successive sectors, which are set apart by their level of consolidation, the socio-demographic characteristics of their inhabitants and the building styles and functions they host:

- Sector I. Porte de Paris-Noisy le Grand (three municipalities, 2063 ha).
- Sector II. Le Val Maubuée-Cité Descartes (six municipalities, 3815 ha).
- Sector III. Le Val Bussy (12 municipalities, 6121 ha).
- Sector IV. Le Val d'Europe (five municipalities, 3215 ha).

The urban development process was progressive from sector I to IV. In sector III, urbanization was not started, and when it was it was only very weak, until the 1980s. Sector IV, where Disneyland Paris is located, was on reserve until 1987. That year, coinciding with the agreement with Disney, urbanization was begun. In addition to the North American company's recreation complex, the planning of the sector includes the Val d'Europe Urban Centre, an international business park, new residential areas and the European food area project. According to the current outline plan, the objectives for sector IV of the 'new town' of Marne-la-Vallée were, at the time of its creation, to reach a population volume in the order of 40,000 inhabitants, 14,000 new dwellings, 700,000 m^2 of office space and 450,000 m^2 of activities, which would mean the total employment of some 65,000.

For the administrative management of the process of the creation of the 'new towns', a special structure, called an Etablissement Public d'Aménagement (EPA), was created for each one. In the 'new town' of Marne-la-Vallée, EPA Marne was created in 1972 and currently oversees the development of sectors I to III. EPA France, created in 1987, manages the development of sector IV. Moreover, in sector IV, the Syndicat d'Agglomération Nouvelle (SAN) of Portes de la Brie is in operation, an association to which the five municipalities located within the perimeter of the project (Coupvray, Chessy, Serris, Magny-le-Hongrie and Bailly-Romainvilliers) have delegated their competencies concerning urbanism, housing, transport, infrastructures, facilities and economic development. In fact, the municipalities' direct competency in the management of the development favoured by Disneyland Paris is limited since, given the size of the investment, the state's involvement is logical. Thus, when the agreement protocol was signed between the French state, the Île-de-France region and the Disney Company in December 1985, the départements and the municipalities where the project was to be located had still not been consulted. Later, the département of Seine et Marne and EPA France joined the process until the signature of the agreement; and, in parallel, in 1987 the SAN of Portes de Brie was created in order to demonstrate their concerns and take part in the negotiations.

The agreement between the different levels of the French public administration and the Disney Company signed on 24 March 1987 establishes the commitment by the North American company to develop a theme park and an 'important area' of recreational and tourist facilities around the park (which may include a second park), the location of the project on a surface area of 1934 ha in sector IV of the 'new town' of Marne-la-Vallée (approximately 60% of the surface area of the sector) and the commitments by the French public administrations as regards the modification of the statute of the 'new towns', the facilities and infrastructures to be financed, the planning programme, the cession of land and the financial conditions of the agreement. The agreement establishes, moreover, the nature and characteristics of the relationships between the private company and the administration and the geographical setting and the process of urban development over the following 30 years, and specifies, significantly, that 'a determining element of the parties' duties is that the global financial equilibrium of the project should stem from the combination of the operation of the park and the other foreseen aspects of the project'. Furthermore, the Disney Company acquired other commitments with regard to the social benefits that the project must bring in for the local communities where it is situated (concerning this, see Caillart, 1987). Finally, it foresees that the development should be done in stages.

It is clear, therefore, that, with Disney's arrival in Paris, private company and public administration agree not just to the development of a recreational and tourist project capable of boosting economic development and territorial re-equilibrium, but they also promise to support mutually the specific strategies of the other party (Maillard, 2003), that is to say, guarantee the business of Disney in the case of the French public administration and create a centre of development that would ensure the state's territorial policy for the east of Paris in the case of Disney (Bagherzadeh, 1988). Hence all of the planning development process that should be favoured by the establishment of the park is to be carried out by the company Euro Disney SCA and EPA France. It was also EPA France that sold to the company Pivot, constituted by Euro Disney SCA, the land it requires to carry out the project in the area set aside for it. In fact, EPA France is a public corporation for territorial development whose mission is to perform all necessary operations so as to facilitate the planning of its area of competency. This is why it is capacitated to acquire, if necessary via expropriation, the necessary spaces to achieve its aims and exercise rights of pre-emptive purchase in accordance with the French urban planning code. It performs planning, programming and financing functions, as well as the building of the facilities, and has powers to manage land and coordinate with other local and supralocal administrations.

8.2.2. The role of Disney in Val d'Europe

Val d'Europe is structured into different units that are organized according to focuses:

1. The tourism and leisure centre. This is mainly concentrated in the area found in the circular boulevard of sector IV. It includes the four large areas of the Disney project (in addition to which, from the point of view of the recreational complex, Golf Disneyland should be added, despite being located outside the circular boulevard):

- Two theme parks. Disneyland, inaugurated in 1992, which recreates the world of Disney characters with the well-known thematic areas of Main Street USA, Frontierland, Adventureland, Fantasyland and Discoveryland, and Walt Disney Studios, inaugurated in 2002, devoted to entertainment through the cinema, animation and television in four different areas: Front Lot, Animation Courtyard, Production Courtyard and Back Lot.
- Seven thematic hotels belonging to Disney (with an area covering 10,500 m² for congresses in the New York and Newport Bay Club

hotels), ranging from two to four stars (from the Disneyland Hotel to Disney's Hotel Santa Fe), with 5165 rooms, and 535 log cabins in a 57 ha wood that make up Disney's Davy Crockett Ranch.

- Three hotels selected by Disney, whose architectural aesthetics are characteristic of the Île de France, operated by external partners (MyTravel, Six Continents and the Envergure Group), ranging from two to four stars and with a capacity of 1100 rooms. This strategy allows the growth of the resort to continue without undertaking investments, and the creation of a new hotel area, Val de France. Another expansion phase is scheduled, which will mean the creation of a further 1100 rooms.

- Disney Village, a street designed by architect Frank O. Gehry with 18,000 m² of shops, bars, clubs and restaurants and 15 cinema screens, which transport the visitors to the leisure atmosphere of the USA. It works as an axis that joins the parks and the hotels, aiming to become one of the night-time leisure centres of the Île-de-France region, with links to RER, TGV and coach stations.

2. The Val d'Europe urban centre. The main urban premises of the whole of sector IV are concentrated in this centre. It includes:

- The International Commercial Centre. Constructed out of iron and glass, its surface area covers 98,000 m² and consists of a hypermarket, ten medium-sized commercial areas and 130 shops. It includes 20 restaurants, a giant aquarium, Sea Life, managed by Merlin Entertainment, and a fitness centre. It is a mall conceived in a way that considers the consumer as a visitor (see Fournié, 2001, and Lemoine, 2001, for further details).

- The Vallée Shopping Village. This is an open-air mall covering 15,000 m², set up as a pedestrian urban artery, with 70 shops selling stock from previous seasons' collections of fashion labels of international renown at a reduced price.

- The station neighbourhood. This is developed around an esplanade and includes urban facilities for commerce, services, residence, a media library, a musical and choreographic area and a second RER and coach station.

- An educational area, made up of a set of school institutions that will be able to take up to 5000 students in 2010 and a campus of the Université de Marne-la-Vallée, which complements in Val d'Europe the already existing one in la Cité Descartes, focusing on the arts, shows, new technologies, health and international relations.

3. The area of industrial, craft and office activities. This is based around the International Business Park. Set on 180 ha of land, 660,000 m² have been built which are to be split 55% for offices, 20% for premises for high-technology activities, 20% for mixed premises and 5% for services. The aim is to generate 20,000 jobs in the context of a high-quality setting and environment.

4. The green spaces, for sports activities and open air recreation. The landscape and green areas have been conceived as basic structural units of the urban area. The original agricultural activities carried out on the land have been greatly transformed due to the 3 million m³ of earth shifted, the 450,000 trees and shrubs planted and the 25 km of communications and electricity lines that criss-cross it. However, this has meant the configuration of a specific landscape where most green and agricultural areas are kept in the municipality of Coupvray, while an 11 ha park has been designed linking the urban centre with the International Business Park. Disney's 27-hole golf course is this sector's main constructed facility. It is divided into three nine-hole courses (par-36, designed by Golfplan Design Group Ltd).

For the development of the sector, an agreement was reached to advance in stages. In February 1989, the detailed programme of Phase I of the project was signed. This phase consisted of the planning of 500 of the 1943 ha set aside for:

1. The major transport infrastructures such as the TGV station, motorway access routes and the prolongation of the RER network.
2. The first theme park.
3. Seven hotels.
4. Eight hundred dwellings.
5. One entertainment centre.
6. One 27-hole golf course.
7. One congress centre.

The Disney Company must consent, in particular, to having train stations at the accesses to the park, despite its initial reluctance due to matters concerning image and accessibility, as well as accepting specific restrictions with regard to signposting, land use, environmental criteria and the consideration that its property is part of the public domain. In December 1997, the detailed programme of phase II was signed, including:

1. The completion of the primary and secondary infrastructures.
2. The start-up of a second theme park.
3. The creation of an urban centre based on the construction of a 90,000 m² mall, a new RER station, a new motorway access, a 33 ha activity park and 1610 dwellings in three sectors on either side of the circular boulevard.

The fact that it is considered a project of general interest capacitates existing localities to be able to keep their current specific characteristics. Phase III of the project dealt with:

1. Reinforcing hotel capacity, together with the opening of the second park, with the opening of three hotels in Magny-le-Hongre run by international companies, the building of two residential time-sharing complexes around the golf course, the opening of hotel L'Elysée in the urban centre of Val d'Europe and the initiative in Montévrain of hotel accommodation mixing business and pleasure.

2. Creating a congress and exhibition centre of between 30,000 and 40,000 m^2, closely linked to the RER and TGV stations.
3. Increasing the project's dimensions with the development of collective and individual housing, the strengthening of the mall's capacity to attract and the expansion of the International Business Park.
4. Completing the network of major infrastructures and developing other public facilities.

The urban nature of the operation is rounded off with the process of the location of housing, which is planned for the urban centres of the five municipalities affected by the project and their surrounding areas, principally to the east of sector IV in the municipalities of Magny-le-Hongre and Bailly-Romainvilliers, and with the creation of Chessy Village.

It is clear, as Belmessous (2002) comments, that, in this process of development, a clear showdown arises between the wish of the state to create not just a new residential periphery around Paris but a veritable new city in the country and the Disney Company's profound aim, which is already explicitly expressed through the development of Walt Disney World in Orlando, to become an urban planning agent in order to thus intervene in the very process of the development of the surroundings of its parks. Meanwhile, Val d'Europe, is becoming consolidated as a unique operation of urban and territorial development in Europe, having repercussions, on different levels, concerning land management systems and collaboration models between the public and the private sectors. There is, however, no lack of criticism, such as Ariès's (2002, 186) when he states that, with the Val d'Europe project, the French state has, for the first time in history, entrusted the development of an urban agglomeration for 40,000 people to a private concern.

Disney, however, justifies its participation in the project on the basis of its will to become territorial and urban planning agents. This is how the company sees its participation in the development of the Val d'Europe town centre, in collaboration with French and international corporations, in the development of hotels, malls, office space and housing (600 dwellings in the neighbourhood of the station, 776 in the east park area and 234 in the south park area), including the construction of subsidized housing in Serris. Among the main Disney collaborators are Arlington Securities plc in the case of the International Business Park, Etoiles d'Europe SAS in the case of the offices in the town centres and Ségécé for the International Commercial Centre. Disney understands, on the other hand, that the municipalities where it is settled already existed prior to its arrival and their needs must be attended to in a long-term plan, up until 2017, as set out in the framework agreement. For Disney, land management, which has come into the hands of the state through EPA France and the planning criteria established in the collaboration agreement, ensures that development takes place according to the priorities of the state. The result for the American company is, consequently, the development of a new urban and territorial model in Paris in which the criteria concerning concentration, density and multifunctionality are better catered for than in its previous urban experiences as planners, in particular, in Orlando.

8.2.3. The economic impact of Disneyland Paris

Advertising of the Val d'Europe presents the place in the following way:

> Born out of the common desire of public and private agents, Val d'Europe is innovative, stimulating and creative. Conceived in accordance with the most demanding requirements, it is carefully integrated into a setting of environmental quality. Conceived both to achieve the success of enterprises and the welfare of those working in them, it invents a new balance between working and private life. Located to the east of Paris, a stone's throw from Disneyland Paris, Val d'Europe has the ambition and the means to become a unique city: one of the principal economic focuses of the 21st century in Île-de-France. Why choose to do business in Val d'Europe? Because in Val d'Europe, in all fields, enterprises have full rights to citizenship.

This literature, which is complemented by a series of specific considerations concerning its geographical situation, connections and the characteristics of its office space, of the International Business Park and of the four activity parks planned by EPA France, provides an excellent summary of the character of Val d'Europe as a centre of strategic development to the east of Paris.

Disneyland Paris acts, therefore, not just as a factor to attract numerous tourists but, through its strategic insertion in the Marne-la-Vallée project, it has become a magnet harnessing flows of capital coming from, in addition to the hotels and recreational activities, other segments of business, industrial and commercial activity, which lead, in short, to the settlement of a residential population. The Val d'Europe urban centre is, with its four central sectors (Quartier de la Gare, Quartier du Parc, Serris and Cottages du Golf in the outskirts of Bailly-Romainvilliers and Magny-le-Hongre) and the peripheral areas of the Quartier du Lac and Quartier du Nord, the nucleus of reference of this growth process. So, in spite of representing just 5% of the total number of inhabitants of the 'new town' of Marne-la-Vallée in 1999, the annual rhythm of growth of the resident population of the five municipalities of sector IV has been exponential (EPA Marne and EPA France, 2000). With 1829 inhabitants in 1968 and 5239 in 1990, if the forecasts are right in 2006 the total population will be 21,000. This dynamic of development has led, on the other hand, to important costs for the five municipal administrations, due to the need to develop new infrastructures and facilities and to adequately manage the local housing market. It must be borne in mind, for example, that, just for the workers of the Disney Company, some 2500 permanent employees have needed to set up residence in the vicinity of the park and some 2000 temporary staff also have housing needs.

In addition to demographic growth and the 'effect' – which is not easy to measure – of favouring the installation of regional or continental headquarters of companies in the surrounding area, Disneyland Paris is having a notable direct impact as regards the generation of resources for local bodies and an indirect impact in terms of the creation of activity and employment. Obviously, the development of Disneyland Paris has also had significant effects on the dynamics of tourism in Paris, as suggested in Chapter 7. In general terms, Table 8.9 shows an estimation of the evolution of the global economic impact of Disneyland Paris in 1999. The added value generated by Disney which is contributed to the Seine et Marne Département, which includes the five municipalities where the recreational complex is located, is estimated at €500 million. In this area, the park purchases mainly agricultural food products, services and energy (concerning this, see STI, 2000). The figure of €500 million, which represents almost a quarter of the total, is especially interesting since it reflects the park's ability to generate an impact on a local level.

On the other hand, although the precariousness, poor working conditions and lack of professional prospects for its workers are sometimes denounced, in 2001 Disneyland Paris generated 11,687 direct jobs, 10,885 indirect jobs (whether as a result of outsourced activities or of expenditure by the Disney workers) and 27,420 induced jobs due to spending by visitors to Disney outside the complex anywhere in France. Of these, the 14,210 that were located in the Département of Seine et Marne, represented 28.4% of the total jobs created by the park. In order to evaluate the magnitude of the park's impact, it can be taken into account that in 1982, according to Vitte (2002), sector IV represented less than 1% of the total jobs of the 'new town' of Marne-la-Vallée (408 jobs), whereas, with 14,210 jobs, it represents 34% of the total 67,000 jobs forecast by the development programme, becoming the main hive of activity of the whole Marne-la-Vallée planning area.

Bearing in mind the evolution of economic, social and territorial indicators of this kind, authors like Handschuch (1998) have qualified Disneyland Paris as a facility for territorial planning that has been a success from the point of view of its local integration. The provision of a complete, multimodal access system, the creation of a system of urban infrastructures that is suitable and the right size for the magnitude of the project and the realization of programmes to supply the necessary collective amenities have kept to a minimum any tensions that could have arisen from a project

Table 8.9. Global economic impact of Disneyland Paris, 1993–2001 (from STI, 2002a).

	1993	1995	1997	1999	2001
Total production (billion €)	2.87	2.82	3.58	3.61	4.39
Added value (billion €)	1.66	1.54	1.84	1.83	2.32
Value-added tax (million €)	124	146	195	212	213
Local taxes (million €)	–	36	41	45	38
Currency exchange (billion €)[a]	1.23	1.25	1.72	1.69	2.01

a. Revenue from foreign tourists.

leading to such vast territorial change as that brought about by Disneyland Paris. In particular, the role of the park in the territorial planning for the metropolitan periphery of Paris translates into: (i) the greatly accelerated growth of sector IV of the 'new town' of Marne-la-Vallée; and (ii) the progressive location of new activities and jobs in the sector's five municipalities, therefore, in the Département of Seine-et-Marne as a whole (for example, of the 400 companies that have participated in the construction of the company's second park, 32% are from the Département of Seine et Marne) and in the eastern sector of the Marne-la-Vallée 'new town'. It is from this viewpoint that Disneyland Paris has been qualified as a 'driving force' of the east of Paris (see, for example, *Les Echos* dated 7 March 2002).

As Celine (2000) remarks, all of the municipalities comprising sector IV have within them one or several activity location zones with the aim of favouring the location of companies and thus taking advantage of the incentive that the Disney park offers for the location of activities. Moreover, it cannot be forgotten that Disney's development has been accompanied by policies aimed at supporting local economic activity. So, for example, as a result of the opening of the International Commercial Centre, measures have been articulated, among others, to give priority to local companies for service and construction contracts, for the promotion of regional and local products, to modernize local commerce and aid the municipalities, for the local recruitment of the workforce and specific training – all of the above in order to combine the location of new activities and maintain existing ones.

Another thing is the risk, as suggested by D'Hauteserre (1997, 29–30), of turning the 'new town' of Marne-la-Vallée into 'Disney Vallée' to the extent that the construction of the territorial identity of this new urban reality is dominated by the cultural capital generated and attracted by Disney. However, the state itself has proposed strategies that try to keep that risk to a minimum, creating social and cultural structures that allow the territorial identity of the place to be defined aside from the Disney brand. Secondly, the inhabitants of the area tend to suggest and articulate organizational solutions that identify them culturally with the specific part of the Brie plain of which they are part. Even so, it cannot be forgotten that, as Bouillot (1993) observed, Disney has brought with it new criteria on issues related to architecture, the environment and town planning that differ substantially from those in force in the quiet rural communities where it has been established. This may be why Charles Boetto, president of the SAN of Portes de la Brie, clearly said in 1995, 'We want to become a city that houses Disney parks, not a city of Disney parks' (cited by Celine, 2000).

8.3. The Emerging Entertainment Economy of the Greater Pearl River Delta

The Pearl River Delta Economic Zone (41,698 km^2) in Southern China was first defined by Guangdong Province in 1984 and was expanded to its present dimensions in 1987. It includes the jurisdictions of Guangzhou (also known as Canton), Shenzhen, Dongguan, Foshan, Jiangmen, Zhongshan, Zhuhai and the urban areas of Huizhou and Zhaoqing. The Greater Pearl River Delta (GPRD) region includes the Pearl River Delta Economic Zone plus the Hong Kong Special Administrative Region (1100 km²) and the Macau Special Administrative Region (26 km²). The total population of the GPRD is 48 million, with 40.76 million on the Chinese Mainland, 6.8 million in Hong Kong and 440,000 in Macau. It is a polycentric region with three major economic cities – Hong Kong, Guangzhou (the historical centre of southern China with a population of 9.9 million) and Shenzhen – and several axes of development between them and other cities. Since the onset of China's economic reform programme the Pearl River Delta Economic Zone has seen unprecedented development and the whole GPRD has emerged as one of the world's economic powerhouses (Enright *et al.*, 2003).

In the early 1970s, the mainland Chinese Pearl River Delta was largely undeveloped. The introduction of the open-door policy and economic reforms in the late 1970s transformed it. In the early 1980s, the areas next to Hong Kong and Macau became the Special Economic Zones (SEZs) of Shenzhen and Zhuhai respectively. These SEZs had special regulations and taxation to attract foreign investment and gain greater independence in international trade activities. Hong Kong was the first to take advantage of the creation of the Special Economic Zones. Its many entrepreneurs moved many manufacturing factories on to the mainland in the 1980s to take advantage of cheaper land, labour and operating costs. Higher value-added activities, such as management, finance, logistics, design, R&D and quality assurance remained in Hong Kong.

In the 1990s a new transformation took place. Guangdong Province developed its service capabilities and increased the proportion of high-tech and other industries such as automobile, petrochemical and equipment manufacturing industries, which feature high growth and long production industry value chains. Hence, currently the Pearl River Economic Zone is changing from a region that was predominantly manufacturing-based to one that is gradually becoming knowledge-based. The resumption of Chinese administration of Hong Kong in 1997 and of Macau in 1999, the entry of the Chinese mainland into the World Trade Organisation and the signature of the successive Closer Economic Partnership Arrangement (CEPA) since 2003 by the Central People's Government and the Government of the Hong Kong Special Administrative Region have provided additional impetus and opportunity to the region as a whole. Nowadays, the Pearl River Delta Economic Zone is a world leader in the production of electronic goods, electrical products, electrical and electronic components, watches and clocks, toys, clothing and textiles, plastic products and a range of other goods.

According to Enright and Scott (2005), the Pearl River Delta Economic Zone GDP grew from just over US$8 billion in 1980 to nearly US$163.92 billion in 2004. During that period, the average real rate of GDP growth in the area was more than 16% while the figure for the whole of China was 9.5%. As the above authors state 'since the onset of China's reform programme, the Pearl River Delta Economic Zone has been the fastest growing portion of the fastest growing province in the fastest growing large economy in the world'. As a result, although the Pearl River Delta Economic Zone encompasses only 0.4% of the land area and only 3.2% of the 2000 census population of the Chinese mainland, it accounted for 9.9% of GDP and 29.6% of total trade in 2004. Moreover, during the last two decades, the composition of the economy has experienced a deep change with tertiary industry increasing its share. Growing affluence on the part of residents has fuelled demand for services such as education, recreation, travel, entertainment and telecommunications. Business services are also burgeoning in the region, together with the rapid growth of secondary industry (Table 8.10). Obviously, the development of the Pearl River Delta Economic Zone has been enormously beneficial for Hong Kong as well (Enright and Scott, 2005).

With the growing economy of the region, a growing consumer market with increasing purchasing power and sophistication is appearing. This is the basis for the development of a new entertainment, leisure and tourism industry. In fact, Hong Kong is a major international tourist destination with more than a half of the world's population within 5 hours' travel, Macau is receiving substantial new investments that could make it a tourism and gaming centre for the entire Asian region. The Pearl River Delta Economic Zone has numerous attractions to clientele from the Chinese mainland, though not as yet to the international tourism market. Attractions include more than 50 amusement theme parks, over 50 golf resorts, two major nature parks and beautiful natural locations mainly on the western side of the Delta. The Greater Pearl River Delta currently has five airports – Hong Kong, Macau, Shenzhen, Zhuhai and Guangzhou – with a capability of handling 210 million passengers per year (see also Leman, 2003).

As reflected in Table 8.11, in 2004, the Pearl River Delta Economic Zone received approximately 71.65 million domestic tourists staying at least one night. Revenue from these tourists reached US$11.51 billion (these figures include all of Huizhou and Zhaoqing). The same year, the Pearl River Delta Economic Zone received 14.91 million international tourists, or 35.70% of the total for the Chinese mainland. Revenue from

Table 8.10. GDP by sectors in the Pearl River Delta Economic Zone (from HKTDC, 2006).

	1980	2004
Primary (%)	25.8	3.8
Secondary (%)	45.3	53.8
Tertiary (%)	28.9	42.4

Table 8.11. Tourism facts and figures in the Greater Pearl River Delta (from Enright and Scott, 2005).

	PDR Economic Zone*	Hong Kong	Macau
Domestic tourists (million)	71.65	N/A	N/A
Revenue from domestic tourists (US$ billion)	11.51	N/A	N/A
International tourists staying overnight (million)	14.91	13.65	8.32
Revenue from international tourists (US$ billion)	5.18	7.84	N/A

*Includes all of Huizhou and Zhaoqing and thus slightly overstates the results.

international tourists was US$5.18 billion, or 20.16% of the total for the Chinese mainland. Hong Kong registered 13.65 million international tourist arrivals in 2004 and US$7.84 billion in international tourism revenue. Macau recorded 8.32 million international tourists staying overnight in 2004 and 16.67 million tourists in total. Mainland China is the largest source market visiting Hong Kong and industry experts project that inbound tourist flows into Hong Kong from the Chinese mainland as a whole will reach 14 million by 2012. On the other side, over 90% of foreign tourists to the Pearl River Delta region come from Hong Kong. In 2000, Hong Kong residents spent an estimated HK$20.3 billion in Guangdong Province on personal travel, with 36% of this spent in Shenzhen (Enright *et al.*, 2003).

Several steps have been taken to facilitate tourism in the Greater Pearl River Delta region. In 1993, the Pearl River Delta Tourism Marketing Organisation (renamed 'Guangdong, Hong Kong & Macau Tourism Marketing Organisation' in 2003) was set up by the Hong Kong Tourism Board, the Guangdong Provincial Tourism Bureau and the Macau Government Tourism Office. The aim of the organization was to jointly develop tourism resources and promotion programmes to attract tourists from the rest of China and elsewhere. Moreover, Hong Kong and Shenzhen have already reached agreements to cooperate in the training of tourism professionals, share tourism-related information, promote each other as a destination and improve the environment for tourism in the region. As Enright *et al.* (2003) states, as a part of coordination, it is also necessary to enhance cross-border facilities.

The fact is that economic growth in the Pearl River Delta Economic Zone has turned the whole Greater Pearl River Delta into a metropolitan region. The development has been facilitated and amplified by massive infrastructure and urbanization initiatives. Road, rail and underground systems are being expanded, connectivity around the region is being enhanced and substantial urban development projects are reshaping the most important cities. Nevertheless, few institutional systems are shared and no metropolitan regional governing bodies exist. Laws are radically different in each part of the GPRD, education systems are different as are tax systems, property rights, planning processes and other matters relevant to the development of an integrated metropolitan region. Equally problematic is the fact that wages, land values and the price of business services are very far apart (Rohlen, 2000).

8.3.1. Hong Kong's tourism and leisure project

The tourism industry is one of the major pillars of the Hong Kong economy. Total tourism expenditure attributed to inbound tourism exceeded HK$100 billion in 2005. Visitor arrivals grew to 23.36 million in 2005. The Chinese mainland is still the largest market with more than 12.5 million arrivals in 2005, increasing moderately by 2.4% on the previous year. According to the World Tourism Organization, Hong Kong was in 2004, for the first time, one of the top ten tourist destinations of the world. By the end of 2005, Hong Kong had 118 hotels, with 43,866 rooms and an average occupancy rate of 86%. The average length of stay of overnight visitors in 2005 was 3.7 nights (Enright *et al.*, 2003).

The Hong Kong Tourism Commission was established in May 1999 to coordinate various tourism development efforts and to provide policy support and leadership for the development of tourism in Hong Kong. The Commission's task was to establish and promote Hong Kong as Asia's premier international city, a world-class destination for leisure and business visitors. The goal of the Tourism Commission was reinforced in 2000, when the Commission on Strategic Development put forth the notion of Hong Kong becoming 'Asia's World City' and several specific sectors were identified as crucial, including tourism. The other sectors were financial and business services; regional headquarters for multinational companies; information services and technology; and trade, transportation and logistics. Since 1999, the Tourism Commission has generated a clear idea as to the city's tourism opportunities, it has fomented greater coordination between the policies affecting tourism, has awarded a HK$100 million loan to the Hong Kong Tourist Association to support the realization of several international events in Hong Kong and has rationalized visitor entry requirements.

According to an article in *Asian Business* in January 2000, what has prompted the Hong Kong Government to promote tourism and high technology industries is the growing competition posed by Singapore, Shanghai and Sydney as financial hubs of reference in the region. Nevertheless, a debate has arisen as to the possible negative impact tourism may have on the island's economic competitiveness. There are positions that uphold that its development could hinder the necessary climate for the development of high technology industries – a proposal to which the government was committed – to the benefit of countries like Singapore. Likewise, from the perspective of Hong Kong as a financial centre, there are those who predict that the development of tourism may deepen the island's loss of weight to the benefit of Singapore, Shanghai or even Sydney.

Hong Kong's tourism strategy aims to strengthen the island's position as a 'must see' destination on the international map of tourism and turn it into the most popular destination in Asia. The implantation of Disneyland and the redevelopment of Ocean Park (in which the Hong Kong government itself has interests) are not, however, the only tourist policy actions undertaken by the government of Hong Kong. Enhancement projects are implemented in the existing popular tourist areas and several other major tourist attractions including Ngong Ping 360 and the Hong Kong Wetland Park. Ngong Ping 360 offers a 20-min cable-car ride that provides an exceptional panoramic view of the many attractions of Lantau Island. The Hong Kong Wetland Park, located near the famous Mai Po marshes, is a 60-ha, world-class conservation, education and tourism facility and is a part of the programme to develop green tourism. Moreover, the government is developing heritage tourism and enhancing its cultural programmes. Hong Kong authorities are also working on the development of new cruise terminal facilities in order to capitalize on the rapid growth of the cruise industry worldwide and become a regional cruise hub. On the other hand, there is special interest in attracting business trips and conventions of global importance to Hong Kong. Finally, apart from making available a wide range of attractions, the HKTB continues to implement the Quality Tourism Services (QTS) scheme and promotes a community-wide hospitality culture.

In this context, the recent development of the Disney theme park has been seen as a key element for the future of the island. Contrary to the critical voices, the park is perceived by the authorities as a clear demonstration of the capacity of Hong Kong to lead the region's development and innovation and hold its position as principal city of reference in Asia for business. Particularly, it must be 'the jewel in the crown' of the new 280-ha tourism, recreation and leisure district on Lantau island. The new park is located on an area covering 126 ha in Penny Bay on Lantau island. It cost HK$14.1 thousand million. Phase I was finished in 2005 and includes a theme park, a thematic hotel complex and a commercial entertainment and catering centre. It expected to generate 18,400 jobs at the time of its opening (35,800 after 15 years). Prior to that, during the construction phase, the project created 6000 jobs, in addition to which one should include the 10,000 jobs derived from government actions concerning infrastructure and the preparation of the land (Whaley, 2001). Knipp (2005) indicates that it is expected that 40% of all visits to the park will come from continental China.

The development of Hong Kong Disneyland and its later management is being carried out by a joint-venture company – Hong Kong International Theme Parks Ltd – made up of the government of the island and Disney, 57–43% participations respectively in the total share capital of HK$5.7 thousand million. Despite the fact that either party may sell its shares, Disney must keep a minimum of HK$1.9 thousand million in shares. In addition to the HK$14.1 thousand million the park will cost, the government will invest HK$13.6 thousand million on infrastructure (roadways from North Lantau to Penny Bay, two piers for public ferries, transport interchanges, police, fire brigade and ambulance posts, drainage and sanitation work as well as preparing the 280 ha of land so that it is suitable for construction to take place). One special element will be an aquatic recreation centre with a large lake which will also serve as a reservoir for irrigation water. According to the government, much of the infrastructure would have been developed anyway in order to facilitate tourist development in the area even if the Disney project had not materialized. Justification for the expenditure by the Hong Kong Government is based on the following points:

- The project is expected to stimulate the economy of the island to the tune of HK$148 thousand million over a 40-year period in terms of added value for companies in Hong Kong.
- Growing visitation is expected reaching 10 million visitors after 15 years.
- It is estimated that Hong Kong Disneyland will attract 7.3 million tourists to the island after 15 years (including 2.9 million additional tourists).
- It is calculated that additional expenditure generated by tourists will total HK$8.3 thousand million for the first year reaching HK$16.8 thousand million per year as of 2020.
- It is understood that Hong Kong Disneyland will lead the way in a new era of tourism in Hong Kong enhancing its international image as a vibrant, cosmopolitan city.
- It is considered that Disney's choice of Hong Kong as its third location for a park outside the USA is a vote of confidence for the future of the city by the best known and most prestigious theme park corporation.

Nevertheless some have criticized the government's participation in the Disney project. *The Economist* of November 1999 disapproved of the fact that the government of Hong Kong assumes 88% of the cost of the park (including the value of the land, transport infrastructure and loans), in exchange for just 57% of the shares and agreeing to pay a management fee to Disney, which has been kept at the maximum. In another sense, in 1999, *Far Eastern Economic Review* criticized the fact that the park could generate, in a similar way to the development of the tourist industry in general, problems in the field of employment and housing. In the former case the construction and operation of the park would require the participation of professionals skilled in English and Mandarin, who do not exist in the city as a result of its traditional separation from continental China. Hence a foreseeable arrival of personnel from continental China and the Philippines who, in the second place, would create a demand for housing which in such a densely populated place as Hong Kong, would by no means be an easy task. A third generalized criticism of the project is in reference to its marked property nature, the traditional activity of the island's most powerful, to the detriment of its supposed touristic 'vocation' and, therefore, its ability to effectively bring about a change to the Hong Kong economic model is being questioned.

Parallel to the development of Hong Kong Disneyland, authorities are redeveloping the 28-year-old Ocean Park to enhance its statutory function as a public recreational and educational park, and to maintain its attractiveness to visitors. In May, 2002, the Government set up an interdepartmental 'Task Force on Redevelopment of Ocean Park and Tourist Attractions in Aberdeen', to oversee the planning for the future of the park. In February 2005, the development group submitted the plans to the task force for consideration. According to the plans, 'Ocean' and 'Animal Encounter' continue to be the key themes of the park. The project is being undertaken by Ocean Park Corporation. This redevelopment is expected to bring net quantifiable economic benefits of HK$40 billion to HK$48 billion over 40 years. The redevelopment project will directly and indirectly generate between 2600 and 4000 additional full-time equivalent jobs in the Hong Kong economy upon the start of Phase I in 2008–2009, rising to between 11,300 and 12,800 in 2021–2022. It will complement Hong Kong Disneyland and enhance Hong Kong's attraction as the prime family destination in the region. The project will be implemented within the existing Ocean Park area.

With this redevelopment, it is estimated that visitors to Ocean Park will increase from 4 million in 2004–2005 to more than 5 million by 2010–2011 and in excess of 7 million by 2021–2022. The redevelopment cost is estimated at HK$5.55 billion. The government is prepared to provide support for half of the funding – HK$2.775 billion – of which HK$1.3875 billion (25% project cost) will be in the form of government guarantees for Ocean Park to secure commercial loans and HK$1.3875 billion (25% project cost) as a subordinated loan. The government is also considering the proposal for the development of hotels at Ocean Park from legal, financial, operational and institutional aspects. Hotel development will further enhance the attractiveness of the Park and induce longer stays. The government has assessed all aspects of the plan in respect of the engineering, technical, land and planning, transport and economic aspects. The environmental assessment of the plans is being dealt with in accordance with the Environmental Impact Assessment Ordinance.

8.3.2. Park development in the Shenzhen Special Economic Zone

Shenzhen was established as China's first Special Economic Zone in 1979. At that time Shenzhen was a sleepy town with no infrastructure and was chosen for its proximity to Hong Kong capital and know-how and because the Guangdong government then contributed very little to the central government's coffers (Gallagher, 2002). In 1988, Guangdong was granted expanded powers to set its own economic direction, and was designated a 'comprehensive economic reform area'. This gave rise to the creation of the Shenzhen Stock Exchange, as well as development of a land lease system and some privatization of housing. Shenzhen became a leader in terms of foreign exchange markets, operation of foreign banks, land reforms and stock market development. Currently, as the city is pushing for substantial economic integration with Hong Kong, with particular regard to cooperation in science, technology, ports, infrastructure, tourism and environmental protection, it may become a part of the entertainment cluster of Southern China led by Hong Kong and completed by neighbouring Macau.

Currently, Shenzhen is a leading city on the Chinese mainland for high-tech industries. In fact, Shenzhen's high-tech output is the highest in China – helped by the fact that an estimated 20% of China's graduates at PhD level reside in the city. In the service sector, Shenzhen's port and logistics industries are also emerging as leaders within China. There is also significant international presence in service sectors such as banking, finance, insurance, shipping, logistics, business services and retailers. Shenzhen also had the greatest number of exports among any city in China – an amount equal to almost one-seventh of the nation's total (Gallagher, 2002). According to Shenzhen's current Comprehensive Plan for 2010 the city will build its economy around finance, trade, commerce, information technology, transportation and high-tech industries. The objectives are for Shenzhen to become a regional economic centre, a garden city and a modernized international city (Niu, 2002). Unfortunately, Shenzhen has also been and still is a great polluter. Air and river water pollution are the most visible issues for residents in the region and may get worse in the short term, due to population growth, rapid industrialization and higher per capita income.

In 1979, Shenzhen's GDP was US$23.6 million. Twenty years later GDP stood at US$17.3 billion. In the same period, per capita GDP jumped from 606 yuan to 35,908 yuan per year, equivalent to US$4,335, six times the national average. With over seven million and more than 90% of the city's residents born elsewhere, Shenzhen has a young population (the average age is 26 years old). Recent surveys show that almost 1 million Hong Kong residents would consider living in Shenzhen within 10 years, and even more (43%) intend to buy property in Shenzhen.

As a result of the development process, Shenzhen hosts a highly attractive, large and sophisticated consumer market. In fact, like Guangzhou, Shenzhen is among the most affluent and trendsetting cities on the Chinese mainland. As a result, in a very few years, there has been a shift in the consumption pattern towards higher level needs as regards accommodation, retail, entertainment and travel and there are a growing number of people who are able to afford better quality leisure time. Complementarily, many tourists visiting the Special Economic Zone also consume leisure and entertainment products during their holidays. So, Shenzhen is also becoming an entertainment and tourist destination. In fact, according to Gallagher (2002) for people from Hong Kong the most common reasons for trips into Shenzhen are shopping and leisure (31%), business (23%), visiting friends/relatives (22%) and sightseeing (14%). In addition, Shenzhen is also home to a number of international trade fairs and exhibitions. The city's 280,000 m^2 international exhibition and convention centre opened in 2004.

In fact, Shenzhen is quickly turning into a Chinese version of Florida (Vittachi, 1995), complete with restaurants, night clubs, resort hotels, golf courses, theme parks and other attractions, and constitutes one of the main entertainment destinations for the Chinese (4/5 of affluence, in addition to visitors coming from Hong Kong and Taiwan). Its major tourist attractions include theme parks and other facilities such as Chinese folk Culture Villages, the Window of the World, Splendid China and the Safari Park in Nanshan district, the SeaWorld in Shekou, the Dameisha Promenade and Xiaomeisha Beach Resort in Yantian district, Zhongying Streak, Xianhu Lake Botanical Garden, and the Minsk Aircraft Carrier World. Honey Lake Country Club, Silver Lake Tourist Center, Evergreen Park and Happy Valley theme park seem to be more attractive to locals. Millions of visitors go there each year. Early in 2006, Shenzhen's Baoneng group and France's Futuroscope Group announced a US$200 million project to build a new Futuroscope in the city.

The development of theme parks got underway in Shenzhen with the building of Splendid China, which was inaugurated in 1989 by the Overseas Chinese Town Group Ltd in collaboration with China Travel Service Ltd. Overseas Chinese Town group, a publicly listed company with interests in electronics, real estate and tourism originally designed a property development project involving residential and factory development named Overseas Chinese Town specifically targeted at overseas Chinese investors. Nevertheless after coming across the theme park idea the initial direction of the master plan was transformed and Splendid China was developed. The park has almost 100 attractions located in three areas devoted to ancient monuments, natural landscapes and traditional dwellings. In successive years, the same company developed China Folk Culture Villages (1991), Window of the World (1994) and Happy Valley (1998/2002), the former two in collaboration with China Travel Service Ltd. They are proposals for recreation which, in most cases have a cultural theme and between 1.5 and 2.5 million visits per year. China Folk Culture Villages displays 24 ethnic peoples from some of the 55 nationalities of China. Window of the World allows visitors to recognize historical places, natural landscapes and customs from all over the world. In 2005, Happy Valley managed to rank among the 10 most visited theme parks in Asia and in the top 50 most visited in the world. According to Ap (2003), the success of the theme parks of the Overseas Chinese Town Group has been as a result of:

- The management philosophy of the OCT group. It consists of 'three insists': on quality (safety, hygiene and comfort); on having its own characteristics (develop and maintain distinctiveness based upon a clear theme); and on maintaining development (ongoing enhancements and regular maintenance and repairs).

- The timing. OCT theme parks were the first of their type to open in China and become market leaders.
- The location in the Shenzhen Special Economic Zone, one of the richest areas in China with salaries among the highest in the country.
- Accessibility. Parks are located in Overseas Chinese Town in places with good accessibility because they are on the main thoroughfare in Shenzhen, approximately 20 km from the town centre and railway station.
- The market-oriented management approach of the OCT group. Being adjacent to Hong Kong, the OCT group took conscientious steps to adopt some of the best practices that market-oriented management had to offer.
- Proper planning, careful attention to detail and maintaining the authenticity of cultural aspects of Splendid China and Chinese Folk Culture Village.
- Travel management. The OCT group is linked up with a major China tour operator, China Travel Service Limited, who provided the necessary expertise for the development and operation of its tourism portfolio, and helped to direct groups to the attractions at the beginning.

8.3.3. The role of Macau in the tourism system of the Pearl Delta

Though it is a small economy, with a GDP of US$10.31 billion, Macau has the second highest per capita GDP in the region after Hong Kong. The potential for closer linkages between Hong Kong and the eastern part of the Pearl River Delta, on the one hand, and Macau and the western part of the Pearl River Delta, on the other, could have an important impact on flows of goods, investment and people. The most important part of Macau's GDP comes from the service sector. Macau is, in fact, an amusement and leisure hotspot in Southern Asia that is visited every day by 45,000 people and has a hotel occupancy rate of 70% year-round. The gaming industry is by far the dominant sector. In 2003, almost one third of the gross value added to GDP came from this sector. It generated US$2.71 billion in 2003 and it is a sector set for further growth, especially because it is open to foreign investors. Currently, Macau is the only location in China to allow casinos, and in 2004 it became the world's second largest gaming market. Its gaming and tourism-related sectors have been targeted for further development and have received massive investment from overseas and local players as Las Vegas Sands (the Sands Macau and Macau Venetian Casino Resort in the 'Cotai Strip'), Wynn Resorts (Wynn Macau), Galaxy Casino Company (Galaxy Waldo Hotel), MGM Grand Paradise (MGM Grand Macau – developed with investors affiliated with Sociedade de Jogos de Macau (SJM)) and Melco International Development Ltd with Publishing & Broadcasting Ltd. of Australia (Enright and Scott, 2005).

Moreover, in 1999, Macau's new governor after the return of the city to the Chinese rule from the Portuguese, decided to pour the taxes that the casinos are paying into preserving and polishing Macau's historic heritage. The total amount spent since 2005 has totalled more than US$18.8 million. In addition, there is also a tendency towards the diversification of entertainment activities such the Sky Jump at the Macau Tower. The most ambitious project (US$320 million) in this respect is the first theme park of Macau, named Macau's Fisherman's Wharf. It will also include Macau's largest convention centre and the world's first purpose built water stunt show pool (Knipp, 2006).

As a result, Macau is undergoing a dramatic transformation, becoming one of the world's premier gaming-and-resort destinations. Complementary to tourism, Macau's public administration, financial intermediation, real estate trade, and wholesale, retail, and repair sectors also play an important part in the economy. The government gives emphasis to improving tourist, recreational, meeting and exhibition facilities, as well as trade-related services. A further long-term goal of the authorities in Macau is to encourage the development of the telecommunications and technology sectors. The government also lends its support to technology-focused investments. Logistics is another priority sector. Macau relies heavily on private sector funding for undertaking such industrial parks. Macau has reached an agreement with the authorities in Zhuhai to establish a cross-border industrial zone on reclaimed land located between the two jurisdictions.

Case 15. The Transformation of PortAventura into a Tourist Destination

Today, PortAventura is enjoying a phase of expansion, which is heading in the direction of transforming the initial theme park into a tourist and recreation complex. Having consolidated the 3 million visitors-a-year threshold during the late 1990s, efforts were concentrated on increasing it. In order to do so, since 2003 new attractions have been developed, the opening timetable has been extended and three 500-room hotels have been started up, as well as a water park and, in 2006, a Beach Club located on the beach front. This backing of investments meant a change in concept since there has been a shift from exploiting a recreational facility to managing a whole productive chain of tourist entertainment (travel, accommodation and a variety of leisure pursuits). Along these same lines, PortAventura's current master plan foresees the building over the next few years of new resort hotels, a bungalow ranch, three golf courses with 45 holes and 2477 dwellings. To do so, bearing in mind its high rate of penetration into the markets residing in its immediate surrounding area of Tarragona and Barcelona, PortAventura is clearly setting its sights on the tourist market as a means to bear potential future growth.

In 1996, the first full year after the park opened, the percentage of international visitors to PortAventura over total attendance was 14%.

In 2005, this multiplied to 35%. A significant proportion of such an increase is due to the greater number of visits to the park by visitors from France and the UK. The number of visits made by the French has gone from the 81 thousand of 1997 to over 383 thousand for 2005, an increase during this period of 472%. More concretely, in 2005, French customers represented 11.4% of the total visitors to the park. However, the number of British visitors in 1997 reached 146 thousand, whereas in 2005 this figure had climbed to 600 thousand. The increase is cited at 411% and the proportional representation by British visitors to the park touched 17.8% in 2005. In both cases, the growth process in visits from both countries has accelerated greatly as of 2000 and, in a second growth phase, as of the start-up of the park's hotels in 2004. Of the overnight stays at the park's hotels in 2005, 11% were by French customers whereas the British accounted for over 30%. More than 90% of overnight stays are translated into visits to the park the following day.

The process of increased international demand at PortAventura has come about in a context of the conversion of the park into a resort but, especially, as a result of the definition of specific marketing strategies focused on the most relevant international markets, namely the French and the British (Table 8.12). To do so, the park undertook specific market studies to help define the most suitable means to achieve their objective of increasing international demand for the park, and, as of 1999, it radically changed its commercialization strategy. It was decided to abandon the single strategy of selling tickets to tour operators, who traditionally sold sun-and-beach package holidays in the adjacent coastal tourist zone – la Costa Daurada or Golden Coast. Communications campaigns run by PortAventura were aimed for the first time straight at the final consumer in selected areas of source demand both in France – with good accessibility to the park via land transport, such as car, coach and train – and in Great Britain – from where tourists have traditionally come to the coastal area where PortAventura is located via flights chartered by tour operators and, especially since 2003, with low-cost airlines.

In the case of France, the communications actions were begun in the largest, regional capitals closest to the destination, Toulouse and Montpellier in 2001, to which Perpignan and Marseille were added in 2002. In 2004, the strategy changed scale and ceased to focus on the cities emitting demand to expand to the four regions that make up much of the region of the south of France. It could be seen that the opening up of new markets provided the desired results and the park decided to extend the strategy to new market areas in 2005, again in the south of France. For the purposes of illustration, it may be said that attendance at the park by visitors from Languedoc–Roussillon rose from 45 thousand in the year 2000 to 120 thousand in 2005. The increase in visitors from the Provence–Alpes–Côte d'Azur region is yet more intense, leaping from 15 thousand visitors in the year 2000 to 96 thousand in 2005. This is why in 2006 the park decided to deploy its media plan in France. A shift from outdoor promotional activities, radio, press and regional TV to a specific campaign on national TV

Table 8.12. PortAventura's marketing strategies for the markets of France and Great Britain. Development between 1999 and 2005 (from company data).

France		Great Britain
Start of public relations activities	1999	
Consolidation of public relations activities	2000	
Communication with the final consumer. Actions in the cities of Toulouse and Montpellier	2001	Sales to tour operators as the main and most effective commercialization action
Consolidation of actions in Toulouse and Montpellier and the first communication action with the final consumer in Perpignan and Marseille	2002	Other actions: family trips, public relations, press and promotions
Communication campaign in the cities of Toulouse, Montpellier, Perpignan and Marseille	2003	Communication with the end consumer. Campaign with outdoor media, press and mailing in the cities of Manchester and Birmingham
Communication campaign in the regions of the south of France: Aquitaine, Midi–Pyrénées, Languedoc–Roussillon and Provence–Alpes–Côte d'Azur	2004	Communication campaign (one wave) via television nationally Mailing
Consolidation of communication campaigns with the final consumer in the regions of the south of France and the first communication action at two cities of the Rhône–Alpes region (Grenoble and Valence)	2005	Communication campaign (one wave) via television nationally in Great Britain and Ireland Mailing
Development of a new media plan incorporating a national TV and radio campaign, a second specific TV and radio campaign in the south of France, a communication plan for Internet and a bartering campaign. Outdoor communication campaign	2006	Communication campaign (two waves) via television nationally in Great Britain and Ireland Specific local radio campaign in cities served by low-cost airline connections Boosting the resort on the Internet Mailing

took place in order to launch the brand throughout France, the coverage and number of weeks' presence on regional TV was reinforced and a specific plan was developed for the Internet (with a penetration of 54% in the 25- to 59-year age range in France), as well as maintaining and strengthening the other media. In all, investment in direct marketing in France between 2001 and 2006 has increased fourfold.

Concerning the British market, PortAventura observes that as of 2002 some changes began to be noticed in the travel habits, especially with regard to the greater use of direct booking systems, the greater use of the Internet as a buying tool and an increase in the amount of independent travel. In this context, in 2003 low-cost flights were already an option at the Reus airport, through which tourists converged on the Costa Daurada. As of this change in conditions, the marketing strategy also changed and in 2003, for the first time, a communications campaign was carried out targeting the end consumer in two cities of Great Britain from which there are the largest number of visitors to PortAventura to date and therefore where the park enjoys a certain positioning. In respect of the symptoms noticed in the market, in 2004 the first nationwide TV campaign was carried out and the Internet was boosted as a means to make the product known. As of then, it has been possible to directly book the recently opened hotels at PortAventura via the Internet. That same year saw the reinforcement of the defined marketing strategy, doubling investment in promotion between 2003 and 2006.

The case of PortAventura illustrates the usefulness of investing in the research into and commercialization of markets for a theme park's positioning as a tourist destination, as well as the transformation of the park into a resort, and as a way to generate solid, stable growth by means of effective strategies.

III   Fundamentals of Theme Park Development and Management

> Essential to the imagery of pleasure-zone architecture are lightness, the quality of being an oasis in a perhaps hostile context, heightened symbolism, and the ability to engulf the visitor in a new role.
>
> (Robert Venturi *et al.*, 1972)

The start-up of a theme park is a complex interactive process of an integral nature. The knowledge that comes into play is linked with project management, creative development, architectural design, market studies, the production of attractions, construction, engineering, financial analysis and operations management. Adjusting matters such as cost, the size of the project, operational needs, product value and the park's market potential is a key element of a project's success. The fundamental starting point requires a clear vision of the recreational concept to be developed, the theme to be recreated and the needs of the potential demand that require satisfying. This means taking decisions as to the location of the activity, the design of the product beyond merely the idea that provides it with meaning and its translation into a series of decisions dealing with the layout of attractions, elements of transport and communication and facilities oriented at the public and logistic service. In order to generate business, the design and management of a park must respond to three sources of needs: customer expectations, operational running requirements and the creative resolution of the planning and management teams.

Once running, good work by the management teams is the basis for a park's success. The main areas of management to be taken into consideration are operations, personnel and marketing, all of which are fundamental in maximizing the experience of the visitors to the park on the basis of a profound commitment to quality. In the field of operations, aspects such as the choice and design of processes, the planning of long-term capacity, the investment to be made in the attractions, infrastructure and theming

and its upkeep, safety and security and technological innovation, quality
and a commitment towards the environment are all critical. A second set
of factors involves human resources management. The design and scale of
labour needs are basic in a service activity and are linked with the profile
and abilities of the employees as well as aspects concerning their specific
training. The staff is a part, therefore, of the thematic product: hence the
importance of the management of their capabilities. Finally, marketing is
clearly another fundamental issue. In particular, critical aspects in this
regard are the variety of the supply, the park's thematic content and the
strategy adopted as regards investment in promotion and advertising. The
park's pricing policy is also highly relevant.

   All decisions as to the aforementioned processes are often interrelated
and the results feed into each other. Given the strategic nature of theme
parks from the point of view of planning and management, all of these
points are dealt with specifically in this third section of the book. Chapter 9
deals with the nature of theme parks as a recreational product and, in particular, the factors that govern their success. Chapter 10 explains the bases
of the planning of a theme park, its operational design requirements and
its main characteristics in terms of operating measures. Chapter 11 tackles
matters concerning form, size, capacity, flow management and the components that make up a theme park. Finally, Chapter 12 explains the main
areas of theme park management.

9 Factors Influencing the Development Process

> Too often entrepreneurs, who are masters of their own art or trade,
> expect to be successful in any location of their choice . . . It does not
> work this way.
>
> (Luigi Salvaneschi, 1996)

The development of theme parks worldwide and in specific regions and countries is conditioned by the global economic climate and the specific economic climate of each country, by the changes in lifestyles and the population's recreational consumption patterns, the increase in available leisure time and international and especially domestic tourism, and the very nature of the demand and operators' expectations. Dozens of projects to develop theme parks throughout the world never actually materialize. There are many reasons for this, ranging from problems of funding to the non-existence of suitable locations for the concept of the project designed. In parallel, among those that are developed, in some cases they must quickly be rescaled as a result of erroneous forecasts as regards matters such as investment needs or the ability to attract demand. Though no *ex ante* guarantee of success exists (even Disney has seen how *a priori* solid proposals like Disney America set for development in the outskirts of Washington, DC, in the USA have failed as early as their pre-design phase), this chapter looks into a series of principles which, if well managed for each specific case, may contribute to a park's success. First, the necessary definition of theme parks as recreational products is analysed. Then a few basic questions concerning their location are considered. Thirdly, the role of the agents that take part in their development is discussed. Finally, the success factors that are to be borne in mind for the development of a park, both at the planning stage and during operation phase, are pursued.

9.1. The Nature of a Theme Park as a Recreational Product

The aim of a theme park is to offer a unique experience to each of its effective consumers. This experience is constructed on the basis of the existence of tangible elements like attractions, shops and restaurants, service activities supplied by the staff of the park, each visitor's own expectations, behaviour and attitudes and a set of other factors that condition the experience at the time it takes place, ranging from the number of visitors at the park at the time it is visited by an individual consumer to the weather or characteristics of the place where the park is located and its accessibility. Scheurer (2002) summarizes these factors in the following key elements:

1. The *main theme* is the starting point of the staging process. It is used to unify the structure and organization of the park through constant visual statements. Theming also means reduction; not all aspects of a theme can be considered. The main theme is synonymous with the story in a theater setting.

2. In the *staging concept* the concrete performance of the main theme is planned. It is important to find the core of the theme, expectations, and images visitors have in their heads.

3. *Attractions* are the focused stimuli of the staging process. There have to be core attractions (rides, shows, games) and supporting attractions (restaurants, souvenir shops and so on) for all visitors, specially all members in families.

4. *Stage design* supports the theming performance and helps to create an atmosphere filled with a consistent stimuli theme. It includes scenery, architecture, landscape and also employees in a theater setting (cleaning personnel, for example). *Stage design* has the function of background stimuli in the atmosphere of experience setting.

5. *Management of visitor flow* ensures that basic needs of visitors (security, information, orientation, hunger, thirst, personal needs) are always satisfied so that higher needs, such as experiences, can occur, as well as lengthening and intensifying experiences by applying dramaturgy.

6. Former experiences and expectations of *visitors* act as residual stimuli. In contrast to a traditional theater staging, the visitors in theme parks are part of the staging and must therefore be considered.

In terms of the well-known definition made by Kotler (1994), according to which 'a product is anything that can be offered to a market for attention, acquisition, use or consumption that might satisfy a want or a need', which 'includes physical objects, services, persons, places, organisations, and ideas', from a conceptual point of view this concept of a park may be defined as a recreational product which, as happens with all service activities, combines tangible goods and intangible services. Establishing the condition of a theme park as a recreational product is fundamental from the standpoint of its development and management. In fact, as can be seen below, its establishment and management are conditioned, fundamentally, by its basic features as a service product, characterized by the following aspects (Swarbrooke, 2002):

- The staff involved in producing and delivering the product are part of the product itself.
- The customers themselves are involved in the production process.
- It is constantly changing – not standardized – depending on a range of factors including the attitude of the staff or the weather.
- It is perishable and cannot be stored because it is produced and consumed at one and the same time.
- There is no tangible product to carry home.
- The surroundings of the service delivery process are a feature of the service.

The set of elements that make up a theme park may be organized following Kotler's (1994) well-known model, according to which every product constitutes three levels: the core product, that is, what the customer is really buying, the tangible product, the entity which customers can purchase to satisfy their needs, and the augmented product, the 'total product bundle that should solve all the customers' problems, and even some they haven't thought of yet' (Lewis and Chambers, 1989).

Applied to a theme park, as proposed in Fig. 9.1, the nucleus of the product is the excitement and/or atmosphere it arouses in its visitors. The tangible product is made up of the elements that the designers and planners' creative capacity transfer to the contents of the park ('white-knuckle' rides, safety, range of rides and on-site attractions, brand name, quality of services, sharing the park with other people). Finally, the augmented

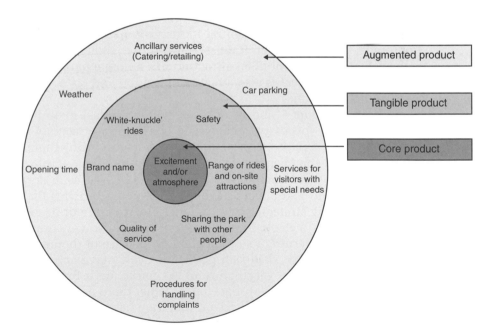

Fig. 9.1. Theme parks as a recreational product (Swarbrooke, 2002 after Kotler, 1994).

product comprises the ancillary services, such as catering and retailing, car parking, services for visitors with special needs, procedures for handling complaints, opening times and the weather. Any visitor might expect a different potential benefit from the visit to a single theme park. It depends on two major factors (Swarbrooke, 2002). The first is the characteristics of any visitor in terms of their age, lifestyle, stage in the family life cycle, past experiences or personality. The second is the type of attraction itself. Although it is a gross simplification, a theme park is usually associated with a particular type of benefits that range from excitement to light-hearted fun, comprising other values such as a variety of on-site attractions or the company of other users. In any case, the key of a theme park development process depends on the ability to match the product to be offered with the benefits that the customer sought from the product. Theming, branding and packaging are some strategies to communicate the benefits that potential consumers can look for in any particular theme park. Theming allows the identification of the narrative argument that articulates the content of the park and therefore its objective in terms of excitement or atmosphere. Branding generates familiarity and safety and encourages people to buy a particular product. Finally, packaging provides information that helps potential visitors to go to the park and facilitates the selling of the product through attractive or accessible combinations.

Wanhill (2005a) uses the 'imagescape' concept to characterize the product nucleus of visitor attractions, which he defines as the combination of tangible objects 'within the context of a specific theme or image in a particular setting or environment' (with regard to this, see also Kirsner, 1988, and Pine and Gilmore, 1999). In this sense, the intangible output of a constructed imagescape is central to the visitor experience (Haahti and Komppula, 2006). However, it must be noted that, though the imagescape is the central component of an attraction like a theme park, it is also true that its ability to attract is also a matter of fashion and taste. Both aspects evolve quickly in time.

Like any product – and in this case with very fast evolution cycles precisely due to successive changes in contemporary society's fashion and tastes – theme parks go through different stages during their lifetime. The well-known life cycle model may be applied to them – introduction, growth, maturity and decline – according to which at each stage of the cycle the park and its demand have different characteristics that require specific marketing strategies (see Kotler, 1994). In spite of its simplicity, this is a generally accepted model, which may, however, present some particularities concerning its application to the case of theme parks. It is clear, in the first place, that each park's life cycle may vary considerably in accordance with the very nature of the parks, their organization and running and their territorial placement. Thus, there are parks that have never entered a growth phase, given that they have failed prior to being able to get that far, whereas it is common for parks to be well planned and rapidly attain the maximum threshold of visitors for which they have been designed. In fact, large parks need to achieve high visitor numbers early because they have to pay back their capital costs over a relatively short period and especially before they have to make new expenditure as relaunches are required. On the other hand, numerous parks may have bimodal or trimodal profiles of evolution, to the extent that, once they have reached a certain state of maturity, they can be relaunched before they enter into the decline stage, changing or adapting the core attraction or developing a new product.

In short, bearing these considerations in mind and the nature of theme parks as a recreational product, matters such as the following must be solved for their successful running:

- A precise definition of the theme.
- A wise choice of location.
- Rigorous *mise-en-scène* (the right handling of volumes and surfaces).
- A good definition of the target demand.
- Appropriate size.
- An appropriate market strategy.
- An appropriate organizational structure.
- Careful financial management.
- A workforce that is committed to the project.
- A suitable running and promotional budget.
- A high degree of quality of service.
- The adequate management of flows and movements.
- Appropriate animation of the themes, places and visitors.
- Integration into the project of a development strategy.

9.2. The Locational Factors in Theme Park Development

The success of a park is conditioned by a large number of variables (Rebori, 1995a) concerning where they are established. Only exceptionally are there situations in which a certain placement is deemed ideal. It is therefore necessary to establish mechanisms of analysis that provide acceptable alternatives for consideration concerning the location of a concrete theme park. It cannot be forgotten, on the other hand, that there are a great many cases that would indicate that one of the main reasons for the failure of a theme park is its location in the wrong place (Brown, 1980).

Generally, different elements exist that may orient location processes (Castán, 2004). Such elements may be understood as cost factors, which may be tangible if they can be precisely calculated (objective market, transport system, human resources, the availability of basic resources such as energy and water, taxation, the cost of the land and of construction work, the possibility of supplies) or intangible, which can hardly be calculated precisely (labour, land and environmental legislation, attitudes towards the project by the authorities and society, political and social stability, geographical and cultural conditions of the place). In this respect, below we deal with three key points regarding the three fundamental factors of orientation: the size and characteristics of the market (concretely, the park's capacity to penetrate into the market areas that can be defined around it), the nature of the product (in particular, the characteristics of the placement that make the development of the proposed activities possible) and the requirements of the productive processes (taking into account the need for the activity to be carried out to be well received socially and to have staff and suppliers available nearby, thus facilitating its start-up and management). The following aspects deal, therefore, with how to establish the size and scale of the market and which are the placement characteristics that condition development and what contribution the public sector could make to render the necessary processes simpler and easier.

9.2.1. The size of the market

The success of a park depends on the response given by the market to the product on offer. With regard to this, Wanhill (2005b) cites a famous sentence attributed to hotel magnate Conrad Hilton: 'There are only three things you need to know about attractions: visitors, visitors, visitors!' Therefore, promoters and planners must attend to and understand the characteristics of the market. Unfortunately, it is not easy to define, identify and measure the size of a park's potential market. From the point of view of operations, moreover, the market depends on and is conditioned by the 'imagescape' and the specific location of the product. Market, imagescape and location are three elements that feed each other and must be considered together. Complementarily, such a basic question as the size of the park – and therefore the size of the investment and resources that are needed for its operation – depends directly on the size of the potential market it can cater for. In order to respond to this need, first it is necessary to delimit the park's potential geographical reach, which may be local, regional, national or even global. In each of the scales of reference there is, in fact, just a percentage of the population that visits recreational facilities like theme parks. This is what may technically be defined as the effective market, which may either visit this kind of amenity occasionally or recurrently. Finally, some subgroups may be established regarding socio-demographic and motivational characteristics, such as age, sex, the stage in the family life cycle, social class, place of residence, the type of transport used to get to the park, personality and lifestyle and expectations. Different sorts of analytical instruments exist, which means that the degree of uncertainty may be improved in respect of the size and characteristics of a theme park's potential market. The main ones are:

• The estimation of the rate of penetration of the park in its sphere of influence, distinguishing between different areas and segments.
• The use of psycho-sociological surveys to ascertain the preferences of the potential demand and the establishment of factors that influence

the levels of visitor numbers to the park (McClung, 1991; Ah-Keng, 1994).

- The use of surveys on spending by the resident population and tourists in order to draft not just elasticity–price indices but also reliable indicators of tendencies (see Lanquar, 1991).

On the basis of the concept that they wish to develop, theme park promoters must have a clear idea of four points concerning the market to which the product may attend: who the park's target market is, how many people are going to visit it, what the park's sphere of influence is and when it may expect its visitors. A theme park's potential markets are normally identified as being the resident population of the geographical area where it is located. As is well known, it is considered that frequentation to a park is in accordance with the rate of penetration of the park among the population residing in its immediate surroundings. Researchers like Oliver (1989) are more precise and claim, for example, that, in Europe, a medium-sized theme park with some 3 million visitors requires a population of 15 million inhabitants within a 90-min radius around the park. This estimate may vary in accordance with whether or not tourist regions exist, bringing large numbers of visitors into a park's immediate area, as well as other variables indicative of social class. An illustration of this may be seen in Table 9.1. However, it must be pointed out that in general terms, little information is available concerning this. Thus, no periodical, systematic studies exist on the population's recreational preferences and the use of leisure facilities like theme parks, among others. On the other hand, parks do not usually make their statistical indicators and information public since they are clearly of strategic, commercial use.

Generally, with regard to areas of the market, for any park different types of potential markets can be distinguished whose importance will vary according to its characteristics. More generally, the following markets must be distinguished:

- Resident market. This is the total number of inhabitants residing in the park's sphere of influence (the area within which a trip to the park can be made without needing to stay overnight). This is normally the main target market of any park. Three sub-areas may be identified and broken down, as shown in Table 9.2, though differences in radius may exist, depending on the parks and concrete territorial surroundings.
- Tourist market at origin. This is the total number of potential visitors who, from their place of residence, may feel attracted to visit the park, staying over at least one night to do so. This is an ad hoc market for each park, which will depend on the park's orientation, theme, characteristics and penetration capacity. In any case, as indicated, it must be highlighted that there are very few theme parks in the world that are capable by themselves of being magnets of attraction for tourist markets in large contingents.
- Tourist market at destination. These are tourists that stay overnight in the vicinity of the park and who can therefore visit it. They may be

Table 9.1. Penetration rate for the main Six Flags (SF) parks, 2004 (from Kan, 2005).

Park	Location	Visitors (million)	Population 0–50 miles (million)	Population household income ($) 0–50 miles	% Penetration
SF America	Washington, DC	1.15	6.9	77,840	13.4
SF Great Adventure	Jackson, New Jersey	2.80	12.6	67,127	17.8
SF Marine World	Vallejo, California	1.45	5.9	84,056	19.6
SF Magic Mountain	Valencia, California	2.70	10.4	65,587	20.8
SF Great America	Gurnee, Illinois	2.30	8.6	71,373	21.5
SF Astroworld	Houston, Texas	1.40	4.9	64,814	23.0
SF Elitch Gardens	Denver, Colorado	1.15	2.8	71,776	32.6
SF Texas	Arlington, Texas	2.20	5.4	68,794	32.7
SF Georgia	Austell, Georgia	1.85	4.6	70,405	34.2
SF New England	Agawam, Massachusetts	1.50	3.2	62,676	36.9
SF St. Louis	St. Louis, Missouri	1.35	2.7	60,102	40.1
SF Darien Lake	Darien Center, New York	1.25	2.2	54,219	45.7
SF Fiesta Texas	San Antonio, Texas	1.40	1.9	54,540	59.9

Table 9.2. Mean radii of the market areas of theme parks in Europe and the USA (from authors' own research).

	Europe	USA
Primary	Up to 50 km	Up to 50 miles
Secondary	Up to 150 km	Up to 150 miles
Tertiary	Up to 250 km	Up to 250 miles

split into sub-areas like those for the residents market, although a park's penetration capacity in these markets is less than its penetration capacity in the residents market. Specific segments may be established according to seasonality, place of origin and the motivation itself of the tourists at their destination.

A fundamental point with regard to design is to determine the park's rate of penetration for each of the areas of the market. This rate depends on the characteristics of each thematic product and the demand motivations. It cannot be forgotten that motivation varies from person to person and is different for each kind of park. For example, the atmosphere of some parks with 'white-knuckle' rides does not correspond to that enjoyed in theme parks based on a cultural idea. Whereas in the former it is important to experience new sensations, in the latter the prevailing vectors are the acquisition of values or nostalgia. It is clear that, in all cases, people visit parks to be entertained, but the key lies in the fact that the very concept of entertainment and its valuation varies from person to person. Personal circumstances exist, such as prejudices or perceptions that affect this process, as well as external determining factors, such as friends and family's opinions and assessment, and the image parks convey to the media all help to condition attitudes. In short, according to the size of the park, how well known it is, its content and orientation, its market objectives and the actual operation of the park, penetration rates may vary greatly. In respect of this, see Table 9.3, which includes rates of penetration for the year 2000 for the five Cedar Fair parks in the USA. There are cases such as Cedar Point, with an exceedingly high rate of penetration among the market of its nearest residents but a very low one at a medium distance.

More generally, by means of a study carried out in order to analyse the value of certain strategic variables for the establishment of a theme park in Quebec (Chassé and Rochon, 1993), based on data from Economics Research Associates, the rates of penetration that appear in Table 9.4 have been established. It can be seen that variations exist between American and European parks and between medium-sized and large parks. It is therefore relevant to consider the need to tailor these general considerations to

Table 9.3. Consolidated rates of penetration of Cedar Fair parks in the USA, 2000 (based on Hovorka, 2000).

	50 miles (%)	100 miles (%)	200 miles (%)
Cedar Point	181.5	50.0	20.2
Dorney Park	42.3	10.1	6.2
Valleyfair	58.8	43.4	24.3
Worlds of Fun	78.6	61.1	28.3
Knott's Berry Farm	49.1	30.3	23.1

Table 9.4. Estimated rates of penetration of theme parks in Europe and the USA (from Chassé and Rochon (1993), based on data from Economics Research Associates).

	Medium park (investment of less than $100 million)	Large park (investment greater than $100 million)	
	USA (%)	USA (%)	Europe (%)
0–50 km	15–28	20–45	25
51–200 km	5–11	10–15	2
201–400 km	1–6	2–35	4
Tourist market	–	2–35	4

each concrete case through specific market research. However, they are indicative of the way things work in reality. Other studies clearly show that for the case of North America it is understood that the primary market area (less than 50 miles or 1 hour's drive away) ought to have a resident population of at least 2 million people in order to ensure the success of an urban or regional park. In the secondary market area (up to 150 miles), the resident population should be at least equal to the primary area. With regard to this, it cannot be forgotten that in the USA, over 80% of visits to most parks that are not destination parks come from these two market areas. Finally, the tertiary area would vary greatly in accordance with the location of each park (see Rebori, 1993).

It is clear, therefore, that correctly estimating rates of penetration for the different market areas and demand segments is fundamental for the success of a theme park. A well-known example of erroneous estimation is the one which formed the basis for the development and later failure of today's Waligator Lorraine park, which started out as Big Bang Schtroumpf and has for many years been well-known as Walibi Lorraine, in the French Lorraine region, a 160 ha park that was inaugurated in 1989 and has had serious problems of survival. The project foresaw that the primary residents market (an estimated population in 1989 at less than an hour's journey of 4 million people) rate of penetration would be 20%; that for the secondary market (an estimated population in 1989 located between 1 and 2 h from the park of 14 million people) the estimated rate of penetration would be 4.5%; and, finally, that the forecast for the tertiary market (an estimated population in 1989 between 2 and 3 h from the park of 34 million people) had a rate of penetration of just 1%. Despite such conservative estimates, that meant potential visitor numbers of close to 1.8 million visitors a year (the project even reckoned it could reach 2.7 million visitors after 10 years). However, in 2002, the number of visitors to the park was a mere 400,000. The mistaken forecast was more than notorious: the results were critical.

Though such deviations in estimating are usually a consequence of mistakes in the studies performed prior to the planning of a park, what is true is that, in general, relatively little is known about how people take decisions as to whether or not to visit a theme park in each sphere of influence. Available results are thin on the ground and particular for specific fields of reference. Thus, a paper by McClung (1991; 2000) identifies a series of factors that potential visitors take into consideration when deciding on a visit to a theme park in the USA. The four most important are climate, preferences for a certain type of park, children's desire to visit the park and cost. The study also identifies, among other things, that the 24–44-year age group and families with children are more likely to visit parks. Nevertheless, the hypothesis cannot be made that such results will be valid in other cultural contexts, such as Europe or Asia/the Pacific. Likewise, it is not clear that the types of theme identified by Wong and Cheung (1999) as being preferable for the demand in Hong Kong – nature, fantasy, adventure, futurism, history and culture, international themes and the cinema, in that order – may be extrapolated to other markets in other geographical areas.

As important as the number of inhabitants residing in the park's sphere of influence are the socio-economic characteristics of their potential visitors, in particular with regard to their social condition and their position in the family life cycle and, concretely, the park's capacity to attract families with children, adults or young people, to cite but three specific cases of interest for parks. Such capacity varies according to a park's thematic content and its characteristics in respect of its attractions. In this regard, it cannot be forgotten that all visitors have special needs, though this idea is often associated with the disabled – from families with small children to visitors from abroad who will require information in their own language. The ability to attract certain segments of the market responds, therefore, not just to marketing objectives but also to the configuration itself of the park's augmented product. Also, as Wanhill (2005b) maintains, certain parks' imagescapes can 'provide passive entertainment for seniors and family members with young children who may not wish to participate in the anchor rides, but enjoy watching others having a good time'. In any case, in that theme parks are family-oriented, bearing the children's preferences in mind is of great importance in a park's decision-making process.

The existence of other attractions in the area where a park is located and its size or scale, nature and image all condition the number of visitors that may go to a park. The key concept in this regard is the already known penetration factor, that is to say, the real number of people from each market segment visiting the park. This value varies greatly, depending on the market segment, which should be specifically estimated for each case. Moreover, it may be highly susceptible to variation according to the time of the year and even the time of day. In any case, it should not be overlooked that, just as it is difficult to precisely establish a park's target market, it is also difficult to ascertain, prior to its opening, its visitors' patterns of frequentation. This is especially true if the park is based on a new concept or incorporates little-known formats.

So an important factor which is likely to influence the success of a theme park from the point of view of its potential markets is the assurance that the concept of the product being developed has a market in the area where it is located. On the basis of such a consideration, success is related to the creativity of the design and the appeal of the imagescape related to a particular market. In this regard, Wanhill (2005a) establishes a market–imagescape mix, which includes four types of attraction that can be recognized in the concrete domain of theme parks (see Table 9.5). The 'me too' attractions are projects with little risk concerning their finance and viability, since they appeal to well-known, common experiences and to formats that are already developed in other locations of similar characteristics. The degree of innovation in this kind of attraction is limited. Replicating a model, however, does not necessarily guarantee success, as has been seen with the city of Shanghai's short-lived experience in the business of parks. The 'grand inspiration' attractions offer a new 'imagescape' for already consolidated markets. They are the result of the work of the main operators' teams of creators and innovators, who conceive of new ways to improve the competitiveness of known products. The innovation process within the 'new version' attractions is based on the opening up of new market opportunities while preserving the existing imagescape in content and format. It is the classic strategy adopted by North American operators for establishing their park format in new market areas such as Europe or Asia/the Pacific. Finally, Wanhill (2005a) uses the term 'wonder' attractions to define

Table 9.5. The attraction market–imagescape mix (from Wanhill, 2005).

	Image	
Market	Current	New
Current	'Me too' attraction	'Grand inspiration' attraction
New	'New version' attraction	'Wonder' attraction

the 'very large projects that have major economic impacts on their location' and are eagerly sought after as flagship enterprises. In these cases, the promoters' uncertainty is usually at its maximum, given that it is a matter of creating a new concept for new markets.

For each case, the requirements and requisites of specific expanding markets in concrete geographical areas can be juggled around. Such is the case, for example, of the senior citizens segment with growing available income and much available free time in Europe, the segments of families with small children who wish to visit parks in order to learn something new, whether a practical ability or some piece of knowledge – which may be related to the boom in parks with cultural contents – especially in Asia/the Pacific, or interest groups focusing on environmental matters and issues related with well-being and lifestyle – which support the appearance of new niche parks and of theme parks linked to ecological values and lifestyles such as the latest ones to be developed by Disney – particularly in the USA. All of the above are growing markets which are likely to become widespread and generalized.

9.2.2. The characteristics of the place

For the establishment of a theme park, studies must be undertaken which, in addition to analysing the size of the resident and tourist markets, assess other locational aspects such as, among other things, accessibility, the area's geographical characteristics, including the availability of water resources, the place's environmental quality, the existence of risk areas, the existence of a critical mass of recreational attraction in its immediate surroundings and the park's own general purpose. Prior to this, however, is the capacity of the location itself. It is well known that theme parks need large areas of land to develop. Locating available land at an acceptable cost in a suitable place is usually a considerable difficulty. A mistake in the decision as to where to locate could definitively hinder the success of the initial project and, just as importantly, its capacity for future expansion.

As regards placement, it is essential for the park to be served by an adequate access system. The relationship between parks and the transport system can be summed up in the following aspects (see also Swarbrooke, 2002, 23–24):

- 'Transport networks are an important factor in determining the number of visitors an attraction is likely to attract.' In this regard, it is important to consider both medium- and long-distance access networks and the existence of a transport system in keeping with the needs of nearby demand. Thus, for example, it has been observed that the existence of airport facilities in the proximity of the Legoland park in Denmark has allowed the attraction's managers to consider the possibility of capturing middle-distance markets by plane in addition to those with access by road. Conversely, several parks in peri-urban Shanghai – so as to benefit from the lower cost of land and its availability – such as the American Dream Park, Frobelland, Universal Park or Cosmos Park, have failed as they did not take into account that much of the population still does not possess cars and that public transport from Shanghai is greatly limited as well as highly time-consuming – between 1 and 2 h.

- 'The existence of major attractions leads to the development of new public transport services to meet the demand of visitors.' If a system does not exist, it will have to be built, taking into account the characteristics of the surroundings as well as the needs of the park. The experience of Disney parks is significant in this field. Thus each park has developed specific transport systems to deal with accessibility requirements. Whereas in California the Disney park is at a motorway exit, in Orlando it is connected straight to the airport, while in Paris it is served both by the TGV high-speed railway line – connecting it to the airport and with the dense railway network of the economic and demographic heart of Europe – and by the RER railway network, which links it with Paris's metropolitan flows. So, despite the fact that in the year 2000 Disney's TGV station only generated on average some 4000 passengers per day, its existence has been considered fundamental by the park's managers, to the extent that they contributed 38.1 million euro of the 126.5 million that the operation cost. The basis was, and still is, to improve the capacity to attract international markets from as far afield as Switzerland or the Netherlands through improved rail connectivity.

- 'Transport is also important within destinations to make travel between attractions, and between attractions and services, as easy as possible and encourage visitors to use as many of the destination's facilities as possible.' Along these lines, the ability of the communications system to absorb rush hour flows especially must be borne in mind. Complementarily, it cannot be forgotten that transport systems connecting different services and facilities at the destination may become elements of attraction in themselves, just as occurs with the Colonial Parkway in Williamsburg or within the parks themselves (for example, the monorail at Alton Towers). Examples such as Universal Studios' concern with the planning and management of the communications systems at its different facilities in Orlando are significant in respect of the importance of transport for the success of a park.

From a geographical point of view, the decision as regards a theme park's placement is usually taken on the basis of the analysis of several climatological, biogeographical and topographical indicators. Thus, for example, in the study for the location of PortAventura, a series of characteristics were evaluated such as temperature, amount and characteristics of rainfall, prevailing winds and the availability of water resources; biogeographical aspects like the characteristics of the soil, vegetation and the landscape and, finally, the morphology of the territory and the slopes (the latter two are basic from the point of view of the effort to be made during the building and construction phase). These characteristics were assessed taking four aspects into consideration: their effects during the process of construction, their effects on the final look of the park, the park's opening periods and their effect on visitor comfort once up and running. The scores for each category were between 1 and 5, 1 being the worst scoring and 5 the best. This is common practice in analysing the characteristics of the potential placement of a theme park. Generally, for the assessment of location alternatives, qualitative analysis techniques are used, in which basic requisites can be distinguished (for example, safety) which, if not achieved, would rule out a certain alternative.

Given that parks aim to develop fundamentally open-air activities, among all of the geographical variables mentioned the climatic ones are, without a doubt, the most relevant from the point of view of visitor comfort. Their role is basic as regards the management of the park, since temperature changes and precipitation often cause decisive fluctuations in attendance. So, for example, it is well known that park operators report rises or falls in attendance according to weather variations between one year and the next. Such is the case of Cedar Fair, for example, which considered that a 5% increase in attendance in June 2002 compared with the previous June was principally due to improved climatic conditions. The effects of meteorological conditions are, however, variable. Thus, conversely, Tokyo Disneyland recorded a decrease in attendance in the summer of 2004 because of the high summer temperatures that hit the region. On the other hand, the matter of the availability and quality of water is especially relevant, whether obtained from the park's own resources or from exogenous resources, as well as access to other public services. The issue concerning water is one of the most sensitive given the water needs usually required by theme parks and given the impact development may have if located in more or less arid areas or where water management systems are not very efficient.

A third environmental aspect which is normally taken into account is that of the quality of the ecology and landscape in the park's surroundings. Thus, the existence of protected areas, though perhaps posing restrictions for the potential development of a park, on the other hand favours the environmental quality of its placement. In the USA, parks like Busch Gardens in Virginia are located in places adjacent to the area managed by the US National Parks Service in the Williamsburg area. Conversely, experience shows that places with low environmental quality may be chosen to set up a theme park – even as a strategy for improvement on the part of the administrations involved – although such conditions will have to be taken into account in the design of the park and for the purposes of establishing the appropriate institutional relationships in order to manage adequately the conflict that underlies the situation. In this regard, Universal Studios' project in Japan is part of the city of Osaka's urban strategy to remodel a stretch of its seafront. This is an especially relevant point for central European countries, whose polluted atmospheres may be the object of improvement precisely on the basis of the conception and development of park-style recreational facilities.

A fourth critical aspect regarding the location of parks concerns the existence of risks in the place of the park's site. The kind of natural disasters that are normally taken into consideration by theme park operators are risks that can occur in concrete areas: specifically, the meteorological events characteristic of the tropics, such as tornadoes and seismic episodes. Along these lines, for example, hurricane Katrina in 2005, in addition to affecting the Florida premises, completely destroyed the Six Flags park in New Orleans and, as a result, it is closed throughout the 2006 season. Oriental Land Co., however, has developed all of the facilities at Tokyo Resort Disney bearing in mind the risk of earthquakes in Maihama; moreover, its annual forecast of results contemplates the fact that the damage caused by seismic movement would lead to a temporary decrease in the number of guests because of a drop in consumer confidence, which might adversely affect performance. Earthquakes also imply periods of nil visiting. In the extreme case, they may cause the destruction of the facilities and, in the event that they are located on the coast and could be affected by a tsunami, their flooding.

With regard to anthropogenic risks, studies usually include, in the first place, maps of industrial risk around certain focal points of industry (cement works, chemical factories and nuclear power stations especially) and airports. Nevertheless, the exclusion zones are usually greatly limited. Normally, the areas of risk are considered to be within a 5 km radius of a cement works, 2 km around the chemical industry, 30 km around a nuclear power station and 2 km around an airport. The role of the administration as an agent acting to control and reconcile the interests of the different activities is deemed fundamental (see, for the case of PortAventura, Anton Clavé and Blay Boqué, 2003). Nevertheless, Phantasialand, in Brühl, on the outskirts of Cologne is a medium-sized park located in the Ruhr petrochemical estate. Similarly, in the USA, Six Flags Fiesta Texas clearly highlights different activities' ability to cohabit. In any case, over and above the environmental measures established by legislation, from the point of view of visitor comfort, in such cases, what is fundamental is to avoid smells, noise, unpleasing views and the perception of industrial risk.

Finally, a basic point concerning the location of a park is whether or not other recreational facilities exist in their immediate surroundings. Prior to embarking on any initiative, there is a need to analyse the park's positioning in comparison with other parks, attractions and leisure amenities (see Chassé, 1993b, for an example of the analysis of the global positioning of the concept of a park devoted to Santa in Quebec). So, for example, the development of today's Six Flags Fiesta Texas in San Antonio stemmed from the ascertainment by its promoters that, given the concentration of parks in Dallas and Houston while in San Antonio at that time there was just one SeaWorld park, the development of a new park in

Texas would only be viable if it was oriented at tourist markets and if it was located in San Antonio (Braun, 1993). Now, this also meant that the park had to offer something unique and beyond the common combination of typical theme park attractions that already existed in other cities and over and above what SeaWorld was already offering in San Antonio: hence the theme of the musical tradition of south-west USA. This experience shows, in short, that analysis of the competitive positioning offered by each location is fundamental. In any case, it cannot be forgotten that a certain concentration of attractions maybe positive for the success of each one.

In conclusion it should not be overlooked that, as recreational products, theme parks may have different purposes from the point of view of their relationship with tourism. In particular, a distinction may be made between the different modalities of parks according to their placement and relationship with tourism:

1. Theme parks that do not give rise to tourist flows. A significant percentage of urban and regional theme parks – especially, but not solely, in the USA and Japan – have a limited capacity to generate tourist flows. In fact, they are conceived and are run as recreational facilities of a metropolitan nature. This is the case of many of the Six Flags parks, which receive between 1.5 and 3 million visitors, and classic parks like the Toshimaen Amusement Park in Tokyo.

2. Theme parks located at popular tourist destinations. Theme parks are proliferating and have become an instrument for the diversification of consolidated tourist destinations and, therefore, an element of a strategy to attract new segments of the market to the destination. Such dynamics have taken place fundamentally at both urban and sun-and-beach consolidated mass tourism destinations. This is the case of medium-sized parks like PortAventura in Salou or the Dreamworld, Seaworld and Movieworld group of parks on the Golden Coast of Australia. Also, the development of parks such as Yokohama Hakkeima Sea Paradise or even Hong Kong Disneyland aims to offer recreational alternatives to metropolitan tourist cities' capacity to attract. Taking as a reference the model of the life cycle of destinations initially presented by Butler (1980), this type of theme park becomes an instrument for the rejuvenation of destinations. Normally, their development goes hand in hand with other initiatives to create new attractions.

3. Theme parks that catalyse the development of tourist activities. These are the numerous parks that have brought about the creation of notable tourist flows in their surrounding areas. In Europe, the best-known cases are those of Parc Astérix in France and Europa Park in Germany, to cite just two examples of medium-sized parks. In Asia/the Pacific, the capacity to attract tourists to parks like Everland in Korea or Suzuka Circuit in Japan is also acknowledged. However, they are parks which, on the one hand, have generated tourist flows especially of regional scope, but which, on the other hand, do not form part of tourist destinations in the style of

those cited above, and neither have they themselves created new tourist destinations.

4.   Theme parks that catalyse the development of tourist destinations. Walt Disney World in Orlando is, without a doubt, the characteristic example of a theme park that has generated a tourist destination to the extent of becoming the actual symbolic referent of the place. This is in spite of the development, even, of new parks at the same tourist destination by competing corporations. There is no doubt that Disney in Orlando is the only existing example with worldwide tourist appeal today. On another scale, there do exist parks like Futuroscope in France that have also proved their capacity to change a city, Poitiers, into a tourist destination on a regional scale.

9.2.3. The support of the public sector

Theme parks are high-risk, capital-intensive investments. The social and environmental interest in the development of a theme park on the basis of its contribution to the improvement to the infrastructure and the generation of income and local and regional job creation normally justifies support from the public sector, especially, though not only, during the construction phase. This is in fact common practice for most parks that have developed since Disney in Orlando, which had a particular institutional system of regulating the process of urbanizing the land it occupies. So, given that on numerous occasions parks act as catalysts of the local economy and even play a major role as key elements for territorial planning, it has been normal, up until now, both in the USA and in Asia and Europe, for their development, despite being a private initiative, to come into close collaboration with the public sector.

In relation to this, according to Hsu (1997), in addition to their suitability in financial terms, the development of a theme park should provide a positive response to some questions which, in addition to favouring support from the public sector, are, in fact, the best guarantee for the project:

- Is it politically reasonable?
- Environmentally speaking, is it run correctly?
- Does it fulfil a socio-economic role in the region?

The systems of support activated by the public sector are various and sometimes, for a particular park, several such systems are combined. For example, Trowbridge (1994) reports in particular the case of the public funding of theme and amusement parks in Arizona through bonds. Along the same lines, see Table 9.6, which shows the main support mechanisms of the different administrations acting in the development of existing theme parks in Spain (Anton Clavé, 2005).

The case of Spain underlines, in any case, the publication of specific legislation for the development of a park, specifically PortAventura. As has

Table 9.6. The main mechanisms of support by the administration in the development of theme parks in Spain, 2005 (from author's own research).

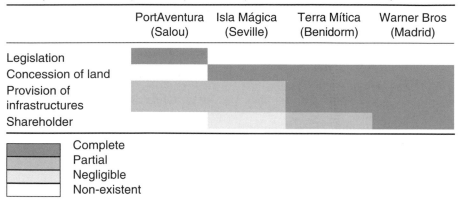

	PortAventura (Salou)	Isla Mágica (Seville)	Terra Mítica (Benidorm)	Warner Bros (Madrid)
Legislation				
Concession of land				
Provision of infrastructures				
Shareholder				

Complete
Partial
Negligible
Non-existent

already been explained (Anton Clavé, 1996), this arose from the political will, on the level of the Autonomous Government of Catalonia and locally, to respond to the need to transform the dominant model of tourism and leisure in Catalonia. This political will translates into the establishment of a novel legal framework for Spain and Europe, which gives an incentive to and regulates the development of theme parks. Law 2/1989 of the Parliament of Catalonia applies the term Recreational and Tourist Centres to leisure complexes that include facilities such as theme parks but also to other uses. This law defines the concept of a Recreational and Tourist Centre and determines the urbanistic requirements that such facilities must comply with in Catalonia and the benefits that will accrue for the developers. On the basis of this law, Decree 26/1989 called a public tender for the adjudication of what was to become the first such centre in Catalonia at the site proposed by the contract winner, provided it came into line with the regulations. Decree 152/1989 awarded the project to Anheuser Busch on an area of 833 ha. Thus, the project, where PortAventura is developed today – officially proposed by Anheuser Busch in 1989 – incorporates by law, and on a surface area of 833 ha, four facets: the recreational, to be developed on a total of 194 ha, the commercial (52 ha), the residential (215 ha) and the sports (307 ha).

There even exist innovative projects that are the result of joint initiatives between the private and the public sectors. This is indeed the case, in France, of the Bioscope project in the Alsace (Boughilas, 2005). The Région Alsace and the Haut Rhin département have joined Grévin et Cie to develop and manage the park. The park foresees 400,000 visitors a year, basically attracting families and tourists, who will potentially prolong their stay in the area thanks to its existence. The public administration has assumed 49% of the direct investment costs and all indirect investment to be made. Grévin et Cie have assumed expenditure of €15 million, which represents 51% of the investment. This initiative, which is the first of its kind in France, lies with the administrative bodies themselves, who have found in Grévin et Cie an expert partner for the conception, execution and management of the park.

More generally, the most common systems for cooperation by public authorities with park promoters are as follows:

- The purchase of land, the concession of land or the awarding of aid towards the purchase of land.
- The provision of public services and improvements to infrastructures outside the park (security/safety, energy, waste management, etc.).
- Aid with the funding of the project.
- A reduction in taxation over a certain period.
- An improvement to the motorway access points and the development of the local road network.
- The building of parking areas.
- The public funding of specific components of the project (for example, an amphitheatre or conventions centre).
- Control over the uses put to the plots of land located around the park.
- Streamlining bureaucratic procedures.
- The funding of training programmes for the employees involved in the project.
- Participation in the shareholding of the project.
- The creation of systems of public/private urbanistic collaboration specific for a project.
- Support for advertising and commercializing the park.
- Adaptation of the legal and urbanistic conditioning factors.
- Support in negotiation with the landowners.
- A stimulus for the establishment of industrial and service activities.

In any case, without the support of the public sector, it is certain that many of the investments made in theme parks would not have materialized. The argument for the authorities is that collaboration benefits all concerned. In fact, a medium-sized park has multiplier effects in complementary economic sectors, generates a large number of jobs, both direct and indirect, and gives rise to the development of new infrastructures and facilities and amenities that benefit the economic environment. Thus, for example, in the case of Disneyland Paris, the French state has managed to continue to stimulate the development process of the new town of Marne-la-Vallée and, via the Disney image, has been able to attract new initiatives, which have brought about new jobs, taxes, transport systems and, in short, new dynamics for the accumulation of capital (D'Hauteserre, 1997, 31). Hence, it is common for parks to tend to seek the collaboration of the authorities in respect of works on necessary infrastructures, regulation of competition in the nearby area and coordination with all of the other economic activities that take place around the park. However, it cannot be forgotten that, at least for the case of Europe, institutional support is being increasingly more seriously scrutinized by the European Union departments overseeing free competition.

9.3. The Business Environment as a Factor of Success

Each theme park's development takes place in a complex context, which conditions it in a variety of ways. Swarbrooke (2002) distinguishes between two main components within the business environment that affect the development of visitor attractions, namely, the macroenvironment and the microenvironment. The macroenvironment exercises a strong influence on organizations but cannot be controlled by them. It may be split into four main types with the initials PEST – political, economic, socio-cultural and technological – although a fifth factor may also be included – natural. The microenvironment includes the structure of the organization itself, its suppliers and marketing intermediaries, existing customers and competitors. The role of each factor in the development of a concrete park is variable in time and specific for each initiative. Table 9.7 illustrates the key factors in the business environment that affect theme park development, according to Swarbrooke (2002). The successful development of a park depends, consequently, on adequate knowledge, anticipation and negotiation of the aspects that are involved in each of them for each specific park. From such a perspective, it cannot be overlooked, therefore, that, in addition to the conditions offered by the business environment that affect each project, the development of a theme park is the result of a public, or more commonly private, business initiative with defined objectives and, therefore, with its own decision-making criteria regarding each of the factors that affect it. So, for example, in the case of the Lego corporation, in addition to ensuring the financial return on the investment, minimizing risks for the company and favouring ease of implementation, an objective has become the generation of synergies with other Lego businesses. Due to this, the development of a Lego park has been conditioned to date not just by issues such as the existence of diversified markets of residents and tourists with spending power, the suitability of the investment to be made, local support for the development project or the existence of possible collaborators, but also and especially by the position of Lego products in the market of reference (Ryder, 1998).

Bearing the factors listed in Table 9.7 in mind, the first ascertainment to be made from the point of view of the microenvironment is that parks' key to success is business management. This is true in three ways. In the first place, one cannot disregard the high negotiating power enjoyed by the suppliers, whether financial institutions, suppliers of services, attractions or products or property developers, over the parks, due, precisely, to the scarcity of suppliers. Something similar occurs with tour operators, in the cases in which the parks have a significant non-resident market. Park operators' ability to negotiate is conditioned by the business strategies of the tour operators. Secondly, and consequently, the success of parks is given by the establishment of an optimal ratio between the capacity of the park, its potential demand and the real mechanisms that come into play to attract visitors. To this end, the role of marketing as a strategy for advertising and commercialization is fundamental. That basically

Table 9.7.   Factors within the business environment that affect the development of a theme park (based on Swarbrooke, 2002).

Macroenvironment	
Political	Political changes around the world
	Legislation (environment, urban planing, health, safety and labour)
	Public-sector policy (utilities, transport, social, educational)
	Deregulation and privatization
	Public support for the development
	Civil unrest and war
Economic	The state of the economy
	The distribuion of wealth
	Taxation policies
	Interest rates – due to the need for constant new product development
	Currency exchange rates
	Newly industrialized and developed countries
	Globalization
Sociocultural	Demographic trends
	The multicultural society
	Changing lifestyles
	Consumer behaviour
	Changing structure of the family
	The growing role of special-interest demand segments
	The desire for corporate social responsibility
Technological	The computer culture
	Growing home-based entertainment systems
	Internet
	Virtual reality
	Management information systems
	New types of rides
Natural	Concern over environmental issues
	Environmental comfort around parks
	The weather – as most theme parks are open-air
Microenvironment	
Organization	The new entrepreneurial culture
	A move towards the empowerment of the staff
	The use of integrated and computerized management systems
	The growing role of quality management systems
	Greater emphasis on marketing
	The role of human resources recruitment
	The motivation of seasonal and part-time staff
Suppliers	The legal concept of product liability
	The quality of products and services
	The rides and on-site attractions
	Catering products
	Souvenirs
	Concessionaires and franchises

Continued

Table 9.7. *Continued.*

Marketing intermediaries	Tourist information centres
	Tour operators and coach companies
	Hotels with display literature
	The growing role of the media
	Targeting the right customers
	Sustainable marketing
Customers	Brand loyalty
	First-time users
	Visits per annum
	Catchment areas
Competitors	Other theme parks
	Other attractions aimed at particular groups
	Other popular activities
	Market uniqueness and placement
	Future plans

means suitably dealing with the research needs the park requires as a product, establishing a long-term strategy of positioning, appreciating the different market segments that are likely to be attracted, dedicating a significant part of the budget to communication and having a professional approach to the needs of the activity. This is especially relevant in that the conditions of the business environment are variable and, therefore, consumers' preferences change and, as a result, so does their behaviour as well as their competitors' strategies to break into the same markets.

With regard to the macroenvironment, what takes on importance in this context is the operational management of the parks and know-how in the sector. Parks' viability and profitability are in accordance with their capacity to dispose of funding, technology and instruments for the development of the necessary attractions so as to satisfy customers' expectations and the appropriate management of the socio-economic and natural conditioning factors. So the crucial type of resources that the management team has to get is financial. Theme parks are very expensive to build and run and, as well as the cost of site acquisition, building work and attraction-buying, there is the need for regular refurbishment, relaunching and remodelling of the existing attractions and regular reinvestment – in many cases annually – in new attractions and products. Finally, the viability and profitability are related to a park's ability to create sufficient brand prestige to increase its penetration capacity. In short, the importance of the experience and stability of the staff holding positions of managerial responsibility concerning the efficacious running of the park must not be disregarded. In fact, the chances of developing a successful theme park are greatly enhanced if the management team has previous experience in the development and management of this kind of attraction. Although there are some exceptions, as the early years of Disneyland Paris show, a human resources team with skills and knowledge is often useful to avoid errors of judgement and to manage the park successfully.

The evolution of the factors mentioned is, in any case, difficult to predict. The development and management of a theme park therefore require both reactive responses and proactive strategies in order to adapt to the future. The critical factor is the perception that the managers have as regards the changes that are continuously taking place in the business environment. This is why it is important to establish the scale of changes, the aspects of the park that can be seen to be most affected by them and which, consequently, will have to be changed and the costs associated with the foreseen changes. As a result, as long as there are no hindrances, adaptations can take place in parks in matters such as the nature of the product, the communication strategy, the channels of commercialization, human resources policies, financial management systems, information management systems, the elements of the tangible product or the organizational structure.

One case that nicely illustrates this is that of Futuroscope, in France. With an increase in demand rising from 225,000 visitors in 1987, its opening year, to 2.8 million in 1997 and later settling at 1.35 million in 2003 (Cochener, 2005), due to critical changes to both the macroenvironment (especially the technological evolution of society during the 1990s) and the microenvironment (especially the role of Disneyland Paris as a competitor and the appearance of new parks in France), since 2004 it has been undergoing a demand recovery process. Two key factors in this process of repositioning in the market have been, in the first place, the identification of the causes and, secondly, the adoption of precise management strategies, which have translated into a specific model known by its director as 10–20–60 (Hummel, 2005). The proposal consists of investing 10% of income each year in order to renew 20% of the supply with the aim of achieving a customer repetition rate of 60%, and, with that, reinventing the park permanently by adapting it to the new expectations of the demand according to the possibilities that the concept and its evolution offer to date. This experience demonstrates that, for the successful management of change, the objectives must be clear and there must be commitment, a precise vision of the business environment and skilful management of staff, available resources and awareness.

More generally speaking, it should be accepted that the theme park industry will evolve quickly over the coming years. Changes will have different effects according to the geographical area, the characteristics of the parks, the nature and strategies of the operators and the type of products they offer. They will be the result of changes to the consumers' motivations, perceptions and expectations, of the growing importance of the concept of value for money in the consumer decision-making process, of the appearance of new systems of communication, promotion and commercialization, of the change in the role played by new technology, of the introduction of new systems to operations management and human resources, of the importance of service quality-related matters, of the awareness of agents and consumers in respect of issues related to environmental impact and social justice in the places of destination and of the improvement to information and decision-making systems.

Case 16. Effects on Attendance of the Addition of a New Gate in a Multipark Destination

Table 9.8 reflects, in absolute values, visitor demand at different multipark destinations during the year prior to the opening of a new park and over the following 4 years. Also indicated are the opening date of the new park, the number of attractions existing at the end of 2004 and absolute demand in 2005, the last year for which figures are available. These data highlight the effects in the fluctuation of frequentation caused by the addition of a new park. The evolution in demand is analysed for three North American cases (Walt Disney World, Disneyland California and Universal Orlando), one case in Europe (Disneyland Paris) and one case in Asia (Tokyo Disneyland) (see also Bilotti and Ksenofontova, 2005).

Analysis of fluctuating frequentation at each multipark destination means that the following statements may be made:

- Total frequentation at existing gates in the year prior to the opening of a new park is normally above the frequentation that these same gates obtain after 4 years. The only case in which a tendency to overcome this is observed, though after 5 years, is that of Disneyland in California, which had 14.5 million visits in 2005, a figure above the 13.9 of 2001.
- Frequentation to existing gates is cannibalized as of the first year of the opening of the new park. The sole exception is Tokyo Disneyland, which in the first year of opening of the new Tokyo DisneySea was situated above the previous year. In this case, the results are explained by the fact that the second gate was started up in the autumn of the year in question.
- Frequentation to the new park tends to level out in a variable range according to the market fluctuations as of the third year of opening.
- Total frequentation at the multipark destination as of the opening of a new gate increases substantially in the cases of Disneyland in California and Tokyo Disneyland, increases slightly in the cases of the multipark destinations of Orlando, Walt Disney World and Universal Orlando and achieves zero increase in the case of Disneyland Paris. Factors that may explain this are the situation of the respective markets and the additional capacity of attraction that the new gates provide. In this regard, Walt Disney Studios in Paris, for example, only contributes a further nine attractions to the 43 of the Disneyland park.
- Specific conditions in the markets and fluctuations stemming from circumstantial aspects may affect the trends expressed above.

Table 9.8. Attendance at multipark destinations after the opening of a new gate (from author's research based on data from *Amusement Business*).

Destination	Opening date	Attractions	Previous year	1st year	2nd year	3rd year	4th year	2005
Walt Disney World, Florida		114	39.3	41.7	42.6	43.2	40.2	43
Existing gates	May 1989[a]	94	39.3	35.7	34.0	34.9	32.2	34.8
Animal Kingdom	April 1998	20		6.0	8.6	8.3	8.1	8.2
Disneyland, California		72	13.9	17.9	17.4	18.0	19.0	21.3
Existing gate	July 1955	49	13.9	12.4	12.7	12.7	13.4	14.5
Disney California Adventure	Feb. 2001	23		5.0	4.7	5.3	5.6	6.8
Universal Orlando, Florida		33	8.9	11.5	14.1	12.8	12.8	11.9
Existing gate	Sep. 1990	17	8.9	8.1	8.1	7.3	6.8	6.1
Islands of Adventure	May 1999	16		3.4	6.0	5.5	6.0	5.8
Disneyland Paris		52	12.2	13.1	12.4	12.4	12.4	12.4[b]
Existing gate	April 1983	43	12.2	10.3	10.2	10.2	10.2	10.2[b]
Walt Disney Studios Paris	March 2002	9		2.8	2.2	2.2	2.2	2.2[b]
Tokyo Disneyland		66	16.5	21.7	25.0	25.3	25.4	25.0
Existing gate	April 1983	43	16.5	17.7	13.0	13.1	13.2	13.0
Tokyo DisneySea	Sep. 2001	23		4.0	12.0	12.2	12.2	12.0

a. Opening date of MGM Studios. Magic Kingdom started in October 1971 and Epcot in October 1982.
b. 2005 was the 4th year after the opening of the second gate at Disneyland Paris.

10 Basic Principles of Theme Park Planning

As for their cities, he that knoweth one of them, knoweth them all: they
be all so like one to another, as farforth as the nature of the place permitteth.
I will describe therefore to you one or other of them, for it skilleth not
greatly which.

(Thomas More, 1516)

The construction of a theme park implies mobilizing a large amount of
resources. Because of this, in addition to having founded expectations on
their capacity to attract visitors, prior to their development precise viability analyses must be carried out to establish the size of the investment to
be made, including the necessary profitability forecasts, which determine
the operations to be done and which translate the resulting parameters to
a layout. The Themed Entertainment Association (TEA) has drafted a
guide for the development of thematic projects, which is made up of four
phases and 11 stages, as summarized in Table 10.1 (TEA, 2000). The project begins with an idea or vision and several feasibility studies. Based on
these, a team of professionals works up a general concept and the master
plan document is created during Phase I. The elements included in the
plan are developed during Phase II of the design process. Phase III concerns
the material construction of the park, including the installation and check-
ing of the attractions. Lastly in the process of the creation of a theme park is
Phase IV, getting ready for the opening of the park. This includes the training of operations and maintenance teams, the installation of furnishings
and fixtures, the inventory, the provision of operations and maintenance
manuals and the resolution of all outstanding issues between the owner
and team members, among other things.

The initial planning of a theme park is normally done within a
5-year time period. Parks must ensure a variety of activities so that the
visitors will wish to stay in them and, yet more importantly, return to them.

Table 10.1. The four phases and 11 stages in the design and construction of a theme park according to the Themed Entertainment Association (from TEA, 2000).

Phases	Stages
I. The project programme	1. Project initiation
	2. Project development planning
	3. Master plan and concept design
II. The design process	4. Schematic design
	5. Design development
	6. Construction/fabrication documents
III. The implementation process	7. Construction/production/fabrication
	8. Show and ride installation
IV. Opening	9. Pre-opening
	10. Grand opening
	11. Project completion

As Wanhill (2005b) states, there are degrees of investment that 'guarantee' penetration into the markets and, especially, repeat visits. At the best parks, repetition rates can be as high as 80% and, in any case, should be no lower than 40% in order to ensure the product is maintained. According to Rector (1997), a theme park project is won or lost precisely at the programming and design stage: hence his insistence on regarding what has come to be known as the 20/80 rule, that is to say, giving over 20% of the cost of a park to its planning as a guarantee of the final success of the remaining 80% of the investment. For this, specific studies must be performed and, finally, a global master plan steering the development of the product must be drawn up. The master plan of a theme park is the basic planning instrument. Together with other complementary, derived documents, its purpose is to establish a strategy which sets out the objectives, the scope, the nature, size, calendar, potential demand, financial parameters and the necessary investment for its development. In this sense, it should be considered that the investment to be made includes both that made in fixed assets (land, buildings and facilities) and that made in working capital, investments in intangibles (studies and projects, works management, start-up, launching) and the necessary investments in replacements and renovation.

10.1. Project Development

The decision to develop a theme park involves drafting a programmatic instrument – the master plan – which sets the targets and steers the development process. Also, in parallel, a project management process must be set up which, on occasions, may be led by the future park operators themselves but which, especially in the case of large-sized parks, is usually contracted out to project managers, who will leave the attraction once it opens.

10.1.1. The design of the master plan

The master plan is a basic instrument for the development, construction and start-up of the park. It is a detailed plan that steers its design, implementation and opening, whose content – together with other specific complementary documents – is the basis of the tasks to be carried out during the phases of programming, design, construction and opening of the park. Consequently, the master plan of a theme park includes the programme of contents determining the concept and theme to be developed, the size, capacity and cost of the different attractions and equipment, development plans for the form and structure of the park (including functional diagrams and outlines of the installation on the terrain) and an architectural programme with illustrational drawings and sketches of the attractions and equipment being developed.

The master plan of a theme park must deal with the provisions made by legislation concerning its location with regard to urbanism, the environment, security and safety, health and employment. Its drafting demands constant revisions. Aspects such as the park's size, the investment to be made and its financial viability once up and running are to be defined in this document, at least in preliminary form, and specific studies and ad hoc market research are needed to allow the setting of parameters. For this, the master plan must also include the results of the park operating plan, that is to say, its basic commercial parameters, measures of operation and the marketing variables which allow the adjustment of the investment to be made to the park's future operation possibilities.

In greater detail, Table 10.2 compiles the points that the master plan of a theme park must consider in different fields of action and in accordance with the objectives to be established, the figures to be analysed, the concepts to be put to the test and the needs to be determined. In any case, it should be stressed that, to the extent that frequentation is directly conditioned by the size of the investment, the correctness of the market studies and the plan of operations, it becomes a fundamental issue for the scaling of the park and therefore a critical element of the master plan.

The operating plan is based on the determination of the park's 'design day' as a fundamental measure. Its drafting requires establishing the scale as regards the number of visitors a day for whom the park is designed. To this end, parameters are resorted to such as the rate of penetration and the rate of recurrence (number of days of visits by visitors). The plan includes estimates as to annual attendance, mean visitor expenditure by item and

Table 10.2. Points for consideration in a master plan for the development of a theme park (from Hsu, 1997).

	Areas				
	Physical	Functional	Social	Legal	Economic
	Location	Areas	Perception	Real-estate law	Real-estate economics
	Surroundings	Proximity	Psychological	Regulations	Markets
	Ecology	Utilities	Historical	Zoning	Financing
	Landform	Services	Symbolic	Jurisdictions	
		Catchment			
		Circulation			
Goals: set	Physical	Building area	Effects	Ownership	Profit
	Physical impact	Utilities	Impact	Political associations	Equity
	Surroundings	Services		Zoning limits	Market limits
	Location	Proximity		Political strategies	Rent
		User			Sales
					Funding
					Budget
					Impact
Facts:	Roads	Area parameters	Statistics	Surveys	Interest
organize	Slopes	Pedestrian	Social structure	Codes	Capitalization
and analyse	Views	Catchment	Behaviour	Zoning	Taxes
	Vegetation	Statistics	Perception	Deed	Land cost
	Geology	Vehicles	History	Easements	Rent/sales
	Soil			Jurisdictions	Transportation
	Climate				Economics
	Ecology				Financing
					Utilities

Concepts: test	Ecological stability Microclimate Ecological analysis	Connectivity Catchment Land use	Lifestyle Behaviour setting	Cooperatives Condominiums Air rights Advocacy Leasehold Joint venture Eminent domain	Economic return Leverage Best use Cost sensitivity Absorption rate
Needs: determine	Buildable area Limitations Ecological analysis	Area requirements Traffic capacity Parking Catchment Utility/service Capacity Access	Sociological Psychological Perceptual		Market analysis Population projection Economic impact Traffic projections Cash flow

the elasticity of the demand to the price, as well as forecasts of the need for staff, supplies and maintenance. It is in accordance with these variables that the theme park may be broken down into tangible elements such as thematic areas, attractions, trajectories, spectacles, animations, services, food points and sales points. The master plan must establish commercial capacities and parameters, architectural characteristics, volumes and surface areas for each tangible element.

Finally, the master plan should consider aspects concerning the funding of the project and, in particular, establish its basic profitability measures. Normally, the viability of the project is measured in terms of its financial results, the return on investment and the depreciation period. In the USA, according to Hsu (1997), the development of a theme park may be justified by a minimum rate of return of some 7 years. The case of Disneyland in Anaheim, where the return period was just 4 years, is, at present, very difficult to match in any geographical and economic context. It is important to point out that a project with positive financial results in the short term, less than 7 years, does not necessarily mean it will be a long-term success. In fact, the inexistence of long-term planning can lead to inertias that hinder the park's adaptation to market changes. Hence the master plan should be understood to be modifiable or adjustable at later stages in accordance with the expansion and growth dynamics of the market.

The master plan must also deal with the need for future reinvestment, as regards both the acquisition of new attractions and the renovation of existing ones. In the USA, these needs have been set at between 4% and 5% of the gross annual income every 3 years and it has even been estimated that a reinvestment deficit according to these parameters of magnitude and time may bring about a fall in attendance of 3.5% per year. Numerous parks reinvest the amount equivalent to their yearly depreciation. On the other hand, carrying out improvements to the park's recreational content usually has highly positive effects on attendance. Thus, Six Flags, for example, claims that a new, big attraction generates on average a 6% increase in attendance (Kaak, 1992). Finally, to involve the public sector in the project, in addition to its direct profitability, the master plan should estimate the economic effects that the development of the park could generate indirectly.

10.1.2. The management of the development process

Managing a theme park's construction project is a complex activity as it involves, as Swarbrooke (2002) observes, managing resources, time and quality in an intricate interrelationship. Two kinds of resources must be managed: people and materials. A variety of types of people are involved in the development process of a park and there are a variety of needs, ranging from architects to decorators through marketing specialists, local authorities and specialized craftsmen. Coordinating them on site is fundamental, given that otherwise delays may be incurred, leading, as Disney found out with its Paris project, to high extra costs. Also, from a resources point of view, materials are managed, that is to say, all necessary elements for the physical construction of the facility. As in the case of the staff, the deficient management of materials may lead to delays and therefore, again, extra costs. Secondly, project management involves setting a work schedule, whose target is the opening of the park on a predetermined day, which is usually widely publicized in advance. Delayed or incomplete opening usually mean a loss of consumer confidence in the park: hence the importance of appropriate management of time and, in particular, a series of tasks in the appropriate order and manner. Finally, the theme park project management team must ensure that its construction takes place with the suitable standards of quality both from the point of view of the resources and time and from the perspective of the demand segments it aims to attract. Good estimation of budgetary needs is essential in this respect. For this, control systems must be laid down.

On the basis of these premises, experience and judgement are usually important for the management of the construction of a theme park. However, useful, well-known project management techniques exist, particularly those like critical path analysis (CPA), 'a time-based technique for managing projects which recognizes and plans the need for interaction between the various players involved in the development process' Swarbrooke (2002), and the programme evaluation and review technique (PERT), a technique that disaggregates the theme park project into a number of tasks and jobs on the basis that the duration of a project does not necessarily coincide with the sum of the times of the activities as a whole that are to be developed between the start time and the end. Obviously it is possible to apply mathematical techniques of linear programming that facilitate the planning of a more effective use of resources during the development process.

In summary, the management of the development of a theme park should take into account some critical points, which, if they have been properly handled, ensure the viability of the project:

1.   The adaptation of investment to the real needs of the project. As demonstrated during the appearance of theme parks in France at the end of the 1980s, underestimating investment needs usually has highly negative results for the viability of the park. One of the most notorious examples is the case of Zygofolis, in which the real investment made was finally double the foreseen (from 150 million francs to 300 million) and led to a financial crisis, which, in conjunction with other design and management factors, brought about the closure of the park. The causes of the lack of foresight concerning the investment are usually a consequence of the non-compliance with planned execution schedules, the need for supplementary work, mistaken valuation of infrastructure costs, the need to create annexed facilities that had not been borne in mind initially or changes to the project itself.

2. Fulfilling the construction schedule and expenditure forecasts during this phase of the project. In other words, the material construction phase of the park is fundamental from the point of view of its economic viability. There are many parks where delays in the process of construction have had important financial consequences that have left them in serious difficulties. As Rector (1997) remarks, it is critical, in this respect, to define on real bases the schedule for the development, the budget to be used and the operations to be performed so as to reasonably fulfil expectations.

3. The conception of contingency plans that allow dealing with the diverse problems that may affect the development process, from those arising due to adverse weather to those that are a consequence of delays in the delivery of materials, as well as other common occurrences, like the non-compliance with commitments to complete certain phases of the project, labour-related problems, increases in labour costs or the price of materials, currency fluctuations, the requirements of inspections or regulations and changes to the project itself, which may be put forward once the construction work is under way.

4. The appropriate scale of the organizational, operations and marketing needs at the time of the start-up of the park. Braun (1993) notes that a multitude of examples exist of parks that have failed as a result of the deficient planning of operations and marketing during the phases leading up to their opening. This is why the formation of a human team trained in general and specialized subjects, according to their role, is a factor that needs careful planning. Also, prior to opening, the relevant park public relations, communications and commercialization programmes should have been activated. Other critical areas that require meticulous planning before opening are general management, operations and the development of shows and entertainment.

5. The necessary training of teams with the right, high level of professional experience, thoroughly committed to the product and visitor satisfaction. It is well known that the running of a theme park generally depends on a large seasonal workforce, presenting high turnover rates. Nevertheless, the personnel are fundamental as regards the operation of the park: hence the need for parks to set out precisely each employee's functions and to have very strict control systems. In this respect, in the mid-1990s, Disney had over 1100 specific job descriptions at its parks. Hence also the importance theme parks give to matters like staff selection and training and the entertainment of the operators at their work posts.

6. The creation of efficient attraction operations and maintenance programmes as a basis for visitor safety and satisfaction. This is one of the most important aspects to be borne in mind, especially as regards the mechanical attractions. It must not be forgotten that the public's behaviour may alter an attraction's operability and give rise to problems. Hence the need for well set-out protocols for the use and upkeep of each one. Though each park has its own operations manual with specific indications for every contingency the International Association of Amusement Parks and Attractions has drafted complete manuals to give guidance on this matter for less experienced operators (see IAAPA, 1993).

10.2. Project Feasibility

In order to determine the operative contents, dimensions and needs of a theme park, specific analyses must be performed so that the viability of the idea may be assessed and to allow the design of the basic strategies of the park, with regard to both the product targeted for offer and its business expectations. Such analyses, which are included as key elements for decision making in the actual master plan, usually include studies on two fundamental matters:

- The planning of services and operations.
- The forecasting of operating measures.

The principal objective of such studies is, basically, to evaluate the potential for success of the project being developed. They are, therefore, systematic analyses of some of the key variables that may come into play in their evolution. Normally, they are rational, logical studies, though sometimes they may also tend to support decisions taken previously on the basis of the strategic options of the agents participating in the process. This is the case, for example, of parks that are developed on the basis of public initiatives, which condition their development on a specific site. Viability studies may be performed either by the promoting corporations themselves or by consultants. It is common practice to produce an initial in-house briefing to allow the clear establishment of the promoter's objectives and expectations and later to contract an external consultant. This, despite usually being distinctly expensive, means that greater objectivity, experience and speed may be gained.

It must not be forgotten that the different development studies required for the start-up of a park are highly complex and challenging. This is due to the fact that constant changes arise in the market, both from the point of view of potential visitors' motivation and behaviour and from the perspective of the formats and characteristics of the attractions. On the other hand, viability studies are usually carried out quite some time before the parks are actually started up, and, in the case of medium and large parks, this may be several years. Also, the related political and economic circumstances, as well as legislation concerning specific matters, may vary during the development process. For instance a particular amenity may be affected by changes made by the authorities governing school holiday periods or by new environmental requirements affecting its development. In spite of the experience gained by the existence of similar parks as regards contents, format and scale, what is true is that each facility is unique and one can hardly be compared with another and, hence, the existence of points of reference of success can never be a guarantee of the success of a new project.

10.2.1. The planning of services and operations

A theme park is a complex facility in which multiple processes are carried out with the purpose of ensuring visitor satisfaction. These processes mean that it is possible to offer different types of services once the visitor has entered the park. In the case of the attractions and shows – in addition to the general services – visitors get a service which they have paid for when purchasing the entrance ticket. In the case of food and beverages and the shops, visitors must pay once they are in the park. The attractions are a standardized service of a continuous nature, whose operational objective is to minimize waiting time. The shows generally take place at previously announced time intervals. Their format is also standardized, though in the production process it is organized as a project. A production process is continuous when production is organized online and idle time is eliminated, always performing the same tasks with the same components obtaining the same product. It is, therefore, a kind of process, typical of the attractions of a park, homogeneous and repetitive. Production by project is useful to elaborate singular products or services (or with unique characteristics) of a certain complexity. In this kind of production, characteristic in filming, there is a sequence of operations at a fixed point to which the people and equipment needed for it have moved. Catering services use a job-shop production system in the case of table service with a menu. In this case, small product units are handled, which vary substantially as regards their form, raw materials and processes. In batch production processes, the same facilities are usually used to elaborate different products. Online production is used when large batches are made with little variety of products, apparently different but technically homogeneous: that is, they require the same type of operations and, therefore, the same facilities can be used – as in the case of the self-service units. The service offered by the shops is more difficult to define on the basis of a theoretical model, given that, in general, the client merely chooses an article from among what is on show and pays for it.

The design of processes has a determining influence on the general layout of the park and that of each facility. The layout serves to determine the best physical arrangement of the different components that make up the park. The processes therefore condition issues such as the location of each facility, its capacity, the size of the waiting areas and its internal structure. So the decisions that are taken as regards the design of the product and its position on ground level are directly governed by the actual design of the park's operations. In this respect, matters should be borne in mind such as the circulation of materials and supplies within the park (linear or zigzag, for example); the quantity and size of the equipment and machinery to be used and the ancillary spaces required around them; the aspects related to the environmental conditions of workers and visitors (security/safety, lighting and ventilation, among other things), the characteristics required for each facility as regards layout, heights and other factors. A good layout of processes should allow the smooth circulation of materials, people, products and information. It should ensure customer comfort, the integration of the activity and other aspects, such as the suitability of the aesthetics and landscaping of the thematic environment designed.

Theme parks present a customer-oriented layout, which, in general terms, includes the parking area, the admissions zone (both ticket sales and ticket validation), customer services, the common services areas (cloakroom, the hire of wheelchairs and a shopping pickup point, among other services), the entrance to the park with shops, restaurants and access to internal transport systems and the animation area (which is in turn usually divided into different thematic areas and concentrates a mixture of all kinds of services available to the customer). At the attractions, it is most important to keep waiting time to a minimum and to have waiting areas that can absorb peak attendance. Also, each attraction must have a suitable operating area in accordance with its load characteristics. In this regard, it must not be forgotten that minimizing visitor waiting time in queues (Castán, 2004) means that visitor satisfaction will be enhanced (since the existence of queues has a negative influence on the visitor's perception of the park), revenue will be maximized (since queuing means that visitors cannot consume other available services at the park) and the large investment involved in the building of a queuing system will be reduced. With regard to the places where shows are put on, a pre-loading area must also be designed where there are guarantees that everyone admitted will have a seat and that waiting will take place in the best possible fashion. In addition to the production areas, the catering facilities must include waiting areas and appropriately sized dining rooms and, for self-service outlets, efficient waiting facilities both in their route (which should be as short as possible) and in the provision of cash registers (shortage of which often leads to unnecessary waiting). As well as the actual shop display space and the cash registers, storage space should be taken into account for shops.

Also, planners of a theme park must consider a series of logistic services – invisible to the customer – which must be incorporated in their design and, therefore, in their layout. Such logistic services involve the human resources (recruitment, candidate selection, contracting and specific training), maintenance (which may be predictive, preventive or corrective and contributes not just to visitor satisfaction but also to safety), the gardening and buildings (whose appearance is fundamental from the perspective of the theming of the park itself), the electrical and electronic installations, the distribution of gas and water, climatization, mechanics, sound and image and information systems, the production of the shows (which, in addition to specialized personnel, involves scenography and furnishings, special effects, sound and image, wardrobe and, quite often, pyrotechnics), the logistics of catering (with common facilities and specific installations at each food and beverage outlet) and the logistics of the shops. Logistics services, in addition to the facilities needed for administration, management and new projects, as well as roadways and technical areas, ensure the running of the park in real time and require, more specifically, concrete spaces, such as general storage facilities, warehouses for goods to be sent out to the shops and play areas, food stores, wardrobe stores, specific storage for shows, maintenance workshops, greenhouses and fuel pumps, among other fundamental facilities. Similarly, parks must consider waste management as something of fundamental importance: take as an example the fact that 50,000 visitors to a large park can generate in 1 day around 30 tonnes of waste, which takes up a huge space.

As can be gleaned from the considerations covered so far, the design of a rational layout that distinguishes the animation areas from the logistics zones, where, for the purposes of illustration, the rear of all customer-oriented facilities is inaccessible, with clear differences between customer access and access for employees and materials and which, especially, suggests an ordered, sequential visit, is an instrument of competitiveness for the company in terms of cost and visitor satisfaction, as they do not see behind the scenes of the business and are not disturbed by its processes. Good layout design ensures the best possible use of the resources that are required in the development process of a park and during its operation, allows turning an idea into a tangible form with the capacity to attract visitors and facilitates the chances of adhesion to the project both by the public sector and by private initiatives. In short, layout stems from the need to render services in accordance with the conceptual nature and the strategy of the park and should be submitted to lengthy, in-depth study and assessment, with the purpose of defining and establishing needs in such a way as to minimize costs and maximize revenue. Also, it means that visitor safety and security standards can be maximized and the generation and handling of waste and the consumption of energy and water can be kept to a minimum and hence be considered environmentally friendly.

It is important, on the other hand, for the layout to take into account the needs of flexibility in the planning of the services and the operations that derive from the continuous changes in the motivation and behaviour of the demand. Thus, the developers of a park ought to bear in mind matters like the incorporation of new attractions and buildings, the ability to operate just one part of the park, or even, as has happened at Futuroscope, for example, the possibility for one pavilion to change its contents in accordance with the evolution of the demand. To this end, it is also important for facilities to attract visitors at any time of the year and under a wide range of meteorological conditions. This is a fundamental measure to combat facilities' seasonality. Finally, it should not be forgotten, from the point of view of generating business, that, generally speaking, the most successful attractions are those that, first, have aesthetic appeal for visitors, which can be based on size, form, colour, appearance or their materials and, secondly, have been designed to be user-friendly because of the sign-posting, access, information displayed, good-quality support services or design adapted to peak crowds and congestion, among other things. A particular point is the park's necessary sensitivity towards visitors with special needs. In fact, any visitor may have special needs, from a customer who does not understand the language to people with some form of physical disability.

The planning of services and operations is, in summary, a fundamental aspect from the point of view of a park's viability, to the extent that it influences their magnitude, characteristics, functioning and aesthetic value and, therefore, directly governs the investment needed for their development. In particular, according to Swarbrooke (2002), it must be taken into account that, from this standpoint, investment includes:

> the acquisition of the site and any restoration or preparatory work on it that is required; construction work to create the buildings and structures that house the attraction; the setting out of the attraction . . . the costs associated with the launch, which are incurred before the attraction starts to earn income, such as staffing and marketing; and any other costs incurred before the attraction opens, such as franchises that have to be purchased or licenses and planning permissions that must be obtained.

In greater detail, it can be said that, in terms of finance, the service life of the different theme park facilities is as follows: between 25 and 40 years for the attractions, 40 years for the buildings and logistic facilities and for furnishings and equipment between 2 and 10 years.

In any case, the result is conditioned by the budget available for the development of the project, the experience and corporate culture of the operator that manages it, the actual conditions of the place itself, especially the physical ones, legal and regulatory conditions, the scale of the project and its size compared with the possibilities and characteristics of the place where it is located, security and safety requirements imposed by the operators themselves, the objectives concerning the beauty of the landscape designed and the perception that the project is, as a whole, coherent with the founding idea of the recreational facility. In short, the planning of services and operations is the basis of the development process of a park since it is directly related: (i) to the internal objectives of the promotional organization of the project; (ii) to the legal restrictions that affect the activity and the location; and (iii) to the expectations of the potential demand.

10.2.2. The forecasting of operating measures

The financial viability of a theme park is established to the extent that its development allows adequate return on the capital invested and the achievement of operating profits. In the case of parks, since some years may be needed before reaching predicted visitor numbers, it is important to estimate income and expenditure in the medium term. Studies carried out prior to the development of the park should clearly set out the capital costs incurred with the park's development as well as, especially, the forecast operating balance in terms of revenue and costs. Given that these are fundamental for the purposes of sizing the park, forecasts that are not within operating measures could lead to its failure and even, to its closure after some time. It is not uncommon for there to be theme parks in a critical situation as a direct consequence of aspects such as an overestimation of frequentation due to the erroneous definition of the market areas and the park's penetration rate and, as a consequence, a mistaken forecast of income. It is therefore necessary to obtain precise estimates as to the results the future running of the park may give. To this end, break-even analysis becomes fundamental. It is also one of the key instruments of the control of results in the management of a park during its operating stage. In general terms, this type of analysis involves calculating the volume of sales of the product needed so as to cover costs, neither generating profit nor incurring losses. As will be seen below, for the case of theme parks this is directly related, on the one hand, to the volume of visitors and the per capita expenditure made by the visitors to the facility and, on the other hand, to the operating costs plus the depreciation that the operators must defray.

Parks generate income in two ways. First, they generate income due to their actual thematic nature by offering meanings to their consumers and, through these meanings, generating 'distinction' among their visitors. The latter are willing to acquire this distinction 'symbolically' through the payment of an entrance ticket (MacCannell, 1976). Thus, visitors to a park pay, since Six Flags introduced it in the 1960s, a single entrance fee to enjoy all of the attractions. The consequence of the 'pay-one-price' concept, that is to say, the payment of a single entrance fee to get access to the park's recreational offer, is the perception of unique meaning as regards what the park represents, ceasing to be a spontaneously consumed attraction and becoming the focus of a planned family excursion. Secondly, theme parks generate income through their truly commercial establishments and facilities. In fact, it is these establishments and facilities that generate a fundamental part of company profit. To this end, Desgue (2005) uses the example of the fact that Parc Astérix, in Paris, directly exploits 17 shops in the park, selling some 7000 different articles and generating close to 25% of the income.

The viability of a theme park is basically conditioned by the number of visitors to it and the per capita expenditure made. In this respect, it cannot be forgotten that attendance is generally seasonal and is highly unstable and that, as can be seen in Table 10.3, important variations exist between parks. Matters such as unusual temperatures, an accident, the appearance of other leisure alternatives or the decrease in the price of air travel, an economy in recession or the holding of world events like the Olympic Games or a universal exposition may have considerable effects,

Table 10.3. Per capita spending at Cedar Fair parks ($) (from Conder and Krecher, 2006).

	1998	1999	2000	2001	2002	2003	2004	2005
Cedar Point	40.28	41.75	44.50	45.61	46.07	48.37	49.34	49.34
ValleyFair	29.10	30.00	32.00	32.80	32.80	33.62	33.96	35.65
Dorney Park	28.24	29.25	30.25	31.76	31.76	32.40	33.23	35.53
Worlds of Fun	25.76	27.00	27.75	28.58	28.58	29.15	30.17	31.08
Knott's Berry Farm	31.99	33.25	34.50	35.54	35.18	36.59	38.42	40.72
Michigan Adventure	31.99	33.25	34.50	34.50	39.68	43.64	45.17	45.62

in addition to the general circumstantial changes that occur in the public's spending habits, on the results of a park in a fiscal year. Also, cultural differences lead to variations in results. Thus, for example, per capita revenue at Disney in Tokyo for 2004 was $87.49 compared with $63.48 at Disneyland Paris and $63.17 at Walt Disney World in Florida. Moreover, in the Tokyo park, income generated by food, beverage and merchandise represents 54.12% whereas in the European park the figure drops to 47.21% and at Walt Disney World in Florida it falls as low as 39.79%. Depending on the risk incurred with the investment, a better or a poorer result during the early years of operation can prove crucial for a park's financial health and the continuity of the project. In this regard, park management becomes a fundamental factor.

Besides matters concerning a park's scale and penetration capacity into the different market areas and the marketing strategies to be implemented so as to improve visitor numbers, there are two points for consideration as regards the attendance of a park: pricing and opening periods. The price factor must be borne in mind as of the early stages of a park's viability analysis (Guyomard, 2005). Going to a park involves a cost to families. Table 10.4 is a summary of the cost of a visit to a selection of theme parks in the USA in 2002 for a family of four and it shows a breakdown of the prices of the main cost elements. Variation between parks can clearly be seen. This is due to the different financial effort which each of them must make in accordance with their investment levels, annual operating costs depending on their size, thematic characteristics and levels of the provision of services and their market positioning strategy. On an international level, price variations also indicate the different purchasing power of the visitors–users of the park for each country. The pay-one-price admission system is generally regarded as the most advantageous for parks and also for customers. Parks try to achieve secondary income equivalent to the revenue gained by admissions, which includes catering, merchandising and other categories, such as sponsorship, corporate hospitality and the rental of facilities. This latter category is difficult to predict.

Table 10.4. Prices ($) of some spending components in a selection of theme parks in the USA and an estimation of the per-family-unit visit cost, 2002 (from *Amusement Business*).

Park	Adult fee	Child fee	Parking	Burger	Beverage	T-shirt	Cost per family (2 adults + 2 children)
Busch Gardens, Tampa	50	41	7	3.5	1.5	15	231
Cedar Point	42	20	8	3.5	2.25	13	170
Disneyland, Anaheim	45	35	7	4.5	2.25	13	227
Dollywood	34	25	5	4	1.75	13	175.5
Frontier City	26	18	6	3.5	2.5	10	144
Paramount's Great America	44	34	10	3	2.5	10	220
Six Flags Fiesta Texas	36	22	7	4.25	2.5	12	181
Universal Studios Florida	50	41	8	4	1.75	16	252
Wyandot Lake	25	19	3	3	2	14	147

Establishing the entrance fees and the prices of consumer products inside parks is fundamental from the perspective of a theme park's viability. Despite the fact that according to classic economic theory demand for parks should have a high price elasticity, data from *Amusement Business* concerning the expenditure made by a family in a North American theme park would indicate the contrary. Indeed, it increased by some 40% between 1993 and 2001. Similarly, between 1987 and 2004 the mean one-day adult entrance fee at Walt Disney World rose from $28.00 to $58.04 and at Disneyland in Anaheim it jumped from $21.50 to $49.75. Key in interpreting this phenomenon is the perception the visitor has of the joint recreational value offered by parks in terms of entertainment and the effort they make to incorporate new attractions and services every so often. On the other hand, concerning prices, it can be seen that one company can have clearly different strategies for its different parks.

In addition to price, for the purposes of estimating a park's attendance numbers and viability another fundamental factor is the operating period. It has already been mentioned that many of the world's theme parks are seasonal. This means that the investment has to be amortized by concentrated visitor attendance at certain times of the year. Operating periods are governed by the behaviour of the market segments that are the subject of the park's commercial strategy, by the magnitude of its market areas in comparison with its size, by its uniqueness and capacity to attract and, as would be logical, by the climatic factors of the area where it is located.

Also, in addition to the annual length of the opening period of a park or the possibility of only opening at weekends at the beginning and end of the season, as is practised by numerous parks, variations exist as to the number of daily opening hours, which may range from the 15 h of opening a day in summer in Gardaland and the 8 h of Efteling in spring and autumn. Such variations are normally accompanied, furthermore, by specific prices for each season of the year. In any case, lengthening the daily stay period in the park is fundamental. There is known to be a non-linear relationship between spending at a park and the duration of the visitor's stay, especially when a stay of 4 h is surpassed, which is when spending soars.

The second key point is that of per capita income. This varies greatly according to each park's magnitude and characteristics. So, for example, Universal in Florida generates per capita income of $48.41 versus the $63.17 generated by Walt Disney World, also in Orlando. What happens, however, is that Disney is able to generate more merchandize and food and beverage revenue per visitor than Universal: $25.14 per visitor for Disney as against $14.79 for Universal. It is understood that, on average, per capita income at a destination park at least doubles that of a regional or urban park. Without a doubt, the length of stay at the park is a critical factor, which would explain such circumstances. The existence of more than one gate at a thematic resort, as well as the availability of on-site hotels, increases per capita spending. In this regard, Table 10.5 shows an improvement in the results at Disneyland in California between 1998 and 2005, according to estimates by Smith Barney. In any case, what is important is that per capita income is in line with the amount foreseen as being necessary to bear the investment made and the operating costs. From the point of view of the management of a park, some of their managers' main objectives are, precisely, to increase per visitor expenditure, as well as the logical target of increasing visitor numbers. To do so, it is common to use mathematical forecasting techniques, such as linear programming or

Table 10.5. Sources of income at Disneyland California, 1998–2005 ($) (from Krutik and Han, 2004).

	1998	1999	2000	2001	2002	2003	2004	2005
Number of gates	1	1	1	2	2	2	2	2
Average effective ticket price	21.41	22.27	23.16	23.16	25.05	26.05	26.73	27.40
Food and beverage per capita	10.02	10.26	10.51	10.76	11.02	11.91	12.15	12.40
Merchandise per capita	10.96	11.25	11.54	11.84	12.15	12.51	12.76	13.02
Total per capita spend	42.40	43.78	45.21	45.76	48.22	50.48	51.65	52.81

systems for the analysis and programming of queues, which aim to improve the park's efficiency as a production area (through consumption).

Although it is not possible to establish a general statistical model, given that there are a variety of geographical zones, visitor behaviour, meteorological characteristics, opening periods, investment size and needs at each park, it can be said that between 50 and 60% of a park's income is generated through entrance fees, whereas the remainder comes mainly through consumption by visitors inside. In the case provided here of the Six Flags parks for 2004, these proportions were exactly 53.6% corresponding to admissions and 46.4% to consumption inside the park (including the games), sponsorship and other income, such as that generated by the parking facilities. At Disneyland in Anaheim, another significant example, the results were 51.8% coming from entrance fees and the remaining 48.2% from consumption inside the park. In greater detail, this latter proportion can be broken down as follows: 23.5% from the sale of food and beverage products and 24.7% from the sale of other goods, fundamentally souvenirs. In addition, parks that have them can manage to generate between 5 and 10% of their income through games.

In addition to sales to their visitors, parks have other sources of income, such as sponsorship and rents. Thus, for example, at the time of opening, JCB Co., Nippon Suisan Kaisha Ltd, House Foods Corp. and Yamazaki Baking Co. purchased the rights to use the Tokyo DisneySea logo in their television advertisements and promotion. In the year 2000, income not coming from visitor consumption at Walt Disney World in Orlando reached $783 million, 22.7% of its total revenue. Parks also let their facilities to other corporations for a variety of activities and, in some cases, to use their scenic image, again for promotional purposes.

Given the great effect that consumption inside the park has on total expenditure made by each visitor, operators are well capacitated to establish entrance discount systems, as the entrance fee becomes less relevant, thus stimulating visits to the park. There are a multitude of types of discount (senior citizens, infants, groups – which may represent over 35% of park admissions – season tickets, working days, evenings, tourist packages, product promotions, among others). In general, they are truly aggressive pricing policies, which translate into highly relevant visitor volumes and, therefore, income. On the other hand, generalized reductions in admission fees have been made up for in recent years by the increase in parking fees. For this, as regards conception, operators conceive the car park as part of the visit to the park and a place of transition from the outside world to the world of thematic recreation. As the profitability threshold is neared, each additional ticket sold produces a high marginal profit. However, one should not overlook the fact that, inasmuch as a park is a facility that is planned to receive an optimal number of visitors, as saturation occurs the marginal profit curve decreases. Material and labour costs increase above what has been foreseen and the actual volume of visitors to the park reduces opportunities to consume (fundamentally due to long queues, dissatisfaction and decreased impulse buying associated with such situations). It may therefore be stated that a park's operating margins are highly sensitive to two key variables: visitors per day and per capita expenditure (Vogel, 2001). In any case, as can be seen in Table 10.6, a notable difference may exist between parks. The figures show the diversity of theme parks' operating margins and results.

Theme parks' operating expenses usually represent up to 80% of total sales. According to Kan (2005, 8):

> the theme park industry is characterized by high operating leverage, with 75% of costs fixed and 25% variable. Labour is the largest portion of total costs (operating expenses plus Selling General & Administrative expenses) at 40% with advertising and marketing costs the second largest at approximately 16% of costs.

In the case of Cedar Fair, for example, in 2004, direct operating expenses accounted for 65% of revenue whereas services and general administration represented 19% and cost of goods sold 16%. Part-time employees' salaries, maintenance, utilities such as electricity and water and insurance are not altered by fluctuations in visitor numbers. Variable costs are provisions (food and beverages, goods and games), marketing and seasonal employment. For the purposes of illustration, see, in Table 10.7, the costs and expenses structure of a sample of 35 parks in North America and Europe according to a survey concerning this performed by the International Association of Amusement Parks and Attractions (IAAPA).

According to IAAPA estimates for different years (see Marketdata Enterprises, 1999), salaries represent by far the greatest cost for all parks (they may reach 50% of costs). The fact that parks are labour-intensive facilities – though basically seasonal and sporadic – leads to this. In this regard, it has been estimated that a theme park employee has an average of 75 personal contacts per day with visitors to the park (Kaak, 1992). This figure signifies the importance of the personnel for the park's success. In the end, the employees are the principal factor contributing to visitor satisfaction.

Table 10.6. Operating margin and EBITDA in a sample of theme park operators (from Ceronkosky and Keller, 2004).

	2001 (%)	2002 (%)	2003 (%)
Operating margin			
Cedar Fair	23.1	24.1	24.5
Six Flags	16.8	19.6	15.1
Anheuser Busch	21.3	21.1	21.5
EBITDA			
Cedar Fair	32.0	33.8	34.4
Six Flags	34.8	33.5	30.2
Anheuser Busch	32.3	31.0	31.0

Table 10.7. Expenses and operating margin for a sample of theme parks (from IAAPA, 2000).

	Total (%) (n = 35)
Personnel	36.0
Maintenance	8.5
Supplies	3.2
Special events	2.2
Promotion	7.0
Public services	3.5
Insurance	1.7
General administration	4.5
Rent	3.9
Taxes	3.1
Interest	4.8
Other	10.6
Operating margin	21.3

According to IAAPA (2000) data, the average number of full-time employees at parks is 160 and the number of employees during the month of greatest attendance is 736.

Unlike personnel costs, maintenance and repair costs remain steady regardless of visitor numbers. The park must be permanently in perfect condition so as not to ruin the expectations of finding a clean, safe, magic atmosphere. Expenditure on marketing is, however, fundamental in order to increase visitor numbers. Timely, significant increases to marketing expenditure are usually associated with novelties in the park. At the bigger parks, whose demand is not so concentrated in the immediate market areas, figures for promotion and commercialization increase. However, once again, significant variations may exist according to the park in question. To illustrate this see, for example, the differences in costs structure between the different Disney parks for 2004 in Table 10.8.

Remaining costs, among which are the provision of products for sale (including food and beverages) and the park's general and administration services, normally represent between 20 and 30%. Of these, insurance and the safety of the attractions may be singled out. These are an essential expenditure due to the risks deriving from the use of attractions and due to the fact that a visitor could suffer a minor accident during their stay at the park, whether while walking through it or while on soft attractions, such as a merry-go-round. As Kaak (1992) reports, the probability of having a minor incident on a roller coaster is 1 : 100,000 (to give an example, the likelihood of having the same incident when riding a bicycle is 253 : 100,000). However, given the repercussions in the media and effect on demand that any incident has, parks tend not just to adopt extreme

Table 10.8. Costs structure of Disney parks in 2004 (% over total income) (from Bilotti and Ksenofontova, 2005).

	Labour	General services	Marketing	Fixed overheads
Disneyland	49	29	7	14
Walt Disney World	49	32	13	6
Disneyland Paris	31	27	14	28
Disney Tokyo	22	35	7	36
Hong Kong Disneyland[a]	35	30	12	23

a. Estimate.

safety measures but also to take out insurance against any possible lawsuits and claims.

Be that as it may, in general terms, the fact that parks usually have high fixed costs makes them financially vulnerable to downturns in the market. As a consequence, providing capital for the development of parks is often difficult. As Wanhill (2005b) states, banks will not usually lend more than 40% of the required sum and so the rest has to be found from equity investors. Sponsorship of attractions also helps.

Case 17. Access for the Disabled at Disneyland Paris

There is a large disabled population and there is a growing number of people suffering some disability (it is estimated that almost 10% of the population has some type of disability, even in Europe). The specific needs of the disabled vary according to the nature of the disability (physical, sensorial or mental) and its degree. On the other hand, different regional and local cultures are at play as regards how these specific needs are responded to. In this context, furthermore, different national regulations exist that increase the complexity of the situation that tour operators and leisure facilities must deal with. In respect of this, Disneyland Paris receives some 40,000 disabled visitors each year. With such a large number of visits it is the number one European destination among the population with special needs and as a result it has received a variety of distinctions, such as the Label Tourisme et Handicap in 2004 among others. However, it has taken 7 years to get 46 accessible attractions (Dequidt, 2005).

From the park's standpoint, Dequidt (2005) admits that lack of knowledge, blinkered vision and individuals' fear of being different make the disabled population normally tolerated rather than welcomed. In any case, it is not usually a priority demand segment as far as marketing is concerned. There are different reasons, according to this author, who is responsible for disability-related matters at Disneyland Paris, that would explain such a lack of enthusiasm. In the first place, there is the necessary obsession with safety held by those in charge of park operations. There are certain attractions that may be considered dangerous for certain groups of people. Moreover, in the event of an emergency, disabled people are often looked upon as being a hindrance, a brake or a reason to boost the degree of anxiety among other users. However, as demonstrated by parks that practise access-for-all policies, it does not have to be so. A second reason comes from the interpretation that visitors with disabilities slow down the park's productivity in that unconventional attraction operation procedures must be implemented, thus decelerating processes. In order to deal with this matter, it is necessary to perform material adaptations to attractions, train the employees suitably and inform visitors. A third reason is to do with customers' potential dissatisfaction if they perceive or feel that the disabled are making the most of classic advantages such as having priority at access points – which is quite common in the traditional conception of dealing with the disabled. This feeling by the visitors to the park can be particularly unsatisfactory if the disability is not all that apparent. At Disneyland Paris, the fast pass system, which is used to get access to the attractions without having to wait, means that the capacitated and the disabled can be treated on equal terms. Finally, the fourth reason is the fear of being different and, therefore, the fear that a large number of disabled visitors may lead to dissatisfaction among non-disabled visitors. Only education and educational policies can help defeat such objections.

The integration of disabled people into a theme park involves applying the principle of non-discrimination, having foreseen specific needs in the design of the park and its attractions and conceiving the special needs as a useful argument, and therefore one that does not demand an additional cost but offers advantages also for other categories of visitor or the employees themselves. The principle of non-discrimination implies that the only causes to prohibit access to an attraction must derive from criteria that exclude a disability (for example, minimum height). This implies, on the other hand, the provision of good information about the attraction, allowing the disabled person to decide whether or not to try out an attraction. The provision for specific needs in the design of the park and its attractions should tackle the different types of disability, which may be physical, sensorial – sight and hearing – or mental. Finally, it should be considered that facilitating accessibility does not imply having to renounce greater profit as a result of a drop in the productivity of the attractions. At Walt Disney Studios Paris, for example, disabled visitors can get wheelchair access to one of Aladdin's flying carpets. Dequidt (2005) proposes the following criteria in order to facilitate access for the disabled to a theme park:

- Think about accessibility prior to building the park.
- Simplify access to and use of attractions as far as possible.
- Previously adequately inform people prior to the visit through leaflets, guidebooks and the Internet (for example, Disneyland Paris has a *Guide for Disabled Visitors* at the disposal of its customers).
- Recommend itineraries, attractions and activities adapted to the different types of disabilities and identify them via specific pictograms.
- Do not overlook allergies.

11 The Architectonic Design of a Theme Park

> The point is that there are new standards, new standards of beauty
> and style and taste. The new sensibility is defiantly pluralistic; it is
> dedicated both to an excruciating seriousness and to fun and wit and
> nostalgia.
>
> (Susan Sontag, 1961)

Universal Studios' second theme park in Orlando, Islands of Adventure, can be characterized as a proposal for recreation in which priority is given to density and compression. It is intense as regards the colours, sounds, vegetation and design of the buildings. It strikes the senses, especially at the entrance gate and, with different modulations, in all of the other thematic nodes. The attractions seek to provide an adrenalin rush, especially the main ones and, in particular, Spiderman. Even those which take a more classic line such as Poseidon's Fury pursue, through the use of a tunnel of water, a clear desire to arouse emotion. On the other hand, the theming shuns authenticity because, in fact, the park themes fantasy: the comic, the legend, landmarks in the film industry or cartoons.

Impressions in the style of those of this first paragraph directly derive from the materialization of a specific design proposal elaborated by narrators and copywriters (Steven Spielberg advised as to the design of the park) and materialized by technicians from a whole range of disciplines. The example highlights the fact that, beyond the development of the necessary infrastructures for its running, the design of a park involves technical considerations as regards its form, size and capacity. After all, according to Hsu (1997), a theme park is a processor of people containing attractions and shows designed on the basis of narrations whose aim is none other than to keep the interest of families and visitors throughout a whole day so that they will consume drinks, food and commercial articles. According to this definition, the relevance of the design, from the strategic point of view, is fundamental for the success of the park.

The establishment of a theme park necessitates therefore, in addition to the definition of its own argumental elements, that is to say, the determination of some specific criteria of positioning and theming, the design of a facility that takes into account matters concerning its physical construction, questions regarding its capacity (in respect of its potential to attract demand) and issues to do with circulation and flow management, both at the access to the park and along its internal routes. These three aspects are dealt with below. The design of a park must respond, in short, to the uses offered by the space both to its visitors and its managers and to the needs that arise from this encounter between visitors and managers in terms of the route, representation and organization. With reference to this, see Table 11.1.

11.1. The Form

Historically, the layout of the attractions at traditional amusement parks made up a maze-like route. The system allowed comings and goings in a relatively limited space. Now, such a layout led to the need to create buildings or attractions with four, equally visible exterior façades. That would be most expensive when, in addition, such façades must be themed. Hence, although it means having to have a greater surface area, as summarized in Fig. 11.1, in today's parks, two characteristic formats can be appreciated (see Rebori, 1993; Hsu, 1997):

- Hub and spoke. The itineraries lead to individually themed nodes of approximately equal size so as to support the same number of visitors. The capacity of the entertainment units of each themed node is usually the same. This is the case of Disney's Magic Kingdom parks. Visitors enter through a corridor which leads them to a hub, from which they disperse to one of the themed nodes set out in circular form around them.

Table 11.1. Uses and needs in the design of the space in a theme park (inspired by Chazaud, 1998).

Aims of the visitor	Aims of the manager	Transect needs	Representational needs	Organizational needs
To escape	To create an atmosphere	To differentiate spaces	Confirm imagined expectations	To create a landscape
To wander	To manage flows	To captivate the attention	Make visual sense	To systematize the route
To be entertained	To manage attractions	To lead from one attraction to another	To induce emotions	To develop a festive feeling

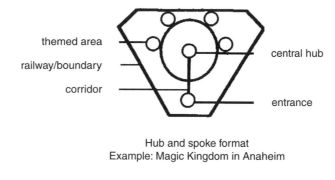

themed area

railway/boundary

corridor

central hub

entrance

Hub and spoke format
Example: Magic Kingdom in Anaheim

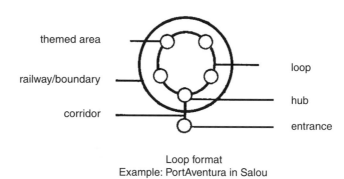

themed area

railway/boundary

corridor

loop

hub

entrance

Loop format
Example: PortAventura in Salou

Fig. 11.1. Basic formats in the design of a theme park (based on Rebori, 1993).

In turn, each of these nodes is circular in structure. Visitors also move in circular fashion finishing their route around the node at the same point as where they entered from the distribution point. In this case, the circle is the dominant factor in the design of the park.

- Loop. An itinerary goes circularly around the whole park approximately two-thirds of the distance from the perimeter. The loop links each of the park's themed nodes. At a distribution point, the visitors choose whether to begin their itinerary around the circle towards the left or towards the right. The layout in the form of a loop ensures that the visitors will pass by all of the attractions. To the outside of the itinerary, the larger attractions are housed and access to them can also be gained via the perimeter service roads. Normally one of the main ones is placed to the outside of the loop from the distribution point so as to encourage the movement of visitor flow. This format is usually known as the Duell Loop in honour of Randall Duell, who designed some of the first parks to have this layout. Small variations may exist in accordance with the concrete positioning of the entrance and the distribution hub with regard to the loop.

Apart from these basic formats, a multitude of different variations may be observed, ranging from the double loop, characteristic of Epcot, to the layout in the shape of Universal Studios' pedestrian urban fabric in Florida (see Fig. 11.2). In any case, some design elements tend to come up again and again: the access corridor (which in Disney's Magic Kingdom parks is the characteristic Main Street), a distribution point (whether to the right or the left of the loop towards each of the themed nodes, which are in the form of rings) and, as a central focal point, a water area – lake – which is used to landscape, as a reservoir and also as a space to put on shows.

On the other hand, the form of the park as a system to mark out the itineraries to be followed by the visitors is useful from the point of view of creating a sequence of perceptions between them. For them, film techniques that are well known in Hollywood are used to create sequences and scenarios. At this point it is essential to deal with scale as a fundamental design element to create the desired appearance and spatial effect for each component, so as to both create visual pleasure and sensory understanding, with the aim of creating visual magnets, characteristic components of the park that integrally guide the itinerary of a visit to the park (the clearest case is Sleeping Beauty's Castle in Magic Kingdom or, though its content is quite different, the Dragon Khan attraction in PortAventura). Finally, it cannot be forgotten that, in designing the form of a park, the transition

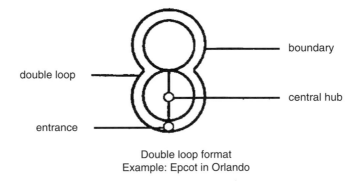

Double loop format
Example: Epcot in Orlando

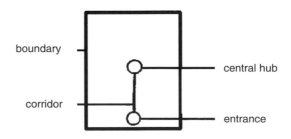

Urban fabric format
Example: Universal Studios in Orlando

Fig. 11.2. Examples of specific formats in the design of a theme park (based on Rebori, 1993).

between themed nodes is fundamental (sequences and scenarios). The suitable design of the landscape in accordance with the theme(s) to be developed is the key to providing a technically sound solution to the problem. That means also taking care of colour design (right for the seasons of the year), the trees planted, the water, the noise, sculptures made of flowers, the furnishings and fittings and the hedges, among other elements.

11.2. Size and Capacity

The surface area of a park is in response to the density of occupation foreseen in accordance with its 'design day'. The 'design day' is an estimated value which must ensure that the degree of satisfaction to be attained by the user is good and that the investment to be made by the promoter is appropriate. Given the variables of opening period and days of greatest visitor numbers, the total annual visits can become an estimate of the figure provided by the 'design day'. A park's 'design day' is usually established on the basis of a forecast of the average number of visits for the 20 days of greatest attendance. This figure must represent around 1.2 to 2% of total estimated annual attendance. The assumption is made that 75% of this mean attendance is in the park during the hours of maximum attendance (this percentage may vary between 65 and 80%, depending on the approaches of the different planners for the different assumptions). The requirements as regards size, capacity, attractions and services are determined on the basis of this figure. For example, a park whose size is designed for a 'design day' of 22,000 visits takes into account a peak day of 33,000. Based on these figures, calculations may be made to obtain the figures of maximum attendance at any given time for the 'design day', which would be 16,500, and for the peak day, which would be 24,750 people simultaneously in the park. Taking these considerations into account, a park is designed with a surface area of 105 ha and attractions with a capacity for 16,780 people simultaneously, which, together with the different types of show (with a capacity of 9960 people simultaneously (see also Swarbrooke, 2002)), can offer a capacity of entertainment opportunities of nigh on 27,000 people simultaneously. Some common work assumptions concerning this are as follows:

- A minimum of between 8 and 10% of attendance during the hours of maximum number of visits will require a place to sit at the same time.
- A minimum of 3 m² of pedestrian surface area per visitor is needed during the hours of maximum attendance.
- Between 1.5 and 2.5 attractions or possibilities of entertainment per visitor are needed per hour during the hours of maximum attendance.
- One toilet is needed per 150 to 200 visitors during the hours of maximum attendance.

Concerning foreseen frequentation, for whose calculation, as we have seen, it is essential to take into account the dimension of the market areas, penetration hypotheses and the investment to be made, the design of the park must apply precise indicators of size and capacity so that, on the one hand, a sufficient sensation of critical mass is generated so that the atmosphere and the animation generated by the visitors themselves are positive when assessing their degree of satisfaction and, on the other hand, its development is bearable from the financial point of view. Real figures indicate that, in the USA, parks are designed to accommodate a mean of 1800 people per hectare at most (Hsu, 1997). In Asia and the Pacific, this figure may reach 2500. See, for example, with regard to the dimensioning and for the purposes of illustration, the size and provision of attractions at the parks operated by Cedar Fair in Table 11.2.

It is clear, however, that these figures cannot be taken as a generalization since parks' dimensions vary in accordance with their very design and the forecasts they have performed with a view to their future enlargement. See, for example, in Table 11.3 the distribution of foreseen uses at Parc Astérix when opened. In the first place, one can observe that the foreseen surface area effectively set aside for the park is substantially reduced in comparison with all of the real and foreseen uses of the land for future expansion, including the development of hotel areas outside the park and yet still integrated within the recreational complex the park catalyses.

11.3. Flows and Transport Systems

A theme park is a *mise-en-scène* that must induce movement. Rebori (1993) specifically states that good circulation of the flow of visitors is fundamental for the success of a theme park. A good park is one that has components that magnetize and provoke journeys to each themed node. The visitors must be continually on the move from one attraction or entertainment opportunity to the next. Therefore, good flow management is fundamental. In this regard, it must borne in mind that, given that the use of theme parks made by their visitors is basically pedestrian, the route to

Table 11.2. Characteristics of the Cedar Fair theme parks, 2005 (based on company reports).

Park	Number of rides	Extra pay attractions	Acreage (developed/available)
Cedar Point + Soak City	65 + 20	8	465/38
Dorney Park and Wildwater Kingdom	80	3	170/30
Geuga Lake	60	3	420/200 (+ 50 acre lake)
Knott's Berry Farm + Knott's Soak City	40 + 21	1	160/0
Michigan's Adventure	70	3	100/150
Valleyfair	35	5	115/75
Worlds of Fun + Oceans of Fun	45	3	235/115

Table 11.3. Planning of land use at Parc
Astérix (from Chassé and Rochon, 1993).

Uses	Surface (ha)
Leisure park	18.3
Expansion area	10.0
Parking	19.7
Car park expansion area	5.0
Staff parking	2.5
Services	3.0
Protection area	20.0
Hotel area	12.0
Green spaces	42.0
Access routes	37.0
Total	169.15

be followed, which is the one that can be taken by a family in a theme park in 1 day, must be of between 3 and 5 km.

The difficulties in handling the visitors to a park are important in that the services to be taken into consideration are not homogeneous (attractions, spectacles, restaurants, shops, animation, etc.), the visitors' preferences are not uniform either, given that the global market may be broken down into different groups, attendance levels at the park vary significantly depending on the time of day, the day and the time of year, the perceptions (for example, their effect on the decision as to whether to queue up) are the main engine in the customers' decision-making process and, finally, all of these conditioning factors are interdependent and are not just not very obvious but are difficult to control. For example, studies exist clearly showing that, in the same way as spending a long time queuing up has a negative impact on visitors, very short queuing times are also negatively valued by users (Ahmadi, 1997).

It is often maintained that the Disney systems for handling the masses are the most sophisticated in existence. Basic questions exist, such as how to avoid congestion, avoid cul-de-sacs and pay special attention to the intersections, which must be duly signposted (Lanquar, 1991). However, flow management in a theme park goes yet further. It is a key element in the day-to-day process, which has repercussions both on customer satisfaction and the park's income and profit. It cannot be forgotten, for example, as Torrado and Sardà (1995) say, that, given that, when opening the gates in the morning, a large park may take some time to fill up, the planners of this park ought to seek different systems to quickly transport the visitors from one end of the park to the other, by means of carriages and trains, so as to fill up the maximum possible space with active people in as little time as possible. Consequently, the transport systems must be designed, in the parks, with the twofold function of managing flows and acting as attractions in themselves. Furthermore, not just the circulation by visitors but also auxiliary circulation flows must be foreseen (Spirn, 1998).

As a whole, a theme park works as a system of systems of movement. There are three critical factors in a park's flow management, which correspond to three scales of different tasks:

1. Mechanical transport systems. Their primary task is to move visitors mechanically (and employees too) from one thematic node to others, once they have left their cars at the car park. They are usually land-based transport systems (either on wheels or on rails) or on water. However, these systems also work as attractions, which, on the one hand, capture the visitors' attention and, on the other, improve their experience of the park. This is why, for example, these systems do not usually cover the distance between two points via the quickest route, but do so along the best itinerary from the point of view of the visual aesthetics.

2. The management of pedestrian movement. The efficient, orderly movement of flows between attractions and throughout the park is fundamental since it is an implicit part of a recreational experience. The existence of visual magnets that generate expectations is the best stimulus for this. However, the approach to the basic control strategy for pedestrian flows considers the space of the parks so that the larger masses break up into increasingly smaller groups as they penetrate each thematic node. Hence the formal layout around a distribution point or a loop from which each themed area derives. Hence also the excentric nature of the main attractions, which are not positioned at the intersections or squares with the greatest capacity as points of transit but are set in places that are explicitly designed for their placement. On the other hand, efficiency can be improved especially by setting timetables for those entertainment opportunities that, like the shows, are only held at certain times of the day. In these cases, the establishment of timetables serves to move masses of visitors from thematic nodes to others and may vary in accordance with the behaviour observed among visitors according to age, the season and other sociocultural characteristics. Thus, for example, in the timetable of SeaWorld's recommendations, which is constantly updated, the shows that may theoretically be full in accordance with the attendance to the park are not included. In general, the parks study the patterns of their visitors' movements during the day in great depth so as to contribute to solving the problems they may lead to. On the other hand, as demonstrated by Rajaram and Ahmadi (2003), the management of visitor flows provides an opportunity to increase store sales by interfacing park operations, which manage visitor flows by setting schedules and capacity of attractions, with the store-level merchandising process, which determines which and how much product to order.

3. Queue management at attractions. This is a minor scale of flow management in a park. This is a problem which is already dealt with in the very design of the attraction itself, which includes the design of the queue, the loading structure and the loading system. The aim is to minimize waiting costs incurred by queuing. To this end, it is usual to theme and make the queue areas comfortable, incorporating visual elements and gradual access systems and preview scenes as a taste of the attraction to come. There also exist design procedures like not allowing the start of the queue to be visible, helping the queue to move continuously or indicating the estimated queuing time. Entertainment and participation while queuing are also common procedures that help to relax the visitor faced with the problem of the queue. Since the end of the 1990s and thanks to the possibilities made available by technology, systems have been incorporated that allow the reservation of an attraction at a precise moment during the day. These are the 'fast pass' or 'express' systems, which are now fairly widespread in a great many parks, or reservation systems.

It is common to establish complex flow management models which attempt to combine these different levels of approach and, in particular, to go from the organization of transport in the park to the optimization of the capacities of the attractions as a whole and individually. Ahmadi (1997) describes a concrete application of such operational instruments for the Six Flags Magic Mountain park in California. It is a model made on the basis of the interpretation of visitors' preferences expressed through their behaviour when planning the route they will take through the park. For its application he develops a mathematical model of the capacity of the attractions, a model of the desirable behaviour when moving between attractions and a model of sequence between attractions. He also develops a neural network model to observe the difference between the theoretical capacities of attractions and those actually observed. This allows the characterization of the real and desirable movements by the users between attractions and, by looking at the adjustments, systems of improvement may be proposed which will affect both the results of the park as well as user satisfaction. For this he proposes specific means to influence the behaviour of the visitors to the park (fundamentally the daily design of show timetables, the use of just-in-time information systems indicating the queue length and the creation of customized or group itineraries to visit the park in accordance with their preferences and expectations).

To this same end, a useful flow management instrument is the creative cartography deployed by parks' information maps. At a point of equilibrium between detail, simplicity and representation, these maps provide visitors with security right from their arrival at the park car park. Whether hand-held or conveniently located at critical intersection points in the park, the maps give key information and facilitate the visit in accordance with the park managers' criteria and priorities. As Minton (1998) observes for the case of Universal Studios, where visitors tend to start their itinerary by heading towards the right once they are inside, by suggesting different routes the park maps help to spread visitors throughout the park and lead to greater satisfaction for all. Colours, itineraries, icons and practical information help to manage flows via the maps.

11.4. Components

The make-up of a theme park's attractions and services reflects its market aims. In addition to some general principles, each park's range of attractions is usually unique and, moreover, also depends on the cultural context of where it is located. Thus, it is different in the USA, in Europe and in Asia. The components of a park must provide a balance between passive activities (shows and spectacles), active ones (the attractions) and services (food and beverage and commerce). There is potentially a multitude of considerations to be taken into account. So, according to a market study by *Amusement Business* at the beginning of the new millennium, 51% of North American adolescents were of the opinion that the final decision taken as to whether to go to one or another theme park was theirs and only 29% visited them without their families. On the other hand, it cannot be forgotten that the number one attractions visited by the almost 12 million tourists of 45 to 65 years of age travelling to Orlando in 2001 (70% of them without children) were theme parks.

The aim of the attractions and services of a theme park is to provide its visitors with sensations. These sensations – which induce visitors to come again – are linked with their ability to arouse emotion, to escape and to share. Other sensations that the attractions of a park may stimulate are to do with their ability to divert and make one laugh or, contrarily, to arouse nostalgia and a feeling of calm. What is important is that the park, via its attractions and services, should be perceived as being unique, entertaining and worthy of being remembered. This is why many parks tend to acquire an identification due to the fact that they have a singular attraction which their competitors do not have. In this way, they offer the possibility of acquiring an experience that cannot be lived at any other park.

In any case, experiencing one or another sensation responds to the park's objective concerning its market orientation and theme. Thus, for example, the range of attractions at Universal Studios in Orlando clearly responds to its 'cinematographic' vocation as a park, with the ability to motivate segments that are not just interested in going on more or less intense rides. Well themed as a film set, the characteristic attractions that relive film scenes from films like *Earthquake*, *King Kong* or *Tornado* are short, while there is a huge range of possibilities of picking up knowledge as to how films and television programmes are made. This is the case of the show dedicated to Hitchcock or, quite differently, the possibilities offered by the Nickelodeon television floor. Finally, the recreation of different films through dark rides differs according to the type of emotions they wish to convey. So, while the Journey into the Future is a bone-shaker, ET is a sweet proposal aimed at infants. It is therefore a park which has little to do, as regards its components, with Six Flags' conventional parks. Even so, there is an attempt at convergence between the one and the other, as can be seen, for example, at the Universal park with the creation of a children's area, out of keeping with the rest, the Woody

Woodpecker Kidzone, which tries to emulate the type of attractions that this age segment may encounter at the neighbouring park, Islands of Adventure.

11.4.1. The attractions and the shows

Despite theme parks differing conceptually, most of them (except the Disney and Universal Studios parks and a few new-generation parks in Europe) contain the same attractions that may be found at amusement parks and even fairs. The differences may be found, in any case, in the use of theming as a strategy to integrate the attraction into the park's argument. In the case of Disney and, more recently, Universal Studios, theming may imply multiplying the price of the attraction several times. On the other hand, most parks tend to give emphasis to emotions and physical impressions as a basic element of their range of attractions. Hence the pre-eminence of roller coasters as the main attraction at numerous parks.

The main kinds of attraction to be found at theme parks today are as follows:

1. Roller coasters. They originate from the wooden carriages built in the surroundings of Saint Petersburg in the 17th century to slide on ice. The mechanism was adapted to a system of ramps and toboggans by 1804 in France, giving rise not just to today's roller coasters but also to water attractions like flumes. Sea Lion Park in Coney Island started up the first water flume and the first 360° loop at the end of the 19th century. In spite of being relatively expensive attractions, they have the advantage of being in great demand and can normally be amortized in very little time. There are some Six Flags parks that specialize in this sort of attraction, with Cedar Point, however, being the Mecca of roller coaster-oriented theme parks. Generally they are configured as parks' visual landmarks and they often arouse emotion as much among those who simply gaze and perceive the sensation of risk from a distance as among those who go on them. They are usually star attractions, created according to the demand for the park. They exist in a variety of forms, as much as regards the materials used in their construction as in the way they move. In fact, the world of roller coasters is a complete one. There are, among others and in addition to the classic wood or steel rides, specific types of roller coaster, such as hypercoasters (great heights and very high speeds), flying coasters (which can carry the passengers horizontally below or above the rail), inverted coasters (circulating below the rail with the passengers' feet hanging down) or vertical coasters (with marked, almost 90° falls). They are always designed well within the limits of safety applicable in the USA, which do not allow a roller coaster to subject a human body to a force of greater than 4.5 times gravitational acceleration (9.81 m/s²). As Green (1999) points out, they are not just an attraction but they have become a sign, a metaphor, of a certain way of understanding entertainment.

2. Dark rides. They are, in fact, show attractions. They are dark circuits inside a building and are the scene of an attraction that combines the classic elements of movement with film and the objectives and techniques used in the theatre. They may incorporate elements of virtual reality, using high-technology simulation, or they may be totally mechanical. Generally they are set in a space with little light and are carefully staged. They usually include the presence of some animatronics (robots characterized as recognizable characters depending on the theme of the attraction). Their simplest precedent is to be found in fairground attractions like the Tunnel of Love or the Tunnel of Horrors, but, in the case of theme parks, the degree of sophistication they have reached is most elaborate. In these attractions, visitors are surrounded by a fictitious situation in which they actively participate. Their inclusion in a park's range of attractions is usually in response to the characteristics of the market. This kind of attraction dominates the Disney parks. Their main characteristic is that they adopt the principles of film production, replacing the camera with a vehicle that moves the users as suitable noises are made so as to create the required atmosphere.

3. Flat rides. These involve the traditional mechanics based on monotonous, repetitive movements (from gyrating teacups to merry-go-rounds), which can also be found at other amusement parks and fairs. There are over 100,000 applications for inventions for theme parks at the North American patents office in response to this idea (Burns, 1988). They are characteristic of the catalogues of the producers of attractions. They are family-oriented and are usually low-cost. Most of them simulate systems of movement (bicycles, cars, aeroplanes, Zeppelins or rockets). The first such circular, wavy attraction was constructed in 1845 in Great Britain and was known as the Venetian Gondolas. Today, these attractions are combined with dark landscapes and tunnels, where mechanical and electrical surprises often occur. Among the classics are the circle swings. The first of the modern era was installed at Elitch's Gardens in 1904. Now, the characteristic example of this type of attraction is the merry-go-round, whose predecessor lies in the rotational structure on which the participants rode in a joust. In reference to this activity, in 1662, Louis XIV named a square between les Tuileries and the Louvre 'Place du Carrousel'. Traditionally, North American merry-go-rounds turn anticlockwise whereas in Europe they turn clockwise.

4. Water attractions. Despite truly belonging to water parks, theme parks' own water attractions industry has developed. The basic kinds are the rapids, flumes and splash rides. The rapids are based on large, circular vehicles which travel along a route of calm water with the odd chance of getting slightly wet. It is basically an attraction for the family. In the flumes, the vehicles travel along waterways with marked ups and downs, causing brusque movements and splashes. Finally, the splash rides are based on the fall of a large-sized boat which slips down a steep gradient, causing it to smash on to the water below, ending up by drenching most of its passengers. Most theme parks tend to have, though with variations, some such attractions, in some cases highly sophisticated ones like the splash at Universal Studios in Orlando, themed around Jurassic Park. Normally, the installation of this sort of attraction requires a large amount of available space.

5. Educational attractions. The last category of attractions combines elements of the above types whose purpose is aimed at informal instruction. So, for example, presentations with an educational content have formed part of Disney's proposal since the start. At Epcot (with presentations like The Living Seas or The Land, among others) and, even more recently, at Animal Kingdom in Orlando, this type of attraction in fact ends up becoming an important part of each of the parks' capacity to attract. Similarly, parks like SeaWorld and Busch Gardens in Tampa, with naturalistic contents and an environmental discourse in both cases, incorporate among their attractions veritable pavilions with an educational penchant and even link entertainment to research activities. On the other hand, this modality has significant precedents as an attraction that was so remarkable and particular in its time as was the Infant Incubator in Dreamland, Coney Island, thanks to which doctor Martin Couney, the attraction manager, saved the lives of 7500 boys and girls born prematurely.

Other specific attractions that can be found at parks are big wheels, whose inspiration was the Ferris Wheel of the Chicago Universal Exposition, Sky Towers and Sky Cars, towers that allow one to view the whole of the park and surroundings from a great height, Walk-throughs like the Temple of Fire at PortAventura, in which the visitor usually walks through several scenes to experience in the first person a story or adventure which usually has real narrators, and free falls, attractions inducing a pure adrenalin rush in which the passengers go to the top of a tower in a wagon which drops freely until an automatic braking system halts it.

Just as important as the attractions are the shows and the animation and, in some parks, they are even more important. Hence, in the Busch Gardens park in Tampa, the range of possibilities for entertainment is 30% attractions, 20% shows and 50% animal exhibitions or specific animal shows. Though the attractions usually grab the interest of the younger age group, the shows usually interest all age groups. Two basic modalities exist:

1. Animations. These may be shows, street animators, ambient animation or technical productions:

- The shows are performed on specially built stages for the specific performance. They may range from stunt shows, that is to say, shows that involve the construction of a decor that simulates a filmset on which the elements may be transformed based on fire, water and explosions during the show, to animal shows, like the flight of birds of prey or the performances of water animals as in the SeaWorld parks, through musical shows (operetta, dance, rock) on covered stages as at Six Flags Fiesta Texas and specific creations for the park such as those that are held at the Great Chinese Theatre at PortAventura.

- Street entertainment is designed as productions that use the street as the stage. Started in Disney in 1955 as a way to keep visitors at the park beyond mid-afternoon, it has become an essential part of the everyday Disney experience and, more profusely, of other theme parks' strategy, especially in the form of special events that take place on the occasion of various celebrations (Carnival or Halloween, for example). It involves the parading of themed carts.

- Ambient animation is performed apparently spontaneously by the characters of the park in the street for the purpose of creating a unique atmosphere. In this regard, the best known are the Disney characters, though it was not until 1968 that they began to form an integral part of the park's entertainment. When the link between the characters and the theme of the park is not so tight, ambient animation is usually performed by actors, who represent a narrative linked to the area where they are acting. So, for example, actors perform animations typical of traditional fairs with characters such as minstrels, tightrope walkers and acrobats, as, for example, at Efteling. In other circumstances, ambient animation may also be represented through the reconstruction of craft workshops, as at Puy du Fou.

- Finally, the technical productions are, fundamentally, shows using light, music and colour, from fireworks to light shows. Thus, lasers and ultraviolet rays that are normally set aside for films and sets have been incorporated into parks to create special effects, ever since Epcot started to use them at the beginning of the 1980s. This means, however, that parks tend to be built that are more attractive at night, when they are lit up, than during the day. This is the case of the technological shows at Futuroscope. This also has repercussions on the facilities' operation strategies. They are essential from the standpoint of keeping visitors at the park, lengthening their stay there and, therefore, providing an incentive to spend more. One such example is the Fábula del Tiempo show at Isla Mágica, which takes place at night on the lake of the park, with the projection on to a 17 m^2 screen of water images created by video, laser and large-scale devices, in combination with pyrotechnics, cybernetic fountains and music.

2. Audio-visual and film presentations. These are highly flexible shows in terms of cost and being up to date. Hence, they have become highly popular ingredients of theme parks. Different types of products may be distinguished:

- Audio-visual presentations, from the classic multimedia attractions to virtual shows introducing special electronic effects like Euforia, the multimedia show based on magic at Isla Mágica.

- Innovative film technologies that allow parks to set themselves apart from conventional cinema studios but also offer their visitors stimulating experiences. Thus, some of the biggest parks have Omnimax dome screen studios to show films in 3D. To this same end, by 1955 at Disneyland, going by the name of Circarama, Circle Vision 360 had been introduced, a circular system of presenting films, which was later developed at all Disney parks although showing different contents. Futuroscope is, without a doubt, the most emblematic park for this kind of show (Wylson and Wylson, 1994).

- The presentation of commercial films. Parks take advantage of their facilities to show previews of films produced by the same film company as operates the park.
- Simulators. The idea behind them is to recreate a journey, adventure or experience using film techniques and systems to create movement. The aim is to give the user a feeling of being immersed in the experience being recreated. Such attractions are characteristic of Universal Studios parks. A clear example of this sort of attraction is Cinemoción at Isla Mágica, with a 600 m^2 screen and the capacity to coordinate the movement of the seats and images that take viewers on a virtual roller coaster, which they live out light-heartedly.
- The programming of explanatory shows. Some parks, such as Universal Studios or Mirabilandia in Italy, programme shows that reconstruct memorable scenes from films, transforming the actors into the main roles of certain films, by Hitchcock, for example, in the former.

Attractions and shows are, in fact, the fundamental component of a theme park. Each spatial and thematic node of the park is organized and activated in accordance with its characteristics and layout and the discourse presented as the axis of entertainment acquires meaning. In general terms, the aim is for the visitors, at the end of their stay at the park, with or without queues, to have been able to go on some ten attractions or entertainment opportunities they enjoyed (Torrado and Sardà, 1995).

Planning a park's range of attractions and entertainment opportunities is linked to the direction wished for it to take but also the total hourly capacity needs of the park in accordance with its size. For this, a per hour rate of attraction or entertainment opportunity is applied for each visitor. In a simple park, this rate may be 0.9 attractions per hour. The mean in the USA is 1.8 attractions per hour and in Europe the figure is between 1.3 and 1.8, according to park typology (Hsu, 1997). The consultants Theme Park Services forecast that each visitor should be able to go on 1.5 to 2 attractions per hour of visit to the park. If it is estimated that the visit lasts 6 h, the park should be sized so that visitors have been on between at least 9 to 12 attractions in order to guarantee that their perception and satisfaction of the park will be positive. As Rebori (1993) indicates, at Paramount Parks, for an 8-h visit, satisfaction is attained when visitors have been on ten attractions and attended between seven and ten shows per day during periods of maximum attendance.

The optimum capacity of a park's attractions must be between one and two times the number of visitors expected during peak visiting times of the 'design day'. Most parks usually have a principal (major) attraction at each of the thematic nodes, together with other smaller-scale attractions to even up the recreational possibilities between thematic nodes and the inside of the node itself. Hence, a high-capacity attraction with big drawing capability should be equal to two lower-capacity attractions with smaller powers of attraction. At Paramount Parks, for example, for each intense, highly emotional attraction, whose capacity is 1500 people per hour, a capacity of 2000 people per hour is planned on smaller, family-oriented attractions (Rebori, 1993). The aim is for the visitor not to move through the park from one thematic node to the next either too quickly or too slowly. In either case, the visitor's experience and satisfaction come into crisis and, consequently, so does their desire to spend. It cannot be forgotten, on the other hand, that, though it depends on the park in question, attractions may represent between 25 and 40% of the total cost of the facilities.

Current trends in this field (Jones *et al.*, 1998; Spiegel, 1999) regarding their design, planning and development are as follows:

- To facilitate visitor participation and interaction. This point is directly related to each park's themed argument. It is understood that priority will increasingly be given to themes related to participative activities such as sport or music than to more passive concepts.
- To attract families instead of proposing attractions that are directly aimed at adolescent and youth groups and to apply this principle even for the case of emotionally and physically more intense attractions like roller coasters or certain dark rides.
- To apply simulation and virtual-reality techniques. Technological advances are allowing the reproduction of virtually any natural or emotional reality. Combining high-quality visual imagery with moving mechanical elements, visitors can today enjoy virtual experiences which until a few years ago were indeed quite rare. The first attraction with such characteristics, which charmed large numbers of the public, was Star Tours at Disneyland. Since then, they have multiplied, especially at the big parks. The case of Spiderman at Universal Florida is a landmark of this kind of facility. From the point of view of the designers, moreover, it is one of the most interesting areas of development. The challenge is, in spite of being a technological creation, for these attractions still to manage to take one's breath away, like the mechanical ones did, and to maintain the spontaneity of individual perceptions of risk and group interaction.
- To increase water attractions. Water as an element for attractions and for the construction itself of the themed areas is gaining ground. Many parks throughout the world combine water attractions, even those which are more typical of water parks, with conventional attractions. This is the case of Ocean Park in Hong Kong; Dreamland in Australia; or Walibi in Belgium. Show parks like SeaWorld resort to the same element. Even more so today, as occurs in the Yucatan, the technology of water attractions is applied not just on constructed areas but on the open sea.
- To design year-round attractions. The new theme parks are tending to incorporate more covered attractions, promenades in environmentally

controlled surroundings and rest areas. The reason is to facilitate the expansion of the operational season and the lengthening of the park's number of daily and seasonal opening hours.

- To move from the concept of emotion to the concept of experience. Technology leads one to think not just of mechanical attractions that generate basic physical sensations, but to apply the technology of movement that is typical of the world of cinema in order to give rise to meaningful experiences in all types of attraction. However, these are generally very expensive attractions, even though they are easily managed and renewable, given that, while they can maintain their material structure, their software and theme can be modified. In any case, this tendency also implies advancing towards the fusion of different types of attraction and towards the incorporation of themes into traditional kinds of attraction.

11.4.2. The services (food and beverages and shops)

Service activities comprise a significant component for theme parks, both in the satisfaction they generate in their customers and in their role in generating revenue. As has already been said, all told, in some cases they may represent over 40% of a park's revenue. Two types of service are provided inside the parks: food and beverages and commerce. Their importance when generating income depends significantly on the number of establishments at the disposal of the public and the uniqueness of the supply. As of the 1980s, in the wake of Disney, numerous parks have also incorporated accommodation services, though they are placed outside the parks, that is to say, in an adjacent area and as a component of a broader corporate concept, that of the resort, of which the park is just one of its components.

Once again, Disney led the way for the food and beverage and shop services. Although, due to a lack of financial and operative capacity, in Disneyland at the start it was decided to hire out the food and beverage and shop services for a 10-year period, once each contract had expired, the park itself took command of the operation and management of such establishments. Currently, this is so at most parks, Disney or not. The reason is not just the importance of their contribution to the park's balance sheet but also the capacity the operator has, by managing these services itself, to also incorporate into them principles, emotions and experiences that are directly linked to the argumental thread of the park. Therefore, restaurants and shops must be understood as complementary support vehicles for the theme park viewed as a whole.

The design of food establishments and shops is based on the principles of durability in order to survive permanent, mass use, thematic integration into the argumental node where they are located in the park, and uniqueness. The aim is, through the creation of a specific atmosphere, to create the visitor's perception of having the chance to experience a unique situation. That implies, in the case of the restaurants, the integral design of all of the elements of the experience, from the colour to the menu. Some restaurants, on the other hand, become entertainment opportunities in themselves. At Epcot, for example, the restaurants emphasize the authenticity and diversity of the different cultures that are represented at the park through its atmosphere, service and the quality of the food.

Restaurants and shops are usually located in accordance with the shopping needs and behaviour of the visitors, principally on the way in/out of the park and at the main distribution hubs of each themed area. So, in the case of the shops, the greatest concentration (up to 70%, depending on the park) is usually situated near the entrance to the park since it is at this point that visitors usually make their purchases as they leave or where they have the need to purchase a certain item (for example, photographic film) once they reach the park, so that they can preserve their experience. Other places for impulsive buying are usually placed throughout the park, while each thematic node usually has its own shop devoted to the narrative argument in which it is established. The location of services at each thematic area, both food and beverages and shops, is associated with the need to satisfy the customers' psychological association of consuming at a place which has been especially satisfactory from the point of view of their entertainment experience. Likewise, the services help in part to delay the transit process from one thematic area to another.

On a very general level, four types of basic catering services may be defined in parks: snack bars, fast, self-service and gastronomic restaurants. Snacks are purchased from small kiosks, generally decorated according to the theme of the node of the park where they are found, and they are consumed while walking around. They respond to impulsive consumption needs. Fast restaurants offer more consistent products for consumption at the restaurant itself or also while strolling around. Self-service restaurants offer a buffet service and are capacitated to serve groups. Finally, gastronomic restaurants, which may be of different standards and also themed, offer a traditional restaurant service. Their distribution within the park is strategically designed in accordance with the estimated capacities and flows for each thematic area. On these bases, there are variations. Thus, Disney differentiates, more concretely, between the following types of catering services: gastronomic restaurants, buffets, fast food, snack outlets, show restaurants, catering for banquets, institutional restaurants and vending.

The planning of the catering needs of a park is also based on the estimated 'design day'. Once the peak of visitors has been calculated for the usual mealtimes (a concept which varies in accordance with cultural setting and, therefore, is different in the USA, Europe and Asia), the proportion of customers that may wish to eat at such times is estimated. For parks in North America, the usual mean figure for this is 35%. This calculation means that the number of food servings needed each hour may be known. These servings must be spread across the different types of establishment. It is clear, on the other hand, that, depending on the type of service, the duration of the meal varies and, therefore, so does the estimated number of service points per hour. For example, in the USA it is estimated that the buffet requires an average of 38 min, gastronomic catering 60 min, snacks 15 min and self-service 22 min. That determines the need for cash registers, seating, queues and space per customer. It also determines the needs of the facilities linked to the services being rendered (supplies, storage, distribution, processing and the setting of menus), as well as their location and operative procedures. In any case, it is important to point out that an aspect such as catering, as has already been mentioned, is conditioned by numerous factors of a cultural nature and that, normally, principles and parameters that are valid for parks in North America cannot be applied to other places in the world. An example of this are the greater predictions, as regards both capacity of service and meal duration, required in Spain for gastronomic catering.

Finally, with regard to the shops, a particular consideration to be made is that, in theme parks, sales are not so much the result of the suitability of the products to satisfy the customers' basic needs but rather of the impulse to consume that visitors have in an environment which is, fundamentally, satisfactory and of which they wish to take home a souvenir. The planning of the sales outlets and their contents is therefore linked with a recreational concept of the buying process. The results depend as much on the ability of the products on offer to satisfy these recreational utilities as on the consumer culture of the visitors, in accordance with economic, social and cultural differences. The main categories of products sold in parks are usually clothing or footwear, souvenirs, sweets, gifts, toys and photographic products.

Case 18. A Flow Management Model to Optimize Retail Profits at Universal Studios Hollywood

Rajaram and Ahmadi (2003) develop a flow management model that sets the capacities and schedules of the major attractions of the Universal Studios Hollywood theme park to conduct visitor flows to high-profit retail areas and to increase park profitability. Before developing the model, the authors performed a statistical analysis based on a field study, which gave them the following main findings: (i) at any given time, total profits are affected by visitor flows in different areas; (ii) schedules and capacity of the main attractions affect visitor flows; and (iii) in addition to capacity, schedule and visitor satisfaction with an attraction, profits at the associated store are strongly influenced by the merchandizing process, which determines which and how much product to order.

The authors represent the flow management model by a linear mixed-integer programme, which they call the Theme Park Profit Maximization Problem (TPPMP). To solve the problem, they develop a two-phase heuristic and decompose the problem into two sub-problems: a Workforce Management Problem (WMP) and a Flow Management Problem (FMP). The WMP determines the best workforce resource allocation to maximize the capacity of the park. The FMP determines the ideal visitor flow patterns to optimize total store profits. Rajaram and Ahamadi tested the TPPMP with data from the field study to determine the schedule and capacity at each major attraction to optimize park profits. The analysis suggested a potential increase in annual profits of $6 million. They found that the heuristic solution suggested more frequent shows with smaller operating capacities at attractions located in high-profit retail areas and less frequent shows with higher capacities in attractions located in low-profit retail areas. This allocation ensures that visitors make more frequent visits to the high-profit areas and less frequent trips to low-profit areas, which, in turn, improves the potential to generate larger total store profits. In addition, the authors point out that a lower operating capacity results in longer queues, offering opportunities for some members of families waiting in line to explore the high-profit stores associated with each attraction. The solution provided by the heuristic also suggests a more staggered closing of the park, in which attractions at lower-profit retail areas close a few hours before attractions at the higher-profit retail areas. The solution also identifies corridors with a consistently high volume of visitor flows and provides guidance to locate carts, kiosks and walking salespeople to further increase retail profits.

12 Management Strategies

> The yardstick for measuring success would seem to be not how much a man
> gets as how much he has to give away.
>
> (Conrad N. Hilton, 1957)

Ford and Milman (2000) maintain that many of the concepts and practices of
management employed today in theme parks were introduced at the end of
the 19th century by George C. Tilyou at Steeplechase Park, Coney Island. In
fact, the authors hold that Tilyou 'was not only a pioneer of amusement
parks, but also developed service-management concepts that are still in use
today'. Steeplechase Park opened in 1897 as an elaborate collection of rides
and attractions in a 15-acre enclosure that was ringed by the gravity-powered
steeplechase racehorses that gave the park its name. Tilyou's key perception
was his appreciation of 'the extent to which guests participate in the service
product'. That is to say, he suitably identified the nucleus of the product it
offered – the satisfaction of people's will to escape from everyday life, the
simultaneous timing of production and consumption and, thirdly, the extent
to which the product is tangible. To this end, as occurs at theme parks today,
careful management of the environment and, especially, the adoption of a
gated park model allowed him to create a sense of place for the typical
demand segments of the Coney Island of the late 19th century, that is, families
heading for the beach. Also, the park's condition as a closed space – a novelty
then – allowed him to guarantee the quality of each individual component of
the global product, among other things. Tilyou considered that, for this, the
stability of available human resources was fundamental and he dealt with
the issues of training and turnover just as managers do today and motivated
employees by maintaining an informal atmosphere and offering benefits.

Though he never wrote on his management principles and practices,
according to Ford and Milman Tilyou's contributions to the contemporary
theme park are considerable. In fact, he introduced commercial yield

management practices, designed strategies for the creation of value on the basis of the symbolic icons the park offered, conceived merchandising as a fundamental part of the business, kept a solid reputation as regards the security and safety and quality of the attractions and stressed the need to have a clean operation. These are a few of the recommendations Tilyou offered to the management of theme parks that are still valid over a century later. In fact, the challenges operators face today are basically to do with operational matters, with the management of human resources, marketing and the strategic vision of the social conditions of development and the processes of change that affect parks: quality and customer satisfaction, attracting and retaining good staff, developing a 'unique selling proposition' and the need for new, competitive advantage strategies. Indeed, it cannot be forgotten that effective management strategies at individual facilities contribute to the success of the entire industry. They elevate facility standards of integrity and professionalism.

Nothing guarantees success but experience suggests that the chances of developing a successful theme park are greatly enhanced if it is effectively managed. In fact, parks without professional management normally achieve poor results. A theme park's corporate strategy and, therefore, its management are directly conditioned by the need to ensure the necessary financial resources to guarantee its running and by the demands that such resources be devoted to achieving the financial results established by the shareholders or, in the case of public or volunteer-run parks, to balancing out the accounted entries. On the other hand, efficient management should be able to respond to changes in the business environment such as technological developments, the evolution of the economy or changing consumer tastes or behaviour.

As stated by Swarbrooke (2002), the aim of a privately owned theme park is generally to generate profit. This is true although there do exist publicly owned parks and even parks managed by volunteer associations, whose objectives may be slightly different. Even so, such parks should also generate sufficient profit to balance the budgets assigned, though they may employ pricing policies that respond to social purposes or other interests. From the point of view of economic and financial viability, the management of a theme park tends to maximize revenue and force costs down to the lowest possible. Though it cannot be forgotten that the time, effort and money which are put into trying to maximize income generation must be cost-effective, some of the park management strategies that are established in order to increase income are as follows (see also Swarbrooke, 2002):

1.   To increase the number of visits. This strategy is closely linked to park marketing operations. With this aim, promotional campaigns are usually carried out, new systems are established to commercialize the product, an increase in the number of visits per visitor is encouraged and the holding of special events is promoted.

2. To design pricing policies with the aim of attracting more visitors. This strategy only works if demand is elastic, as in fact occurs with theme parks. It is useful during the off-peak season. This may involve specific price offers for groups or specific segments of demand, such as families with children or groups of schoolchildren, among others.

3. To stimulate secondary visitor expenditure at the park. It has already been seen in previous chapters that income coming from admissions to the park only represents a part of the total revenue generated by a visit. The sale of products related to the park brand, its characters and its symbolic value is the main means to increase expenditure by visitors to the park. Complementarily, to the extent that a theme park offers entertainment opportunities for the whole day, consumption at restaurants, cafeterias and other outlets also present business opportunities.

4. To boost the use of the park by corporate clients. A source of income that is in the process of growing at numerous parks is due to making the different spaces of the park available to companies and individuals to hold congresses and exhibitions, to launch new products, for receptions and other such events. Also, parks can be used as film sets for advertisements and television series or films.

5. To obtain income through other means such as letting, franchises, concessions, grants, sponsorship or consultancy services.

At the same time, the control and reduction of costs are a fundamental management strategy from the standpoint of maximizing profits. However, the most useful procedures to comply with this aim are substantially more complex than those used to increase income. Among them are the following (see also Swarbrooke, 2002):

1. Appropriately managing human resources. Especially operating the park with strictly the necessary provision of staff in order to increase productivity. Productivity can be raised by using multi-skill trained employees who can be moved around or can perform several tasks in a particular attraction or ride, including, for instance, maintenance.

2. Reducing costs deriving from the purchase of products for sale at the park's shops or in its restaurants. This requires the establishment of purchasing, supplies and distribution policies that ensure the best prices, the highest turnover of products and minimum storage.

3. Reducing general communications, water, electricity and gas costs through the efficient use of available resources.

4. Establishing energy-saving measures, promoting waste recovery and reuse programmes, outsourcing services such as laundry, window cleaning, gardening or insurance, selling off unproductive assets that are a liability or rescheduling loan repayments.

5. Adjusting park operation periods during the off-peak season in such a way that start-up costs do not exceed the income coming from the number of visitors effectively attracted to the park. To this same end, it should not be forgotten that, to the extent that the daily opening of the park generates costs related to personnel and production factors, it is strategic to maximize the use of the facilities so that the park will tend to withstand for as long as possible the volume of attendance for which it was designed – not forgetting, of course, that seasonality is without a doubt one of the biggest challenges in the management of a visitor attraction (see Goulding, 2003).

In any case, bearing in mind, as we have seen in previous chapters, that theme parks have relatively high fixed costs, from the point of view of their management it should not be overlooked that a cost reduction strategy could lead to a drop in the quality of the service provided for visitors. Such a result would be undesired and could lead to important problems of competitiveness and positioning, which should therefore be avoided. On the other hand, as in the case of income, it cannot be forgotten that the expense involved in cost reduction must itself be cost-effective.

So as to facilitate a park's operation and, especially, decision making in the short and medium term, its management usually establishes periodical – sometimes daily – information systems concerning its results regarding visitor numbers, income, stock levels, budgetary variations, labour costs and so on. In addition to facilitating immediate decision making, this information is useful for the purposes of evaluating the park's evolution, to have available data to make predictions, to provide information for potential investors, to inform shareholders or to identify the magnitude of the fiscal contributions to be paid to government agencies. In accordance with the information available for each item, performance indicators are established which allow the assessment of the park's financial state of health. According to Swarbrooke (2002), some of the most common are:

- Payroll cost per revenue generated.
- Income per profit centre per staff involved.
- Net operating expenditure per number of visitors.
- Net cost of marketing per number of visitors.
- Admission income per total operating costs.
- Visitor spend per head.
- Income per operating expenditure (recovery rate).

The evaluation of the financial results of each unit of cost and each unit of profit is of special interest, whether for attractions, shows, restaurants or shops. Cost centres are the main areas of the park that incur costs. Profit centres are the main elements of the park that attract income, including entrance charges, the shops and meeting room hire. Though it is relatively easy to assign a portion of income to the profit centres, it is more difficult to decide the proportion of total costs that may be assigned to each of the park's components. For example, in the case of a restaurant, there are costs that are easy to identify, such as those deriving from purchases or on staff. However, there are also general administration and financial costs. Another difficulty comes from the existence of overheads (for example, insurance), semi-fixed costs (for example energy) and variables (for example, products on sale to the public). An indicator of the measurement of results in respect of this is as follows: individual profit centre income as a fraction of total park income per individual cost centre expenditure as a fraction of total attraction expenditure. If the top fraction is higher than the lower, the centre is performing well, and vice versa.

Anyway, the performance indicators allow decision taking at the time of drafting the park's annual budget. In fact, the budget allows the viewing of a theme park manager's corporate objectives. The budget is the point of reference for financial evaluation and, therefore, the results of the park's management, it guides financial management and allows the establishment of internal dynamics of improvement by means of the involvement of the different departments. In fact, the budget provides the working framework of the park during the year for which it is valid. Matters concerning the management of a theme park such as the design of operations, the provision of human resources, marketing strategies and the company's social responsibility are reflected in the budgetary forecast.

12.1. Operations Management

Part of the success of the management of a theme park lies in the suitable design – practical and effective – of its operations programme. Operations management involves the design, operation and control of the system that assigns the resources of the organization to satisfy the needs of the consumers. In a theme park, the right operations programme is fundamental from the point of view of the safety of employees and guests (it also increases employee safety awareness), guest satisfaction, comfort and security, the upkeep of the thematic environment and the park's competitiveness. Operations programmes also allow a reduction in the time needed to perform a certain task and facilitate communication between line operating staff, supervisors and management team. Each park must have its own organizational and operations structure in accordance with its location, size, seasonality and typology. On a basic level, operations management is the day-to-day management of the site. In this light, generally speaking, it should be considered that all employees of a park are involved in the management of operations in that, in a service activity, each employee forms part of the operations of the facility. According to Swarbrooke (2002), it may be stated, on the other hand, that the aims and functions of operations management seen from the point of view of the organization are different from those which may be defined from the point of view of the visitors to the park (Table 12.1). It is observed that some objectives may be contradictory. This illustrates the paradox that forms the basis of operations management: adjusting the productive factors available to the organization to the visitors' needs and expectations.

Operations management is therefore a complex, fundamental task that requires a variety of skills and attributes, such as in-depth knowledge of the park and the uses made of it by both employees and visitors, the ability to perceive the needs of the park as a whole without overlooking the details,

Table 12.1. Operations management from the viewpoints of the organization and customers (from Swarbrooke, 2002).

The organization	The customer
Maximizing throughput and opportunities for visitor spending	Minimizing delays, crowding and queuing
Safety of visitors and staff	Safety of visitors
Minimizing operating costs (labour, energy and so on)	Maximizing quality of service and optimizing visitor enjoyment
Looking after the needs of those groups who are described as 'visitors with special needs' such as the disabled	Treating every visitor as if they are unique and special
Ensuring quality standards are as high as possible within resource constraints	Optimizing quality regardless of costs
Problems solved quickly and as cheaply possible	No problems occurring in the first place but, if they do, being solved quickly without regard to the cost to the organization
Compliance with the law	

the ability to establish plans and procedures prior to its start-up, flexibility to adjust systems in the event of changes in the behaviour of the visitors, the ability to communicate with the other members of staff and the customers of the park, deep knowledge of the principles of management control and financial management, firmness and resolution, the ability to work under pressure and act with common sense and effectively when problems arise, empathy and the ability to see problems from the customers' point of view or from the standpoint of other managers in the management team. In fact, operations management should assume that multiple variables exist which affect the normal operation of the park, some of which are controllable, such as the volume and quality of the products acquired for customers to purchase in the shops or at catering outlets, others may be influenced, such as the degree of motivation, commitment and behaviour of the employees, and others are clearly uncontrollable, though real, such as visitors' attitudes towards and their expectations of the park or, yet more evidently, the atmospheric conditions at the park on any given day.

Operations management has to deal with a great variety of circumstances – some problematic such as certain mechanical hitches with rides, for example – in the day-to-day management of the park. However, most of the needs to be attended to are long-standing and continuous: for example, long queues or 'bottlenecks' on the site or the need to reduce and treat waste. This is why logistics systems are established that aim to set up standardized systems of functioning for the facility and mean that the most common problems can be solved procedurally. This is why theme parks, as they establish logistics systems concerning the production process, procurement and logistics, maintenance and security, also tend to document the processes and draw up help systems for decision making in irregular circumstances. In short, the purpose of the system is to ensure quality in the park and at the same time maintain its competitiveness. Even so, there are times of crisis that require general or specific solutions that have not been foreseen in the design of the logistics systems and, hence, in the operations manuals.

One special circumstance to be overseen by operations management derives from situations of crisis that attract the attention of people and organizations from outside the park, such as, for example, a fire, a fatal accident, a bomb scare or an explosion, a case of intoxication or a violent incident in the park. When such events occur, operations management must deal with the crisis – for example, by evacuating the area or closing an attraction – but also, and especially, it must deal with the media keen to pursue the situation. Larger theme parks with greater management capacity must have protocols drawn up as to how to act in such situations of crisis as mentioned. In such circumstances, it is not just a question of solving a minor problem but of dealing with an emergency, which may cost the park's image and positioning dear: hence the need to have to hand formal, planned solutions.

12.1.1. The logistics of operations

Logistics are of fundamental importance in the development of processes in theme parks. As in other service enterprises, in theme parks the moments of production, distribution and consumption overlap each other. The result is that in fact, in theme parks, momentary excess demand cannot be dealt with by increasing the capacity of an attraction or a show. The following section deals first with the differential aspects of parks as regards the operation of a park's productive components. Secondly, the design of the operations that satisfy the specific needs of the procurement and distribution of the goods and services of a park are dealt with. Thirdly, it looks at the logistical aspects associated with the maintenance of the facilities. Finally, this section looks at questions that are specifically linked to safety and security as a guideline for a theme park's operations logistics.

(A) Production

The production of unique experiences by means of attractions at a theme park is based on an operations programme whose recurrent principles are the following: safety, integrity, control and quality. Given their ludic nature and the confidence they arouse among their visitors, safety is the highest priority in the process of the operation of attractions at a theme park. As the IAAPA would insist, aside from the differences between parks and between management styles, in the theme park industry the guideline is 'the safe way is the right way'. Integrity is linked to the challenge facing theme parks to make available to their visitors the best products and services every day and to provide, consequently, the best possible experiences also every day. Control is the internal procedure that links the different departments of the park and allows them to work together. Quality is a process that is conditioned not just by the characteristics of the facility but fundamentally by the standard operational procedures that are really effective in parks.

The shows are an activity of an exceptional nature in theme parks as a result of their singularity as a service but also in respect of other conventional spectacles, due to their iteration and continuity in time and in their capacity as fundamental elements from the viewpoint of a park's capacity to attract and its efficiency and productivity. It is an activity in which the production stage should be distinguished from the operation stage. From the logistics point of view, aspects must be taken into account such as the scenography and furnishings, the special effects and pyrotechnics, image and sound, the wardrobe and the characters.

In theme parks, catering is a large-scale, heterogeneous, complex production process. As we have seen, parks, within their supply, tend to include as many catering options as possible. The results obtained from an economic standpoint are linked to the established purchasing policy, personnel costs, the size and type of services, the availability of suppliers and the flexibility of the overall system. Similarly, though the rendering of the service presents significant differences, in a theme park's shop operations logistics, the purchasing policy is greatly influential. It should be borne in mind that many parks go straight to the producers, eliminating intermediaries, due to reasons linked to the type of product (artisan or thematic) and price. Likewise, there are huge differences between products according to the timing of their purchasing cycle. Thus, products with an annual purchasing cycle due to the distance from the supplier and supply periods may present problems in determining stock levels.

(B) Procurement and distribution

The production process in a theme park first requires performing all activities necessary in order to provide each work unit with the productive factors required for the fulfilment of its functions. For this reason it is important to minimize all operations in the productive process that do not add value to the product. The first step in the process is to obtain the necessary productive factors, which is why the production process is highly dependent on the park's procurement policy, especially as regards suppliers' flexibility, agility, accessibility and capacity to respond. Secondly, to keep a suitable production rhythm, it is important to establish a system of storage, transport and handling that will allow each work unit to have the necessary productive factors available to them. A park's production capacity is directly linked, therefore, with a theme park's layout.

A theme park must negotiate with suppliers and take decisions as to the purchase of goods and services concerning such diverse items as bin bags, ice cream, T-shirts, attractions and shows. Purchasing processes are crucial from the point of view of the operation of a park. Bad procurement logistics could lead to tension between departments, excessive prices, the absence of supplier guarantees and dissatisfaction among visitors. Procurement consists of establishing the needs of productive factors, determining the amounts to buy, analysing alternatives for acquisition, choosing the most appropriate and negotiating delivery dates, guarantees, end prices, purchasing the factors, properly storing them if necessary and supplying them at the right time to the right place. Moreover, it is understood that procurement plays an important role in managing the quality of parks. It is therefore basic to establish systems that facilitate the purchase of any good or service necessary in the park, specifying the stages involved in the process and the people responsible for them. The following stages are common: the identification of the suppliers of the good or service (for example, a Polynesian dance company), the establishment of selection criteria with regard to the supplier (who may already have been positively vetted by the park if a regular supplier) and the product or service (via any necessary specifications), a request for provisioning, the formalization of the contract and the delivery of the good or service. If it is a material product, its storage and/or distribution will have to be considered. Parks' purchasing policies are increasingly tending towards establishing cooperation systems or even partnerships with their most critical suppliers of the services that are rendered to the end consumer. Cooperation means collaborating with suppliers in specific fields and over limited periods of time, with a price negotiation process that may be defined as being objective. A partnership means the joint construction with the supplier of some aspect of the product which the visitor to the park will eventually consume, with transparency of costs. In fact, numerous parks have partner companies that supply them with a whole variety of products and services.

The distribution of goods and services inside the park often demands decentralized logistic organization so as to be able to attend to the needs of their end customers, their visitors. The seasonality of the activity, the big differences between peak and trough times and the different magnitudes of frequentation inside a park itself (which may range from 5000 to 50,000 people a day in some cases) pose great difficulties in optimally scaling distribution systems. However, this does mean that flexible logistic organization and specific agreements with suppliers must be available. A good layout of the storage system and service facilities of a park as well as adequate planning of the routes to keep them to a minimum and the optimization of transport systems are, from this standpoint, a fundamental instrument of competitiveness.

(C) Maintenance

A theme park's maintenance policy is established on the basis of people's safety (as much clients' as employees') in the use of the attractions, transport systems and the facilities in general of the park, customer satisfaction during their visit, the legal aspects deriving from existing regulations in each country governing leisure facilities, recreational activities and safety, the cycle of each facility and the economic cost. The maintenance systems to be set up may be predictive, when techniques are used that help foresee problems before they arise, preventive, when periodical inspection activities are scheduled in order to detect problems before they materialize, and corrective, which consists of righting problems when they occur. Given the heterogeneity of parks, the functions to be carried out as regards maintenance are diverse and heterogeneous. This poses one of its biggest problems. In addition to this is the fact that, occasionally, maintenance operations to be implemented are little standardized. This, though positive from the point of view of the quality of the processes, implies high associated costs. On the other hand, a part of such processes must be scheduled to take place at times or on days when the park is closed (either in the winter or at night). A good maintenance system – in terms of response capacity and flexibility – has, however, immediate effects on customer satisfaction and revenue. This is why, for proper implementation, parks usually have specific maintenance divisions:

1. Attractions. They are usually inspected periodically – daily – following preventive criteria and dealing, fundamentally, with matters of safety and customer satisfaction (one of the main causes of dissatisfaction is the impossibility for visitors to be able to enjoy an attraction regarding which they had expectations during their visit to the park).

2. Buildings and gardens. This includes the maintenance of the park's civil works, buildings, gardens and theming. The idea is to maintain elements that, though they may be considered structural, contribute value to the visited space as well as improving the conditions of the visit (shade, rest areas, visuals, etc.).

3. Cleaning and disinfecting. Cleaning is one of the aspects to receive the most attention in theme parks. In fact, it forms part of the very concept. On the other hand, the logistics of maintenance must be able to prevent and, if this is not possible, react to plagues, especially of insects (this factor must be taken into due consideration in parks located in the tropics, subtropical and mild temperate areas), in addition to maintaining the good condition of such classic components for parks as water elements.

4. Waste. Park maintenance logistics must consider the collection and recovery of the different types of waste generated every day. Parks like PortAventura in Spain have certified such processes within the framework of its environmental policy.

5. Installations. A theme park must ensure the supply of high-, medium- and low-voltage electricity, water and gas. This must be foreseen in the park's contingency plan. Also, the logistics of maintenance must ensure the correct functioning of the electronic systems – which are fundamental for the working and control of the processes in the park – as well as other basic aspects from the point of view of visitor comfort, such as heating, cooling and ventilation.

6. New projects. It is responsible for the implementation of new projects in terms of cost, time and quality. Its duty is to keep possible delays in the start-up of a new attraction – with a view to renewing and expanding what the park has to offer – to a minimum, as delays could lead to problems with advertising campaigns, lost visitors and income, contractual difficulties with operators and a tarnished image.

(D) Safety

Safety at a theme park is an across-the-board objective. As Gélis (2005) maintains, safety is an imposed necessity – and not just for human reasons but also economic ones. It is, in fact, the critical factor for the survival of parks, both individually and collectively. That means that safety must be incorporated at all levels, from the formulation of operative programmes to strategic decision making, passing through the actual execution of the tasks assigned to all employees. Nothing must be overlooked, in order to avoid an accident. If few accidents occur, this is not by chance. The installations are of good quality, flows inside the park are carefully studied and all possible steps are taken to avoid the slightest problem, far more than in any other space of everyday life. Today, parks are increasingly tending to automate the processes, keeping, however, elementary human control systems.

The most positive action to take in order to guarantee safety is to provide training for the employees, to promote safety skills, to develop safety awareness and to model good safety practices. According to Liebrenz-Himes and Ramsay (2000), studies show that employees fail to follow safety procedures if they do not have proper instructions or if they misunderstand, disregard or minimize the instructions. So sound orientation programming is one of the best ways to involve employees. Orientation sessions should emphasize general company rules and benefits and safety rules in the accident prevention programmes, including specific hazards and precautions on the job.

Programmes, policies and procedures must be drawn up by the safety manager or designer, who has to be assisted by a safety committee, which reports directly to the head of operations or the park's general management. To this same end, the IAAPA has continuously insisted for its associates that 'a strong, clearly defined, well communicated, and effective safety philosophy is a necessary component for a successful park . . . the safety commitment must be, through management policies and directives, a top priority of the entire organization' (IAAPA, 1993). From this standpoint, each employee can benefit from and is responsible for the success of the safety programme. The attitude of employees is therefore fundamental. Recognized standards exist among the sector's agents which affect the development of the industry and ensure that risks are kept to a minimum. Some of these standards are voluntary and others are applicable by law. For this purpose, the USA has developed an important and diverse specific standard, which aims to guarantee safety in parks and attractions. The existence of standards, whether for voluntary or imposed implementation, has

legal repercussions in that those responsible for a park may be held responsible in the event of a lawsuit. Large parks usually have their own regulations which are even more advanced than national legislation.

12.1.2. The documentation of processes

All processes carried out inside a theme park must be documented. As
Castán (2004) indicates, to this end there is a need to create a hierarchical
documentation structure that includes the following components:

1. Operations manual. This must include the general aspects of the
operation of the park and of coordination between the different services,
the operative organization that guarantees its smooth running and the
company's organization policies.
2. General procedures. They must outline how the processes related
with general operation of the facility or those that are common to different
areas of activity are carried out.
3. Specific procedures. These must give a detailed explanation of how
the different operations in the park's different installations are carried out
in accordance with the criteria defined in the above documents. The purpose of the operations manual of a specific attraction is to facilitate the
training of employees and to document procedures and responsibilities.
4. Instructions. They explain in detail how a certain task is performed,
considering its complexity, importance and/or hazard potential.
5. Specifications. These define the characteristics a certain product or
service must fulfil.
6. Checklists. Checklists of the processes to be carried out for the execution of a certain task or function.

The operations manuals for a ride or attraction may include the following information. Organizations such as the IAAPA possess generic
models that may be applied to the operation of parks, attractions or
specific rides (see IAAPA, 1993):

1. A general description specifying: (i) the goals and objectives of the ride
or attraction; (ii) the employee policies, including pertinent standards in
areas such as employment requirements, identification cards, employee
uniforms, grooming standards, rules of conduct, employee services and
incentive bonus plans, pay schedules, holidays and vacations and termination procedures, complementary guidelines on the manner in which guests
have to be treated by the operating staff and measures with respect to providing access to persons with special needs or with a disability; and (iii) a
description and history of the ride or attraction, including information on
its manufacturer and the date of manufacture, how it works, capacity and
limitations and approximate speed and cycle time, as well as detailed
information to assist employees to operate and control it and specific guest
or rider policies that are to be enforced by the operating staff.

2. Specific instructions for each operating or attendant position. This information, combined with on-the-job training, provides the employee with complete operating instructions. The information included in this section may vary depending on the type of ride, its size and its complexity. This section may include: (i) the ride leader or foreman responsibilities; (ii) duties of the main control operator, including a description and explanation of the main control panel and the function of the controls; (iii) the typical duties for the person in charge of loading/unloading, including the enforcement of rider restrictions when necessary before admitting guests; and (iv) the procedures of the person responsible for the turnstile/grouper with regard to the monitoring and control of lines and typical duties concerning the ride queue area.

3. The operating procedures section of the manual should cover the following responsibilities: (i) pre-opening cleaning; (ii) pre-opening safety; (iii) specific operation (includes procedures or policies that are only necessary for an individual ride); and (iv) procedures for closing the ride. Control of procedures scheduled in this section is assessed through a daily inspection and checklist for each attraction or ride.

4. Instructions as to the use of the public address system as a way to inform and advise a large number of guests. Prepared scripts containing directions for loading, unloading, safety or other procedures ensures consistency and accuracy. Many parks use pre-recorded announcements.

5. Shutdown/breakdown procedures. This section of a typical manual addresses the two types of shutdowns/breakdowns that may occur. It is planned when a ride is scheduled to close and no vehicles are stranded, such as normal closing. It is unplanned when a ride must be stopped and vehicles may be stranded in locations that are not normal, such as in the event of a power failure. The manual should address the necessary procedures to be followed.

6. Safety information relative to the ride or attraction. This is the most critical aspect of the operation of an attraction. Documentation must consider issues concerning procedures, checklists, systems, emergency situations such as shutdowns, other incidents, such as fire, and first aid. It must also include emergency contact numbers.

The documentation available for the planning and execution of operations must integrate all aspects concerning the quality of the processes and their management. As indicated in the next section, for their drafting, the use of models such as IN-ISO 9000 general standards and an adaptation thereof (9004) for service companies is highly recommended. These standards help to achieve the integral development of the system and can help guide decisions to be taken on such matters. Moreover, documentation must include the processes to be implemented in conditions other than the habitual, albeit temporarily (when factors occur that affect the normal running of the facility, such as inclement weather, technical breakdowns, cuts in basic supplies such as electricity, water or gas, or greater visitor attendance than expected), or in an emergency (situations must be foreseen which could pose a risk to people and their belongings).

12.1.3. Quality assurance

Good operations management is basic, not just from the point of view of the smooth operation of the park but especially from that of the quality of the visitors' experience. Thus, the logistics systems and documentation that determine the procedures to be implemented for the operation of the park are also basic for the purpose of helping ensure the quality perceived. The quality of the visitors' experience at a theme park depends, in the end, as is known for all service activities (Grönroos, 1983), on the technical and functional quality of the service, that is to say, not just the element or elements that are the object of consumption but also their implementation or, in other words, on the process through which the outcome is produced. Therefore, quality assurance means establishing complex control systems to evaluate how the service is produced and consequently consideration is given to highly important critical aspects from the point of view of visitors' perception of a park, such as queue management and prevention, the good state of the attractions, the effective management of complaints, the rapid resolution of problems and the feeling of safety and security, to name but a few.

From a general standpoint, according to O'Neill and Palmer (2003), the key aspects that a theme park's operations management should tackle in order to ensure the quality of a theme park are as follows (see Berry *et al*, 1985; Tenner and DeToro, 1992):

- Reliability: the ability to perform the promised service dependably and accurately.
- Assurance: the knowledge and courtesy of employees and their ability to inspire trust and confidence.
- Tangibles: the physical facilities, equipment and appearance of personnel.
- Empathy: caring, individualized attention.
- Responsiveness: the willingness of staff to help customers and provide prompt service.

For these to be dealt with, a system of measures must be established – on the basis of the definition of quality adopted, the performance standards and measurement system to be used and, finally, what management system the park adopts to achieve quality – which mean that it is possible to ascertain the degree of quality of the park as a whole and its processes in particular. Although over time four main quality management approaches have emerged: quality control, quality assurance, total quality control and total quality management (TQM), TQM has emerged as an important way in which many contemporary park managers refocus their organizations on quality (Jay, 1998). This system is concerned with trying to achieve constant, continuous improvement to meet both the organizational objectives and customer needs. It involves the whole organization, all departments, every activity and every employee at all levels, including those worst paid or with few promotion or career prospects. To adopt it in practice, parks have to be able to develop their own quality objectives and performance standards and to plan how quality will improve in the future. To be effective, the system must cover every aspect of the management of the park: (i) the tangible elements, such as buildings, in terms of aesthetics, cleanliness, maintenance, reliability, safety, comfort and security; (ii) the characteristics of service delivery, including the competences and attitudes of the staff or the frequency with which the normal product is not available; (iii) the human resource management, comprising how the staff is recruited, trained, motivated, rewarded and disciplined; (iv) the pricing of the product; (v) the content of the information available about the park; (vi) the financial management; (vii) the relationships with the suppliers, with the intermediaries and with the customers; (viii) the relations with the local community; (ix) the social and environmental corporate responsibility; and (x) the effectiveness of management systems and operational procedures. Although there is little consensus on a methodology which is of general applicability to measure quality in the service business, in the absence of any other objective measure, disconformation models dominate the literature on service quality from the early 1980s. Pre-eminent among these studies is SERVQUAL (Parasuraman *et al*, 1985), an instrument based on the belief that service quality is measurable but only in the eyes of the consumer.

Ensuring the quality of a park, not just from the viewpoint of the definition of its processes but especially putting them into practice adequately and thereby generating customer satisfaction, is a complex goal. This is so because, first, for the case of a theme park it is necessary to appreciate that quality is not an absolute concept but, rather, the opposite: it is usually connected to matters such as its relationship with the price and cost of the service, visitors' expectations, the improvements that may be made to the management processes, changes to legislation and regulations, the actions pursued by competing parks, technological possibilities to be implemented in production systems or even fashion. So an attraction, especially one that incorporates an advanced technological system could have been considered high-quality a decade ago but be perceived as being of medium or low quality today. Updating the catalogue of cinematographic attractions in a park like Futuroscope is a good example of this process. In addition, there exist numerous impediments that may hinder not the assurance of quality but the implementation of the management systems. Guaranteeing certain levels of quality brings about costs and it is therefore necessary to have available, direct and prioritize specific funds for such a function. Other factors may also exist, such as little committed corporate culture on the part of the management team or little interest and even opposition by employees to different positions adopted by the different stakeholders, with the capacity to influence the process, whether the parent companies, investors or managers.

In this regard, it cannot be forgotten that, in general terms, experience with quality management systems applied to the services, theme parks particularly, is relatively scarce. The very condition of the leisure and entertainment sector as a producer of services that are non-standardized, intangible, non-stockable and highly dependent on the interactive and simultaneous process of production–consumption leads to yet more difficulties in their materialization. It must also be taken into account that perceptions as to the quality of the services supplied at parks and as to parks as a whole (which is the basis of the measurement of the quality of a leisure facility) decline with the passage of time. The consequence of this, for example, is that, whereas customer perceptions of the quality of a service are traditionally measured immediately after the person has consumed the service, the consumer's remembered perception of service quality at the time when she or he decides whether or not to buy the service may better explain repeat buying behaviour (Palmer and O'Neill, 2003). It is probably as a result of all of these circumstances that quality in general terms, but especially with regard to aspects such as a theme park's operations management, is also currently a marketing tool for these facilities. So, for example, many people who have never been to a Disney park have the perception that they are well managed, clean, safe leisure facilities, with well-trained, motivated employees. Other examples are related to questions concerning the sustainable management of waste or, for example, the park's ability to welcome disabled visitors.

Experiences such as the Enchanted Kingdom park in the Philippines highlight the importance of the development of TQM systems as a strategy for operations management at a specific theme park. They have had important implications as regards customer satisfaction but, yet more importantly, they have proved key from the standpoint of the very profitability of the park. In fact, the Enchanted Kingdom Service Quality Enhancement programme was launched – following a strategy of a labour–management cooperation approach – to combat a progressive slump in income and profit as of 1997, which almost led to the closure of the park in 2001. On the other hand, this is an interesting example to illustrate the importance of the commitment of all of the levels of a theme park's staff in a quality improvement process. Prior to the implementation of the scheme, relations between management and employees were poor. Data also revealed rampant pilferage, theft and cheating, this indicating a developing culture of dishonesty. The scheme which established systems to measure the improvements as regards quality, profitability and competitiveness, started with developing a shared understanding of the company's vision, mission and goals among all stakeholders and defined the work phases, which are given in Table 12.2. Significant gains started to be observed in an unprecedented manner and within a relatively short period of time. The system has galvanized the management and employees of the park and the company was able to achieve the goal of a significant business turnaround by 2005 (see Gatchalian *et al*, 2004).

12.2. Human Resources Management

The quality of the operations in a theme park and therefore of its visitors' experience depends on the facility managers' ability to employ the best possible human resources for each available work post. Given that it is a labour-intensive service activity, the importance of the management of

Table 12.2. Phases of the Enchanted Kingdom TQM programme (from Gatchalian *et al*, 2004).

Phase I. Assessment of quality practices and the climate for TQM
Role of top management in quality development company-wide
Presentation of results to company leaders (employees and management)

Phase II. Development of a quality language company-wide
Strategic planning for quality vision–mission–policy–goals–objectives–activities–monitoring development and sharing
Company-wide quality campaign
Principles and practice of total quality management (TQM)

Phase III. Planning for quality (continuing activity)
Review and development of strategic plans for quality (short- and long-term)
Organize short- and long-term human resource management programme

Phase IV. Development of 'quality-mindedness' (continuing activity)
Partnership for quality, profitability and competitiveness (QPC)
Mobilizing quality improvement teams or task forces
Review/organize monitoring approaches for business results
Monitoring continuous quality improvement programmes
Documentation and internal quality audit, financial analysis (aiming at ISO 9000 certification)

Phase V. Effective communication and teamwork
Team building and communication for effective partnerships
Development of supervisory leadership
Measurement of customer satisfaction (internal and external)

Phase VI. Building the capability for sustaining quality
Statistical thinking (including quantified approaches to decision making and design of experiments)
Supervisory leadership training programmes
Continuous training and updating for quality (quality management systems, training of trainers, evaluating and monitoring training programmes, job evaluation and wage determination, performance appraisal)
Other quality programmes necessary to sustain commitment to partnerships within the company, with suppliers, stakeholders, family, community and the country as a whole

human resources is fundamental. It cannot be forgotten, with regard to this, that, in parks, the cost of work is the biggest budgetary item. Watson and McCracken (2003) single out three essential issues for a theme park's human resources (HR) management strategy:

- Selecting and retaining quality staff.
- Training and development to meet new and changing demand.
- Managing the employee–employer relationship to meet organizational objectives.

According to Storey's (1995) model, for the case of theme parks the following basic principles should be considered for the management of human resources: that people are fundamental for the success of a business, that the management of human resources must be done by the highest level in the organization, that the line managers are the key players in managing people and ensuring the successful delivery of human resource management strategies and, finally, that the culture of the organization and integration of people management procedures enhance effective people management. Applying such principles, it may be said that only organizations that are committed to the personal and professional development of their human resources obtain the best results of HR management. From this stance, human resources management is, therefore, a strategic function. Theme parks' main challenges as regards HR management are:

• The vast quantity of seasonal and part-time jobs with minimum wage earnings.
• The high percentage of employees within the industry with no formal education beyond secondary school, the majority under the age of 35.
• The need to perform monotonous operational functions of little value and yet crucial from the point of view of rendering a service. Since 2002, Disneyland Paris, for example, has employed over 12,000 workers per year, leading, in 2004, to a consolidated cost of €366 million. College students represent a sizeable portion of the employee population in many theme parks.
• The fact that a high number of jobs perform customer service responsibilities and, therefore, there is a need to be able to work with people.
• The diversity of professional functions and profiles required for the running of the facility. For instance, Florida theme parks use over 3000 job titles.
• The high personnel turnover within the industry, which can reach 50%, creating numerous opportunities for growth in employment.
• The difficulties that exist to define attractive career plans for all functions so that employees may combine professional improvement with training for the work post. Conversely, an excellent way to attract the best people is to be known as the preferred employer in a particular place due to a variety of reasons.
• The inexistence, in a great many parks – especially small and medium-sized ones – as well as in the field of the leisure industry in general, of training schemes and recognized qualifications.
• The need to make compatible the demands of human resources management with the assignation of funds in the organizational budget.
• The problem of establishing demand volume prediction systems so as to efficiently adjust the number of staff necessary to manage the park. Parks with more advanced technological implementations automate the planning of working timetables, mobility between functional units and payments through real-time control systems (RTCS). The system continually updates its prediction as to the business volume to be experienced throughout the day. The system would also receive real-time information from all point-of-sale systems and from other data-tracking services, such as the queue-length monitor (Thompson, 1999).

- The difference in rhythm between the inertias of the park management systems and structures – and, in particular, of the procedures and practices of human resources management – and the rapid changes that the industry experiences and the continuous transformations of the tourist market's motivation and behaviour.
- The difference in labour laws between countries, as well as the different human resource management traditions in different cultural contexts and the need to establish procedures adapted to the local conditions of personal and professional development.

Another aspect is that theme parks need systems that ease the relationship between the organization and the employees and allow managing disciplinary and grievance procedures consistently and fairly. In the countries where it is possible, agreements exist between the unions and park management. When this is not so, the problems are usually solved by means of informal agreements. When some kind of disciplinary action is required or if it is understood that the organization has acted unlawfully, matters are taken to court. In the event that disciplinary action is required as a result of unacceptable behaviour or inadequate performance, there is usually, before resorting to the courts, a sequence of actions ranging from verbal and written warnings to eventual dismissal.

The proper management of human resources, therefore, is fundamental as regards the park's positioning. That is why parks have become committed to the development of good practices, from the point of view of both staff recruitment and hiring (objective processes, equal opportunities, suitable training, remuneration that rewards the contribution of employees' value to the organization, among other things) and their loyalty (good induction, motivational management and effective staff development schemes).

12.2.1. The hiring process

Theme parks establish specific human resources management structures that look after the process of personal and professional development in the heart of the organization, right from the identification of a new work post and its description to the design of the training procedure and the assignation of a concrete operative function (for complementary material, see Castán, 2004). The objective of the process is to provide qualified candidates for any organizational job. Operating costs are directly affected by the process. According to Aragon and Kleiner (2003), this process is essential because how well an employee is matched to a specific job greatly influences the quality and quantity of the employee's work and affects the company:

1. Identification. When a theme park acknowledges the need to create a new work post, the job design and description process is begun. Each work post is designed in accordance with the needs of the organization. This means deciding what the purpose of the job will be and where it will fit in with other people's jobs. Once defined, the process continues with

the description of the post, which is as honest, lawful and detailed as possible. This part of the initial process is fundamental, not just for the recruitment process but also for training, reward systems and performance appraisals. In addition, it allows potential applicants to be aware of the nature of the job. Though there is no universal system for the description of a work post, the following should be indicated: the nature of the job, the department to which it is assigned, the salary range and remuneration package, an outline of the main duties and responsibilities of the post, the post-holder's line manager, the post-holder's subordinates, the limitations to decision-making power, working relationships, details of the terms and conditions that go with the job – for example, holidays – and the date of the job description. Finally, the personal characteristics of the potential candidates for the post should be indicated in respect of aspects such as age range, physical attributes, qualifications/education, personal skills and qualities, experience in a similar post and technical knowledge. It is important to point out that the description of the work post and the characterization of the personal specifications should be made with equal opportunities in mind, in terms of both general principles and the law.

2. Recruitment. The staff recruitment phase usually gets under way with the publication of the available work posts among potential candidates. The procedure of advertising, of the content of the advertisement and of the choice of media in which the park advertises the post forms part of the recruitment strategy. In general, the publication of the vacancies serves not just to attract the attention of potential candidates but to identify the park as a good employer. It therefore has a public relations function. Most jobs and attractions are advertised in the printed media. The services of specialized companies are also used. Finally, some of the work posts are taken up by people that existing staff have met in a work context. Occasionally, medium- and large-sized parks carry out specific annual recruitment campaigns. For instance, Florida theme parks recruit from far outside the central Florida area. Once the advertising is done, the process is usually followed by the completion by candidates of a written application. This usually includes information concerning previous work experience, the nature of the position the candidate would prefer, time available and other matters. This phase usually poses difficulties, given the varying personnel needs at different times of the year. In fact, the seasonality of the activity and its intensity necessitate seasonal and temporary contracting, making the staff recruitment stage a truly complex one. The Internet is a very convenient tool in looking for potential candidates. An example of computerized tools is the company databases containing information and curricula vitae of candidates.

3. The selection of candidates. The selection process is based on the assessment of the written application, first taking into account the appropriateness of the information available about the candidate for the needs of the park. When the number of applications is high or is defined as such, a shortlisting process is usually carried out to preselect the candidates that a priori best suit the job description and meet the desired specifications.

The selection process continues with an in-depth, person-to-person interview covering the applicant's past experience, attitude and qualifications. Though there is growing recognition that the traditional interview is no longer a satisfactory way of selecting people, it does have a role to play. The interview should be conducted by staff who are knowledgeable of the qualities required to perform the duties of the position. Some of the important applicant qualities include, as the IAAPA (1993) states, 'enthusiasm, initiative, dedication, integrity, effort, involvement, responsibility, honesty'. Hickman and Mayer (2003) identify six core competences that have to be scrutinized when job applicants are interviewed: a team player attitude, a guest service orientation, business savvy, leadership potential, personal and professional style, and communication skills. Other activities may be set up to ascertain the candidates' suitability, such as individual practical exercises, formal presentations, personality tests or social events to see the people when they relax. It is also necessary to find out whether the candidate is physically capacitated and meets the necessary health conditions to be able to perform the required activity. Hence, the candidate's suitability for the essential tasks performed in his or her potential job is analysed. Last in this phase, references – written or verbal – of the candidate made by previous employers may be taken into account. Based on all of the information gathered, the selection itself is made. However, this is a formal process which cannot be carried out without a certain degree of subjectivity as regards the perception of the abilities of each candidate as to whether 'he or she will fit in' or 'can work with' the other employees. This phase in the process finishes when recruiting staff write definitive letters to all unsuccessful applicants.

4. Hiring. This is the administrative process of incorporating the chosen candidate into the staff of the organization. It consumes both time and resources, which are multiplied in the case of parks, since, generally, for the one work post there is usually a high degree of staff turnover. This circumstance is usually the employees' response to the nature of the work posts – fundamentally the manual and hands-on ones in the park – offered by the parks and their seasonality in general. The fact that many of the jobs in a theme park are perceived as being of poor status makes it difficult to keep hold of the good employees and increases turnover in a work post. Once taken on, the new employee is usually given an Employee Policy Manual or Employee Handbook, which contains important information as to the company's policies. Depending on the park, such manuals may include information on: (i) the park's employment policies, such as equal employment opportunities, personnel classifications, recruiting, selecting and hiring, relocation, training and development, promotions, transfers, physical examinations; (ii) benefits, such as holidays, transportation, bereavement leave, insurance programmes and medical plans, pension plans, voting, service awards or educational reimbursements, among others; (iii) wages and salaries; (iv) standards of performance and conduct, such as identification, computer usage, security, discipline, rest and meal periods, jury service; (v) emergency procedures; and (vi) contract termination procedures. The manual may include other general issues like an overview of the park's organization and other, more specific matters, such as policies governing work posts. Occasionally, some of these aspects may be included in other specific documents for the purposes of information. According to the regulations for each country governing workers' affiliation to trade unions, these manuals also often include specific information concerning employees' rights in this respect.

5.   Training. Having selected and hired the candidate, he or she must be trained. In an initial training period, the park will inform its employees as to the characteristics of the facility, its business philosophy and, in particular, also its commitment and sensitivity to all matters concerning safety. Personnel policy guidelines covering aspects concerning conduct, dress code, facility rules, benefits and other policies and procedures, written in a basic employee manual, should be included in this orientation. Likewise, now is the time to explain the facility's chain of command for new employees to understand how they fit into the overall park operation. A second stage deals with the training needed so as to be able to perform the specific tasks required of the work post for which the candidate has been selected. From the park's point of view, this is a complex process given the volume and diversity of functions to be performed in the park. Normally, parks tend to approach the initial training phase as a time to convey the organization's values, its mission, its vision and beliefs regarding basic aspects, which may later result in the improved satisfaction of the customers' expectations. So, for example, parks tend to demonstrate their commitment to total quality management processes as a near-fanatical commitment to satisfy the guests' needs. They also insist that their guest-driven philosophy acts as a catalyst for innovation and improvements in quality and that the role of the staff (whether salaried, regular, part-time or casual) and that of the contractors is to promote the mission, value the beliefs and pursue the vision of the future of the park.

6.   Authorization and empowerment. Once trained, the employees are authorized to perform the duties of a particular position. At this point, a fundamental matter is the employee's familiarity with the attraction manual outlining the various procedures and policies that he or she should follow. If problems exist with the performance of an employee at a work post, systems should be set up for retraining and re-authorization, which may be advisable on a periodic basis. The employee has to understand that the theme park organizational processes have been designed with customer value and customer satisfaction in mind. It is in this regard that theme parks develop extensive systems of standard procedures. This allows control of the quality of service. With regard to this, as Hickman and Mayer (2003) state, many theme parks have discovered that effective empowerment strategies usually lead to happy, motivated employees. To be truly responsive to customer needs, front-line employees need to be empowered to accommodate customer requests and to act on the spot when things go wrong.

12.2.2. Employee loyalty strategies

In addition to the recruitment procedures, it is important for theme parks to draw up management strategies whose aim is to build up the loyalty of the organization's workers. This involves setting up effective systems and globally conceiving the needs of the park and employees' capacity given that they participate in its running. Four procedures exist which may help to keep hold of the good staff at a park (see also Swarbrooke, 2002):

1. Induction. This is carried out right from the moment a potential candidate comes into contact with the organization. The point is to offer opportunities to employees not just to find out about the responsibilities involved in their work post but to have information and contact concerning the job opportunities the park can offer in general. This means that the human resources management team should have a specific programme that includes issues such as: information on the organization's work posts, advice as to housing, education and social services that may prove useful for new members of staff moving in from another area or the assignment of a 'mentor' who takes responsibility for orienting the new employee. Also, the new employees must feel they have the chance to learn and find out more about the organization, whether through meeting members of the team of managers, their own line manager, guided tours or other procedures.

2. Motivation. The management of human resources once they are involved in the running of the park must promote the upkeep of employees' enthusiasm and motivation, including those performing less gratifying tasks and with lower salaries, whether casual or part-time employees. Two types of action are needed for this:

- Personal. The post-holder's line manager should tend to be sensitive to employees' needs and expectations, value a job well done, encourage improvement on the basis of constructive criticism and offer support in critical external circumstances.
- Corporate. The organization may offer incentives to boost staff job satisfaction: financial incentives in the form of pay rises linked to increased results or customer satisfaction; non-financial incentives, including gifts, trips to conferences and award schemes (Disney in Orlando offers over 50 different reward and recognition programmes); empowerment; job rotation to prevent boredom caused by doing monotonous tasks; the incorporation of employees into teams or quality circles or the establishment of a professional career structure allowing progression within the organization itself or the creation of group dynamics. Finally, if the organization treats employees as customers and they feel valued, they are more likely to stay within the park (Hoai Anh and Kleiner, 2005). For instance, in an in-depth study on hourly employee retention in the Orlando attraction industry, Milman (2002) shows that employees who had a sense of fulfilment with their job exhibited little inclination to move to another employer because of different

management style, and those that were given clear job responsibilities and had consistent working hours were more likely to remain with their current employer.

3. Support. As Hickman and Mayer (2003) point out, when employees do not have the right equipment or their equipment fails them, they can easily be frustrated in their desire to deliver service quality. To be efficient and effective, employees require internal support systems aligned with their need to be guest-focused. Tools such as performance appraisals and performance surveys measure service quality and encourage supportive internal services because they give employees the chance to discuss ideas for improvement. As a result, employees feel that they are an important part of the team and their opinions really matter to management.

4. Training. Training has been a traditional tool in motivating the employees of an organization. Being chosen to attend a training course may be understood as an incentive and acknowledgement since the organization is committed to the employee and values their work to the extent of providing an incentive to improve on it. To take such decisions, the park's human resources management system may have systems to assess the performance of each employee at their work post. Now, besides motivation, a singular way of boosting staff loyalty is to create training opportunities within the park itself, leading to employees' professional improvement. This approach is being explored by some of the big park operators and some of the medium-sized ones too. The idea is not just to help employees perform better in their job but also develop their potential in general. To achieve this, parks may draw up different strategies, which can be broken down into two broad groups:

- Training not associated to a system of professional qualification. This includes mentoring programmes, on-the-job training under the supervision of an experienced person, reading manuals or textbooks, group problem-solving, short on-site courses run by the organization's own trainers and professional off-site courses in specific areas, such as those organized by the International Association of Amusement Parks and Attractions.

- Training associated with a system of professional qualification. The idea is to guide employees to follow specific training programmes, which may be held by educational institutions with which the park may have training agreements or by the park itself (Mayer, 2002). In this case, it will be the park's task to ensure that the system of professional qualifications of the country where it is located will acknowledge the value of the qualification issued. This has been, for example, the case of Disneyland Paris since 2001. The park offers a small number of its employees a specific professional qualification programme, known as Hôte d'Accueil Touristique (HAT) (see Mercier and Lasbleis, 2005), which is carried out within the framework of a permanent contract and provides the qualification (grade V in the French system) of Agent de Loisirs, or Leisure Agent. It lasts 15 months, during which specific training is offered on each of the three major areas of the park's activity: attractions, shops and light catering, as well as other generic and complementary training. The main purpose of the programme is the professionalization of the park's employees, as well as the development of their abilities. The second aim is to pave the way for future improvements in the employees' employment prospects through training. The third is to boost recognition of the trades related to leisure and to stress that it is a qualifying sector in the labour market. The programme has a later specialization module lasting 18 months, available to the employees, known as HAT SPE, which allows them to achieve a grade IV qualification. The HAT programme takes some 300 people a year, whereas the HAT SPE programme some 100. With this specialized programme, employees perform several functions of short duration which allow them to know their chances of evolving in their careers. Complementarily, Disneyland Paris is considering a system to allow the HAT SPE employees to join team leader courses, which prepare future team leaders. At the end of 3 years as team leader, employees can validate their professional knowledge by means of another official qualification, this time grade III. To run this programme, Disneyland Paris has over 500 tutors at its disposal.

12.3. Marketing Strategies

Swarbrooke (2002) insists on the fact that successful attractions are usually those which have a systematic approach to marketing. He characterizes this by factors such as giving adequate attention to market research, recognizing that marketing is not just about producing brochures, taking a long-term strategic view, employing specialist marketing staff, appreciating that there are lots of different market segments, spending a significant proportion of turnover on marketing each year and accepting the importance of word-of-mouth recommendation. Theme parks constitute, therefore, a challenge for strategic marketing. In a context of the growth and/or sustained renewal of the supply, of the appearance of new recreational leisure opportunities and of the evolution of the markets, both in their demographic characteristics and in aspects concerning consumer behaviour, miscalculating which groups might be a park's potential customers could lead to an important loss of income. The processes of change are, furthermore, much more intense as the economy grows more quickly. This is especially so in the new industrialized countries of Asia/the Pacific.

A useful general approach to theme park consumer markets can be based on the classification drawn up by Rohde (cited by Bray, 2005). Rohde identifies four types of consumer according to their age and their relationship with new technologies: the computer game generation, the search generation, the stress society and the 50-plus market (see Table 12.3). Each of the groups' consumer needs and expectations are

Table 12.3.   Theme park consumer generations (from Bray, 2005, based on Carl Rohde).

Computer game generation
- Market includes pre-teens and teens
- This category is growing as computer entertainment becomes more entrenched
- Looking for 'the perfect moment'
- Looking for the interactive experience
- Australian Idol and Big Brother, both heavily interactive television shows, great examples of change in TV

Search generation
- Young adults between 16 and 27
- World made up of 'us' and 'them'
- Brands defining belonging
- Cell phones connecting them to friends and family

Stress society
- Includes those in late 20s to early 50s
- People more stressed now because time is more valuable now
- Must be on call 24 h a day
- 'Just in time' global economy operates continuously and does not go on vacation
- Attractions make it possible to 'get away' in a world with fewer places to 'get away' to

50-plus market
- Group with taste
- Likes to travel
- Recent retirees have grown up with the modern theme park
- Know a quality experience when they see one

linked, especially, with the variable condition of the family in the social structure of the different areas of the world, with the distribution, use and value of leisure time, with the incorporation of young people in the mass use of new technologies and with the role of the groups and brands as points of reference in people's identity. Identifying suitable market segments is primordial for the management of a theme park. This is why it is fundamental to know the market in terms of demographics, geography, behaviour, benefits and psychographics. In any case, it should be borne in mind that segments of the market exist which are growing, such as the older age groups with disposable income as well as leisure time, the segments of demand that are interested in learning something new or families with children who seek to spend a good time together. It is worth highlighting the fact that the family segment increasingly includes a growing number of non-traditional family types: grandparents, single parents and friends and family. There is also a growth in multigenerational family travel parties (grandparents, parents, kids, in-laws, aunts, uncles and cousins who travel together) (Garfield, 2004).

Defining a marketing strategy for a theme park is governed by market conditions, competitors' actions, the legal framework, the corporate culture of the organization and its history, the training, experience and attitudes of the staff, the budget available, ethical considerations and the very nature of parks as places of entertainment. Thus, whereas on the one hand a great number of parks become places of entertainment for all generations and develop exciting attractions for both young and old, other parks with offerings tailored to specific segments have the park's ability to compete precisely in their specialization. So competition in the theme park industry requires a better understanding of consumer choice processes. For example, as Kemperman (2006b) have demonstrated, consumers exhibit some degree of variety-seeking behaviour, which leads them to visit different parks on different choice occasions. This means that the managers need to emphasize or add distinctiveness in the services they offer to consumers. Likewise, knowledge of specific variety-seeking effects could help managers to focus their competitive promotion and advertising campaigns.

12.3.1. Marketing plans

Marketing strategies are usually developed on the basis of the drafting of marketing plans. Marketing plans aim to ensure that the organization's objectives are met. They incorporate proposals at strategic and tactical levels. They involve the use of a wide range of techniques of analysis in order to identify the strengths and weaknesses of the organization, threats and opportunities of the markets, the effective allocation of resources, the evaluation of performance, day-to-day marketing activities and responsibilities of all of the members of the planning and development team. It is currently perceived as a horizontal function that must be coordinated with the rest of the functions of the park in order to ensure the coherence of the messages conveyed with the nature and characteristics of the product. Their purpose is to enhance the satisfaction of customers' expectations in terms of quality, price and availability. Therefore, marketing plans define, for each specific park, the functions of investigation, the design of the marketing mix, product development, campaigns, budget, evaluation and control. In this connection, it should be stressed that it is especially important to have at one's disposal a system to evaluate and control the marketing strategy. To do so, the plan must contain measurable objectives and information systems must exist.

When drawing up a marketing plan, the basis is often the analysis of the current situation. It is common to employ specific techniques for its realization, including SWOT (strengths, weaknesses, opportunities, threats) analysis, in order to evaluate the situation of the organization as a whole, tools like the product positioning study – which allows observing where customers perceive each park in the marketplace – or models such as the product life cycle (see Swarbrooke, 2002). At this stage in the process of elaboration, market research and the existence of information management systems are of crucial importance. In fact, they are basic in order to comprehend questions such as how visitors decide which attractions to visit, factors that influence customer satisfaction, and customer perception of attractions. Also, in addition to improving their knowledge of consumers, market research allows the identification and analysis of potential competitors, the prediction of changes in the context of the development of the park and the measurement of the effectiveness of the actions undertaken. Having analysed the current situation, a theme park's marketing plan should define future goals – including the mission statement of the park – the strategy options and tactical plans – including the resources required to achieve its goals – and the strategy for the evaluation of its performance. For the generation of strategies, parks may establish options like market penetration, product development, market development and diversification. Market penetration is a low-cost alternative that involves the use of promotional techniques. Product development can be expensive, because it usually involves the buying of new on-site attractions or rides. Market development is also expensive, because it implies considerable expenditure on advertising. Finally, diversification implies a large amount of investment with risk. In any case, as Porter (1985) remarks, each park should establish the bases for its competitive edge: cost leadership, product differentiation or market focus.

In greater detail, as mentioned, marketing plans usually use the set of variables of the marketing mix in order to respond to the market objectives that each specific park has set itself. Though authors like Booms and Bitner (1981) include more categories, traditionally the marketing mix has meant the four Ps: product, price, promotion and place. The three remaining Ps (people, physical evidence and process) in fact concern concrete aspects regarding the conditions of the product.

(A) Product

Theme parks are a key figure in the global entertainment industry within the framework of the experience business. The product includes the park's material characteristics, the service, the image, the brand, the positioning, the benefits it offers its visitors, the quality of the management systems and the guarantees and after-sales services. Given that customers are increasingly expert and selective and that they have at their disposal complementary or replacement products, the configuration of the product and the communication of its characteristics are fundamental in the case of theme parks. Issues such as the recognition of the quality of the service at parks such as Disney's, the reputation of the brand in potential markets as is the case of Ocean Park in Hong Kong or Alton Towers in Great Britain, market leadership like PortAventura in Spain or SeaWorld in Australia or the clear perception of the benefits that each park may offer, such as excitement in the case of Cedar Fair or cultural contents in the case of Window of the World in China, are all key elements for communication for each of the cited parks. At developments that are enjoying success today, what are important are innovative approaches to a concept, the variety of the on-site attractions, a high-quality environment and unique ideas. Consumers want totally immersive, realistic, intense, personalized, convenient and diverse services (Lounsberry, 2004). Also, the most successful parks are those that are perceived not just as 'places for consumption', but as concepts, as labels associated with experiences – with lifestyles. This is the case, for example, of parks like Legoland, which, as Johns and Gyimóthy (2002) have demonstrated, compete on the basis of the values they convey. According to them, visitors to the Legoland park at Billund, Denmark, perceive the park in terms of a hedonic experience rather than simply as a commercial service and respond to emotional content rather than to the provision of a utility service.

The recent trends in attendance patterns, the changing expectations of family members related to amusements and relaxation, and the market conditions underline the need for family activities that provide a learning environment with enjoyment. Also, there is a call for parks and facilities that challenge adults and provide experiences. Now, it should not be overlooked that this is a characterization that refers to a concrete cultural and geographical context. Different levels of development, different generations of consumers and different systems of cultural representation offer different opportunities for the development of parks. Thus, for the case of Taiwan, for example, Tomes and Hwang (1995) indicate that 'the factors of overriding importance in determining choice of theme park were found to be picturesqueness, quietness and clean environment, cultural/educational attributes and low admission prices'.

Anyway, from the point of view of the product, for theme parks attracting clients implies the periodical renewal of the supply. It should not be forgotten that the very nature of the product in the theme park sector is subject to quick changes, principally due to technological developments. So, as Brault and Brouzes (2005) state, some European parks announce annual investments of €10 to 15 million, the purpose of which is to maintain their positioning. Such investments do not generate a lasting competitive edge, although they are indispensable from the viewpoint of maintaining their ability to compete. An example of how a lack of innovation can have a negative effect on a park, as we have seen, is the evolution of Futuroscope during the 1990s. On the other hand, innovation means gaining customer loyalty, and that, in general terms, is a basic condition in order to ensure the long-lasting profitability of the business.

(B) Price

Correctly defining a theme park's pricing policy is fundamental from the point of view of the business (Guyomard, 2005). On the other hand, it is a complex task. There are two basic issues to be taken into consideration when setting prices in parks:

- That theme parks have defined rates of penetration in their market areas, which, when in a situation of maturity of the supply, are difficult to raise.
- That each segment of potential customers is sensitive to prices in different ways. The preferences of potential customers are governed by the overall budget their visit requires and the psychological investment they have to make. For example, an 8-h visit to a theme park at a weekend in spring for a family that resides in a market area away from the park could well cost more than twice what it would cost the same family to go on a half-day excursion to a rural area near their place of residence, and yet they consider it money well spent.

On the basis of such principles there are a further two elements to be taken into account when setting the price of a park:

- The prices of the competition, bearing in mind its characteristics (number and type of attractions, visit duration, positioning), the base price and the pricing structure, including its profitability.
- Customers' susceptibility to establish a relationship between the price of the service and the utilities satisfied during the period of use and consumption in the park. These utilities vary in accordance with each customer, although demand segments may be established.

Parks' revenue managers face the challenge of delimiting the relevant demand segments in order to favour the park's optimal revenue opportunities. Hence, they have at their disposal a variety of tools, ranging from the setting of a standard tariff to discounts and concessions. Discounts are normally used to attract visitors during the low season or to attract specific demand segments like families, groups or repeaters. There are three types: reduced cost or added value (such as 'two for the price of one' offers), concessions and packages. Concessions are reductions in the standard price which are carried out by attending to social objectives. It is common, for example, for there to exist special tariffs for the elderly or disadvantaged segments. Other criteria often considered when establishing prices concern the creation of packages that include the travel and/or stay plus the visit or the use of advanced-purchase methods, such as the acquisition of tickets through the Internet.

The ability to define complex pricing structures in accordance with the product on offer allows the consideration of a number of innovations and maximizes business figures. In any case, the price should be in accordance with the quality of the product and the value for money perceived by the visitor. Together with the different pricing structure for admissions to parks according to the season, the most developed practices are the different systems to stimulate repetition, ranging from yearly passes, or season tickets, to special offers for residents in the park's area of influence to the possibility of getting a discount for the next visit (for further information, see Table 12.4). The use of new technology means, furthermore, that novel pricing systems can be studied. This is the case of debit charging cards for 'pay-per-ride' model parks as well as games and concessions. However, as segmentation criteria become finer, parks still have at their disposal an important potential for solutions to be exploited for the periods of less attendance. The use of yield management techniques, which are commonplace in the travel industry, is a practice to be exploited further.

(C) Promotion

To the extent that visitors cannot inspect a theme park before purchasing tickets, the use of promotion and communication instruments is basic to attract custom. To do so, theme parks use common techniques such as advertising, brochures, press and public relations, sponsorship, or the use of the Internet, among other methods (see Diamond and Smith, 2000). Complementarily, despite not forming part of the traditional functions of marketing, for the case of theme parks, it is fundamental to create merchandise and concessions as an effective method for extending the brand of the park. This includes souvenirs, consumables, novelties such as unique items to be displayed or used after leaving the park and participatories (items that enhance the customer's experience).

Parks have to understand their media options (print media, electronic media, outdoor advertising, flyers, product placement, transit advertising, specialities such as T-shirts, calendars or other printed items and

Table 12.4. Examples of pricing practices that favour multiple visits at European parks (based on Brault and Brouzes, 2005).

Practice	Example
Unlimited evening pass	Gardaland
Packages for stays of over 2 days	Europa Park
Entrance for several days with flexible dates	PortAventura
Package with special service for customers in the hotels	PortAventura
Discount for a second visit on a date that can be chosen	Phantasialand
Annual passes for other parks, even abroad	Efteling
Packages that include transport and the stay	Disneyland Resort
Student discounts	Futuroscope
Loyalty club	PortAventura
Specific offers for pensioners	Europa Park
Tickets that exclude the access to attractions	Tivoli Gardens
Discounts for online buying	Parc Astérix

unconventional advertising such as bus display ads or banners). Major parks can afford expensive television advertising because they tend to have a relatively high advertising budget. In general terms, however, medium-sized and small parks tend to be present only in the media through paid advertisements in the local, regional and/or specialized press. Radio is less used. In any of these cases, for an advertisement to be successful, its good design is key and it must be placed in the right media at the right time. It is also interesting and substantially less costly to target potential customers in a particular geographical area according to the strategies of the park. The success of brochures and leaflets depends on their design and contents, the size of the print run and how well they are distributed. There should be different brochures for different purposes, the design should grab the attention of the target market and the content should provide the information required by the potential customer. Strategically, parks use other promotional tools, such as the following:

- Free coverage in the media through press and public relations. For this, parks need to provide the media with information content of interest in the form of press releases.
- Direct marketing strategies for dealing with each different market segment (Lafuste, 1998).
- Sponsorship of events, people or organizations. It is basic for them to be present at sports and/or media events such as the Tour de France and to give support to people and organizations that are coherent with the characteristics of the product. Thus, parks with animals, like SeaWorld, often sponsor environmental protection groups and activities.
- Agreements between parks to run joint advertising campaigns (Fyall, 2003).
- Finally, as will be seen in a specific section, the Internet has become a key tool for promotion. Parks take advantage of the growing tendency for consumers to perform extensive holiday and travel planning and research via the Internet and to compare products and features.

Within this framework, there is a great deal of interest in the initiative taken by the International Association of Amusement Parks and Attractions' 'Ticket for fun' (see www.ticketforfun.com). It is the only theme park industry-wide consumer media campaign. It serves as an information resource on travelling to theme parks, amusement parks and other attractions. It was developed in 2004 and contains a worldwide database of parks and attractions, industry news and promotions, fun facts and safety tips. The website received more than 1.8 million visitors and two awards in 2005. In September 2005 the website introduced interactivity pages for children and families with games/activities and a mascot was also created, a friendly new character shaped like a ticket and fashioned with a big smile and sports shoes, named Stubs.

(D) Place

Place is how the customer has the opportunity to purchase the product. In the case of theme parks, visitors travel to the product to use it. Nevertheless, distribution channels do exist. Thus, for example, tour operators put together parks and package holidays, acting as intermediaries. The parks that have accommodation facilities are at an advantage in this respect since they can negotiate jointly the prices of the stay and the park admission fee. Also, attraction booking agencies operate in local, regional and – some – worldwide markets. They guarantee no price increase and no queuing at the ticket kiosk, among other things.

Today, the Internet has revolutionized the concept of place. Numerous medium- and large-sized parks let people book and purchase tickets prior to travelling. Nevertheless, as is explained in the next section, when dealing with the Internet it is often difficult to distinguish between promotion and place.

12.3.2. The role of new technologies

According to Gonzalez (2005), the Internet is an opportunity for parks to make themselves known beyond the local area, to make recreational proposals, to show the evolution of the product and to respond to a more demanding public that requires complementary services. The Internet provides a unique opportunity for the efficient testing and experimentation of new products, added value and pricing, to react quickly to consumer trends and events that impact travel, tourism and leisure and to provide the most cost-effective distribution system for sales transactions, fulfilment, information distribution and communication. We should not forget that the information revolution has changed the way people work, play and communicate:

- Potential guests get their first impression from the park website.
- Parks have more sources of news on the Internet than on their own website.
- Younger generations are online on a daily basis, many of them are in contact with peers all over the world and they acquire a transnational culture.
- Customers are talking on the Internet through weblogs (blogs), online message boards, chat groups, travel websites and personal websites.
- News travels faster (Internet anonymity makes rumours easier to spread).
- Advances in telecommunications are producing an on-demand generation.

In this regard, certain Australian parks make creative use of the Internet by means of interaction systems that prepare customers for the visit and persuade them to visit them again through information in real time on the attractions. For this they use webcams or interactive virtual mascots.

However, not all parks make the most of the possibilities offered by the Internet. Thus, on numerous occasions the website is merely another space to convey information (although on occasion in a highly sophisticated manner, as occurs with the sites that offer virtual visits). In this field, significant differences exist between parks according to their size, operator, market area, geographical location and technological incorporations of reference. Such utilities are highly developed, for example, among the parks of the main North American operators. In fact, in the USA, the Internet is at the centre of park operators' marketing strategies. For them, the Internet is a means to perform customer relationship management (Garfield, 2004). Hence, the possible uses of the Internet by parks are far superior to being merely informative:

- Online reservation.
- Online ticket purchasing (often with special tariffs and management systems that are typical of low-cost companies).
- Obtaining information on the characteristics of customers through an online questionnaire that must be filled in to see any transaction through.
- Queue enhancement management through fast-pass offers.
- Customer feedback via newsletter, email or bulletin board.
- New ways to incorporate guests through interactive tools such as design contests, games and trivia, which may offer prizes in the form of free tickets.
- Communication campaigns on the occasion of the launching of new attractions.
- Generating viral marketing strategies (electronic word of mouth, or 'word of web'), making available downloadable games, screen savers or information as to happenings and novelties in the park, which are disseminated vigorously.
- Dispelling misinformation quickly.

Such uses not only affect sales and customer satisfaction but, especially with regard to booking and purchasing admission tickets online, mean that tighter operations management can be practised thanks to better frequentation forecasting. Likewise, it means costs can be reduced: the visitor buying online does not need to queue up at the park, though the price is usually lower, the park economizes the cost of issuing and printing the ticket and, in short, the number of reception and sales staff can be brought down. Moreover, the interactive use of the Internet arouses emotional empathy and facilitates customer loyalty. To sum up, the use of new technology allows the product to be customized to each individual customer. Hence, as Lounsberry (2004) claims, the Internet is causing theme park operator corporations to rethink sales and marketing channels and pricing and product strategies.

12.4. Operators' Corporate Social Responsibility

An increasing number of companies are drawing up social responsibility strategies and they voluntarily assimilate commitments that go beyond conventional regulations in order to raise the levels of social development, environmental protection and respect for human rights. Nevertheless, corporate social responsibility should not be seen as a substitute for legislation concerning social rights or environmental standards, including the development of appropriate new legislation. Thus, in countries where such regulations do not exist, efforts should focus on putting the proper regulatory or legislative framework in place in order to define a level playing field, on the basis on which socially responsible practices can be developed. According to the Commission of the European Communities (CEC, 2001), several factors are encouraging this move forward in companies' social responsibility:

- New concerns and expectations from citizens, consumers, public authorities and investors in the context of globalization and large-scale industrial change.
- Social criteria are increasingly influencing the investment decisions of individuals and institutions, both as consumers and as investors.
- Increased concern for the damage caused by economic activity to the environment.
- Transparency of business activities brought about by the media and modern information and communication technologies.

While the following initiatives are not legally binding, an approach to corporate social responsibility within the theme parks industry must reflect and be integrated in the broader context of the various international initiatives concerning the matter, such as the UN Global Compact (2000), the International Labour Organization's (ILO's) Tripartite Declaration of Principles concerning Multinational Enterprises and Social Policy (1977/2000), and the Organisation for Economic Co-operation and Development (OECD) Guidelines for Multinational Enterprises (2000). In particular, see the ten principles of the UN Global Compact agreement:

1. Businesses should support and respect the protection of internationally proclaimed human rights.
2. Businesses must ensure that they are not parties to the violation of human rights.
3. Businesses should uphold the freedom of association and the effective recognition of the right to collective bargaining.
4. Businesses should uphold the elimination of all forms of forced and compulsory labour.
5. Businesses should uphold the effective abolition of child labour.
6. Businesses should uphold the elimination of discrimination in respect of employment and occupation.
7. Businesses should support a precautionary approach to environmental challenges.

8. Businesses should encourage initiatives that promote greater responsibility towards the environment.

9. Businesses should encourage the development and diffusion of environmentally friendly technologies.

10. Businesses should work against corruption in all its forms, including extortion and bribery.

Table 12.5 shows the components of the two dimensions – internal and external – of corporate responsibility. The fact that there are two dimensions is relevant for the case of theme parks since sometimes the paradox arises that they may have well-developed and well-implemented environmental and social policies – and even, in some cases, environmentalist discourses as a business strategy – at the same time as in their most immediate surroundings they bring about unsustainable territorial dynamics, also in terms of the environment (the case of certain property development processes and the consumption of limited resources such as land and water). In more general terms, within the company, socially responsible practices primarily involve employees and relate to issues such as investing in human capital, health and safety, and managing change, while environmentally responsible practices relate mainly to the management of natural resources used in the production. Corporate social responsibility extends outside the company into the local community and involves a wide range of stakeholders in addition to employees and shareholders: business partners and suppliers, customers, public authorities and NGOs representing local communities, as well as the environment.

Companies' approaches in dealing with their responsibilities and relationships with their stakeholders vary according to sectoral and cultural differences. At the start, companies tend to adopt a mission statement, code of conduct or credo where they state their purpose, core values and responsibilities towards their stakeholders. These values then need to be translated into action across the organization, from strategies to day-to-day decisions. This involves practices such as adding a social or environmental dimension in plans and budgets and evaluating corporate performance in these areas, creating 'community advisory committees', carrying out social or environmental audits and setting up continuing education programmes. Nowadays, many companies are issuing social responsibility reports. So, environmental and health and safety reports are common. On

Table 12.5. Dimensions within corporate social responsibility (from CEC, 2001).

Internal	External
Human resources management	Local communities
Health and safety at work	Business partners, suppliers and consumers
Adaptation to change	Human rights
Management of environmental impacts and natural resources	Global environmental concerns

the other hand, a growing number of social and eco-labelling initiatives have originated from either individual producers (self-declared labels or brands), industrial sectors, NGOs or governments. These are a market-based (rather than regulatory) incentive, which can help to deliver positive social change among enterprises, retailers and consumers. Finally, in recent years, socially responsible investing (SRI) has experienced a strong surge in popularity among mainstream investors. Socially and environmentally responsible policies provide investors with a good indication of sound internal and external management. They contribute to minimizing risks by anticipating and preventing crises that can affect reputation and cause dramatic drops in share prices.

The experience with investment in environmentally responsible technologies and business practice suggests that going beyond legal compliance can contribute to a company's competitiveness. Noteworthy along these lines is the value of the PortAventura theme park water management and reuse system which includes a weather station that monitors the different irrigation needs of the park's gardened areas, a system that takes advantage of rainwater and the use of recycled water for irrigation puropses. Going beyond basic legal obligations in the social area, e.g. training, working conditions, management–employee relations, can also have a direct impact on productivity. On the other hand, it cannot be forgotten that implementing corporate social responsibility not only needs commitment from top management, but also innovative thinking and, thus, new skills and closer involvement of the employees and their representatives in a two-way dialogue that can structure permanent feedback and adjustment.

For the control and development of corporate social responsibility, classic quality management systems can be used as a basis such as the International Organization for Standardization's ISO 9001 standard. However, specific internationally recognized tools are available to businesses that are useful in order to boost and develop their social responsibility in other fields:

1. SA 8000. Elaborated in 1998 by the Council for Economic Priorities, this tool determines social responsibility with regard to employees, suppliers, customers and society. It involves the direct participation of the workers and groups of interest from outside the enterprise and deals with issues such as the prohibition of forced child labour, the prohibition of racial, gender and religious discrimination, the right to the organization and freedom of association, the establishment of a maximum of 48 hours' work per week with 1 day off, the guarantee of a minimum salary that covers basic needs, humane working conditions, systematic improvement of the situation of the business and external dissemination and documentation through certification.

2. EMAS (Eco Management and Audit Scheme). Drafted on the basis of the European Union regulation on environmental audits, it is a voluntary instrument created in 1993 which can be used as a tool for the continuous improvement of environmental management. PortAventura theme park in

Salou, for instance, has established procedures to certify all of its processes, through the EMAS evaluation system. All of the park facilities, including the Costa Caribe water park and the company's hotels as well as PortAventura itself were environmentally certified in 2003 and 2004. Moreover, the hotels have specific Guarantee of Environmental Quality marks issued by the Autonomous Government of Catalonia.

3. ISO 14001. Standard by the International Organization for Standardization in 1996 establishing the international requirements for an environmental management system. It is a component of the EMAS ordinances.

For the case of tourist activities, in 1999, the World Tourism Organization drafted the Global Code of Ethics for Tourism, a broad set of principles that are reflected in ten articles aimed at enhancing tourist development processes in a responsible way, ecologically, socially and culturally speaking, which are directly applicable to the development of recreational facilities such as theme parks. They deal with issues such as the role of tourism for the mutual understanding and respect between peoples and societies and as a vehicle for individual and collective fulfilment. They approach tourism as a factor of sustainable development, as a user of the cultural heritage of humankind and a contributor to its enhancement and as a beneficial activity for host countries and communities. They determine the obligations of stakeholders in tourism development, the right to tourism and the liberty of tourism movements and, finally, they establish the rights of workers and entrepreneurs in the tourism industry.

As for organizations like the World Travel and Tourism Council, they acknowledge that companies have social responsibilities that go well beyond their commercial duties and the traditional role of wealth generation and profit making, and stress, for the field of travel and tourism, that the new standard is for business to exercise corporate social responsibility, adopting open and transparent business practices that are based on ethical values. From this standpoint, large corporations have already begun to express their results in the form of a triple bottom-line report and following the idea that the overall performance of a company should be measured on the basis of its combined contribution to economic prosperity, environmental quality and social capital. The adoption of such practices, moreover, has concrete results in terms of cost reduction, the improvement of the organization's public image and answering the consumers' concerns and, indirectly, achieving competitive advantage in the marketplace. However, it cannot fail to be mentioned that the development of this kind of practice may be conditioned by the park management's lack of strategic vision, by an inability to bring about the necessary changes in the staff's attitude and commitment and even by the impossibility of having the financial resources available to develop the necessary programmes of corporate social responsibility.

In the case of theme parks, the development of socially responsible practices principally includes the following areas:

1. Creating sustainable human resource management through strategies such as practising positive discrimination in terms of recruiting local people wherever possible, even if they are not skilled, keeping in line with local culture and employment practices, training local managers and staff to understand the importance of corporate social responsibility issues. In this sense, PortAventura, for instance, has a Green Team in which employees of all levels define, treat and focus on environmental issues and a Sustainability Committee which is made up of volunteer employees. In fact, the park has been, since 2001, a founder partner of the Spanish Excellence in Sustainability Club promoted by some of the largest companies in Spain. However, it cannot be forgotten that, unlike other business strategies, corporate social responsibility strategies have no immediate results and, therefore, may take time to be implemented. Nevertheless, to the extent that they can be capitalized on in the medium term, they do prove to be of interest to operators.

2. Developing sustainable operation processes such as, among others, lowering energy consumption, reducing waste and ensuring that recyclable materials are used wherever possible, minimizing water, air and noise pollution, buying from local suppliers and/or suppliers who also behave in a responsible manner wherever possible, reducing packaging and maintaining the environmental quality of the park. For this, some parks have drawn up specific policies whose purpose is to see that environmental legislation is met, making progress towards the minimization of negative impacts and the maximization of positive impacts and arousing awareness both within the departments of the company and among employees and visitors. Thus, for example, in 1999, Parc Astérix started a coherent environmental policy on the basis of three priority axes: resource management, impact management and the management of the communication of information within the framework of ISO 14001. Along the same lines, one should also acknowledge Disney's ongoing environmental programmes. They include everything from innovations in firework launch technology, using compressed air and virtually eliminating the need for smoke-producing chemicals, to proactive strategies in the management of energy and water resources, air quality, waste minimization and the development of educational programmes.

3. Sponsoring sustainable projects. Parks like SeaWorld incorporate an environmental and social commitment strategy which involves the development of specific projects beyond the park. In this way, Anheuser Busch, a major supporter of environmental conservation organizations, has established a Budweiser Conservation Scholarship Program with the National Fish and Wildlife Foundation and other environmental excellence programmes and has created an environmental charity, the SeaWorld and Busch Gardens Conservation Fund. Moreover, it is concerned with human needs and quality of life and provides support for many charitable social organizations, such as the Hispanic Scholarship Fund and the Budweiser Urban Scholarship Program for African American Students. Similarly, PortAventura in 2005 became committed to landscape restoration activities for public use, took part in the recovery of a system of fossilized dunes in an area of the park next to the coast and participated in the recovery of 17 ha of wetlands of great value to local biodiversity.

In addition to the many charitable contributions made periodically by individual parks to the local communities where they are located, the International Association of Amusement Parks and Attractions (IAAPA) has made a commitment to support two worldwide organizations that serve those in need and promote world peace: Give Kids the World and the International Institute for Peace through Tourism. IAAPA's support for the Give Kids the World Village in Kissimmee, Florida, is important for children with life-threatening illnesses. Children and their families arrive at the Village and for 6 days they can visit the Central Florida attractions and stay at the Village for free. The International Institute for Peace through Tourism is a not-for-profit organization established in 1986 in response to concerns as to the effect of terrorism and conflict on the travel and tourism industry. It fosters and facilitates tourism initiatives that contribute to international understanding and cooperation, an improved quality of environment, the preservation of heritage and, through these initiatives, a more peaceful and sustainable world.

From a critical standpoint, according to Davis (1997), these corporate social responsibility strategies represent an enormous paradox since, through them, entertainment, recreation, social relations, marketing, mobility and environmental concerns are all mixed together. So, for example, programmes such as DisneyHand is a public service in the areas of compassion, learning, the arts and the environment that includes the Disney VoluntEARS programme. VoluntEARS visit children's hospitals to deliver – in conjunction with Starlight Starbright Children's Foundation – DisneyHand packages filled with toys, books and games provided by Disney businesses. In any case, parks shape themselves as educational and philanthropic mechanisms and become, for their visitors, symbols of environmental and social commitment, contributing value to their act of consumption.

Case 19. The Safety of the Attractions at Six Flags Parks

Statistics show that a visit to a theme park – including the excitement of a roller coaster ride – is a safe choice (Exponent, 2002). Six Flags, the world's largest regional theme park company, has explained to consumers some of the systems and procedures at their parks that have produced the finest roller coaster safety record in the world (see Six Flags, 2005). With more than 40 million guests, Six Flags provides hundreds of millions of thrilling roller coaster rides, each year – more than anyone else on the planet. Because of that, safety is an across-the-board matter within the planning of the park, the training of employees, the operation of attractions and their maintenance schemes. In the case of Six Flags, its safety statement points out that the company:

is dedicated to providing the safest possible environment for everyone to enjoy our family entertainment. Every member of the Six Flags team is committed to the safety of our guests, his or her own personal safety, and the safety of our fellow employees as our first job priority.

It is through a complete universe of practices behind the scenes that parks like those of Six Flags can achieve the goal of making extraordinary thrills extraordinarily safe. These practices include (based on Six Flags, 2005):

- Park planning. Park design and construction take into account the specific location characteristics of each park, including climate, weather patterns, topography, local demographics and culture. All of them might affect the safety needs for rides within the park.
- Ride design. Six Flags insists on partnering only with time-tested manufacturers using only the finest materials. Every contract prescribes Six Flags' specific standards for each ride, especially regarding safe and comfortable restraint systems. Six Flags standards always exceed long-standing industry standards. All materials used in critical applications must achieve safety factors of 8 to 10, meaning the material can endure eight to ten times the expected load without starting to fail.
- Training of employees. Every Six Flags employee has been trained to manage their specific duties through handbooks, formal training courses, departmental certifications and extensive experience operating specific rides without passengers for hundreds of cycles. In addition to the training scheme, each operator must pass a written exam. Only then can the operator become certified for a designated ride. This process has to be completed for each ride on which the operator works. Moreover, all Six Flags operators must pass a 'catch-all' exercise, in which they are trained to anticipate emergency situations and are drilled in rapid, appropriate response.
- Equipment. Six Flags employees are provided with safety equipment and are trained to use it. Six Flags management strictly adheres to manufacturers' recommendations for worker safety in the operation and maintenance of rides, and encourages alert vigilance for any potential hazard.
- Technological monitoring. Technologically advanced rides are controlled by redundant industrial computers, constantly monitoring the condition and location of every coaster train through hundreds or thousands of sensors built into the track. If any one of the sensors reports a fault and there is not 100% agreement reported by all the sensors as to every train's location, then all the trains are stopped in a safe place. Sometimes the ride must be brought to a controlled shutdown until the discrepancy is resolved, including the safe unloading of all passengers.
- Ride loading. Six Flags operators and attendants are also trained to conduct checks on every restraint on every passenger on every ride.

There are dozens of redundant safety systems in place to protect the well-being of their passengers no matter what happens.

- Restraint systems. Coasters that create a temporary lift employ restraint systems that include passenger fit, safety factors and extensive testing. Generally, the carefully calculated forces generated by a coaster keep passengers in their seats throughout the ride. Over-the-shoulder coaster restraints are locked in place by ratchet mechanisms that cannot be released until activated by the computer in the station or manually by ride operators or maintenance personnel.

- Inspection procedures. Each season, Six Flags safety teams generate more than a half million handwritten ride inspection reports. At Six Flags each park and each ride have a comprehensive inspection and maintenance programme with specific guidelines that comply with international standards, with industry standards, with local regulations, and with Six Flags internal regulations. In all cases, rides are personally assessed daily by Six Flags employees. In the USA, for government agencies and insurance companies, inspections are further conducted by experts certified by the National Association of Amusement Ride Safety Officials (NAARSO). The American Society of Testing and Materials (ASTM) has established rigorous standards for amusement park rides that are the benchmark for inspection and maintenance around the world. All Six Flags parks and rides strictly adhere to these ASTM standards.

- Ride testing. Each of the 1500 Six Flags rides is subjected to several tests, checks and evaluations each year. These include:

  - Modelling tests during the course of design.
  - Tests at key stages of construction.
  - Stress testing once construction is complete.
  - Daily tests once the ride is in operation.
  - Regular testing by regulatory agencies.
  - Underwriting guidelines inspections by insurance companies.
  - Unannounced safety audits.
  - Operator and attendant safety inspections.
  - Regular, documented maintenance testing.
  - A comprehensive annual maintenance inspection by Six Flags corporate engineering staff.

- Maintenance. Every year the Six Flags coaster trains are dismounted and rebuilt to manufacturers' specifications. Every critical component is examined and any suspect parts are replaced. During the off season, all the rides again undergo rigorous examination, maintenance and, if necessary, repair or replacement. Key components of rides are taken into buildings for the winter, where they are dismounted, inspected and overhauled, with new wheels, bearings, wiring, harnesses or other components being fitted.

Case 20. The International Association of Amusement Parks and Attractions

Created in 1918, according to its own definition (see http://www.iaapa.org) the International Association of Amusement Parks and Attractions (IAAPA) is the largest international trade association for permanently situated amusement facilities worldwide and is dedicated to the preservation and prosperity of the amusement industry. IAAPA represents nearly 4500 facility, supplier and individual members from more than 95 countries. Approximately two-thirds of IAAPA members are located in the USA. Member facilities include theme parks, amusement parks, water parks, attractions, family entertainment centres, arcades, zoos, aquariums, museums and miniature golf venues. Approximately two-thirds of IAAPA members are manufacturers and suppliers and the rest are facilities. Amusement/theme parks represent 37% of facility membership. Since 1950 the Association adopted a code of ethics.

IAAPA's Global Alliance partnerships include ALAP (Latin American Association of Amusement Parks and Attractions), AALARA (Australian Amusement, Leisure and Recreation Association serving Australia and New Zealand), ADIBRA (Brazilian Association for the Amusement Industry), CAAPA (China Association of Amusement Parks and Attractions), IAAPI (Indian Association of Amusement Parks and Industries) and ASEAN (the Association of South-East Asian Nations, serving the Philippines, Thailand, Vietnam, Indonesia, Singapore and Malaysia). IAAPA also has collaborative relations with the existing national associations in Belgium, Denmark, France, Germany, Spain, Sweden, the Netherlands and the UK. IAAPA hosts three trade shows worldwide focused on the amusement park and attractions industry: IAAPA Attractions Expo, IAAPA Asian Expo and Euro Attractions Show. Each of them is the largest trade show in the entertainment industry in its region. Among the most important of IAAPA's areas of activity are (based on http://www.iaapa.org):

- Training. IAAPA offers training for every aspect of the amusement industry and provides all members with opportunities to educate their personnel through workshops, on-site seminars, videotapes/manuals and the IAAPA Management School. At each trade show, IAAPA also offers educational seminars that cover topics important to every aspect of the industry. Moreover, IAAPA is developing an Amusement Industry Institute Program and the IAAPA education division has launched an online learning service. IAAPA's online bookstore carries almost 300 titles in 15 categories covering all the operational areas of the amusement and attractions industry.
- Safety. IAAPA promotes safety standards, as a main priority, and maintains a constant partnership with the American Society for Testing and Materials to develop and update stringent safety and maintenance requirements. To further enhance safety IAAPA has also been an active promoter of International Standards harmonization.

- Publications. *Funworld* is the association's monthly publication and includes the latest amusement news spotlighting IAAPA members worldwide. The *Online Industry Resource Guide* is the industry's most complete source for product and service information.
- Charity. Since 1995 IAAPA has partnered with Give Kids the World (GKTW), a non-profit organization that provides 'wish vacations' to Central Florida for children with life-threatening illnesses. IAAPA members donate gifts, toys and supplies to GKTW, and more than 330 facilities provide complimentary admission to their parks for GKTW children through the World Passport for Kids Program. IAAPA also supports the International Institute for Peace through Tourism.
- Research. Periodically IAAPA develops or commissions several studies on the performance of the different sectors of activity within the industry, including all the operational and management aspects of the activity.

In 2004 the International Association of Amusement Parks and Attractions (IAAPA) developed a consumer website (http://www.ticketforfun. com), where visitors can find more than 1200 theme parks and attractions, safety tips, trivia, games and more, all to ease travel planning as well as learn about the many dimensions of the worldwide amusement industry. More than 1.8 million people visited the website in 2005.

Bibliography

ACFCI (Association des Chambres Françaises de Commerce et Industrie) (1993) *Les Parcs de Loisirs en France.* ACFCI, Paris.

Adams, J.A. (1991) *The American Amusement Park Industry. A History of Technology and Thrills.* Twayne Publishers, Boston.

Adelson, N (2001) El modelo Xcaret viaja a Chipas. *La Jornada,* 15 April.

Adorno, T.W. and Horkheimer, M. (2000) [1944] The culture industry: enlightenment as mass deception. In: Schor, J.B. and Holt, D.B. (eds) *The Consumer Society Reader.* New Press, New York, pp. 3–19.

Ah-Keng, K. (1994) Assessing the market receptivity of a new theme park in Singapore. *Journal of Travel Research* 32 (3), 44–50.

Ahmadi, R.H. (1997) Managing capacity and flow at theme parks. *Operations Research* 45 (1), 1–13.

AlSayyad, N. (2001) Global norms and urban forms in the age of tourism: manufacturing heritage, consuming tradition. In: AlSayyad, N. (ed.) *Consuming Tradition, Manufacturing Heritage: Global Norms and Urban Forms in the Age of Tourism.* Routledge, London, pp. 1–33.

Alfino, M., Caputo, J.S. and Wynyard, R. (eds) (1998) *McDonaldization Revisited. Critical Essays on Consumer Culture.* Praeger Publishers, Westport.

Alphandéry, P. (1993) L'insoutenable développement d'Euro-Disneyland. *Ecologie politique* 5, 51–76.

Alphandéry, P. (1996) La nature de Disneyland Paris. *Courrier de l'Environnement de l'INRA* 28, 27–34.

Altman, Y. (1995) A theme park in a cultural straitjacket: the case of Disneyland Paris, France. *Managing Leisure* 1, 43–56.

Anton Clavé, S. (1996) El parque temático PortAventura. Estrategia de producto para la reestructuración de núcleos turísticos consolidados en Cataluña. *Estudios Turísticos* 130, 7–36.

Anton Clavé, S. (1997) *Diferenciació i reestructuració de l'espai turístic. Processos i tendències al litoral de Tarragona.* El Mèdol, Tarragona, Spain.

Anton Clavé, S. (1998) La urbanización turística. De la conquista del viaje a la reestructuración de la ciudad turística. *Documents d'Anàlisi Geogràfica* 32, 17–43.

Anton Clavé, S. (2001) Variaciones sobre el concepto de parque temático. In: *Diversificación del sector turístico, desestacionalización e internacionalización.* Tirant lo Blanch, Valencia, Spain, pp. 237–253.

Anton Clavé, S. (2005) *Parques temáticos. Más allá del ocio.* Ariel, Barcelona, Spain.

Anton Clavé, S. and Blay Boqué, J. (2003) La petroquímica al Tarragonès. Indústria, seguretat i activitat turística. In: Nello, O. (ed.) *Aquí No! Conflictes territorials a Catalunya.* Empúries, Barcelona, Spain, pp. 353–378.

Ap, J. (2003) An assessment of theme park development in China. In: Lew, A.A., Yu, L., Ap, J. and Guangrui, Z. (eds) *Tourism in China.* Haworth Hospitality Press, Binghamton, New York, pp. 195–214.

Aragon, E. and Kleiner, B.H. (2003) Hiring practices in the amusement park industry. *Management Research News* 26 (2–4), 20–26.

Archer, K. (1996) Packaging the place. Development strategies in Tampa and Orlando, Florida. In: Demazière, C. and Wilson, P.A. (eds) *Local Economic Development in Europe and the Americas.* Mansell, London, pp. 239–263.

Archer, K. (1997) The limits to the imagineered city: sociospatial polarization in Orlando. *Economic Geography* 73 (3), 322–336.

Ariès, P. (2002) *Disney Land. Le royaume désenchanté.* Golias, Villeurbane, France.

Atkins, P., Simmons, I. and Roberts, B. (1998) *People, Land and Time. An Historical Introduction to the Relations between Landscape, Culture and Environment.* Arnold, London.

Atkinson, J. (1984) *Flexibility, Uncertainty and Manpower Management.* Institute of Manpower Studies, University of Sussex, Falmer, UK.

Augé, M. (1995) *Non-places. Introduction to an Anthropology of Supermodernity.* Verso, London.

Ault, S. and Wiktor, G. (2001) California dreaming. *Attractions Management* 6 (3), 24–27.

Bagherzadeh, F. (1988) Eurodisney resort, Marne-la-Vallée. *Cahiers du CREDIF* 22, 107–122.

Barber, B.J. (1996) *Jihad vs McWorld.* Ballantine Books, New York.

Barnes, J. (1998) *England, England.* Vintage Books, New York.

Barrado, D. (1999) El proyecto de parque temático de San Martín de la Vega en el contexto de la periurbanización de los equipamientos de ocio en Madrid. *Boletín de la Asociación de Geógrafos Españoles* 28, 135–145.

Baudrillard, J. (1983) The ecstasy of communication. In: Foster, H. (ed.) *The Antiaesthetic. Essays on Postmodern Culture.* Bay Press, Port Townsend, Washington, pp. 126–134.

Baudrillard, J. (1998) *America.* Verso, London.

Baudrillard, J. (2000) [1969] The ideological genesis of needs. In: Schor, J.B. and Holt, D.B. (eds) *The Consumer Society Reader.* New Press, New York, pp. 57–80.

Belmessous, H. (2002) La ville rêvée des anges. *Urbanisme* 323, 14–19.

Benckendorff, P. (2006) Attractions megatrends. In: Buhalis, D. and Costa, C. (eds) *Tourism Business Frontiers. Consumers, Products and Industry.* Elsevier, Oxford, UK, pp. 200–210.

Bennet, A. and Huberson, S. (2005) Le Snelac, un syndicat professionnel au service de la grande famille des parcs de loisirs. *Cahier Espaces* 86, 19–26.

Bentham, J. (1979) [1822] *El panóptico.* Ediciones de La Piqueta, Madrid, Spain.

Benz, M. (2002) Parks industry re-calibrates growth rates. *Amusement Business,* 8 June, p. 6.

Berman, M. (1997) Signs of the times: the lure of 42nd Street. *Dissent* 44 (3), 76–83.

Berry, L.L., Zeithaml, V. and Parasuraman, A. (1985) Quality counts in services too. *Business Horizons* 28 (3), 44–52.

Beyard, M., Braun, R.E., McLaughlin, H., Phillips, P.L. and Rubin, M.S. (1998) *Developing Urban Entertainment Centers*. Urban Land Institute, Washington, DC.

Bilotti, R. and Ksenofontova, S. (2005) *The Economics of Theme Parks and Resorts*. Morgan Stanley, New York.

Blair, R.D. and Rush, M. (1998) Economic impact statement of Universal Studios Florida on the Central Florida Region. Universal Studios Florida, Orlando, Florida. Not published.

Blank, D. (2000) A tale of two cities: Orlando's rapid hotel growth continues despite slight drop in area's occupancy. *Hotel and Motel Management* 215 (4), 81.

Boniface, P. and Fowler, P.J. (1993) *Heritage and Tourism in the 'Global Village'*. Routledge, London.

Booms, B.H. and Bitner, M.J. (1981) Marketing strategies and organisation structures for services firms. In: Donnely, J.H. and George, W.R. (eds) *Marketing of Services*. American Marketing Association, Chicago, Illinois, pp. 47–51.

Boorstin, D.J. (1964) *The Image: a Guide to Pseudo-events in America*. Harper, New York.

Bostnavaron, F. (1999) Les projets de nouveaux parcs de loisirs se multiplient en Europe. *Le Monde*, 6–7 June, p. 70.

Botterill, J. (1997) The 'fairest' of the fairs: a history of fairs, amusement parks and theme parks. Master of Arts Thesis, Simon Fraser University, British Columbia.

Boughilas, Z. (2005) La légalité des aides publiques au regard du droit européen. L'exemple du Bioscope. *Cahier Espaces* 86, 157–164.

Bouillot, P. (1993) La dynamique Euro Disney. *Espaces* 119, 24–26.

Bourdieu, P. (2000) [1979] The aesthetic sense as the sense of distinction. In: Schor, J.B. and Holt, D.B. (eds) *The Consumer Society Reader*. New Press, New York, pp. 205–211.

Bourguignon, P. (2005) *Hop!* Editions Anne Carrière, Paris.

Branch, M.A. (1990a) Story time. *Progressive Architecture* 3, 77–82.

Branch, M.A. (1990b) Why (and how) does Disney do it? *Progressive Architecture* 10, 78–81.

Brault, F. and Brouzes, S. (2005) Les nouveaux défis du marketing des parcs de loisirs. *Cahier Espaces* 86, 114–119.

Braun, B.M. and Milman, A. (1990) Localization economies in the theme park industry. *Review of Regional Studies* 20 (3), 33–37.

Braun, B.M. and Milman, A. (1994) Demand relations in the Central Florida theme park industry. *Annals of Tourism Research* 21 (1), 150–153.

Braun, B.M. and Soskin, M.D. (1999) Theme park competitive strategies. *Annals of Tourism Research* 26 (2), 438–442.

Braun, B.M., Soskin, M.D. and Cernicky, M. (1992) Central Florida theme park pricing: following the mouse. *Annals of Tourism Research* 19, 131–136.

Braun, R. (1993) Theme park development case study. Fiesta Texas. Prepared for the Second Annual Asia Pacific Theme Parks and Attractions Congress, Hong Kong. http://www.erasf.com/erasf/papers.

Bray, C. (2005) IAAPA and AALARA into the future. In: *12th Annual AALARA Conference*. Gold Coast, 11 pp. http://www.iaapa.org.

Brill, L.M. (1993) From concept to concrete: theming parks. *Funworld*, November, 24–28.

Britton, S. (1991) Tourism, capital, and place: towards a critical geography of tourism. *Environment and Planning D: Society and Space* 9, 451–478.

Brown, D.L. (1980) Thinking of a theme park? *Urban Land*, February, 5–11.

Brown, J. and Church, A. (1987) Theme parks in Europe. Riding high in the 1980s. *Travel and Tourism Analyst*, February, 35–46.

Bryman, A. (1995) *Disney and his Worlds*. Routledge, London.

Bryman, A. (1999a) Theme parks and McDonaldization. In: Smart, B. (ed.) *Resisting McDonaldization*. Sage, London, pp. 101–115.

Bryman, A. (1999b) The Disneyization of society. *Sociological Review* 47 (1), 25–44.

Bryman, A. (2003) McDonald's as a Disneyized institution. Global implications. *American Behavioral Scientist* 47 (2), 154–167.

Burns, C. (1988) Amusement parks. In: Wilker, J.A. and Packard, R.T. (eds) *Encyclopedia of Architecture. Design, Engineering and Construction.* John Wiley, New York, pp. 199–208.

Burnside, M.W. (2005) Coasters or condos. *Amusement Business* 117, 18–20.

Butler, R. (1980) The concept of the tourism area cycle of evolution: implications for management of resources. *Canadian Geographer* 35, 287–295.

Caillart, E. (1987) *Euro-Disneyland en France. Dossier de presse*. Mission de Négociation, Paris.

Camp, D. (1997) Theme parks in Europe. *Travel and Tourism Analyst* 5, 4–21.

Camp, D. and Aaen, C. (2000) *Big Fun*. Economics Research Associates, London, 3 pp.

Canogar, D. (1992) Ciudades efímeras. Exposiciones universales: espectáculo y tecnología. Julio Ollero, Madrid, Spain.

Capel, H. (2000) Los jardines y el diseño urbano: el jardín formal renacentista y neoclásico. *Debats d'Arquitectura i Urbanisme* 12, 66–83.

Cartier, C. (1998) Megadevelopment in Malaysia: from heritage landscapes to 'leisurescapes' in Melaka's tourism sector. *Singapore Journal of Tropical Geography* 19 (2), 151–176.

Castán, J.M. (coord.) (2004) *Operacions i processos de producció*. Universitat Oberta de Catalunya, Barcelona, Spain.

Castells, M. (1998) *La era de la información: economía, sociedad y cultura*. Alianza Editorial, Madrid, Spain.

Cazes, G. (1988) Les grands parcs de loisirs en France. Reflexions sur un nouveau champ de recherches. *Travaux de l'Institut de Géographie de Reims* 73–74, 57–89.

CEC (Commission of the European Communities) (2001) *Green Paper. Promoting a European Framework for Corporate Social Responsibility*. COM (2001) 366 final. Commission of the European Communities, Brussels.

Celine, L. (2000) Eurodisneyland en France. Phase 2. Cinq communes rurales associées à un gigantesque projet urbain. Memoire pour l'obtention de la Maîtrise de Géographie, Université Paris 1, Paris.

Cerankosky, C.E. and Keller, W.J. (2004) Cedar Fair, L.P. KeyBanc Capital Markets, Cleveland, Ohio.

Chang, T.C. (2000) Theming cities, taming places: insights from Singapore. *Geografiska Annaler*, 82B, 35–54.

Chang, T.C., Milne, S., Fallon, D. and Pohlmann, C. (1996) Urban heritage tourism: the global-local nexus. *Annals of Tourism Research* 23 (2), 284–305.

Charmes, E. (2005) Celebration: une horreur urbanistique? *Etudes foncières* 115, 25–29.

Chaspoul, C. (2001) Thématisation. Une nécessité marketing? *Espaces* 183, 21.

Chassé, S. (1993a) Les parcs thématiques et le tourisme. *Téoros* 12 (3), 2.

Chassé, S. (1993b) D'un concept de parc thématique sur la cité du Père Noël à un parc sur la nordi-cité. *Téoros* 12 (3), 32–36.

Chassé, S. and Rochon, P. (1993) Analyse de certaines variables stratégiques pour l'implantation d'un parc thématique au Quebec. *Téoros* 12 (3), 10–14.

Chazaud, P. (1998) Le parc à theme, production touristique hors sol. *Cahier Espaces* 58, 88–96.

Cochener, C. (2005) Le marché français des parcs de loisirs est arrivé à maturité. *Cahier Espaces* 86, 17.

COCIN (Cambra Oficial de Comerç, Indústria i Navegació) (1996) *El turisme i l'impacte de PortAventura. Anàlisi econòmica.* Cambra Oficial de Comerç, Indústria i Navegació de Tarragona, Tarragona. Not published.

Colquhoun, L. (1999) Hong Kong buys into Disney's magic world. *Evening Standard*, 2 November, p. 39.

Coltier, T. (1985) Les parcs à thèmes. *Espaces* 73, 18–20.

Conder, T.A. and Kreher, W.C. (2006) *Cedar Fair, LP.* AG Edwards and Sons, Inc., London.

Conseil Régional d'Auvergne (1999) Le chantier de Vulcania. Une opportunité de communication. *Espaces* 163, 20–22.

Corbin, A. (1993) *El territorio del vacío. Occidente y la invención de la playa (1750–1840).* Mondadori, Barcelona, Spain.

Córdova Lira, F. (2005) *Modelo de Responsabilidad Medioambiental y Social en la Empresa.* II Inter-American Conference on Corporate Social Responsibility. InterAmerican Development Bank, Mexico City. http://www.iadb.org/csramericas/2004/doc

Corliss, R. (1999) Thrill park. *Time*, 21 June, pp. 88–90.

Crawford, M. (1992) The world in a shopping mall. In: Sorkin, M. (ed.) *Variations on a Theme Park. The New American City and the End of Public Space.* Noonday, New York, pp. 3–30.

Csikszentmihalyi, M. (2001) Ocio y creatividad en el desarrollo humano. In: *Ocio y desarrollo. Potencialidades del ocio para el desarrollo humano.* Universidad de Deusto, Bilbao, Spain, pp. 17–32.

Cuenca, M. (2001) Perspectivas de nuevos hábitos en Ocio y Turismo. In: IV Congrès de Turisme de Catalunya. Tarragona. Not published.

Cuvelier, P. (2000) La fin du tourisme fordiste. *Espaces* 177, 32–37.

Cybriwsky, R. (1999) Changing patterns of urban public space. Observations and assessments from the Tokyo and the New York metropolitan areas. *Cities* 16 (4), 223–231.

Czarnecki, J.E. (2001) Disney strengthens Anaheim presence with planning and pixie dust. *Architectural Record* 189 (4), 49–52.

Darling, L. (1978) On the inside at parks à la Disney. *Washington Post*, 28 August, p. A10.

Davis, S.G. (1997) *Spectacular Nature. Corporate Culture and the SeaWorld Experience.* University of California Press, Berkeley, California.

DBK (2002) *Parques de ocio.* DBK, Madrid, Spain.

de Araújo Rodrigues, A.M. (2004) Estudo de metodologias para formataçao de empreendimentos voltados para o segmento de parques de diversoes. Masters thesis, Escola Politécnica da Universidade de São Paulo, São Paulo, Brazil.

Debord, G. (1967) *La Société du spectacle*. Buchet-Chastel, Paris.

Dequidt, S. (2005) L'accessibilité des parcs de loisirs aux personnes handicapées. Un enjeu et une necessité. *Cahier Espaces* 86, 103–111.

Derrida, J. (1972) *Les Marges de la philosophie*. Minuit, Paris.

Desgue, R. (2005) La boutique, un enjeu majeur pour les parcs de loisirs. *Cahier Espaces* 86, 130–132.

de Villiers, P. (1997) *L'Aventure du Puy du Fou*. Albin Michel, Paris.

D'Hauteserre, A.M. (1997) Disneyland Paris: a permanent economic growth pole in the Francilian landscape. *Progress in Tourism and Hospitality Research* 3, 17–33.

Diamond, M.E. and Smith, S. (2000) *Amusement and Attraction Marketing*. IAAPA and the George Washington University, Alexandria, Virginia.

Díaz, A. (2000) Parques temáticos: ¿Qué son? ¿A dónde van? *Editur* 2087, 16–20.

Didier, S. (1999) Disney urbaniste: la ville de Celebration en Floride. *Cybergeo* 96. http://193.55.107.45/culture/didier/didier.htm

Dietvorst, A. (1998) Tourist landscapes: accelerating transformations. In: Scraton, S. (ed.) *Leisure, Time and Space: Meanings and Values in People's Lives*. Leisure Studies Association, Eastbourne, UK, pp. 13–24.

Donaire, J.A. (1999) I nuovi spazi del turismo. Tempo libero e territorio nella società post-industriale. *Archivio di Studi Urbani e Regionalli* 65, 7–27.

Dumazedier, J. (1962) *Vers une civilization du loisir?* Seuil, Paris.

Duncan, E. (1998) Technology and Entertainment: a brand new strategy. *The Economist*, 21 November, Vol. 349, Is. 8095, p. 55.

Dunlop, B. (1996) *Building a Dream. The Art of Disney Architecture*. Harry N. Abrams, Inc, New York.

Eco, U. (1986) *Travels in Hyperreality*. A Harvest Book, San Diego, California.

Eco, U. (1989) *La Guerre du faux*. Le livre de poche, Paris.

Emmons, N. (2002a) Long-awaited Taiwan park set to open. *Amusement Business* 114 (18), 1 and 9.

Emmons, N. (2002b) China's amusement industry eyes future. *Amusement Business* 114 (22), 3.

Enright, M.J. and Scott, E. (2003) *Hong Kong and the Greater Pearl River Delta: The Economic Interaction*. The 2022 Foundation, Hong Kong.

Enright, M.J. and Scott, E. (2005) *The Greater Pearl River Delta,* 3rd edn. Invest Hong Kong, Hong Kong.

EPA Marne and EPA France (2000) *Ville nouvelle de Marne-la-Vallée: Les premiers résultats chiffrés du recensement général de la population. D'après INSEE, RCP1999. Fascicule 1*. Observatoire économique et social, Noisiel.

ERA (Economics Research Associates) (2003) *Big Fun 2003*. Economics Research Associates, Los Angeles, California.

Exponent (2002) *Investigation of Amusement Park and Roller Coaster Injury Likelihood and Severity*. Exponent and Six Flags, Alexandria, Virginia.

Eyssartel, A.M. and Rochette, B. (1992) *Des mondes inventés. Les parcs à thème*. Les Éditions de la Villete, Paris.

Fainstein, S.S. and Gladstone, D. (1998) Evaluating urban tourism. In: Judd, D.R. and Fainstein, S.S. (eds) *Places to Play: the Remaking of Cities for Tourists*. Yale University Press, New Haven, Connecticut.

Farrell, D. and Watson, N. (2005) *Village Roadshow Ltd*. Deutsche Bank, Sydney.

Findlay, J.M. (1992) *Magic Lands. Western Cityscapes and American Culture after 1940*. University of California Press, Berkeley and Los Angeles, California.

Fjellman, S.M. (1992) *Vinyl Leaves. Walt Disney World and America.* Westview Press, Boulder, Colorado.

Fletcher, J. (1989) Input–output analysis and tourism impact studies. *Annals of Tourism Research* 16 (4), 514–529.

Foglesong, R. (1999) Walt Disney World and Orlando. Deregulation as a strategy for tourism. In: Judd, D.R. and Fainstein, S.S. (eds) *The Tourist City.* Yale University Press, New Haven, Connecticut, pp. 89–106.

Foglesong, R. (n.d.) Walt Disney World: une ville privée modele. Not published. 13 pp.

Ford, R.C. and Milman, A. (2000) George C. Tilyou. Developer of the contemporary amusement park. *Cornell Hotel and Restaurant Administration Quarterly* 41 (4), 62–71.

Formica, S. and Olsen, M.D. (1998) Trends in the amusement park industry. *International Journal of Contemporary Hospitality Management* 10 (7), 297–308.

Foucault, M. (1979) *El ojo del poder.* Ediciones de la Piqueta, Madrid, Spain.

Foucault, M. (1988) *La arqueología del saber.* Siglo XXI, Mexico.

Fournié, A. (2001) Val d'Europe: un centre commercial régional de troisième génération. *Urbanisme*, November–December, 25–31.

Francaviglia, R. (1999) Walt Disney's Frontierland as an allegorical map of the American West. *Western Historical Quarterly* 30 (2), 155–182.

Francis, D.D. and Francis, D. (2004) *Cedar Point.* Arcadia Publishing, Mount Pleasant, Michigan.

Fyall, A. (2003) Marketing visitor attractions: a collaborative approach. In: Fyall, A., Garrod, B. and Leask, A. (eds) *Managing Visitor Attractions. New Directions.* Elsevier Butterworth–Heinemann, Oxford, pp. 236–252.

Galbraith, J.K. (1958) *The Affluent Society.* Hamish Hamilton, London.

Gallagher, M.R. (2002a) Shenzhen introduction. In: *National Planning Conference Proceedings.* American Planning Association, Chicago, Illinois.

Gallagher, M.R. (2002b) Shenzhen and Hong Kong: links and challenges. In: *National Planning Conference Proceedings.* American Planning Association, Chicago, Illinois.

García Canclini, N. (1995) Consumidores y ciudadanos. Conflictos multiculturales de la globalización. Grijalbo, Barcelona, Spain.

Garfield, R.A. (2004) How Disney targets the familiy vacation market. In: *The Complete 21st Century Travel and Hospitality Marketing Handbook.* Pearson and Prentice Hall, Upper Saddle River, New Jersey, pp. 169–179.

Garreau, J. (1991) *Edge City. Life on the New Frontier.* Anchor Books, New York.

Gatchalian, M.M., Gatchalian, J.C., Mamon, M.O. and Torres, L.C. (2004) Partnerships for quality, productivity, profitability: a reprise. In: *Quality Congress. 58th ASQ's Annual Quality Congress Proceedings.* American Society of Quality, Toronto, pp. 439–448.

Gélis, P. (2005) La sécurité, un enjeu majeur pour les parcs de loisirs. *Cahier Espaces* 86, 100–102.

Gilling, J. (1998) Dan Aylward. *Attractions Management*, October, 20, 22.

Gilling, J. (2001) Otto Wachs and Cornelius Everke. *Attractions Management* 6 (3), 14–17.

Goffman, E. (1970) *Internados.* Amorrortu Editores, Buenos Aires.

Gonzalez, A. (2005) Parcs de loisirs et internet. *Cahier Espaces* 86, 138–142.

González Reverté, F. and Anton Clavé, S. (2005) Fundamentos de la planificación territorial. In: Anton Clavé, S. and González Reverté, F. (coords) *Planificación territorial del turismo.* Edicions UOC, Barcelona, Spain, pp. 15–62.

Goodey, B. (1994) Interpretative planning. In: Harrison, R. (ed.) *Manual of Heritage Management*. Butterworth–Heinemann, Oxford, pp. 303–311.

Gottdiener, M. (1997) *The Theming of America. Dreams, Visions and Commercial Spaces*. Westview Press, Boulder, Colorado.

Gottdiener, M., Collins, C.C. and Dickens, D.R. (1999) *Las Vegas. The Social Production of an All-American City*. Blackwell Publishers, Malsen.

Goulding, P. (2003) Seasonality: the perennial challenge for visitor attractions. In: Fyall, A., Garrod, B. and Leask, A. (eds) *Managing Visitor Attractions. New Directions*. Elsevier Butterworth–Heinemann, Oxford, pp. 140–158.

Goytia, A. (2001) El fenómeno del ocio. ¿Amenaza para el patrimonio y el turismo cultural? *Boletín ADOZ* 21, 28–38.

Green, B. (1999) Sign, space and story: roller coasters and the evolution of a thrill. *Journal of Popular Culture* 33 (2) 1–22.

Grönroos, C. (1983) *Strategic Management and Marketing in the Service Sector*. Report No. 83-104. Swedish School of Economics and Business Administration, Helsinki.

Grover, R. (1997) *The Disney Touch. Disney, ABC and the Quest for the World's Greatest Media Empire*. Irwin Professional Publishing, Chicago, Illinois.

Gunn, C. (1994) *Tourism Planning. Basics, Concepts, Cases*. 3rd edn. Taylor and Francis, New York.

Guyomard, G. (2005) Définition des prix dans un parc de loisirs. Le cadre théorique. *Cahier Espaces* 86, 124–129.

Haahti, A. and Komppula, R. (2006) Experience design in tourism. In: Buhalis, D. and Costa, C. (eds) *Tourism Business Frontiers. Consumers, Products and Industry*. Elsevier, Oxford, UK, pp. 101–110.

Hachache, N. (1999) Les parcs à thèmes redémarrent. *Le Moniteur*, July, 26–29.

Handschuh, E. (1998) Disneyland Paris. Un équipement d'aménagement du territoire qui a resussi son intégration locale. *Cahier Espaces* 58, 97–106.

Hannigan, J. (1998) *Fantasy City. Pleasure and Profit in the Postmodern Metropolis*. Routledge, London.

Harvey, D. (1990) *The Condition of Postmodernity*. Blackwell, Cambridge, Massachusetts.

Hawkins, D. and Cunningham, J. (1996) It is 'Never-Never Land' when interest groups prevail. Disney's America Project, Prince William County, Virginia, USA. In: Harrison, L.C. and Husbands, W. (eds) *Practicing Responsible Tourism. International Case Studies in Tourism Planning, Policy and Development*. John Wiley and Sons, New York, pp. 350–365.

Hendry, J. (2000a) Foreign country theme parks: a new theme or an old Japanese pattern? *Social Science Japan Journal* 3 (2), 207–220.

Hendry, J. (2000b) *The Orient Strikes Back. A Global View of Cultural Display*. Berg, Oxford.

Herbert, D. (2001) Literary places, tourism and the heritage experience. *Annals of Tourism Research* 28, 312–333.

Hiaasen, C. (1991) *Native Tongue*. Ballantine Books, New York.

Hickman, J. and Mayer, K.J. (2003) Service quality and human resource practices: a theme park case study. *International Journal of Contemporary Hospitality Management* 15 (2), 116–119.

Hildebrandt, H.J. (1981) Cedar Point: a park in progress. *Journal of Popular Culture* 15 (1), 87–107.

Hill, C. (1999) Wax works. *Business Life*, November, 80–84.

Hilton, C.N. (1957) *Be my Guest*. Simon and Schuster, New York.

Hitchcock, M., Stanley, N. and King Chung, S. (1997) The South-east Asian 'Living Museum' and its antecedents. In: Abram, S., Waldren, J. and Macleod, D.V.L. (eds) *Tourists and Tourism. Identifying with People and Places.* Berg, Oxford, UK, pp. 197–221.

HKTDC (Hong Kong Trade Development Council) (2006) *PDR Economic Profile.* http://www.tdctrade.com

Hoai Anh, N. and Kleiner, B.H. (2005) Effective human resource management in the entertainment industry. *Management Research News* 28, 100–107.

Holt, D.B. and Schor, J.B. (2000) Do Americans consume too much? In: Schor, J.B. and Holt, D.B. (eds) *The Consumer Society Reader.* New Press, New York, pp. vii–xxiii.

Hood, G., Bachmann, B. and Jones, D.B. (1997) *Orlando. The City Beautiful.* Towery Publishing, Memphis, Tennessee.

Houellebecq, M. (2002) *Plataforma.* Anagrama, Barcelona, Spain.

Hovorka, J. (2000) *Cedar Fair.* Raymond James and Associates, Inc., St Petersburg.

Hsu, C.T. (1997) Master planning for successful theme park development. In: *Asia Pacific Theme Parks and Attractions '97 Conference.* Singapore. Not published.

HTR (1999) Les parcs de loisirs. L'apogée des forts en themes. *HTR,* December, 15–21.

Hummel, D. (2005) Futuroscope. La stratégie du 10,20,60. *Cahier Espaces* 86, 199–201.

Huxtable, A.L. (1997) *The Unreal America.* New Press, New York.

IAAPA (International Association of Amusement Parks and Attractions) (1993) *Guidelines to Establish Effective Operations Programs for Amusement Parks and Attractions.* IAAPA, Alexandria, Virginia.

IAAPA (International Association of Amusement Parks and Attractions) (2000) *Amusement Facility Operations Survey 2000.* IAAPA, Alexandria, Virginia.

Ibelings, H. (1998) *Supermodernism. Architecture in the Age of Globalization.* NAi Publishers, Amsterdam.

Jacques, C.J. (1997) Hersheypark: The Sweetness of Success. *Amusement Park Journal* Jefferson

Jacquin, J. (1993) Parcs de loisirs et développement local: deux expériences divergentes: le Futuroscope et Euro Disney. *Cahiers (Institut Français d'Urbanisme),* Vol. 5, 37–54.

Jamal, T. and Tanase, A. (2005) Impacts and conflicts surrounding Dracula Park, Romania: the role of sustainable tourism principles. *Journal of Sustainable Tourism* 13 (5), 440–455.

Jameson, F. (1984) Postmodernism, or the cultural logic of late capitalism. *New Left Review* 146, 58–92.

Jay, L.E. (1998) Total quality management within descentralized orientation process of the Walt Disney World Company. Thesis of Master of Arts in Education, Mount Saint Vincent University, Halifax, Nova Scotia.

Jenner, P. and Smith, C. (1996) Attendance trends at Europe's leisure attractions. *Travel and Tourism Analyst* 4, 72–93.

Johns, N. and Gyimóthy, S. (2002) Mythologies of a theme park: an icon of modern family. *Journal of Vacation Marketing* 8 (4), 320–331.

Jones, C.B., Robinett, J. and Zito, T. (1998) *The Future Role of Theme Parks in International Tourism.* http://www.erasf.com/erasf

Jones, T.S.M. (1994) Theme parks in Japan. *Progress in Tourism, Recreation and Hospitality Management* 6, 111–125.

Ju, C. and Li, S. (2005) *China Travel. Hot Spring for a Bright Future.* JP Morgan, Hong Kong.

Kaak, K.T. (1992) Theme parkarama. Thesis of Master of Science in Community and Regional Planning, University of Texas, Austin, Texas.

Kan, A.L. (2005) *Six Flags Inc. Initiating Coverage.* Morgan Stanley, New York.

Kazdoy, A. (2005) Cultural divide. *Funworld* 21 (2), 47–49.

Keil, R. (1994) Global sprawl: urban form after Fordism? *Environment and Planning D: Society and Space* 12, 131–136.

Kellner, D. (1999) Theorizing/resisting McDonaldization. A multiperspective approach. In: Smart, B. (ed.) *Resisting McDonaldization.* Sage, London, pp. 186–206.

Kemperman, A. (2000a) Temporal aspects of theme park choice bahavior. Modelling variety seeking, seasonality and diversification to support theme park planning. PhD, Technische Universiteit Eindhoven, Netherlands.

Kemperman, A. (2000b) Consumer choice of theme parks: a conjoint choice model of seasonality effects and variety seeking behaviour. *Leisure Sciences* 22, 1–18.

Kirsner, S. (1988) Hack the magic: the exclusive underground tour of Disney World. *Wired*, March, 162–168 and 186–198.

Klein, N. (1999) *No Logo. Taking Aim at the Brand Bullies.* Picador, New York.

Knipe, T. (2005) In Dubai, the situation is developing. *Amusement Business* 118 (1), 6–9.

Knipp, S. (2005) The Magic Kingdom comes to the Middle Kingdom. *Funworld* 21 (2), 32–37.

Knipp, S. (2006) Booming Macau. *Funworld* 22 (3), 60–64.

Koranteng, J. (2002) Future development to be centered on attractions, museums. *Amusement Business* 114 (27), 6.

Kotler, P. (1994) *Marketing Management: Analysis, Planning, Implementation and Control.* Prentice Hall, Englewood Cliffs.

Kotler, P., Hamlin, M.A., Rein, I. and Haider, D.H. (2002) *Marketing Asian Places. Attracting Investment, Industry and Tourism to Cities, States and Nations.* John Wiley & Sons Asia, Singapore.

Krutic, J. and Han, S. (2004) *Walt Disney Co. The Mouse Roars On.* City Group Smith Barney, New York.

Kurtti, J. (1996) *Since the World Began. Walt Disney World. The First 25 Years.* Hyperion, New York.

Kwong, H. (2005) *China Travel International. No Disney Magic for CTI.* GK Goh Research Pte Ltd.

Lafuste, P. (1998) Le role du marketing direct dans le développement d'un parc de loisirs. L'exemple du Futuroscope. *Cahier Espaces* 44, 103–106.

Lanchester, J. (2002) *Fragant Harbour.* Faber and Faber, London.

Lanquar, R. (1991) *Les Parcs de Loisirs.* PUF, Paris.

Lanquar, R. (1992) *L'Empire Disney.* PUF, Paris.

Lazzarotti, O. (1995) *Les Loisirs à la conquête des espaces périurbains.* L'Harmattan, Paris.

Lefebvre (1976) *The Survival of Capitalism.* Allen and Unwin, London.

Leman, E. (2003) Can the Pearl River Delta Region still compete? *China Business Review*, May–June, 6–17.

Lemoine, N. (2001) Quand Val d'Europe sert de laboratoire. *L'Hôtellerie*, March, 42–47.

Lewis, B.R. and Clacher, E. (2001) Service failure and recovery in UK theme parks: the employee's perspective. *International Journal of Contemporary Hospitality Management* 13 (4), 166–175.

Lewis, R.C. and Chambers, R.G. (1989) *Market Leadership in Hospitality.* Van Nostrand Reinhold, New York.

Liebrenz-Himes, M. and Ramsay, A. (2000) *Amusement and Attractions Operations.* IAAPA and the George Washington University, Alexandria, Virginia.

Lipietz, A. (1987) Un projet sans intérêt public? *Études Foncières* 34, 3–8.

Lockwood, C. (2000) Anaheim's excellent adventure. *Planning* 66 (12), 4–9.

Lodge, D. (1991) *Paradise News.* Penguin Books, London.

Lopes, E. (2002) El reto de la conservación ambiental y la diversificación del turismo masificado de balneario: el diseño de una estrategia para Caldas Novas, Brasil. PhD thesis, Department of Geography, Universitat Autònoma de Barcelona, Bellaterra, Spain.

Lounsberry, F. (2004) The theme park perspective. In: *The Complete 21st Century Travel and Hospitality Marketing Handbook.* Pearson and Prentice Hall, Upper Saddle River, New Jersey, pp. 181–189.

Lusignan, M.J. (1993) Romanticisme, féerie, fête et jeu: les origines des parcs d'amusement thématiques. Extraits de la thèse de doctorat d'Yves Robillard. *Téoros* 12 (3), 3–4.

Lynch, R. (2001) Ocio comercial y consumista. In: *Ocio y desarrollo. Potencialidades del ocio para el desarrollo humano.* Universidad de Deusto, Bilbao, Spain, pp. 167–203.

Lyon, R. (1987) Theme parks in the USA. Growth, markets and future prospects. *Travel and Toursim Analyst*, January, 31–42.

Lyotard, J.F. (1984) *La condición postmoderna.* Cátedra, Madrid, Spain.

MacCanell (1976) *The Tourist. A New Theory of the Leisure Class.* Schocken Books, New York.

McClung, G.W. (1991) Theme park selection. Factors influencing attendance. *Tourism Management* 12 (2), 132–140.

McClung, G.W. (2000) Theme park selection. Factors influencing attendance. In: Ryan, C. and Page, S. (eds) *Tourism Management: Towards the New Millennium.* Pergamon Press, New York.

MacDonald, G.F. and Alsford, S. (1995) Museums and theme parks: worlds in collision? *Museum Management and Curatorship* 14, 129–147.

McEniff, J. (1993) Theme parks in Europe. *Travel and Tourism Analyst* 5, 52–73.

Mack, R. (2005) Europa-Park vit l'innovation. *Cahier Espaces* 86, 60–63.

Mackenzie, E. (1994) *Privatopia: Houseowners Associations and the Rise of Residential Private Government.* Yale University Press, New Haven, Connecticut.

Maillard, J.P. (2003) La maîtrise foncière d'Euro Disney à Marne la Vallée. In: *Best Practices in Land Administration. Regional Perspectives. FIG Working Week.* International Federation of Surveyors, Paris. 8 pp.

Mangels, W.F. (1952) *The Outdoor Amusement Industry. From Earliest Times to the Present.* Vantage Press, New York.

Marcus, G. (1997) Forty years of overstatement: criticism and the Disney theme parks. In: Marling, K.A. (ed.) *Designing Disney's Theme Parks. The Architecture of Reassurance.* Canadian Centre for Architecture, Montreal, pp. 201–208.

Marcy, L.B. (1994) The evolution of Walt Disney World. *Urban Land*, October, 36–41, 84.

Marketdata Enterprises (1999) *The US Amusement and Theme Parks Industry. A Marketing, Operational and Competitive Analysis.* Marketdata Enterprises, Inc., Tampa, Florida.

Martí, J. and Comas, A. (1994) *La quiebra de la 'idea Disney' en París.* Tibidabo, Barcelona, Spain.

Martínez, L.D. (2001) Parque temático de Alicante, ocio o especulación. Negocios inmobiliarios en los alrededores de Terra Mítica. *El País*, 25 November.

Mason, D. and Opperman, J. (1996) The business of accounting for theme parks. *Bottomline* 11 (7), 11–22, 24.

Mayer, K.J. (2002) Human resource practices and service quality in theme parks. *International Journal of Contemporary Hospitality Management* 14 (4), 169–175.

Mercier, E. and Lasbleis, J.M. (2005) Disney, enterprise apprenante et diplômante. Le programme Hat. *Cahier Espaces* 86, 94–97.

Miller, R.K., Walker, T. and Pursell, C.E. (1999) *The 1999 Entertainment and Leisure Market Research Handbook.* Richard K. Miller & Associates, Inc., Norcross, Georgia.

Milman, A. (1993) *Theme parks and attractions.* In: *VNR'S Encyclopedia of Hospitality and Tourism.* Van Nostrand Reinhold, New York, pp. 934–944.

Milman, A. (2001) The future of the theme park and attraction industry: a management perspective. *Journal of Travel Research* 40, 139–147.

Milman, A. (2002) Hourly employee retention in the attraction industry: research from small and medium sized facilities in Orlando, Florida. *Journal of Leisure Property* 2 (1), 40–51.

Minca, C. (1996) *Spazi effimeri.* CEDAM, Padua, Italy.

Minton, E. (1998) Maps. *Funworld*, May, 70–75.

Mintz, L. (2004) In a sense abroad: theme parks and simulated tourism. In: Gmlech, S.B. (ed.) *Tourists and Tourism. A Reader.* Waveland Press, Long Grove, Illinois, pp. 183–192.

Mitrasinovic, M. (1996) *Theme Parks. Postmodern Landscapes.* http://web.nwe.ufl.edu/miodrag/postland.html

Molitor, G.T.T. (1999) The next 1,000 years: the 'big five' engines of economic growth. *The Futurist*, December, 13–18.

Mongon, E. (2001a) Le complexe français. *Espaces* 183, 22–24.

Mongon, E. (2001b) Commerce et loisirs. Des fiançailles à consomer! *Espaces* 178, 24–27.

Monory, R. (1992) Futuroscope: un concept de loisirs dynamique pour régénérer l'économie locale. *La Gazette Officielle du Tourisme*, 14 September, 5–12.

Montpetit, R. (1993) Sites historiques, musées de plein air et parcs thématiques: une recette américaine. *Téoros* 12 (3), 26–32.

More, T. (1977) [1516] *Utopia.* Bosch, Barcelona, Spain.

Mulard, C. (2003) NBC se donne les moyens de rivaliser avec les majors de la communication. *Le Monde*, 4 September, p. 16.

Mullins, P. (1991) Tourism urbanization. *International Journal of Urban and Regional Research* 15 (3), 326–342.

Münch, R. (1999) McDonaldized culture. The end of communication? In: Smart, B. (ed.) *Resisting McDonaldization.* Sage, London, pp. 135–147.

Murphy, P.E. (1997) Attraction land use management in Disney theme parks: balancing business and environment. In: Murphy, P.E. (ed.) *Quality Management in Urban Tourism.* John Wiley and Sons, Chichester, UK, pp. 221–223.

Nevin, T. (2005) At least, Africa to get its own theme park. *African Business* 308, 40–41.

Niu, H. (2002) Planning for rapid growth in Shenzhen, China. In: *National Planning Conference Proceedings*. American Planning Association, Chicago, Illinois.

Nogué, J. (2000) Paisatge, escala i percepció. La creació d'identitats territorials. *Debats d'Arquitectura i Urbanisme* 12, 29–35.

Nogué, J. and Vicente, J. (2001) *Geopolítica, identidad y globalización*. Ariel, Barcelona, Spain.

Norcliffe, G. (2001) Canada in a global economy. *The Canadian Geographer* 45 (1), 14–30.

Nye, R.B. (1981) Eight ways of looking at an amusement park. *Journal of Popular Culture* 15 (1), 63–75.

NYT (*New York Times*) (1994) Should Disney pave over our real past to promote a commercial fantasy? *New York Times*, 17 May, p. A9.

Oakes, T. (1998) *Tourism and Modernity in China*. Routledge, London.

O'Brien, G.M. (1981) The parks of Vienna. *Journal of Popular Culture* 15 (1), 76–86.

O'Brien, T. (1994) The parks. Of mice and men and machines. From Coney Island to Pleasure Island, the public's love affair with amusement parks endures. *Amusement Business. 100th Anniversary Special Edition,* November, 86–94.

O'Brien, T. (1998) Universal Studios Experience Beijing opens as culturally sensitive facility. *Amusement Business*, 28 September, 35.

O'Brien, T. (1999) Taiwan's $180 mil Discovery World set to open in 2001 with 24 rides. *Amusement Business*, 12 July, 36.

O'Brien, T. (2001a) Africa: North and South are bright spots. *Amusement Business* 113 (26), 22.

O'Brien, T. (2001b) Light at the end of the tunnel? *Amusement Business* 113 (26), 23.

Ogilvey, J. (1990) This postmodern business. *Marketing and Research Today* 18, 4–20.

Oliver, D. (1989) Leisure parks: present and future. *Tourism Management* 10, 233–234.

O'Neill, M. and Palmer, A. (2003) An exploratory study of the effects of experience on consumer perceptions of the service quality construct. *Managing Service Quality*, 13 (3), 187–196.

Ortiz, R. (1994) *Mundializaçao e cultura*. Brasiliense, São Paulo, Brazil.

Ouset, B. (1986a) Les parcs de loisirs. *Monuments historiques* 143, 67–71.

Ouset, B. (1986b) Les parcs d'attractions americains. *Monuments historiques* 143, 72–75.

Packman, H.M. and Casmir, F.L. (1999) Learning from the Euro Disney experience. A case study in international/intercultural communication. *Gazette* 61 (6), 473–489.

Paes de Barros, M. (1996) The Brazilian amusement industry. *Funworld*, June, 50–52.

Palmer, A. and O'Neill, M. (2003) The effects of perceptual processes on the measurement of service quality. *Journal of Services Marketing* 17 (3), 254–274.

Parasuraman, A., Zeithaml, V.A. and Berry, L.L. (1985) A conceptual model of service quality and its implications for future research. *Journal of Marketing* 49 (3), 41–50.

Parent, F. (1998) La famille des parcs s'est considérablement agrandie. Des parcs d'attractions aux écomusées, en passant par les parcs à thème et les aquariums. *Espaces* 58, 8–13.

Pelli, C. (1999) *Observations for Young Architects*. The Monacelli Press, New York.

Pine, B. and Gilmore, J. (1999) *The Experience Economy: Work is Theatre and Every Business a Stage.* Harvard Business School Press, Cambridge, Massachusetts.

Porter, M.E. (1985) *Competitive Advantage: Creating and Sustaining Superior Performance.* Free Press, Detroit, Michigan.

Powers, S. (2006) Parks in India, China's Future. Disney CEO: Lack of infrastructure, other issues in the way. *Knight Ridder Tribute Business News.* 2 March, p. 1.

PricewaterhouseCoopers (2004) European theme park wars: hotels help refresh park revenues. *Hospitality Directions. Europe Edition* 9.

Puydebat, J.M. (1998) Un centre d'interpretation n'est pas un parc à thème! L'exemple du château d'Auvers. *Cahier Espaces* 58, 46–51.

Rajaram, K. and Ahmadi, R. (2003) Flow management to optimize retail profits at theme parks. *Operations Research* 51 (2), 175–184.

Raz, A.E. (1997) The slanted smile factory: emotion management in Tokyo Disneyland. *Studies in Symbolic Interaction* 21, 201–217.

Raz, A.E. (1999) *Riding the Black Ship. Japan and Tokyo Disneyland.* Harvard University Press, Cambridge, Massachusetts.

Rebori, S.J. (1993) Theme parks: an analysis of Disney's planning, design and management philosophies in entertainment development. Thesis for Master of Science in Planning, University of Tennessee, Knoxville, Tennessee.

Rebori, S.J. (1995a) *Theme and Entertainment Park Developments: Planning, Design, Development, and Management.* Council of Planning Librarians, Chicago, Illinois.

Rebori, S.J. (1995b) *The Influence of the Disney Entertainment Parks on Architecture and Development.* Council of Planning Librarians, Chicago, Illinois.

Rebori, S.J. (1995c) *Disney and the Development of Vacation Destination Resorts.* Council of Planning Librarians. Chicago, Illinois.

Rector, K.R. (1997) Theme park project management for international design and construction. In: *Asia Pacific Theme Parks and Attractions '97 Conference.* Singapore. Not published.

Ren, H. (1998) Economies of culture: theme parks, museums and capital accumulation in China, Hong Kong and Taiwan. Thesis of Doctor of Philosophy, University of Washington, Seattle, Washington.

Richards, G. (2001) The experience industry and the creation of attractions. In: Richards, G. (ed.) *Cultural Attractions and European Tourism.* CAB International, Wallingford, UK, pp. 55–69.

Richards, G. and Richards, B. (1998) A globalised theme park market? The case of Disney in Europe. In: Laws, E., Faulkner, B. and Moscardo, G. (eds) *Embracing and Managing Change in Tourism. International Case Studies.* Routledge, London, pp. 365–378.

Rifkin, J. (2000) *The Age of Access. How the Shift from Ownership to Access is Transforming Modern Life.* Penguin Books, London.

Ritzer, G. (1996) *The McDonaldization of Society.* Pine Forge Press, Thousand Oaks, California.

Ritzer, G. (1999) *Enchanting a Disenchanted World. Revolutionizing the Means of Consumption.* Pine Forge Press, Thousand Oaks, California.

Ritzer, G. (2001) *Explorations in the Sociology of Consumption.* Sage, London.

Ritzer, G. and Liska, A. (1997) 'McDisneyization' and 'post-tourism'. Complementary perspectives on contemporary tourism. In: Rojek, C. and Urry, J. (eds) *Touring Cultures. Transformations of Travel and Theory.* Routledge, London, pp. 96–109.

Robathan, M. (2005) Creating Dubailand. *Leisure Management* 25 (5), 50–54.

Roberts, K. (1999) *Leisure in Contemporary Society*. CAB International, Wallingford, UK.

Robertson, R.W. (1993) Theme park development in S.E. Asia. *World Travel and Tourism Review* Vol. 3, pp. 151–155.

Robillard, Y. (1993) *Du jeu au développement économique: technopoles et parcs thématiques*. *Téoros* 12 (3), 39–42.

Robinett, J. (1992) *An Analysis of U.S. Theme Park Industry*. http://www.iaapa.org

Robinett, J. (1998) The fast show. *Attractions Management*, October, 9.

Robinett, J. (1999) Orlando: how high is up? *Attractions Management* 26–28.

Robinett, J. and Braun, R. (1990) A bumpy road building the European theme park industry. *Urban Land* 49 (9), 15–19.

Rohlen, T.P. (2000) *Hong Kong and the Pearl River Delta: one country, two systems in the emerging metropolitan context*. Working Paper, Shorenstein APARC, Stanford University, Los Angeles, California.

Rojek, C. (1985) *Capitalism and Leisure Theory*. Tavistock, London.

Rojek, C. (1993) *Ways of Escape. Modern Transformations in Leisure and Travel*. Rowman and Littlefield Publishers, Lanham, Maryland.

Rubin, J. (1997) Clash of the titans. *Leisure Management* 17 (10), pp. 20–27.

Rybczynski, W. (2001) Disney's new theme park in Anaheim tells a tale of California's history. *Architecture. The AIA Journal* 90 (3), 84–93.

Ryder, M.H. (1998) Legoland. In: *IAAPA Annual Convention and Trade Show*. IAAPA. Dallas, Texas. Not published.

Rymer, R. (1996) Back to the future. Disney reinvents the company town. *Harpers Magazine*, October, 65–78.

Salomao, M. (2000) *Parques de diversoes no Brasil: entretenimento, consumo e negócios*. Mauad, Rio de Janeiro.

Salvaneschi, L. (1996) *Location, Location, Location. How to Select the Best Site for Your Business*. The Oasis Press/PSI Research, Grants Pass, Oregon.

Samuels, J.B. (1996) Trends in growth and segmentation of the theme/amusement park industry. *Visions in Leisure and Business* 15 (3), 6–12.

Samuelson, D. and Yegoiants, W. (2001) *The American Amusement Park*. MBI Publishing, Saint Paul, Minnesota.

Sánchez, A. (1998) Le concept de parc à thème. Définition, évolution et perspectives. *Cahier Espaces* 58, 14–23.

Sargent, P. (2001) Divine Inspiration. *Attractions Management* 6 (3), 44–47.

Sasaki, K., Harada, M. and Morino, S. (1997) Economic impacts of theme-park development by input–output analysis: a process toward local industrialization of leisure services. *Managing Leisure* 2, 29–38.

Savage, V.R., Huang, S. and Chang, T.C. (2004) The Singapore River thematic zone: sustainable tourism in an urban context. *Geographical Journal* 170 (3), 212–225.

Schaffer, S. (1996) Disney and the imagineering of histories. *Postmodern Cultures* 6 (3). http://muse.jhu.edu/journals/postmodern_culture/v006/6.3schaffer.html

Scheer, M. (2000) *Der themenpark 'Universal PortAventura' von Salou, Provinz Tarragona. Entwicklung eines modernen Grossprojectes für Freizeit und Erholung und seine Auswirkungen auf den Tourismus in der Region Katalonien*. Katholischen Universität Eichstätt, Eichstätt, Germany.

Scheurer, R. (2002) Theme park tourist destinations: creating an experience setting in traditional tourist destinations. In: Weiermair, K. and Mathies, C. (eds) *The Tourism and Leisure Industry Shaping the Future*. Research

Institute for Leisure and Tourism, University of Berne, Berne, Switzerland, pp. 227–236.

Schiller, H.I. (1973) *The Mind Managers*. Beacon Press, Boston, Massachusetts.

Schoolfield, J. (2005) Three of a kind. *Funworld* 21 (11), 50–56.

Scott Brown, D. (1976) On architectural formalism and social concern: a discourse for social planners and radical chic architects. *Oppositions* 5, 99–112.

Scully, V. (1996) Disney: theme and reality. In: Dunlop, B. (ed.) *Building a Dream. The Art of Disney Architecture*. Harry N. Abrams, New York, pp. 7–11.

Shaw, G. and Williams, A.M. (2004) *Tourism and Tourism Spaces*. Sage, London.

Shields, R. (1991) *Places on the Margin. Alternative Geographies of Modernity*. Routledge, London.

Six Flags (2005) *The Technologies of Six Flags Rollercoasters: Safety by Design*. Six Flags, Oklahoma City, Oklahoma.

Smith, M. (2006) Entertainment and new leisure tourism. In: Buhalis, D. and Costa, C. (eds) *Tourism Business Frontiers. Consumers, Products and Industry*. Elsevier, Oxford, UK, pp. 220–227.

Smoodin, E. (1994) Introduction: how to read Walt Disney. In: Smoodin, E. (ed.) *Disney Discourse: Producing the Magic Kingdom*. Routledge, New York, pp. 1–20.

Sofield, T.H.B. (2001) Globalisation, tourism and culture in Southeast Asia. In: Teo, P., Chang, T.C. and Ho, K.C. (eds) *Interconnected Worlds. Tourism in Southeast Asia*. Pergamon, Oxford, UK, pp. 103–120.

Sontag, S. (1961) *Against Interpretation and Other Essays*. A Delta Book, New York.

Sorkin, M. (1992a) Introduction: variations on a theme park. In: Sorkin, M. (ed.) *Variations on a Theme Park. The New American City and the End of Public Space*. Noonday, New York, pp. xi–xv.

Sorkin, M. (1992b) See you in Disneyland. In: Sorkin, M. (ed.) *Variations on a Theme Park. The New American City and the End of Public Space*. Noonday, New York, pp. 205–232.

Spiegel, D. (1999) Challenging rides. *Attractions Management* 4 (10), 36–37.

Spirn, A.W. (1998) *The Language of Landscape*. Yale University Press, New Haven, Connecticut.

Stern, R.A.M. (1992) The pop and the popular at Disney. *Architectural Design* 62 (7/8), 20–23.

Stevens, T. (2000) The future of visitor attractions. *Travel and Tourism Analyst* 1, 61–85.

Stevens, T. (2003) The future of visitor attractions. In: Fyall, A., Garrod, B. and Leask, A. (eds) *Managing Visitor Attractions. New Directions*. Elsevier Butterworth–Heinemann, Oxford, UK, pp. 284–298.

STI (Société de Tourisme International) (2000) *Analyse des retombées économiques et sociales de Disneyland Paris. Bilan 1999*. EPA France, Paris.

STI (Société de Tourisme International) (2002a) *Analyse des retombées économiques et sociales de Disneyland Paris. Bilan 2001*. EPA France, Paris.

STI (Société de Tourisme International) (2002b) *Analyse des retombées économiques et sociales de Disneyland Paris. Rapport sur l'impact hotelier de Disneyland Paris. Actualization pour l'année 2001*. EPA France, Paris.

Storey, J. (1995) *Human Resource Management. A Critical Text*. Routledge, London.

Storey, J. (1998) *An Introduction to Cultural Theory and Popular Culture*. University of Georgia Press, Athens, Georgia.

Stynes, D.J. (1997) *Economic Impacts of Tourism.* Illinois Bureau of Tourism, Chicago, Illinois.

Sudjic, D. (1992) *The 100 Mile City.* Harcourt Brace and Company, San Diego, California.

Swain, M. (1989) Developing ethnic tourism in Hunnan, China: Shilin Sani. *Tourism Recreation Research* 14, 33–9.

Swarbrooke, J. (2001) Key challenges for visitors attraction managers in the UK. *Journal of Leisure Property* 1 (4), 318–336.

Swarbrooke, J. (2002) *The Development and Management of Visitor Attractions.* Butterworth-Heinemann, Oxford, UK.

Swartzman, E. (1995) Main attractions. *Leisure Management* 15 (9), 65–67.

Taylor, R. and Stevens, T. (1995) An American adventure in Europe: an analysis of the performance of Euro Disneyland (1992–1994). *Managing Leisure* 1, 28–42.

TEA (Themed Entertainment Association) (2000) How to design and build a themed attraction. Guidelines to project development and team building process. In: *IAAPA 2000 Convention and Trade Show.* Georgia World Congress Center, Atlanta. Not published.

Tenner, A.R. and DeToro, I.J. (1992) *Total Quality Management: Three Steps to Continuous Improvement.* Addison Wesley, Cambridge, Massachusetts.

Teo, P. and Yeoh, B.S.A. (2001) Negotiating global tourism: localism as difference in Southeast Asian theme parks. In: Teo, P., Chang, T.C. and Ho, K.C. (eds) *Interconnected Worlds. Tourism in Southeast Asia.* Pergamon, Oxford, UK, pp. 137–154.

The Project on Disney (1995) *Inside the Mouse. Work and Play at Disney World.* Duke University Press, Durham, North Carolina.

Thompson, G.M. (1999) Labor scheduling, Part 4. Controlling workforce schedules in real time. *Cornell Hotel and Restaurant Administration Quarterly* 40, 85–96.

Tocqueville, A. de (1985) [1835] *La democracia en América.* Orbis, Barcelona, Spain.

Tomes, A.E. and Hwang, S.J. (1995) A study of visitors' attitudes to theme parks in Taiwan. In: Jobber, D. (ed.) *Making Marketing Work.* Marketing Education Group Annual Conference, University of Bradford, Bradford, UK, pp. 806–815.

Tomlinson, A. (1990) Consumer culture and the aura of the commodity. In: *Consumption, Identity and Style. Marketing, Meanings and the Packaging of Pleasure.* Routledge, London, pp. 1–38.

Torrado, A. and Sardà, A. (1995) Parques temáticos: la atracción del siglo. *Anuario de los temas*, Planeta Barcelona, pp. 416–433.

TRM (1995) *Theme Parks. UK and International Markets.* Tourism Research and Marketing, London.

Trowbridge, E.H. (1994) Public sector funding for theme and amusement parks through bond financing in Arizona (a case study). In: *Proceedings of the Environments for Tourism Conference.* William F. Harrah College of Hotel Administration, University of Nevada, Las Vegas, Nevada, pp. 490–496.

Tuan, Y.-F. (1998) *Escapism.* Johns Hopkins University Press, Baltimore, Maryland.

Tuan, Y.-F. and Hoelscher, S.D. (1997) Disneyland: its place in the world culture. In: Marling, K.A. (ed.) *Designing Disney's Theme Parks. The Architecture of Reassurance.* Canadian Centre for Architecture, Montreal, pp. 191–200.

Tyrell, B. and Mai, R. (2001) *Leisure 2010. Experience Tomorrow.* Jones Lang La Salle, Henley, UK.

Urry, J. (1990) *The Tourist Gaze. Leisure and Travel in Contemporary Societies.* Sage, London.

Urry, J. (2002) *The Tourist Gaze. Leisure and Travel in Contemporary Societies,* 2nd edn. Sage, London.

Valenti, M. (1997) The fantastical meets the practical. *Mechanical Engineering,* December, 66–71.

Valls, J.F. and Mitjans, A. (2001) El futuro de los parques temáticos en Europa. In: *IV Congreso de Turismo Universidad y Empresa.* Benicàssim, Spain.

Van Assendelft de Coningh, R. (1994) Marketing a theme park: Efteling. *Journal of Vacation Marketing* 1 (2), 190–194.

Van Eeden, J. (2004) The colonial gaze: imperialism, myths and South African popular culture. *Design Issues* 20 (2), 18–33.

Veal, A.J. (1998) Leisure studies, pluralism and social democracy. *Leisure Studies* 12 (1), 33–44.

Veblen, T. (1953) [1899] *The Theory of the Leisure Class.* Mentor, New York.

Venturi, R., Scott Brown, D. and Izenour, S. (1972) *Learning from Las Vegas. The Forgotten Symbolism of Architectural Form.* MIT Press, Cambridge, Massachusetts.

Vittachi, N. (1995) Global Village (surreal Shenzhen brings the world's wonders to China). *Far Eastern Economic Review* 158, 36–37.

Vitte, P. (2002) *Le Pole urbain Val-d'Europe–Disneyland–Paris dans l'aménagement de l'est francilien.* Conseil Economique et Social, Région Ile de France, Paris.

Vogel, H.L. (2001) *Entertainment Industry Economics. A Guide for Financial Analysis.* Cambridge University Press, Cambridge.

Walsh, D.J. (1992) The evolution of the Disneyland environs. *Tourism Recreation Research* 17 (1), 33–47.

Wanhill, S. (2005a) Interpreting the development of the visitor attraction product. In: Fyall, A., Garrod, B. and Leask, A. (eds) *Managing Visitor Attractions. New Directions.* Elsevier Butterworth–Heinemann, Oxford, UK, pp. 16–35.

Wanhill, S. (2005b) Economic aspects of developing theme parks. In: Fyall, A., Garrod, B. and Leask, A. (eds) *Managing Visitor Attractions. New Directions.* Elsevier Butterworth–Heinemann, Oxford, UK, pp. 39–57.

Ward, M.E. (1997) Orlando's Cinderella story. *Funworld,* October, 70–77.

Warren, S. (1996) Popular cultural practices in the 'postmodern city'. *Urban Geography* 17 (6), 545–567.

Watson, S. and McCracken, M. (2005) Visitor attractions and human resource management. In: Fyall, A., Garrod, B. and Leask, A. (eds) *Managing Visitor Attractions. New Directions.* Elsevier Butterworth–Heinemann, Oxford, UK, pp. 171–187.

Weedon, G. and Ward, R. (1981) *Fairground Art: the Art Forms of Traveling Fairs, Carousels and Carnival Midways.* White Mouse Editions, London.

Weinstein, R.M. (1992) Disneyland and Coney Island: reflections on the evolution of the modern amusement park. *Journal of Popular Culture* 26 (1), 131–164.

Whaley, F. (2001) Move over Mickey. *Asian Business* 37 (5), 28.

Willis, S. (1993) Disney World: public use/private space. *South Atlantic Quarterly* 92 (1), 119–137.

Wolf, M.J. (1999) *The Entertainment Economy. How Mega-media Forces are Transforming our Lives.* Times Books, New York.

Wong, K.K.F. and Cheung, P.W.Y. (1999) Strategic theming in theme park marketing. *Journal of Vacation Marketing* 5 (4), 319–332.

Wong, Y.C. and Tan, K.L. (2004) Emergence of cosmopolitan space for culture and consumption: the New World Amusement Park–Singapore (1923–70) in the interwar years. *Inter-Asia Cultural Studies* 5 (2), 279–304.

Wootton, G. and Stevens, T. (1994) Staying alive. How will future trends affect theme parks? *Leisure Management*, December, 43–44.

Wylson, A. and Wylson, P. (1994) *Theme Parks, Leisure Centres, Zoos and Aquaria.* Longman, London.

Xie, P.F. and Wall, G. (2005) Authenticating visitor attractions based upon ethnicity. In: Fyall, A., Garrod, B. and Leask, A. (eds) *Managing Visitor Attractions. New Directions.* Elsevier Butterworth–Heinemann, Oxford, UK, pp. 107–123.

Yeoh, B.S.A. and Teo, P. (1996) From Tiger Balm Gardens to Dragon World: philanthropy and profit in the making of Singapore's first cultural theme park. *Geografiska Annaler* 78B, 27–42.

Yoshii, C.L. (2002) *International Theme Park Development and Trends, Implications and Lessons Learned for China.* Shenzhen. http://www.erasf.com/erasf/papers.

Young, T. and Riley, R. (eds) (2002) *Theme Park Landscapes: Antecedents and Variations.* Dumbarton Oaks Research Library, Washington, DC.

Zins, M. (1993) Enjeux stratégiques des parcs thématiques: Amérique du Nord et Europe. *Téoros* 12 (3), 5–9.

Zoltak, J. (1998) China: theme park market for new millennium? *Amusement Business*, 14 September, pp. 2 and 60.

Zukin, S. (1991) Disney World: the power of facade/the facade of power. In: *Landscapes of Power: from Detroit to Disney World.* University of California Press, Berkeley, California, pp. 217–250.

Zukin, S. (1995) Learning from Disney World. In: *The Cultures of Cities.* Blackwell, Cambridge, Massachusetts, pp. 48–77.

Index

ageography 155, 193, 214
amusement parks 4, 5, 6, 7, 8, 10, 11, 12–16,
        18–20, 21, 24, 26, 38, 46, 60, 64, 90, 107,
        121, 191, 385
    as a theme 37
    trolley parks 15
amusement scape 4
aquariums 129, 168
art galleries 169
attractions and rides 14–15 169, 318, 352, 365,
        374, 379, 391, 398
    flow management 383–384
    operation and maintenance 350, 396
    risks 362
    roller coasters 39, 47, 51, 71, 121, 150, 152,
        362, 375
    safety 424–426
    trends 380–381
    types 110, 320, 375–377
attendance 323, 325, 326–327, 357, 358
    effects of the addition of a new gate 341–342
    effective market 322
    influencing factors 327, 331, 345, 348, 413
    market areas 239, 246, 248, 322, 323, 325,
        326–327, 357, 370
    market penetration 322, 323–325, 326, 344
    market size 322–329
    potential market 64, 286, 310–313, 322,
        323–324, 356
    recurrence rates 345, 348
    repetition rates 344–345
authenticity 21, 158, 167, 168, 169, 178, 186, 208,
        212, 217, 218, 220, 222, 260, 264

brand 108, 119, 160, 412, 415
    branded chains 169
    branded cities see cities
    branded environments 164, 299
    branded lifestyle 213, 299
    branding 42, 320
    corporate lands 95
    theme parks as brands 38–39, 95, 135, 151
business environment 186, 337–340

casinos 168, 169, 176

cathedrals of consumption 21, 167, 168, 169, 181,
        182
centres for scientific divulgation 168
characters 24, 123, 169, 181, 189–190, 261
cities
    as theme parks 191
    as tourism hubs 76
    branded cities 213, 221
    compact cities 192, 205
    crisis of traditional cities 205
    edge cities 204, 233
    fragmented cities 275
    French new towns 291, 299
    heteropolis 204
    hypercities 208
    incremental cities 193, 194
    postindustrial cities 208
    problems 192, 204–205, 206
    suburbs 204–205, 240
    themed cities 165
City Walk 61, 115, 120, 181, 199, 204, 213, 232,
        276, 280
commodified spaces 169
consumption 1, 3, 10, 12, 21, 23, 104, 156, 157,
        160, 161, 165, 166, 167, 191, 205,
        208–209, 260, 262–263, 409–410
corporate social responsibility 189, 419–424
    and quality management systems 421
    charities 423, 424, 427
corporate visitor centres 168
cruises 168, 169, 176
cultural impact 261–264, 287, 290–291
cultural theme parks 34, 36, 77–78, 169, 183, 220,
        242, 260, 263, 268–269
culture 156, 158
    commodification 160, 163, 192, 194, 220,
        240, 244, 260, 261, 268–269
    cultural capital 42, 159, 160, 161, 170, 240,
        244, 269
    cultural studies 156, 264
    identity 183, 262, 263
    international popular culture 160, 181, 261
    mass media culture 160
    popular culture 160–169, 263
    stereotypes 163
    suburban culture 23

Disneyfication 156, 180
Disneylandization 156
Disneyization 156, 177–187, 220

ecohistorical theme parks 71, 147, 187–189
   see also cultural theme parks
economic impact 233, 234–238, 243, 246,
      273–285, 285, 297–299, 305–306, 329
   job creation 150, 152–153, 225, 226, 233,
      234–235, 239, 276, 285, 294, 298
entertainment architecture 191, 194, 198, 199, 208
entertainment economy 299–310
entertainment experience 3, 5, 24, 30, 121, 158,
      159, 160, 161, 163, 164, 166, 182, 191,
      198, 205, 205, 374
entertainment society 23, 150, 151, 155, 161, 163
environmental impact 250–257
Environmental Impact Assessment 252, 253, 257,
      265–268, 306
environmental protection measures 264–268
environmentally sustainable practices 45, 127,
      132, 224, 252, 253, 255, 256, 257, 332,
      421, 423

fairs 1, 3, 4, 5, 6, 8, 12, 13, 21, 24
festival market places 169
film and TV production 104–105, 116–117, 119,
      124, 128, 145, 165, 236, 283
film exhibition 16–18, 145–146
film techniques 5, 16–18, 160, 169, 195, 233, 368,
      374
financial aspects
      costs 355, 356, 362
      feasibility analysis 351, 355
      investment 82, 345, 349, 355
      operating plan 345
      operation measures 345, 355, 356, 360, 361,
         362
      performance measures 388–389
      profit 348, 382–384
      profit centre 388
      rate of return 348
      reinvestment 70, 71, 109, 348
      resources 186
      sources of income 355, 356–361
      sponsorship 360–363
      strategies to increase income 386–387
      strategies to reduce costs 387–388
      visitor per capita expenditure 50–51, 66, 73,
         356, 357, 360
      visitor per capita income 50–51, 66, 73,
         357, 359
      yield management 386
flows management 211, 318, 354–355, 366,
      370–373, 379, 383–384
Fordism 23, 170, 172, 186, 187
      crisis 170, 171
      transition to post-Fordism 177
Frankfurt School 160, 260
fun shopping 179

gaming 309–310
gardens 5, 5–8, 13, 24, 168, 193, 194, 195, 201, 219
      and natural parks 8
      picnic groves 8
      pleasure gardens 6, 7, 8, 15
      royal and aristocratic gardens 6, 7, 15
global–local relations and influences 76–77
globalization 1, 48–92, 160, 183, 189–190, 192,
      220, 261–264
government support 72, 225, 230–233, 241–243,
      244–246, 249, 273, 290, 334–336

heritage sites 35, 147, 168, 217, 220, 242, 259,
      263, 310
hotel business in theme parks 70, 278–279, 289,
      311–313
human resources management 175, 182, 350, 353,
      361, 385, 386, 400–409, 422
hyperreality 168, 184, 186

imagescape 320, 322, 327–328, 328–329
Industrial Revolution 5, 161, 162
information management system 171, 388, 412
internet 312, 313, 404, 416, 417, 417–418, 427

landscape of consumption 159, 162, 168216
landscape of production 159
late-modern society 4, 21
      see also postmodernism
leisure 1, 18–20, 23, 157, 158, 159, 160, 161–166,
      167, 178–179
leisure complexes 30, 61–62, 198, 200, 244, 272
      as corporate environments 293–297, 310–313
      as policy tools 227–228, 233
      development 200, 221–223, 248
      evolution model 200–201, 202
      themed 166–170
lifestyles 161, 164, 165, 413
location 64, 317, 321–336
      in Asia/the Pacific 75
      in Europe 66, 68
      in Latin America 87
      in USA and Canada 61–62
      metropolitan 60
      periurban 227–228, 233
      trends 240

Main Street 26, 194, 196, 205, 206, 211, 368
maps 373
marketing 193, 386, 409–417
      channels 312, 418
      customer complaints 182, 398
      customer loyalty 418
      customer relationship management 418
      customer satisfaction 352, 386, 389
      market analysis and research 311, 322, 409,
         412
      market–imagescape mix 328
      market segmentation 171, 358
      marketing mix 412, 412–417
      merchandising 211, 386, 415
      plans 350, 411–412
      promotion and advertising 312–317
         415–417
      strategies 311–313, 357, 411, 417–419
McDonaldization 170–177, 180, 182, 187
means of consumption 166
mobility 198, 206, 207, 211, 254
museums 160, 168, 169, 182, 191, 208, 220

natural resources 168
nature theme parks 169, 187–189
      see also ecohistorical theme parks
neo-Marxists 161–260
      see also post-Marxism

operations management 350, 358, 389–400
      procurement and distribution 392–393
      production processes 352
      purchasing processes 392
      Real Time Control Systems 174–175, 402
      storage 393

place 158, 193, 208, 329–334, 413
  corporate places 201, 209, 217
  identity 71, 183, 206, 209, 215–220, 261, 268
  leisure places 193
  non places 216
  on the margin 194
  place marketing 169
  privatization 209, 210–215, 215
  sense of place 197, 201, 206, 207, 385
  total design places 193, 194, 205, 212
post-estructuralism 156
post-Fordism 158, 164, 170–171, 172, 174, 177, 186,
post-Marxism 156
  see also neo-Marxists
postmodernism 156, 158, 167, 177, 181, 183–187, 187, 264
  see also late-modern society
pricing policies 109, 356, 357, 358, 359, 360, 414–415, 418
privatopia 214
product life cycle 320, 333, 411
project management techniques 349, 350
property development 44–45, 153–154, 165

quality 386, 390, 391–392, 393, 396, 398–400, 401 406, 412
  quality management systems 360, 398, 399
queue management systems 101, 371, 372–373, 398, 418

regional development 170, 225, 238–246, 249, 269, 273–285, 299
resort 191, 199, 248

safety 192, 391, 393, 395–396, 397, 398, 424–426, 427
  safety standards 395
  see also security and safety
science parks 168
seasonality 393, 402
security and safety 177, 350, 355, 375, 386, 389
  see also safety
service product 385
shopping malls 76, 165, 169, 176, 182, 191, 205
shows 352, 372, 374, 377–379, 392
  animators 377
  audiovisual 378–379
  simulators 379
  street entertainment 378
  technical productions 378
social construction of space 165, 201, 209
social impact 257, 258–260
  opposition 259–260, 263
  social benefits 258
  social perception 259–260
social organization of work 162
society of spectacle 157
spatial innovation 198, 203, 209–220
spectacle 5, 11, 21, 169, 183
sports parks 168
stadiums 168
sustainable development 187, 187–189, 250–251, 252–253, 257, 258–259, 400, 419–424
SWOT analysis 411
symbolic capital *see* cultural capital

taste 161, 164, 386
theme 32, 33, 33–34, 36, 37, 193, 195, 198
theme parks
  and media industry 41–43, 119

and regional policy 225, 226, 239–240, 249, 256, 296
and tourism development 333
and urban planning 191–220
as cultural creations 1, 3, 17, 21, 22, 24, 43–44, 194, 195
as 'good image' 228, 242, 245
as imaginary worlds 17, 193, 195, 196, 197, 203
as invented/symbolic/closed spaces 6, 31–32,168, 169, 176, 193
as a product 317, 318–321, 322, 328, 412
as tourist destinations 64, 272, 273, 278, 286, 310–313
challenges 40–41
concept and definition 5, 12, 21–22, 23, 27–28, 28–29, 31 49, 107–110, 117–118, 168
construction 349–351
corporate operators 57–58, 93, 96–97, 98, 100–128, 128, 129–137, 137–144, 145–146, 147, 147–149
design 22, 191, 194–195, 196–197, 315, 344, 345, 365
  design day 345, 369, 379, 382
  hub and spoke 366–367
  layout 352–254, 366, 372, 393
  loop 367
  peak day 369
development phases 343, 350
emerging country markets
  Brazil 86–87, 90–92
  China 81–83, 308–309
  India 83–84
  Japan 79–81
global market evolution 49, 56–64, 71
history 23–36
  opening dates of Asian/Pacific parks 80–81
  opening dates of Brazilian parks 91
  opening dates of European parks 67–68
  opening dates of USA/Canada parks 54–55
logistics 353–354, 390–391, 391–396
maintenance 192, 353, 393–395
management 101–102, 315–316, 385–424
models in Asia 77–78
multipark destination 30–31, 100, 112, 341–342
planning 343–344, 344–351, 355
  Master Plan 345–348
regional markets
  Asia 51, 53, 72–84, 85, 137
  Australia 84
  Europe 53, 64–72, 93, 109–111, 150, 159, 180, 249, 413, 415
  Latin America 85–90
  USA and Canada 51, 53, 56–64, 94–98
restaurants 352, 356, 381–383
risks and emergencies 102, 291, 332, 396
shops 352, 356, 372, 381–382, 383, 383–384
success factors 37–41, 159, 317, 337–340, 386
transportation 329–330
types 29–31, 57, 56, 61, 69, 246, 325
visitors per regions 52
  Asia/Pacific 74
  Europe 65
  Latin America 86, 88
  USA and Canada 58–59
  world 54–55
world distribution 53, 55, 56, 57
world market 49, 49–56
themed architecture 181
themed environments 168, 169, 175
themed landscapes 168, 169
themed spaces 168, 169

theming 16, 35, 125, 168, 169, 181, 211, 260, 269,
    318, 320, 365,
theories of consumerism 183–185
theories of consumption 180
theories of regulation 177
theory of rationalization 176, 180
three-minute culture 167
tourism 11, 165, 167, 169, 185, 193, 194,
    208–209, 220, 422,
tourism impact 3, 224, 242–243, 245–246,
    246–250, 272–273, 280–282, 305–306,
    310–313

universal expositions 5, 8–12, 28, 201
    chronology 9
    of Chicago 10–11, 14, 151, 377
    of New York 11–12, 211
    of Saint Louis 46, 125
universal fairs *see* universal expositions

urban entertainment centres 179, 199
urbanism
    and theme parks 201–209
    corporative urbanism 198, 201, 285–299
    urban design 193–195, 270–271
    urban development 198, 251, 292
    urban impact 224
    urban life 192, 194
    urban order 197
    urban planning 156, 191, 192, 194, 201,
        203, 210, 228, 270–271
    urban renovation 233
visitor
    attractions 168, 185
    experience 197, 398
    management tools 257
    services 159
    with special needs 327, 353–355, 363–364
water parks 136–137, 141, 168
world fairs *see* universal expositions

PARKS AND ATTRACTIONS INDEX

(Only when parks and attractions appear in text)
Adventure Dome 53, 57
Adventure World 89
Africa the Park 89
AgroTourism Resort 78
Alhokairland 89
Al Shallal Festival 89
Alton Towers 66, 70, 71, 129, 330, 412
American Dream 230
Anheuser Busch, 57, 59, 63, 93, 94, 121,
        124–128, 129, 240–243, 335, 361, 423
    Adventure Islands 127
    Busch Entertainment Corporation 125, 126,
        189, 226
    Busch Gardens Conservation Fund 127–128
    Busch Gardens Europe 35, 126, 150, 226,
        239, 240, 240–243, 264, 331
    Busch Gardens Tampa 126, 176, 226, 377
    corporate social responsibility 423
    Discovery Cove 127, 63
    financial data 128
    history 125
    number of visitors 127
    SeaWorld parks *see* SeaWorld
    Sesame Place 31, 126, 189, 190
    Water Country USA 127
Aqualand 168
Aquarium de La Rochelle 168
Asia-Pacific Family Centre 78
Autostatd 71

Baba Nonya Heritage Village 215
Bakken 15
Bandar Sunway *see* Sunway City
Beijing Amusement park 82, 138
Big Bang Schtroumpf *see* Walibi Lorraine
Bioscope 136, 335
Blackpool Pleasure Beach 15, 53, 55, 64, 70, 129
Boardwalk and Baseball 126
Bonfante Gardens 31, 71
Boomers 95

Cable Sports World 84
Canada World 78
Caribbean Bay 141
Carthago Adventureland 89
Castle Park 95
Cedar Fair 23, 57, 63, 94, 109, 121–124, 361, 412
    Castaway Bay Indoor Waterpark Resort 124

Cedar Point 121, 124, 325, 375
    history 45–47
    roller coasters 47
Dorney park 121
financial data 123
Geuga Lake 107, 122
history 121–123
Knott's Berry Farm 23, 121–122, 123
Knott's Soak City 124
Michigan's Adventure 122
number of visitors 122
Paramount Parks *see* Paramount Parks
parks 59, 93, 95, 98, 325, 331, 357, 370
portfolio of parks 124
Valleyfair 122
Worlds of Fun 121, 124
Chessington Zoo 131
Chicago Railroad Fair 25
China Travel International Investment Hong Kong
        Ltd 137, 142–144
    China Folk Culture Village 36, 78, 308, 309
    financial data 143
    Happy Valley 73, 142, 308
    number of visitors 144
    Splendid China 77, 180, 260, 308
    Window of the World 308, 412
Chinese Ethnic Culture Park 82, 263
Chinese Garden 77, 220
Church Street Station 276
Cité de la Bière 183
Cité des Insectes 168
Colonial Virgina Historic Triangle 241, 243
Corporación Interamericana de Entretenimiento
        85–86, 128, 147–149
    La Feria de Chapultepec 86, 149
    Planeta Azul 149
    Salitre Mágico 86
    Selva Mágica 86
    Wanadoo City 149
Corrumbin Sanctuary 84
Cosmos Park 330
Cypress Gardens 126, 276

Dadda 87
Daneishe Promenade 308
Delivery and Event 71
Dinópolis 72
Discovery World 76
Disney *see* Walt Disney Company
Donjon des Aigles 168

Dorney park 60
Dracula Park 262
Dragon World 35, 180, 219 *see* also Haw Par Villa
Dreamland 14, 15, 380
Dreamland park, Nara 101
Dreamworks 63
Dreamworld 78, 84, 333
Dubailand 89, 130, 221–223
Dutch Wonderland 152

Ecomusée d'Alsace 168
Eden Project 168
Efteling 35, 43–44, 64, 69, 129, 149–151, 217,
        239, 264, 333, 415
Enchanted Kingdom 30, 400
Europa Park 30, 64, 69, 70, 129, 149–151, 217,
        239, 264, 333, 415
Evergreen Park 308
Everland 55, 73, 137, 139, 141–142, 333

Fox Studios Park 84
Freedomland 26
Frobelland 330
Futuroscope 41, 69, 72, 168, 183, 239, 240,
        243–246, 248, 334, 340, 308, 354, 378,
        399, 413, 415

Gardaland 64, 70, 359, 415
Gene Autry Heritage Museum, Los Angeles 211
Gold Reef City 89
Grand Parc du Puy du Fou 34, 71, 268–269, 378
Great World and New World, Shanghai 19
Grévin et Cie 71, 129, 133–136, 236, 335
        Bagatelle 133
        Bellewaerde Park 134
        Bioscope *see* Bioscope
        Parc Astérix *see* Parc Astérix
        porfolio of parks 134
        Walibi parks *see* Walibi
Grupo Xcaret 187–189
        Garrafón 86, 187–189
        Parque Ecoturístico Cañón del Sumidero 188
        Xcaret 86, 169, 187–189, 253, 259
        Xel-Ha 86, 187–189

Happy Valley Park, Singapore 19
Haw Par Villa 169, 219–220
Henderson Centre 120
Henry Ford's Greenfield Village 25
Hershey Gardens 153
Hershey Park 60, 151–153
Hesdin 6
Holyday Land 23
Holyland Experience 31
Honey lake Country Club 308
Hong Kong Wetland Park 304
Hopi Hari 86, 190
Hot Park 92
Huis Ten Bosch 44–45, 78

Ildewild Park 23
Inner Harbor, Baltimore 170, 203
Ironbridge Museum, Telford 169
Isla Mágica 30, 35, 335, 378, 379

Jardin des Découvertes 168
Jewelry City 41
Johnson Space Centre, Houston 211
Jungle Land 89

Kennedy Space Center 100, 274, 276
Korean Folk Village 208
Kurashiki Tivoli Park 79
Kyongju World Tradition Folk Village 78

La Bambouseraie 168
La Cité de l'Espace 168
Labyrinthus 71
Legoland parks 35, 79, 129, 131, 132–133, 329, 413
Leoland Central City 83
Linear City 83
Liseberg 64, 70, 71
Little India 218
Lost City 89, 263
Lotte World 31, 55, 73, 81
Luna Land 14
Luna Park, Sydney 84

Macao Tower 310
Macau Fisherman's Wharf 310
Madrid Xanadú 31
Magic Mountain 26
Malay Village 34, 77, 220
Malaya Borneo Exhibition 19
Mall of America 31, 124
Manassas National Battlefield 259, 260
Marine Park Nixe 78
Marineland 168
Martha Vineyard Camp Meeting 8
Maruyama Shakespeare Park 78
Meiji Museum Village 79
Merlin Entertainment 129, 131–133
        Dungeon 132
        Earth Explorer 132
        financial data 131
        Gardaland *see* Gardaland
        Legoland parks *see* Legoland parks
        portfolio of parks 132
        Sea Life 132–133
Mersal Village 89
Mexico Mágico 149
Mines Resort City 77, 138
Miniature Park 208
Minsk Aircraft Corner World 308
Mirabilandia 379
Mirapolis 69
Morey's Pier 57
Mountasia 95

Nagasaki Bio Park 45
Nagasaki Holland Village 44
Nagashima Spa Land 73
New World, Singapore 18–20
Nijinosato 78
Nong Ping 360

Ocean Park 30, 73, 81, 264–268, 304, 306, 380, 412
Oceanile 168
Oceanópolis 168
Opryland 234, 247, 254
Oriental Land 137, 138–139, 140, 332

Pacific Ocean Park 26
Paramount Parks 57, 59, 63, 93, 94, 95, 98, 100,
        121, 122, 239, 379, 380
        Carowinds 123, 124
        history 122–124
        Paramount Canada Wonderland 84, 123, 124
        Paramount Great America 124, 257
        Paramount Kings Dominion 123, 124, 239

Paramount Kings Island 123, 124
Paramount Wonderland Park Australia 123
portfolio of parks 125
Parc Astérix 35, 69, 70, 133, 168, 184, 333, 356,
    370, 415, 423
Parc du Vegetal 71
Parque da Monica 86
Parque do Ibirapuera 90
Parque España 78
Parque Fluminense 90
Parque Plaza Sésamo 190
Parques Reunidos 129, 135–137
    Bobbejaanland 137
    Bo Sommerland 137
    cable cars 137
    Madrid zoo 136
    Oceanogràfic 137
    Parque de Atracciones de Madrid 136, 137
    portfolio of parks 135, 137
    water parks 137
    wildlife projects 136–137
Phantasiland 68, 70, 239, 332, 415
Planet Pogo 84
Playcenter 86, 90
Pleasure Island, Boston 26
Polynesian Cultural Centre 250
PortAventura 50, 64, 70, 71, 115, 120, 126, 129,
    131, 184, 249, 332, 368, 394, 412, 415
    as tourism destination 310–313
    attractions 368, 377
    corporate social responsibility 421, 422,
        423, 424
    economic impact 236–237
    environmental enhancement 256
    layout 367
    legislation 334–335
    leisure complex 248
    location study 330–331
    tourism impact 333
Porto Europa 120
Prater 7, 15–16
Premier Parks 107, 108, 109, 134

Ravensburger Spielelandpark 70
Roshia Mura 78
Ruggieri Gardens 7

Safari Park 308
Sanrio Company Ltd 137, 138, 146–147
    Harmonyland 147, 253
    Sanrio Puroland 147
Santa Claus Land 23
Santa Cruz Beach Boardwalk 57, 60
Santa's Village 23
Santa's Workshop 23
Santaland USA 23
Sarawak Cultural Village 77, 138, 180
Sea Lyon Park 14–15, 375
SeaWorld, Sheoku 308
SeaWorld 7, 22, 30, 56, 126, 377, 380
    SeaWorld Ohio 108, 109, 127
    SeaWorld Orlando 55, 127, 186, 246, 276,
        280, 282, 371, 377
    SeaWorld San Diego 114–225, 236, 252, 423
    SeaWorld Texas 61, 332–333
    Silver Dollar City 60
Silver Lake Tourist center 308
Singapore River thematic zone 217
Six Flags 22, 26, 38, 39, 59, 60, 63, 85, 94, 98,
    106–112, 113–115, 121, 127, 131, 181
    333, 348, 356, 360, 361, 374
    corporate strategy 108–110
    European division 109–110, 134

financial data 112–115
Frontier City 107
history 106–108
La Ronde 108
markets 112
name 26
number of visitors 123–124
parks 30, 93,95, 312, 342
portfolio of parks 110–112
Reino Aventura *see* Six Flags Mexico
rides 110
roller coasters 375
safety 424–426
Six Flags Astroworld 63, 107, 110, 254
Six Flags Darien Lake 108
Six Flags Elitch Gardens 30, 60, 108, 376
Six Flags Fiesta Texas 61, 332–333, 377
Six Flags Great Adventure 107
Six Flags Great America 60, 107, 123
Six Flags Kentucky Kingdom 108
Six Flags Magic Mountain 107, 373
Six Flags Mexico 108
Six Flags Mid America 107
Six Flags New Orleans 35, 108, 332
Six Flags over Georgia 26, 107
Six Flags over Texas 22, 26, 106, 107
Six Flags White Water 108
Six Flags World of Adventure 63, 109, 110
    The Great Scape and Splashwater
        Kingdom 108
    Wild Waves and Enchanted Village 108
    Wyandot Lake 107
Southport Pleasureland 129
Southstreet Seaport 213
Space World 79
Star Parks 133, 136
Steeplechase Park 14, 385
Storybook Land
Suncity 89, 263
Sunway City 78, 84, 85, 153–154, 183
Sunway Lagoon *see* Sunway City
Suzuka Circuit 7 73, 79, 333

Taman Mini Indonesia Indah 36, 79
Tatawako Swiss Village 78
Terra Encantada 90
Terra Mítica 255, 335
The Beach Park 92
Tivoli Gardens 7, 64, 66, 71, 79, 415
Tjapukai Cultural Theme Park 77
Tokyo Sesame Place 190
Toshimaen Amusement Park 333
Transmontagne 168
Tropical Fruit World 84
Tuilleries Gardens 6
Tussauds 64, 129, 130–131
    Alton Towers 131
    Chessington World of Adventures 131
    Heide Park 131
    London Eye 130
    Thorpe Park 131
    wax museums 130–131

Universal Park 330
Universal Studios 17, 29, 38, 51, 53, 56, 57, 61,
    62, 63, 73, 76, 93, 94, 95, 98, 112–120,
    121, 181, 199, 205, 226, 236, 246,
    270–271, 275, 276, 279–280, 282, 286,
    365, 374, 379, 380
    City Walk *see* City Walk
    corporate strategy 120
    financial data 105–106
    history 16, 115–119

in Asia/the Pacific 120
in Europe 69, 115, 120
Islands of Adventure 27–28, 35, 120, 276
   365, 374
number of visitors 116
Universal Creative 186
Universal Experience Beijing 115, 183
Universal Parks and Resorts 118
Universal Studios Hollywood 57, 115, 116,
   117, 120, 383–384
Universal Studios Japan 30, 50, 73, 81, 115,
   120, 257, 262, 331
Universal Studios Orlando 115, 120, 199,
   341–342, 359, 368, 377

Vauxhall Gardens 7
Village Roadshow 84, 137, 145–146
   Australian outback Spectacular 145–146
   financial data 146
   Paradise Country 145–146
   SeaWorld 84, 145–146, 333, 412
   see Warner Bros Australia
   Warner Roadshow Studios 145–146
   Wet'n'Wild Water World 84, 145–146
Vulcania 72

Walibi 380
   history 109, 134–135
   parks 109, 134
   Walibi Aquitaine 134
   Walibi Lorraine 69, 133, 134, 326
   Walibi Rhône Alpes 134
   Walibi Wavre 134
   Walibi World 134
Walt Disney Company 17, 21, 22, 29, 31, 38, 42,
   56, 57, 59, 60, 61, 62, 63, 73, 76, 77, 78,
   81, 84, 98, 93, 94, 95, 100–106, 107, 108,
   112, 121, 128, 137, 138–139, 169, 182,
   191, 194, 195, 196, 197, 198, 199, 201,
   203, 204, 205, 208, 210–213, 218–219,
   226, 228–233, 234, 235, 242, 246, 247,
   248, 256, 259–260, 261, 262, 270, 271,
   272–285, 330, 362, 363, 376, 378, 381,
   400, 412
   corporate social responsibility 424
   corporate strategy 98–100, 106
   culture and ideology 183, 186, 211
   Disney America 259–260, 317
   Disney development companies 211
   Disney effect 228, 242
   Disney participation in non USA theme
      parks 104
   Disneyland 1, 3, 22, 23, 24, 25, 27, 32, 35,
      46, 53, 56–57, 60, 61, 100, 101, 121, 178,
      181, 184, 185, 195, 196, 198, 199, 206,
      228–233, 240, 251, 256, 300, 341–342,
      348, 358, 359, 360, 378, 380, 381
   Disneyland California Adventure see
      Disneyland
   Disneyland Paris 51, 55, 64, 70, 101, 102,
      129, 159, 168, 193, 194, 227, 247,
      285–299, 330, 339, 340, 341–342, 349,
      350, 402
   disabled access 363–364

effects in the European theme parks
   industry 69–70
government support 338
job creation 235
tourism impact 249
training 408–409
environmental practices 255–256, 277, 423
financial data 105–106
history 100–101, 276–279
Hong Kong Disneyland 85, 101, 102, 104,
   142, 143, 233, 250, 304, 304–306
Main Street see Main Street
number of visitors 102, 103
style 63, 169, 191
Tokyo Disneyland 73, 81, 100, 101, 102,
   139, 159, 331, 332, 341–342, 357, 360
Tokyo DisneySea see Tokyo Disneyland
urban planning 277–278
Walt Disney Imagineering 101
Walt Disney International 104
Walt Disney Studios see Disneyland Paris
Walt Disney World 100, 101–102, 133, 173,
   174, 175, 176, 181, 197, 198, 203, 214,
   217, 221, 240, 250, 273, 375, 333,
   341–342, 357, 358, 359, 360, 407
   Animal Kingdom 101, 184, 253, 377
   Epcot 100, 174, 195, 203, 210–211, 277,
      278, 367–368, 377, 378, 382
   Magic Kingdom 60, 100, 172, 186, 203,
      366, 367, 368
   MGM Studios 100
Walygator Park see Walibi Lorraine
Warner Bros Parks 39, 100, 107, 135, 145, 249,
   262,
   characters 109
   history 109
   Warner Bros Australia 84, 109, 145–146,
      150, 333
   Warner Bros Germany 109, 133
   Warner Bros Madrid 72, 109,134, 253–254,
      335
Waterworld USA 108
Welfan Fushua Amusement Park 76, 138
Wild Animal Park, San Diego 224
Wisconsin Dells 23
Wonderland of the Southwest 82
World Landscape Park 82
World Park 82

Xianhu Lake Botanical Garden 308
Xiomeisha Beach Resort 308

Yokohama Hakkeima Sea Paradise 55, 73, 333
Yong In Farmland 141
Yoshikuni Kamichika 44
Yunnan Nationalities Villages 82, 263

Zhongying Streak 308
Zion Natural Park 164
Zygofolis 69, 349

GEOGRAPHICAL INDEX

(Only when places appear in text)
Abu Dhabi 89
Acapulco 86, 148
Africa 87–88, 126, 159, 263
Albany 108

Alsatia 217, 335
Amsterdam 134
Anaheim 3, 24–25, 57, 60, 100, 199, 211,
   228–233, 252, 257, 348, 358, 360
Anjou 71

Aquitaine 312
Argentina 126, 148
Arizona 178, 334
Armetières 183
Asia/The Pacific 1, 18–20, 48, 53, 93, 94, 137,
    145, 159, 167, 169, 180, 183, 200, 207,
    208, 213, 220, 221, 225, 227, 264, 273,
    299–310, 327, 328, 329, 333, 334, 370,
    374, 382, 409
Atlanta 60, 108
Atlantic City 107
Australia 78–79, 145–146, 252, 380, 412, 417
Austria 51
Auvergne 72

Bahamas 42
Baja California 186
Bangkok 75, 76, 83
Barcelona 18, 207, 310
Barhain 89
Beijing 78, 82, 120, 263
Belgium 129, 133, 134, 137, 380
Benidorm 335
Biarritz 18
Billund 132, 413
Birmingham 312
Bloomington 124
Bogotá 86, 148
Boston 136, 169, 203
Bourgogne 6
Branson 60
Brazil 49, 53, 85, 126, 148, 159, 190, 270
Brisbane 84
Bruhl 332
Brussels 109
Buffalo 60, 108
Burbank 24, 25, 77

Cabo San Lucas 187
Cairns 77
Caldas Novas 92
California 13, 24, 31, 56, 57, 59, 60, 62, 77, 84,
    95, 100, 101, 121, 138, 178, 198, 228,
    230, 240, 257, 280, 286, 359, 373
    as a theme 35
Canada 56–64, 84, 109, 169, 182
Cancún 86, 188
Capetown 89
Caribbean 187–189
Carlsbad 132
Catalonia 126, 137, 335
Ceará 92
Celebration 105, 211–213
Cergy Pontoise 291
Chantilly 6
Chemuyil 189
Chengdu 82
Chiapas 187, 188
Chiba 139
Chicago 10–11, 60, 148, 149, 283
Chile 148
China 49, 51, 72, 73, 78, 104, 126, 128, 137,
    142–144, 183, 220, 240, 263, 264,
    299–310, 412
Cincinnati 123
Clearwater 227
Cleveland 46, 60, 107, 126
Colombia 148
Columbia 203
Columbus 108
Concord 108
Coney Island 8, 14–15, 16, 25, 123, 375, 377,
    385

Copenhagen 7, 15, 66, 132
Cornwall 168

Dallas 26, 60, 332
Daytona Beach 274
Deerborn 25
Delhi 84
Denmark 7, 132, 329, 413
Denver 26, 69, 108
Department du Maine et Loire 70
Detroit 46
Dongguan 300
Dorset 132
Dubai 89, 221–223

England 53, 126
Europe 1, 5, 7, 15, 16, 30, 31, 39, 48, 51, 56, 63,
    94, 98, 109, 120, 131, 133, 136, 167, 179,
    184, 200, 207, 208, 213, 221, 225, 227,
    235, 243–246, 251, 252, 262, 264, 269,
    273 285, 299, 325–326, 327, 328, 329,
    331, 333, 334, 335, 336, 361, 363, 374,
    376, 379, 382
Evry 291

Florida 56, 59, 61, 95, 100, 101, 102, 126, 127,
    129, 187, 191, 199, 208, 210, 221, 226,
    227, 228, 230, 236, 237, 240, 242, 243,
    256, 260, 273, 274, 308, 332, 334, 357,
    359, 404, 423, 427
Flushing Meadows 10
Fort Lauderdale 46, 148
Foshan 300
France 5, 51, 60, 69, 70, 71, 133, 134, 168, 236,
    239, 240, 243–246, 249, 269–270, 308,
    311–313, 326, 333, 335, 336, 340, 349,
    375

Georgia 95
Germany 68, 70, 84, 131, 132, 133, 149, 264
Gold Coast, Australia 84, 145, 333
Golden Coast, Europe 311
Göteborg 71
Great Barrier Reef 186
Great Britain 5, 68, 129, 131, 132, 133, 311–313,
    376, 412
Greater Pearl River Delta 73, 82, 142, 273,
    299–310
Greece 145
Grenoble 312
Guadalajara, México 86, 148
Guangdong 138, 142, 299, 300, 302, 306
Guangzhou 79, 82, 273, 300, 301, 307
Gunzburg 132
Gurnee 60, 107

Hainan 220
Hawaii 250
Hershey 60, 151–153, 179
Hollywood 368
Hong Kong 30, 53, 73, 78, 81, 82, 101, 120, 137,
    142, 199, 250, 264–268, 173, 300, 301,
    302, 303–306, 307, 327, 380, 412
Houston 60, 63, 254
Huizhou 300, 301

Ile de France 290, 291
Illinois 60
India 312, 313, 404, 416, 417, 427

Indochina 73
Indonesia 79, 137, 138, 220
International Drive, Orlando 205, 270–271, 275, 282
Ireland 312
Irving 190
Isla Mujeres 188
Italy 70, 133, 379

Jackson 107
Jakarta 83, 208
Jalan Besar 19
James City County 239, 240, 240–243
Jamestown 241
Japan 44–45, 55, 56, 72, 73, 78, 79, 126, 128, 137, 138–139, 146–147, 165, 180, 185, 190, 198, 237, 253, 264, 270, 333
Jeddah 89
Jiangmen 300
Johannesburg 89

Kissimmee 278, 423
Kitakhyushu 237
Korea 55, 56, 72, 73, 77, 78, 81, 137, 139, 140–141, 147, 333
Kuala Lumpur 76, 77, 78, 83, 138, 153, 183
Kunming 82, 263

Lake Buenavista 210, 270, 275, 278
Lake County 275
Lake Eire 12, 46
Lancaster 151–152
Languedoc Roussillon 168, 311–312
Lantau Island 304
Las Vegas 11, 34, 53, 57, 107, 109, 182, 194, 208, 211, 221, 228
Latin America 51, 90, 94, 108, 128, 147–149, 189
Lille 133, 179, 291
London 7, 130
Long Beach 211
Long Branch 8
Longhorne 126
Lorraine 133
Los Angeles 16, 23, 56, 57, 60, 77, 199, 204, 217, 228, 284
Louisville 108
Luxembourg 129
Lyon 291

Macau 142, 273, 300, 301, 307 309–310
Madrid 72, 235, 249, 253
Maihama 332
Malaka 215
Malaysia 49, 78, 78–79, 83, 137, 153, 183, 215, 220
Manchester 312
Manila 83
Marne-la-Vallée 227, 285–299, 336
Marseille 291, 311, 312
Martinique 129
Maryland 107
Melaka 215
Melbourne 84
Melun Senart 291
Metz 153
Mexico 49, 85, 108, 126, 128, 147, 149, 159, 169, 187–189, 190, 224, 253, 259, 262
Miami 187, 204, 280, 284
Michigan 25
Midi Pyrenées 312
Minneapolis 31, 133

Mission Bay 225
Missouri 60
Miyazaki 185
Monterrey 190
Montpellier 312
Montreal 108

Nashville 234, 247, 254, 257
Netherlands 3, 43–44, 68, 69, 133, 148
New Jersey 8, 57, 60
New Orleans 108, 332
New York 8, 14, 16, 26, 60, 95, 206, 213, 217
New Zealand 145, 169
Newport 8
Nice 18
Norfolk 243
North Carolina 123
Norway 137

Ohio 60, 63, 84, 121, 124, 127
Oita 147
Oklahoma City 107
Oman 89
Ontario 89
Orange County 199, 205, 271, 274, 275, 276, 277, 282
Orlando 22, 31, 56, 57, 61, 63, 89, 102, 117, 120, 121, 126, 127, 131, 133, 181, 198, 199, 203, 204, 205, 210–213, 221, 226, 227, 228, 234, 236, 242, 246, 248, 250, 256, 270–271, 273, 273–285, 286, 330, 333, 359, 360, 365, 374, 377, 407
Osaka 30, 50, 120, 257, 331
Osceola County 199, 212, 275, 276, 277, 282

Palm Springs 124
Panama 148
Paris 6, 18, 55, 129, 199, 227, 244, 249, 273, 285–299, 356, 376
Pasadena 125
Penang 78
Pennsylvania 60, 123, 151–153
Penny Bay 305
Perpignan 311–312
Petaying Java 153
Philadelphia 8, 51
Phillippines 30, 83, 305, 400
Playa del Carmen 188
Poitiers 243–246, 239
Poole 132
Portes de la Brie 292
Portugal 129
Prince William County 259–260
Provence-Alpes-Côte d'Azur 311, 312
Puebla 148

Qatar 89
Quebec 325, 332
Queensland 77
Quintana Roo 187, 189

Ravensburg 70
Red Coast
Reno 107
Rhode Island 8
Rhône Alps 312
Rhur 184, 332
Richmond 123, 239, 241
Rio de Janeiro 90, 92, 250
Riviera Maya 188

Riyadh 89
Romania 262
Rome 205
Rouen 291
Russia 15, 51, 101
Rust 149, 264

Sacramento 60, 108
Saint Louis 60
Saint Quentin en Yvelines 291
Saint Petersburg 375
Salou 50, 126, 236, 256, 335
San Antonio 60, 61, 126, 332–333
San Diego 124, 126, 224, 228, 236
San Francisco 228
Sanduski 46–47, 124
Santa Clara 123, 257
Santa Fe 178
Santa Monica 26
Sao Paolo 86, 90, 92, 190
Saratoga Springs 8
Saudi Arabia 89
Seaside 191, 208
Seattle 62, 179, 211, 218–219
Seine et Marne Departement 290, 292
Seminole County 275, 276
Seoul 31, 81
Seville 335
Shandong 76, 138
Shangai 19, 79, 82, 138, 142, 303, 304, 329–330
Shenzen 35, 78, 79, 82, 142, 180, 300, 301, 302,
        306–309
Silver Springs 95
Singapore 4, 18–20, 34, 35, 76, 77, 78, 83, 84, 85,
        137, 146, 169, 180, 218, 219–220, 220,
        221, 303, 304
South Africa 41, 89, 263
South Korea *see* Korea
Southampton 18
Spain 71, 126, 129, 131, 148, 236, 249, 334, 360,
        383, 412
Springfield 108
Switzerland 129, 133
Sydney 84, 303, 304

Taiwan 77, 137, 142, 308
Tama City 147
Tampa 226–227, 274, 284, 377
Tarragona 236, 310
Tennessee 234, 247
Teruel 72
Texas 61, 95, 110, 190, 323
Thailand 49

Thousand Oaks 62
Tokyo 101, 138, 147, 213, 214, 333
Toledo 46
Toronto 77, 123
Toulouse 312
Tunis 18
Tunisia 87, 89, 159

United Arab Emirates 130
UK 69, 132, 311
Urasayu 138
USA 1, 5, 8, 10, 14, 16, 23, 30, 35, 41, 42, 48, 49,
        56–64, 93, 94, 95, 101, 138, 148, 150,
        167, 179, 192, 195, 200, 201, 202, 204,
        205, 206, 207, 210, 211, 213, 214, 224,
        225, 227, 230, 235, 236, 237, 239,
        240–243, 246, 249, 252, 253, 254, 260,
        264, 273–285, 317, 325–326, 327, 328,
        329, 333, 341, 348, 357, 361, 370, 373,
        374, 375, 376, 379, 382, 383, 413, 417,
        425, 426

Val d'Europe 286, 287, 289, 291, 292, 294, 296,
        297
Valence 312
Valencia 137
Vancouver 77
Vendée 269
Versailles 6
Vienna 15–16
Vienne 243–246, 248
Vila-seca 126, 236
Virginia 126, 127, 150, 226, 239, 240–243, 259–260
Virginia Beach 241, 243

Wakayama 120
Waldkirch 150–151
Washington DC 60, 241, 259
Williamsburg 126, 240, 240–243, 264, 330, 331
Windsor 132
Winter Haven 276
Wolfsburg 71

York County 241
Yorktown 241
Yucatan 380

Zhaoqing 300, 301
Zhongsha 300
Zuhai 82, 142, 300, 310

COMPANY INDEX

(Organisations, people and companies)

ABC 25
Advent International 136
AIG 275
AMC Theatres 232
America Online 275
American Society of Testing and Materials 425,
        427
Amnesty International 260
Amusement Industry Institute Program 427
AOL Time Warner 39, 106
Architecture 77
Arpegio 72
Aspro Ocio 129

Association of South East Asian Nations 427
Australian Amusement Leisure and Recreation
        Association 426

Bally Manufacturing Collaboration 26, 107, 121
Bank of New York 275
Baonang Group 308
Blackstone 120, 131
BMW 71
Boston Ventures 107
Brazilian Association for the Amusement
        Industry 90, 426

BRC Imagination Arts 77, 186
Bruntland report 250
Burke, Graham 145
Burke, Kierkan 107
Burnham, Daniel 201

Caisse de Dêpots et Consignation
    Développement 133
Canal+ 117
CBS 63, 94, 121, 122, 124
Charter of the Earth 189
Charterhouse Capital Partners 130, 131
China Association of Amusement Parks and
    Attractions 427
China pan Tourism Industry Development Co 138
China Travel Service 142, 308–309
Clinton, Hillary 262
Compagnie Général des Eaux 117
Constande brothers 188
CT Hsu International 189

Darden restaurants 274
Dasmal, Salem Bin 212
Décathlon 179
Descartes 6
Disney, Roy 100
Disney, Roy, E. 100
Disney, Walt 1, 10, 17, 18, 23, 24, 99, 100, 191,
    198, 199, 203, 210–211, 212, 274
Donghwa Real State 141
Dubai International Capital 130, 131
Duell Corporation 76
Duell, Randall 26, 367

Ecologistas en Acción 253
Economic Development Commission of
    Mid-Florida 283
Economics Research Associates 49–50, 86, 159,
    325
Eisner, Michael 100, 101, 211
Emirates 222
EuroPools 84

Ferris Wheel 11, 14
Florida Department of Environmental
    Regulation 256
Florida Hospital 285
Forrec 77, 84, 86
Fort-Brescia, Bernardo 198
Funtime Parks 107
Funworld 427

Gameworks 62
Garland Entertainment 234
Gas Research Institute 255
General Electric 118–119
General Motors 12
Ghery, Frank O. 294
Give Kids the World 423, 427
Graves, Michael 198
Greenpeace 132
Grévin Development 236
Grimon-Sanson, Raoul 18
Grupo Ecologista del Mayab 259
Grupo Mágico 148–149
Gwathmey, Charles 198

Hannah Barbera 123
Harcourt Brace Jovanovich 121, 126, 127
Hard Rock Cafe 61
Harry Potter 186

Heineken 179
Henderson Land Development Co 120
Hermes Private Equity 131
Hershey Chocolate Company 151
Hershey Entertainment and Resorts Company 153
Hershey Entertainment Group 152
Hershey, Milton 151–153
Hershey Trust 153
Hewitt and Associates 275
Hong Kong International Theme Parks 304
House Foods Corp 360
House of Blues 232
Howard, Ebenezer 12, 201

IAAPA 40, 160, 200, 235, 350, 361, 391, 395, 396,
    405, 408, 416, 423, 426–428
Iger, Robert 101
India Association of Amusement Parks and
    Industries 427
Instituto Nacional de Antropología e Historia 188
International Drive Chamber of Commerce 205,
    270–271
International Institute for Peace through
    Tourism 423, 427
International Labour Organization 419
International Organization for
    Standardization 421
International Theme Park Services Inc 76, 186
Intra Asia Entertainment Corporation 76, 138
Isozaki, Arata 198
ITEC 89

Jacobs, Jane 201
Jahn, Helmut 198
JCB Co 360
Jerde, John 120, 199, 204, 207
JoongAng Development Co 141
JPI Design 89

Keisei Electric Railways Co. Ltd. 139
Kellogg's 179
Kerzner, Sol 263
King's Entertainment company 123
Kingsmill Resort 127, 241, 242
Kirby, Roc 145
Königreich, Glüks 78
Kroger Company 123
Kumagai Gumi Co 138

La Caixa 120
La Compagnie des Alps 133–136
Laemle, Carl 16, 115
Landmark 76
Latin America Association of Amusement Parks
    and Attractions 426
Law Olmstead, Frederic 201
Le Corbusier 12, 201
Lego 59, 132–133, 337
Lego Imagination Center 133
Leisure Resources International Ltd 129
LHA 77
Lockheed 274, 285
Loews Hotels 120
Longhurst, John 84
Lord of the Rings 169
Louis XIV 6

Mack family 150, 151
Mack Rides 151
Management Consultants 84
Manila Declaration on the Social Impact of
    Tourism 257

Marriott 107, 121, 123
Matsushita 117
Maxwell, Robert
MCA Inc 115–117, 120
McCullough, David 259
McDonald's 108, 161, 165, 173, 181, 226
Meeus, Eddie 109
Mersal Entertainment 89
Messier, Jean Marie 118
Microsoft 161
Miller, Ron 101
Mills Corporation 149, 254
Minute Maid 274
Mitchell, George 101
Mitsubishi Heavy Industries 275
Mitsui Fudosan Co Ltd 139
Mondavi, Robert 181
Moses, Robert 201
MVA 84

NASA 255, 274
National Association of Amusement Ride Safety
    Officials 425
National Trust for Historic Preservation 260
NBA 166, 284
NBC 106, 188–119, 120
New Urbanism 212, 213
News Corp/Fox
Nickelodeon 123, 283
Nike 108, 161
Nippon Suisan Kaisha Ltd 360
Northrop Grumman Electronic 285

Olive Garden 182
Ong brothers 19
Online Industry Resource Guide 427
Opel Live 71
Opry Mills 254
Oracle 275, 286
Organization for Economic Cooperation and
    Development 419
Orlando Convention and Visitor Bureau 282, 283
Overseas Chinese Town Group 142, 308
Oxford Valley Mall 189

Palace Entertainment 95
Palamon capital partners 109, 133, 134
Pascal 6
Pearl River Delta Economic Zone 300, 301
Pepper, John E. Jr 101
Phoenix Seagaia Complex 185
Prince Al Waleed 286

Quincy Market 169, 203
Quintana Pali, Miguel 187

Rainforest Cafe 61
Rank Group 120
Recreational Equipment Inc 179
Reedy Creek Improvement District 210–211, 212,
    256, 277, 278
Rodeo Drive 217
Roose, George 46

Samsung 77, 137
Seacon Square Mall 83
Seagram 117
Sega 63

Sesame Place 31, 189–190
Shaw brothers 19
Shin Nippon Steel 237
Shunde Jiaxin Realty Development Co 138
Siegel, Robert 198
Siemens 275, 285
S. Pearson and Son 131
Speedzone 95
Spielberg, Steven 265
Starbucks 169
Stein, Jules C 115
Stern, Robert A.M. 198
Suncity Group 153–154
Syndicat National des Espaces de Loisirs,
    d'Attractions et Culturels 168

Taft Broadcasting 84, 12, 123
Theme Park International Services 84, 379
Themed Entertainment Association 343, 344
Tieman, Jurgen 69
Tilyou, George C. 14, 385
Time Warner 84, 107
    see also AOL Time Warner
Tolkien 169
Tupperware Brands Corporation 275
Turner Broadcasting System 84
TUV 84

UNESCO 251
UNICEF 147
United Nations 251
    United Nations Commission on
        Environment and Development 250
    United Nations Conference on Environment
        and Development 250
    United Nations Global Compact 419,
        419–420
Universidad Nacional Autónoma de México 189
University of Central Florida 285
University of the Caribbean 189
Urban Land Institute 274

Veblen, Thorstein 161
Venturi, Robert 198
Via Delphi 187, 189
Viacom 106, 123, 124
Vivendi 117
Vivendi Universal 117
Vivendi Universal Entertainment 11, 118
Volskwagen 71, 179

Walt Mart 161
Wasserman, Lew 116
Water Hyacinth Project 255
Wesray Corporation 107
West Edmonton Mall 31, 169, 182
World Code of Ethics in Tourism 257, 263
World Tourism Organization 221, 251, 257, 263,
    422
World Travel and Tourism Council 251, 422
Worldwide Fund for Nature 151
Wyne, Angus 106, 107

Yamazaki Backing Co 360
Yue-mei International Development Corp 77

Zistel, Louis 46
ZN Mexico 149